Labour in Southeast Asia

Given the transformations taking place in many parts of Southeast Asia, the question of labour remains as pertinent today as it has ever been. Labour issues are central to the social tensions marking the transformations taking place in both rural and urban areas, and underscore the myriad ways people have responded to economic and political crisis. In aiming to understand the multiple and specific dimensions of labour in this region, this book offers a collection of empirical studies of labour across a range of time-frames (colonial and contemporary), economic sectors, labour processes and community contexts. In seeking to provoke debate, the book reveals the variety of experiences evident in countries and regions marked by capitalist and (post) socialist regulatory frameworks, and contrasting labour regimes, histories and cultures. The contributions show the importance of critically examining both the complex nature of global–local links and the particular ways economic processes are refracted through culture and locality in Southeast Asia. Clustered around the themes of labour regimes, labour processes, labour mobility and labour communities, the essays show how economic development is not only shaped by market forces but is also interlocked in systems of meaning.

Rebecca Elmhirst is Senior Lecturer in the School of Environment, University of Brighton, UK

Ratna Saptari is Senior Researcher at the International Institute of Social History, Amsterdam, The Netherlands

CHANGING LABOUR RELATIONS IN ASIA
Series editors: Marcel van der Linden and Ratna Saptari,
International Institute of Social History, Amsterdam

Labour in Southeast Asia
Local processesses in a globalised world
Edited by Rebecca Elmhirst and Ratna Saptari

Labour Contracts and Labour Relations in Early Modern Central Japan
Mary Louise Nagata

Subcontract Labour in Asia
Historical and contemporary perspectives
Edited by Jan Lucassen and Ratna Saptari

Labour in Southeast Asia

Local processes in a globalised world

Edited by Rebecca Elmhirst
and Ratna Saptari

RoutledgeCurzon
Taylor & Francis Group
LONDON AND NEW YORK

International Institute
of Social History
Amsterdam

First Published 2004 by RoutledgeCurzon
2 Park Square, Milton Park, Abingdon, Oxon, OX14 4RN

Simultaneously published in the USA and Canada
by RoutledgeCurzon
270 Madison Ave, New York NY 10016

RoutledgeCurzon is an imprint of the Taylor & Francis Group

Transferred to Digital Printing 2006

This publication was made possible with the generous support of the International Institute for Asian Studies, Leiden

Typeset in Bembo 11/12 pt by Bert Heesen Produkties, Utrecht, The Netherlands

British Library Cataloguing in Publication Data
A catalogue record for this book is available from the British Library

Library of Congress Cataloguing in Publication Data
A catalog record for this book has been applied for

ISBN10: 0–700–71420–0 (hbk)
ISBN10: 0–415–40599–8 (pbk)

ISBN13: 978–0–700–71420–9 (hbk)
ISBN13: 978–0–415–40599–7 (pbk)

Contents

Preface

In recent times, the assumed certainties of globalisation, economic growth and the rise of the 'new rich' in Southeast Asia have given way to economic contraction, new forms of poverty and a less assured development path for many parts of the region. As scholars and activists document and attempt to challenge Southeast Asia's new political, social and economic realities, it has become imperative to rethink ways of representing and challenging this new state of affairs. Nowhere is this more the case than with respect to changing labour relations in Southeast Asia where shifts in the relationships between work, community and resistance politics appear to be pivotal to the kinds of transformations now taking place. In bringing together a diverse collection of papers that examine labour issues from a variety of angles, our aim is to illustrate the complexities of labour in Southeast Asia, as these are forged through global-local links and constructed in and through various cultural frames.

The book initially grew out of a panel on 'Changing Labour Relations in Southeast Asia' at the 1998 meeting of the European Southeast Asian Studies Association in Hamburg, convened by Ratna Saptari and Willem van Schendel of the International Institute of Social History (IISH) in Amsterdam, and with the support of the Changing Labour Relations in Asia (CLARA) programme. There followed a series of discussions between Ratna Saptari and Rebecca Elmhirst on cold, windy beaches in Brighton and Scheveningen in which the broad conceptual framework for an edited book was hatched. Several of our contributors met again at a panel on Labour, Employment and Development at the 1999 meeting of the European Association of Development Institutions in Paris in which we refined our discussions and developed a focus for the book. From these beginnings, we sought revised papers from our original contributors, and invited contributions from other scholars working in this field, which were in turn revised and finally edited. We are grateful for the cheerful hard work of everyone involved in this long and drawn out process, and for their patience in seeing it through to completion. We should also like to acknowledge the generous support provided by the International Institute for Asian Studies in Leiden and in particular Wim Stokhof, without whose support the various meetings and workshops needed for the preparation of this book, would not have been possible. We are also grateful for the intellectual and practical support offered by the CLARA programme at IISH, in particular, the work of Marcel van der Linden, Willem van Schendel, Ben White. Marcel van der Linden as co-editor of the CLARA Labour in Asia series has been particularly supportive and confident enough that this book would, despite all the hiccups, eventually meet completion. Dick van der Meij has worked hard to make this book readable and Aad Blok has given valuable advice and time to prepare this book for camera-ready format.

It is our hope that this collection of essays will further stimulate interest in this important area.

List of Tables and Figures

Tables

FIGURES

Contributors

Jennifer Alexander is a former Australian Research Council Fellow at the University of Sydney. Her numerous publications are based on field work in Indonesia, Malaysia and Sri Lanka. She is author of *Trade, Traders and Trading in Rural Java* (Oxford University Press, Singapore, 1987). With Paul Alexander she is currently engaged in research on the export furniture industry of Indonesia and the destruction of small-scale communities in Central Borneo.

Paul Alexander is a social anthropologist, formerly based at the University of Sydney. He has conducted extensive fieldwork in Indonesia, Malaysia and Sri Lanka, and has published widely on petty commodity production and trade. He is editor of *Creating Indonesian Cultures* (Oceania Publications, Sydney 1989) and *In the Shadow of Agriculture. Non-Farm Activities in the Javanese Economy, Past and Present* (with Peter Boomgaard and Ben White, Royal Tropical Institute, Amsterdam 1991).

Daniel Arghiros has written widely on rural change and politics in Thailand and is the author of *Democracy, Development and Decentralisation in Provincial Thailand* (Curzon Routledge, 2001). Formerly a lecturer in Southeast Asian Studies at the University of Hull, he is now the representative of the UK's Department for International Development in Cambodia.

Chan Fong Yin is a graduate of the Honours programme in Southeast Asian Studies at the National University of Singapore, where her research focused on the political economy of development in the Philippines.

Rebecca Elmhirst is Senior Lecturer in Human Geography at the University of Brighton. Her research centres on labour migration, ethnicity and the politics of place in Indonesia. She has published articles in journals such as *Political Geography, Journal of Development Studies, Women's Studies International Forum* and *Area*.

Erwiza Erman is Senior Researcher at the Research Center for Regional Resources, Indonesian Institute of Sciences (PSDR-LIPI) in Jakarta. Her research centres mainly on labour conditions and labour politics in Indonesia especially in the mining sector. She is author of *Manager, Coolie and the State: Belitung Tin-mines, 1892-1942* (published in Indonesian by Sinar Harapan, Jakarta, 1995).

Shirlena Huang is Associate Professor at the Department of Geography, National University of Singapore. Her research interests focus mainly on gender issues (with specific interest in transnational labour migration in the Asia Pacific) as well as urban conservation and heritage. Her publications include articles in *International Migration Review, Women's Studies International Forum, Urban Studies* and *Geoforum*.

Richard T. Jackson is an independent scholar, formerly with James Cook University, Townsville, Australia.

Amarjit Kaur is Professor of Economic History at the University of New England, Armidale, Australia. Her research centres on labour systems, wage labour, women workers, labour standards and labour migration in Southeast Asia and Asia. Her most recent publications include *Wage Labour in Southeast Asia since 1840* (Palgrave 2002) in 'The Economic History of Southeast Asia' series and a forthcoming edited book *Women Workers in Industrialising Asia: Costed, Not Valued* (Palgrave 2003).

Philip F. Kelly is Assistant Professor of Geography at York University in Toronto. His research focuses on the political economy of industrialising localities, labour market processes and international migration in Southeast Asia. He is author of *Landscapes of Globalisation: Human Geographies of Economic Change in the Philippines* (Routledge 1999).

Irene Nørlund is Associate Professor in the Department of Geography and International Development Studies, Roskilde University, Denmark. Her research interests centre on labour regimes, trade unions and development in Southeast Asia, with emphasis on Vietnam. She is author of several journal papers and edited books, including *Asian Values and Vietnam's Development in Comparative Perspective* (NIAS, with Nguyen Van Thanh 2000) and *Vietnam in a Changing World* (Curzon Press, with Vu Cao Dam and Carolyn Gates 1995). She is currently involved in a major research programme on sustainable livelihoods and food security in Vietnam, Laos and Thailand.

Xavier Oudin is researcher for the French 'Institut de Recherche pour le Développement'. He has conducted research in Thailand, Vietnam and West Africa on employment and micro-enterprises. His published work includes *Micro-enterprises and the Institutional Framework* (OECD Development Centre, 1994) with Christian Morrisson and Henri-Bernard Solignac-Lecomte. He is now attached to the Faculty of Economics, University of Montpellier, France.

Bernadette P. Resurrección is Assistant Professor in Gender & Development Studies at the Asian Institute of Technology, Thailand. Her research has focused on gender and natural resource management, environmental policy processes and labour migration in the Philippines, Thailand and Vietnam. She has contributed articles to journals such as the *Bulletin of Concerned Asian Scholars, Gender, Technology & Development, Alternatives: Local Transformations* and *Human Governance.*

Jonathan Rigg is Reader in Geography at the University of Durham. He has worked on and in Southeast Asia since the early 1980s, mostly in rural Thailand but latterly in Laos. His current interests revolve around rural-urban interactions, agrarian transitions, and deagrarianisation. His publications include *Southeast Asia: the Human Landscape of Modernisation and Development* (Routledge 1997, with a second edition published in 2002) and *More Than the Soil: Rural Change in Southeast Asia* (Pearson Education 2001).

Edsel E. Sajor is Assistant Professor in the School of Environment, Resources and Development (SERD) at the Asian Institute of Technology, Thailand. He obtained his MA and PhD degrees in Development Studies at the Institute of Social Studies, The Hague. He has published on the subjects of state-society relations in rural livelihoods and environmental politics. His current research focus is on urban governance and land policy, as well as on state-community relations in environmental management in developing countries.

Ratna Saptari is Senior Researcher at the International Institute of Social History (IISH) in Amsterdam and 'Coordinator of the Changing Labour Relations in Asia Programme' based at the IISH. Her current research focuses on the cigarette industry, trade unions, and social movements in Indonesia. She has published in journals such as *Asian Studies Review, International Review of Social History* and in a number of edited volumes. She is co-editor of *The Household and Beyond: Cultural Notions and Social Practices in the Study of Gender in Indonesia*, (Curzon Press-NIAS 2000). She is currently preparing a book on labouring communities in the East Javanese cigarette producing areas.

Peter Wad is Associate Professor at the Department of Intercultural Communication and Management, Copenhagen Business School. His ongoing research focuses on the impact of the East Asian financial crisis on trade union structures in Malaysia and South Korea, and the importance of international linkages for the competitiveness of national auto manufacturers in developing countries. His publications include articles in the *Copenhagen Journal of Asian Studies* and the *International Journal of Business and Society*, and in the anthology *Political Business in East Asia*, edited by E.T. Gomez (Routledge 2002).

Ben White is Professor of Rural Sociology at the Institute of Social Studies, The Hague. He has been involved in research on rural society in Indonesia since the early 1970s, and also has a special interest in the sociology/anthropology of childhood. Books and (co-)edited volumes include *Rural Household Studies in Asia* (Singapore University Press 1980); *Agrarian Transformations: Local Processes and the State in Southeast Asia* (University of California Press 1989); *In the Shadow of Agriculture: Non-Farm Activities in the Javanese Economy, Past & Present* (Royal Tropical Institute 1991); *Child Workers in Indonesia* (Akatiga 1998); *Understanding Child Labour* (Sage 1999); *Forests: Nature, People, Power* (Blackwell 2000); *Child Labour: Policy Options* (Aksant Academic Press).

Brenda S.A. Yeoh is Associate Professor, Department of Geography, National University of Singapore. Her research foci include the politics of space in colonial and post-colonial cities; and gender, migration and transnational communities. She has published over 50 scholarly journal papers and is author/editor of a number of books including *Contesting Space: Power Relations and the Urban Built Environment in Colonial Singapore* (Oxford University Press 1996); *Singapore: A Developmental City State* (John Wiley 1997, with Martin Perry and Lily Kong); *Gender and Migration* (Edward Elgar 2000, with Katie Willis) and *Gender Politics in the Asia-Pacific Region* (Routledge 2002, with Peggy Teo and Shirlena Huang).

1

Studying Labour in Southeast Asia: Reflections on Structures and Processes

RATNA SAPTARI AND REBECCA ELMHIRST

In the so-called 'aftermath' of the economic crisis of the 1990s, social relations and tensions that have until recently been masked under a blanket of capitalist 'success' and immutable political authoritarianism have come under scrutiny, both by policy makers, political activists and scholars. The large increase in unemployment across sectors, a reduction in wage levels, an increasing number of migrants both within and between countries and rising social tensions between social groups as its consequence, are some of the manifestations of the economic and political crisis occurring in the region (World Bank 1998, ILO 1998, McLeod and Garnaut 1998). Labour has been a strong component in the discussions linked to issues of unemployment, welfare schemes and the building of 'democratic institutions [...] central to the post-crisis economic model' which were 'essential for ensuring greater social equity in the development process' (ILO 1998: 2). In view of this, there is a compelling case for reinvigorating the study of labour and its embeddedness in local structures and global markets, particularly as Southeast Asian scholarship on the political economy of labour lags behind that of other developing regions such as Africa and Latin America (Taylor and Turton 1988, Rodan et al. 2001).

Given the transformations taking place in many parts of Southeast Asia, the question of labour (and land) remains as pertinent today as it has been in the past and certainly cannot be separated from any discussion of capital accumulation and social differentiation in the region. The recent economic crisis has reminded us of two important dimensions in the study of labour. Firstly, the geographically diverse impacts of the crisis are rooted in the differing nature of 'global-local links' of particular areas and nation-states of Southeast Asia. Secondly, the underlying structures through which labour relations are forged are strongly influenced by how these have been shaped in the past. The range of experiences of the 1997 crisis has indeed ignited the need to examine carefully the processes and relations that give shape to labour relations in the region. This book aims to provoke discussion about labour in Southeast Asia by offering a collection of empirical studies that address a range of time-frames (colonial and contemporary), economic sectors, labour processes and labour contexts. The chapters consider the variety of experiences across Southeast Asia, in countries and regions marked by capitalist and (post)socialist regulatory frameworks, labour regimes, histories and cultures. Our emphasis is thus upon history, diversity and context, and these empirical themes are developed, to different degrees, in each of the studies.

Amidst this variety of empirical experience, the chapters help us to re-examine two significant analytical positions. Firstly, they show the importance of critically examining the complex nature of global-local links. Studying these connections enables us to move away from sharp dichotomies of the global and local, of the modern and traditional, of universalism and particularism. Much of the literature on globalisation continues to revolve either around general statements about globalisation and its social consequences, or on the particular exigencies of bounded localities as they evade global processes. In the first case, generalisations tend to be made about the adoption of global (western) cultures and life styles and the destruction of local traditions and ways of life (Jameson 1999).[1] Emphasis is given to the increasingly dominant role played by transnational corporations and international institutions in shaping national economies and politics and the reduced relevance of nation-states in shaping political economies (McMichael 1996, Strange 1996).

In contrast to this more universalist approach, a second thread to the literature focuses on the particular: how local communities have evaded global incorporation and been shielded from global processes that might otherwise have transformed traditions and local cultural practices. Within this perspective, there is a tendency to view communities as closed and bounded systems with their own economic and political dynamics: carried over from traditional structures. This dualistic framework, much in fashion in the past (Furnivall 1939, Geertz 1967), echoes in debates among policy makers and civil society in many parts of Southeast Asia.[2]

Yet any attempt to construct a narrative regarding Southeast Asian labour regimes and relations has to deal with the dialectics between the general and particular. Most parts of Southeast Asia share the general experiences of colonialism, the Depression of the 1930s, the Japanese Occupation, independence movements

1 Although globalisation is not a new phenomenon, as the mobility of capital, goods and labour has been a feature of human history for some centuries, it is also recognised that the velocity and scale of globalisation have grown significantly in the last few decades (Sassen 1996).

2 But also some streams of the subaltern school, as developed in India, underline the essentialist nature of local communities, which are perceived as having a 'pre-modern catholicity of inchoate, pluralistic traditions' (Sarkar 2000).

and post-colonial development projects. The colonial project was wrought through hegemonic constructions of European cultural superiority and non-European backwardness and traditional thinking that echoed through labour relations. The gradual development of modern bureaucracies through colonialism often went together with religious crusades and 'civilising' missions that affected the way labour regimes were regulated, both in work and domestic spheres. However, scholars have pointed out that such seemingly common events were not universally experienced and did not produce common responses across the region (Hart et al. 1989, Boomgaard and Brown 2000, Tarling 1992a, Tarling 1992b). The global-local links fostered through colonialism need to be historically situated in order to read their implications for labour in different parts of Southeast Asia.

Whilst local kingdoms, traditional forms of land tenure, the social division of labour and cultural ways of life were transformed, remoulded and geared to accommodate to the rapid and overarching changes imposed from 'above', such processes were shaped, interpreted and incorporated in particular ways in different localities. This reflects not only the manifold ways different colonial powers chose their strategies of increasing revenues and controlling the various resources available in particular local settings, but also the diverse ways communities responded, accommodated and resisted colonial demands. In this way, factors such as the diversity of natural resources, the different periods in which local economies were incorporated into the international system, the position of diverse factions of capital in the world system, and the constitution of local ruling elites and their relations with different segments of the populations, are but a few of the elements shaping different forms of 'articulation' between the global and local, and therefore local labour experiences in a globalising world (Cooper et al. 1993).

An important factor shaping the nature of 'local' response is the historically emergent class structure, which intersects with other social factors such as gender, ethnicity and religion. Class structure refers to the diverse economic locations or positions that make up a society and is considered to set objective limits to the nature of class struggle. However as social and political struggles are often waged over symbols, terms and concepts, economic positions are also culturally embedded. Therefore workers' identities are often simultaneously shaped in conjunction with identities of gender, ethnicity and communal loyalties (Bourdieu 1980, Steinberg 1991, Therborn 1983). This diverse nature of the 'articulation' of the global and local is, in different degrees, emphasised in the contributions to this book.[3]

3 In the discussion of 'the local' most of the chapters in this volume, whether examining state policies on labour, labour processes, labour markets, agrarian relations, or labouring communities, look at locality as a spatial entity, bound to certain geographical places. However, 'the local' may also be defined in a non-spatial manner, meaning specific social groupings, or networks which may cross spatial boundaries, such as networks of migrant workers.

A second analytical thread that runs through this book concerns the ways that cultural constructions have played a role in giving shape to various aspects of labour control, relations and markets. Culture has often been seen as basically essentialist and static where communities and social actors build relationships and institutions within bounded cultural entities, based around coherent cultural elements that share a common logic (Chandavarkar 1997, Pinches 1999). However, culture must not be regarded as timeless and monolithic: rather, cultural order is a 'construction or maintenance of belief, value and meaning [...] in a context of shifting social, political and economic relations' (Pinches 1999: 6). Therefore struggles over meaning and identities can be seen, for instance, in policies on labour regulation, definitions of worker categories, or definitions of skill, and such representational tensions draw on both global and local repertoires. This brings us inevitably to the complex issue of how culture and economy are linked. Past disciplinary traditions have frequently seen one as separate from the other.[4] Attempts to bring economy and culture together within one analytical framework have often retained a conceptual distinction between the two, with one viewed as external to the other. Here, we follow the view that culture should be defined as a system of meanings that both structures and is structured by relationships, groups and society, and may also change over time and place as it is struggled over. As economic activities are culturally embedded, this implies that the logic of economic development is not only shaped by market forces but these same market forces interlock with certain systems of meaning. In turn, cultural notions of domination, which are represented in discursive fields, are grounded in specific relations of production and exchange (Cooper and Stoler 1997). It has also been argued, especially within feminist scholarship, that 'work' is not separable from other spheres of life. Prevailing gender notions and ideas about the family (and anxieties about childhood) shape state regulation, worker protection and the control of particular groups of labour, namely, women and children (White, this volume). These ideologies intersect also with conceptions of 'the oriental', ethnicity and nationalism (Locher-Scholten 1987, Stoler 1995, Clancy-Smith and Gouda 1998). As material circumstances change, shifts have also occurred in these definitions.

Working around these themes of global-local links, economy and culture, this book is divided into four parts that focus on particular dimensions of labour in Southeast Asia. The first part focuses on the regulation of labour and labour regimes, drawing on cases from Malaya, Indonesia, Vietnam and the Philippines. In different ways, the chapters address the issue of how various dimensions of labour

4 In anthropology, economic systems have been seen as following a trajectory of kin-dominated systems towards more market-dominated ones. Culture is often associated with kinship, which preceded the more rational market-based system. See Sahlins (1974) and Cheater (1986) for a discussion of these classifications.

are constructed through colonial and post-colonial discourses of ethnicity, personhood and work, and the implications of this process for both formal and informal labour regulation, and the social fabric of labour markets. Kaur's chapter deals with how labour regimes were created in colonial mining and plantation economies, how ethnicity was constructed and capitalist control resisted. White looks at how constructions of childhood are debated in the Dutch metropole and how this shapes legislation on children and child labour in the Netherlands Indies and later on in post-colonial Indonesia. Nørlund examines the changing definitions of labour and unions in the Vietnamese constitution and how these are shaped by external and internal political struggles and debates. Fong Yin and Kelly look at the discrepancy between the Philippines' institutional framework on labour and the actual practice of labour regimes shaping local labour markets and labour relations as personalised and informal power relationships condition the enactment of labour regulation, giving particular shape to labour markets and labour relations in a specific locality.

The second part of the book examines labour processes and work relations in the agricultural and industrial sectors in the Philippines, Indonesia and Malaysia. Sajor focuses on the prevalence of 'traditional' forms of production in a highly commercialised upland economy in the Philippines. Also in the Philippines, Resurrección follows changing divisions of labour and gendered identities in an agricultural community, once based on a swidden economy but rapidly shifting into a sedentary economy as large capital enters the locality. Alexander and Alexander also look at how seemingly old forms of production relations and cultural idioms are manufactured and retained but within highly commercialised structures. Focusing on the development of unions in Malaysia, Wad examines the process of decentralisation in the automobile industry and how it has affected the position of unions in the automobile sector. A common theme running through these chapters concerns the ways that labour relations are refracted through a complex mix of 'reinvented traditions' that echo local practices but are created within the labour discourses of transnational economic relations.

In the third part of the book, attention is directed towards labour mobility and how this has transformed work relations and occupational structures in different parts of Southeast Asia. Looking at the brick industry in Thailand, Arghiros shows how a combination of factors defines labour recruitment policies in the brick industry and social relations in the workplace. Occupational mobility, namely, the shift from agricultural to non-agricultural occupations, particularly for the younger generation in Thailand is Rigg's theme for his chapter. Oudin concentrates on the post-socialist period in Vietnam where new occupational structures are emerging, with traces of the incomplete nature of the socialist policy still leaving their mark. Shifting to an increasingly significant form of spatial mobility, namely transnational migration, Huang, Yeoh and Jackson look at transnational

Philippine female workers and examine the views of the Philippine public, the nature of labour demand in Singapore and the perceptions of the migrants and their families.

The last part of this book looks at labouring communities, and the gendered politics internal and also external to these communities. Erman traces the historical development of a mining community in Indonesia, the changing face of the enclave community and how this social history has shaped miners' labour politics. Elmhirst looks at the social networks of an ethnic community in Indonesia, which has shaped the actions of young women who migrate from rural Lampung to an industrial centre in Jakarta, and the ambivalent nature of such networks for these migrants and their labour activism.

The remainder of this introductory chapter situates the different points highlighted by the authors within the Southeast Asian historical context, focusing on the aspects of labour around which the book is organised: labour regulation and labour regimes, labour processes and work relations, labour mobility and labouring communities.

The Regulation of Labour and Labour Regimes

In both colonial and postcolonial conditions, the labour question has always been a source of contention for a number of competing interests and claims between states, different factions of capital, and competing political elites. Underlying these tensions are also the different goals that frame the need to regulate labour. State regimes face the problem of guaranteeing and regulating a supply of cheap and compliant labour for state enterprises or capitalist ventures, whilst at the same time they also have to deal with the problem contending moralities and rationales regarding economic development, political stability, social order and social justice. As one scholar puts it, the question raised is not only 'how many low-paid workers could be obtained' but also 'how much coercion could a "civilised" government legitimately deploy to make people [...] perform work for public or private employers'.[5] Ideological arguments which frame the notions of civility and ethical conduct overlap with the need to balance the amount of labour that could be compelled to work for the colonial state and settlers, and the amount of labour necessary to reproduce the households of those performing labour services (Stoler 1985, Bernstein et al. 1992). For these reasons the state's role in the regulation of labour is beset with potential contradictions: the goals of political stability although closely related, often do not coincide with that of economic growth.

5 See Cooper (1996: 5) for an excellent analysis of the intersection of French and British colonial bureaucracies with African labour movements.

The former is closely linked to nation-state formations, territoriality, legitimacy and citizenship, whereas the other is linked more with increased integration into regional or global economies.

In the sixteenth and seventeenth centuries, long before the introduction of colonial rule, attempts to harness the thinly dispersed population were already part of the local landscape, and achieved mainly through the control of labour (often through land) and the appropriation of heavy taxes or tributes.[6] Citizenship here meant the obligation to pay taxes and occasionally to be conscripted, but also the right to obtain patronage and protection. The most fertile areas in the lowlands of Southeast Asia, namely in Siam, Burma, Cambodia, Java and North Sumatra experienced the most elaborately imposed taxation schemes and these were the areas where centralised bureaucracies or kingdoms, emerged.[7] As the needs of these centralised kingdoms grew, a combination of tribute, bondage and slave labour became a crucial feature of the social reproduction of these kingdoms.[8]

When the western powers arrived, their first attempt was to shift tribute payment from the local elite to themselves. This, among other factors, became the basis of the Cultivation System introduced in the Netherlands Indies by the Dutch in 1830–1870, where land rent imposed first by the British, and later on taken over by the Dutch was primarily paid by workers through providing labour services on village land that had been allotted to crops specified by the colonial government (van Niel 1990: 74, Elson 1994: 193).

In other cases it was a matter of eliminating the local powers and bringing an area under direct control such as the subjugation of the old Burma heartland in 1886 by the British where they then eliminated existing traditional structures, and directly governed the territory through its Indian colony. Thereafter, the British actively promoted the migration of farmers from India to Burma both directly and through private agencies where the provision of land grants was used to stimulate Indian farmers to migrate (Thompson 1947). The emergence of large-scale capitalist enterprises in the extractive and agricultural sectors which took place in the early to mid-nineteenth century for most parts of Southeast Asia came together with various regulations which allowed the migration of Chinese and In-

6 Therefore since many centuries ago, land surveying was a common activity within the administrative system of a kingdom (van Setten van der Meer 1979: 35).

7 For instance, in Central and East Java one calculation found that during periods of peace, tax levies could amount to one-sixth of the harvest whereas in war time this could amount to one-fourth (van Setten van der Meer 1979: 77-9).

8 As Reid has shown, the distinction between bondage and slave labour was not so sharply made as found in the West. There were different degrees of bondage. One could distinguish between the voluntary type of bondage (because of poverty/debt, search for merit or escape from capitation tax/corvee labour) and the involuntary type (war and conquest). The term 'slavery' could be misleading since a slave could be a debtor, dependant or subject. Slaves were never entirely under the control of their masters (Reid 1988: 132–3).

dian workers to fill the mines and plantations in different areas. In Malaya in the earlier periods when Malays were still cultivating their own plots of land with rice, the estates at first brought Chinese workers who were recruited from mainland China. However, when the supply of Chinese workers dried up, the British colonial government started to recruit Tamil workers from South India instead to work as indentured labour (Heyzer 1986: 69).

In the Sumatran plantations workers were initially obtained from mainland China. However, when recruiting Chinese workers was considered to be too expensive, labour was then provided by Javanese indentured labour (Stoler 1985: 39).[9] These workers were regulated under the Coolie Ordinance of 1880, in which labour contracts were given on the condition that workers were obliged to work for three years in exchange for a passage to Deli. These workers lived in barracks at the fringes of the plantations. A penal sanction was imposed on coolies who left work without a recognised excuse. They were the 'runaways', 'deserters' who were subject to punishment by law. Even the early mining laws enacted in the mid-nineteenth century, foresaw beating (thirty strokes with a rattan cane) as punishment for deserters (Heidhues 1992: 115). Regulations to facilitate supply of labour to the companies were concurrent with the possibility to discipline and control them, a function, which was often supplemented by the armed forces. In the Netherlands Indies an Ordinance was enacted in 1914 allowing the use of the military on civil functions 'for the preservation of public order or the maintenance of essential services in the public or private sectors'.[10]

In her chapter, Amarjit Kaur gives an overview of the development of the plantation and mining industry in Malaya and the Netherlands Indies from the nineteenth until the mid-twentieth century. She shows how government ordinances and immigration laws not only provided companies with labour but also defined which social group was allowed to enter which sectors. The entrance of Indian (Tamil) male workers into Malayan plantations, Chinese male workers (which gradually shifted to Javanese male workers) to the plantations in Sumatra and to the tin and gold mining industry in Kalimantan, Bangka, Belitung, Malaya and southern Thailand were all manifestations of careful planning but at the same time accommodations to local circumstances. Thus for instance the exclusion of other social categories, such as the Malayans from the plantations and mining sector, the

9 In late nineteenth-century Netherlands-Indies, 90 per cent of the labour force consisted of Chinese indentured labour. However both the restrictions imposed by the Chinese government and the high costs involved in maintaining Chinese workers brought a change in the labour policy of the Dutch colonial government. The supply of cheap labour was then obtained from Java, where in 1911 more than 50,000 coolies were imported from Central Java (Stoler 1985: 39).

10 See Ingleson (1986: 71). However the government at this time was relatively 'neutral', not overly reactive to labour disputes and only intervening when the situation was considered to 'get out of hand'. See also Hawkins (1971: 198).

Batak and Malays from the Sumatran plantations, were 'accidents' of history that reflected the often 'unfree' condition of workers unable to sell their labour to the companies. Kaur's chapter reminds us that the way in which labour was regulated was to a certain extent strongly coloured by the coloniser's view of different types of workers and by the stereotypes attached to certain categories of workers, which in turn stimulated racial and ethnic tensions. Taking other examples from Southeast Asia, in colonial Burma for instance the Indians were considered good for administrative posts whereas the indigenous population were the farmers (Thompson 1947: 20). In Indochina, the Annamites were considered the most industrious, the Cambodians, religious and artistic but indifferent farmers, Laotians were 'more skilful as boatmen and merchants'. It was reported that 'the Cambodians fear the aggressive and prolific Annamites and their land hunger' (Thompson 1947: 168-70). Through such illustrations one is made to ponder how these stereotypes emerged, to what extent they were based on the daily experiences of colonial rule and how the images emerged and dissipated during and after the independence struggles.

Related to this, Erman shows that in Ombilin, West Sumatra the emergence of a labour force followed a different route. Being from the beginning a monopoly of the Dutch, the exploitation of the coal mines and recruitment and control of labour was regulated by the penal sanction. Since local workers were unwilling to work in the mines, the Dutch brought in convicts and political prisoners from Java to work on the mines. Therefore the mines were known for their use of convict labour, and anyone associated with the mine was in one way or another associated with 'criminality'.

Labour policies constructed by the state not only relied on the creation of 'free labour' but were also predicated on the existence of semi-proletarianised labour.[11] Smallholder peasants were part and parcel of the large push towards capital accumulation. For instance, in Burma the British encouraged the growth of Burmese smallholder rice producers. This also occurred with the Malaysian peasantry where they were given the task of producing food crops for the rest of the population. To regulate this process land tenure laws were made to ensure the possibility of smallholder ownership (Brown 1997: 16, Stivens 1985). Encouragement and the preservation of 'independent' smallholder production can also be seen in the sugar haciendas of Pampanga, Luzon where share tenancy prevailed (Brown 1997, McCoy 1992: 115).

The emergence of small-scale production alongside large-scale enterprises, was not always the result of careful design. When around 1909 large scale rubber plan-

11 'Free' here can mean two things: a) workers are freed from various bonds of servitude, where they are 'owned' by others which means they are free to sell their labour in anyway they please; b) workers are also 'freed' from their means of production and subsistence, which means that they in the end are compelled to find other means of livelihoods to sustain their own survival.

tations emerged in Malaya, rural Malays started to take up rubber cultivation so that eventually a portion of peasant land was devoted to rubber trees, while another portion was reserved for subsistence production (Brown 1997: 17). The development of smallholder rubber cultivation caused a certain amount of resentment towards smallholder production, since this meant that with less peasants cultivating rice, there was an anxiety that this would lead to a reduction in food supplies for the workers in the tin mines (Brown 1997: 152).[12] Similarly, many Javanese indentured workers who were supposed to be repatriated to Java set up their own living quarters outside the Sumatran estate grounds. Ex-coolies living on the fringes of plantation land either purchased or rented land from the surrounding Malay or Batak villages and became the basis for a resident labour reserve for the plantations, a situation which the colonial authorities faced with much ambivalence. As Stoler pointed out, the question was 'how to make workers available when needed but not wholly dependent on estate wages during periods of slack' (Stoler 1985: 39). This ambivalence emerged from the fact that the colonial government had difficulty maintaining the balance between production levels and labour supply. The problem of supervision was greater because of the scattered locations of the settlements. This concern was reflected in the stipulations emerging in 1910 which allotted small plots of land to married workers who would live in estate 'villages' under supervision for the duration of the workers contract. However, the size of the allotments was a source of constant debate as opinions differed concerning how much was 'too much' or 'too little' to allow for the balancing of these goals

The concern of colonial regimes to regulate the movement of workers often brought them in conflict with each other or with the regime who had the authority to control the labour supply from the sending area. For instance, the supply of Chinese workers to the mines and plantations in Malaya, Netherlands Indies and Indochina was thwarted by the Chinese government when, being aware of the abuses towards coolies recruited for the mines, it pressurised both governments to guarantee decent treatment and the right to repatriate recruits. Recruiters during the Dutch period were reputed to be responsible for blatant abuses so that the Governor General of Guangdong-Guangxi used 'a combination of threats and show of force' to stop coolie trade from Macao (Heidhues 1992: 56-7).[13] As Javanese workers were seen as cheaper alternatives for the plantations, there was a move from the British in Malaya and the French in Indochina to attempt to recruit them. This plan was hindered by the colonial Dutch government, which

12 In 1921, the area of smallholder rubber in Malaya amounted to 37 per cent of total area under rubber cultivation (Brown 1997: 151-2).

13 The British colony of Hong Kong also forbade all recruitment for Bangka. However the administration in Bangka managed to contravene these policies by having coolies sign a different contract in Bangka from the one signed before embarking from Singapore (Brown 1997: 56-7)

was reluctant to grant the channelling of Javanese workers to other territories.

The shaping of labour regimes not only involved the construction of ethnic and working class formations; such formations were built upon hegemonic ideas of gender with clear distinctions between masculinity and femininity, and which, to a certain extent, were instrumental in shaping gender divisions of labour. In Sumatra, the recruitment of women in plantations and the regulations concerning where they were to work and live were embedded in notions regarding indentured labour and later on, 'the family'. Women who came to plantations were initially seen as functional for single male indentured workers. In the mid-nineteenth century debt bondage came together with prostitution and the opium trade and these were all seen as a means to keep wages down. However, rising medical costs and the increasing difficulty in stopping high labour turnover rates being felt by the early twentieth century, made management and the colonial regime later on reconsider their policy of recruiting single males (Stoler 1985).

Eventually family-based units were considered more conducive to the shaping of a stable environment for any community in the colonies, European or Asian (Stoler 1985, Thompson 1947). The shift from the single male indentured labourer to the creation of family-based workers' communities was considered preferable by the government but for many companies too costly. With changing material circumstances in many parts of Southeast Asia, family formation became more of a possibility. The Indian immigration act of 1922 stipulated that for every three males who were allowed to emigrate to Malaya two females were required. Measures were also taken to make immigration more attractive to families and this included incentives for the employment of women, differential recruiting allowances in favour of married couples, Hindu marriage legislation and the employment of women travelling inspectors (Thompson 1947: 100). Whether the settlements were based on actual kin-related family units was not as relevant as the fact that they showed some semblance of the family. In Indochina in the 1920s, for example, women workers were recruited and became the foundation upon which a semi-permanent plantation labour community was built. Individual dwellings were allotted a small garden for vegetables and these dwellings were generally occupied by 'three or four unmarried coolies, between 20 and 30 years old, and a woman who does the cooking, and who may or may not be the wife of one of them' (Murray 1992: 54).

It is within the context of the moralities concerning family life and women's and children's roles within it that the debates concerning the regulation of child labour, which is the focus of White's chapter, emerged. Underlying debates were fought out in an ideological battleground particularly in the metropole, and represented contending streams of thought regarding children and childhood, namely those that viewed children either as a threat, as victims, or as learners. White shows that in the early twentieth century Netherlands Indies government regulation was in principle very selective. In practice only certain forms of protection for child workers were enacted and for the sake of expediency, specific forms of work and places of work were excluded. The first Child Labour Ordinance, which was a much diluted version of the International Labour Organisation's 1919 convention was enacted in 1925. Debates concerning the position of child labour was conducted in the *Volksraad* (People's Council) where the native elite regularly assembled to advise on crucial issues. Afterwards it was only in post-colonial Indonesia in the 1990s that this issue came to the surface again, when non-governmental organisations, as a result of their links with international trade unions, became attentive to 'children's rights'. This chapter shows that global-local links are reflected in the way moralities originating in the West institutionally define who has the right of entry into the labour market and who needs to be protected. His analysis raises the question of the contentious nature of universalism versus particularism, of how ideas are disseminated by colonial governments and how they are adopted and rephrased by national unions. We are also left with the question as to why groups within the former colonies decide to raise this issue at particular moments in time, and why certain groups advocate prohibition of child labour while others do not.

Shifting our focus to the role of unions in labour regimes, the emergence of unions in Southeast Asia, as with many parts of the developing world, was in the early stages also a manifestation of resistance against colonial rule that in turn, prompted states to endorse 'a politics of containment'. Thus, in the early twentieth century as labour supply became more stabilised, workers started to show more overt forms of collective action at times culminating in the establishment of organised labour. Colonial governments introduced labour legislation to allow workers' participation in bargaining work agreements, albeit in a controlled form.[14] Many unions emerged when anti-imperialist ideology went in line with the desire to improve workers' lives. Strike activities were often staged in the face of rising inflation and expanding markets, and the proliferation of unions came also with occasional spells of liberalism seeping through the edifice of colonial state regimes.[15]

Government intervention into labour institutions in the post-World War II period was primarily shaped by cold war politics where the creation of non-communist federations or unions were geared not only to facilitate government control but also to obstruct the expansion of communist-affiliated unions. Since these

14 The emergence of labour inspectorates all over Southeast Asia preceded the formation of unions and labour institutions. Established initially to ensure the enactment of labour ordinances and penal sanction, these labour inspectorates became the arenas in which labour arbitration was crafted.

15 Deyo argues that labour exclusion regimes (where state intervention to exclude labour from the decision-making bodies went together with employer strategies to control labour at the workplace) *preceded* industrial transformation in all these countries (Deyo 1989).

unions usually had a strong foothold in the expanding working population, governments were eager to interfere in the balance of power between communist and non-communist unions.

With the collapse of left-wing unions in the 1950s and 1960s, there came also a rapid reconstruction of labour regimes in most of Southeast Asia. Labour reform has mainly concentrated on the procedures for labour disputes, whose form and content may often differ. Some governments prefer bipartite settlements (but prohibit industrial action before a dispute has failed to be arbitrated), some establish tripartite arrangements, and others create arbitration courts. These repressive regulations are sometimes combined with welfarist schemes. Trade unions were eventually seen not only as a symbol of workers' organisation but also of their domestication. Trade unions and workers' federations emerged under different circumstances depending on the political configuration in each country.

Within this discussion on unions and their relations with the state, the definition of labour and the regulation of labour unions have not been the prerogative of capitalist regimes only. Nørlund focuses on the changing definitions of labour and trade unions in the constitution of Vietnam. The way in which the Vietnamese Communist Party and the Vietnamese Federation of Trade Unions formulated their programme for social transformation, although rooted in the experiences of Vietnamese politics, was also influenced by the leaders' exposure to their international links. The changing emphasis on the proletariat as the vanguard of the revolution in the late 1920s, a shift in emphasis to the peasantry during the Japanese Occupation and then to the proletariat and peasantry after independence, were all caused by the exchange of a combination of local and international orientations. As Vietnam is in a period of transition again since the introduction of reforms (*Doi Moi*) in the 1980s, changes in the role of the state vis-à-vis labour can also be clearly seen. A remaining issue for research is how these changing definitions within the constitution influence labour relations and labour markets in practice.

The disparity between an institutional framework existing at the national level and its implementation in different sub-national localities is clearly outlined in Fong Yin and Kelly's chapter. Here they show that personalised and informalised power relationships in local political arenas are more significant than the institutional frameworks that exist. Such power relations become a decisive force in shaping definitions of labour and labour systems, particularly in the distinctive environment of an industrial enclave. The recruitment of 'volunteer' labour that is unpaid with the promise of future employment security reminds us of the indentured labour recruited for the colonial plantations. Fong Yin and Kelly's study looks at how labour markets and the process of labour recruitment in turn shape dispute resolution and unionisation, which are constructed primarily at the local level and through the personalised politics of the local elite, where the manipulation of traditional symbols plays an important role. They caution that an understanding of local symbolisms should avoid essentialist characterisations, which in the past have coloured Western (North American) scholarship in the Philippines. Apart from the fact that such symbolisms are often negotiated, contested and utilised in different ways, a closer examination of the labour process and the shaping of labour communities would bring us closer to an understanding of the way the construction of symbols and forms of labour relations may represent and underlie diverse forms of labour relationships.

Labour Processes: Old Forms, New Meanings

If labour regulation and legislation is often a site of struggle between state, capital and different segments of organised labour, and is a response to changing local and translocal labour markets, analysis of the causes and consequences of changing forms of the labour process in the workplace is no less problematic. Within the labour process the main foundation underlying its organisation is the question of how to convert 'labour power' (i.e. the potential of workers to work) into 'labour' (the actual work effort itself). In other words, the struggle revolves around the issue of how to make people work within the time and work content as defined by the employer. In conventional structural terms, the labour process is seen to evolve in a linear progression, i.e. from a situation where feudal ties based on 'unfree labour' (where labour may be under conditions of debt bondage, tribute or slavery) develop into wage relations based on 'free labour' where workers voluntarily sell their labour in the labour market. Others argue that labour strategies are embedded in a combination of circumstances, such as investment strategies, product markets, policies of trade unions and employers and existing labour markets. Economic units, even in the same sector, never take only one form. Although this was less so in the case of the Southeast Asian mining sector, in the plantation and industrial sectors, large modern capitalist enterprises existed side by side with smaller-scale units, which were often producing for the larger units in a subcontractual relationship, or had their own commercial relations with local traders. Therefore the use of 'semi-proletarianised' labour was often seen in capitalist agricultural and industrial enterprises. Quite often workers combine production using their own means of production with wage labour for local farms and industrial enterprises. This includes small farmers who, even since colonial times, had to combine their earnings from their land or small scale enterprise with wage labour to allow the payment of taxes and other obligations imposed on the citizens of a particular system of authority. In short, whether as part of intra-sectoral or inter-sectoral linkages, different forms of production may emerge and be maintained at the same time.

This holds true also for the different categories of labour. Even in the pre-colonial period when bondage and slave labour played a large role in the social reproduction of these kingdoms, the boundaries between and within these categories often overlapped. As Reid has shown, the degree of coercion within one type of labour relation often varied. One could distinguish between the voluntary type of bondage (because of poverty/debt, search for merit or escape from capitation tax/corvee labour) and the involuntary type (war and conquest) Also the term 'slavery' could be misleading since a slave could be a debtor, dependant or subject. Reid mentions various examples such as women who wove for their masters, men who opened up new agricultural land, worked in mining, were sailors or construction workers. Of these, many worked certain days for their master and certain days for themselves. Not unlike the large commercial enterprises that later on operated in these areas, the king left them free for half of the time to earn their own livelihood so that he could spare himself the burden of feeding this labour force (Reid 1988: 132-3). Despite the term used to describe it, 'unfree labour' did not necessarily mean total subjection.

On the other hand, the large scale recruitment of indentured labour for the plantations and mines often classified as 'free labour' was based on various forms of coercion. The Chinese immigrants who arrived in Malaya in the nineteenth century and early twentieth century came on three-year contracts. This system allowed the employer to forfeit payment until the ore gained had been smelted and sold. Sales occurred after a period of six months, which meant that workers had to find a means to live without the wages. The employer provided workers with food, which was later deducted from their wages (Loh Kok Wah 1988: 8). This is also the case with the plantation workers in Malaya and Sumatra mentioned in the previous section. Employers' strategies to control their labour in the workplace also varied. For instance in Negros, the Philippines, planters used a mix of paternalism, paramilitary control, and debt bonding to secure a permanent workforce on a labour deficit frontier in the 1880s. Living in a mono-crop province with little alternative to sugar work, hacienda owners were able to offer free housing, extremely high-interest loans, bringing workers, their children and their children's children into debt (Eviota 1992: 52, McCoy 1992: 111).

Sajor in this volume, shows us a number of seemingly contradictory processes in his study of a Philippine upland village, which he conducted in the late 1990s. On the one hand commercialisation of agriculture became a main feature of the village economy. However, two factors contributed to the shape of the commercial economy that emerged. The process of land fragmentation was arrested by the particular nature of the inheritance system, which followed the rule of primogeniture (where the eldest child should inherit the family land) therefore the younger children had to seek their fortunes elsewhere. Secondly, reciprocal labour in crop cultivation was much more common than wage labour. Therefore this case illustrates the fact that 'traditional' customs considered as constraints to the functioning of the market have been retained. He argues that this contradicts the view which reigned in the 1980s which held that the 'decomposition' of rural areas, i.e. full proletarianisation, is needed for the full development of capitalist production (see Friedman 1980: 163). Sajor's argument is similar to that made by the Alexanders in their chapter on labour relations in the furniture industry of Java, as will be discussed further below. The study of reciprocity and labour exchange is a terrain that deserves much attention, particularly in the present period. Since such a phenomenon is often linked with 'traditional' forms of relationship, its existence is often interpreted as symbolising the traditional nature of the society involved, with its linked characteristics assumed to be constitutive of traditional societies.

The disjuncture between ideological constructions and actual practice and how this is created both as intended and unintended consequences of capitalist penetration can be seen in Resurrección's chapter. This study is also based on research in an upland village in the Philippines. Unlike Sajor's study village, the presence of modern capitalism was physically more distinct, with the introduction of a sawmill company in the area. Available forest land was utilised for logging activities. Access to land, which previously was based on communal rights, where men and women had complementary roles in agricultural work, became the prerogative of men after commercial logging increasingly dominated the local scene. The classical account of women being marginalised with the entry of large capital seems to hold true in this upland village. Cash income and sedentary rice agriculture were associated more with male work. Despite the fact that women were active in paddy rice farming and petty trade, they were still, however, associated with swidden farming. This demonstrates that swidden farming, as a former social activity reproduces social identities, which occurs via symbolically mediated, norm-governed social practices, with implications for familial relations. This study raises the issue of how these women themselves view and experience such constructions, and how they are confined within such constructions or manage to manipulate them for their own purpose.

Within labour studies there is growing awareness of the importance of examining the role of familial relations within and also outside the workplace. In the past, caste, kinship and religious loyalties of workers were considered insurmountable obstacles to the growth of class consciousness and that as far as these primordial ties were still in operation, class consciousness would not develop. On the other hand, other scholars have shown how family and neighbourhood became sources of solidarity for the development of collective action and the emergence of class consciousness. As Kwan Lee has shown in her study of women workers in East Asia, the culture of familialism allowed smoother implementation of labour control among management but on the other hand promoted accommodation to women's family-based identities through company policies. In other words, management considered family problems to be legitimate reasons for emergency leave. In turn, women workers took care to police themselves and not abuse managerial tolerance (Kwan Lee 1998: 128–30).

Paul and Jennifer Alexander follow along a similar vein, arguing that the persistence of locally owned small businesses cannot be equated with an industry that is 'backward' or 'traditional' but should be seen as part and parcel of the growth of a newly-industrialising nation. Their study examines how the furniture industry operates through a series of production chains forming an intricate web of interlinked workshops, each producing a limited range of components, and each having to keep track of their own overlapping orders and cash flows. They show how such production relationships function through culturally specific relations of reciprocity, which are not in themselves clearly defined entities, but are continuously redefined and adjusted to changing circumstances. The reworking of kinship metaphors, a state-induced policy that appropriated local kinship terms and applied them in employer-labour relations, is beneficial to the process of capital accumulation. It is suggested that the identification of small scale industries with household economies would lead to a misinterpretation of the functioning of these enterprises, as family members are seldom involved in the running of the enterprise.

In contrast to the Alexanders, Wad focuses on the politics of unions in a large scale industry, i.e. the automobile industry. He explores the dynamics of industrial relations behind the trend towards decentralisation of union organisation in the Malaysian auto industry. As with unions in many other developing countries with strong state regimes, in Malaysia, after a period of relatively strong unionisation in the auto industry which reached its peak in the 1940s and 1950s, the post-independence period saw a gradual strengthening of state control over union activity, the declining role of centralised unions and a decrease in union density. The introduction of the enterprise union came together with this process. Instead of providing a simplistic and deterministic picture, Wad shows a complex web of negotiations, contention and political conflicts in the process of restructuring. These dynamics are placed within the ambiguities of increasing awareness of national identity on the one hand, and a deep immersion in the global economy on the other. Wad's argument brings up a range of questions concerning the desirable forms of union organisations and their functioning within modern capitalist structures.

Although previous authors on trade unions have tended to draw a sharp line between 'political' and 'economic' unions, Wad's analysis reminds us of the need to examine the interlinkages between the organised and unorganised, the politically sanctioned unions and those working outside state endorsement, in understanding the operations of trade unions. It must not be forgotten that only a small percentage of workers are incorporated in unions. Thus for instance even in the Asian Newly Industrialising Countries in 1990-1991, union membership only reached 33, 24, 19 and 17 per cent of total non-agricultural employees in Taiwan, Korea, Hong Kong and Singapore respectively (Frenkel 1993: 311). The percentage would be even lower in the other countries of Southeast Asia. This has to do not only with the ability of unions to attract lower echelons of workers, but reveals also the structure of industries in most Asian countries. The right to form unions, independent or otherwise, is usually based on a minimum number of workers within one enterprise. In many Asian countries, although economic growth may be driven by large, capital-intensive enterprises, the majority of enterprises are small, employing less than 30 workers. Such a situation forces us to question what roles unions can play in bringing about political and economic improvement to workers. This condition is exacerbated by the high degree of subcontracting relations between large factories – workshops and homeworkers, or the common recruitment of casual labour which is now evident not only in the 'traditional' domestic industries but also in the modern export-oriented ones.

Labour Mobility and Work Transformations

A glance into Southeast Asian history reveals that labour mobility has been an inherent feature of daily life. Pre-colonial and colonial regimes have always been involved in regulating the movement of people or in spreading out the population in frontier settlements whether to fill the labour needs for development projects; or as part of state formation and creation of loyal subjects (Reed 1990). At the same time as has been discussed above the movement of labour has often been unregulated, with state subjects and those on the fringes of state rule intentionally or unintentionally eluding the immediate dictates of state authorities. Not only those who practise shifting agriculture but also cultivators of relatively permanent settlements situated within the parameters of a given state would quite often be on the move because of a combination of factors: the desire to flee from heavy burdens, political conflict and warfare, and subsistence crises which they experience regularly (Reed 1990, Taylor and Turton 1988).

The bulk of the literature on migration has attempted to distinguish different motivations, structural features and conditions under which migration occurs, whether collectively or individually; and the economic impact of migration, whether in areas of destination or in areas of origin. Conventional migration literature sees the migration process as primarily an economic phenomenon, i.e. the interplay between factors 'pushing' individual migrants from the sending community and factors 'pulling' individuals toward their destination. Such an approach has however, been much criticised, since factors such as political constellations and struggles, social networks, changing perceptions and identities of race, gender and ethnicity are equally important in understanding why, how and under what conditions people migrate (Basch et al. 1994).

In the nineteenth century, as Kaur in her chapter has shown, it was primarily the Chinese, Indian and Javanese who filled the slots in the plantation and mining areas. However, although these groups may carry certain ethnic identities, how these identities are redefined and constructed depends on the specific political constellations both at their places of origin and places of destination. For instance, as Mackie explains, overseas Chinese have borne different identities: in some areas they become western colonial subjects, in others they are loyal citizens of the adopted countries, revolutionary communities or modern multinational capitalists. The possibility of the overseas Chinese being integrated in their new places of residence or to take up citizenship, an issue which was evidently very much debated in various Southeast Asian countries from the 1950s onwards, was not taken up in the colonial period or the period prior to that, except in the Philippines and Thailand (Mackie 1996). Similarly, resentment towards a particular immigrant group by the host community is not necessarily an inherent feature of race relations in multi-racial populations, but may alternately emerge or submerge, depending on local circumstances. In the early twentieth century, when the British colonial state actively promoted the entry of Indians to fill segments of the Burmese labour market, initially there was no competition between the two racial groups. The Indians were in the industrial, commercial and administrative sectors as well as providing seasonal labour during peak agricultural seasons. However, the rise of a landless Burmese proletariat created by various land grants appropriated by the British state, increased the resentment of the Burmese peasantry towards Indians in the country, culminating in the riots of 1938 (Thompson 1947: 20–5).[16]

In looking at patterns of migration, Huang, Yeoh and Jackson remind us it is no longer the case that people migrate from 'the periphery' to 'the centres', nor necessarily from areas with a labour surplus to those with a labour shortage. Definitions of periphery and centre have changed throughout history, not only as assumptions of which countries are central or peripheral are being redefined, but also as the criteria forming such definitions are questioned. The history of transnational migration has shown that where previously it was the South Asians and East Asians who used to migrate in large numbers to different parts of the world during the colonial period,[17] it is currently the Southeast Asians, particularly the Filipinos and Thais who predominate in transnational migration. Also

16 About 2.6 million Indians migrated to Burma between 1852 and 1937; by 1931 10 per cent of lower Burma's population was Indian (Elson 1997: 159).

17 In nineteenth-century Burma for instance the opening of the Burma delta in the south stimulated the immigration of poor, young, male peasants (sometimes seasonal labour) from upper Bur-

classifying a country as either a sending or receiving country may be misleading as those that used to receive migrants may later on become major senders of migrants, or they may receive migrants at the same time as send migrants out. Examples of the latter are for instance, Thailand, which receives migrants from Cambodia, Burma, Laos and Vietnam but at the same time sends its nationals to Taiwan, Europe and the United States. Similarly Malaysia, receives migrants from Indonesia, Sri Lanka and the Philippines, but at the same time sends out workers to the Middle East or to East Asia (Battistella and Paganoni 1996, Chin 1998, Chantavanich et al. 2001, Wille and Passl 2001). In a wider context, Sassen has shown that migrants take jobs in both declining and expanding industries therefore undermining the assumption that migrants flow only to expanding economies (Sassen 1994). Who or which social group fills which kinds of jobs and how different social groups are associated strongly with what kinds of skills and attributes, is also a shifting and contested process.

The meaning of social networks has often been understated in migration studies. It has also been argued that different forms of social networks have mediated the movement of different types of labour, shaped different patterns of migration, and allowed different trajectories of the movement of individuals and groups. Elmhirst's chapter shows networks can be both constraining and enabling factors for individual migrants where gender and age play a large role in how they position themselves vis-à-vis these networks. It is through such 'spider-web' networks that migrants' lives are lived simultaneously within two or more nation-states, where the flows of material goods and information on labour markets and jobs occur and are embedded in equally complex power relations (Basch et al. 1994). How workers have participated in the shaping of their destinies and the cultural and political consequences of migrant labour movements cannot be seen separately from these networks (Bates 2001: 8).

As a growing number of studies have concentrated on such networks a debate has emerged concerning the concept of borders and territories. Spatial borders are created through the process of political struggle and whether these borders have separated nation-states, different economic zones or different ethnic groups, they have experienced distinctive shifts throughout history. In this process the making of boundaries becomes an important conceptual tool. As Wallman has argued, boundaries have separating as well as integrating dimensions. This means that the redefinition of boundaries has to do with the reconstruction of identities but also with what one does with these identities for political or economic gain (Wallman 1978).

ma's dry zone. In 1901, 10 per cent of lower Burma's 4.1 million population was made up of people born in upper Burma (Elson 1997: 160).

Therefore an understanding of processes of labour migration should take into account a complexity of factors, the dynamics of which may change over time. The chapters in this section underline these complexities in different ways. Arghiros, Rigg and Oudin directly or indirectly define the concept of labour mobility in two ways: spatial mobility (or migration), and sectoral mobility which may or may not involve spatial mobility. Arghiros argues that the 'push-pull' framework does not help us to understand the dynamics of state structures and capital requisites. Focusing on the rise and fall of the brick industry in Thailand, he examines the changing categories of labour entering the industry following structural shifts in the economy. In the early period of its development the brick industry competed with the agricultural sector in obtaining its labour. Local labour for the brick industry was available during the agricultural slack season. With an increased integration of local economies with national and international markets, both the brick industry and the agricultural sector experienced a boom, resulting in increased competition for labour and an insuffiency of local labour markets. Labour for the brick industry was then obtained through the recruitment of migrants from the north east of Thailand. However, when export-oriented factories started to appear in the vicinity, even this supply of migrant labour started to dry up as the brick industry had to compete with factories for workers. Labour was then obtained from outside Thai borders, namely from Burma and Cambodia. Although the Thai government initially opened the borders to these foreign migrants, with the monetary crisis in the mid 1990s preference for employment of Thai nationals pushed the government to close its borders to foreign migrants, resulting in a the shift in their status to illegal migrants.

The changing nature of labour markets and local economies has affected the nature of work within the brick industry. In times of labour shortage, employers have adopted a number of strategies, such as changes in work regimes, the introduction of mechanisation and the manipulation of local rituals and symbols. In turn workers have also tended to work in groups, conducting negotiations collectively rather than individually. Since the link with global and national economies has been highly uneven, the impact of the monetary crisis has varied significantly. Some export industries have fared better than others. Whilst the agricultural sector expanded because of an increase in rice exports, the brick industry has collapsed because of the decline of the construction sector with the reduced spending of the urban middle class and the private sector on building or house constructions. The crisis has affected different segments of the population differently, but this in turn cannot be analysed separately from preceding forms of labour markets and regimes.

Focusing on different parts of Thailand, Rigg underlines the conditions that Arghiros has illustrated. However, he emphasises the tensions between the agricultural and non-agricultural sector in looking at rural labour markets. Multiple factors underlie the movement of labour out of agriculture, namely the mechanisation of wet-rice agriculture, competition between non-farm and farm work, and for certain layers of the rural community, the abandonment of land as rural communities are increasingly incorporated into the wider economy and land is no longer the main basis for survival or accumulation. Rigg also brings up a number of interesting points, namely, that the household is considered an important component in terms of remittances and the wish of migrant workers to settle back in their natal villages. The community and family are no longer space-bound units, and although migrants have moved out of the village, social networks maintain community and family ties, which support household economies but also the finding of jobs. He argues also that the 'culture of modernity' should not be underestimated in defining the choices men and women make when searching for employment opportunities.

Complementing Arghiros and Rigg, Oudin looks at changes in labour markets and recruitment in the state and non-state sectors after the reform (*Doi Moi*) period in Vietnam. He shows that the transformation of labour relations is accompanied by the distribution of human resources by gender, educational level and industries. However, changes occurring after the reform cannot be understood without understanding the trajectory of socialism in Vietnam, and Vietnamese politics vis-à-vis neighbouring countries. When in 1976 the north and south became integrated, the wealthy areas in the south were also integrated into the collectivisation process. Private land ownership was abolished, private trade prohibited, and state enterprises managed the economy through the co-operatives. In the first ten years, attempts to stimulate rural areas were manifested in resettlement of urban refugees in rural areas, and redistribution of land to families. Because of these policies the increase in the labour force (partly due to increase of the working-age population) was initially absorbed in agriculture in the rural areas. However, in the following ten years the absorption capacity of agriculture has decreased and there has been a marked movement of the younger generation into non-farm occupations upon finishing school.

These changes have partly been due to the inability of the state sector to prevent and regulate the emergence of non-agricultural occupations. Oudin argues that one must not ignore the fact that collectivisation even prior to the reform period was never fully functioning.[18] Own-account workers existed at the same time as the prohibition of private trade. Even though they were not operating under free market conditions but under the control of state enterprises, segmentation of the labour market already existed prior to the liberalisation of the economy. More recently those who remained in the state sector have been better educated

18 That socialist regimes, as capitalist ones, never could entirely control the direction of their economic policies has often been argued by scholars. See for instance Rigg (1997: 20-2)

and male workers, while those who were absorbed in the agricultural and non-state sector were the less educated and in particular, women workers.

Focusing more on labour mobility as a transnational phenomenon, Huang, Yeoh and Jackson point out that globalisation has not destroyed the importance of localities and geography but has created new definitions of localities. They underline the contradiction of barrier control, i.e. although trade barriers are being removed, barriers restricting the free movement of people remain. They distinguish between different types of migrants, through their different degrees of legality defined by whether the migrants themselves, their agencies or their types of work are legal/illegal. The disjuncture between how the general public views the phenomenon of female migration overseas and how the families themselves experience the migration of their family members is a question that this study invites. Indeed if we deconstruct the 'public' into state officials and politicians or civil society, it would be interesting how these views change, are contested and under what conditions they change. The authors also examine how the gender component of overseas domestic workers, and the origin and destination areas of migrants have shifted throughout the history of Philippine transnational migration. This underlines the transitory nature of social categories, patterns of migration and the social consequences of migration. Finally, they stress the need to look not only at structural explanations for migration but also at the perceptions, motivations and needs of the migrants and their families.

Reproducing Workers: The Boundaries of Community

Since the 1970s and 1980s, feminist scholarship has contributed significantly to our theoretical understanding of the links between home and work, between family and work relations and how relations of production, class consciousness and solidarity among workers cannot be understood without a knowledge of the dynamics of the different spheres and how they are interrelated. Feminists have elaborated further the concept of reproduction as a critique of existing scholarship which looked solely at social relations in economistic terms and placed too great an emphasis on the forces of production (Harris and Young 1981: 111). They particularly emphasised the different levels on which conditions are created

19 The distinction was made between social reproduction, the reproduction of labour and biological reproduction. To recapitulate, social reproduction refers to the systemic continuity of production meaning the cycle of production-circulation-consumption-production; the reproduction of labour refers to 'the reproduction of adequately socialised, adequately nourished labour [...] which is the condition of existence for the reproduction of any social system'; biological reproduction refers to the production of children which feeds into the demographic balance of the labouring population. See Harris and Young (1981: 111-3).

to allow the continuation and maintenance of particular forms of production (Chatterjee 1995).[19]

Our discussion above, has suggested that family formation, domestic life and sexual relations are all part and parcel of state formation and productive life, whether in capitalist or socialist configurations. As we have seen, the recruitment of labour hinged on whether or not one was married; the ability to increase one's mobility was also largely dependent on the existence or non-existence of familial links. Therefore family and work were two inseparable units, the relationship of which is important to understand. As one scholar put it 'devising a family recruitment policy was premised on the belief that the presence of women and children would "stabilise" men and prevent new male migrants from "absconding" back to their [...] homelands'.

Labour studies have also been enriched by the study of community and workplace, and examining how they are interrelated. Community here may be defined in terms of a spatially defined social entity or that of a socially constructed unit that may not be based on a particular territory. The latter has been much under scrutiny within flows of transnational migrants, where those sharing particular ethnic and religious backgrounds are defined as members of a community bound together within a common distinctive identity (Basch et al. 1994: 33).

Although demarcations of community may be generated by the larger society, or the state, the constructions of such boundaries have a definite effect on the identities of members of that community. But to understand how these constructions are negotiated and contested one has to look at the workings of power within these communities. Since women are usually the bearers and reproducers of their families and family membership is an important criteria for community membership, they are directly concerned with either ensuring the maintenance of their community, or using its social support networks to guarantee the reproduction of themselves and their families. This means also looking at the interplay of gender, class and kinship in shaping the social structure of the community.

Many studies have shown how social networks may both constrain and enable individual enhancement and agency. In other words, social networks may ensure the attainment of jobs; maintain certain levels of security (through) reciprocal obligations as well as expectations of support. In the negative sense social networks may imply 'kinship obligations' (Smith 1978: 106). Kin-based networks may also place certain moral restrictions to the movement of particularly young unmarried women.

Couched within the framework of an enclave society created by Dutch colonial rule, in Erman's chapter 'community' is placed within clearly defined spatial boundaries. However, the changing gender, ethnic and class composition of the Ombilin mining community in Sumatra is a reflection of the changing policies of the Dutch colonial state and the exigencies of global markets. Here, the mining community was first populated by single men, like the plantations in Kaur's chapter: specifically Javanese convicts and contract workers whose maintenance and reproduction became the responsibility of the state company. Whether by company design or not, women, who were brought by the company as prostitutes to provide sexual services to these men, became a source of conflict between workers, underlining the weakness of class-based solidarity. In the first decades of the twentieth century in conjunction with the emergence of left-wing political parties and trade unions, strikes became a familiar phenomenon in the mining scene. Partly in response to this a family formation policy was introduced and women came either as wives or as workers. The company's main policy was to recruit free labourers with families and create a mining community. It was expected that establishing a mining community would favourably affect reproduction of future generations of labourers. Within this, women played a variety of roles, namely as worker, as wife, as entertainer, thus underlining the diversity of the category 'woman'. When labour organisations and political parties started to appear on the scene, some of these women became also politically involved in the women's wing of such organisations.

Elmhirst, focusing on present day industrial labour in Indonesia looks at migrant networks that link young female factory workers who work in Tangerang, near Jakarta with their home villages in Lampung, South Sumatra. In contrast to Erman, Elmhirst views communities, although originating from particular territories, as social entities unrestricted by territorial boundaries. She focuses on how ethnic identities are constructed through the creation of institutionalised social networks, demarcating a boundary between Lampungese migrants and 'other' workers, and maintaining a common origin-based identity among these migrants. She refuses to view these communities as 'either-or' entities where the networks either constrain or stimulate workers' consciousness and activism, preferring to focus more on how identities are shaped and community links maintained, with specific consequences for labour activism. An ability to fall back on parental contributions of rice meant women were able to risk unemployment by engaging in labour protests. However, in the context of severe drought and depleted harvests, the direction of support among young women from North Lampung was from city to village, engendering a strong sense among factory migrants that they should avoid actions that might jeopardise their jobs.

Both contributions give us some reflection on the relationship between women, their communities and the political struggles they do/do not engage in. The women in the mining community illustrated by Erman remind us not only of the changing policies of labour and family formation but also of the diverse experiences of different categories of women. For those working in the mine and for the wives of male workers, their politics seem to coincide with that of the men. Women were not only important in helping to alleviate the economic difficulties of the household, but also in defining the forms of their husband's political participation. However, it would be interesting to pursue further the underlying tensions women experience when endorsing the politics of the 'male breadwinner', when their interests may not necessarily always coincide with those of their husbands. The experience of the Lampungese migrant workers examined by Elmhirst provokes questions regarding those seemingly marginal instances when daughters do leave their network's control. What happens when enough poor households who have been cut off from the right to cultivate land are able to create a disjuncture in patron-client relations? Can those who try to use the state ideology to counter the strictures of local custom manage to introduce a different sphere of influence?[20] Such processes would certainly not come as a sudden onslaught but are built on the small instances that may become recurrent in conditions of change. Would this lead to a clear disintegration of the moral order of kin-based networks or would there be a 'reinvention' and reformulation of tradition which might benefit different groups of women?

At the same time feminist scholars have reminded us of the need for caution in looking for action that can be coined as 'resistance'. The domination versus resistance binary is currently being challenged since actions are saturated with 'ambivalences and ambiguities which emerge from the intricate webs of articulations and disarticulations that always exist between dominant and dominated' (Ortner 1995: 120). Or as Fernandes has argued, 'on the one hand, the struggle of women workers simply to survive cannot be adequately conceptualised in terms of the category of resistance. On the other, women workers interpret their labour as a means to provide a better future for their children [...] This imagined future and this investment in children prevent us from reducing women workers' practices to an individualistic form of survival. They do not perceive their labour as merely serving the needs of capitalism or patriarchy even while they are acutely aware of the implications and effects of such larger structures' (Fernandes 1997: 157). Thus we should neither romanticise resistance (Abu-Lughod 1990) nor present women as passive victims of structures of oppression (Mohanty 1991).

Conclusion

This book examines the complexities of global processes as they interact with and are also shaped through localities. Although it cannot be denied that an array of 'global' processes has swept over many parts of Southeast Asia, generating signifi-

20 In a case study on the networks of Minangkabau women in West Sumatra, Blackwood (2000) has used the terms 'the logic of commodification' in looking at the forces of production and 'the logic of relatedness' in referring to the forces of familial networks.

cant transformation in the lives and structures of labouring communities, we argue that global-local articulations involve a multitude of factors which are historically contingent. The first section of this book focuses on how different states have dealt with 'the labour question'. Such interventions were not just colonial inventions but have occurred prior to the colonial experience. Much has been written on the imposition of colonial rule on local hierarchies and feudal structures. Reference to the pre-colonial reminds us that existing local structures play a significant role in shaping systems of surplus extraction and labour regimes in subsequent periods. The examples provided above hint at the rich collection of studies examining different forms of production system in these pre-colonial monarchies and also those living on the fringes of centralised state control, namely in the uplands, forest areas and borderlands. Policies aimed at regulating labour frequently constitute contradictory processes and generate ambivalent effects. These may be due to conflicting state interests, where the need to extract local surpluses may come up against the necessity to provide a 'human face', legitimising state rule. Rather than assuming a monolithic position of the state in relation to society, we should sensitise ourselves to conflicting interests within the state and how this often manifests itself in contradictory policies. In the same way, 'capital' should also be seen as consisting of different fragments where the interests of one may collide with the other. As is dealt with more elaborately in the chapters, the need for labour, and the timing of when and which types of labour are needed may often generate tensions between different fractions of capital. Where the state decides to position itself vis-à-vis these different interests is also subject to historical circumstances. Important in the discussion is the fact that state design may often not have the intended results. The persistence or emergence of semi-proletarianised labour, the escalation of undocumented workers, the growth of prostitution, gambling and opium or the drug trade, may both be a curse and blessing seen from the eyes of the state apparatus. When initially these were and could be instruments for state control and capital accumulation, under different circumstance they also could diminish capital reserves and endanger administrative and political control.

Moving away (or moving down) from the discussion of state regulation and labour policy, the labour process itself has often been seen as the crux of the production system and labour relations. Yet an understanding of the labour process cannot be framed in evolutionary terms, neither can it be separated from the exigencies of the labour market nor of state policies. Again, multiple forms of workplace relations may emerge within a given historical conjuncture. The co-existence of different types of labour and labour relations may be the result of a combination of factors. Such a situation complicates both the task of researchers but also policies to improve workers' conditions. Existing legislation and also union policy, usually take into account workers who are employed permanently or on a long-term basis and exclude other categories. Where in the West, the history of the labour movement has been characterised by the struggle for a family wage, in most Third World countries, and Southeast Asia in particular, the individual wage is more typical and political struggles have been carried out to fight for a minimum individual wage. After agreements are reached, legalised by labour contracts or collective labour agreements, workers still have to struggle for the actual implementation of such agreements. Other forms of wage relations, such as contract, piece-rate and casual labour are still marginal to such struggles. There has been much research done on how ethnic and gender identities are constructed in the formation of national identities. As various chapters in this collection suggest, how ethnic and gender identities interact with the politics of labour is still much neglected in Southeast Asian labour studies and requires further attention.

Migration studies in Southeast Asia have significantly enriched the understanding of transnational and intra-national labour mobility. Indeed the movement of labour is an age-old phenomenon. Yet most studies have attempted to explain such phenomena only in terms of labour shortage and labour surplus. The motivation to move from one place to another, or to shift from one type of work to another may stem from different interests. The degree of proletarianisation and availability of other sources of livelihoods are but a few of the reasons. Images of certain ways of life, redefinitions of one's identity and the increasing need to be able to cater to modern consumption needs of different members of the family are other factors that may interact with the need for physical reproduction.

Critical studies on labour mobility nowadays prefer to examine the whole range of social phenomena which shape the conditions under which workers move or take up new occupations, life styles and identities. Cultural constructions of particular types of skills, ethnic groups, men or women workers, or particular nationalities contain their own histories but are also liable to change as circumstances also change. Many issues still intrigue us when we consider the complexities of migration processes. Most studies on migration focus either on internal migration or international migration and very few attempt to look at the links between the two. Such an approach invites contributions by those studying social networks in migration studies: how workers' experiences and identities change or are strengthened when crossing borders dividing nation-states should be compared with what happens to those who remain within such boundaries. Thus far, cross-border migration literature has tended to overlook internal migration (rural-rural or rural-urban). There is much to be gained by sharing conceptual frameworks and looking at the linkages between the two types of mobility, particularly as state boundaries are becoming both more variable in some cases and inflexible in others, and as new forms of 'internal' boundary emerge within countries.

Studies of the politics of labour have in the past concentrated on workplace relations and workers' consciousness, focusing on issues such as under what circumstances such consciousness emerges and how it is shaped in the workplace. The existence of solidarities and consciousness operating outside the parameters of class were considered as hindrances to the shaping of class consciousness. More recently, local ethnographies of labouring communities have directed attention towards the construction of communities based either on residential solidarities, on ethnic or religious affiliations, or on kin-based networks, and the intermeshing of class with other social groupings. This linkage between cultural studies and labour studies has provided us with the tools to look beyond the material and class dimensions of labour relations. Yet at the same time our knowledge of the role of symbols and the creation of multiple and negotiated identities should not lead us to overlook the political economy of surplus extraction and accumulation of capital with labour as a valuable means of production, particularly as material and political inequalities grow ever more apparent in Southeast Asia (Dragsbaek Schmidt et al. 1998).

The gendered dimension of the shaping of labour communities, particularly in the scholarship of Southeast Asia is still very limited. Particularly when we are now starting to break the dichotomies of the public and private sphere, women and men must be seen as mediating household and work, or community and workplace in different ways. Communities and kinship networks are closely bound, and women are often the bearers of community and kin relations. The chapters in the last section remind us also of the need to transgress boundaries of space and time. Interestingly if one chapter shows the relatively 'timeless' nature of social networks as these are maintained and constructed to preserve community loyalties and allegiances, the other chapter looks at how a territorially-bound community may change over time as the composition of the workers change. Both studies indicate that as we move towards integrating the analysis of work and community, we should also understand that the dimensions of space and time bring a more insightful comprehension to the workings of class, gender and ethnicity. The contributions to this volume help us to reflect on the complexities of labour relations and remind us of the need for more research on Southeast Asian labour that is able to offer a robust analytical framework for addressing the issues confronting workers in the context of capitalist expansion and crisis.

References

Abu-Lughod, L. (1990) 'The romance of resistance: tracing transformation of power through Bedouin women', *American Ethnologist* 17: 41–55.

Basch, L., Schiller, N.G. and Blanc, C.S. (1994) *Nations Unbound: Transnational Projects, Postcolonial Predicaments and Deterritorialized Nation-States*, Basel: Gordon and Breach.

Battistella, G. and Paganoni, A. (1996) *Asian Women in Migration*, Quezon City: Scalabrini Migration Center.

Bates, C. (2001) 'Introduction: community and identity among South Asians in dispora', in C. Bates (ed.) *Community, Empire and Migration,* London: Palgrave.

Bernstein, H., Johnson, H. and Thomas, A. (1992) 'Labour regimes and social change under colonialism', in T. Allen and A. Thomas (eds.) *Poverty and Development in the 1990s,* Milton Keynes and Oxford: Open University Press and Oxford University Press.

Blackwood, E. (2000) *Webs of Power: Women, Kin and Community in a Sumatran Village,* Lanham: Rowman and Littlefield Publishers.

Boomgaard, P. and Brown, I. (2000) *Weathering the Storm: The Economics of South East Asia in the 1930s Depression*, Leiden and Singapore: KITLV Press & ISEAS.

Bourdieu, P. (1980) *The Logic of Practice*, Cambridge: Polity Press.

Brown, I. (1997) *Economic Change in South-East Asia, c.1830-1980*, Oxford: Oxford University Press.

Chandavarkar, R. (1997) '"The making of the working class": E.P. Thompson and Indian History', *History Workshop Journal* 43: 177–196.

Chatterjee, P. (1995) '"Secure this excellent class of labour": gender and race in labor recruitment for British Indian tea plantations', *Bulletin of Concerned Asian Scholars* 27, 3: 43–56.

Cheater, A. (1986) *Social Anthropology: An Alternative Introduction*, London: Routledge.

Chin, C.B.N.(1998) *In Service and Servitude: Foreign Female Domestic Workers and the Malaysian 'Modernity' Project'*. New York, Columbia University.

Clancy-Smith, J. and Gouda, F. (1998) *Domesticating the Empire: Race, Gender and Family Life in French and Dutch Colonialism,* Charlottesville: University Press of Virginia.

Cooper, F. (1996) *Decolonization and African Society: The Labor Question in French and British Africa*, Cambridge: Cambridge University Press.

Cooper, F., Isaacman, A.F., Mallon, F.E., Roseberry, W. and Stern, S.J. (eds.) (1993) *Confronting Historical Paradigms: Peasants, Labor, and the Capitalist World System in Africa and Latin America*, Madison: University of Wisconsin Press.

Cooper, F. and Stoler, A.L. (eds.) (1997) *Tensions of Empire: Colonial Cultures in a Bourgeois World*, Berkeley: University of California Press.

Deyo, F. (1989) *Beneath the Miracle: Labour Subordination in the New Asian Industrialism,* Berkeley: University of California Press.

Dragsbaek Schmidt, J., Hersch, J. and Fold, N. (1998) 'Changing realities of social transition in Southeast Asia', in J. Dragsbaek Schmidt, J. Hersch and N. Fold (eds.) *Social Change in Southeast Asia*, London: Addison Wesley Longman.

Elson, R.E. (1994) *Village Java Under the Cultivation System, 1830-1870*, Sydney: ASAA and Allen and Unwin.

Elson, R.E. (1997) *The End of the Peasantry in Southeast Asia: A Social and Economic History of Peasant Livelihood, 1800-1990s*, London: Macmillan.

Eviota, E.U. (1992) *The Political Economy of Gender: Women and the Sexual Division of Labour in the Philippines*, London: Zed Books.

Fernandes, L. (1997) *Producing Workers: The Politics of Gender, Class and Culture in the Calcutta Jute Mills*, Philadelphia: University of Pennsylvania Press.

Frenkel, S. (1993) 'Variations in patterns of trade unionism: a synthesis', in S. Frenkel (ed.) *Organized Labor in the Asia Pacific Region*, Ithaca: ILR Press.

Friedman, H. (1980) 'Household production and the national economy: concepts for the analysis of agrarian transformations', *Journal of Peasant Studies* 7: 158–184.

Furnivall, J. (1939) *Netherlands India. A Study of Plural Economy: A Sociological Approach,* Cambridge: Cambridge University Press.

Geertz, C. (1967) 'Social change and economic modernization in two Indonesian towns: a case in point', in G. Dalton (ed.) *Tribal and Peasant Economies: Readings in Economic Anthropology,* Austin: University of Texas Press.

Harris, O. and Young, K. (1981) 'Engendered structures: some problems in the analysis of reproduction', in J.S.Kahn and J.R. Llobera (eds.) *The Anthropology of Pre-Capitalist Societies*, London: Macmillan.

Hart, G.,Turton, A. and White, B.(1989) *Agrarian Transformations: Local Processes and the State in Southeast Asia.* Berkeley, University of California Press.

Hawkins, E. (1971) 'Labor in developing countries: Indonesia', in B. Glassburner (ed.) *The Economy of Indonesia,* Ithaca: Cornell University Press.

Heidhues, M.S. (1992) *Bangka Tin and Mentok Pepper. Chinese Settlement on an Indonesian Island: Social Issues on Southeast Asia*, Singapore: Institute of Southeast Asian Studies.

Heyzer, N. (1986) *Working Women in South-East Asia: Development, Subordination and Emancipation,* Milton Keynes: Open University Press.

ILO (1998) 'Report of the High-Level Meeting on Social Responses to the Financial Crisis in East and South-East Asian Countries', GB.272/4, Geneva: International Labour Organisation.

Ingleson, J. (1986) *In Search of Justice: Workers and Unions in Colonial Java, 1908-1926*, Singapore: Oxford University Press.

Jameson, F. (1998) 'Notes on globalization as a philosophical issue', in F. Jameson and M. Miyoshi Jameson (eds.) *The Cultures of Globalization*, Durham and London: Duke University Press.

Kwan Lee, C. (1998) *Gender and the South China Miracle: Two Worlds of Factory Women*, Berkeley: University of California Press.

Locher-Scholten, E. (1987) 'Female labour in twentieth century Java: European notions-Indonesian practice', in E. Locher-Scholten and A. Niehof (eds.) *Indonesian Women in Focus: Past and Present Notions,* Dordrecht: Foris Publications.

Loh Kok Wah, F. (1988) *Beyond The Tin Mines: Coolies, Squatters and New Villagers in the Kinta Valley, Malaysia, c. 1880-1980,* Singapore: Oxford University Press.

Mackie, J.A.C. (1996) 'Introduction', in Reid, A. (ed.) *Sojourners and Settlers: Histories of Southeast Asia and the Chinese,* St. Leonard: Allen and Unwin.

McCoy, A.W. (1992) 'Sugar barons: formation of a native planter class in the colonial Philippines', in V.E. Daniel, H. Bernstein and T. Brass (eds.) *Plantations, Proletarians and Peasants in Colonial Asia*, London: Frank Cass.

McLeod, R.H. and Garnaut, R. (eds.) (1998) *East Asia in Crisis: From Being a Miracle to Needing One?* London: Routledge.

McMichael, P. (1996) *Development and Social Change: A Global Perspective,* London: Sage Publications.

Mohanty, C. (1991) 'Under Western eyes', in A. Russo, C. Mohanty and L. Torres (eds.) *Third World Women and the Politics of Feminism*, Bloomington: Indiana University Press.

Murray, M.J. (1992) '"White Gold" or "White Blood"?: The rubber plantations of colonial Indochina, 1910–1940', in V.E. Daniel, H. Bernstein and T. Brass (eds.) *Plantations, Proletarians and Peasants in Colonial Asia*, London: Frank Cass.

Ortner, S. (1995) 'Resistance and the problem of ethnographic refusal', *Comparative Studies in Society and History* 3: 173–193.

Pinches, M. (ed.) (1999) *Culture and Privilege in Capitalist Asia*, London: Routledge.

Reed, R.R. (ed.) (1990) 'Patterns of Migration in Southeast Asia', Berkeley: Center for South and Southeast Asia Studies, Occasional Paper no. 16.

Reid, A. (1988) *Southeast Asia in the Age of Commerce, 1450-1680: The Lands Below the Winds*, Volume One, New Haven: Yale University Press.

Rigg, J. (1997) *Southeast Asia: The Human Landscape of Modernization and Development*, London: Routledge.
Rodan, G., Hewison, K. and Robison, R. (eds.) (2001) *The Political Economy of Southeast Asia: Conflicts, Crises and Change*, Oxford: Oxford University Press, second edition.
Sahlins, M. (1974) *Stone-Age Economics*, London: Tavistock.
Sarkar, S. (2000) 'The decline of the subaltern in *Subaltern Studies*', in V. Chaturvedi (ed.) *Mapping Subaltern Studies and the Postcolonial*, London: Verso.
Sassen, S. (1994) *Cities in a World Economy*, California: Pine Forge Press.
Smith, J.E. (1978) 'Our own kind: family and community networks', *Radical History Review* 17: 99–120.
Steinberg, M. (1991) 'Talkin' class: discourse, ideology and their roles in class conflict', in S.G. McNall, R.F. Levine and R. Fantasia (eds.) *Bringing Class Back In: Contemporary and Historical Perspectives*, Boulder: Westview Press.
Stivens, M. (1985) 'The fate of women's land rights: gender, matriliny and capitalism in Rembau, Negri Sembilan, Malaysia', in H. Afshar (ed.) *Women, Work and Ideology in the Third World*, London: Tavistock Publications.
Stolcke, V. (1988) *Coffee Planters, Workers and Wives: Class Conflict and Gender Relations on Sao Paulo Plantations, 1850-1980*, London: Macmillan Press.
Stoler, A. (1985) *Capitalism and Confrontation in Sumatra's Plantation Belt, 1870-1979*, New Haven: Yale University Press.
— (1995) *Race and the Education of Desire*, Durham: Duke University Press.
Strange, S. (1996) *The Retreat of the State: The Diffusion of Power in the World Economy*, Cambridge: Cambridge University Press.
Tarling, N. (1992a) *Cambridge History of Southeast Asia: From c.1800 to the 1930s*, Vol. Three, Cambridge: Cambridge University Press.
— (1992b) *Cambridge History of Southeast Asia: From World War II to the Present*, Cambridge: Cambridge University Press.
Taylor, J. and Turton, A. (eds.) (1988) *Sociology of 'Developing Societies'*, London: Macmillan Education.
Therborn, G. (1983) 'Why some classes are more successful than others', *New Left Review* 138: 37–55.
Thompson, V. (1947) *Labor Problems in Southeast Asia*, New Haven: Yale University Press.
van Niel, R. (1990) 'The legacy of the cultivation system for subsequent economic development', in A. Booth, W.J. O'Malley and A. Weidemann (eds.) *Indonesian Economic History in the Dutch Colonial Era*, New Haven: Yale University Southeast Asia Studies.
van Setten van der Meer, N.C. (1979) *Sawah Cultivation in Ancient Java: Aspects of Development During the Indo-Javanese Period, 5th to 15th Century*, Canberra: Australian National University Press.
Wallman, S. (1978) 'The boundaries of "race": processes of ethnicity in England', *Man* 13, 2: 200–217.
Wille, C. and Passl, B., (eds.) (2001) *Female Labour Migration in South-East Asia: Change and Continuity*, Bangkok: Asian Research Center for Migration.
World Bank (1998) *Social Impact of the East Asian Crisis*, Draft January 1999, Washington D.C.: The World Bank.

2

Labour Dynamics in the Plantation and Mining Sectors in Southeast Asia, 1840–1950: A Historical Perspective

AMARJIT KAUR

The ability to organise the production of goods and services has been an integral factor in the evolution of social and political structures in Southeast Asia. The social order rested on the personal authority of the ruler and customary obligations to the state. Since the availability and control of labour formed the basis of a state's wealth there were several forms of servitude, which persisted in Southeast Asian societies until the late nineteenth and early twentieth centuries.

Starting from about 1840, the peripheral economies of Southeast Asia were linked more directly to the economies of Europe and the United States. This 'imperial-led' globalisation, trade, and capital flows from Europe, and migration, principally from China and India, resulted in commodity specialisation and the international division of labour. More importantly, it led to equally dramatic labour transformations and the emergence of a wage labour force in Southeast Asia.

The region therefore provides important insights into the development of wage labour in the context of capitalist production. Three outstanding historical features were associated with wage labour. The first was the recruitment of migrant workers, principally from China and India on a contract basis, to labour on the mines, plantations, and in urban occupations. The vast majority of these migrants were regarded as sojourners and were not expected to remain on completion of their contracts. The second was the design of an ethnic division of labour maintained by the use of political and economic mechanisms. This resulted in labour differentiation along ethnic and occupational lines. The third was the emergence of a gendered division of labour, both in the domestic and commercial spheres, as the region became more integrated into international trade.

This paper examines labour transformations in Southeast Asia in the context of the global market place. The focus is on how transnational economic processes

Political and Economic Structures in Early Nineteenth-Century Southeast Asia

In contrast to India and China, one of the most important characteristics of Southeast Asian demographic history before 1750 was a low population density. According to one scholar, population growth in the seventeenth and eighteenth centuries did not exceed 0.2 per cent (Reid 1987: 35). This was primarily due to the effects of war as a check on fertility and not so much through direct loss of life. War campaign losses were relatively small due to the type of weapons used but principally because the aim of warfare was to capture populations (mainly male) as slaves and captives. Generally, settlement and production in Southeast Asia prior to the nineteenth century can be roughly divided into two regions: the long settled, relatively densely populated areas and the sparsely populated areas. In the first category were mainland regions based on the major river valleys of the Irrawaddy, Chao Phraya, Mekong, and the Hong (Red) rivers. Here wet rice cultivation had resulted in sedentary population groupings and civilisations centred on the river valleys. In the second category, populations were generally smaller and were located mainly along the coasts with relatively less suitable land for extensive agriculture. These were also the maritime regions (with the exception of volcanic-soil rich Java). In both categories, there were sparsely populated upland regions. States in Southeast Asia were 'informal, impermanent, personal [...] and prey to contestation [...]' (Elson 1992: 131-2). Political and social organisation were diffused and decentralised and the bulk of Southeast Asians lived in subsistence-oriented rural communities or in fishing villages.

Three main features determined the character of production relations during this period. First, lower population densities in Southeast Asia compared to other regions meant that control of people was more important than control of land. Second, society was organised along vertically shaped personal relationships with inherent superior and inferior roles. The patron-client and bondage systems played a key role in the mobilisation of labour before the advent of high colonialism. Third, wage labour developed relatively late in Southeast Asia. In most societies, whether Muslim, Christian, or animist, manual labour was synonymous with servility and people were reluctant to carry out manual tasks for persons other than their legitimate 'patrons' or 'lords.' The principal sources of wage labour were Chinese settlers or Indian sailors, though the Dutch East India Company often employed indigenous people on a casual basis, for example.

Increasing western intrusion and the demand for unskilled labour resulted in a transformation of existing labour relations. Although the abolition of slavery had its origins in European consciousness, slavery also declined due to gradual changes in the nature of Southeast Asian society. These included impoverishment and the inability to maintain slave retinues; the advance of Christianity and Islam in the region which tended to 'restrict the scope of slavery' and the 'rise in power of the absolutist states' (Reid 1993: 69-71). In all regions, slavery's demise 'was much a result of legislation [...] than of changing social and political realities [...]' (Elson 1992: 175). As slave trading and some varieties of forced labour were gradually eliminated, 'disguised' forms of corvée or unpaid labour were still prevalent, particularly in Java. The *cultuurstelsel* (cultivation system) introduced by the Dutch colonial government represented the most systematic form of exploitation of labour. During the period 1830-60, Javanese peasants were required to produce export crops designated by the Dutch. These crops included coffee, sugar, and indigo, which were delivered to the Dutch officials in Java at very low cost, enabling the Javanese sugar industry to compete with slave labour-produced sugar from the West Indies (Ricklefs 1981, Elson 1984, Van Niel 1992). The Dutch claimed the labour of the Javanese as a sovereign right. Forced labour was also utilised by the colonial state for a myriad of public works, including the construction and maintenance of roads, bridges, canals, and the construction of houses etc. Reliance on this form of labour was gradually decreased as the cultivation system was dismantled in stages, beginning with the least profitable crops. Alongside obligated labour or corvée, colonial governments also relied on convict labour. For example, the British colonial authorities in the Straits Settlements relied on convict labour transported from India to carry out public works in these settlements. Another source of unpaid labour comprised short-term minor offenders who were sentenced to work on a variety of public projects (Kaur 1994). Thus the underlying issue within the labour process was the problem of how to convert the inhabitants' potential to work.

The International Economy, 1840-1914

The period from around 1840 to 1914 saw the spread of the industrial system in Europe and North America and the integration of world markets. An important element in this globalisation process was the acquisition of colonies in Asia and Africa by European powers. The process began around 1850 and climaxed between 1870 and 1914. Great Britain annexed Lower Burma in 1852 and by the 1880s had taken over all of Burma. From the Straits Settlements (acquired between 1786 to 1824), Britain also brought the Malay states under formal control between 1874 and 1914. Indochina came under the French. In the Indies, the Dutch extended their control over the islands of the 'Indonesian' archipelago while the United States took over the Philippines from the Spaniards in 1898. Thailand remained outside formal colonial rule but the Thai state acceded to free trade demands from Britain and other western countries.

Thus a new political order was created in Southeast Asia which resulted in new economic structures, the creation of new primary production centers, and the international division of labour. The colonial states 'forcibly' integrated their Southeast Asian colonies into the international economy through transfers of capital and labour and later commodities. While capital was of European origin, migrants were drawn from neighbouring regions to meet the demand for labour, especially in the case of Malaya, Sumatra, Sabah, Sarawak, Burma, and Thailand.

The creation of new states represented new departures within the regions. The new states had precisely delineated boundaries; an internal dynamic which possessed a permanency that indigenous states had lacked; a new style of administration and institutional structures to oversee the various aspects of government; and an intensity in governance not hitherto experienced in these states.

First, the formation of a global market shaped by the needs of the industrial economies generated an accelerated demand for Southeast Asian primary commodities, particularly those associated with industrial processing and manufacturing.

Second, lowered freight rates associated with technological changes in transportation dramatically lowered the costs of long distance bulk transportation and the opening of new transport routes facilitated the movement of these commodities to Europe and the United States.

Third, falling transport costs were reinforced by a simultaneous liberalisation of trade policy which was initiated by Great Britain. Indeed, it has been argued that British hegemony during this period was responsible for the rise in late nineteenth century liberalism that saw commodity prices across the world converging.

Fourth, just as migration from Europe to the New World had an enormous impact on the global economy, so too did migration from China and India have an impact on the Southeast Asian states. This migration swelled the labour force of most of the colonies and led to their increased importance in the world economy. More significantly, it resulted in a dramatic transformation of labour relations and a shift to wage labour.

Fifth, capital too flowed from Europe as never before. Prior to the 1840s, small-scale Chinese capital dominated, especially in the tin-mining industry. But now European and British savings in the form of portfolio investment financed plantations, mines, and in some areas, transportation lines. Although the proportion of this capital flow to Asia was relatively small in comparison to capital flows into the New World, it filled a vacuum in the region. For example, British overseas investment during 1907-13 to 'other empires i.e. China, and Japan totalled £50 million or about 18 per cent of the total share of investment' (O'Rourke and Williamson 1999: 211).

These transformations affected labour processes in three main ways. First, the colonial powers brought a wholly new approach to the ownership and usage of land. Ultimate control was vested in the State and legal systems of tenure developed that granted prescribed rights. This led to the introduction of new food and industrial crops associated with industrial production in Europe. The commodification of land also affected the dynamics of large-scale mining and commercial agriculture in the region. Consequently, property rights in land became more important than property rights over persons impacting not only on the indigenous people but also on the migrant communities.

Second, the extension of European control over the two great Asian population centres, India and China, had two implications for overcoming the labour shortage created by the abolition of slavery through the empire-wide sourcing of labour. One, there was a switch in the sourcing of the labour supply from Africa to Asia, and two, there was a switch in the form of labour from unfree to indentured labour.

Third, the development of rail and road networks, and the growth of cities to service the export sector created a demand for an urban labour force to carry out administrative, technical, and other tasks. These urban workers had many characteristics in common with agricultural and mining workers. Moreover, the construction of modern transportation facilities (railways, roads) facilitated the transfer and movement of labour from the ports to the interior. As transport connections were extended, labour mobility also increased.

Migration Flows and the International Division of Labour

Although migration into the region was not new, this new migration between 1840–1914 was different. It involved two other groups in the migration process apart from the migrants. These were the private labour brokers and other parties who organised travel arrangements and employment, and state officials. The process also involved the setting up of labour depots (warehouses) and earmarking funds for migration. Three migration networks are associated with the labour diaspora in Southeast Asia. These were the Chinese, Indian, and Javanese networks and the recruitment of workers from China, India, and Java facilitated a rather elastic use of the migrant labour force.

The workers who came through these networks had many characteristics in common. First, they were young, unskilled adult males. Second, they emigrated as individuals, carrying both high labour force participation rates and low dependency burdens with them. Three, they comprised mainly illiterate peasants who had spent hardly any time away from their village roots. Four, they were regarded as sojourners, to be repatriated when the demand for their services no longer existed. Fifth, the diversified recruitment policy adopted by colonial regimes meant that migrant labour could be manipulated easily.

All these factors ensured that the workers (with the exception of the Javanese in Malaya and Sumatra) were not easily assimilated nor readily accepted by the local inhabitants. They were transported into alien surroundings where their language, religion, and cultural norms kept them apart, a process that was 'pushed' by the colonial authorities in pursuit of a 'divide and rule' policy. This helps to explain the legacy of ethnic divisions and fragmented visions in the post-colonial era.

Table 2.1: Migration to and from Southeast Asia, 1880-1939

Annual Averages	Migration Flows (x 1000)			1900–19 as % of 1920 population
	1880–99	1900–19	1920-39	
Burma				
Arrivals	122	268	333	
Departures	93	232	300	
Net migration	29	36	33	0.2
Thailand				
Arrivals	22*	84	122	
Departures	12*	64	87	
Net migration	10*	21	35	0.2
Malaysia / Singapore				
Arrivals	153	244	300	
Departures	56	85	214	
Net migration	97	159	86	4.9
Indonesia				
Arrivals	7	41	38	0.1
Philippines				
Arrivals	9	15	13	
Departures	7	2	8	
Net migration	2	13	5	0.1
Indochina				
Arrivals			62	
Departures			46	
Net migration			16	0.0

Note: *Chinese migrants only.
Source: Personal communication – Pierre van der Eng.

Two important points may be noted about Chinese migration which comprised the largest migration stream. First, although until the 1890s there were periodical bans on emigration by the Chinese government, there was nevertheless a constant flow of emigrants, especially during periods of droughts, floods, and natural calamities. Consequently, estimates of the numbers of migrants embarking at ports along the South China Sea coast in this period must be viewed with caution. Second, there was a high incidence of 'repeated' or circular migration.

Although at the receiving end colonial administrators kept fairly reliable records of immigration, repeated migrations tend to make the data unreliable. In the case of Indian migrants, from the late 1830s the British authorities in India regulated all assisted migration. Furthermore, the Indians went to two main countries – Burma and Malaya – and the census identification of the Indian population was considerably more straightforward since few of them moved outside their community, unlike the Chinese. Migration flows to and from Southeast Asia for the period 1880–1939 is shown in Table 2.1.

Migrant workers were typically associated with the growth of enclaves of capitalist production – mining, plantation agriculture, and urban occupations. In Burma, they worked as agricultural labourers in rice cultivation. The first two enclaves were often located in remote areas and although the labourers were voluntary migrants, the use of the indenture contract in reality restricted mobility and prevented the free operation of market forces. Consequently, migrants who worked on plantations or mines were basically 'unfree.'

Labour Dynamics in the Mining Sector

As early as the eighteenth century, Southeast Asian rulers had encouraged the migration of groups of Chinese workers as one means of offsetting the labour shortage in their territories. The Chinese pioneered tin and gold mining in Kalimantan, Bangka and Belitung (Indonesia), Malaya, and southern Thailand. A number of factors account for this situation. First, the traditional farming technologies and communal organisation, coupled with an aptitude for hard work, certainly helped the success of Chinese migrants. For example, the 'primitive' types of drainage and washing techniques used in the Chinese operated tin mines could be organised on a similar basis as that already familiar in rice technology (such as the bucket-chain), with the miners gathered in a *kongsi* (business cooperative) as a virtually self-contained unit. Also significant was the influence of Chinese 'clans' or societies, which often organised and controlled migration, and facilitated such matters as the provision of capital.

From the start, Chinese mining labour recruitment, whether for the tin fields of Bangka and Belitung, southern Thailand or the western Malay States (see Figure 2.1), was essentially a personal system of recruitment, reflecting varying recruitment networks. Workers bound for Malaya, Indonesia, and Thailand were initially recruited through the only channel of the Straits Settlements (mainly Singapore) where British firms and *Baba* (*peranakan*) Chinese coolie brokers handled the trade. Their networks extended from Singapore to the South China port cities and even to the home towns of the Chinese sub-brokers.

This system of indirect recruitment later gave way to a direct recruitment policy whereby coolie foremen and middlemen, such as Chinese officials closely associated with the mines, were entrusted with the job. In Indonesia, Dutch recruiting firms entered the labour market in the early twentieth century to ensure that the recruiting business was not monopolised by the Chinese. This was concomitant with the recruitment of people from different regions and the breaking down of traditional bonds of kinship and brotherhood.

The new immigrants (*sinkheh*) were transported under the credit-ticket system and were held on arrival in Singapore. The coolie brokers, who also functioned as agents for the prospective employers in the new lands, organised employment for the migrants whereby these employers settled the *sinkheh*'s travel costs or obtained their labour by way of an advance on wages. Subsequently, the indentured worker was bound by a contract to serve for a specified period – usually three years – until the debt incurred by him was paid off to his employer. In effect this meant that the employer had a contractual obligation on the *sinkheh*'s services for the specified period. The transaction was conducted between broker and prospective employer with the worker usually unaware of his employer, place, or conditions of work. He was not allowed to change employers until he had repaid his steamer-passage ticket or allowance. This meant that employers exercised a strong control over their employees that amounted to *de facto* property rights, rather than the customary rights over person, for example, to extract labour (corvée) in many Southeast Asian societies.

Mining was organised through the *kongsi*. The *kongsi* was a business co-operative or an association of miners who carried out the commercial working of a mine under a fairly 'democratic' system where leaders were elected. The *kongsi* was a resilient organisation in a frontier society, based on bonds of brotherhood and partnership in economic activity. The isolation of the tin mines from settlement areas or towns meant that the *kongsi* had to provide a multiplicity of ancillary services needed by the workers (and their dependents).

The *kongsi* also provided an institutional framework with which new arrivals were inducted. More significantly, it allowed mining operations to continue unhampered by the fluidity of workers. The *kongsi* thus offered a sense of security and identity – it relied on a variety of mechanisms including a personal recruit-

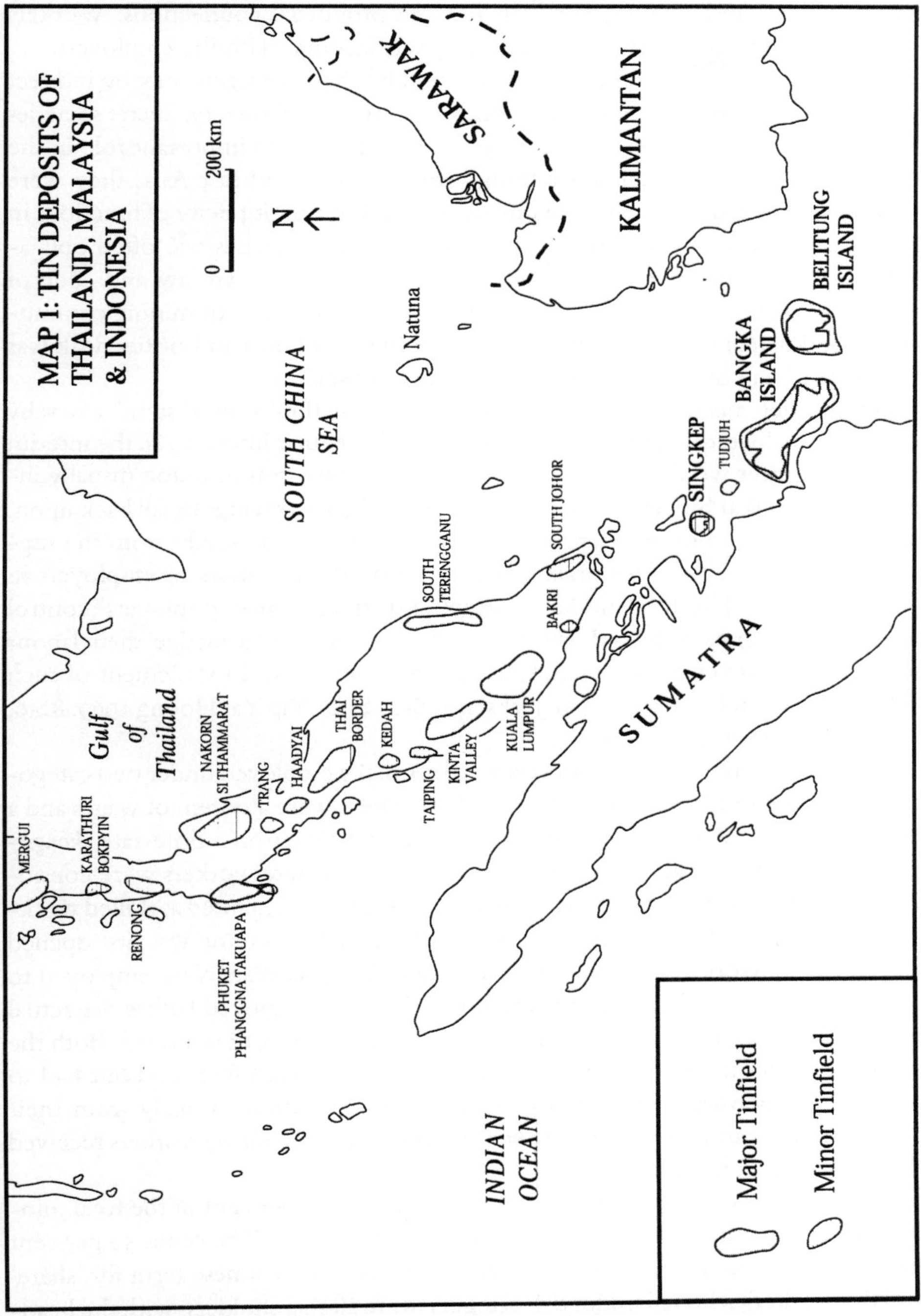

Figure 2.1: Map of Tin Deposits of Thailand, Malaysia and Indonesia

ment system, kinship links, and clan ties and provincial connections. Workers were essentially locked into a 'dependency relationship' with the employers.

In the frontier areas, workers could be held by their contracts only by indirect social controls. An important social control was the secret society. Secret societies had emerged in China on a quasi-religious basis to play an important role in the resistance against the Manchu (Ching) Dynasty. In Southeast Asia, they were transformed into quasi-welfare organisations serving a multiplicity of functions in the uncertain frontier society. Membership of secret societies was often obligatory – the society offered protection and established its own law and code of conduct while receiving complete loyalty from the workers. In mining communities the *Kapitan Cina* (mine head) with whom the colonial authorities dealt was usually the head of the most powerful local secret society.

Yet another means of indirect social control was the 'truck system' whereby workers usually received their wages at long and irregular intervals. In the interim period a worker would be advanced items for personal consumption (usually including opium) at higher than usual prices. As he had no savings to fall back upon, he had no choice but to meet his needs by taking items on credit from the supplier-cum-mine boss. This practice often bound the labourers to employers in perpetual debt. The revenue farm system also strengthened employers' control over labour. Once indebted, the labourers were forced to pledge their labour service to the revenue farmer (in this case the mine boss) in settlement of such debts (Wong Lin Ken 1965: 43–9, Jackson 1969: 42–52, Yip Yat Hoong 1969: 82–6, Heidhues 1992: 8–12, 71–81).

In terms of remuneration, workers were normally employed under two categories in the late nineteenth century in Malaya. These were a system of wages and a tribute system. Wage-earning labourers were paid either on a time-rate (*kongsi-kung*) or on a piece rate (*naik chiang*) basis. The piece-rate workers were considered unskilled workers while the time rate workers were regarded as skilled workers. *Kongsi-kung* labourers were usually employed when a mine was first opened and normally worked a seven-hour day. *Naik chiang* workers were employed to remove the overburden of earth which had first to be removed before the actual mining was carried out. They were paid by the *chiang* of earth removed. Both the *kongsi-kung* labourers and the *naik chiang* workers received free food but had to purchase their own opium, tobacco, and other provisions, usually from their employer. In contrast to the *kongsi-kung* workers, the *naik chiang* workers received their wages on a monthly basis.

This category of wage workers represented about 50 per cent of the total mining labour force in Malaya in the early twentieth century. The other 50 per cent worked under the tribute (or *hun*) system. *Hun* was the Chinese term for 'share' and the workers who fell under this category were all shareholders, with the headman usually holding two or three shares in contrast to the single share held by a worker. Workers under this system received no fixed wages but were entitled to a share of the mining enterprise's profits. There was also a division of labour based on gender. Women workers were usually employed as *dulang* washers (or panners). *Dulang* washing was essentially a method of recovery rather than a mining method and the workers were considered marginal miners, who sold the tin to the tin ore dealers.

Chinese dominance in tin-mining, whether in Bangka, southern Thailand, or the western Malay States, was largely due to the fact that, until the first decade of the twentieth century, technological conditions favoured Chinese mining methods and the Chinese organisation of mining and labour. Between 1900 and 1913, the number of Chinese workers employed in the tin mining industry in the Federated Malay States (FMS) was estimated to be about 200,000. In 1913, the Chinese workers totalled 200,000 out of a total of 225,405 mining workers (Yip Yat Hoong 1969: 79–82, 30–1). Employment by ethnic group in the tin mining sector in Malaya is provided in Table 2.2 below.

Table 2.2: Employment in Tin Mining in Malaya, by Ethnic Group, 1911, 1931–65 (annual average)

Quinquennial Average	*Chinese*		*Indian*		*Malay*		*Others*		
	No	% of total	No	% of total	No	% of total	No	% of total	Total
1911	189,100	96.2	4,630	2.4	2,580	1.3	210	0.1	196,520
1931-5	44,530	85.1	5,130	9.8	2,270	4.3	430	0.8	52,360
1936-40[a]	61,310	81.3	9,420	12.5	4,010	5.3	650	0.9	75,390
1941-5	n.a.	-	n.a.	-	n.a.	-	n.a.	-	n.a.
1946-50	30,980	68.5	6,660	14.7	6,690	14.8	880	2.0	45,210
1951-5	n.a.	-	n.a.	-	n.a.	-	n.a.	-	41,350
1956-60	n.a.	-	n.a.	-	n.a.	-	n.a.	-	30,443
1961-5[b]	26,700	60.9	5,060	11.5	11,470	26.2	610	1.4	43,840

Notes:

[a] Average for three years, 1936–8; the figures for other years are not available.

[b] Average for two years, 1962 and 1964.

Source: Yip Yat Hoong (1969: table V-19, p. 384).

In Thailand, tin mining was overwhelmingly in the hands of the Chinese. Phuket, the richest mining area (it produced nearly 80 per cent of the tin mined in Thailand) had a Chinese population of over 40,000 in 1884, most of whom worked in the mines (Skinner 1957).

Detailed statistics on the ethnic background of workers in the tin mining industry in Indonesia (Bangka, Belitung and Singkep) are not available. Nevertheless, the mining labour on Bangka and Belitung was almost exclusively Chinese (See Table 2.3).

Table 2.3: Indonesia, Total Labour Employed in Tin Production 1866-1938

Period	Bangka Average No.	Belitung Average No.	Average Total	Singkep % of Chinese	Indonesian
1866-70	7,787	2,747			
71-75	7,951	4,323			
76-80	8,023	4,094			
81-85	7,224	5,175			
86-90	8,099	7,507	n.a.		
91-95	10,695	8,600	n.a.		
1896-1900	14,088	7,815	n.a.		
1901-05	12,581	8,473	n.a.	647	n.a.
1906-10	17,514	12,679	n.a.	1172	n.a.
1911-15	21,209	14,919	n.a.	752	n.a.
1916-20	18,830	16,353	n.a.	478	n.a.
1921-25	18,784	19,582	n.a.	612	n.a.
1926-30	19,004	18,407	1,305	n.a.	n.a.
End of year					
1931	16,366	15,514	975	544	431
1932	9,473	9,712	621	314	307
1933	3,932	3,855	402	210	192
1934	5,300	3,143	645	300	345
1935	6,529	3,664	853	386	467
1936	9,325	6,568	1613	914	699
1937	14,625	8,360	1732	n.a.	n.a.
1938	12,638	7,134	2321	n.a.	n.a.

Note: Often different sources give different figures without stating whether these are annual averages, end of production year or end of financial year figures.

Source: *Koloniaal Verslag* (*Colonial Report*) annually 1866-1929; *Indisch Verslag* (*Indian Report*) annually 1930-1938.

As is shown in table 2.4 below, these three countries (Malaya, Indonesia, and Thailand) accounted for 59 per cent of total tin produced in 1913; 60.2 per cent in 1922; 59.9 per cent in 1929; and 64.3 per cent in 1937. In Malaya, tin was the largest commodity export earner until the 1920s, giving way to rubber in the 1930s. In Indonesia, tin also represented an important export earner – it was the third largest export earner until 1900 (after sugar and coffee) and was also displaced by rubber.

Table 2.4: World Tin Production in 1913, 1922, 1929 and 1937

	1913		*1922*		*1929*		*1937*	
Producing Countries	*Tons*	*%*	*Tons*	*%*	*Tons*	*%*	*Tons*	*%*
Malaya	51,377	38.4	37,226	30.4	69,366	36.1	777,542	37.3
Nigeria	3,872	2.9	5,123	4.1	10,734	5.6	10,468	5.0
Bolivia	25,939	19.4	27,685	22.6	46,338	24.1	25,024	12.0
Indonesia	20,921	15.6	29,532	24.1	35,920	18.6	39,825	19.1
Thailand	6,748	5.0	6,979	5.7	9,939	5.2	16,494	7.9
Others	24,943	18.7	16,055	13.1	20,303	10.4	38,847	18.7
TOTAL	133,800	100.0	122,600	100.0	192,600	100	208,200	100

Note: These production figures differ slightly from those given in later statistical year books prepared by the International Tin Study Group.
Source: *International Tin Research and Development Council, Statistical Year Book, 1939*, cited in Yip Yat Hoong (1969: 276).

As the Southeast Asian countries became increasingly integrated into international trade, western technology and global capital shifted the new and more productive mines beyond the small-scale diggings of the earlier period.

The entrepreneurial role of the miners also shifted from those who toiled to others who capitalised technology and organised labour systems. Consequently, as the miners were forced to change and adapt, their toil was now seen as a cost to be minimised by both employers and colonial states which now competed with one another to keep wages low in order to influence investment decisions.

In Malaya, the credit-ticket system of indentured labour recruitment was abolished in Perak in 1894, and in 1895 in Selangor and Negeri Sembilan. It was replaced in the Labour Code 1895 by written contracts for specified periods. In 1881, 36.7 per cent of Chinese immigrants arriving at Singapore and Penang had their fares paid by their employers; by 1890, the percentage had dropped to 10.9 per cent.

Whether in Bangka and Belitung, the Malay States, or Thailand, employers increasingly turned to the system of private recruitment whereby trusted foremen or employees were sent back to China to recruit fellow villagers and kinsmen who came nominally as 'free labourers' but were obligated to their employers.

To summarise, 'cheap' Chinese labour enabled Chinese-owned mines to produce at low cost, making less labour-intensive techniques uncompetitive. The banning of secret societies, the exhaustion of known accessible surface deposits, and the increased demand for labour led to a lessening of the control over the workers, exercised by *kongsi* leaders.

This 'freeing' of labour especially followed in the wake of the ban on the importation of Chinese indentured labour in 1914, the passing of control of the industry to western capital and technology and the decline of the *kongsi* system (Yip Yat Hoong 1969: 70). Coincidentally, the rise of protectionism after World War I also saw the passing of control of the industry to western capital and technology.

Labour Dynamics in the Plantation Sector

The trade in minerals formed an important component in regional specialisation, but the spread of plantation crops had a far bigger impact, both in terms of the commodities produced and labour specialisation. The plantation system involved the insertion of cash crops into what had been predominantly subsistence agriculture. Plantations represented tree or related crops planted and cultivated systematically for cash purposes. The most important of these plantation crops were rubber, coffee, oil palm, tobacco, sugar cane, and coconut and they made substantial contributions to the gross domestic product and export earnings of Malaya, Indonesia, Thailand, and the Philippines.

The rapid expansion of plantation production in Southeast Asia was a direct consequence of the expansion of the international economy, especially the growth of the automobile industry in the United States, incentives provided by the colonial states such as cheap land, infrastructure, and above all the availability of low-wage labour. This plantation labour was predominantly of South Indian (Malaya), Chinese (Malaya, Sumatra, North Borneo, Sarawak), Javanese (Sumatra, Sarawak, North Borneo and Malaya), and Vietnamese origin (Vietnam and Cambodia).

The state was the most important single factor in structuring labour use/mobilizing labour, especially in Indonesia, Malaya, Sabah, and Sarawak. The entire process of labour market functioning and organisation was regulated through legislation, recruitment systems, and migration policies which served largely to protect capitalist interests and maintain work force fragmentation. Plantation labour regimes were based on two important considerations. The first was the mobilisation of a largely migrant labour force which facilitated the use of economic and extra-economic means to maintain low wage bills. The second was an ethnic differentiation of labour that permitted the state to manipulate both workers and wages. Migrant workers were treated like disposable commodities who were subjected to medical and 'political' screening. For example, all migrant workers in Malaya underwent a comprehensive medical examination in migration depots or special immigration camps. In Indochina, 'the Sûreté became involved in [the worker health] screening process in order to weed out workers deemed politically undesirable and potential trouble-makers' (Murray 1992: 52). Immigration controls were also used in Malaya to deport Chinese or Indian 'labour activists' and 'trouble-makers.' An important instrument for control of workers was the indentured labour contract system. The indenture contract was usually a written one, but verbal agreements (especially in the case of Chinese workers) were quite common. Many migrants signed these contracts in ignorance of employment terms or under coercion. Breaches of written contracts were regarded as criminal, not civil offences.

Three principles underlay colonial labour policy. The first was the provision of a limited amount of protection for workers. This was accomplished mainly through the establishment of labour departments, labour inspectorates, and for the Chinese, Chinese Protectorates which also functioned as 'screening bodies' to identify trouble-makers. The role of these three agencies centred on the supervision of migration principally to satisfy governments of sending countries and to conduct comprehensive medical examinations of workers. Workers were housed in depots or migration centres manned by security guards and kept in 'quarantine' until they were deemed healthy to be transported to their place of employment. Moreover, all places of employment were subject to periodical checks by health inspectors. This ensured that records were maintained for sending countries and at the same time 'infectious diseases' were kept in check.

The second principle was the establishment of working conditions and wage rates in consultation with employer associations. These employer associations emerged in the early stages of the expansion of capitalist production and aimed at dealing with labour issues, namely, how to keep wages low; to block worker protest and action; to regulate competition among employers by fixing wages; and to act as a lobby group. The wage rates invariably favoured employers. In times of depressed economic conditions, wage rates were lowered and workers assisted to return to their place of origin. However, in times of economic upturn, wages were restored but rarely raised. Moreover, the maintenance of a divided labour force, hired on the basis of ethnicity, permitted employers to pay differential wage rates based on a worker's ethnicity. This precluded any co-operation among workers for a united stand on wage bargaining and fixing. Employers were also allowed to hire replacement workers in the event of a strike, thus reducing effective collective action by workers.

The third principle underlying labour policy, which permitted intermediaries to maintain social control over the workers, effectively ensured worker docility and discipline. Thus the 'free' and 'unfettered' labour contract was nullified by the hold of *kanganis, maistries* and the Vietnam *cais* over the workers. This 'hold' was based on kinship links, village ties, the debt relationship, and 'power' relations. Moreover, at the next level in the administrative hierarchy, the European supervisors had at their disposal an extensive system of fines that invariably led to wage deductions. Physical punishment for infractions and violations of mining or plantation rules was also common. Plantations and mines were in remote areas, and workers were isolated from contact with the outside world. They thus lived in enclaves or 'micro-societies' with strict hierarchical divisions. Their lives and accommodation contrasted sharply with those of the management, but the fear of losing their livelihood and housing kept workers 'captive' to the dictates of capital.

The State and Processes of Recruitment of South Indian Plantation Labour in Malaya

For a variety of reasons European planters preferred South Indians. Chinese workers could only be hired through contractors and were relatively 'expensive' to employ. South Indians (Tamils) were cheaper, and could be recruited easily because India was under the same imperial government. Equally, India's proximity to Malaya and Burma was an additional consideration. Tamil labour was also preferred because it was considered docile and fitted well into the dependent relationship between management and employee. The dominant motive of the European plantation owners was to retain the greatest degree of control possible over the work force. However, the South Indians lacked funds to migrate spontaneously and there were more attractive opportunities in other British colonies that offered higher wages, better living conditions and a greater chance of landing as free men. Consequently, from the start, the recruitment of Indian labour was both regulated and sponsored by the colonial administration. South Indian plantation labour was hired either as 'assisted' or 'unassisted' labour. Under the category of 'assisted,' there were two types of recruitment systems – indenture and *kangani*. Indenture was more important in the sugar cane plantations in the first half of the nineteenth century. It gave way to *kangani* – assisted labour in the coffee plantations in the second half of the century and in turn was replaced by 'unassisted' labour. In rubber plantations, all three types of recruitment systems were utilised by planters.

Under the indenture system of recruitment, immigrants could be recruited through either labour recruitment firms in India or through agents sent to South India to recruit labourers directly. The agents advanced money to persons wanting to emigrate to Malaya and other colonies. The advance was conditional on the intending migrants signing a contract. They were then deemed to be under 'indenture' to their employer for a fixed period, varying from three to five years. They could not change either employer or place of employment. When their period of indenture was completed they could be re-indentured for a further period or released from indenture, provided they had paid off the expenses incurred in their recruitment. Wages were fixed at the time of recruitment and were not subject to change. The charges for recruitment and the expenses involved in the transport of labour were borne by the employer and the wages calculated after deducting this initial outlay.

The *kangani* system was essentially one of personal recruitment and became popular when the coffee and later rubber planters hired labour through this avenue. The word *kangani* means overseer or foreman in Tamil and under this system, the *kangani*, usually a labourer already employed on the plantation, was sent by his employer to recruit labour from his village. This system was preferred because of the lower cost involved in sending a *kangani* to recruit labour compared with the cost of indentured labour obtained through recruiting agencies. Moreover, the monopoly of Indian recruiting firms, which were believed to be responsible for restricting labour supply, was broken. The *kangani* system also appealed to the planters because the prospect of absconding was less likely compared with the indenture system especially as the *kangani* usually had a vested interest in ensuring that the labourers did not abscond. The *kangani* was not only a powerful intermediary but also received 'head money' from each recruited worker for every day worked, which was forfeited if the worker absconded (Sandhu 1969: 101). The *kangani* also related to the labourer as shopkeeper and moneylender, and the labourer was frequently indebted to him, often unable to repay his debts. The *kangani* system, it has been argued, was a 'variant of the indenture system, as in effect, the debt-bondage relationship between servant and master still remained, although indirectly' (Arudsothy 1986: 75).

At the height of the expansion of the rubber industry, *kangani* recruitment was still inadequate to meet the labour needs of the plantations. The problem was intensified by desertion of the indentured and *kangani*-recruited labourers. This resulted in direct government intervention to systematise the recruitment of free labour from India under a common recruiting system. Under this system, free labourers who volunteered themselves at Malayan depots in India were assisted to migrate to Malaya. The Indian Immigration Committee operated this system. All employers of Indian labour were required to contribute annually to a fund to subsidise the costs of immigration to Malaya. Technically, this was to be the migration of free labourers whose emigration was assisted. The system was cheaper than the *kangani* system because no inducements had to be made to the *kangani* and the hold of the *kangani* over the worker was diminished. This was an inexpensive system of labour importation: it appealed to employers because it kept wages low. Two distinct types of labour immigration emerged out of this 'assisted immigration system.' These were 'recruited independent labour immigration' and 'non-recruited independent labour immigration' (Sandhu 1969: 103). Indian workers represented between 65 to 80 per cent of the plantation labour force in Malaya between 1907 and 1938 (see Table 2.5 below).

Indian workers lived on the plantations which they were forbidden to leave without passes, they worked unlimited hours, were subjected to penalties for misconduct and attempts to run away were punishable (in Indonesia, Chinese, and Javanese workers were subject to a penal sanction). In return, they received basic wages which were tied to the prices of commodities (but never revised upwards), basic free accommodation in labour lines, subsidised food, and return passages.

Plantation workers were categorised into three groups according to job classification: factory workers, rubber tappers, and field workers. Factory workers were employed on the preparation of the latex or liquid rubber for initial moulding. Rubber tappers were employed to tap rubber, collect the latex and transport it to collecting stations or to the factory. Field workers were employed on various tasks on the estates, but mainly on weeding. Indian men were normally employed as tappers while Indian women were generally hired as weeders. Of the three categories, tapping was regarded as skilled work, while fieldwork was considered unskilled. In addition to this wage differential based on job classification, labour differentiation also existed along ethnic and gender lines.

Indians and Javanese were hired under direct employment – the planter and his staff kept work records, paid wages directly to the workers and supervised the tasks performed by them. Chinese workers were employed through a labour contractor and consequently came under an indirect system of employment. The contractor kept workers' work records and paid and supervised them.

Table 2.5: Malaya, Breakdown of FMS Estate Labour Force by Ethnic Group, 1907–1938

Year	Indians	Chinese	Javanese	Others	Total	Indian as % of labour	No. of Estates
1907	43 825	5 348	6 029	2 872	58 073	75.5	287
1908	43 515	6 595	4 999	1 961	57 070	76.2	300
1909	55 732	12 402	6 170	2 778	77 524	71.9	n.a.
1910	n.a.	n.a.	n.a.	n.a.	128 446	-	n.a.
1911	109 633	331 460	12 795	12 127	166 015	66.0	711
1912	n.a.	n.a.	n.a.	n.a.	188 050	-	n.a.
1913	142	25 081	12 197	8 496	188 250	75.7	n.a.
1914	120 144	24 000	10 115	7 120	161 379	74.4	n.a.
1915	126 347	27 446	8 356	8 592	170 741	74.0	719
1916	138 295	42 831	7 485	7 496	196 123	70.5	797
1917	148 834	55 240	7 746	8 902	220 758	67.4	920
1918	139 480	46 372	8 249	7 821	201 954	69.1	1003
1919	160 658	61 089	7 861	7 492	237 134	67.7	1087
1920	160 966	40 866	8 918	5 808	216 588	74.3	1105
1921	121 644	25 712	5 732	3 353	156 341	77.8	1001
1922	122 589	27 575	4 906	3 724	158 794	77.2	1052
1923	121 463	31 957	4 791	4 894	163 105	74.5	1 204
1924	119 242	30 884	4 516	4 715	159 357	74.8	1 068
1925	137 761	37 879	4 165	4 549	184 354	74.7	1 206
1926	176 114	61 064	4 760	4 822	246 760	71.4	1 403
1927	172 466	44 239	4 550	3 963	225 218	76.6	1 421
1928	162 460	50 647	5 149	4 788	223 044	72.8	1 509
1929	181 205	65 617	5 316	6 642	258 780	70.0	1 651
1930	132 745	30 860	3 665	2 411	169 681	78.2	1 757
1931	104 767	32 916	2 464	2 357	142 504	73.5	1 800
1932	90 003	31 349	1 920	2 328	125 600	71.7	1 912
1933	96 138	35 188	2 207	3 318	136 851	70.3	2 030
1934	119 443	43 305	2 521	4 153	166 422	71.8	2 178
1935	118 591	29 950	1 941	2 658	153 140	77.4	2 345
1936	123 595	30 760	1 924	2 979	159 258	77.6	2 419
1937	155 725	37 200	2 371	3 823	199 119	78.2	2 519
1938	137 353	28 925	1 762	2 892	170 932	80.4	2 388

Source: J.N. Parmer 1960: 273.

There was differentiation too in the methods of remuneration. There were three principal methods of remuneration, namely check-roll, task, and result. The check-roll labourer was paid a fixed daily wage, provided a whole day's work was completed. Under the task method of remuneration the worker was assigned a certain amount of work (by law the equivalent of a day's work of no more than nine hours) and paid according to the number of tasks completed. The task of the rubber tapper was fixed at a certain number of trees to be tapped a month. The number of trees varied according to the terrain, distance from the factory and the height of the tapping cut on the trees. In the category of remuneration by result, the tapper was also given a task but was paid at so much per pound of dry rubber contained in the latex obtained from the task. Although Indians and Chinese worked on similar tasks, generally the Indians were employed under the check-roll system, whether as tappers or field workers. The Chinese were usually remunerated on the payment by result method. Consequently, in prosperous times Chinese labourers' wages usually ranged well above Indian and Javanese workers' wages. Planters justified this wage differential on the grounds that the Chinese were healthier and more hardworking than the Indians and employment through contractors meant that the planters could save on housing and other facilities (Kaur 1998).

In the Netherlands East Indies, the Dutch had only one labour regime or system for the mining and planting sectors, covering both Chinese and Javanese coolies. After 1850 the extension of mining to Belitung and later Singkep necessitated a more regular labour supply while the expansion of commercial agriculture to Sumatra and the other sparsely populated Outer Provinces after 1870 required the use of coercion to tie workers down in the frontier regions.

Subsequently, Dutch firms entered the labour recruitment market to ensure and regulate labour supply and Javanese labour migration formed a substantial branch of this migration stream. In 1880 the Dutch colonial administration passed the coolie ordinance of 1880 (it was repeatedly revised thereafter) to regulate coolie-working conditions. Coolies signed a contract varying from one and a half to three years in exchange for a cash advance and transportation costs.

The plantation/mine owner's obligation was to provide employment for the worker, pay a wage and bear the costs of medical expenses. This ordinance incorporated a penal sanction clause – if a coolie defaulted on the service bond, he was arrested by the police, and gaoled. After serving his sentence, he was taken back to his employer at the latter's request to work out the rest of his contract. To ensure the smooth functioning of the system, each coolie was issued with a work card bearing his photograph, thumbprint, and the results of his medical examination. The sanctions were used not only in the case of desertion but also to punish laziness and refusal to perform specific tasks.

Similar regulations were introduced for workers recruited to serve on the plantations in French Indo-China and in Sabah. The authorities believed that coercion served the interests of workers because it fostered the work ethic and conditioned them to be useful. In time, coercive measures were replaced by more indirect controls as supervisor-foremen functioned as a link between the capitalist employer and the worker. The supervisor-foreman imposed the work discipline and thus relieved the state of this task.

These coercive legal measures were repealed after World War I. Nevertheless, the Sumatran planters continued to rely on them until external pressure in the form of protectionist measures passed by the United States led to a ban on tobacco imports produced under coercion.

Gender and Plantation Labour

Malaya

An important point on the composition of the Indian plantation labour force in Malaya that needs to be made is that it was predominantly male. Part of the explanation for this trend lies in the cultural traditions of the Indians. But the ideology of the authorities – that a woman's role was largely a reproductive one – also played its part in this development. Moreover, the nature of the rubber plantation was different from the tea plantation of Ceylon where women were considered 'suitable' for tea picking. All these factors had important repercussions for women workers, determining the gender-based division of labour on the plantations and a differential wage scale, with women paid lower wages than men.

The character of the new industry and agitation for a more stable Indian society on the plantation frontier led to an increasing emphasis on female labour recruitment in the twentieth century. From 1920 onwards, the Indian government began to focus on the gender imbalance among emigrants and its concerns were embodied in subsequent legislation. By far the most important piece of legislation in this regard was the Indian Emigration Act of 1922. This Act was an attempt to regulate the ratio of male to female emigrants by the stipulation that 'the number of male emigrants unmarried or unaccompanied by their wives [was] not [to] exceed one in every five persons over 18 years, in any one year' (Ramachandran 1994: 23). However, Malaya was repeatedly exempted from the gender ratio provision of the Act. Generally, nevertheless, the *kangani* recruitment system encouraged the migration of families and this was reflected in the census figures for 1901, 1911, 1921, 1931 and 1947. The proportion of females for these census years for every 1,000 males were: 171 in 1901; 308 in 1911, 406 in 1921, 482 in 1931 and 637 in 1947 (Ramachandran 1994: 32). As noted previously, these statistics also help explain the trend towards permanent settlement by Indian labour by the 1930s. Hence the possibilities for female employment on estates and elsewhere, the provisions of the 1922 Act, and the establishment of families, resulted in more permanent settlement in Malaya and the part-peasant, part-proletariat positioning of the Indian workforce. This was similar to the situation in Sumatra, and contrasted with the situation of the mining workforce for whom the process started during the 1930s and accelerated during the World War II period.

Sumatra

In Sumatra, all the initial Chinese workers were male while the Javanese workers who were recruited included a small number of women. At the beginning of the twentieth century, women workers comprised only about 10–12 per cent of a total labour force of 55,000 workers (Stoler 1985: 31). The women, who earned lower wages than the men (in 1894, their wages were 50 per cent of men's wages), and often had no housing allocated to them, were thus coerced to prostitute themselves in order to survive (Stoler 1985: 31). They were also used as a 'lure' in the recruitment of male workers. In both Malaya and Sumatra, both the European and Asian managers had 'first pickings' of these women workers (see, for example, Fauconnier 1931 and Lulofs 1993).

Wages and Conditions of Work of Indian Plantation Workers in Malaya

Institutionalised Indian labour recruitment enabled both the state and employers to manipulate a key factor in production depending on their immediate economic needs. Consequently, Indian labour possessed very little bargaining power. Demand varied with the widely fluctuating price of rubber. There was a sudden drop in the employment of Indians on estates in 1920–21, and of nearly 100 per cent in 1930–32, then an increase of 61 per cent in 1933–34, as shown above in Table 2.5, reflecting market conditions. During the depression of 1930–33 part of the labour 'surplus' was shipped back to India under the aegis of the Tamil Immigration Fund. Labour unrest and the cost of unemployment relief were largely avoided. We should not forget that as in all migrant labour forces, the Southeast Asian plantation labour force had its origins elsewhere, and it was in the countless, poverty-stricken South Indian villages that the costs of bearing and rearing the future migrants was met.

Wage Policy

The fact that Indian labour supply could be manipulated through immigration controls was to have important implications for the wage structure. Indeed the socially necessary wage for South Indian labour was deliberately kept low. In the late nineteenth century, the wages of estate workers were fixed by Indian Law. The Straits Settlements Ordinance of 1884 stipulated the following rates for Indian labourers on three year contracts: 12 cents a day for the first year and 14 cents a day for subsequent years for adult males; 8 cents a day for the first year and 10 cents a day for subsequent years for females and males under 21 years of age (Arasaratnam 1970: 57). In 1886, for example, indentured sugar workers received 14 cents a day against 18–20 cents for free Indian labourers and 24 cents for Javanese, who also cost two to three times as much to recruit (Chanderbali 1983: 53). Women were placed on the same footing as 'young' males (i.e. not adults) reflecting the ideological bias of the colonial state (in Sumatra, women earned half the wage paid to male workers). Under the provisions of this law, employers were permitted to deduct wages for infringement of contracts. Indeed, freedom of movement of workers was hedged around with legal constraints carrying fines (which added to constant indebtedness) and imprisonment. European employers also used various practices of dubious legality to avoid paying contract rates. Moreover, while the legislation provided for wage fixing and laid down the number of days labourers had to work, it did not take into account the well-being of the workers and failed to alleviate the poverty and misery experienced by workers (Jackson 1961: 61, 67). Migrant labour's contribution to the rubber industry is shown in Table 2.6 below. Malaya and Indonesia were the top two producing countries (see Figure 2.2), while Thailand and Indochina were not far behind.

The distinguishing feature of the labour market in Southeast Asia during this period was that it remained in a state of flux. In all labour systems, labour continued to be on the move because in most cases employment was 'permanently casual,' conditioned by short-term arrangements and contingent on economic conditions. As noted previously, many workers were contracted through advance payment, binding them to an employer or her/his agent. Others remained attached to systems of delayed payment permitting them to leave only at the end of

Table 2.6: Percentage Distribution of Natural Rubber Production of Principal Rubber Producing Countries (1910, 1920, 1930, 1940, 1950 and 1960)

Country	1910	1920	1930	1940	1950	1960
Malaya	6.7	51	53.6	38.7	37.3	35.4
Indonesia	2.9	22.1	29.2	38.4	37.4	31.5
Ceylon	1.7	8.6	9.2	6.4	6.1	4.8
(Big Three)	(11.3)	(81.7)	(92.0)	(83.5)	(80.8)	(71.7)
Thailand	0.001	0.1	0.5	3.1	6.0	8.4
Indo-China	0.2	0.9	1.2	4.5	2.6	5.6
Sarawak	0.001	0.5	1.2	2.5	3.0	2.5
North Borneo	0.03	1.2	0.9	1.2	1.3	1.1
India	0.2	1.9	0.2	1.2	0.8	1.2
Brazil	40.3	6.8	1.4	1.3	1.0	1.1
Africa	21.4	1.6	0.6	1.1	2.9	7.1
Others	26.0	1.2	2.0	1.6	1.6	1.3
Total	94,100	341,900	825,400	1,415,000	1,860,000	2,000,000

Note: Malaya includes Singapore, though Singapore's rubber production throughout was very small.
Source: Lim Chong Yah (1967: 94).

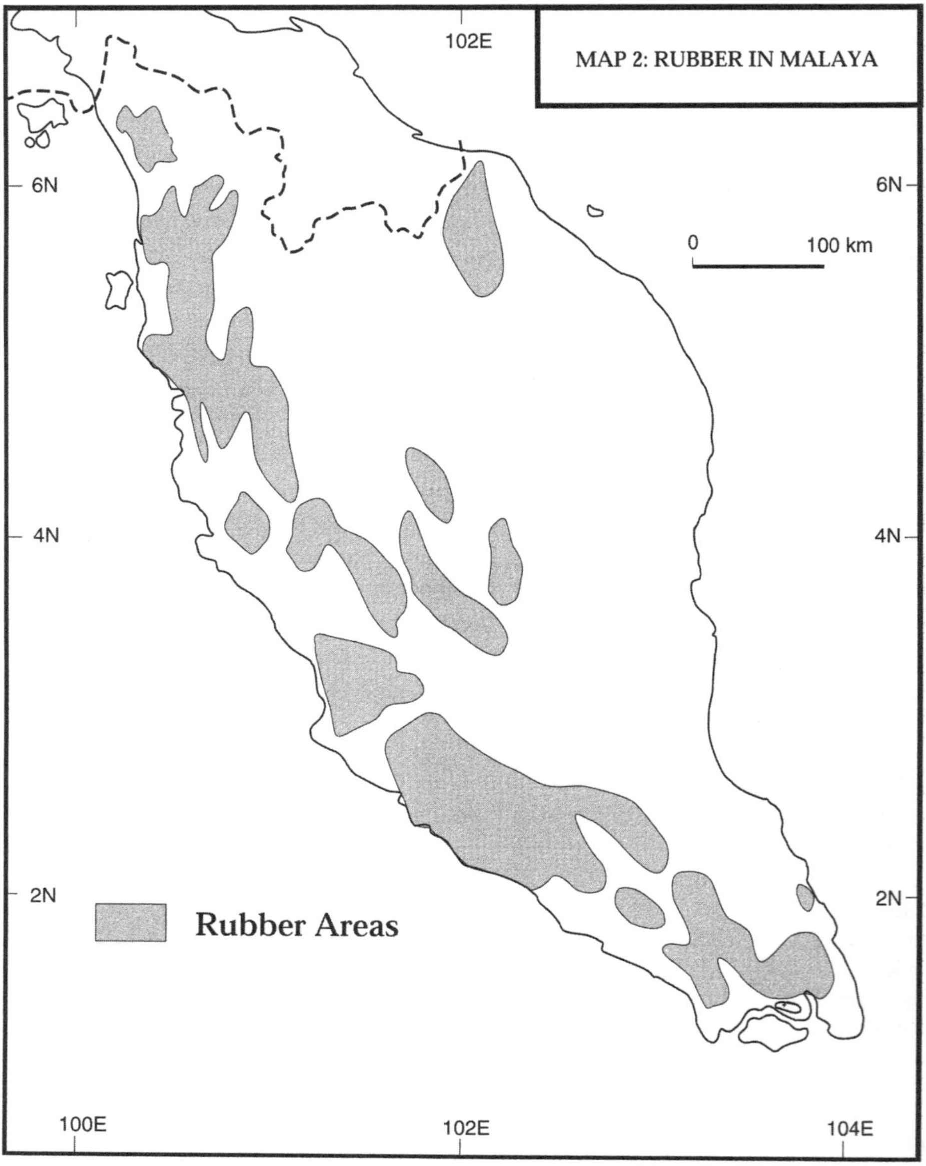

Figure 2.2: Map of Rubber Areas in Malaya

the 'contract' or when the season was over. Colonial regimes were thus both complicit and acquiescent in the exploitation of labour and consequently played a key role in structuring labour institutions (Kaur 2000).

To summarise, colonial labour policies centred on the acquisition of a plentiful and cheap supply of labour, the assurance of the worker's freedom of movement through the abolition of indenture, and the provision of a limited amount of protection for workers through the agency of labour departments, labour inspectorates, and Chinese Protectorates. To a large extent, the success of these agencies in ensuring basic rights for workers depended on the character and attitude of the administrators and the co-operation of the leading planters. Notwithstanding this, the colonial administrations gave no thought to the possible effects of labour policies on the social life of the coolies and bequeathed what is termed as 'plural societies' on them.

An Era of Trade Restrictions and Protection (1914-45)

After World War I, there was a backlash against globalisation and a rise in protectionism associated principally with commodity restriction schemes in Southeast Asia. This had important consequences for the region. One, it stemmed the cross-border flows of goods, capital and migrants. Indentured labour migration was banned. There was also mass repatriation of workers to their countries of origin. The ending of direct state involvement in labour recruitment also led to a decline in authoritarianism, paternalism, and a reliance on official bodies to protect labour's interests. Some colonial states (for example, Malaya) restricted labour migration but allowed the migration of women and children, thus enabling the formation and reconstitution of families. In Burma and Thailand, there was a political backlash against migrant labour and restrictions on foreign labour. In other areas a more stable labour force emerged, resulting in the formation of a 'free ' or a 'freer' labour force (Kaur 2000).

Individual and Collective Responses by Workers

Workers were not compliant or docile all of the time, nor did they submit to the arbitrary rule of capitalist interests without a struggle. On the whole they avoided direct and open confrontations against those who harassed and exploited them. Invariably, they relied on what some scholars have termed 'everyday forms of resistance' (Scott 1985). The nature and character of these largely spontaneous actions show a remarkable similarity in most countries owing to the fact that they were largely defensive acts. Moreover they required little or no 'co-operation' and were not meant to directly challenge the power of the plantation or mine management. Essentially, the workers wished to vent their frustration, to ensure their survival, and also to wreak their anger. Their actions often took the form of destruction of property, or of rubber trees, or equipment. Desertion was a popular choice, and often involved 'crimping' by neighbouring estates. Nevertheless, these acts by their very nature had their limitations. The strike action by workers was an offensive weapon in contrast to these defensive tactics. One, it represented collective action on the part of the workers. Two, it involved a much greater calculated risk because it meant a temporary halt to production with its attendant retaliation by the management. Three, there was a clear connection between economic conditions and the necessity to 'have a voice.'

In most Southeast Asian countries, the 1930s stands out as the decade of concerted action by workers. There were two main reasons for this. The first was the greater number of 'freer' wage workers entering the labour market and the decline of assisted labour migration. This decline was concomitant with the ending of direct state involvement in labour recruitment and it also heralded a decline in authoritarianism, paternalism, and a reliance upon official bodies (e.g. the Labour Department) to protect labour's interests. Second, some states (for example, Malaya) restricted labour migration but allowed the migration of women and children, thus enabling the reconstitution of families in the host countries. Third, a more stable labour force emerged in most countries. Whether in Malaya, Sumatra, Sabah, or Sarawak, a substantial number of workers chose not to take up repatriation offers but to settle in these states, and sought alternative ways to make a living on the land. For example, earlier legislation that had provided for land allocation for workers on estates was enforced and workers were given small allotments. Some plantations in Malaya even leased land to their workers. Tin miners became 'squatters' in larger numbers than before. This process helped create 'settled' workers; reduced their dependence on the wage economy of the plantation and mining sectors, and facilitated the permanent settlement of workers in these states. When economic conditions improved, labour realised that it was not getting its share of the new prosperity and workers became better organised and more militant. In Malaya, for example, vernacular newspapers, cultural organisations, and social action groups mushroomed among the different ethnic groups. Labour organisations were formed and strikes occurred in a number of undertakings and enterprises employing Indian labour separately and alongside Chinese workers. The apparent boldness of semi-skilled and skilled workers can be attributed to the fact that they enjoyed greater mobility and were more willing to co-operate with the more militant Chinese in joint-strike actions to demand better working conditions. Such activities soon spread to other sectors.

Case Study – Labour Organisation in Malaya

Prior to the 1930s, the number of labour organisations in Malaya was small. Most of them were confined to Chinese workers and were organised initially through trade guilds, secret societies, and mutual benefit groups which were not primarily labour organisations. Moreover, during the 1920s, trade union organisation and collective action among the Chinese community in Malaya was directly related to political events in China. Local branches of the Kuomintang and the Malayan Communist Party helped to organise Chinese labour (Yeo Kim Wah 1976).

In the second half of the 1930s, both Chinese and Indian labour became more militant. As noted previously, where there was a concentration of Chinese and Indian labour in a relatively 'closed' environment – for example, the railway workshops in Sentul and the Batu Arang Colliery, the Indian workers acquired some of the industrial militancy of their Chinese co-workers. Consequently, they were prepared to shed their communal separateness for the common good of all workers (Kaur 1990a, Kaur 1990b). In the late 1930s, plantation workers used the strike weapon to express their dissatisfaction and anti-colonial sentiment, and a spate of strikes took place in the plantation sector in Malaya. The colonial government retaliated by deporting the leaders to India and China and enacting banishment ordinances. Thereafter, only organisations for religious activities were permitted while working-class based and politically-oriented groups were disallowed. Thus in the closing years of the 1930s, there were substantial developments in labour organisation. These were reflected in the emergence of trade unions and the use of collective industrial action in a number of workplaces – the Collieries, the Railway Workshops, and the Plantations.

The growth of both Chinese and Indian nationalism also helped to stimulate labour organisation. For example, the influence of political events in the subcontinent and the Indian community's ascribed role in Malaya made the community aware of the necessity to safeguard its cultural identity. Large numbers of Indians joined the Indian National Army and the Indian Independence League, intent on attaining independence for India. These nationalist groups therefore provided the framework for labour organisation and sometimes for industrial action. After World War II, the tradition of militant leadership being provided from outside the plantation structure continued. The leaders appeared to have originated from the groups that had retreated into the jungles during the War to fight the Japanese or were disillusioned leaders of the Indian Independence League who had become disenchanted with Japan's objectives.

World War II, the influence of Gandhi and the Indian National Congress, a succession of Labour Party and Labour Coalition governments in Great Britain, and Britain's desire to improve its colonial image allowed the possibility of trade unions in the Colonies. The Trades Union Ordinance was passed in Malaya in

1940, and stipulated compulsory registration of unions, emphasised 'conciliation procedures,' denied the right to picket and prohibited political and sympathy strikes. Thus although the Malayan Administration was obliged to recognise trade unions, it bound them to restrictive rules. In the context of global struggles and independence movements, the labour movement in Malaya gathered momentum after 1945. Between 1945 and 1947, over 25 per cent of wage workers and 85 per cent of unions were federated under the new Pan-Malayan General Labour Union. However, a spate of strikes after 1945 resulted in further repressive measures by capital and the Malayan Administration and labour legislation became more draconian. In 1948, following the Declaration of Emergency, new legislation was enacted which 'in effect destroyed Malayan trade unionism.' The anti-union stance was played out against the background of the red menace and the discovery of a new source of cheap labour – Malay labour. Both capital and government were therefore relieved from the task of improving working conditions for labour. The restrictive paternalism of the pre-war period was restored and workers were no better off than before.

In summary, migrant and other workers undoubtedly had a choice in the expanding global market for labour, but that choice was 'exercised' in an environment determined by historical and political circumstances and economic structures. At no stage were workers able to escape exploitation, particularly since they were divided along ethnic and occupational lines in most countries. There was no real alliance of class – class consciousness was limited or heavily influenced by communist or nationalist ideologies. The colonial authorities frowned upon worker organisations and ensured that only compliant organisations were allowed to survive. They viewed labour's struggle for industrial rights as a threat to the social order and the development process. In effect, colonial governments pursued a range of policies and practices designed to ensure that worker organisations, militancy and opposition remained subordinated to the logic and dictates of capital. They were aided in this by both the nature of capitalist economic relations and the specific management practices of employers. Notwithstanding this, and despite their positioning as a part-peasant and part-proletariat group, many migrant workers were able to adapt and survive, saving money for relatives and becoming a part of the recruitment system. In the process, they constituted new identities which enabled them to maintain their links with their homelands.

Conclusion

The international economy, which linked almost all parts of the world through open trade and capital, and labour flows, impacted on the different ways in which labour relations were played out across the Southeast Asian region during the period under study. The interlocking of Southeast Asian economies with the global market place, particularly the global market place for labour, lay at the very heart of Southeast Asian economic growth. In this 'imperial-led' globalisation, the colonial state played a central role in securing the conditions for the utilisation and domination of wage labour. Consequently, in the first part of the twentieth century, a 'free' labour market did not really exist in Southeast Asia.

References

Arasaratnam, S. (1970) *Indians in Malaysia and Singapore*, Kuala Lumpur: Oxford University Press.

Arudsothy, P. (1986) 'The Labour Force in A Dual Economy', PhD Thesis, Glasgow University.

Breman, J. (1989) *Taming the Coolie Beast: Plantation Society and the Colonial Order in Southeast Asia*, New Delhi: Oxford University Press.

Chanderbali, D.S. (1983) 'Indian Indenture in the Straits Settlements 1872–1910. Policy and Practice in Province Wellesley', PhD Thesis, Australian National University.

Elson, R. (1984) *Javanese Peasants and the Colonial Sugar Industry: Impact and Change in an East Java Residency, 1830-1940*, Singapore: Oxford University Press.

— (1992) 'International commerce, the state and society: economic and social change', in: N. Tarling (ed.) *The Cambridge History of Southeast Asia Volume 2*, Cambridge: Cambridge University Press.

Fauconnier, H. (1931) *The Soul of Malaya* (trans. by E. Sutton), London.

Heidhues, M.S. (1992) *Bangka Tin and Mentok Pepper: Chinese Settlement in an Indonesian Island*, Singapore: ISEAS.

Jackson, J.C. (1969) 'Mining in eighteenth century Bangka: The pre-European exploitation of the "Tin-Island"', *Pacific Viewpoint* 10, 2: 42–52.

Jackson, R.N. (1961) *Immigrant Labour and the Development of Malaya*, Kuala Lumpur: Government Printer.

Kaur, A. (1990a) 'Hewers and haulers: a history of coal miners and coal mining in Malaya', *Modern Asian Studies* 24, 1: 75–113.

— (1990b) 'Working on the railway: Indian workers in Malaya 1880-1957', in P.J. Rimmer and L.M. Allen (eds.) *Pullers, Planters, Plantation Workers: The Underside of Malaysian History*, Singapore: Singapore University Press.

— (1994) 'Hantu and Highway: transport in Sabah 1881-1963', *Modern Asian Studies* 28, 1: 1–49.

— (1998) 'Tappers and Weeders: South Indian Plantation Workers in Malaysia, 1880-1970', *South Asia* XXI [Special Volume, L. Brennan and B.V. Lal (eds.) *Across the Kala Pani*]: 73–102.

— (2000) 'Sojourners and settlers: South Indians and communal identity in Malaysia', in C. Bates (ed.) *Community, Empire and Migration: South Asians in Diaspora*, Basingstoke: Macmillan.

Lim Chong Yah (1967) *Economic Development of Modern Malaya*, Kuala Lumpur: Oxford University Press.

Lulofs, M.H. (1993) *Coolie: If Allah had Ordained it Thus* (trans. by G.J. Renier and I. Clephane), Singapore: Oxford University Press.

Murray, M.J. (1992) '"White Gold" or "White Blood"? The Rubber Plantations of Colonial Indochina, 1910-40', in E.V. Daniel, H. Bernstein and T. Brass (eds.) *Plantations, Proletarians and Peasants in Colonial Asia*, London: Frank Cass.

O'Rourke, K.H. and Williamson, G.J. (1999) *Globalisation and History: The Evolution of a Nineteenth Century Atlantic Economy*, Cambridge, Mass.: MIT Press.

Parmer, J.N. (1960) *Colonial Labour Policy and Administration: A History of Labour in the Rubber Plantation Industry in Malaya*, New York: Locust Valley. J.J. Augustin for the Association for Asian Studies.

Ramachandran, S. (1994) *Indian Plantation Labour in Malaya*, Kuala Lumpur: S. Abdul Majeed & Co. for Institute of Social Analysis (INSAN).

Ramasamy, P. (1996) *Plantation Labour: Unions, Capital and the State*, Basingstoke: Macmillan.

Reid, A.J. (1983) 'Introduction: slavery and bondage in Southeast Asian history', in A.J. Reid (ed.) *Slavery, Bondage and Dependency in Southeast Asia*, St Lucia: Queensland University Press.

— (1987) 'Low population growth and its causes in pre-colonial Southeast Asia', in N. Owen (ed.) *Death and Disease in Southeast Asia: Explorations in Social, Medical and Demographic History*, Singapore: Oxford University Press.

— (1988) *Southeast Asia in the Age of Commerce, 1450-1680*, Vol. I, New Haven: Yale University Press.

— (1993) 'The Decline of Slavery in Nineteenth-Century Indonesia', in M.A. Klein (ed.) *Breaking the Chains: Slavery, Bondage, and Emancipation in Modern Africa and Asia*, Madison: University of Wisconsin Press.

Ricklefs, M.C. (1981) *A History of Modern Indonesia*, Basingstoke: Macmillan.

Sandhu, K.S. (1969) *Indians in Malaya: Some Aspects of their Immigration and Settlement*, Cambridge: Cambridge University Press.

Scott, J.C. (1985) *Weapons of the Weak: Everyday Forms of Peasant Resistance*, New Haven: Yale University Press.

Skinner, G.W. (1957) *Chinese Society in Thailand: An Analytical History*, Ithaca: Cornell University Press.

Stenson, M. (1970) *Industrial Conflict in Malaya: Prelude to the Communist Revolt of 1948*, Kuala Lumpur: Oxford University Press.

Stenson, M. (1980) *Class, Race and Colonialism in West Malaya: The Indian Case*, St. Lucia: University of Queensland Press.

Stoler, A.L. (1985) *Capitalism and Confrontation in Sumatra's Plantation Belt, 1870–1979*, New Haven: Yale University Press.

Van Neil, R. (1992) *Java under the Cultivation System: Collected Writings*, Leiden: KITLV Press.

Wong Lin Ken (1965) *The Malayan Tin Industry to 1914: With Special Reference to the States of: Perak, Selangor, Negri, Sembilan and Pahang*, Tucson: University of Arizona for the Association of Asian Studies.

Yeo Kim Wah (1976) 'The Communist Challenge in the Malayan Labour Scene, September 1936–March 1937', *Journal of the Malayan Branch of the Royal Asiatic Society* XLIX, 2: 36–79.

Yip Yat Hoong (1969) *The Development of the Tin Mining Industry of Malaya*, Kuala Lumpur: University of Malaya Press.

3

Constructing Child Labour: Attitudes to Juvenile Work in Indonesia, 1900–2000

BEN WHITE[1]

The study of 'child labour' falls analytically at the intersection of labour studies on the one hand, and the sociology/anthropology of childhood on the other. From both these angles, we would expect research to focus on the changing social construction and re-construction of childhood, work and labour and in turn of 'child labour.' Much contemporary research on child employment, however, draws on neither of these traditions but is understandably more concerned to establish and document the facts of abuse and exploitation of juvenile workers.

Indonesia, and the Southeast Asian region generally, show the problem of 'labeling' or stereotyping in relation to children's work. Since the 1980s 'child labour' in Southeast Asia has evoked two principle images, particularly from Thailand and the Philippines, in which children are seen as the passive victims of commercial exploitation in labour-intensive export manufactures and in the sex trade. Some other accounts of children working in conditions of extreme exploitation or hardship reach the international media: forced labour in Burma, pearl-divers, and scavengers in the Philippines, 'street children' everywhere.[2] Until quite recently no particular label was attached to child work in Indonesia: there have been no international exposures of large mass concentrations of child employment, except in one recent case (the *'jermal'* children working on fishing platforms off the coast of Sumatra). In the 1990s however, as we shall see, international media have presented a picture of millions of Indonesian children working

1 Thanks to the editors for helpful comments, and to the Netherlands Institute for Advanced Studies in the Humanities and Social Sciences for a Fellowship which made possible the completion of this study. All translations from Dutch and Indonesian sources are by the author.

2 Good sources of such cases are the Bangkok-based bulletin *Child Workers in Asia* and the London-based *Anti-Slavery reporter*.

in factories and thereby categorised child employment, in line with dominant global stereotypes, as a phenomenon linked primarily to industrialisation and globalisation (Bessell 1999: 353).

These labels on the one hand serve the important purpose of highlighting and exposing the 'worst forms'[3] of child exploitation. On the other hand they can be too easily transferred to all forms of child employment, promoting an inaccurate picture of the realities and problems of child work generally. The great majority of working children, in Indonesia as in other Southeast Asian countries, are employed in agriculture or other rural occupations, and in family farms or ther small-scale enterprises. Many combine work and school; for some (including many so-called 'street children') work is the only way to stay in school. In Indonesia as in other countries, the neglect of the majority of working children, in both statistics and research, reflects the way 'child labour' has been constructed over time.

This chapter explores the ways in which juvenile employment has been perceived and addressed in Indonesia during the period (roughly) 1900-2000. Although available historical information is scarce, prevailing discourse on child work and education since the early twentieth century in the Netherlands Indies and (after 1945) Indonesia both reflects, and in some ways contrasts with, the preoccupations and tendencies seen in Europe. Various themes run through the account which follows. First, the history of discussion and concern on child employment (or the lack of it) tells us much about the specific and changing interests that adults had in children. Discourse on child work and schooling, and the notions of childhood constructed by adults in this discourse, have always shown a tension between three coexisting images of children, all of them infused by adult interests and perspectives: the child as threat to adult society (in this case, often with implicit reference to the boy-child); the child as victim of adult society; and the child as learner of adult culture (Thorne 1987: 89). Second, in the history of interventions on juvenile employment, and in perceptions of the 'child labour' problem by both officials and activists, international influences have been the main motive force; finally and related to this, children's own interests have been, and remain, relatively marginalised in child labour discourse and policy, leaving children as 'pawns in a game in which they are quite peripheral' (Bessell 1999: 370-1).

Historical work on juvenile employment, anywhere in the world, encounters special difficulties. Even in Europe and the United States information is scarce and fragmentary, and heavily biased towards industrial work in factories and mines; sources are especially weak on child work in agriculture and in small-scale enterprises (Cunningham 1990, Cunningham and Viazzo 1996, de Coninck-Smith et

3 To use the phrase ultimately adopted in the ILO's new Convention 182 of 1999, after earlier drafts had successively tried the terms 'intolerable' and 'most extreme' forms of child labour (White 1999).

al. 1997, Sjoberg 1997). They also lend themselves to stereotyped interpretations of the history of child labour in which urbanisation and industrialisation are seen as the main causes of the mass exploitation of child workers and laws prohibiting child employment, prompted by social concern for the welfare of children, as the main instruments for its elimination.

Recent research on Europe has challenged every aspect of this traditional view. It is now better understood, for example, that early public concern about child employment in Europe was often based on the perceived need not to prevent, but to *provide* employment for children. Similarly, early arguments for the provision or universalisation of primary education were often based not on pedagogical grounds but on that common theme in European history, the fear of children's idleness and the threats which this was thought to pose for the social order during early industrialisation and urbanisation (Gardarsdottir 1997: 161). Children who worked in factories were not necessarily worse off than those who did not, and factory employment may even have meant an improvement in working conditions, particularly after the introduction of powered machinery (Brugmans 1978: 102, Nardinelli 1990: ch. 4).

In any case, child labour historically has been primarily a non-industrial, and certainly a non-factory phenomenon; the regions in which child employment in factories became widespread – notably nineteenth century Britain, and the American South – are exceptions to the general pattern, even in the West (Nardinelli 1990: 153). Debates and social conflicts on child labour essentially concerned the issue where it was best for children to spend their years of growth. The choice was between 'the home, the street, work and school' (Sandin 1997: 43), but also between different sites and sectors of child work; in those debates and ensuing state regulation, the interests of employers and parents often ensured that restrictions on child employment made exceptions for precisely those sectors and scales of production in which child employment was most common (for example, agriculture, domestic service, small-scale enterprise), often going to great contortions to re-define 'employment,' 'workplace' etc. to exclude specific forms and places of work, for reasons of pure expediency. Child labour laws themselves are now thought to have played a rather minor role in the decline in numbers of full-time child workers; researchers now are more concerned to explore and debate the relative importance in specific cases of compulsory education, increasing household incomes and changing family livelihood strategies, and in some cases changing technologies of production (Nardinelli 1990, Weiner 1991, Cunningham 2000).

These ideas provide food for thought for researchers interested in the history of childhood and work in other national contexts. The few historical studies available touch on many similar themes (Cunningham and Viazzo 1996). In colonial export economies of sub-Saharan Africa for example, the need to keep native boys and girls out of 'idleness and mischief' was an important theme in early twentieth century policy and debate on child labour; in Zimbabwe, legislation regulating child employment was designed to enhance employers' access to and control over the labour of children (Grier 1994), and in Tanganyika, years of pressure from Whitehall for child labour legislation on the ILO model resulted in a version so watered down as to leave the employment of children under 12 years in coffee, pyrethrum and tea estates, and the widespread practice of long-distance migration of children with families to estate work, virtually undisturbed (Shivji 1985).

In the following section we sketch some basic features of child work and official attitudes towards it in the late nineteenth and early twentieth century Netherlands Indies, when very few children were in school, child employment was unregulated, and its discussion uninfluenced by international developments in this field. The early twentieth century provides a stark contrast between the relative indifference to child work in the colony, and the active debate and law-making on child employment and education in the Netherlands itself. The next section focuses on a specific and instructive moment, the discussion and enquiries leading to the passage in 1925 of the Netherlands Indies' first child labour ordinance. This period is of particular interest in relation to issues of the (re)construction of child labour, since the law eventually passed – a much-diluted version of the ILO's 1919 'Convention on the Minimum Age for Admission to Industrial Employment' – incorporated argued re-definitions of the notion of both 'child,' 'labour' and 'workplace,' and even of 'night' and 'day,' mainly in response to the concerns of employers' associations. We then look at the efforts of the newly-established Labour Office to implement the ordinance in the last decade of colonial rule. After looking (more briefly, since so little was done) at various interventions in the subsequent fifty years when the 1925 ordinance remained on the books (until 1997), the final section jumps to the last years of the twentieth century, a period in which the issue of child labour, having failed to attract attention and concern for some decades, again became the focus of widespread international attention. We close with a brief discussion of the impact of Indonesia's current 'total crisis' on the realities and perceptions of juvenile employment.

Childhood and Work around 1900[4]

The late nineteenth and early twentieth centuries were periods of quite active government intervention in labour matters in both the Netherlands and the Netherlands Indies. There are however some instructive contrasts. In the Netherlands,

4 Some parts of the narrative in this and the following sections are drawn from earlier work (White 1994a, White 1994b, White and Tjandraningsih 1998).

both state- and civil society-based enquiries and proposals concerned mainly the need to restrict and/or regulate women's and children's employment, together with (in the early twentieth century) efforts by labour unions to restrict the length of the working day for all workers. It was a busy time for debate and legislation on child labour in particular, with van Houten's largely ineffective law of 1874 being replaced by successive new labour laws in 1889, 1909, and 1919, each one placing greater restriction on child employment and each preceded by one or more official enquiries and a host of unofficial enquiries and pamphlets by professional unions and political parties (White 1994b, White 2001).

In the Indies however labour regulation began with adults, and with another set of issues, in particular the prohibition of slavery and the prohibition or regulation of various other forms of unfree labour such as debt-slavery, corvée and coolie-indenture (Tjoeng 1948: chs. 1, 2 and 4); thus focusing mainly on promotion of Marx's second freedom (of the person, to operate in markets for 'free' labour) which had already been largely dealt with in northern Europe. In further contrast with Western legislation which focused mainly on manufacturing and particularly factory labour, 'original' Indies regulations of the nineteenth century (those not derived from Dutch law) were if anything more focused on agriculture (Boeijinga 1926: 4-5); the labour problem in the Indies, as in other Asian colonies such as British Ceylon and Malaya (Butler 1938b: 39, 56) was seen as mainly a plantation problem (Breman 1989, Stoler 1985).

Available sources from the late nineteenth and early twentieth centuries (mainly from Java) suggest large-scale involvement of children and youth in both peasant and plantation agriculture and in non-farm work, both as family workers and as wage-workers.. In rural crafts and small industries, children were commonly employed both as family helpers and for wages. The very low earnings in this sector – much less than prevailing agricultural wage rates – meant that all family members including children had to participate in production in order to attain a survival income for the household, in conditions reminiscent of those which we have seen described for European 'proto-industries' in the early industrial revolution. A good example is the hat-weaving industry in Tangerang (West Java), which in 1908 produced about ten million hand-woven pandanus hats mainly for export to Europe and the USA, and was looked on by officials as a dynamic success story. For the pessimistic researcher Pleyte however, the industry only served as an example of the impoverishment of workers that came with the emergence of a world-market product:

> In households with no other income sources than hat weaving, all are compelled to help, including very young children, and one finds even the tiniest children, still dependent on mothers' care, already fellow-slaves in the struggle for their daily food (Pleyte 1911: 59).

Apart from this single author there are few indications that the employment of children was considered a social issue in the Indies before the first World War; children's work generally was considered 'natural,' and their wage-employment in particular seems to have been considered desirable. In the massive 'Inquiry into the Declining Welfare of the Native Population of Java and Madura' of 1904-5, officials in all of Java's seventy-two districts received a thick instruction manual containing 533 questions on economic and social conditions. These include quite detailed questions on access to education (which at the time was largely non-existent except for the sons of native officials) but only one question on children's employment which asks: '74. Is there generally *sufficient opportunity for wage-employment for men, women, and children?*' together with two follow-up questions, '75. Do many people take advantage of these opportunities? If not, why not?' and '76. How much can they earn per day, in cash (day- or piece-rates), working: a. for government (public) works, b. for Europeans, c. for natives, d. for foreign orientals?' (Leidraad 1904: 4, emphasis added).

The answers to these questions indicate that not only native Javanese and 'foreign Asiatic' enterprises, but also the colonial government and European enterprises (in nearly all cases, plantations) employed children on a large scale In general, the working-day for children was reported as being the same as that of adults (most commonly between eight-ten hours), and children's wages were generally about one-half those of adult men, and 65-75 per cent of those of adult women (Onderzoek 1911, VIf 1-17, Onderzoek 1912, IXc 94-101). In terms of both working hours and their relative wages compared to adults, Javanese children seemed better off than their counterparts in the farms and factories of Holland had been a few decades earlier (White 1994b: 10-11).[5]

Children's involvement in productive work , and the general feeling that work was a natural or desirable element in children's lives, are not surprising if we recall that at the beginning of the twentieth century only about one in two hundred native children attended formal school of any kind. It was not until the so-called 'ethical policy' and the gradual establishment of village schools from 1907 onwards that villagers in most regions had any prospect of access to education; even by the 1930s only about one-third of native children went to primary school (which they attended for only three years, and only two and a half hours each day). An early experiment with village schools in Ambarawa (Central Java) in the 1890s was cynically reviewed by Pott, the Director of Education:

5 Even in 1908 the Dutch trade unions were campaigning for a maximum work-day of ten hours, and in many branches of both agriculture, industry, trade and services, work-hours for both adults and children were commonly twelve-fourteen hours (Vakverenigingen 1908).

> the intention was certainly a good one, namely to keep the young boys busy, who otherwise did nothing except tend the buffaloes [...] Mr. Steinmetz has told me [...] that the schools indeed were of some use: the boys were kept out of mischief, such as setting things on fire (they had caused some serious fires in the past) (Brugmans, 1938: 307, note the emphasis on the boy-child).

In some eyes then, even those of a Director of Education, the introduction of schools for the children of the poor was justified mainly by concern to structure the time of the idle, in the Indies as in Europe (Cunningham 1990: 121).

As we have noted, the Welfare Enquiry reports show child employment was common in European plantation enterprises in Java. It is reasonable then to assume that it was also common in the plantations of Sumatra and other islands; however, in its annual reports covering the years 1913 to 1925 the Labour Inspectorate (which prior to the establishment of the Labour Office in 1921 dealt only with the islands outside Java) made not a single mention of child work. They do however note the half-hearted attempts of some plantation companies on Sumatra's East Coast to establish 'company schools' for the children of their coolies. In 1913 the companies' flagging interest in providing schools was explained by the fact that the boys who had learned to read and write didn't stay on the estate, but tried above all to find clerical work: '[...] moreover the coolies themselves have little interest; in many schools more children of the local population than of the coolies come to school (Arbeidsinspectie 1913: 85).

Similar reports were made in 1914 (when it was also reported that some recently opened plantation schools had since been closed) and 1917 (Arbeidsinspectie 1914, Arbeidsinspectie 1917). Only in 1919 could they report that the Inspector of Education and the Planters' Committee in Medan had generated some interest with the promise of limited government support for the establishment of plantation schools, and that it was expected that numbers of company schools would increase rapidly (Arbeidsinspectie 1919: 39-40); and indeed, by the 1930s the proportions of '*schoolrijpe kinderen*' (those over six years of age) enrolled in plantation company schools had risen to about 30 percent (Kantoor van Arbeid 1937: 156-7).

Regulating and Re-Defining Child Labour in the 1920s

The measures eventually taken for the limited restriction of juvenile employment in the Netherlands Indies were not stimulated by social concern in the Indies or the Netherlands, but by the international obligations deriving from the Netherlands' membership of the League of Nations and the new International Labour Office established at the Treaty of Versailles. The Treaty required member states to apply all conventions which they ratified to their colonial possessions, although modifications to adapt the convention to local conditions could be proposed (Van Zanten 1927: 103-5, 148).

The ILO's convention no. 5 on 'Minimal Age for Admission of Children to Industrial Employment' (1919) stipulated that:

> Children under the age of fourteen years shall not be employed for work in any public or private industrial undertaking, or any branch thereof, other than an undertaking in which only members of the same family are employed (Article 2).

The Convention applied only to industry (thus excluding the agriculture, trade, and service sectors), reflecting the tendency in Europe and North America to associate the 'child labour' problem with urban industries. Article 1 defined 'industrial undertaking' to include mining/quarrying, manufacture, construction and transport (though excluding 'transport by hand'), but added that 'the competent authority in each country shall define the line of division which separates industry from commerce and agriculture.' The Convention made specific exceptions for Japan (Art. 5) and India (Art. 6), lowering the minimum age to twelve years in both cases and restricting 'industrial undertaking' to 'those working with power and employing more than ten persons.'[6]

This Convention is the first significant step in the internationalisation of child labour regulation, which resulted in the introduction of derivative child labour legislation in many Asian countries, each making their own modifications to the ILO convention. Japan, China, Hong Kong, the Philippines, Ceylon, the Straits Settlements and Federated Malay States, and British India all introduced new child labour laws or ordinances in 1923 (Butler 1938a, Volksraadstukken 1925: 14-6).[7]

The Netherlands Indies government was more cautious in responding to these new international initiatives.[8] In 1924 preparations were made for the drafting of a new Ordinance to regulate child employment and the night-time employment of women (thus combining the two new ILO conventions which had been ratified in the Netherlands in 1922).[9] The recently-established Labour Office circulated an Inquiry on the feasibility of applying the Conventions on Child Labour

6 The exceptions were to avoid conflict with existing national legislation in each country, but in the case of Japan stipulated that 'the provision in the present law admitting children under the age of twelve to certain light and easy employment shall be repealed' (Art. 5).

7 The processes and argumentation with which the different colonial powers (Britain, France, the Netherlands, Portugal) adjusted the ILO Convention to colonial conditions would make a fascinating comparative study.

8 But by no means the last among colonial possessions; British Tanganyika for example procrastinated until 1940 before introducing a much watered-down ordinance (Shivji 1985).

9 Locher-Scholten (1987) provides an interesting discussion of the debates on the 'female nightwork' articles of this ordinance.

and Female Night Work to various departmental heads, regional and district authorities and a number of employers' organisations: the Indies Business Association (*Indischen Ondernemersbond*), the Java Sugar Industry Employers' Association (JSWB), the Netherlands Indies Agricultural Union (*Nederlandsch Indisch Landbouw Syndicaat*), the General Association of Rubber Planters on Sumatra's East Coast (AVROS), the Deli Planters' Association, and the Agricultural Association for the Principalities (*Vorstenlandsch Landbouwvereniging*). These employers' organisations in turn circulated the Inquiry among their members. The Inquiry specifically asked:

> whether there are industrial undertakings as defined by the Convention which made significant use of the labour of children below twelve years, or where such children are employed at night (between 10 pm and 5 am) and whether enterprises can be identified which would be rendered unviable or seriously inconvenienced by a prohibition on child labour (Volksraadstukken 1925: 3).

Workers' organisations were not consulted; when asked in the *Volksraad* why this had not been done, the government lamely stated that while there were no objections in principle, this had not been done 'because the matter to be regulated gave no occasion to do so' (Volksraadstukken 1925: (6,5) 1).

The results of this Inquiry, their use by the Labour Office in preparing an ordinance for the regulation of child labour, and the discussion on this ordinance before its approval by the *Volksraad* in 1925 provide interesting insights into attitudes to child employment at the time. In fact, the decision to introduce some local adaptations to the text of the standard ILO convention had already been made before the Inquiry was carried out. As shown in the quotation above, it had already been decided to re-define 'night-time' from the Convention's original 'rest-period of eleven consecutive hours, which includes the hours between 10 pm and 5 am' to a period of only seven hours between 10 pm and 5 am (in defiance of the realities of the equatorial Indies, where night-time lasts roughly from 6 pm to 6 am, constantly through the year); more importantly, 'childhood' itself was redefined by lowering the minimum age from fourteen to twelve years, although in the Netherlands itself the minimum age had just been raised to fourteen in the new Labour Law of 1919. Here, no doubt, the Indies' Labour Office followed the pointers provided by the ILO Convention which introduced specific modifications in the case of Japan and British India, and the regulations adopted in 1923 by other Asian countries; these had been studied by the Labour Office and had all, with the exception of Ceylon and the Philippines, lowered the minimum age to twelve or even lower. The official reason given for this change was simply the 'earlier maturity of Eastern peoples' (Volksraadstukken 1925: 9).

In Java's leading export sector, the board of the sugarcane employers' association (JSWB) had already preempted the anticipated government ordinance by issuing a prohibition on the employment of any 'children, who may reasonably be supposed not to have reached the full age of twelve years,'[10] beginning with the harvest campaign of 1924. The JSWB advised the Labour Office that:

> the exploitation of children, insofar as it amounts to an abuse, must be sought chiefly in small-scale enterprises which would have difficulty under the proposed regulations, and definitely not in the large European enterprises (Verslag 1925: 46).

The JSWB thus made clear that while they had prohibited child employment in their factories (not in the fields!), they did not consider it particularly necessary to do so. Explaining the decision in their annual report, they admitted that social legislation in general was the obvious means to bring about reforms, and therefore to counter the idea ('which had captured not only socialist theoreticians and communist hotheads') that the end of the First World War must bring radical changes in the structure and working of society; such reforms however tended to affect precisely those enterprises where they were least needed:

> it is always simplest to apply social legislation to those enterprises in which labour relations are most regulated, most easy to monitor, most systematic and therefore almost always the best. In consequence, particularly in the Indies, abuses are first combated in the places where they do not exist at all, or scarcely so (Verslag 1925: 45).

In fact, the sugar industry did rely extensively on juvenile labour, not mainly in its factories (which were covered by the prohibition) but in the sugarcane fields (which were not), in such tasks as fertilizing, planting, watering and weeding. One year after the ban, the sugar association's 138 factories reported using no less than 14.4 million person-days of so-called 'half-adult' labour, with this category comprising as much as 23 per cent of all hired labour days in some districts (Levert 1934: 126).

The Netherlands Indies Agricultural Union reported objections to the proposed prohibition from many upland plantations, including some rubber estates but particularly the tea estates, which employed children in many kinds of work. Labour Office officials made repeated visits to tea factories to convince them that they could easily do without the labour of children under twelve, which was in any case not often used inside the factories; in one factory which did make widespread use of children, calculation of the costs of replacing children by adults

10 The awkward wording reflects the absence of any system of civil registration and hence of a means of establishing the precise age of young workers.

showed that production costs would increase only by one-tenth of one cent per pound of tea (Volksraadstukken 1925: 4).

In the tobacco belt of Besuki (East Java) a study commissioned by the Labour Office found widespread employment of children below twelve years; the total number of underage children at work during the campaign season (August-April) was estimated at 5,000, almost entirely girls. They worked in both drying- and packing-sheds, particularly the latter, fetching and carrying bundles of tobacco leaf to the sorting- and stacking-women and bringing the sorted bundles to the weighing-scales and packing-chests. These often very young girls worked from 6 am to 5 or 5.30 pm, with rest breaks totaling 1-2 hours, for a daily wage of about 10 cents (Volksraadstukken 1925: 4).

These employers, arguing against prohibition of child labour, pointed – with the support of local government officials – to:

> the absence of a civil registration system for natives [which made it difficult to ascertain the age of young workers – BW], the fear that older workers might damage the tobacco through rough handling, and the difficulty of replacing children by adults, particularly in the sparsely-populated districts of South Jember (*ibid.*)

Summarising the results of the Inquiry the Labour Office concluded:

> that with one single exception, application of the convention on child labour as specified in the proposed ordinance would provoke few objections from industries in the Indies and certainly would not seriously inconvenience them [...] (*ibid.*)

The single exception was the tobacco industry; their objections according to the government:

> had been partly overcome by formulating the definition of 'workplace' in such a way that the mainly open drying-sheds were not included, and only work in the closed fermenting-sheds would be covered by the prohibition (*ibid.*)

By re-defining 'workplace,' then, the only serious objections to the proposed ordinance could be circumvented, but with the consequence that some of the largest concentrations of child employment in export production (in field work and in the drying-sheds) would be left undisturbed.

Introducing the proposed Ordinance to the Volksraad in 1925, the government underlined its position that there was not really a child labour *problem* in the Indies: the Ordinance 'was thought desirable as a preventive measure, to ensure that abuses such as Western countries had known would never arise in the Indies' developing industries' (Boeijinga 1926: 149). In Governor-General Fock's explanatory note various other actual or possible objections to the provisions were also addressed, often with reference to the experience of the Netherlands or other Western countries. The objection that women and children had to contribute to family income, and that state intervention in this matter would lead to serious popular resistance, was brushed aside:

> There is no need for concern about popular resistance, when children below twelve years may no longer work inside factories and enclosed workplaces; they may still work in the rice-fields, as buffalo-herds and in all fieldwork [...] and for the present the employment of older boys will not be interfered with at all (Volksraadstukken 1925: 4 – note again the emphasis on the boy-child).

Some Volksraad members had objected (with reason) that the limitation of child labour made no sense if it was not linked to compulsory education, as it had been in the Netherlands and other Western countries:

> The argument that [...] this ordinance will only impel children who don't attend school to hang around the kampungs, instead of accustoming themselves to labour through regularly undertaking light and educative work, thus nurturing habits of idleness and sloth, could only be accepted if (1) there were no opportunity for education and (2) all forms of child employment were banned; neither of these is the case, since education facilities are ever increasing and only that labour is prohibited which gives grounds for concern for accidents, health and growth, while work in the fields, and with livestock, work which the young native has done for centuries, is totally untouched.
> Keeping small children away from places where machines are working, from long and monotonous work in closed places, from carrying and breaking stones in road construction, where abuses can and indeed do easily occur, cannot be equated with banning children from useful employment in other activities or preventing them from earning some extra money (Volksraadstukken 1925: 4).

This remark should be weighed against the reality that in the 1920s, although education facilities were increasing, more than 60 per cent of all Indonesian children were not yet attending school of any kind, and the great majority of those who did attend school remained there only for three years, leaving at age nine or ten (Brugmans 1938: ch. XI, Ricklefs 1981: 150–1).

The government also claimed that the proposed Ordinance had not simply copied the original ILO Convention or the Netherlands Labour Laws of 1911 or 1919, but had been carefully adapted to local conditions, in particular by carefully defining 'industrial undertakings' in a more restricted way than the Convention's much more general formulation which would have led to serious objections.[11] In the

11 As '1. factories, that is enclosed places or places considered as closed, where one or more powered machines are used in or for an enterprise,' and '2. enclosed workplaces where ten or more persons undertake manual work in or for an enterprise'.

case of 'workplaces' the phrase 'considered as closed' had been specifically omitted so as to exclude from regulation many activities of an agricultural character which took place in open spaces, for example, workplaces under a simple roof, open-sided sheds like the tobacco-drying sheds and other open-air activities without powered machinery all fell outside the prohibition (Volksraadstukken 1925: 9-10).[12] The government's adaptation to local conditions was of course a highly selective one, with no attempt to shift the Convention's industrial focus to the conditions of the Indies' overwhelmingly agrarian economy, and conceiving of 'industrial undertaking' even more narrowly so as to place known (agro) industrial concentrations of full-time child employment outside the definition of 'child labour.'

In the Volksraad debate, some members expressed disappointment that the subject of child labour had only arisen from considerations of 'international propriety,' even though the Volksraad itself had been responsible for the installation of a committee to enquire into labour conditions in 1918. They also were disappointed that European and native employees' associations had not been included in the Inquiry. Others asked why, even though the Netherlands' own child labour laws had been much more widely opposed by manufacturers than this proposed Ordinance, still the government proposed to concede far more exceptions in the Indies than in the Netherlands, why was no consideration given to limiting children's working-hours, for example to a maximum of eight hours excluding rest-breaks, and why were no regulations proposed to protect young workers of thirteen-fourteen years of age? Others suggested that *all* workplaces, including those with less than ten workers, should be included, excepting only 'pure' household enterprises where only members of the same household were at work, many native and Chinese enterprises, it was argued, would fall outside the Ordinance while it might be precisely in such enterprises that prohibition was most needed, for example in the batik workshops where it was known that serious abuses abounded (Volksraadstukken 1925, (6, 4): 2-3). Some of these interventions, then, could be seen as attempts by the more progressive members in the Volksraad to adapt the ordinance much more fundamentally to local realities.

The government answered these reservations in a *Memorie van Antwoord* of 11 June 1925. Limitation of working-hours in the case of child employment would fit only in a framework of protective regulation of the labour of so-called 'young persons,' while the suggestion to raise the minimum age to fifteen years was also

12 The minimum limit of 10 workers was borrowed from the Indian Factories Act of 1922 (Volksraadstukken 1925: 9-10); in fact, many of the definitions of prohibited kinds of employment besides 'factories and workshops' (for example, construction, transport, freight handling etc. as defined in articles 2c, 2d and 2e) were derived either from the ILO Convention or from the Netherlands' own Labour Law of 1919.

considered inadvisable, since 'natives of fifteen years are in physical development much closer to adults than to children.' And as to extending the prohibition to enterprises with less than ten workers:

> Besides the fact that it would be unenforceable without a huge number of inspectors, these small enterprises with less than 10 workers are anyway ruled more by family-relations and popular custom, and need more time to adapt themselves than the larger, more businesslike establishments (Volksraadstukken 1925, 6, 5: 2).

The Ordinance was approved in the Volksraad, signed by Governor-General Fock on 17 December 1925 and came into force on 1 March 1926 (Staatsblad 1925).

Enforcing Restrictions on Child Employment: The Late Colonial Years

In the following years the Labour Office seems to have been quite active in investigating and prosecuting violations of the new Ordinance- at least, in comparison to post-colonial Indonesia – and to have had some limited success. In the years 1933-1938 for example no less than 444 cases were brought to court, all of them in Java and nearly all involving Asian (that is, Chinese/Indian/Arab) employers, with fines of between fifty and seventy-five guilders being applied in most cases. The most commonly-prosecuted enterprises were (in descending order of frequency): batik workshops (139 cases); tobacco sorting and processing (73); kapok processing (56); textile-weaving (48); rice or maize milling (26); tea processing (21); ground-nut sorting (19); tapioca-making (7); coffee roasting (5), with smaller numbers (less than 5 cases) in bakeries, leather tanneries, cotton sizing, copper-beating, mosquito-coils, floor-tiles, fireworks, can factories, copra-drying, printing shops, glassworks, hat-weaving, kerupuk-making, cooking-oil, cigarette-papers, and tofu processing (Kantoor van Arbeid 1937, Kantoor van Arbeid 1939). It is interesting to note the relative frequency of agro-processing, alongside the expected craft and manufacturing industries, in this list.

The inspectors also found children working in many other enterprises besides those prosecuted; generally, if only one or two children were involved, the employer was merely issued a warning (Kantoor van Arbeid 1937: 130). In some cases the children simply ran faster than the inspectors:

> In several Chinese cigar or cigarette-factories, batik workshops etc. we found that each time we visited, many children simply took to their heels through the many passages which such factory-complexes have [...] making it difficult if not impossible to establish a violation (Kantoor van Arbeid 1939: 177).

In the plantation enterprises outside Java it was reported that 'child employment is limited to light garden- and fieldwork for a few hours only, such as picking caterpillars, collecting seeds and also – in tobacco farms – stringing up tobacco leaves in the drying sheds' (Kantoor van Arbeid 1937: 131).

At least in some corners of the Labour Office, voices were raised in favour of extending child labour regulation to enterprises with less than ten workers. De Kat Angelino's extensive report on the batik industry noted that most batik workshops where child workers were found fell outside the 1925 regulations, since they were generally in the parental home and sometimes in 'completely open spaces, under a roof on some poles in the parental compound, a shady spot in the yard'; nevertheless the workshops were:

> very unhealthy places, where the labour of children under twelve years of age can no longer be permitted [...] Given the very unhealthy conditions in this industry, it seems desirable to prohibit the employment of children in even the smallest batik-enterprises (de Kat Angelino 1930–1: 122).

One interesting aspect of implementation is that the Labour Office sometimes went beyond the strict provisions of the Ordinance and persuaded employers' associations to enter voluntary agreements restricting the employment of juvenile workers even when these were not covered by the Ordinance. In the East Javanese tobacco regions of Besuki and Pasuruan, the tobacco companies agreed after long negotiations to restrict work-hours of children under twelve (insofar as their work fell outside the 'closed workplaces,' and thus outside the ordinance), to seven hours per day in normal months and eight hours in the harvest season. The Inspectorate was also active in monitoring the conditions of work of 'young persons,' although these were not covered by any state regulations. In the tobacco-drying sheds of East Java for example, where agreements had been made to limit work-hours of 'half-adults' (*halfwassenen*) of twelve-sixteen years to eight hours per day during harvest and seven hours at other times, it was found that the agreements had generally been adhered to. The Inspectors noted that persons of this age-group 'were found in almost all kinds of enterprise, both inside and outside factories and workshops'; in some cases, where long working hours, hazardous work or unhealthy conditions suggested action, employers were urged to replace their young workers, even when these were working legally, with adults (Kantoor van Arbeid 1939: 178).

In the Central Javanese principalities of Yogyakarta and Surakarta, where tobacco was also a major crop, the Principalities' Agricultural Association (VLV) in 1926 objected to voluntary restrictive agreements on the technical grounds that limitation of juveniles' work-time to eight hours (including one hour's break) would make timely processing of the harvested leaves – 'an absolute necessity in this industry' – impossible, and urged the Labour Office to verify these practical objections for itself. In 1927 however the VLV planters agreed to a temporary measure: juvenile workers would either be divided into two part-time shifts, or replaced with adult workers, except in some tasks (particularly the sorting and smoothing out of the dried leaves) where the VLV insisted that restrictions would bring the enterprise into serious problems. To assess the VLV's claims, the Labour office carried out a survey in 1928 covering both the enterprises and the villagers where tobacco growers lived. The resulting report (de Kat Angelino 1929) provides fascinating details of the labour process; while most of these are not of interest for our present purpose, some of the conclusions drawn by Labour Controller Raden Iskander from his village-level interviews are quite revealing of prevailing views of the adults and children involved.

Having never considered the age of their workers to be a matter of concern, and in the absence of any civil registration system, the administrators often reported problems in establishing the age of their younger workers. In Klaten, Raden Iskandar brought together a collection of children (from age eight and above) and young persons, male and female, and an adult man and woman for comparison, and invited a committee of five persons to estimate their ages (the local village head, schoolteacher, policeman, a foreman of the tobacco company and himself). With the ages arrived at by this consensus pinned on placards to their shirts they were lined up in various combinations against a 1.60 metre measuring rod, and photographed against a 1.60 metre measuring to provide a guideline for the administrators.[13] Iskandar concluded that 'considering their build, facial expression and general *habitus*, serious errors in estimating the age limits would be impossible' (de Kat Angelino 1929: 134).

On the attitudes of the local population, Iskandar concluded:

> It can not be expected that people would understand that the prohibition of child labour is intended to promote the child's physical and mental development [...] If you ask [the villager] what he thinks about it, he will answer that he was ordered to keep the children at home, and that's why he does it.
> A woman overseer explained that the children were sent home because it was not good for them to be in the sorting-sheds [...] She had also noticed that small children in the sorting-sheds were often sick and vomited (de Kat Angelino 1929: 143-4).

On the attitudes of the children themselves, it was reported that some children came home in tears when turned away from the tobacco sheds [...] Some (adult) villagers jokingly remarked that they only cried at the loss of their *snoepcenten* (lit. pennies for candy) and maybe also because they were not yet seen as grown-up.

13 Three of these photos are reproduced in the report (de Kat Angelino 1929: 133-4).

Children's interest in earning money and their consciousness as workers were also manifested in other, not so childish ways, as experienced by a nursery foreman who had sent for some children to pick caterpillars off the young tobacco leaves. When the children appeared for payment, in what he thought to be too large numbers, their hands full of infested leaves, he tore them out of the children's hands and stamped on them, refusing to pay. Some of the disappointed children, whether in tears or not, then set a drying-shed on fire in protest.

As for the possible dangers of condemning children to idleness: there was no indication, Raden Iskandar reported, that children barred from the packing-sheds would be hanging around idle, at the mercy of the 'demoralising influences of the village':

> Besides the fact that the child is an appreciable source of domestic help, there is always something to do in and around the village that brings in cash or saves on expenses [...] The young child can look after little brothers and sisters, whose working mother might otherwise have to hire help for this; the girls can cook rice and vegetables, clean the house and yard, bring meals to the parents [in the fields], gather firewood that otherwise would have to be bought, look for wild vegetables in the fields; the boys can graze the animals or ducks, cut fodder, help their fathers in all stages of rice and tobacco cultivation; many children earn money selling snacks, serving in foodstalls, or running errands for neighbours [...] (de Kat Angelino 1929: 140).

These remarks, besides offering a fine stereotype of gender divisions, underline the point that the child labour ordinance, and its enforcement apparatus, were not intended to keep children away from the world of work, from agricultural production or even from earning money, and certainly not to push them into school – the latter, interestingly, is hardly mentioned in the entire report – but only to ban them from the world of industry and large-scale, formal sector agro-processing in enclosed buildings.

The 1925 Ordinance remained in force without changes for more than twenty years. In the late 1940s, on the eve of transfer of sovereignty to the Indonesian Republic, two parallel developments left the legal status of child workers in Indonesia in a state of some confusion. In 1948, in the heat of the revolution the provisional Republican government formulated a new Labour Act (re-enacted as Act no. 1 of 1951 shortly after the transfer of sovereignty) which included a (total) prohibition on employment of children under fourteen, defining 'employment' for this purpose as work performed by a labourer with an industrial relation to an employer. The 1951 Act however included the provision that enactment of specific articles could be postponed; and this provision was applied to the child labour clause, which was never subsequently brought into force by announcement of implementation regulations and procedures. Meanwhile, in 1949 the beleaguered (colonial) Indies government amended its 1925 Ordinance, raising the minimum age to fourteen years (but only, as explained above, applying to factories and enclosed industrial workplaces employing more than ten persons). Since the 1951 Act had no validity in the matter of child employment, most observers agree that, formally speaking, the amended 1925 Ordinance is the regulation that remained in force (Bessell 1999: 358–9, ILO 1994: 16–7). The question is mainly academic however, since as we shall see, not a single case was prosecuted during the ensuing half-century until (and, so far as I know, since) passage of Indonesia's new Labour Law in 1997.

Attitudes to Juvenile Work and Education in the Late Twentieth Century

During the past half-century since independence, the lives of Indonesian children have changed in many ways. While the formal age of (political) majority remains unchanged, 'childhood' itself has become extended and redefined through a combination of rising age at first marriage, the rapid spread of primary and junior secondary education, and correspondingly changed patterns of involvement in work for most children, both boys and girls.

Dramatic growth in access to education meant that by the mid-1980s (before the introduction of compulsory education in 1984), more than 90 percent of boys and girls aged seven–twelve, and just under 70 percent of girls and just over 70 per cent of boys between thirteen–fifteen were already attending school (Oey-Gardiner 1991)[14]; by the end of the twentieth century attendance had risen to 96 per cent (in the seven–twelve age group) and 79 per cent (thirteen–fifteen) (Oey-Gardiner 2000: 127). The number of children under fifteen who are employed and not attending school is therefore relatively small, according to most estimates probably somewhere between two and three million, or roughly one in ten children in the ten–fourteen age group, most of these in the upper years of that age group (White and Indrasari Tjandraningsih 1998: 17–8).

School attendance, (although occupying only four–five hours per day in the first six years) places limits on the kinds of work available to children, and of course restricts employment to a part-time activity. A good example is given by the Akatiga Foundation's recent research in East Java's tobacco industry. Older respondents (who were of primary school age roughly from Indonesian independence to the mid-1970s) recall working childhoods similar to those which we

14 Despite this remarkable progress significant numbers of impoverished children remain outside the formal education system: in the poorest quintile of Indonesian households in 1999, 8 per cent of primary age and 34 per cent of junior secondary age children were not in school (Oey-Gardiner 2000: 127).

have already outlined for the late colonial period: not going to school at all, working full-time in the drying sheds helping their mothers (who earned piece-rate wages) from the age of five-six years until they got married (sometimes as early as age twelve for girls) and started to work on their own account. While today's tobacco companies, both state-owned and private, still make widespread use of child labour it is now on a rather different basis. All children attend school for at least some years; many, particularly girls, begin working in the drying or sorting sheds before they are twelve years old, but the majority combine this with school attendance, working four hours or less on school days; only about one in ten left primary school before completion. Also in contrast to earlier times, child workers generally earn their own wages although some give part or all to their parents. Other aspects of child work in this sector however have not changed; more than half the children complained of headaches and nausea from the heavy, tobacco-laden atmosphere of the tobacco sheds.[15]

Compared to many other Asian countries there was comparatively little public concern, and correspondingly little research on Indonesian child labour until the 1990s. From various small-scale studies it appears that child factory workers and domestic servants are predominantly female, while those in the rural or urban small-scale, informal sector enterprises are more commonly male. Very few children in factory employment or domestic service are still in school, but most of them have completed at least some years of primary school. In contrast, most studies suggest that more than half of all children in informal-sector employment, including 'street children,' are still attending school (Irwanto et al. 1995, White and Tjandraningsih 1998: ch. III).

'Real' street children – those who literally live on the streets of Indonesian cities – are a very small proportion of urban working children. Street-based working children – those who make a living in urban street occupations, but do not actually live there – are much larger in number but are not necessarily more vulnerable than other categories of working children, in fact probably less so. A comparative study in Jakarta found that two-thirds of street children were attending school compared to one-half of urban scavengers and only one-fifth of factory workers; street children's earning were also higher than in these other occupations (Irwanto et al. 1995). A recent anthropometric study among Jakarta street children found a very low prevalence of indicators of current nutrition or disease problems compared to a control sample; the street children in fact were both taller, and weighed more, than their non-street children peers (Groos et al. 1996). The relatively great attention paid by policy makers and NGOs to street children – out of all proportions to their numbers, for example in comparison to child industrial workers and domestic servants – reflects no doubt the perception that

15 Information is from the draft report (Tjandraningsih and Anarita 2001).

street children are either particularly vulnerable and in need of 'rescue,' or more simply a dangerous nuisance, prone to immorality and criminality and beyond adult control: to middle-class adults, both Indonesian and foreign, they appear as 'children out of place' who do not fit the modern image of childhood (Ennew 1994: 14).

There are few documented cases of extreme abuse of child workers. Bonded labour, the virtual kidnapping of children, mass concentrations of children working for long hours and in appalling conditions (such as reported from South Asian carpet, matchstick of glassworks industries or in sweatshops and prostitution as often reported for Thailand and the Philippines) have rarely if ever been brought to light in academic research or the mass media. Isolated cases of extreme abuse of smaller numbers of child workers certainly do occur (some examples are mentioned in White and Indrasari Tjandraningsih 1998: 31), and international attention was recently attracted to the case of several thousand children working in harsh conditions close to forced labour on the off-shore fishing platforms *(jermal)* in the Malacca Straits.

It also appears from various studies – again, in Asian comparative terms and with some exceptions – that children below fifteen years are not employed systematically or on a large scale in Indonesia's labour-intensive export manufacturing sector (garments, footwear, toys etc.). The US Department of Labour, mandated since 1994 by the US Congress to identify countries and industries using child labour in US imports, mentions 'credible allegations' of child employment in Indonesian US-destined exports but its reports could provide surprisingly few details compared to many other countries (US Department of Labour 1994, US Department of Labour 1995). Factory recruitment generally aims at lower secondary school graduates (i.e. from fifteen years upwards) although employers are certainly not insistent on barring entry to younger children who may have forged their school diplomas.

For the first three decades after independence the child labour problem as such was given little if any attention by the government or the labour movement, although sporadic reports appeared in the media. No efforts were made to straighten out the unclarity surrounding child employment legislation, nor have any employers been prosecuted for employing underage children (ILO 1994: 19), in contrast to the relatively energetic interventions of the Labour Office in the 1930s. Much greater efforts were directed to rapidly extending access to primary and secondary school, both before and after the formal introduction of compulsory education (for children aged 7-12) in 1984. By the mid-1980s however we can detect the emergence of both some concern and some ambivalence on the child labour issue in government circles, with a tendency on the one hand to deny reports of child employment (particularly in factory industries, and particularly in statements directed at the outside world), and on the other for specific departments to recognise the existence of a child labour problem and the need to find new ways of addressing it.

In January 1983 *Newsweek's* international edition, for a special report on child labour, used as its glossy front cover a coloured photo showing a very young boy (perhaps five-six years old) carrying a brick on his head, and captioned 'on the job in Indonesia' (*Newsweek*, 24/1/83). In response a Ministry of Labour spokesman said that there was no child labour problem in Indonesia, since children under fourteen were forbidden to work,[16] any children seen working in a factory were 'not actually working but accompanying their parents' and the *Newsweek* photo was 'probably of a child helping in his parents' brickyard' (*Asia Record*, March 1983: 4). In the following year however, while introducing the new compulsory education programme[17] the Minister of Home Affairs directed special attention to the problems of working children:

> In the framework of compulsory education attention must be paid to school-age children who because of socio-economic circumstances are compelled to work in factories, agriculture/plantations etc. who should be accommodated in non-formal education groups (Ministry of Home Affairs, Instruction 421/7519/SJ para. 2c).

In 1987, in a similar spirit of realism (or protection of child workers rather than denial of child employment) the Minister of Labour issued a controversial regulation 'For the Protection of Children Who Are Compelled to Work.' The regulation recognised that children under the legal minimum age of fourteen may be compelled by circumstances to enter employment, but stipulated that in such cases children should not work more than four hours daily or at night, should be paid at least the legal minimum wage, and should be provided with opportunities for basic education (Ministerial Regulation no. 1/1987). Some legal experts and NGOs disputed this Decree, on the grounds that it contradicts both the 1925 Ordinance and the 1951 Act.

In 1989 the government had rejected an ILO proposal to establish a small child labour programme; three years later, in a significant shift in response to new external pressures Indonesia agreed to launch one of the first six country programmes in the ILO's new International Programme for the Elimination of Child Labour (IPEC), and adopted a National Plan of Action at a well-publicised National Conference in 1993. The Action Plan recommended revocation of the 1987 Decree and the issuance of regulations for implementation of the 1951 Act. The old

16 As we have seen, due to the unclear status of child employment regulations there is some doubt whether this was formally the case (an open-air brickyard, including the partly-open sheds in which the firing kilns are housed, would not fall under the amended 1925 ordinance).

17 In fact, by the time compulsory education for the 7-12 age group was introduced in 1984, already about 97 per cent of children in that age group were enrolled in school (Booth 1998: 275).

ambivalence however remained: on the same day that he inaugurated the Indonesian component of the IPEC programme the Minister of Labour took care to make a public denial of reports of child employment in Indonesian industry (*Kompas*, 8/12/92).[18]

Such ambivalence is not hard to understand in face of the threatening and quite distorted picture of child labour in Indonesia that was emerging at this time, due to the lobbying particularly of US Trade Unions and the AFL-CIO's affiliate the Association of Asian Free Labour Institutes (AAFLI). This may be seen in exaggerated form in the following fragment from a 1994 article in *American Prospect* magazine highlighted by Bessell:

> Indonesia in 1949 prohibited children from working. But in 1987, to attract more investment, the country abolished this prohibition [...] By 1991 there were 2.8 million children 'bonded' to factories – that is, mortgaged by parents to employers (Rothstein, 'The global hiring hall: why we need worldwide labour standards' quoted in Bessell 1999: 353).

These few lines embody at least five gross inaccuracies: first, that in 1987 the prohibition on child labour had been abolished (the Minister's 1987 Regulation is explicitly stated not to replace existing legislation); second, that the 1987 Regulation was intended to attract foreign investment (there is no evidence of this); third, that 2.8 million children were working in factories (as we have seen above, this is actually closer to most estimates of the total number of full-time employed children in Indonesia; most of these are not in the industrial sector but in agriculture, trade and service sectors; and among those working in industry, most are not in factories but in small-scale industries); fourth, that these children are 'bonded' (most research suggests that children in industrial employment enter simple work agreements, whether written or unwritten, and are free to leave), and fifth that their parents have 'mortgaged' them to employers (research in several industries has shown that most children have made their own decision, with or without their parents' consent, to enter factory employment and in most cases also retain their own wages).[19]

The reasons why it became so important for foreign observers and lobbyists to portray Indonesian child employment conditions in this exaggerated way can be found in the momentum of international discourse and policy on child labour

18 Recall the colonial government's attitude almost 70 years earlier, pushing through a Child Labour ordinance while at the same time insisting that it was not really necessary except as preventive measure.

19 It is possible that ideas of children 'bonded' or 'mortgaged' by parents, if not transplanted from South Asia, have been transposed from reports on the off-shore fishing rigs in northern Sumatra, where such practices do indeed occur (White and Tjandraningsih 1998: 52–6).

through a succession of (overlapping) waves, and the emergence around the beginning of the 1990s of a third wave (on top of 'abolitionism' and 'protectionism'), in which the child labour problem is 'identified as an extreme example of the abuses of labour standards and human rights that will go unchecked within an unregulated trade regime'; juvenile employment then, in countries defined like Indonesia as having a child labour problem, is represented as primarily industrial, homogeneous, always inhuman and abusive (Bessell 1999: 353, 356). It is also identified as primarily a global trade issue, although even the ILO estimates that less than 5 per cent of the world's working children are involved in export production. Concrete measures stemming from this perspective include Senator Harkin's bill (introduced in 1993) to ban imports into the United States of goods produced wholly or partly by child labour (Rahman et al. 1999), and a number of non-governmental initiatives in 'social labelling,' the labelling of products to provide a 'child labour free' guarantee (Hilowitz 1997). Such interventions then represent the demand-side face of abolitionism, working to prohibit the employment of children rather than to improve conditions for child workers. Children, when asked their opinion, are overwhelmingly against the boycott of products made by children.

In this new context the last years of the twentieth century saw some important developments in the regulatory framework, both internationally and in Indonesia. As the Suharto regime was already faltering and the Indonesian economy plunging into deep recession, Indonesia's new Labour Law (UU 25, October 1997) basically combined and re-enacted two previously existing – and in the eyes of some, incompatible – regulations. Clause 95 states bluntly and uncompromisingly 'the employment of children by any employer is prohibited,' thus reflecting the old Labour Law no. 1 of 1951 and bringing legislation into line with the ILO's comprehensive, abolitionist Convention 138 of 1972 (which Indonesia, and many other developing countries, had not yet ratified). Clause 96 however (like the old Ministerial regulation of 1987) establishes an exception to this general prohibition for 'children who for certain reasons are compelled to work'[20]: these are to work for not more than four hours daily, not in certain types of work (including in 'factories in enclosed places where machinery is used'), not between 6 pm and 6 am,[21] and not to be paid below the legal minimum wage rate, but without any obligation on employers (in contrast to the 1987 Regulation) to ensure their access to education. 'Employment of children' is further defined in the Explanatory Note to Clause 95 (1) as 'causing a child to work in a relationship

20 These are defined in the Explanatory Note to Clause 96 (1) as 'children who for certain reasons are compelled to work because of economic reasons in order to increase their family's or their own income, because of parental neglect or an insufficiently harmonious family environment which results in neglect of the child'.

21 Note how an equatorially realistic notion of 'night-time' has finally been reinstated.

bound by working hours and payment of a wage' thus apparently (but perhaps unintentionally) excluding all piece-rate labour arrangements, as well as domestic service (in which working hours are generally extremely long, but not specified in work agreements) (White and Tjandraningsih 1998: 29).

Meanwhile, two important international developments should be included in the picture. The first is the UN Convention on the Rights of the Child (1989), enthusiastically signed and ratified by Indonesia,[22] which is important in various ways. It does not forbid child employment; it establishes the child's right of access to education, to protection from economic exploitation and from involvement in work harmful to the child's development. Furthermore, it establishes the principle that in any matters affecting children, the 'best interests of the child' (rather than, for example, Trade Unions, globally leveled playing fields, or whatever) should be a primary consideration, and further that children have the right to have their own views heard in such matters. Secondly, the ILO after several years of preparation and intense debates at regional and international level during the years 1996–99, adopted Convention 182 (1999) on elimination of the 'worst forms of child labour,' defining these to include prostitution, forced labour, use of children in criminal activities and a final category of work which, by its nature or the manner in which it is carried out, is likely to harm the child's development; this last category is to be identified and defined by member states themselves, with the help of some recommendations attached to the Convention (White 1999). This Convention was also signed and quickly ratified by Indonesia.

Although several new organisations promoting child rights have emerged, there are few signs that they have gone beyond the rhetoric of the UN Convention or considered the practical implications of adopting notions of children as active subjects with the right to express their views and to have them heard. Specifically in the field of child labour, with the overwhelming majority of NGO child labour interventions funded by ILO-IPEC or USAID it is perhaps not surprising that rather conventional views on child employment, and old views of child workers as either threats or victims to be rescued and 'rehabilitated,' still tend to prevail.

In 1998, during the transitional regime of President Habibie and at the height of Indonesia's economic crisis, the Indonesian Institute for Child Advocacy organised a large 'National Workshop on Legal Protection of Child Workers.' The contributed papers, panel discussions and recommendations collected in the workshop's proceedings (Maiyasyak Johan et al. 1998) overwhelmingly discuss the issue not in terms of protecting child workers (although, as we have seen, Indonesia's 1997 Labour Law provides for this) but of abolishing child employment, in revealingly militant language which in places actually talks of 'eliminating child

22 As by all ILO members excepting the United States and Somalia.

workers' and 'abolishing child workers,' as if the children themselves are some kind of scourge or disease.[23] The Conferences' final recommendations begin with '1. Pressurise the Indonesian government to ratify ILO Convention no. 138' [i.e., to re-establish a blanket prohibition on child employment, thus outlawing rather than protecting child workers].[24] Fears of criminality and deviance among urban street children are expressed (Maiyasyak Johan et al. 1998: 80, 128); there is no proposal, even any mention of any needs to realise street or working children's rights to protection.

While it is to be expected that government officials will remain for some time in old modes of child labour discourse it is surprising that so many civil-society activists also appear so out of touch with more recent ideas and approaches focusing on children's needs, interests and rights. Indonesian NGO involvement in child labour issues is relatively recent; since the early 1990s relatively dominated by ILO-IPEC (and more recently USAID) funding; tends in most cases to pay only lip-service to notions of children's rights, and perhaps for these reasons has a rather disappointing record of contributing to any fundamental public re-thinking of child labour issues.

Indonesia's current crisis underlines the need for such re-thinking. Early indications that the crisis would result in mass school drop-outs and corresponding increases in numbers of child workers seem now to have been largely unfounded.[25] By mid-1999, school attendance in both primary, junior and senior secondary school were actually slightly higher than before the crisis (Stalker 2000). While there may have been many more children looking for work (sometimes in order to earn money to stay in school), jobs in most sectors will not have been easy to find; as Hardjono has pointed out, there is no evidence that the crisis has significantly reversed the long term trend to declining work-involvement of children, and there is actually evidence of significant job losses for children in some sectors (particularly manufacturing) as enterprises fail or contract. While it is generally agreed that numbers of children in street trades are increasing, they now have to compete more with adults in these activities. The real challenge is to reduce the

23 '*Mengeliminasi pekerja anak*,' '*menghapuskan pekerja anak*' (Maiyasyak Johan et al. 1998: 43, 132). Possibly the authors used these phrases because of the difficulties in finding an equivalent for 'labour' (as distinguished from more neutral 'work') in Indonesian language, as in most other world languages. Hence one (European) participant's note that we should distinguish 'child work' and 'child labour' has in translation become the confusing '*kita bedakan antara "pekerja anak" dan "anak yang bekerja"*' (literally: 'we distinguish "child worker" and "[a] child who works") (Woodhouse 1998: 42).

24 These or other pressures seem to have worked: Indonesia ratified ILO Convention 138 in the following year (Law no. 20 of 1999).

25 Most claims of higher incidence of child employment, even when recently made, refer to statistics from 1998 (for example Dewanto 2001).

real costs of school and to make it a more rewarding experience, to reduce the numbers of children who continue to drop out of primary and secondary school, even if in no greater numbers than previously (Hardjono 2000: 177–81).

As in other countries which have now ratified both ILO Conventions 138 and 182, those concerned about issues of child work and education in Indonesia face a strategic choice between attempting to enforce a blanket ban on child employment or a more focused effort on the 'worst forms' of child labour. Hardjono correctly questions both the desirability and feasibility of the first: even if it made sense to attempt to remove children from all types of paid employment the Department of Manpower, already overstretched dealing with a host of crisis-related labour disputes 'are unable to give time and attention to the question of working children unless cases of very obvious exploitation or mistreatment are reported to them, or publicised in the media' (Hardjono 2000: 182). While it may be criticised in some details, the focus on 'worst forms' in the new ILO Convention 182 – particularly when viewed in the context of the Convention on Rights of the Child – does provide a potentially workable basis for approaching problems of child workers in ways more attuned to their interests and needs. Apparently the new 'National Action Committee for Elimination of the Worst Forms of Labour,' established by Presidential Decree (no. 12 of 2001) already has its eyes on some specific 'worst forms': child trafficking, debt bondage, use of children in armed conflict, prostitution and pornography, underground mining, pearl diving, and other forms of child work (such as full-time domestic service and factory work) which deny children their fundamental right to education (Dewanto 2001). Rather than insisting on the need to chase children out of all corners of the labour market, this narrower focus on 'worst forms' reflects, ultimately, a better set of priorities where the target is those forms or relations of work which seriously compromise children's rights to health, education and development.

References

Arbeidsinspectie (1913) *Eerste Verslag van den Dienst der Arbeidsinspectie en Koeliewerving in Nederlandsch-Indië: Deel I, Oostkust van Sumatra*, Batavia: G. Kolff & Co.

— (1914) *Derde Verslag van den Dienst der Arbeidsinspectie en Koeliewerving in Nederlandsch-Indië*, Weltevreden: Filiaal Albrecht & Co.

— (1917) *Vierde Verslag van den Dienst der Arbeidsinspectie in Nederlandsch-Indië*, Batavia: Landsdrukkerij.

— (1919) *Verslag van den Dienst der Arbeidsinspectie en in Nederlandsch-Indië over de jaren 1917 en 1918 (Vijfde Verslag)*, Weltevreden: Boekhandel Visser & Co.

Bessell, S. (1999) 'The politics of child labour in Indonesia: global trends and domestic policy', *Pacific Affairs* 72, 3: 353–371.

Boeijinga, K. (1926) *Arbeidswetgeving in Nederlandsch-Indië*, Leiden: Drukkerij Nieuwe Leidsche Courant.

Booth, A. (1998) *The Indonesian Economy in the Nineteenth and Twentieth Centuries: a History of Missed Opportunities*, Basingstoke: Macmillan Press in association with the Australian National University.

Breman, J.C. (1989) *Taming the Coolie Beast: Plantation Society and the Colonial Order in Southeast Asia*, Delhi: Oxford University Press.

Brugmans, I. (1978) *De arbeidende klasse in Nederland in de 19e eeuw 1813-1970*, Utrecht: Het Spectrum.

Brugmans, I.J. (1938) *Geschiedenis van het Onderwijs in Nederlandsch-Indië*, Groningen & Batavia: J.B. Wolters.

Butler, H. (1938) *Problems of Industry in the East: With Special Reference to India, French China, Ceylon, Malaya and the Netherlands Indies*, Geneva: International Labour Office.

Cunningham, H. (1990) 'The employment and unemployment of children in England c. 1680-1851', *Past & Present* 126 (February): 115–150.

— (1995) *Children and Childhood in Western Society Since 1500*, London: Longman.

— (2000) 'The decline of child labour: labour markets and family economies in Europe and North America since 1830', *Economic History Review* LIII(August): 409-428.

Cunningham, H. and Viazzo, P. (eds.) (1996) *Child Labour in Historical Perspective* 1800-1985*: Case Studies from Europe, Japan and Colombia*, Florence: UNICEF International Child Development Centre.

de Coninck-Smith, N., Sandin, B. and Schrumpf, E. (1997) 'Introduction', in N. de Coninck-Smith, B. Sandin and E. Schrumpf (eds.) *Industrious Children: Work and Childhood in the Nordic Countries 1850-1990*, Odense: University Press.

de Kat Angelino, P. (1929) *Vorstenlandsche Tabaksenquete*, Publicatie No. 5 van het Kantoor van Arbeid, Weltevreden: Landsdrukkerij.

— 1930-1931 *Batikrapport*, 3 Vols., Weltevreden and Batavia: Landsdrukkerij.

Ennew, J. (1994) *Street and Working Children: a Guide to Planning*, London: Save the Children.

Gardarsdottir, O. (1997) 'Working children in urban Iceland 1930-1990: ideology of work, work-schools and gender relations in modern Iceland', in N. de Coninck-Smith, B. Sandin and E. Schrumpf (eds.) *Industrious Children: Work and Childhood in the Nordic Countries 1850-1990*, Odense: University Press.

Grier, B. (1994) 'Invisible hands: the political economy of child labour in colonial Zimbabwe, 1890-1930', *Journal of Southern African Studies* 20, 1: 27–52.

Groos, R., Landfried, B. and Herman, S. (1996) 'Height and weight as a reflection of the nutritional situation of school-aged children working and living in the streets of Jakarta', *Social Sciences and Medicine* 43, 4: 453–458.

Hilowitz, J. (1997) 'Social labeling to combat child labour', *International Labour Review* 136, 2: 215–232.

ILO (1994) *Child Labour in Indonesia*, Jakarta: International Labour Office, International Programme on the Elimination of Child Labour.

Irwanto, S., et al. (1995) *Pekerja Anak di Tiga Kota Besar: Jakarta, Surabaya, Medan*, Jakarta: Pusat Penelitian Unika Atma Jaya.

Kantoor van Arbeid (1937) *Zestiende verslag van de Arbeidsinspectie (1933, 1934, 1935 en 1936)*, Batavia: Landsdrukkerij.

— 1939 *Zeventiende verslag van de Arbeidsinspectie (1937 en 1938)*, Batavia: Landsdrukkerij.

Leidraad (1904) *Leidraad voor het gewestelijke onderzoek naar de oorzaken der mindere welvaart van de inlandsche bevolking op Java en Madoera*, Batavia: Landsdrukkerij.

Levert, P. (1934) *Inheemsche arbeid in de Java-suikerindustrie*, PhD dissertation, Wageningen: H. Veenman.

Locher-Scholten, E. (1987) 'Female labour in twentieth century Java: European notions – Indonesian practice', in E. Locher-Scholten and A. Niehof (eds.) *Indonesian Women in Focus: Past and Present Notions*, Dordrecht: Foris (KITLV Verhandelingen 127).

Maiyasyak, J., et al. (eds.) (1998) *Perlindungan Hukum Pekerja Anak di Indonesia*, Medan: Lembaga Advokasi Anak Indonesia.

Nardinelli, C. (1990) *Child Labour and the Industrial Revolution*, Bloomington: University of Indiana Press.

Oey-Gardiner, M.L. (2000) 'Schooling in a decentralised Indonesia: new approaches to access and decision-making', *Bulletin of Indonesian Economic Studies* 36, 3: 127-134.

Oey-Gardiner, M.L. (1991) 'Gender differences in schooling in Indonesia', *Bulletin of Indonesian Economic Studies* 27, 1: 57-80.

Onderzoek (1911) *Onderzoek naar de mindere welvaart der inlandsche bevolking op Java en Madoera. IXc: Overzicht van de uitkomsten der gewestelijke onderzoekingen naar de economie van de desa, Deel III: Bijlagen*, Batavia: Kolff & Co.

— 1912 *Onderzoek naar de mindere welvaart der inlandsche bevolking op Java en Madoera. VI: Overzicht van de uitkomsten der gewestelijke onderzoekingen naar den niet-Inlandsche handel en nijverheid, Deel IV: Eigenlijk overzicht, Deel VI: Bijlagen*, Batavia: Drukkerij Papyrus.

Pleyte, C. (1911) *De inlandsche nijverheid in West-Java als sociaal-ethnologische verschijnsel*, Batavia: Javasche Boekhandel & Drukkerij.

Rahman, M., Khanam, R. and Absar, U. (1999) 'Child labour in Bangladesh: a critical appraisal of Harkin's Bill and the MOU-type schooling programme', *Journal of Economic Issues* XXXIII, 4: 985–1003.

Ricklefs, M. (1981) *A History of Modern Indonesia*, London: Macmillan.

Sandin, B. (1997) '"In the large factory town": child labour legislation, child labour and school compulsion', in N. de Coninck-Smith, B. Sandin and E. Schrumpf (eds.) *Industrious Children: Work and Childhood in the Nordic Countries 1850-1990*, Odense: University Press.

Shivji, I. (1985) 'Law and conditions of child labour in colonial Tanganyika 1920-1940', *International Journal of the Sociology of Law* 13: 221–235.

Sjoberg, M. (1997) 'Working rural children: herding, child labour and childhood in the Swedish rural environment 1850-1950', in N. de Coninck-Smith, B. Sandin and E. Schrumpf (eds.) *Industrious Children: Work and Childhood in the Nordic Countries 1850-1990*, Odense: University Press.

Staatsblad (1925) *Staatsblad van Nederlandsch-Indië no. 647*, Batavia: Landsdrukkerij.

— (1928) *Staatsblad van Nederlandsch-Indië no. 515*, Batavia: Landsdrukkerij.

Stoler, A. (1985) *Capitalism and Confrontation in Sumatra's Plantation Belt, 1870-1979*, New Haven: Yale University Press.

Thorne, B. (1987) 'Re-visioning women and social change: where are the children?' *Gender & Society* 1, 1: 85–109.

Tjoeng, T.F. (1948) *Arbeidstoestanden en arbeidsbescherming in Indonesië*, Den Haag: Van Stockum.

US Department of Labour (1994) *By the Sweat and Toil of Children, Vol. I: the Use of Child Labour in American Imports*, A report to the Committee on Appropriations, United States Congress. Washington DC: Bureau of International Affairs, US Department of Labour.

— (1995) *By the Sweat and Toil of Children, Vol. II: the Use of Child Labour in US Agricultural Imports and Forced and Bonded Child Labour*, A report to the Committee on Appropriations, United States Congress. Washington DC: Bureau of International Labour Affairs, US Department of Labour.

Vakverenigingen, Nederlandsch Verbond van (1908) *Arbeidersleven in Nederland: Resultaten der Enquete ingesteld door het Nederl. Verbond van Vakverenigingen in het Najaar van 1907 naar de*

Wenschelijkheid en Mogelijkheid van Beperking van den Arbeidsduur voor Volwassenen tot 10 Uren per Etmaal en Afschaffing, respectievelijk Beperking van Nacht- en Kinderarbeid, Amsterdam: Soc. Dem. Arbeiderspartij/Ned. Verbond van Vakverenigingen.

van Zanten, H. (1927) *L'influence de la Partie XIII du Traite de Versailles sur le developpement du droit international publique et sur le droit interne des Etats (L'Organisation Permanente du Travail)*, PhD. Thesis, Leiden University.

Verslag (1925) *Verslag van het Algemeen Syndicaat van Suikerfabrikanten in Nederlandsch-Indië over het 30e jaar*, Surabaya: Van Ingen.

Volksraadstukken (1925) *Volksraad, Eerste Gewone Zitting 1925: Onderwerp 6, Stukken 1–3*, Batavia: Landsdrukkerij.

Weiner, M. (1991) *The Child and the State in India: Child Labour and Education Policy in Comparative Perspective*, Princeton, NJ: Princeton University Press.

White, B. (1994a) 'Children, work and "child labour": changing responses to the employment of children', *Development and Change* 25, 4: 849–878.

— (1994b) *Children, Work and 'Child Labour': Changing Responses to the Employment of Children*, Dies Natalis Address, The Hague: Institute of Social Studies.

— (1999) 'Defining the intolerable: child work, global standards and cultural relativism', *Childhood* 6, 1: 133–144.

— (2001) 'Children, work and education; the Netherlands and Netherlands Indies/Indonesia compared, 1900–2000', *Brood & Roozen* 2001/4 (Special issue on child labour): 105-119.

White, B. and Tjandraningsih, I. (1998) *Child Workers in Indonesia*, Bandung: AKATIGA/International Working Group on Child Labour.

Woodhouse, S. (1998) 'Implementasi Konvensi Hak Anak dalam hukum pekerja anak di Indonesia', in Maiyasyak Johan, Muhammad Joni, M.S. Ritonga, Zahrin Piliang and Edy Ikhsan (eds.) *Perlindungan Hukum Pekerja Anak di Indonesia*, Medan: Lembaga Advokasi Anak Indonesia.

4

Trade Unions in Vietnam in Historical Perspective: The Transformation of Concepts

IRENE NØRLUND

Since World War II the world has undergone a number of significant changes, particularly during the cold war, which became a hot war in Asia, in Korea and Vietnam in the 1950s and into the 1970s. This was followed by a period of accommodation and reform in the 1980s, and finally a period of détente and increased cooperation in the 1990s. The war was a conflict between the two major social systems: socialism and capitalism, each functioning according to its own logic. The capitalist system was based on the principle of a market economy and liberalism, and the socialist system was based on state intervention in both the economic and the political spheres. Obviously the realities were much more complex than the stereotypes, and conflicts between countries often had much deeper historical roots under the superficial national participation in one or the other camp. In all cases there were gaps between the ideology of the state and the realities. It should not be overlooked, however, that ideologies and self-image also had an impact on the way the state acted.

In the case of Vietnam the reforms that began in the early 1980s also signalled the end of classical socialist central planning, which was replaced by a system in transformation that is a combination of the perceptions and rules of the classical socialist system and the increasing impact of the market. It is still too early to call the present system a post-socialist one, and it is also too early to predict that part of the socialist system will not survive in a 'neo-socialist' type of society in a state policy with a social emphasis. If ownership of land - private or collective - is the main determinant for distinguishing a type of society, certainly, individual private property is the reality in Vietnam today. If, on the other hand, political system and identity are the main criteria for determining social systems, the dichotomy between capitalism and socialism seems to fade away. The state is not only an important actor in socialist countries, because even in the capitalist parts of East and Southeast Asia it is now obvious that the market and liberal politics are not the only determining factors. In most of Asia the state has been and is of prime importance.

The evolution of the current social systems can be better understood in their historical perspective, combined with the context of increasing globalisation in the most recent decades. Added to the historical perspective and globalisation is the emphasis on liberal ideas.

The purpose of this paper is to analyse labour and trade unions in Vietnam in their historical perspective. From this analysis we hope to point out some of the continuities and discontinuities in Vietnamese socio-political history to elucidate some of the dilemmas facing the Vietnamese trade unions in their transformation. Labour and trade unions are particularly important in the Vietnamese context, because they were part of the broad social organisations of the Communist Party, and in the party's view, they constituted the most important power base of the (party) state. This history will be described through the role of the working class and the trade unions in the four Vietnamese constitutions: 1946, 1959, 1980, and 1992. The constitutions are of significance because each was formulated at a specific time, and shed light on the type of regime in existence at that particular period. Of course, the constitutions reflect the ideology the party-state pursued and promoted at various times. Our task in this context is to follow and analyse the perception of the party, or in modern terms, to analyse the discourse of the party.

With the opening of the Vietnamese economy to foreign investment in the late 1980s and the 1990's, new conditions were developing for the labour force and the trade unions, and their perceptions were also changing. But even before this, many of the older ideas had begun to change. One important new issue was the perception of women in the labour force, for they constituted a significant share of the labour force in foreign-funded enterprises. The changes in concepts and perceptions must be seen as a process subject to continuous change – it is an issue that will be even more important under the impact of globalisation.

Trade Unions in Historical Perspective

The trade unions in Vietnam, closely connected with the party from the very beginning of the revolution in the 1920s, passed through various stages of revolution. At first they were opposed to the (colonial) government, from the 1920s to the 1940s. Following the August revolution in 1945, the party became a counter-power to the colonial government, but in an 'established state'. After the Geneva agreement in 1954, it held formal power in the north of the country. The unions were one of the mass organisations that carried out party policy. Then, in the 1980s, the reform process started, at first by means of small steps but later having a broader goal of 'market-socialism' or 'neo-socialism'. Even if it is not yet clear where this development will lead, the capitalist relationship between production and foreign influence have been accepted by the party-state. New contradictions have been inherited in the present society, because it is a combination of socialist state and a society influenced by market forces. The role of trade unions is also important because through them some of the interests in society are manifested. In addition, they enable us to judge some of the intentions and real changes taking place.

When the Red Workers' Association was established in 1929, it was an integral part of the revolutionary movement's attempt to win power and create a socialist state. In the neighbouring country, China, the peasants began to play a leading role in the revolution after the slaughter of the workers in Shanghai in 1927, especially after Mao Zedong took the leadership in the long march in the early 1930s.

In Vietnam the path of revolution took a somewhat different direction. Ho Chi Minh, who became one of the leading figures in the Communist movement, was inspired first by the Second International, and in the early 1920s he came to know the people who organised the Third International in France. Because it espoused much stronger anti-colonial ideas, he was attracted by the new movement and started to work for the Third International – first in Paris and later in Moscow. Although he himself was probably more anti-French nationalist than hard core communist, he believed the anti-colonial policy was essential. The political direction that determined the revolutionary path in Indochina occurred in the late 1920s and the early 1930s; it clearly emphasised the role of the proletariat, and many of the (intellectual) communist cadres took jobs as workers in the large French enterprises to join the rising proletariat. It was only after the Japanese occupation in 1941 that the strategy changed to participate in the resistance of the peasantry in the countryside, and the peasants were accepted as equal partners in the revolutionary task.[1] The changed strategy was not a fundamental change of ideology, but rather a tactical change, because the resistance had to move from its base in the cities to the countryside.

In the Communist Party's history of the Vietnam Worker's Party (published in 1970), we see the following analysis of the importance of the social forces at the time the Vietnam Communist Party was established in 1930 (later that year it became the Indochinese Communist Party):

> The founding of the Vietnam Communist Party marked a momentous turn in the history of the Vietnamese revolution and heralded a new era, the era of the Vietnam-

1 The literature on Vietnamese communism is vast and will not be referred to here. See Huynh Kim Khanh (1982).

> ese revolution under the leadership of the working class and its vanguard, the Marxist-Leninist party.
>
> The Vietnamese working class, though not large in number, was geographically concentrated to a relatively high degree, and was a homogeneous class without a stratum of aristocratic workers thus not subject to the influence of reformism. Moreover, it had a close ally, most reliable and highly combative: the peasantry. Both the workers and the peasants are the main revolutionary forces of our people, a heroic people with a tradition of resolute and unbending struggle. These are the favourable circumstances, which allowed Marxism-Leninism to take root firmly among the masses of our country.
>
> Because of these characteristics of our working class and our people and its basically just line, our Party, although newly founded, had all the requisites of a new-type revolutionary party of the working class and soon became the only leader of the Vietnamese patriotic movement (Anon. 1975: 15).[2]

Even if it is not valid to say that history in and of itself is not important, how history is perceived, especially from today's perspective, is just as important as what actually took place. No doubt the proletariat has played a very central role in the consciousness of the Communist Party: it influenced classical Marxist-Leninist thinking, and the leadership of the party was convinced of the basic validity (in a modified form) of the communist analysis for the conditions in Vietnam. The innovation of the party was to see the party as a 'new-type' of revolutionary party based both on the working class and the peasants.

After the August revolution in 1945, the Democratic Republic of Vietnam was proclaimed. The first constitution was adopted on 9 November 1946, and was largely inspired by the American Declaration of Independence. It was very liberal, emphasising equal rights for all citizens and guaranteeing fundamental freedoms. Moreover, the right of property was guaranteed, as were free elections, social security, and education. The trade unions were not mentioned directly. The only paragraph that dealt with the workers was 'The rights of intellectual and manual workers are guaranteed' (Anon. 1992: 15, chapter II, art. 13).

The Vietnam Federation of Trade Unions (VFTU), based on the union movement of the 1920s, had only just been established in July 1946, immediately before the adoption of the first constitution. The first congress met in 1950 in Viet Bac, the northern liberated provinces, during the resistance against the French (Anon. 1990: 10–11). The task of the VFTU was to encourage workers to evacuate the cities and move the machines and equipment into the mountains to produce sup-

2 First edition appeared in 1970, written by the commission to write the history of the Vietnam Workers' Party. A second edition appeared in 1975 on the occasion of the 44-year anniversary of the VWP. Foreign Language Publishing House, Hanoi, 1978, p. 15.

plies for the military and the necessary consumer goods for the civilian population.

Campaigns to increase production were launched under slogans like 'One hour more work for the national liberation', 'Produce more arms', or 'Increase production to make enough food and clothes'. In the occupied areas the trade unions organised workers to sabotage the economy of the French. The number of supporters increased from 140,000 in 1947 to 310,000 in 1949 (Anon. 1990: 11).

After the defeat of the French army at Dien Bien Phu in 1954 and the peace accord in 1954, Vietnam was de facto divided in two parts. The division was only meant to be temporary, but because reunification did not come about,[3] two different political systems, one in the north and another in the south, became a fact. The party state was established and Leninist institutions were set up on the model of the USSR. The state was called a workers' and peasants' state, but as in the early phase of the Vietnamese revolution, the workers were the core of the revolutionary movement. The state-owned enterprises, most of them taken over after the French retreat in 1954, were the organisational units of the working class, with the trade unions as the bridge between party and workers.

In the south the trade unions had to operate illegally, but in a few years the workers constituted 'one of the most important movements for the struggle in Saigon, Da Nang and other cities which could gather millions of people', claimed the History of the Trade Union Movement (Anon. 1990: 13).

In the trade union law of 1957 in the north (Democratic Republic of Vietnam - DRV), the trade unions were supposed to take part in the economic management of the state and economic enterprises, which accorded them an official position in the corporatist institutions of the party-state. This law obliged the state to establish the necessary conditions for trade union activities, and to create a fund from the 2 per cent tax on salaries, which was to be earmarked for trade union activities (Anon 1990: 23).

The period from 1954 to 1960 was a time of transition; production relationships were gradually socialised, including the land reform and the first phase of collectivisation. Ownership by individuals and national capitalists was still protected by the state. By 1960 the 'socialist construction' was considered to have begun. In 1959 a second constitution was adopted, with new chapters covering the economic and social system and much more detailed paragraphs on the role of the state.

3 This was due to obstacles by the southern Republic of Vietnam and the US government, which feared to lose an election to Ho Chi Minh.

The 1959 Constitution

Labour and trade unions were mentioned directly in this constitution in several paragraphs (quoted below). Contributions to social legislation and the labour code are integrated in the constitution, which is one of the core legal documents of the state in this period. The largest part of the new document is devoted to the structure of state and local administration (which we not deal with in this paper), for its principal focus was to define the political and economic character of the state. One of the main goals - outlined in the first sentence - was to show that the government did not recognise the division of Vietnam into North and South: 'The territory of Vietnam is a single, indivisible whole from North to South' (article 1).

> The Economic and Social System
>
> Art. 10
> The State leads all economic activities according to a unified plan.
>
> The State relies on the organ of State, trade union organisations, co-operatives and other organisations of the working people, to elaborate and carry out the economic plans.
>
> Fundamental Rights and Duties of Citizens - and Women
>
> Art. 24
> Women in the Democratic Republic of Vietnam enjoy equal rights with men in all spheres of political, economic, cultural, social and domestic affairs. For equal work, women enjoy equal pay with men. The state ensures that women workers and office employees have fully-paid periods of leave before and after childbirth.
>
> The state protects the mother and child and ensures the development of maternity hospitals, creches and kindergartens.
>
> The state protects marriage and the family.
>
> Art. 30
> Citizens of the Democratic Republic of Vietnam have the right to work. To guarantee to citizens enjoyment of this right, the state, by planned development of the national economy, gradually creates more employment and better working conditions and wages.
>
> Art. 31
> Working people have the right to rest. To guarantee to working people enjoyment of this right, the State prescribes working hours and holidays for workers and office employees, and gradually expands material facilities to enable working people to rest and build up their health.

It is important to note that the state is responsible for both work and guaranteeing rights and social benefits of the citizens. Moreover, women are to enjoy equal rights, and special care should be taken of women and children. Ho Chi Minh is probably one of the first leaders in Asia to be concerned about women as an important segment of the working population. The type of equality promoted was similar to the individual rights within the collective population in other socialist states. It was based on the perception and expectation that women were full participants in the labour market, and enable them to do that they must be supported. In addition, the family was also mentioned as protected by the state, which differed from some other socialist countries of the time - but even in Vietnam it was a period where the family not emphasised.

The War Period and Liberation

The trade unions' goals were changing according to the historical circumstances. During the Vietnam War (1964-75) the emphasis on the ideological role increased; and after the reunification in 1976, the trade unions' role was 'to mobilise, organise, educate and train the workers', but it was also mentioned that they should 'protect the legitimate interests of the workers and employees and take care of their living conditions' (Vietnam Federation of Trade Union 1978: 213).

In general enterprises in the socialist countries had a double function: they were economic and production units as well as social and political units. According to Pravda and Ruble the trade unions were organised on the Leninist principle of dualism: they were expected to mobilise workers for production, maintain discipline, and educate them about production, management, and ideology, as well as defend labour interests and guard members' legal rights against management (Pravda and Ruble 1986: 2-3).

In the Stalinist ideology the second aspect of the dual function (defending labour interests and guarding members' rights against management) was reduced because there should be no contradictions between labour and management in a socialist state. The state enterprises were those organisations that contained the core 'proletariat' of the revolution; they were also the new experiments of the revolution. It was in the factories that workers came in contact with the party and its officials. They were the origin and the pillar of the new industrial (capital) accumulation, intended to take the country into the communist society of the next century, and whose goal was to create a society of equality.

The 1980 Constitution

The third constitution of the Socialist Republic of Vietnam (the official name was changed from the Democratic Republic of Vietnam in 1976), was adopted 18 December 1980, a few years after the reunification of the country in 1975. At that time the conflicts with China and Cambodia had become open warfare (1978–79), and the party approved the start of the first limited economic reforms in August 1979. The early reforms were still perceived as temporary, and thus are not reflected in the constitution, which was drafted over a longer period, before the reform ideas had become mature.

The Political System

Art. 1
Article 1 of the 1980 Constitution reflected the political situation, as the earlier one had, but under new conditions. The country was now united, and the conflict with China was centred around the offshore islands in the South China Sea:

The socialist Republic of Vietnam is an independent, sovereign and united country comprising its mainland, air space, territorial waters, and off-shore islands.

Art. 2
Human exploitation should be abolished, and the goal is to build socialism successfully to advance to communism.

Art. 3
In the Socialist Republic of Vietnam, the collective master is the working people, comprising the working class, the collective peasantry, the socialist intelligentsia and other labouring people, with the worker-peasant alliance led by the working class as the core.

Art. 4
The Communist Party of Vietnam, the vanguard and general staff of the Vietnamese working class, armed with Marxism-Leninism, is the only force leading the State and the society, and the main factor determining all successes of the Vietnamese revolution.

Art. 9
The Vietnam Fatherland Front, which comprises the various political parties, the Vietnam Confederation of Trade Unions, the Vietnam Association of Collective Peasants, the Ho Chi Minh Communist Youth Unions, the Vietnam Women's Union, and other member organisations, is a firm prop of the state.

The Front promotes the tradition of national unity, strengthens political and moral unity among the people, takes part in building and consolidating the people's power, educates and motivates the people to raise their sense of collective mastery, and to emulate one another in building socialism and defending the country.

Art. 10
The Vietnam Confederation of Trade Unions is the largest mass organisation of the Vietnamese working class, a school of communism, of economic management, and management of the state.

Within the limits of their competence, the Trade Unions take part in State affairs and supervise the work of State bodies, and participate in the management of factories. They educate workers and office employees; organise socialist emulation movements, and, together with the State bodies, care for the lives of workers and office employees and protect their interests.

The Economic System

Art. 15
The Socialist Republic of Vietnam (SRV) is advancing directly from a society in which small-scale production predominates to socialism, bypassing the state of capitalist development to build a society with modern industrial-agricultural economy, advanced culture, science and technology, a strong defence potential and a civilised and happy life.

The economic policies of the SRV are aimed at progressively satisfying the increasing material and cultural needs of the whole society by continuous developing production and raising social labour efficiency, on the basis of socialist collective mastery and modern science and technology.

Art. 16
The central task throughout the period of transition to socialism is the socialist industrialisation of the country [...]

Art. 30
The State educates and motivates the entire people to build socialism with industriousness and thrift; it defines and closely controls the use of the labour force, materials and capital in all economic activities and in the management of the state.

Art. 31
The State and collective economic organisations apply the principle: 'From each according to his ability, to each according to his work', while gradually increasing the social benefits of development of the national economy.

Art. 32
The State, in coordination with the trade-unions and other people's organisations, combines political education and the enhancement of labour discipline with material incentives with the aim of promoting the socialist emulation movement.

Art. 33
The State guides the national economy according to unified plans [...] it mobilises all labour forces, national resources, and material and technical resources of the country, so as to ensure a comprehensive economy at a rapid pace and with a high level of efficiency.

Basic Rights and Obligations of Citizens - and Women

Art. 58
Work is the primary right, obligation and privilege of citizens.

Citizens have the right to work. People fit for work must work as provided by the law.

The State creates jobs on the basis of economic development plans, employs people according to both their personal aptitudes and desires, and social requirements. It fosters professional skill, preserves the health of the work force, and constantly improves working conditions for both mental and physical labour.
The State institutes and enforces regulations aimed at preventing industrial accidents and occupational diseases.

Art. 59
Working people have the right to rest. The state regulates the conditions related to work, rest and recreation for workers and office employees. Working people are entitled to social insurance benefits in retirement, old age, sickness, or disability.

The state guarantees the working people's right to social insurance and gradually extends the system as the national economy expands.

Art. 60
Education is a right and obligation of citizens. The state gradually enforces free compulsory general education, and grants scholarships to create favourable conditions for citizens to pursue their studies.

Art. 61
Citizens have the right to health care. The state provides free medical examination and treatment.

Art. 62
Citizens have the right to housing. The state has a responsibility to improve the rate of housing [...]

Art. 63
Women and men have equal rights in all respects - in political, economic, cultural, social and family life. The state and society are responsible for raising the political, cultural, scientific, technical and professional standards of women, and constantly improve their role in society.

The State establishes work conditions suited to women's need. Women and men receive equal pay for equal work. Women are entitled to pre- and post-natal paid leave if they are workers or office employees, or to maternity allowances if they are cooperative members.

The state and society ensure the development of maternity homes, creches, kindergartens, community dining-halls and other social amenities to create favourable conditions for women to produce, work, study and rest.

> Art. 64
> The family is the cell of society. The state protects marriage and the family. Marriage is based on the principles of voluntariness, progressivism, monogamy, and equality between husband and wife.
>
> Parents have an obligation to bring up and educate their children to become citizens useful to society. Children have an obligation to respect and care for their parents.

The 1980 constitution reflects the *classical socialist system* in Vietnam at its most developed stage: in the 1970s, and after the peace in 1975. One reason the state to drafted this constitution was the need to integrate South Vietnam: the socialist transformation in the South was intensified, especially in the years 1978-80. The new ideas of limited reform, which were accepted in the summer 1979, are not reflected in the constitution. The main task was the building of socialism. The intelligentsia was referred to in this constitution as the collective masters and the worker-peasant alliance, but it is really the workers who lead the revolution at this stage, under the direction of the party. The trade unions were considered as the most important of the social mass organisations, and they were expected to teach the workers the communist ideas, management skills, as well as management of the state. The party-state was still an inseparable unit.

The paragraphs in the constitution that deal with the economy reflect the contemporary party line: to develop a socialist society, bypassing the capitalist stage in order to advance the economy, to go directly from small-scale production to a large-scale socialist production/industrialisation. Each person was supposed to contribute to society 'according to ability' and receive 'according to his work', an indication that the society was not communist (with equal distribution of goods), but socialist (individual work counted). A system of work points for each task in agriculture was the basis of payment, although the industrial wages were based mainly on seniority. The state guided the national economy and the mobilisation of labour. The task of the trade union was not given a great deal of attention, but political education, enhancement of labour discipline, and promotion of labour productivity were mentioned. In the 1980 constitution this role was more vaguely defined than at the Congress of the VFTU in 1978, where the trade unions were to protect the legitimate interests of the workers and had responsibility for the living standard. They functioned in latter role during the bombing war, when the trade unions had to evacuate the workers to the countryside and secure the basic living conditions.

Work has become a more central issue, not only as a right, but also as an obligation and privilege. The state is the agency not only responsible for the economy, but also for work, rest, and welfare. This includes all areas covered under social insurance, health, education, and housing. According to the constitution, the state was a welfare state, but it occasionally acknowledges that the state does not yet completely fill its role in this regard, and will increase this with the development of the economy.

The attitude towards women has not changed much in the period between the 1959 and the 1980 constitutions: they are still considered full partners in the labour market and other fields. What is new in this constitution is that women are expected to work under conditions suited to their needs. The discussion about gender was beginning, albeit on a very low level, and here the solution was that special attention should be given to women. The family was given a more prominent role on the official agenda as the 'cell of society'. Parents were responsible for educating their children, and the children should not only respect their parents, but also take care of them; it was not the obligation of the state to do this.

Nguyen Van Linh was elected president at the fourth congress of the Vietnam Federation of Trade Unions (VFTU) in May 1978 for a period of five years, but he only served for two years. He is famous for his reformist ideology in the party committee in the South; it was he who introduced the '*doi moi*' reform program at the sixth party congress in 1986 as the new Secretary General of the Communist Party. The turning point for VFTU was its sixth congress in 1988. It was held in a spirit of 'renewal, openness and democracy'. One of the main speeches was delivered by Nguyen Van Linh, the Secretary General of the party, who pointed out the main challenges ahead for the trade unions: they had to renew the content and methods of their activities, their organisation and staff; they had to expand their work to the emerging private sector in a 'multi-component society'; the trade union federation changed its name to Vietnam General Confederation of Labour (VGCL), in line with the organisation's new goals. The trade unions' independent character must be ensured organisationally; moreover, Linh demanded that the trade unions voice their own ideas, not simply borrow ideas from party committees or from management. He also stressed that trade union cadres need not necessarily be party members, provided they had been trained through grass-roots activity or trade union work (Nguyen Van Linh 1989: 6–7).

The speech marked a revolution from above, and had the stamp of the highest authority of the Communist Party, who knew well the situation of the trade unions. Grass-root pressure had not yet succeeded in changing the organisation. The following year, 1989, saw some retrenchment from the openness, which was partly the effect of the insurrection at Tienanmen and the first collapses of the European socialist regimes. But the reforms of the trade unions had begun and were confirmed by laws such as the Trade Union Law of 1990, the state constitution of 1992 (see below), the Constitution of the VGCL of 1993, and the major Labour Code of 1994. The separation between management, party, and trade unions is one of the important underlying themes. In the trade union law of 1990, the trade unions were still expected to participate in management of the enterprises, but the state constitution and the later laws changed that; the unions were assigned a new role as 'controllers and supervisors of state organs and economic units'.

The 1992 Constitution

The Political Regime

Art. 2
The Socialist Republic of Vietnam is a State of the people, from the people, for the people. All State power belongs to the people and is based on an alliance between the working class, the peasantry, and the intelligentsia.

Art. 4
The Communist Party of Vietnam, the vanguard of the Vietnamese working class, the faithful representative of the rights and interests of the working class, the toiling people, and the whole nation, acting upon the Marxist-Leninist doctrine and Ho Chi Minh's thought, is the force leading the State and society.

All Party organisations operate within the framework of the constitution and the law.

Art. 6
The people make use of state power through the agency of the National Assembly and the People's Councils, which represent the will and aspirations of the people, are elected by them and responsible to them.

Art. 9
The Vietnam Fatherland Front and its member organisations constitute the political base of people's power. The Front [...] participates in the building and consolidation of the people's power, works together with the state for the care and protection of the people's legitimate interests, encourages the people to exercise their rights to mastery [...] and supervises the activity of the state organs, elected representatives, and state officials and employees.

The State shall create favourable conditions for the effective functioning of the Fatherland Front and its component organisations.

Art. 10
The Trade Unions, being the socio-political organisation of the working class and the toiling people, joint State organs, economic and social bodies in looking after and safeguarding the rights and interests of cadres, workers, employees and other labouring people; it participates in State administration and social management, in the control and supervision of the activity of State organs and economic bodies; educates workers, employees and other labouring people to work well for national construction and defence.

The Economic System

Art. 15
The State promotes a multi-component commodity economy in accordance with market mechanisms under the management of the State and following the socialist orientation. The multi-component economic structure with various forms of organisation of production and trading is based on a system of ownership by the entire people, by collectives, and by private individuals, of which ownership by the entire people and by collectives constitutes the foundation.

Art. 19
The state sector shall be consolidated and developed, especially in the key branches and areas, and play the leading role in the national economy.

Art. 21
In the private individual and private capitalist sectors people can adopt their own ways or organising production and trading; they can set up enterprises of unrestricted scope in fields of activity which are beneficial to the country and the people. Encouragement shall be given to the family economy.

Art. 25
The state encourages foreign organisations and individuals to invest funds and technologies in Vietnam in conformity with Vietnamese law and international law and usage; it guarantees the right to lawful ownership of funds, property and other interests by foreign organisations and individuals [...]

Art. 26
The state manages the national economy by means of laws, plans and policies; it makes a division of responsibilities and devolves authority to various departments and levels of the administration [...]

Fundamental Rights and Duties of the Citizen - and Women

Art. 55
The citizen has both the right and duty to work.

The state and society shall work out a plan to create ever more employment for the working people.

Art. 56
The State shall enact policies and establish regimes for the protection of labour.
The State shall establish working times, wages scales, regimes of rest and social insurance for State employees and wage earners; it shall encourage and promote other forms of social insurance for the benefit of the working people.

Art. 57
The citizen enjoys freedom of enterprise as determined by law.

Art. 59
The citizen has both the right and the duty to receive training and instruction.
Primary education is compulsory and dispensed free of charge.

The citizen has the right to get general education and vocational training in various ways [...]

The State shall enact policies regarding tuition fees and scholarships.

Art. 61
The citizen is entitled to a regime of health protection.

The State shall establish a system of hospital fees, together with one of exemption from and reduction of such fees [...]

Art. 62
The citizen has the right to build dwelling-houses according to zoning regulations and the law [...]

Art. 63
Male and female citizens have equal rights in all fields - political, economic, cultural, social and family.

All acts of discrimination against women and all acts damaging women's dignity are strictly banned.

Men and women shall receive equal pay for equal work. Women workers shall enjoy a regime related to maternity. Women who are state employees and wage-earners shall enjoy paid prenatal and post-natal leaves during which they shall receive all their wages and allowances as determined by law.

The State and society shall create all necessary conditions for women to raise their qualification in all fields and fully play their role in society; they shall see to the development of maternity homes, pediatric departments, creches and other social-welfare units so as to lighten housework and allow women to engage more actively in work and study, undergo medical treatment, enjoy periods of rest and fulfil their maternal duties.

Art. 64
The family is the cell of society.

Parents have the responsibility to bring up their children to good citizens. Children and grandchildren have the duty to show respect for and look after their parents and grandparents.

The 1992 constitution outlined a fundamentally new political and economic system, although there were many points that were taken from the earlier constitutions/systems. The state is no longer the one and only actor in society. There is a new emphasis on 'the people', despite the fact that the Communist Party was still considered the leader of the working class. The working class, supported by the toiling people and the whole nation, is the core of the social forces. A new theme has been added to Marxist-Leninist doctrine: ideas adopted from Ho Chi Minh. Ho Chi Minh was now promoted to strengthen unity, because he was perceived as a symbol of unity and national honour, even in the south of Vietnam. What is more important, though, is the stress on the law and legislation. Now even the party operates within the constitution and the law. From the early 1990s and up to the present, there has been an 'explosion' of new laws passed by the National Assembly, giving the National Assembly a new and important role in society. The division between the party and the administration was in principle decided by this constitution.

The Fatherland Front, with the trade unions as its most important organisation, constitutes the political base of popular power. The government urges the need for this organisation to work together with the state to care and protect the people's interests. The role of trade unions is to be quite different: they must now fulfil a caring as well as controlling function. In addition, they must also protect the interests of the workers and employees. The state was withdrawing from any direct responsibility; its role was to create the conditions for the mass organisations.

The economic system has now changed from one having only state and cooperative land and enterprises to one having many different components, including private, joint venture, and family enterprises. The market plays a prominent role, even if the state is still supposed to manage it. The emphasis will be on the state's development of key areas. Thus, even though the state sector will not be abolished, there is a clear acceptance that there will be other forces as well. The private and individual sectors of production are allowed to produce as they like, and the new opening to the world is reflected in state encouragement of investment by foreign organisations and individuals.

The rights and duties of citizens have undergone a number of changes, which in many ways are the outcome of the other changes, particularly the new limits on the state's obligations to citizens. People no longer have the 'privilege' of work, only the right and duty, although the state and society are to work out plans for creating more employment. The state is still the institution that decides on the basic regulation of the labour market, work hours, wage scale, and social insurance for state employees and wage labour, but it must promote other forms of social insurance for the working people. A clearer distinction is now established between the insiders of the state system and the outsiders: there are state employees and wage labour on the one hand, and other types of employment on the other; those who were self-employed or engaged in family labour were not guaranteed insurance by the state.

The new welfare state has other limitations, for only primary education was guaranteed by the state. There was no longer free access to higher education, as there is a charge for tuition, and the granting of scholarships is not automatic. Nor is health care free to all. Moreover, housing is no longer the state's concern and obligation.

For women, not much has changed from the earlier constitutions. The basic idea that women have equal rights receives somewhat greater emphasis, and women participate in the labour market on an equal footing with men. But there is acknowledgment that since women have a special reproductive task, they are granted a number of allowances related to childbirth. Also, for women, there is a distinction between state employees, wage earners, and other types of labour (which are not mentioned).

The legislation dealing with the trade unions attempts to separate the various institutions (management, party, and union) from one another, both in organisation and formulation of goals. The purpose of this separation may be to establish a system with the same interests in the different sectors of the 'multi-component' economy. And the components or interests in this system tend to be divided between outsiders and insiders of the state, especially in the labour market, where labour in state sector enjoys more privileges than does the growing small-scale sector. The state can more easily regulate the foreign sector, as it is more well-defined than the private sectors, and the workers will have some of the same privileges as in the state sector.

The 1992 constitution clearly recognises a number of differences in society, with the new multi-sector economy and the market being established facts. This created segmentation in the labour market among the various sectors. From a comparison among the various constitutions, we can see that the official concept of the role of trade unions has also changed: unions, which had been perceived more as disciplinary and ideological educational forces, are now intended to take care of workers' and employees' interests and control the functions of administration. It is no longer the state that directly protects the workers, trade unions must work more proactively – in an environment that is not always friendly. The interests of the state and the unions are no longer united; in an increasingly market oriented economy where competition with the foreign and private sectors has forced restructuring of the state sector, their interests are now separate.

Although most of the changes in society were established facts when the constitutions were promulgated, the change in the status of the trade unions is especially clear: the unions were expected to fulfil a number of functions that had not yet been established. The 1992 constitution is not the final step in the transformation of this society, and in the last section of this paper we will focus on how the trade unions and conditions have changed in the 1990s, both conceptually and practically.

Trade Union Structure

Since the Vietnam Confederation of Trade Unions changed its name in 1988 to the Vietnam General Confederation of Labour the number of industrial unions has increased from 17 to 26, an indication of the increasing importance of the industrial unions and new types of unions in the private sector (these are called professional and trade or occupational unions) (Vietnam Courier 1, 1989: 5).[4] Two new industrial unions were established in the 1990s, including the Banking Union and the Public Sector Union, which were formally constituted in January 1996 (the other new unions since 1988 consist of the Petroleum Workers Union, unions for the police, aviation, commerce, and tourism, medical workers, and sailors). In 1997 some of the industrial unions merged, yielding the present number of 18 industrial unions.[5] One of the main reasons for the merger was to accommodate the ministerial structure, linking the unions. For instance, the Ministry of Light Industry and the Ministry of Heavy Industry merged into the Ministry of Industry, and the same was true for a number of unions in the productive branches. Other unions are expected to accommodate the new state corporations, which include all state enterprises for the major trades (petrol, rubber, textile and garments, etc.). Another reason new industrial unions were established was to represent new trades in a society that was developing along with the reforms. These sectors - aviation, tourism, banking and petroleum - now operated more independently.

By mid-1998, 3,621,500 people were organised trade union members at the national level. Of this number, there were 407,500 members (11 per cent) working in the non-state enterprises (Tong Lien Doan Lao Dong Viet Nam 1999: 29). The rest belonged to the hierarchical system of trade unions organised in provinces, cities, and districts, or the 18 industrial unions. Most of the organised members in industrial unions belonged to the state sector.

More important, there has been a proliferation of primary level unions both in the state and in the non-state sectors. Organisation of trade unions in the non-state sector has been a difficult task, and only 20 per cent of the foreign enterprises had organised trade unions in 1995 (Far Eastern Economic Review 25 january 1995: 22). In the national private sector there were even fewer. In 1996 and 1997 the number of primary level unions in the non-state sector increased considerably: 485 basic unions were established in the foreign funded enterprises. VGCL considered this the equivalent of 60 per cent of the eligible operational businesses

4 Industrial unions cover over a number of professionally oriented unions, not only within industries but also other professions such as teachers, doctors, banking employees. These unions are enterprise/company-based, and each is the sole bargaining agent for that group.

5 Interview with Nguyen Van Dung, Director of the International Department of VGCL, Hanoi, 2 May 1997.

(but this is probably an overestimate). In private enterprises, limited liability companies, and joint ventures the number of primary level unions had increased to around 30 per cent of the enterprises by 1997 (Vietnamese Trade Unions 3, 1997: 6). In 1998 the official figure was 5,644 basic trade union units established in the private sector – or as much as 12 per cent of the total number of basic trade unions (Tong Lien Doan Lao Dong Viet Nam 1999: 31).

A new trend is the establishment of non-state professional associations, an area in which VGCL is less informed and involved, even though it has some contacts with this type of associations. Such groups are fully dependent on their own income. The professional associations, for example, have been established among cooks, street sweepers, porters in the large market places, and cyclo drivers. The structure is still not well established, only in some of cases do the associations go beyond the boundary of the work sites. The VGCL's main emphases by the close of the 1990s was to establish unions in the foreign sector and to build strong primary unions, i.e. enterprise unions based on written labour contracts and collective agreements. The regional union structure (i.e. in provinces and the district level) is still dominant compared to the industrial union structure, and in many cases an enterprise-based union will relate both to the regional structure and the industrial/professional union. Moreover, in the newly established state industrial corporations, including most of the large-scale core industries, the plan is to set up trade unions at the general corporation level. In 1998, 68 unions were established at this level, which strengthens the professional aspect of trade union work, but probably weakens the more independent and branch oriented industrial unions.

The Tasks of the Trade Unions

At this point of the development in Vietnam the trade unions face several challenges: they must transform the unions in the state-owned enterprises (SOEs) and create new unions which are able to defend the workers' interests in the foreign funded sector and in the private national sector.

In the SOEs the trade unions were traditionally part of management, and in fact they still have a large role in the economic management of an enterprise and how the surplus should be divided among the various employees. The tendency in coming years will be to emphasise a larger number of equitisation (a type of privatisation where the enterprise is put out shares, but the shares may be bought by state, employees, and other non private interests) for an increasing number of SOEs, which may lead to a reduction in direct union influence.

In the joint ventures and the 100 per cent foreign-owned enterprises, the trade unions play a role more like that of Western trade unions, where the interests of the employers and trade unions are more clearly separated, but this is a new and difficult challenge for unions accustomed to the corporate type of negotiation. The VGCL has focussed strategically more on the joint ventures than on the national private enterprises. No doubt it has been easier to mobilise both workers and the public because of the increasing number of cases of poor treatment of workers, especially by management from some Asian countries (e.g. Nike). Moreover, this focus is considered more 'politically' correct because the foreign enterprises represent the capital that only recently had been viewed as dangerous and exploitative.

The discussion about the management of workers in the foreign funded enterprises may actually have facilitated the work by the VGCL, because it sparked an almost national reaction against poor treatment of workers. Here international interests for labour may under certain circumstances help the unionisation. Most of the investments in the labour intensive processing industries comes from South Korea and Taiwan, which have moved their labour intensive factories to Vietnam and other low wage areas in the 1990s.

Conclusions

A comparison of the different Vietnamese constitutions makes it obvious that the framework of Vietnamese society has changed. This includes labour relations as well as the organisation of welfare. Even though the state sector is still dominant economically, most labour is employed outside the state sector. The employees in the state sector (and according to the Labour Code) in the foreign sector still retain a number of privileges, including regulated labour relations, but labour in the non-state sector is largely unregulated by anything other than the authority of the employer. The state no longer assumes direct responsibility for welfare, but the trade unions do not carry out this role either (as they had earlier done). In the 1990s the basic regulations about working conditions and social conditions are written in the Labour Code. Welfare schemes have moved to state-run private agencies for health and medical services. Education is no longer free beyond the primary school. Housing is now increasingly a private matter and not the concern of the enterprises. Women are increasingly employed in the foreign funded sector in the labour-intensive industries; they are increasingly younger, and will probably not work more than a short time in these enterprises.

Ideologically the trade unions remain one of the core forces of society: they are the most important basis for the state and party, but the state takes less interest in trade unions than before, and the balance (or political struggle) between the interests of the foreign investors and the workers sometimes results in policies that support the investors as well as those supporting the workers. Nevertheless, the historical legacy makes it difficult for the state and party to dismiss the interests of the labour force, and in a number of respects working conditions are not as bad as in some other Asian countries. At the same time, the unions are supposed to fulfil a very diversified role: to protect workers' interests, oversee their welfare, and function as controlling institutions. This is a situation in which legislation is somewhat ahead of reality. The trade unions are still involved in the management of the state-owned enterprises, although much of this influence is through informal structures that have survived changes in the formal ones. The informal structure supports a policy of consensus among the various partners: management, party and trade union. The unions also function as 'controllers' and supervisors of labour relations, but when defending the interests of the employees, much depends on the particular trade union in the individual enterprise. In contrast, the privately owned and foreign funded enterprises have trade unions whose main influence is in areas such as working conditions and social concerns.[6]

Open conflicts in the state-owned enterprises are reduced through the corporatist structure, and solutions are usually found before it comes to open conflict and strike. The majority of the conflicts in Vietnam since 1989 have taken place in the foreign funded enterprises. The trade unions are to some extent caught in a social bind between a constituency that has become increasingly diversified: the issue is between the state sector workers' demand for security and the emerging proletariat in the non-state sector who need a more innovative policy to defend themselves. The trade unions are only beginning to learn how to handle trade union work under the new conditions.

In Vietnamese society before the reforms trade unions were an integrated part of the party-state, functioning as a mediator between the party and the working class (also called a 'transmission belt'). Pravda and Ruble point to the fact that trade unions in socialist countries mobilise rather than defend labour, but they have a dual role to protect the interests of their members and to promote production, often called the 'classical dualism'. Moreover, the unions are far from uniform, and in their experience economic and social change make the 'classic dualism' less cost effective (an urgent task in emerging systems of market competition), which tends to cause the unions to move away from this type of dualism. They suggest various new types of unionism: corporatist dualism, which is usually sponsored from above by the unions and party officials aware of the need for more effective policy making; participatory dualism, which attracts the support of union officials, technicians, skilled workers, managers, and party officials who wish to further economic reforms; and finally, adversarial non-dualism, which is usually a result of pressures from the grass-roots for more radical modifications of

6 This is based on experiences from field work and visits in 1994, 1996, 1997, and 1999 in both the north and the south of Vietnam.

the proposals by party and union leaders. In Vietnam elements of all three types seem to be at stake in the present period, depending on regional differences, sectors, and enterprises (Pravda and Ruble 1986: 18–19).

References

Anon. (1975) *An Outline History of The Vietnam Worker's Party (1930-1975)*, Hanoi: Foreign Language Publishing House (second edition).

Anon. (1990) *Le Movement Syndicale au Vietnam: Experiences Vietnamiennes*, Hanoi: Edition en Langues Étrangèrs.

Anon. (1995) *The Constitutions of Vietnam, 1946, 1959, 1980, 1992,* Hanoi: The Gioi Publishers.

Far Eastern Economic Review 1995, 25 January.

Huynh Kim Khanh (1982) *Vietnamese Communism 1925-45*, Ithaca: Cornell University Press.

Nguyen Van Linh (1989) 'The trade unions must renew their activities', *Vietnam Courier* 1: 6–7.

Pravda, A. and Ruble, B. (1986) 'Communist trade unions: varieties of dualism', in A. Pravda. and B. Ruble (eds.) *Trade Unions in Communist States*, Sydney: Allen and Unwin.

Tong Lien Doan Lao Dong Viet Nam (1999) *Congdoan Viet Nam. Li su ñ phat trien (The Vietnamese Trade Unions. History-Development).*

Vietnam Courier (1989) 'The Sixth Congress of the Vietnamese Trade Unions', no. 1.

Viet Nam Federation of Trade Unions (1978) 'Rules of the Vietnamese Trade Unions' in *Fourth National Congress of the Vietnamese Trade Unions,* Hanoi.

Vietnamese Trade Unions (1997) *Three Years of Mobilisation and Development of Trade Unions in Non-State Sector, No. 3.*

5

LOCAL POLITICS AND LABOUR RELATIONS IN THE PHILIPPINES: THE CASE OF SUBIC BAY

CHAN FONG YIN AND PHILIP F. KELLY

It is well established that labour markets are socially regulated institutions rather than neutral mechanisms to bring together the supply of, and demand for, human labour power (Peck 1996).[1] In addition, it is increasingly recognised that such social regulation of the labour market is locally constituted not just in the absolute space of 'journey-to-work' areas, but also in a more sophisticated sense through the geographically distinct constitution of social processes (Hanson and Pratt 1995). The social and cultural dimensions of the *local* labour market have therefore been a topic of much discussion in recent years. These discussions focus, however, on North American and Western European experiences, and tend to emphasise the institutional distinctions of various locales and their consequences for labour market processes. In the Philippines, and Southeast Asia more generally, this chapter will suggest that a further dimension must be added to local labour market studies. The nub of this extra ingredient lies in the disparity between the institutional frameworks that exist at a national scale and their implementation in practice in multiple localities. National level labour laws in the Philippines, enshrined in the Labour Code of 1974 and numerous subsequent amendments, often bear little resemblance to the actual practices of employers, industrial estate managers and local government officials. Local labour market practices are dependent only in part upon the institutional frameworks that exist. Perhaps more significant are the personalised and informalised power relationships in local political arenas and privately managed industrial estates. It is in these contexts that actual experiences of labour market regulation are constituted.

1 We gratefully acknowledge the fieldwork and research support provided by the Southeast Asian Studies Programme at the National University of Singapore, and NUS Academic Research Grant #RP970013.

Local labour regimes are, moreover, especially important in Southeast Asia, where new growth has tended to be geographically concentrated in industrial enclaves variously designated as Free Trade Zones, Free Ports, Export Processing Zones, or Special Economic Zones. These localities, which include both government-owned and privately managed industrial estates, often form distinct environments with an administrative autonomy and specific set of regulatory conditions designed to attract global capital.

This chapter examines one such distinct economic zone at Subic Bay in the Philippines. The withdrawal of the US Navy from its base at Subic in 1991 left approximately 42,000 people unemployed. The response was a concerted effort to convert the military base into a Freeport and industrial estate, administered by the Subic Bay Metropolitan Authority. The first chairman of the Authority was Richard Gordon, then mayor of the neighbouring town of Olongapo. From 1992 until 1998, Gordon administered the new Freeport Zone in an autocratic, and, in economic terms at least, a very successful manner. By 1998, more than 34,000 people were employed in the zone. Over this period, however, access to the labour market and collective representation of workers were closely controlled by Gordon's administration. Only with the election of a new President in 1998 did Gordon's power wane, as Joseph Estrada orchestrated his removal and replacement. Even then, the new regime headed by Felicito Payumo has not been immune from personalised forms of labour market regulation. Subic thus provides a vivid illustration of the power that local government officials can wield over the labour market, often in defiance of national regulatory frameworks.

This chapter explores the nature of labour market relations at Subic within an understanding of Philippine local politics in the following way. The first section examines how certain tendencies in Philippine local politics have been conceptualised through notions such as patron-client relations and bossism. The second part then relates these ideas to the local political economy of Subic and its neighbouring city of Olongapo, primarily through the dominant personalities of Richard and his wife Kate Gordon, respectively Chairman of the Subic Bay Metropolitan Authority and Mayor of Olongapo during most of the 1990s. The third section establishes the connections between this local power structure and labour market practices, highlighting the processes of volunteerism, recruitment, dispute resolution and unionisation. Finally, we consider the implications of this example for the ways in which local labour markets are conceptualised and studied. In particular, we argue that the importance of personalised power relations in a local political setting implies that labour market studies need to take account of how institutional frameworks become warped, mediated and informalised in local settings, particularly in the context of a relatively 'weak' state in the Philippines. This does not, however, represent the thorough subversion of formal institutional frameworks by 'personality politics,' but rather the negotiation of a tension between the two that exists within the Philippine local state. Furthermore, this negotiation is unevenly and differently resolved across space and time, generating a complex and shifting geography of political environments at multiple scales.

PHILIPPINE LOCAL POLITICS

The workings of local politics in the Philippines have conventionally been interpreted through a framework highlighting the phenomenon of patron-client factionalism. Power relationships are understood as constituted not through formal mechanisms of institutional rationality, but through personalised bonds of allegiance and loyalty. Scott and Kerkvliet (1973:502) define this patron-clientelism in the following terms:

An exchange relationship or instrumental friendship between two individuals of different status in which the patron uses his own influence and resources to provide for the protection and material welfare of his lower status client and his family, who, for his part, reciprocates by offering general support and assistance, including personal services, to the patron.

Scott (1972) argues that while a patron-client link originates in an unequal power relationship, genuine affective ties reinforce this link and help to legitimise its inherent inequality. The relationship also relies heavily on cultural values that stress personal loyalty and indebtedness. Hence Varela (1995) relates patronage to certain essentialised Filipino cultural traits of personalism, familism, and particularism (or popularism), rooted in Tagalog concepts of *utang-na-loob* (debt of gratitude) and *pakikisama* (sociability or good inter-personal relations). These personal ties become aggregated into a social structure in which the personal, the political and the economic are inextricably linked (see Hollnsteiner 1968, Hutchcroft 1991, Hawes 1992, Magno 1993, Putzel 1995). Networks of patron-client relationships form factions that bind together actors from the village level up to the presidency. Gutierrez (1994), for example, shows in some detail how electoral contests and the exercise of state power at both local and national scales are frequently articulated through personalised factions based on these 'ties that bind.' A link is thus created between prosperous patrons and poor dependent clients that transcends class-based or other social cleavages in the dynamics of Philippine local politics.

While early interpretations of patron-clientelism implied a relatively harmonious relationship between those involved, Gutierrez (1994: 229) is careful to note that such ties are not always smooth and mutually beneficial. This point forms the basis for John Sidel's (1995) contribution to the debate, in which he argues that local politicians also rely heavily on impersonal and coercive mechanisms and resources to entrench themselves in power. Similarly, Rocamora (1995: xxi) asserts that the *patron-client* framework gives insufficient attention to the inequality of such relationships, resting too heavily on 'valorised reciprocity, smooth interpersonal relations, and kinship and fictive kinship bonds.' Both writers therefore advocate an approach in which 'bossism' forms the fundamental mechanism for the exercise of political power. Sidel's 'bosses' are predatory power brokers who achieve monopolistic control over coercive and economic resources within given territorial jurisdictions or bailiwicks (1997: 952). These bosses include 'para-statal mafias,' small town mayors, provincial governors, congressmen, and even presidents.

Such local bosses and their dynastic families, or something approximating to them, have been identified across the Philippines. Sidel focuses on municipal and provincial politics in the provinces of Cebu and Cavite, while McCoy (1994) brings together examples from Ilocos in the North to Davao in the South (see also Lacaba 1995). Sidel (1997) notes how local politics in Cebu, for example, has been dominated by local families who activate networks of dependants and vote-brokers, manipulate alliances with other local notables and politicians, dispense private and public funds, and engage in election-related violence, fraud and vote-buying. When not acting on their own behalf, they have often engineered the election of their scions to political offices in the province. Thus, even when new factions emerge, such families are already deeply entrenched, making their displacement difficult (see also Doronila 1985).

Kerkvliet (1995), however, contends that while patron-clientelism and bossism, or tendencies towards them, undoubtedly exist in the Philippine political system, we must also look at the full range of interaction that occurs within the political arena, which includes both genuinely altruistic intentions and the pursuit of ideas and ideologies rather than just personal gain. Beneath Kerkvliet's criticism of over-generalised understandings of Filipino politics lies a broader point. The implication in many accounts of patron-client relationships or bossism is that these characterisations represent a vestige of pre-colonial (and pre-modern) Filipino political organisation carried over into a context of modern statehood. This is an argument developed in some detail by Ileto (1999) who suggests that much American scholarship, in particular, is loaded with colonial preconceptions of the essentialised nature of Filipino political life. This essence is customarily identified in the implied inferior half of several dualisms – private versus public, particularistic versus nationalistic, violence versus law, family versus state, clientelism versus genuine democracy, anarchy versus order, and warlords versus statesmen. Needless to say, the ideal of American democracy is found in the latter half of each binary opposition, while the Philippines is represented as an aberration from this model. Ileto's complaint is not simply with the essentialisation and denigration of Filipino politics, but also with the dualisms themselves, which imply mutually exclusive categories. Instead, he prefers to view Filipino politics as a system unto itself, in which many of these binaries are negotiated and transcended, thereby rendering them meaningless. What many American writers share, according to Ileto, is 'a propensity to spot a particularistic, familial tie in just about every Filipino political relationship they encounter' (1999: 61). Genuine political ideologies, such as nationalism, are' [...]made to look plain silly in the avalanche of classmates, friends, relatives, bodyguards, protégés, and patrons all out to further their narrow, selfish, Hobbesian agendas' (ibid 1999: 61).

There are, therefore, dangers in seeking to derive a consistent characterisation of Filipino local politics. Attempts to generalise in this way are open to both frequent empirical refutation and accusations of colonialist discourse. What the literature on Philippine local politics has taught us, however, is that there exists at least the tendency and the potential for patrons or 'boss'-like figures to emerge in the structure of the Philippine local state. Moreover, these figures and families often transcend the binaries that Ileto has noted. The lines between family and state, public and private, violence and law, legal and illegal, are frequently blurred in a system of governance that usually leaves outside observers reaching for adjectives such as corrupt, nepotistic, coercive, and anarchic. It is, perhaps, more useful, following Ileto, to view Philippine political processes (and probably those elsewhere as well) as existing in a dialectical tension between the binary oppositions of state versus family, law versus violence, democracy versus clientelism and so on. Moreover, the manner in which these tensions are resolved will vary across space and time, creating a complex and shifting geography of political contexts to be understood. The implication of this conceptualisation for the concerns of this chapter is that local labour market processes need to be linked to the nature of political power as it is exercised in specific localised contexts, which, in turn, must be understood as situated in larger scales of political power.

The Personal Politics of Development at Subic

Before Subic was a US naval base, its potential had been recognised by the Spanish explorer Juan de Salcedo as early as 1572. Lying on a deep inlet of Manila Bay it was a location with great strategic and logistical importance (see Figure 5.1). It wasn't until 1884, however, that the Spanish constructed a naval shipyard on the site. After the Spanish left in 1898, the Americans took over and used Subic as a naval base providing support to the US Asiatic Fleet (SBMA 1996).

The 1991 eruption of nearby Mount Pinatubo covered Subic in a thick layer of ash. This raised the question of whether the base would be reclaimed or not, a decision that was ultimately made not by the US military but by the Philippine Senate which, in September 1991, refused to renew the ten-year Treaty of Friendship, Peace and Cupertino that provided for the leasing of Subic Naval Base, Clark Air Base and other installations by the US military.

While seen as a victory for nationalist sentiment, the closure of the base at Subic left 42,000 people abruptly unemployed. To address this problem and to make

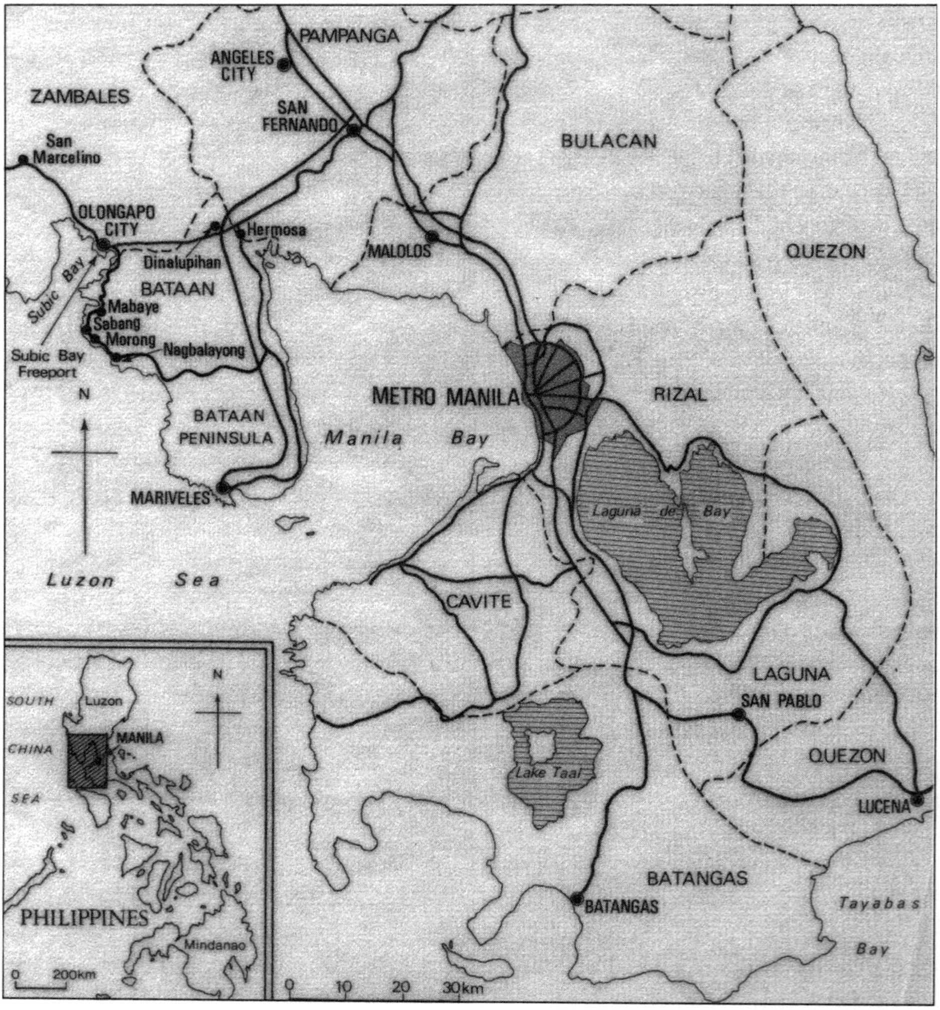

Figure 5.1: Map of Metro Manila and Surroundings, the Philippines

use of the infrastructure left behind by the Americans, the Bases Conversion and Development Act (Republic Act 7227) was passed in March 1992. This established the Bases Conversion Development Authority (BCDA), which then formed the Subic Bay Metropolitan Authority (SBMA). Under the SBMA a Freeport and Special Economic Zone were designated at Subic, providing tax and duty free imports of capital equipment and raw materials for enterprises within the secured area. Firms were also exempted from all national and local taxes, paying only a five per cent flat corporate tax on gross income. The intention was to use these incentives, together with facilities left by the Americans (including a port and airstrip) to attract industrial and commercial investment to provide employment for those left jobless by the closure of the naval base. The Subic Bay Freeport (SBF) has been a great success. By the end of 1999, the SBMA had approved 368 projects representing over $2.5 billion worth of investments.

Table 5.1: Subic Bay Freeport & Special Economic Zone Investment Approvals

Year	*Amount (US$)*	*No. of Approved Projects*	*Projected Employment Generation*
1992	4,072,621	4	519
1993	351,717,702	25	3,476
1994	339,521,915	39	1,373
1995	525,853,882	56	9,657
1996	531,313,823	64	12,622
1997	270,519,367	55	7,922
1998	260,129,688	47	5,111
1999	248,146,000	78	14,540
Total	2,531,274,998	368	-

Source: SBMA Investment Centre; SBMA website: www.sbma.com

The upward trend of Subic's growth figures was interrupted in 1997 and 1998, reflecting both a local crisis within Subic to be described later, which undoubtedly deterred potential investors for several months in 1998, and, at a larger scale, the regional economic recession in Southeast Asia, which dampened investment from foreign sources.[2] Whether or not previous levels of investment will be reached again remains to be seen - increasing competition from other Asian locations and limited room for expansion within the Freeport area itself may set limits. Like investment flows, new employment generation in the Freeport was impressive in the years following its establishment, but it too declined in 1997-98, with an apparent rebound in 1999. On balance, however, the employment generation by the Freeport since its inception has been impressive. In 1998, over 30,000 were employed in the zone - a decline from its peak a year before at 42,807 (see Figure 5.2).

Much of the Freeport's success has been ascribed to its ability to attract 'big names' such as FedEx, Acer, and Hitachi. FedEx in particular represented an early coup for Subic, which was adopted as the company's Asia-Pacific hub following agreement from the SBMA that modifications would be made to the runway to

2 The devaluation of the Philippine currency in 1997, from approximately 27 to 40 pesos to the dollar, must also be reflected in the figures in Table 5.1, giving locally sourced investments a lower value in US dollars.

Figure 5.2: Subic Bay Freeport Employment Levels, 1993–1998

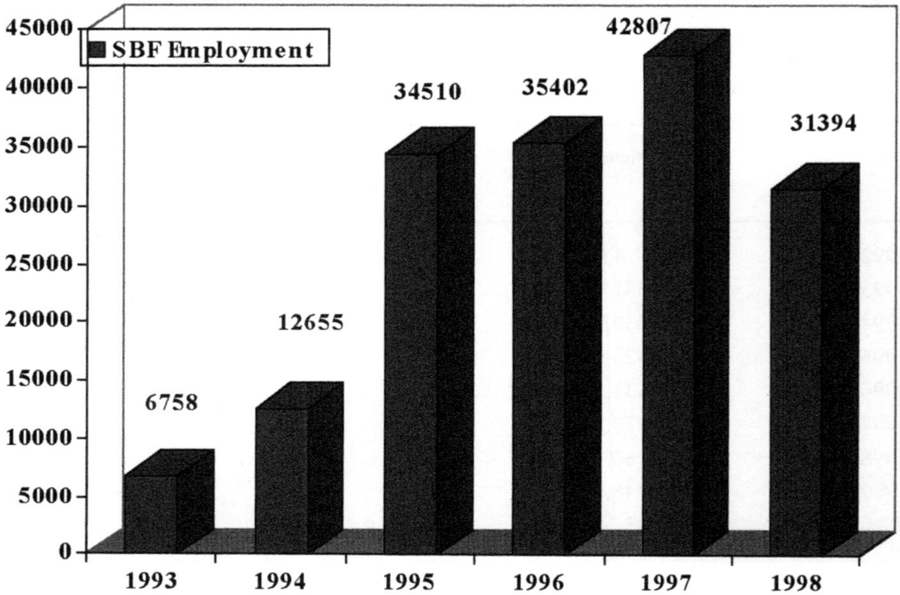

Source: SBMA Chairman's Office, *SBMA 100 Days Accomplishment Report*, 1998

allow the company's wide-bodied planes to land. More recently, some observers have cast doubt upon the future viability of the Freeport, with the French electronics transnational Thomson pulling out in December 1999 and Acer's plans to do so averted only because of a need for extra capacity after an earthquake damaged its facilities in Taiwan (Napack 2000).

If Subic's prospects now seem uncertain, it is not for the first time. The period after the relinquishing of American control and before the establishment of the new Authority was one of even greater concern for the future of a town, whose economy was estimated to be up to 95 per cent dependent on the military base. While Clark Air Base, which had closed at the same time, was subject to extensive looting, Subic was protected by a force of volunteers mobilised by Richard Gordon, then Mayor of the City of Olongapo, located just outside the gates of the military compound. These volunteers, numbering around 8,000, were rallied to protect the base, and have since become part of Subic's officially promulgated folklore.[3] The volunteers were said to have worked willingly without pay (the

3 A flagpole and monument now provide a memorial to this service and it is a story of survival and self-reliance that is oft repeated for visitors to the area.

government had not, at that time, released funds for the conversion of the Base), and their roles included staffing the Base's power plant, working in the petroleum tank facilities, patrolling forest reserves, maintaining barracks and houses, and tending to lawns and landscaping. According to the official version of the tale, every item left by the Americans, from office equipment down to the last light bulb, refrigerator, and bedsheet, was kept intact. Gordon has frequently referred to this 'creation myth' as not just an episode of popular mobilisation, but a source of national redemption as well: 'Subic achieved what no other city had done [...] and it's all because of the volunteers [...] they not only preserved the base, but also the integrity of the Filipino people.'

If Philippine politics a whole can be viewed as a tension between several contradictory tendencies, then Gordon himself epitomised that tension. Indeed, even his family background was a hybridised conjunction of two cultures. As the key figure in the politics of development at Subic it is worth exploring Gordon's background and career in more detail. He was the grandson of an American serviceman who had settled in Olongapo after the Spanish-American war and married a local Spanish mestiza. Their son (Richard's father) James Gordon was elected as the first mayor of Olongapo in 1963,[4] and held the post until his assassination in 1967 at the hands of a political rival (Kirk 1998). Richard's mother, Amelia, then took over as mayor, as her son was considered still too young to replace his father. It was in 1979, on reaching the age of 34, that Richard Gordon contested and won the mayoralty, having already served as the youngest member of Marcos' constitutional convention in the early 1970s. Like Marcos himself, then, Gordon was recognised as intelligent, talented and fluent in the language of development and modernisation. When, in 1992, the Subic Bay Metropolitan Authority was established, Gordon was appointed by President Ramos as its first Chairman. A condition of his appointment was that he relinquish his position as Mayor of Olongapo, which he did, only to be succeeded by his wife, Kate.[5] Once again, then, Ileto's binaries are transcended, with a formal separation of powers duly respected, but in practice a blurring of boundaries as the mayoralty and chairmanship were held in the same household. This familial, and by now familiar, succession allowed Gordon to integrate easily the needs of the nascent industrial zone with the services and human resources available in Olongapo.

Kate Gordon remains (in 2000) Mayor of Olongapo City, but Gordon's tenure as Chairman of the SBMA ended flamboyantly after the election of Joseph Estrada to the presidency in 1998. Gordon's style had always been confrontational. One example was his attitude towards those areas neighbouring Subic that fell outside his political bailiwick. The Morong gate, providing access to the Subic Bay Freeport

4 The town had been governed by the US military as part of its Naval Reservation area until 1959.

5 See Gutierrez (1994: 161) for a brief review of Kate Gordon's background.

from the province of Bataan was kept closed during Gordon's tenure as Chairman, making it difficult for the province's residents to access the Freeport. This meant that employment at the Freeport was, in practical terms, more easily available to those living in Gordon's own 'turf' of Olongapo City in the province of Zambales.[6] This strategy led to calls for Gordon's removal as early as 1996 by the governor of Bataan, who accused him of lacking perception of the needs of multinational investors and being 'too politicised.'

Gordon's politicisation of local development thus won him some powerful enemies. These included Estrada, who, as a Senator in 1992 had been one of the national legislators who vocally, and ultimately successfully, opposing the renewal of the Bases Agreement that Gordon was fighting to retain. This difference of opinion apparently developed into a longer-term antipathy and upon assuming the Presidency, one of Estrada's first acts was to dismiss Gordon as SBMA chairman.[7] Unsurprisingly, it was a member of Bataan's political establishment, Congressman Felicito Payumo (representative for the First District of Bataan in the national legislature), who succeeded Gordon. The choice of Payumo was, according to one SBMA Director, not without some element of malice: 'It's simple. Because the President simply hates Gordon and Payumo is Gordon's number one enemy!'[8]

Gordon refused to accept his dismissal, arguing that his appointment to a new six-year term by Fidel Ramos towards the end of his Presidency was irrevocable. The Chairman and hundreds of his supporters barricaded themselves inside the SBMA's administrative headquarters.[9] Police initially moved in on July 26 1998 to clear the building. The operation was unsuccessful and left around 60 injured.[10] The new administration subsequently decided to establish itself elsewhere in the Freeport, leaving Gordon entrenched and fighting his dismissal through the courts. Tourism came to a standstill for about 2 months, FedEx diverted its planes to Manila for 2 days, and Acer shut down for a day at the height of the crisis – partly due to security concerns, but also because, according to one manager in the Zone, 80 per cent of its employees were absent defending Gordon's position in the administration block.[11] Gordon lasted only until 1 September 1998 when the

6 See *Manila Standard*, 28th November 1998; *Sun-Star Clark*, 1st April 1996.

7 Through Administrative Order No. 1, of 1998.

8 Interview, SBMA director, 24th December 1998.

9 *The Asian Wall Street Journal*, 17th November 1998. Gordon and his supporters encamped with brown-bag lunches, banners and enthusiastic pronouncements that it was business as usual at the port. One young public-relations executive compared the atmosphere to Woodstock in the 1960s: 'everyone was singing and felt so sure about the cause.'

10 *The Straits Times*, 15th July 1998. Even before the clash, it was said that Gordon had told his supporters that if Estrada insisted on replacing him, 'blood will flow.'

11 SBMA Chairman's Office, *100 Days Accomplishment Report*, 1998. It was also noted in *The Straits Times*, 30th January 1999. Interview, General Manager, US company, 25th December 1998.

Supreme Court ruled against him, demanding that he vacate the headquarters and make way for Payumo.[12] Gordon then called on his supporters, who included hundreds of SBMA workers and Olongapo residents, to peacefully remove their barricades and end the 'vigil.' Interestingly, then, despite the personalisation of local politics and Gordon's embeddedness as a 'boss' or 'patron,' it was through the formal legal system that he attempted to defend his tenure. It was also the rejection of his case by that system that ended his resistance (although whether such a rejection would have been forthcoming without a determined President so closely involved in the issue is debatable).

This episode did not, however, represent a sudden politicisation of control over the Subic economic zone, nor did Gordon's removal bring about a sudden depoliticisation. Personality politics and economic development had, all along, been closely integrated in Gordon's administration. This applied in particular to those employed by the SBMA. As the President of a British company in the Freeport commented: 'Networks? Absolutely! It's a line-up. Nepotism rules!'[13] Many investors were also acutely aware that in order to get registration and other documents processed efficiently, it was important to be on good personal terms with Gordon, which often meant providing work for Gordon loyalists. Nevertheless, the legitimacy and power of Gordon's administration rested upon its ability to deliver economic growth and employment. For this to happen, the needs of investors had to be satisfied:

> The bottom-line is that, maybe people are just in office because of relationships and political pay-backs, but you cannot stay long in this community and not perform. You still have to be competent or you will be scrutinised. People have done business all over the world and if they are doing business here, they have their demands and expectations [...][14]

Thus while Gordon exerted a great deal of power in the local context, this was checked by a key foundation of that power, which was his ability to deliver development and, particularly, employment opportunities to loyal followers. To do this it was necessary to abide by the expectations of international investors represented by, among others, the SBF Chamber of Commerce.

Can, therefore, Gordon be seen as a 'patron' or 'boss' in the mould described by various authors in the previous section? His ability to mobilise thousands of 'volunteers' in the early stages of Subic's conversion, and hundreds of supporters in the final days of his rule, gives some indication of the personal loyalty that he

12 'The Cost of Fighting over a Public Office', from http//www.celtel.org/subicnews/politics.

13 Interview, December 1998.

14 Interview, Vice-President, British Company, also a sub-committee member in the Subic Bay Freeport Chamber of Commerce, 21st December 1998.

commanded among a sizeable following. His earning of this loyalty through 'granting' employment in either the SBMA administration or the operations of investors within the Zone, would seem to be reminiscent of classic patron-clientelism. The intersection of economic and political power is also redolent of Sidel's bossism, but the extent to which coercion or violence were involved is unclear. Another characteristic of bossism, territoriality, was however evident in Gordon's closure of the Morong gate in order to favour those living within his political bailiwick of Olongapo. At the same time, Gordon had to play by the rules of international business and deliver the goods, so to speak, in terms of local economic development – his status as patron was not unconditional. Furthermore, it was through formal legal mechanisms that he was eventually brought down, albeit under the watchful eye of the arch-patron, the President.

These practices are identified with Gordon as an individual, but the extent to which they are systemic is perhaps indicated by their continuation under the new regime:

> When the new guys came in, they asked me to change my canteen operator... my canteen operators, doctors, and contractors have all been given trouble. They are trying to move in their own people, own network. The old administration was like that, this new one also. No difference [...] But they cannot be too obvious because they have to show the government and the people who are watching that they are fine administrators [...]'New broom sweeps clean,' right?[15]

Interestingly, then, personalism and particularism are tempered by continued discursive adherence to impartiality and administrative rationality.

The opening of the Morong gate was represented as the symbolic opening up of Subic to benefit more than a small coterie of cronies and clients. President Estrada himself dramatically opened the gate, breaking the lock with bolt cutters and dismantling what one newspaper described as 'Subic's Berlin Wall.'[16] Indeed one of Payumo's stated aims on taking over the chairmanship of the SBMA was to spread the benefits of growth to neighbouring provinces. This episode could therefore be plausibly read as either the laudable overcoming of narrow patronage-based politics in the labour market, or alternatively, as the reorienting of the Freeport towards employment for those in the bailiwicks of the new administrators in Bataan province.[17]

The continued tension between the personal/particularistic and the rational/administrative is seen in staffing changes during the transition from Gordon to

15 Interview, General Manager, Singaporean company, 22nd December 1998.

16 'Erap opens Subic's "Berlin Wall" today.' In *Manila Standard*, 28th November 1998.

17 As noted earlier, Payumo represented a district of Bataan in Congress. His nephew is the mayor of Dinalupihan, Bataan.

Payumo. Only 25 employees (all of them top management) of the SBMA's 1519 staff actually left the organisation with Gordon's departure.[18] Most of these were forced to leave so that Payumo's own people could be brought in, rather than doing so in an act of loyalty to their 'patron.' Evidently, for Gordon's other 'clients,' allegiance to an individual was not as secure as the patron-client framework suggests. As one interviewee, a representative of an international multilateral organisation assigned to Subic, noted:

> I'm very amazed at how people can be so loyal to Gordon one day, but the next day they can suddenly turn their loyalty to Payumo. But that is how things work here. Payumo is the one who can provide and deliver to these people now. Gordon is out and has no power.

Patron-clientelism is itself, then, tempered by a rationality among 'clients' who carefully calculate the costs and benefits of loyalty. Equally, however, we should not preclude the possibility that the stability of the SBMA workforce reflected loyalty to the institution and the job to be done, rather than simply a switch in patronage.

In summary, it seems clear that the boundaries and binaries identified by Ileto – family versus state, private versus public, personalism versus rationalism, clientelism versus democracy and others – are indeed transcended in distinctive ways in the case of Subic. While features of patronage and bossism, which dwell upon one side of these binaries, are evident, there is enough inconsistency that such easy labels are difficult to sustain, and it is more appropriate to view local politics as being in tension between these opposing tendencies. There is, however, plenty to suggest that the institutions and actors of the SBMA and surrounding political jurisdictions are closely involved in the processes of investment and economic growth in the Freeport, that such processes became intimately identified with the personalities involved, and that such personalisation may not have ended with Gordon's removal. The caricature of personalised strong-man politics must, however, be reconciled with the checks which existed upon the exercise of such power. In the next section we turn to examine how these local political circumstances have shaped and regulated Subic's labour market.

18 Interview, SBMA Employees Welfare & Protection Department, December 1998; also *BooM Magazine*, Vol. 3, Issue No. 5, 1998.

Labour Market Regulation at Subic Bay[19]

The local politics of development at Subic have intersected with the labour process in important ways. The first instance of this connection was in the much-heralded volunteer labour mobilised to protect the facilities of the Subic base immediately after the American withdrawal. The second, and related, instance is in the recruitment process for new enterprises in Subic. Thirdly, and perhaps most obviously, the selection of staff for the SBMA itself is a process in which personal ties and political loyalties are crucial. The fourth aspect of the labour process that is influenced by local politics is the resolution of workplace disputes. Finally, the process of unionisation, while legitimate according to national constitutional and legislative provisions, has also seen significant informal involvement by the local political leadership. Each of these areas will now be considered in turn.

Volunteerism

As noted earlier, the mythology and publicity surrounding the development of Subic has tended to glorify the role of the volunteers who 'saved' the base from looting and disrepair. Several monuments now exist in the Freeport to commemorate the efforts of these 8,000 volunteers. One sculpture stands 7.5 feet tall and attempt to depict the story of the volunteers, which Richard Gordon called the 'Spirit of the New Filipino.' The monument comprises a family of four gaining 'true freedom' through the fruits of their volunteerism. The four are striding forwards and at the same time removing blindfolds. They hold high a torch, and are, according to a press release at the sculpture's unveiling in 1996, taking away the blindfold of ignorance, pettiness, tunnel-vision, tribalism and envy, facing the dawn of a 'New Age' filled with hope. The family represents two generations – father and mother are farmers, while their son is dressed as a young city professional. The fourth member of the family is a baby – a symbol, according to the official discourse, of the future generations that will enjoy a bright future because of others' sacrifices.[20]

Gordon's ability to mobilise unpaid labour on this scale is intriguing. Some have argued that it was due in no small part to coercive strategies. Donald Kirk, for example, suggests that:

> [Gordon's] grip on the levers of local government and his political resources enabled him to compel thousands to volunteer on the promise that some day, if they did well

19 Fieldwork for this study was conducted in December 1998 and January 1999 and consisted of interviews with key informants in the corporate, administrative and labour sectors at Subic.
20 SBMA, 'Monument Honours Volunteers' Role in Subic Miracle', in *Press Release*, Public Affairs Office, 1996.

> and the base prospered in its reincarnation as a free port and industrial zone, they would all be offered paying jobs (Kirk 1998: 101).

If Kirk is correct, then Gordon's coercion was at most conditional rather than absolute, and based upon the promise of future employment opportunities. More damning is the uncorroborated claim by a local union organiser that Gordon had embezzled funds intended to pay for the Base's maintenance:

> The people of Olongapo are very deprived because all the Gordons conspired to exploit the workers [...] Although there was supposedly no salary, it was rumoured that there was actually a budget of 900 million pesos. Where did the money go to then?[21]

Stories of missing millions are, of course, a staple of Filipino political lore, but more concrete testament is provided by a former volunteer who now works for the SBMA. In an interview she described her experience with the Gordon machinery:

> I volunteered and worked without pay for three months. I was lucky to start getting paid after three months because there were some from the Trade and Tourism Department who had to work for more than one year before they got paid. There was no guarantee for us at all, we just worked [...] Although I'm a college graduate, I'm only earning 5,800 pesos a month [...] Gordon was also very domineering, for celebrations involving the Gordons, he forced us to attend [...][22]

It appears, then, that even when the SBMA was fully functional, volunteers were still being retained on the promise, or at least the possibility, of a 'promotion' to paid employment. Gordon's ability to command the labour market in this way was due in part to his close control over the recruitment process at the SBMA itself and in local private enterprises (to be discussed below). Through this control, he was able to make voluntary work an effective prerequisite for employment. The creation of an unpaid labour force at Subic was also, however, a product of Gordon's own charisma and salesmanship. This is illustrated in the testimony of one worker at the Freeport:

> Gordon was able to rally people well and we believed in his vision and plans. I volunteered as a tour guide. There were a lot of volunteers who worked for Gordon without pay and I'm proud to be one of them. He was a charismatic leader and it is a pity that he has left [...][23]

21 Interview, Officer, Trade Union Congress of the Philippines, 29th December 1998.
22 Interview, SBMA secretary, also a SBMA volunteer, 24th December 1998.
23 Former SBMA volunteer, now SBMA employee, Interview, December 1998.

Three factors, then, appear to lie behind Gordon's creation of a wageless labour force: the coercion of a well-established local political figure; second, the charisma of a leader with a vision; and third, the enticement of paid employment that he was able to deliver upon, in some cases at least, through control over local hiring practices. It is to these recruitment practices that we now turn.

Recruitment of Industrial Labour

The skills demanded by investors in manufacturing and tourism industries were not so different from those of a workforce servicing a military installation. More important, therefore, than the retraining or recreating of a labour force, was the process of new allocating jobs among the unemployed. A significant, and unique, feature of this process was the preference given to former volunteers. Indeed, in inviting applications for vacancies in the private sector, the SBMA's Labour Centre requests that applicants produce documentation to certify their voluntary work in the Freeport. The rationale is explained in the SBMA's Labour Manual for new companies:

> They were the ones who 'volunteered' to 'protect' and 'preserve' this facility, thus making it possible for business enterprises like your company to invest in Subic. Hence, it is just fair that they should be given the first crack at the jobs which become available.[24]

In addition, under the Gordon administration, residents of Olongapo City were strongly favoured in the recruitment process. This was made explicit in the terms under which investors leased property from the SBMA:

> The investors will hire employees from the City of Olongapo and adjoining municipalities [...] as far as practicable.[25]

This basis for selection is also corroborated in the experiences of industrialists:

> Recruitment requires the people to show their volunteers' certificates and voters' affidavits, so these people were somehow related to the Gordons. Especially with Kate Gordon as the Olongapo Mayor, it is very easy for Richard Gordon to co-ordinate with her to pull the labour from Olongapo. Now with the new guy, more are from Bataan.[26]

24 SBMA Labour Centre, The Labour Manual, 1997.
25 Section 2, Article IV, 'Business and Employment', *SBMA-Investors Lease Agreement.*
26 Interview, General Manager, Shipping company, 25th December 1998.

The SBMA could, moreover, enforce this approach through its Labour Centre, which acted as a recruitment agency to supply a workforce to new investors. The Centre itself asserts that investors are able to freely hire their own labour, and that the process of recruitment through the Centre operates according to standard impartial procedures. If employers wish to, the Centre argues, they are free to recruit independently.[27] Investors, however, disagree with this representation. Many argued that there was little alternative to recruiting through the SBMA:

> We can hire directly, but you then have to go to the Labour Centre to approve it. You can still hire someone you like but you still need approval from the SBMA and go through all this paper chase to make up. It was probably worse with the last chairman. You have to hire everybody from the SBMA so that they knew who you were hiring.[28]

After posting an advertisement in local media on behalf of a company, the Labour Centre would screen and sort applicants, and then send the files of those they deemed qualified to the firm. The data required from applicants included a photograph, volunteer's certificate, voter's affidavit, birth certificate, diplomas, police and *barangay* clearance, and a specific request to give a clear indication of middle name. From this information, a very clear picture emerges of a candidate's location and acceptability in the local political scene – even down to their middle name, which indicates maternal family connections. In addition, any interviewee or applicant requires a gate pass issued by the SBMA to enter the Freeport. From *this* pool, the investors themselves were free to choose.

> It's not that simple to hire someone directly and we had to go through the Labour Centre again to make sure that they are OK. We also have to get passes for them and all these loads of things. It's a bit more complicated and it's not completely free and workable. Well, you are free to hire who your like but you will have to go through all the paper chase [...][29]

The recruitment procedure under the new administration remains the same except that the policy of giving priority to ex-volunteers no longer holds. Indeed, the Payumo administration has now shifted the focus of employment from Olongapo to Bataan and hence rendered this policy redundant. But those favoured for employment are no less a reflection of the political territoriality of the personalities in charge. As two managers noted:

27 Interview, Officer, SBMA Labour Centre, 15th December 1998.

28 Interview, General Manager, British company, 16th December 1998.

29 American General Manager, SBF firm, Interview, December, 1998.

> Definitely more labour are now from Bataan. Payumo is from Bataan! Previously, no chance. Now, a lot of Bataan people. And what the SBMA do is that they put in a lot of applications and give them to the factories and sometimes they even follow up to see whether these people are employed or not. The previous guy was concentrating in Olongapo and now this new guy is bringing in his own Bataan people [...] the higher authorities will give them a recommendation letter [...] if you have someone in the family to help, it's no problem. If not, you need recommendations from this mayor or that mayor.[30]

> Although we can determine the people to be recruited, there are still lots of 'under-the-table' transactions. More applicants are from Bataan now because Payumo is from Bataan.[31]

Once again, however, the needs of investors must be satisfied. Most firms appear to be fully aware of the way in which the local political scene was affecting their recruitment practices, but had no reason or incentive to resist. Where the candidates submitted by the SBMA were unsuitable, one manager described going ahead with interviews regardless in order to keep the local authorities happy.

> The people that the SBMA got for us were not suitable, but we interviewed the people anyway just so as to satisfy the SBMA, to play the game [...][32]

Ultimately, however, investors would not allow unqualified patronage appointments to compromise their operations.

Personalised politics thus exerts a significant, but negotiated, influence on who gets access to employment within the Freeport. Moreover, the institutions of the Freeport, such as the Labour Centre, are evidently vulnerable to being used to reflect the political interests of incumbent power holders.

Recruitment of SBMA Administrative Staff

Not surprisingly, the recruitment of SBMA administrative employees is also very much regulated by political affiliation. An SBMA Human Resource manager described the situation in the following terms:

> Under the Gordon Administration, everything goes by vote. You just have to vote for Gordon and you get the job. They don't go by qualifications and educational level. I even have subordinates in this Labour Department who are not qualified but got their jobs because they volunteered to cut the grass or be security guards for 6

30 Interview, General Manager, Singaporean company, 22nd December 1998.

31 Interview, Manager, 18th December 1998.

32 British Vice-President, SBF firm, Interview, December 1998.

months! Chairman Payumo is different, he is objective and wants things to be done professionally. Now, we only employ people who are good.[33]

While this new direction might be the ideal, informal information gathered during fieldwork did not suggest that the new administration was a great deal more 'professional.' Personal networks were still prevalent in the recruitment process, including the appointment of several SBMA directors from Bataan who were old allies of the new Chairman. This applies even more to those in lower level secretarial or administrative positions. Thus, while recruitment into the private sector at Subic has been determined by political affiliation, loyalty exhibited through a willingness to work for nothing, and residence within the Chairman's bailiwick, employment in the SBMA itself is also based upon personalised relationships and networks. This is not to say that those appointed are incompetent or unqualified for the work at hand, as the binary oppositions discussed earlier would imply. Instead it suggests that institutional procedure can indeed co-exist easily with personalised and politicised agendas. Moreover, the discourse still espoused by these institutions is one of professionalism, impartiality and efficiency. Thus even if this only vaguely reflects the reality, it is a discursive counterweight to the excesses of personalism, favouritism etc. that provides a check upon these practices when the disjuncture between discourse and reality becomes too wide. This point should not be overstated, since practices and their representation can clearly be widely discordant, but as long as an organisation such as the SBMA attempts to project an image of rational efficiency then there is an incentive to live up to that image.

Table 5.2: Subic Bay Freeport Establishments Inspected on General Labour Standards, 1995-97*

Particulars	*1995*	*1996*	*1997*	*Total*
SBF Establishments Inspected	88	29	157	274
With Labour Standards Violations	59 (67%)	9 (32%)	96 (61%)	164 (60%)
SBF Establishments with Corrected Violations	42	8	82	132
SBF Establishments with Minimum Wage Violations	46%	89%	52%	52%

Source: Current Labour Statistics, *SBMA-LIDO*.
* No inspections were conducted in 1998 due to the disruptions caused by the transfer of power from Gordon to Payumo.

33 Interview, Officer, SBMA, 11th December 1998. Note, however, that this officer had been employed after the changeover to the Payumo administration.

Labour Relations and Dispute Resolution

The institutional mechanism within the SBMA for resolving labour disputes is the Labour Inspection and Disputes Office (LIDO). Indeed, the absence of trade unions from the SBF leaves LIDO as the only formal channel for settling disputes, usually arising from issues such as non-payment of benefits, violation of minimum wage laws, illegal dismissal and poor health and safety provisions.

When a labour dispute arises, LIDO attempts to mediate between the parties using voluntary arbitrators. When an agreement cannot be reached locally, the dispute must be forwarded to the National Labour Relations Commission (NLRC) of the Department of Labour and Employment (DOLE). The NLRC would then assign arbitrators to carry out compulsory arbitration or assumption of jurisdiction to resolve the dispute.

The dispute resolution mechanism is well used, and much needed, as Table 5.2 indicates. During the three-year period 1995-97, 60 per cent of establishments in the SBF were found, upon inspection, to be in breach of nationally mandated labour standards.

Table 5.3 shows the stage at which various labour disputes were resolved. It is worth noting that just a handful ever reached the national scale of jurisdiction, while the vast majority was resolved locally.

Table 5.3: Labour Dispute Settlement, 1995-98.

Particulars	*1995*	*1996*	*1997*	*1998*
Labour cases received at LIDO	96	254	553	728
Cases resolved through LIDO mediation	94	206	494	607
Cases resolved through LIDO voluntary arbitration	2	6	16	31
Cases endorsed to NLRC for assumption of jurisdiction	0 (0%)	1 (0%)	4 (0.7%)	17 (2.3%)
Cases remaining in process as of year-end	0	37	39	24

Source: Current Labour Statistics, *SBMA-LIDO*; SBMA Chairman's Office, *SBMA 100 Days Accomplishment Report*, 1998; and SBMA Investment Centre, *The Subic Bay Freeport: A Guide for Investors*, 1997.

With just a handful of cases proceeding to national level institutions, SBMA-LIDO retains effective local control over the mechanism for dispute resolution. This need not be interpreted as sinister – inevitably the majority of disputes are minor affairs and are resolved either within the firm or through mediation by LIDO. Equally, the ascent of a complaint to the national scale needn't necessarily imply that it will be dealt with in a more impartial manner. The workings of the local dispute resolution mechanism must therefore be assessed.

Officials at LIDO claim that the dispute resolution mechanism works according to impartial institutional procedures.

> We follow the [national] Labour Code to help both the employers and the employees [...] We are cutting down on corruption and do not accept bribes here. We are professional [...][34]

Many disagree with this self-assessment, including employers. As one Taiwanese manager complained:

> There is a lot of corruption in the SBMA-LIDO. We had a case of labour dispute [...] the LIDO asked us to pay damages to the employees, we refused because we felt we were right [...] the LIDO people then told us that we would go to court and we would lose, finally they said that if we were willing to pay them 'under-the-table' money, they will forget about the whole thing!'[35]

Two points of interest emerge from this statement. First, it is notable that LIDO ruled in favour of the employees in the dispute in question. It would, therefore, be inappropriate to depict the office as simply doing the bidding of firms and managers. Some degree of professionalism and impartiality is clearly implied. But the willingness of LIDO to abandon a position if a bribe was paid shows the vulnerability of labour relations procedures to corruption. A significant issue here is the absence of a labour sector representation in LIDO's dispute resolution process, which would serve to discourage the kind of incident described above. This leaves the SBMA administration with a free hand in the field of industrial relations and a danger that procedures will be undermined by either petty corruption or countervailing local priorities to serve the needs of investors. Thus, while the resolution of disputes at the local level does not necessarily imply the dissolution of due process, the lack of checks upon the procedure at that scale does leave it vulnerable.

Unionisation in Subic Bay

The formation of trade unions in the Philippines is legal under The New Labor Relations Law (Republic Act 6715) of the Philippine Labour Code (see Foz 1998).[36] Nevertheless until 1998, no unions existed in the Subic Freeport. One

34 Interview, SBMA Labour Officer, 15th December 1998.

35 Interview, HR Manager, Taiwanese company, 18th December 1998. This accusation was also levelled by a former SBMA department head, 26th December 1998.

36 See RA 6715, Sec. 17, Art. 243 - Coverage and Employees' Right to Self-organise. The article states that 'All persons employed in commercial, industrial and agricultural enterprises and in religious, charitable, medical, or educational institutions whether operating for profit or not, shall

SBMA employee rationalised this state of affairs in the following way:

> Labour unions are not banned in SBF. But we don't have an organised union for SBF because the labour saw no need for unions. The SBMA-LIDO is very efficient in helping labour solve their disputes. We satisfy both the employers and employees. And if there are unions, investors will feel threatened. So having LIDO is enough.[37]

According to a number of reports, however, the absence of unions suggested not harmony but the enforcement of a 'No-Union' policy by Gordon to attract foreign investment. One newspaper suggested that:

> The story behind Subic's success is the espousing of anti-labour practices by the SBMA headed by Gordon [...] the 'no-union' policy is the 'come-on' to investors.[38]

If this were indeed the intention, then it would appear to have worked as planned. Many investors and early tenants cited the unofficial banning of unions in SBF as one of the main incentives for locating there:

> Trade unions had been banned under the old administration. When Gordon invited investors to invest here, he gave the assurance of no unions.[39]

The Gordon Administration kept the unions out in various ways. One was a strategy of direct intimidation against workers wanting to form a union. Another was the harassment of union organisers. The Trade Union Congress of the Philippines (TUCP), the country's mainstream union umbrella organisation, reported the following:

> We are not allowed access in SBF. We were being closely monitored. In fact, our office has been under close surveillance by four SBMA Intelligence persons [...] likewise, our core groups and workers who visit our offices were also under surveillance and were subjected to harassment. The SBMA intimidated, persecuted and even coerced workers to prevent them from organising unions [...] When workers of the Good Speed Garments Corporation decided to form their union, Chairman Gordon personally intervened and initiated a meeting with the employees. Gordon told the

have the right to self-organisation and to form, join, or assist labour organisations of their own choosing for purposes of collective bargaining.'

37 Interview, SBMA Labour and Inspection Office (LIDO) Senior Officer, 15th December 1998.

38 *Philippine Daily Inquirer*, 3rd August 1997. The paper suggested that SBMA officials were exerting extreme anti-union pressure on Subic's 35,000 workers. See also *SunStar Clark*, 15th January 1997.

39 Interview with a general manager of a Singaporean company, 22nd December 1998. All other investors and TUCP official interviewed re-affirmed the *de facto* banning of unions in SBF by Gordon.

> employees that if a union was formed, he would close down the company and he assured that whoever went against him would no longer be employed in SBF [...] hence they were forced to agree to the forming of a LMC instead.[40]

A third measure against the formation of independent unionisation, was thus to encourage the development of 'in-house' unions or Labour-Management Councils (LMCs).[41] While LMCs are in principle intended to provide employees with greater bargaining power, in reality they have represented workers only nominally because of the tight control over them exerted by the SBMA. As a TUCP official noted:

> Gordon also formed LMCs so that TUCP would have no chance because these LMCs would act to solve disputes. But these LMCs have no voice of their own to speak up for the workers. They are controlled by Gordon [...][42]

This strategy was also recognised by early corporate tenants at Subic:

> The SBMA had been promoting their LMCs [...] because this will pre-empt the formation of unions through the frustrations of the employees who do not have a voice. Their governance is assisted and processed by the SBMA [...][43]

There is, however, evidence that this strategy against unions was personal rather than systemic. The attitude of the SBMA to unionisation appears to have undergone a sea change under Chairman Payumo, with ten unions having registered in 1998 (see Table 5.4). Many, however, are unaware of this shift in circumstances:

> Actually Chairman Payumo is now secretly supporting the TUCP. He instructs LIDO to assist the TUCP, but all these are unofficial. In the old administration, LIDO was against us because of Gordon's instructions, but now they have to help us because of Payumo's orders [...] Also, my boss is a good friend of Chairman Payumo [...] Chairman Payumo cannot openly support us because it will scare off the investors [...] although most are registered, their existence are not disclosed yet.[44]

It would seem that there is good reason to suppress this information. A 'fear' of trade unions was a consistent theme in the reactions of industrialists to the new administration:

40 Unpublished TUCP General Report, 1996.
41 RA 6715, Book V, Rule XXI, Sect. 1 on Labour-Management Councils.
42 Interview, TUCP Paralegal Officer, Olongapo City, 29th December 1998.
43 Interview, Vice-President, British company, 21st December 1998.
44 Interview, TUCP Paralegal officer, Olongapo City, 31st December 1998.

Table 5.4: Unions Formed in Companies in SBF*

No.	Names of Companies Organised	Date registered/ Number of Workers	
1	T & H Shopfitters Corp.	1st January 1998	50
2	Subic Bay Golf Course	8th August 1998	50
3	Jaylee Subic Corp.	20th September 1998	500
4	BICC Brand-Rex, Inc.	27th September 1998	70
5	Subic Telecommunications, Inc.	2nd November 1998	70
6	Subic Water & Sewerage	11th November 1998	211
7	Ocean Pacific Service, Inc.	14th November 1998	50
8	Vision Air Philippine, Inc.	23rd November 1998	27
9	Coastal (Rank-and-file)	July 1998	200
10	Coastal (Supervisory level)	July 1998	50

Source: TUCP-LECC Olongapo Office.
* As of 6 January 1999.

> The old chairman may not like unions, but the new chairman may be pro-labour. I don't know yet. But there is a fear of a growth of trade unions.[45]

> There is always a fear that unions will come in. The new chairman didn't promise the investors anything. He had never said that he will keep the unions out, so he's not committed either way. So, that's still a big question mark.[46]

> Our greatest fear is the formation of trade unions [...] Payumo is pro-trade unions because there are a number of unions in Bataan and Payumo is pro-unions there. Although the Chairman says that he is not encouraging unions, but he is also not discouraging them too! But our stand is - no unions. If there are unions in our company, we will pull out of Subic.[47]

The change in administration at Subic has, therefore, served to highlight the importance of personalised politics in the regulation of the labour process. While the formal institutional mechanisms remain the same, the operating environment for unionists has changed dramatically due to a shift in attitude attributable only to a change in the individual involved. This example, along with the other elements of a labour market regulated according to personalised politics highlights the need to look beyond the formal institutional composition of labour market regulation.

45 Interview, General Manager, British company, 16th December 1998.
46 Interview, General Manager, Singaporean company, 22nd December 1998.
47 Interview, HR Manager, Taiwanese company, 18th December 1998.

Local Politics and the Labour Market

Existing literature on local labour markets acknowledges the importance of institutions, historical antecedence, personal identity, and cultural change (Massey 1995, Hanson and Pratt 1995, Peck 1996, Kelly 1999, Coe and Kelly 2000a). The Subic example suggests that this must be expanded to include not just local institutions, but the ways in which they may be used to further political goals of particular factions or individuals.

The much-heralded volunteerism at Subic highlighted the remarkable ability of the Gordons to mobilise human labour based broadly upon an assumed relationship of patronage that would ultimately culminate in paid employment. The disaffection of many volunteers, however, suggests that this was not a relationship forged in the classic mould of the patron and client, although personal charisma did play a part. Instead it was largely based on the desperation of many local people for employment and their consequent willingness to do what was necessary to secure it. In many cases, while their labour was not provided freely and willingly on the basis of affection for, and faith in, their patron, nor was it delivered under the coercive duress of a local 'boss.'

Other dimensions of local labour market practices highlight the difficulty of jumping to conflate local and sometimes informal types of regulation with personalistic and corrupt practices. Rather, the two sides of Ileto's dualisms appear to co-exist in a tension that creates distinctive local outcomes that may change over time (for example, with the appointment of a new Chairman at the SBMA). In the case of recruitment at Subic's private sector enterprises, effective control has been assumed by the SBMA's Labour Centre and the preference given to former volunteers and to residents of Olongapo highlights the way in which an institutional mechanism for matching qualified individuals with employment vacancies can be harnessed for personal political purposes. This system appears to persist under the new administration, albeit reoriented to a different political bailiwick. Nevertheless, these possibilities for personalisation and politicisation are held in check by a combination of formal rules governing labour market practices (which, while not adhered to in all cases, do provide a pull towards administrative rationality), and, importantly, the requirements of investors whose presence ultimately provides the basis for local political power and patronage.

In the case of recruitment to the SBMA itself, we see less the politicisation of institutions and more their personalisation, such that appointments are made on the basis of connections, kinship and personal loyalty. To return once again to Ileto's dualisms, though, it does not follow that this is automatically antithetical to the efficient operation of the state machinery. The impact of this system upon the equity and efficiency of labour market regulation is, in fact, an empirical question based on individual cases, rather than a structural weakness due to a departure from the ideal of a rational objective institution.

The mechanisms for dispute resolution also create opportunities for informalised control at the local scale, but again these are negotiated in a contingent manner. The localisation of dispute resolution does not conclusively imply their manipulation either for or against workers' interests, although the lack of labour representatives in Subic's labour office leaves the process open both to political manipulation and petty corruption. In these circumstances, and given the foundation of local power upon the attraction and retention of investors, the possibility that the Freeport's industrial relations will diverge from their legislated path is ever present.

The final case presented here, relating to the suppression of unionisation in Subic, encompasses several of the points made above. While national level labour laws permit the free association of workers into independent trade unions, this right was apparently undermined at the local level by the Gordon administration. The rationale for doing so was clear enough – foreign investors were evidently looking for an environment in which they could be guaranteed the freedom to operate unhindered by the demands of an organised workforce. The mechanism for fostering such an environment, however, owed much to the personal style and power of Richard Gordon, which extended beyond his formal powers as a state functionary. Intimidation and threats, along with the pre-emptive formation of 'in-house' Labour Management Committees were among the strategies employed to discourage independent unionisation. The appointment of a new administration, apparently more sympathetic to organised labour, illustrates a two-sided check upon personal power. On the one hand, Gordon's tenure proved to be contingent on the support (or lack of it) of political players at other scales, notably the President. On the other hand, Payumo's support of the TUCP has been low profile in order to avoid disaffection among investors, whose opinions clearly matter, and upon whom local power holders ultimately depend.

In conclusion, it seems that political actors and institutions, constituted at the scale of the local labour market, appear often to subvert, mediate or circumvent the provisions for labour regulation enacted at the national scale. This is a feature of labour market regulation that is far from unique to Subic, or indeed to the Philippines (see Kelly 2001). It implies that our understanding of the social regulation of the local labour market has to be broadened to include such local political manoeuvrings. In the Philippines, however, models of how local politics works, usually based upon patron-clientelism or bossism, inadequately account for the intersection of politics and the labour process. As Ileto argues, we do not find unchecked personalism, particularism and corruption in every relationship, although these are clearly present in many instances. Instead, we find these tendencies in tension with their opposites – institutionalism, impartiality and administrative rationality – in the construction of the labour market. This tension, played out differently in various contexts creates a complex geography to labour market regulation that demands empirical attention.

References

Coe, N. and Kelly, P.F. (2000a) 'Connections and constructions in the local labour market: the case of Singapore', *Area* 32, 4: 413–422.

— (2000b) 'Distance and discourse in the local labour market: the case of Singapore,' *Area* 32, 4: 413–22.

Doronila, A. (1985) 'The transformation of patron-client relations and its political consequences in post-war Philippines', *Journal of Southeast Asia Studies* 16, 1: 99–116.

Foz, V.B. (1998) *The Labour Code of the Philippines*, Manila: Philippine Law Gazette.

Gutierrez, E. (1994) *The Ties that Bind: A Guide to Family, Business and Other Interests in the Ninth House of Representatives*, Manila: The Philippine Centre for Investigative Journalism.

Hanson, S. and Pratt, G. (1995) *Gender, Work and Space*, London: Routledge.

Hawes, G. (1992) 'Marcos, his cronies, and the Philippines' failure to develop', in R. McVey (ed.) *Southeast Asian Capitalists*, Ithaca, N.Y.: Cornell University Southeast Asia Program.

Hollnsteiner, M.R. (1968) *The Dynamics of Power in a Philippine Municipality*, Quezon City: The Community Development Research Council, University of the Philippines, Diliman.

Hutchcroft, P.D. (1991) 'Oligarchs and cronies in the Philippine state', *World Politics* 43, 3: 413–450.

Ileto, R. (1999) *Knowing America's Colony: A Hundred Years from the Philippine War*, Centre for Philippine Studies, University of Hawaii, Philippine Studies Occasional Paper Series No. 13.

Kelly, P.F. (1999) 'Rethinking the "local" in labour markets: the consequences of cultural embeddedness in a Philippine growth zone', *Singapore Journal of Tropical Geography* 20, 1: 56–75.

— (2001) 'The political economy of local labour market regulation in the Philippines', *Economic Geography* 77, 1: 1–22.

Kerkvliet, B. (1995) 'Towards a more comprehensive analysis of Philippine politics: beyond the patron-client framework', *Journal of Southeast Asian Studies* 26, 2: 401–419.

Kirk, D. (1998) *Looted: The Philippines after the Bases*, Basingstoke: Macmillan.

Lacaba, J.F. (ed.) (1995) *Boss: Five Case Studies of Local Politics in the Philippines*, Manila: Philippine Centre for Investigative Journalism.

Magno, F.A. (1993) 'Politics, elites and transformation in Malabon', *Philippine Studies* 41: 204–216.

Massey, D. (1995) *Spatial Divisions of Labour: Social Structures and the Geography of Production*, Basingstoke: Macmillan (second edition).

McCoy, A. (1994) *An Anarchy of Families: The Historiography of State and Family in the Philippines*, Quezon City: Ateneo de Manila University Press.

Napack, J. (2000) 'Stuck at Base', *Far Eastern Economic Review* 19 October 2000.

Peck, J. (1996) *Work-Place: The Social Regulation of Labour Markets*, New York: Guilford.

Putzel, J. (1995) 'Democratisation and clan politics: the 1992 Philippine elections', *Southeast Asia Research* 3, 1.

Rocamora, J. (1995) 'Introduction: classes, bosses, goons, and guns: re-imagining Philippine political culture', in J.F. Lacaba (ed.) *Boss: Five Case Studies of Local Politics in the Philippines*, Manila: Philippine Centre for Investigative Journalism.

SBMA (Subic Bay Metropolitan Authority) (1996) *Map and Guide to Subic Bay Freeport*, Subic: SBMA.

Scott, J.C. (1972) 'Patron-client politics and political change in Southeast Asia', *The American Political Science Review* 66, 1: 91–113.

Scott, J.C. and Kerkvliet, B. (1973) 'How traditional rural patrons lose legitimacy: a theory with special reference to Southeast Asia', *Cultures et Developpement* 5, 3: 482–512.

Sidel, J.T. (1995) 'Coercion, Capital and the Post-colonial State: Bossism in the Post-war Philippines', PhD Thesis, Cornell University.

— (1997) 'Philippines politics in town, district, and province: Bossism in Cavite and Cebu', *Journal of Asian Studies* 56, 4: 947–966.

Varela, A.P. (1995) 'Different faces of Filipino administration culture', in P.D. Tapales, N.N. Pilar and L.D. Romblon (eds.) *Public Administrator by the Year 2000: Looking Back into the Future*, Quezon City: University of the Philippines Press.

6

Are They Incompatible? Modern Farming and Non-Market Labour in the Northern Philippine Uplands

EDSEL E. SAJOR

A major trend in agrarian change during the nineteenth and twentieth centuries in many countries of Southeast Asia has been the disappearance of reciprocal labour and its replacement by hired labour. Elson, reviewing the literature on the Southeast Asian region, notes that while the spread of hired labour was in the first instance a replacement for co-operative labour, in time the former 'began gradually to replace tasks which had previously been the preserve of household members of the farming unit' (Elson 1997: 164). Thus, hired labour has grown and in the process substituted both reciprocal and family labour in farming (Horri 1981, Turton 1989, Ganajapan 1989, Hefner 1990). Scholars on Philippine agrarian issues reach a similar conclusion (Castillo 1982: 348, Fegan 1989a: 131, Boyce 1993: 135-6). While the clear trend in farming villages all over Southeast Asia has been a general decline of reciprocal labour and family labour, this change is nonetheless uneven. Various studies have noted the pervasiveness of reciprocal labour exchange and family labour in wet rice farming in the north-western plains of Malaysia (Dong 1987: 118-21) and in swidden and wet rice farming among forest and upland farmers of Thailand (Hamilton 1976: 62-7, Kunstander 1978: 74-131) up to the 1960s and 1970s. In the Philippines, some local case studies have also noted the persistence of reciprocal labour exchange in remote upland areas occupied by indigenous communities such as the Buhids of upland Mindoro (Lopez-Gonzaga 1983), the Kalingas (Lawless 1975), and the Kankanais of Sagada (Voss 1983).

Scholars of agrarian change in Southeast Asia have directly related the persistence/decline of reciprocal labour and family labour to the degree of market penetration or level of commercialisation of a particular agrarian economy (Hamilton 1976: 226, Chulasai et al. 1986: 168-69, Hirashima and Muqtada 1986: 5-6, Elson

1997: 164). While both forms of labour have been negatively affected by the deepening market penetration in agriculture, reciprocal labour in particular is seen as the one most incompatible with the commercialisation of agriculture (Hefner 1990: 137). Most findings in upland areas in the Philippines are similar. Duhaylungsod (1989), in her study of an upland village in the province of Laguna where farming is not mechanised, observed that the local reciprocal labour-exchange institution has been confined to slashing and clearing swiddens, clearing undergrowth from coconut farms, and building ricefields, and is excluded from the domain of tomato production for the market where wage labour is used instead. Studies in the upland province of Benguet have also noted that since the shift from subsistence food production to commercial vegetable gardening after the War, reciprocal labour declined dramatically, rarely applied to vegetable harvesting and was confined to a few remote communities where money is scarce (Voss 1983: 231, Lewis 1992: 146, 154). Wiber's labour study (1985) in Kabayan, Benguet also suggests this incompatibility. There is a significant persistence of *oboan,* a reciprocal labour-exchange arrangement in rice production, but its absence is noticeable in commercial vegetable gardening where both household and daily wage labour are employed.

However, such observed negative correlations between the commercialisation of agriculture on the one hand, and reciprocal and family labour on the other hand, may not be straightforward and simple. There may be other mediating factors which stymie the growth of hired labour and the demise of family and reciprocal labour. Such factors, for example, may be relative remoteness and sparseness of population of an area, little or no landlessness and equality among partners in the exchange relationship, absence of mechanisation and low use of modern inputs.

But while some authors have correctly identified the role of certain mediating factors, still the overall perspective underscores a decline, or at least, the inevitability of the demise of family and reciprocal labour exchange, expressed in such terms as 'survival' and 'persistence' of these forms (Castillo 1982: 321, Elson 1997: 164). Thus, incompatibility of these forms of labour with market-orientation is implied, although it is conceded that such trend cannot be an accomplished fact overnight. This view is founded on an influential notion in agrarian studies that regard social institutions and traditional customs as constraints to the functioning of the market by setting up barriers to mobility of factors of production (Basu 1984: 179). The complex institutions existing in peasant reproduction are seen as resistant to commoditisation, a drag on capitalist development in rural areas, and inevitably have to 'decompose' for the full development of capitalist production (Friedman 1980: 163).

However, such presumed 'decomposition' of pre-existing non-market institutions as family and reciprocal labour as an inevitable and necessary path prior to market integration of local agriculture may be an overly dichotomised view. It does not always follow that reciprocal and family labour diminishes in proportion to the penetration and growth of commercialism in agriculture. It may be, as in the case in highland Sulawesi, Indonesia, as argued by Schrauwers (1999), that optimal utilisation of non-market inputs of 'kin labour' and 'traditional labour exchange' shapes the condition wherein it becomes feasible for local peasants to engage in market-oriented production and produce cash incomes. Hence, such non-market forms of labour could not be interpreted to be mere vestiges of a 'natural economy' on the way out, but rather as creative and strategic forms of engagement by marginalised upland peasants enabling them to engage in commercial production. They may not be obstacles to commercialisation but essential assets of local peasants sustaining their participation in the process. This underscores the importance of looking into the terms of the local community's engagement with the market, or the conditions under which its livelihoods and agriculture have articulated with the broader market forces outside

This article examines the pervasiveness and dominance of family and reciprocal labour (*obbo*)[1] in an upland village of Duit, in Kiangan municipality in the province of Ifugao belonging to the Cordillera Region[2] of northern Philippines in the introduction and spread of a two-cropping system comprising modern rice varieties and the commercial cultivation of snap beans (*Phaseolus vulgaris. L.*) since the early 1980s. Adoption of modern rice variety by local farmers has not only retained the pre-eminence of these two forms of labour *vis-à-vis* hired labour. These forms have also expanded and gained prime importance in the domain of the recently cultivated highly commercial vegetable crop. In explaining the present-day pervasiveness and much-enhanced importance of these labour arrangements, this paper examines the particular terms of engagement of local farming with the broader market in the last two decades of the twentieth century. Two factors

1 A reciprocal labour group or *obbo* is launched informally in Duit when at least three farmers decide to start such a group by rotating their collective work among their fields. In the process, more individual farmers might join in, enlarging the original group. In Duit, some *obbo* groups may form for only one crop season, but many remain intact all year, covering a number of seasons in both rice and vegetable crops. In the author's random survey (1997) of 92 families, 82 (or 89 per cent) reported participating regularly in reciprocal labour-exchange groups.

2 Aside from the Ifugao province, the five other provinces comprising the Cordillera Region are Benguet, Mt. Province, Kalinga, Apayao and Abra. The Ifugao are the indigenous inhabitants of the present-day province of Ifugao and are one of the seven major ethnolinguistic groups known by their popular generic name as Igorot who inhabit the mountainous Cordillera Region. Much of this mountainous region remained independent from the Spanish colonial administration lasting from 1565 to 1897 in the rest of the country. Cordillera Region is bordered in the east, west and south by lowland provinces inhabited by the Ilocano who have been long Christianised and had been subjects of the Spanish colonial administration prior to the occupation of the Americans in 1898.

serve as important contexts which exert great influence in the current pervasiveness of traditional or non-market forms of labour arrangements in the uplands: a) the persistence of a smallholding pattern and absence of a mass of landless farmers who can serve as potential army for hired labour recruitment; and b) the lack of state patronage of the village elite during the late 1970s and 1980s when local agriculture was being modernised and profoundly commercialised. Both contexts are outcomes of particular trends in local agricultural history shaped by the forces of the state and market intersecting with local culture and social autonomy[3] of an indigenous upland village society. The chapter discusses these trends and the influence of these two contexts to argue why and how local farmers have managed to fit non-market labour arrangements within modern and commercialised farming in the uplands.

New Farming and Non-Market Forms of Labour

According to older informants, from the early 1900s up to the 1970s the core of farming and livelihood activities in the village of Duit were pondfield rice farming and the cultivation of sweet potatoes in swiddens, a common characteristic of wet-rice terracing indigenous communities in the mountain region of the Cordillera in northern Luzon. Pondfields or *payo*, located in the vicinity's gentler mountain slopes and stream depressions, were planted with single-crop, late-maturing indigenous rice varieties.[4] All households in varying degrees, on the other hand, engaged in swidden farming of sweet potatoes in clearings on steeper slopes. Households without or with only small rice pondfields had the most extensive swiddens. They coped with their lack of rice by substituting sweet potato during the lean months. Swiddens were also an important food source for raising pigs and chickens, an important economic activity which allowed households to meet their need for animals for ritual sacrifice.

Various types of labour were employed in these two farming activities. Family, reciprocal labour exchange, and hired labour were used in varied proportions based on the specific phase of cultivation, and on the particular economic status of

3 I am using 'social autonomy' in the way James Scott has referred to it as the degree of relative freedom from state control enjoyed by non-state social units such as the household, the kinship group, the village, or settlement (as distinct from the individual freedom of the citizen) 'to determine their own residence, their community forms, their own forms of property and production as opposed to the imposition of state-mandated forms of residence, social organisation, property, and production' (Scott 1995: 1-3). For an excellent and thorough discussion of this subject see Scott (1998).

4 Traditional mountain rice varieties required five months to ripen, much longer than the shorter four-month maturation period of the modern rice varieties adapted for mountain areas.

the household. Rice cultivation employed reciprocal labour exchange most intensively. This type of labour was augmented by family labour, principally done by the male and female spouses in the farms which a couple operate. Only a few households employed hired labour in this farming activity. The field preparation phase, requiring heavy labour in repairing dikes and irrigation canals, was done by all-male reciprocal labour groups. The adult female member(s) of the household operating the farm however also contributed in this phase, doing the less heavy tasks of cleaning and weeding paddy walls. Seed bed preparation was done by family labour, with both the male and female spouses doing the work. Rice transplanting and harvesting were done through large reciprocal labour groups composed of men and women. In between transplanting and harvesting, various tasks related to crop maintenance, mostly weeding, were done through a combination of all-female reciprocal labour and, in less work demanding phases, the individual labour of the female spouse.

Family labour clearly dominated in swidden farming. In this activity hired labour was totally absent. Clearing of grasslands for opening swiddens, done during the dry summer months, was performed by both the male and female spouses of the households. Oftentimes, grown-up children also helped their parents in this task. According to older informants, in a few cases reciprocal labour group of mixed male and female compositions was employed in this task. But this was not the common practice. Family labour was clearly the dominant type of labour in all phases of work in swidden farming. Planting sweet potato and other minor cultivars such as ginger, mongo beans, and sugarcane was done solely by the female spouse. So too was weeding and the general maintenance work for the growing crops. Harvesting of sweet potato was also a task the female spouse performed.

In addition to these three types of farming labour, a type of festive co-operative labour (*dang-a*) was also practised in the community outside of regular farm tasks, except in hauling rice-bundle harvests from the fields to the owner's granary.[5] *Dang-a* was commonly used in house construction, timber hauling, and, in the case of female-headed households, for gathering and chopping firewood.

In the early 1980s, two important changes in farming activities in Duit caused the intensification of labour use in village farming: first, the shift from single-cropping cultivation of the traditional, late-maturing rice variety to the double-cropping system using a modern, early-maturing variety; and second, the introduction and spread of commercial vegetable gardening, particularly, snap bean

5 Unlike in the practise of reciprocal labour (*obbo*), immediate and exact repayment of labour was not required of the host by the participants in *dang-a*. Moreover, the festive mood in the dang-a contrasted with the obbo where each participant's work was far more efficient and strict. Unlike the reciprocal-labour exchange, the dang-a usually lasted for only a day, with every able-bodied male in the village participating in heavy tasks of hauling or cutting firewood. Women participated in the occasion generally in food preparation with the host providing food and rice wine.

cultivation. Such agricultural changes were catalysed by very limited livelihood intervention projects in the uplands in the late 1970s and early 1980s by the Philippine state that historically has constructed mountain agriculture as unproductive and marginal (Contreras 1990: 13–4, see also Li 1999: 5). Though limited to a few demonstration farms, free seed distribution, and initial marketing assistance, these official projects were seized by a few enterprising farmers of Kiangan municipality, including some from Duit, who in turn initiated the spread of the new rice varieties and vegetable crops (some of these projects were actually unintended spill-overs from an earlier Green Revolution programme intensively implemented in the nearby lowland province of Nueva Viscaya). This type of low-level state intervention shaped a relatively autonomous trajectory of agrarian change in the village in the 1980s up to the present. Its social consequences largely contrast with that of strong rural development intervention program implemented by the state in the lowlands during this era, a point which will be discussed later.

In the upland village of Duit, the introduction of the modern rice variety, which has a shorter 127-day cycle, allowed for a two cropping system.[6] This cropping intensification did not displace but absorbed farm labour. A previous labour-slack period of six months was shortened to two and a half months. This development is much unlike what occurred in rice farming areas of lowland Philippines where the increase in cropping intensity attributed to the introduction of the non-photosensitive, quick-maturing varieties in the 1960s at first caused farm employment to rise. But later, by the 1970s to 1980s, these initial employment gains gave way to declines in farm employment as a result of labour-displacing technological change accompanying the Green Revolution rice variety (Boyce 1993: 150).[7]

The spread of the double-cropping system of rice farming coincided with the growth of commercial vegetable gardening in 1981 in the village. This other major change in local agriculture quickly mobilised local labour to cultivate idle lands. Snap bean has a short crop cycle of 45 to 50 days and can be grown at any time of the year. Local farmers therefore could easily squeeze it into the labour-slack periods in rice farming, whenever household labour capacity and access to farm land allow. In addition, the cultivar requires much less water than rice. It is therefore adaptable to the many pondfields that had been abandoned due to perennial drying up. Hence, snap bean cultivation ideally complements local rice

6 A second crop right after the May to June first-crop harvest, would be harvested in October or November, still leaving ample time to prepare the field immediately, between November and December, for a new round of rice cropping.

7 The new rice varieties of the Green Revolution programme which were propagated in the lowland Philippines did not inherently require that human labour be replaced by tractors, power tillers, herbicides or threshing machines. However, as Boyce (1993: 145) argues, in the particular political economic landscape observed in the lowlands, the Green Revolution and mechanisation were bound together. Thus, farm labour under these conditions was inevitably displaced.

farming both in terms of labour and land use. It has become a virtual year-round activity for many local households. Based on the author's survey of cultivation schedules involving a sample of 160 vegetable plots operated by sixty-six households, planting and harvesting of the plots are more or less spread evenly in eleven months of the year. On the other hand, swidden farming has been virtually wiped out.

Based on the author's survey of 102 households (1997), 72 per cent cultivate snap beans. Local farmers buy their fertilisers, insecticides, and seeds from local merchants in Kiangan municipality who in turn purchase their vegetable produce from them. These vegetables are then resold to big trading centres in the nearby lowland province of Nueva Viscaya which ultimately brings these vegetables to the large markets in Metro-Manila. For the majority of local households who regularly experience rice deficiency, snap bean cultivation serves mainly to provide cash for purchasing additional rice outside.[8] It is also their source of cash for other necessities such as food condiments, medical expenses, basic household articles and school children's matriculation and transportation .

In present-day Duit, both family labour and reciprocal labour have remained pillars of farming labour arrangements in the village. In the author's survey of ninety-two farming households (1997), ninety-one (99 per cent) contribute family labour to their farms. Only one person, who derives income from ownership of several hectares of irrigated farm in the lowland and from farm equipment services in the village operates as a pure farm manager, relying entirely on hired labour to cultivate his farm in the village. In this same survey, eighty-two out of ninety-two families (89 per cent) reported regular participation in reciprocal labour-exchange groups.

The significance of both family labour and reciprocal labour in local farming is demonstrated in the figures in Table 1 drawn from the author's survey of a sample of 125 rice farms and 115 garden plots operated by ninety-two households. In both the subsistence sector of rice farming and the market-oriented sector of snap bean cultivation, hired labour trails reciprocal labour and family labour in significance. Reciprocal labour comprises 62 per cent of all labour input in rice farming. Hence, despite the village's shift to the double-cropping modern rice variety in the early 1980s, reciprocal labour continues to dominate rice farming overwhelmingly as in the pre-war and early post-war decades. Family labour (21 per cent) and hired labour (17 per cent) lag far behind labour exchange in rice farming. On the other hand, in snap bean farming family labour constitutes the biggest chunk of labour input (45 per cent). But even in this commercial endeavour, reciprocal

8 In the village of Duit, rice cultivation today, as in the past, is commonly for a household's own consumption. The community does not significantly export rice padi outside. With the decline of sweet potatoes in swidden and its substitution by vegetable gardens, more households today, 63 per cent, are dependent in varying degrees on purchased rice outside.

labour contributes the next biggest share (33 per cent), and hired labour again occupies the bottom rung.

Table 6.1: Types of Labour, by Major Crop (1997)

Crop	*Family labour*	*Hired labour*	*Reciprocal labour*	*Total*
Rice*	1409 person-days (21%)	1147 person-days (17%)	4235 person-days (62%)	6791 person-days (100%)
Snap Beans**	2300 person-days (45%)	1109 person-days (22%)	1705 person-days (33%)	5114 person-days (100%)

* Based on the author's survey of 125 rice farms operated by 75 households.

** Based on the author's survey of 115 garden plots operated by 82 households.

In Duit, despite the shift to double-cropping using a modern, early-maturing rice variety, the same gender division of labour as in the Pre-War period prevails today in various phases of work in rice cultivation. Moreover, the profile and mix of family labour and reciprocal labour in various phases earlier discussed have held basically, with large work groups employed for phases requiring great bursts of energy over a short time to finish up work at once in critical periods such as transplanting and harvesting. In Duit today as in the Pre-War period, such large work gangs have been formed mainly under reciprocal labour arrangements, and not by hiring wage workers. However, family labour (mainly participation by the female and male spouses) continues to be employed in low-intensity crop maintenance work such as periodic weeding before harvest: which remains the task of the female spouse.

In snap bean cultivation, family labour is generally the more dominant type of labour. Compared to pondfield rice cultivation, the former does not have as many labour-intensive phases where a large concentrated work force is needed to finish the task quickly. But still, in certain tasks, such as those during peak pod-cutting days, group labour power, albeit to a lesser degree, is necessary. It is here that reciprocal labour is significantly employed. Field preparation for planting snap beans involves clearing a plot by cutting grasses and uprooting weeds (*gabut*) and then hoeing the soil and forming two-metre-long mounds where the seeds are planted (*gabion*). These tasks are commonly done by small reciprocal labour groups. The next phases of work after field preparation are usually done by family labour. These are: application of chemical fertiliser or chicken dung (*abono*) and planting (*panagmula*); setting up of trellises (*luhad*) to support the growing creeper; and various types of crop maintenance work including turning up the soil around the plant (*sirado*) and weeding. In addition, family labour is employed in spraying the plant with chemical insecticide and fungicide one and a half weeks after planting and, thereafter, regularly at six-day intervals and at four-day intervals when the plant is 31 to 35 days old. Snap beans harvesting consists of about seven cuttings performed in separate days. The third, fourth, and fifth cuttings have the highest yields of pods and require the most number of labourers. In these cuttings, reciprocal labour groups are commonly employed. However, hired labour is employed solely or in combination with family and reciprocal labour by the richer households. The last two cuttings give a much lower yield and family labour (i.e. the male and female spouse and, at times, with their grown-up children) would suffice. All of the tasks in vegetable gardening are done by both men and women, except the spraying which is definitely regarded as male work.

In present-day Duit there is no great divide in the allocation of reciprocal labour between the two major crops. The traditional *obbo*, which was originally employed in rice farming – and to a certain extent to swidden farming before the War – is strongly utilised today to serve commercial vegetable gardening as well. When commercial vegetable farming spread in the village beginning in 1981, the practise of *obbo* dominant in rice farming merely extended into the domain of the new crop. Local farmers recruited extra labour to augment family labour in the cultivation of snap beans not by labour hiring, but by employing reciprocal labour. Moreover, current deployment of reciprocal labour in the village easily alternates between rice and snap bean cultivation. It is not uncommon for a reciprocal labour group which started work in rice cultivation to end up in subsequent rounds working in each member's vegetable plots. It is a usual occurrence too that hosts of *obbo* in rice harvesting would detach two or three people from the group after midday to shift their work to the hosts' vegetable gardens. According to local informants, it is entirely up to the *obbo*'s host to shuffle the some labourers between rice and garden plots as long as all members of the work group are dismissed by five o'clock in the afternoon.

Employment of the three types of labour varies not only by crop but also by size of the total farm holding of a household. In rice cultivation, the proportion of utilisation of family labour is substantial and fairly consistent, irrespective of farm size (Table 6.2).

In present-day Duit, virtually every household which operates a rice farm also works on the land. As a rule, those who are unable to work due to old age or engagement in urban-based livelihood let others operate their farms in a sharecropping arrangement. Nonetheless, in commercial vegetable gardening while the per cent of family labour is also fairly consistent among farms of twenty-four *bettek*[9] or less, family labour drops substantially for families with farm holdings

9 *Bettek* is a local measure of pondfield area traditionally used in Kiangan, Ifugao. Six *bettek* (abbr. btk) is roughly equal to 0.2 hectares.

Table 6.2: Type of Labour, by Farm Size Group and by Major Crop (1997)

Rice *Farm size group*	*0 btk.*	*1-5 btk.*	*6-12 btk.*	*13-18 btk.*	*19-24 btk.*	*> 24 btk.*
Per cent of family labour	22	28	14	21	19	25
Per cent of hired labour	3	10	8	9	35	41
Per cent of reciprocal labour	75	62	78	70	46	34
Snap bean *Farm size group*	*0 btk.*	*1-5 btk.*	*6-12 btk.*	*13-18 btk.*	*19-24 btk.*	*> 24 btk.*
Per cent of family labour	45	61	45	52	54	33
Per cent of hired labour	7	4	19	8	31	47
Per cent of reciprocal labour	48	35	36	40	15	20

N = 92 households operating 125 rice farms and 115 garden plots.

greater than twenty-four *bettek*. In this group a number of households in this farm size group contribute only a token share of family labour in their garden plots, relying heavily on hired labour to operate them. On the whole, however, despite the introduction of the double-cropping modern variety and commercial vegetable gardening, the current situation in this upland village is one of stable dependence on family labour. This phenomenon is quite unlike the general trend in Philippine (mostly lowland) agriculture in which, according to IRRI[10] data, hired labour increasingly substituted family labour during the height of the Green Revolution years from 1966 to the mid-1970s (Boyce 1993: 148).

While reciprocal labour's percentage to total labour input generally declines as the size of farm holding rises,[11] overall it occupies a dominant position in labour arrangements in rice farming and a secondary position in commercial vegetable gardening. In rice cultivation, households with farm holdings of eighteen *bettek* or less have a range of dependency on reciprocal labour between 62 per cent and 78 per cent (Table 6.2). In this sector, its dominant position is maintained in all farm size groups, except in the group of households owning more than twenty-four *bettek*, where it is displaced by hired labour. On the other hand, in vegetable gardening, family labour dominates for all farm size groups, except among farm-

10 International Rice Research Institute (Laguna, Philippines).

11 On the other hand, Duit data on hired labour demonstrates the opposite trend. Share of hired labour generally rises as the household's farm ownership increases. This trend is shown clearly in rice farming (Table 6.2). While the shares of hired labour in the total farming labour of households belonging to farm size groups from zero to 18 *bettek* ranges only from three per cent to nine per cent, this figure rises dramatically to 35 per cent and 41 per cent in the groups owning 19-24 *bettek*

ers without land ownership where reciprocal labour dominates. In this sector, reciprocal labour retains its secondary importance to family labour (from one *bettek* to eighteen *bettek* farm size groups), dislodged only in farms above twenty-four *bettek* in size, where land rich farmers depend primarily on hired labour. The present situation of reciprocal labour in Duit thus tends to support similar findings in northern Thailand in the 1980s (Ganajapan 1989), in West Malaysia in the 1970s (Horri 1981) and in southern Vietnam in the 1950s (Elson 1997) that mutual exchange and co-operative labour have been most common among poorer villagers or lower-scale farmers.

A roughly consistent major dependence on reciprocal labour by all farm-size groups from zero to eighteen *bettek* reaffirms the point that the arrangement works easily among farms and farmers of roughly equal size and social status. In land control figures, these particular ownership size groups comprise 79 per cent of all households, representing a large concentration of farmers whose size of land control and status do not greatly differ. They comprise the foundation of the smallholding pattern of land control in local village agriculture. Roughly speaking, each member of this large group of smallholders controls just enough land for their own family labour to maintain and operate during low-intensity work periods.[12] However, both in rice cultivation and commercial gardening, in peak work seasons, these households also need large enough work groups to finish up quickly critical phases of work in either crop cultivation (e.g. in rice harvests and in cutting peaks in snap bean harvest). Since the family labour of an overwhelming majority of households is tied up all year round to various activities revolving around each household's own rice and vegetable farms, on the supply side, there is a general scarcity of local idle labour lying around available for wage hiring. (The demand side of the potential labour market is, of course, also seriously constrained by the inadequacy of capital for labour hiring, a point which will be discussed later). In this particular environment, therefore, a reciprocal labour institution, strongly practised historically in the village, was simply extended by local farmers into the domain of commercial gardening to accomplish such tasks requiring group work. As a result, both reciprocal labour and family labour have to date remained the strongest pillars of major farming activities.

I now turn to a discussion of this small holding pattern in the village, an important variable underpinning pervasiveness of family labour and reciprocal labour despite modern changes and commercialisation of local agriculture of this upland village.

and more than 24 *bettek* respectively. A similar trend is evident in snap bean cultivation – the two largest farm size groups exhibit the highest degree of utilisation of hired labour.

12 Examples of regular low-intensity work in small farm operations where family labour is adequate and fit are the following: post-planting light weeding in rice cultivation, sowing snap beans seeds, weeding in snap beans cultivation, and final cuttings in snap bean harvesting.

Dynamics of a Local Smallholding Pattern

Empirical village-level studies have noted the greater prevalence of smallholdings[13] in the uplands compared to the lowlands (Cornista et al. 1986). In the upland village of Duit in particular, landholding is certainly less skewed than in Philippine lowland areas. Based on the author's survey of 100 households, only 29 per cent own no farm land. This is obviously less severe compared with the lowlands, where 50–64 per cent of rural families own no farm land at all (Riedinger 1995: 76). In 20 of the 29 households which do not own any farm land in the village, one or both spouses is an immigrant from other Ifugao municipalities.

Land ownership alone, however, gives an incomplete picture of the reality in the village that most households make their living by having access to a piece of farm land. In Duit, a smallholding pattern predominates (see Table 6.3 below). Such a pattern can be seen in Table 3 below by focusing on the land control[14] profile in each farm size group and the percentage of households and land area within each group. In the table, the columns between land ownership[15] and land control show significant differences. While 29 per cent of all surveyed households have zero farm ownership, only 3 per cent have actual zero land control. This indicates that the number of households having no land is drastically smaller due to arrangements which provide access to and control of a piece of land. Moreover, while 7 per cent of households own land between 31 to 40 *btk* in area, only 2 per cent of households actually control farm lands in this size group, indicating that some of the biggest local landowners have relinquished control of a significant part of their owned land to other households. Percentages of owned and controlled land in certain land size groups also vary significantly. For instance, size group six to 12 *btk* comprises only 14 per cent of all owned farm lands while making up 32 per cent of all controlled lands. On the other hand, size group 19–24 *btk* comprises 25 per cent of all owned farm land while making up only 18 per

13 Typical farm sizes in the Philippine uplands vary. They have been estimated to be as low as one hectare in overcrowded areas, and two to three hectares in less densely populated areas (World Bank 1989:22).

14 On land controlled, I have adopted Benjamin White's reference to it as 'a measure of the area of land to whose yields the household has access, regardless of ownership' (White 1976: 132). Following White's method of computation (White 1976: 126–34, see also Hart 1986: 96, Hefner 1990: 116), a household's land controlled in the case of Duit is made up of the area of land cultivated by the household as owner or mortgagee, plus half the area of land that the household has rented in and also half the area it has rented out (in sharecropping involving ½: ½ sharing of yield) and/or, plus 2/3 of the area that the household has rented in and 1/3 of the area it has rented out (in sharecropping with a 2/3: 1/3 sharing of yield).

15 By land ownership in this study, I refer to the land over which a household has legal rights of ownership, use and disposal, as recognised in the community and defined by normative order on land property rights existing in the local community at that time.

cent of all controlled land. This indicates that in farm-size group six to 12 *btk*, the percentage of controlled farm land is more than double that which is actually owned. The reverse is true for size group 19-24 *btk*. That is, land control on the basis of ownership is of less importance, indicating that many farm lands owned by the respondents in this group are actually operated by others, most likely land-poor households.

Table 6.3: Land Ownership and Control (1997)

		Ownership		*Control*	
Size Groups (btk)		% All Households	% All Farm land	% All Households	% All Farm land
0		29	0	3	0
1-5 *btk*	(0.03 to .16 ha)	11	6	18	5
6-12 *btk*	(.20 to .40 ha)	32	14	39	32
13-18 *btk*	(.43 to .60 ha)	12	17	19	16
19-24 *btk*	(.63 to .80 ha)	12	25	10	18
25-30 *btk*	(.83 to 1.0 ha)	7	17	9	22
31-40 *btk*	(1.03 to 1.33 ha)	7	21	2	6

N = 100 households.

Sharecropping has been the principal mechanism for expanding land control beyond what is owned or, in the case of large land-owning households, relinquishing land to other households. The other mechanism for this is a leasehold arrangement, which is usually done in commercial vegetable cultivation. Leasehold is secondary to sharecropping as an instrument for gaining control of land for land-poor households. Through both sharecropping and leasehold, skewedness of land control is mitigated. In the same random survey by the author, aggregate size of all sharecropped-in farms and all leased-in farms comprises 24 per cent of the total size under land control.

Present-day dominance of the smallholding pattern in Duit can be understood by looking into the particularity of local history and kinship practices affecting land access and distribution. The combination of developments since the War in local agriculture and population mobility, and the strong mediation on the latter of indigenous land inheritance practices among kin have sustained the dominance of smallholding in the village that existed before the War.[16]

16 According to elder informants in Duit, most households in the 1930s were one of three types: owners of ricefields of insufficient size for annual grain support who were at the same time share-

In the late 1950s to the 1970s many local farmers in Duit moved out to resettle in the remaining frontier areas of the neighbouring lowland provinces of Nueva Viscaya and Isabela. Based on the author's recall interviews, 53 per cent of the total of 74 households in the 1960s had at least one adult member migrating out to resettle elsewhere. On the one hand, this outmigration was an outcome of internally generated processes. In particular the natural growth of the local population that survived during the War,[17] combined with the extreme farm degradation due to perennial problems of worm and rat infestations,[18] have forced many local farmers to look for alternative farming elsewhere. On the other hand, the government's aggressive programme to promote resettlement of the Ifugaos living in remote upland villages into the province's lower areas of Lamut or in the frontier areas of Nueva Viscaya and Isabela have provided the external incentives for local farmers to emigrate. During this period, too, successful government anti-malaria campaigns in lowland resettlement areas finally removed the fear of many Ifugaos, a factor which hitherto has historically constrained them from opting to reside in

croppers on other people's ricefields, owner-cultivators who owned just enough ricefields to support more or less their annual rice requirement for the year, and a handful who were absolutely without ricefields who became pure sharecroppers. There were no non-cultivator ricefield owners in Duit. This description of the pattern of landholding in the 1930s in Duit is consistent with an earlier description of ricefield ownership in central central Kiangan in the 1910s, which noted that only a handful of families were landless while an overwhelming majority had an acre or two or more (Barton 1922: 412). Moreover, sharecropping was highlighted as an important mechanism for those with little or no land in expanding their land control. In addition, according to local elder informants, in the 1920s and 1930s, all households in Duit operated swiddens of varying sizes The relatively poorer members of the village were the ones who had the largest swiddens since these constituted their major fallback for staple food provisioning. Swiddens served this purpose either directly, by consuming camote harvests during the lean months, or indirectly, by enabling a poor household to raise swine and chicken and using these, in turn, to purchase rice among grain-rich households during the lean months. Swiddens could be opened in open-access lands, which was still sizeable in the village during the Pre-War, or simply by exercising usufructory rights on privately owned fallowed swidden fields.

17 Present-day Ifugao province was the site of the fiercest battles between the Japanese Imperial Army and the Filipino guerrilla forces fighting with the USAFFE (United States Forces in the Far East) troops during the last months of the World War Two in the archipelago. Kiangan municipality was one of the hardest hit by epidemic and famine. In 1945-46 in Duit, out of the 130 households in the village, 87 households (67 per cent) lost on average two to three members to disease and malnutrition. The extent of depopulation in the village during the War might have staved off a burgeoning problem of population pressure on existing local ricefields in the 1930s and early 1940s. But by the 1950s, local population had recovered. According to local informants, total number of households in Duit had already reached 75 per cent of its former total household number before the War.

18 To a large part due to the loss of labour force and abandonment of many actively operated farms resulting from War depopulation, several municipalities of Ifugao would be plagued by rat and worm infestations that heavily damaged the crops in the remaining fields under cultivation. This problem was to last for more than a decade after the War. According to local farmer inform-

lower geographical zones. Moreover, the government promoted emigration by openly declaring certain areas of public lands in the adjacent provinces of Nueva Viscaya and Isabela for resettlement and formal titling, and by assisting would-be settlers with grant of land patents. Such state initiatives in the northern Luzon region coincided with the Philippine government's widespread campaign, which began in 1948 when it expanded land resettlement projects, public health facilities, and improvements in the transportation network, resulting in a dramatic rise in the rate of migration within the archipelago (Simkins and Wernstedt 1963: 202).

During this period many local ricefields in Duit were abandoned due to lack of tillers. Many swiddens too were left untended or simply changed into woodlots over time. Abandoned swiddens in open-access zones generally became private woodlots since they were kept fallow for a decade or two, allowing valuable tree species to grow and be nurtured by individuals who on this basis laid claim to private ownership on the land. Privately owned swiddens were also deliberately planted with coffee trees and shade species by local people who chose to remain in the village. Once private fallowed swiddens were converted to woodlots with coffee trees, access to them also became restricted. It was also during this period that local people who opted to remain aggressively planted coffee trees and staked off areas for this purpose in the last remaining open-access forest of the village. By the 1960s, all lands in this open-access zone had been privately claimed as woodlots planted with coffee. Hence, even as people were moving out *en masse*, many abandoned swiddens (including those lying in open-access zones) were being individually developed as woodlots, leading to the decline in fallowed swiddens and the associated practice of free usufructory access to them.[19] More importantly, outmigration during this period also had the impact of preventing the fragmentation of small farmholdings in the village and the emergence of a near-landless mass of households. Those who stood to have very little farm lands or no lands at all took resettlement out of the village as their alternative livelihood strategy. As a consequence, this outmigration further reinforced the position of the smallholders in the village. Later on, the development of commercial vegetable gardening in the 1980s and the 1990s further rigidified the local smallholding pattern in significant ways by completely wiping out the traditional practice of granting temporary free tillage of idle farms, greatly enhancing the commercial value of local farms, and creating a farm lease market in the village.

ants in Duit, massive rat infestation became a chronic problem in the locality from the 1950s to the 1960s. Often their rice harvest would be reduced by two-thirds.

19 According to older informants, in pre-war Duit, ricefields (*payo*) were privately owned by individuals. This type of land was inherited and could be sold. As in other places in the Cordillera, *payo* was the most valuable property by local criteria. Swiddens or *habal* were also privately owned by individuals. However, unlike in ricefields, tillage of abandoned but privately owned swiddens was generally allowed rent-free by the owners. Owners had no right over the camote harvest of

Generally speaking, the spread of double cropping with the modern rice variety and cultivation of snap beans for the market vastly improved the livelihood opportunities of farmers in Duit. Rising incomes of local families were soon invested, among others, in financing secondary and tertiary education of children. By the 1980s, local farmers had stopped migrating out to farm elsewhere. This does not mean however that the local emigration phenomenon ceased or was radically reduced following the transformation of local agriculture. The author's random survey (1997) of families with emigrants who left the village since the 1950s suggests that the outmigration rate of 23 per cent from 1975 to 1979 would be basically sustained in the next three five-year periods (i.e. in 1980–84, 23 per cent; in 1985–89, 16 per cent; in 1990–94, 21 per cent). What has happened in the village in the last 15 years of turnaround of local agriculture is that, in contrast with the 1970s, many local farmers have stayed in the village, engaging in modern rice variety two-crop farming and in commercial vegetable gardening as their main livelihood activity. However, these same farmers' households who are experiencing a farming boom, income gains, and rising standard of living, have also been producing high school- and college-educated members who have increasingly sought to make a living in non-farming, salaried jobs in the Philippine urban centres and abroad. Thus a major stream of outmigration continues to date in the village.

Outmigration in the late 1950s to 1970s involved a stream of farmer-resettlers, while the outmigration of the 1990s is a stream of job-seekers in the non-farming occupations in the urban centres. What is common between the two is that both are composed largely of people who have inherited or stand to inherit very little or no farm land at all from their parents. This is of major significance since in Duit, inheritance is the single most important mechanism for acquiring land ownership in the village. Inheritance far outstrips land purchase as a means of acquiring land.[20] Couples who have not inherited farm land from their parents seldom accumulate enough resources within their lifetime to be able to purchase one. These couples may be people who grew up in the village, but whose parents did not have enough land to bequeath to them. Or one or both of the spouses might have migrated to the village from a neighbouring municipality. A random survey (1997) done by the author of 98 households showed that only seven of the 40 couples without an inheritance to start with were able to purchase farms.

In the village, therefore, the phenomenon of outmigration since the 1950s is embedded in the cultural norms and practices of inheritance. This indigenous system is based on the principle of primogeniture, a tradition among the Ifugaos

the tillers they allowed to work their idle land, just as the tillers did not acquire ownership rights to such land they cultivated.

20 Based on the author's random survey (1997) of 69 households owning farms, 78 per cent gained part or all of their current land through inheritance. The aggregate size of all farms inher-

wherein regulation in land inheritance is governed by the ordinal rank of the children in birth. Eldest children inherit a greater proportion of the property than the younger ones, and if there be but one rice field, the eldest takes it (Barton 1919: 51). If the number of children exceeds the number of rice fields, the eldest children take the fields. This Ifugao custom of primogeniture does not discriminate between male or female children (ibid, see also Goldman 1937, Eggan 1967, Kikuchi 1989a, 1989b). Among the Kiangan Ifugaos, benefits of the practice of primogeniture extend to the second child since the inherited property of the male and female spouses are not united in their marriage. The first child is bequeathed the larger set of ricefields inherited by either of the two spouses; the second child gets the smaller set of ricefields inherited by the other spouse. Thus either the father or the mother's inherited property goes to the eldest child (male or female) with the rest of the kinship property going to the second child.

In Duit, the reproduction and the continuing strength in the last several decades of the indigenous inheritance custom based on primogeniture has mediated the process of outmigration, with the net effect of leaving only those with viable smallholdings to stay and make a living through farming in the village. Contrary to the commonly held notion that primogeniture creates a family centre for assistance to poorer siblings (Barton 1919: 40, Goldman 1937: 163, Dumia 1979: 10), in practice the custom has disadvantaged the younger siblings in local land possession. In post-war decades at least, it has been the mechanism shaping the phenomenon of a large part of the local population being 'purged' from the community, unable to make a living in the village. With many without inheritance being forced into emigration, the net impact of this cultural institution is actually to counter tendencies towards land polarisation and fragmentation in the locality by 'exporting' landlessness. Hence in this way it has served to more or less level out land ownership, a stabilising force in maintaining the dominance of smallholding among the native population[21] over generations.

Based on the author's random survey (1997) of 71 couples with spouses averaging 41 years of age and with a least one spouse who was born of local parents in the village, nearly 60 per cent are actually couples with the husband or wife having a birth-order rank of first or second child. This category of couples make up the majority of the native population of the village. They have managed to sustain a living in the locality based on their ownership of small farms and have thus

ited outstrips the aggregate size of all purchased farms by a ratio of 1 to 3.5. Moreover, the average size of farms gained through inheritance is larger than those acquired through purchase.

21 Most of the present population of Duit are descendants of Tuwali-speaking Ifugaos who settled in the place long before even the American colonial administration at the turn of the century. Only about 15 per cent of local households belong to the Kalanguya ethno-linguistic group, mostly from the adjacent municipality of Asipulo who started to settle and farm in the village in the early 1980s, attracted by the livelihood opportunities offered by commercial vegetable gardening.

opted to stay. At present, these couples comprise the foundation of the village's small landholding pattern. On the other hand, those with birth-order rank of third, fourth or fifth child are usually among the land-poor couples in the village.

Strong evidence of this 'pushing out' of siblings with low birth-order ranks that allows mainly those with higher birth-order rank to stay in the village as small-farm owners can be seen in another survey of the author of couples who have siblings who permanently migrated out of the village between 1950 to 1995. In this random survey of 80 couples who have at least one spouse born in the village, 48 per cent have two or three siblings who have settled permanently elsewhere and who are mostly of younger age, with a birth-order rank of mostly fourth and fifth child. On the other hand, at least half of these spouses who stayed in the village are actually eldest or second-eldest child.

Although primogeniture-based inheritance has been long practised by the Ifugaos of Kiangan since before the coming of the Americans in 1900, it did not necessarily lead to major out-migration of people from the settlement. Elder informants in the village recall that before the War, local people in Duit did not migrate out in significant numbers to settle in other areas. A normal response to rice insufficiency was to cultivate sweet potato in open-access lands or on borrowed lands (private owners at that time still readily lent out parts of their woodlots or fallowed swiddens free of charge to anyone who wanted to use them for sweet potato cultivation). Such a form of staple food cultivation rested on the relative availability of local land and less restrictive private ownership practices, and in effect tied farmland-poor people to the locality by enabling them to secure their food security. Thus in the pre-war period, the primogeniture-based institution of inheritance did not lead to a 'purging' of the local people without inherited farm lands.

The fact that this particular cultural norm and practice took the form of a sustained outmigration of a section of the local population is clearly a post-War phenomenon. As mentioned earlier, internally generated changes as demographic changes, and the exhaustion of open-access land and the rise of more restrictive access to farm lands due to the forces of commercialisation, combining with external processes such as active state promotion and breakthroughs in resettling the uplanders in neighbouring lowland areas in the 1950s up to the 1970s, shaped the decision of people with low-birth order rank to farm elsewhere. Roughly two decades later, with the onset of a local farming boom from the late 1980s to the present, local farmers' increased earnings from double cropping and snap bean cultivation have been increasingly invested in children's higher formal education, enabling the latter to take the option to make a living in non-farming occupations in the urban areas, most especially in cases when s/he, being one of the youngest, stands to inherit no farm land.

In recent years, an increasing number of parents have actually postponed the bequeathal of farm lands to elder children upon their marriage, particularly in situations where the latter have attained tertiary education and therefore stand a good chance to successfully obtain office employment in the urban centres. This option is taken by parents seeking to optimise earnings from their farm land in order to continue supporting the higher education of the rest of their younger children. Lately, there are also cases where the expenses incurred by parents in the college education of elder children who have already found employment in local government agencies have been counted as their inheritance (*tawed*) in lieu of farm lands. While this is a clear digression from the indigenous practice of inheritance, the principle of primogeniture is still invoked by the parents in such cases: such elder children did not inherit prized farm land, but their parents' large investment in their higher education has still given them the most privileged wealth status vis-à-vis their younger siblings. By preventing land fragmentation and by easing farming household population in the locality, the recent adjustments and flexibility in inheritance norms tend to reproduce and reinforce the system of smallholding in the village even though the ultimate inheritor of the farmland might not exactly be the child with the highest birth-order rank.

In sum, since the 1950s up to the present, both internal and external developments such as demographic shifts, commercialisation of agriculture and land, trends towards more restrictive land access in the locality, and the state's active role in the resettlement of upland farmers have shaped a culturally-mediated sustained outmigration process in Duit that has sustained the dominance of the small-landholding pattern in the village. Such a pattern of land ownership has precluded the burgeoning of a local class of landless farmers who would have been a convenient recruiting pool for hired labour, and the dominance of wage hiring in local farming. This landholding pattern has therefore served as one important context underpinning the contemporary dominance of family and reciprocal labour despite market-related local transformations of farming. I now turn to a discussion of the other important context also related to the uplands' historical social autonomy – the absence of state patronage accompanying contemporary modernising trends and commercialisation of farming in the locality.

Local Agricultural Change Without State Patronage

In rural lowland Southeast Asia, the imperatives of increasing rice production by transforming the production base of rural society and gaining greater agrarian control promoted state patronage of the rural elite. The latter were to become the political and economic agents of the state in the countryside - overseers, conduits and implementers of the state's agricultural policies as well as the police force maintaining peace and stability (Hart 1989: 33). In most parts of the region, the rural elite became the state's favoured clients. From the mid 1960s, they had privileged access to the torrent of resources which flowed into the villages – subsidised credit, inputs, licenses, guaranteed prices on farm produce, and infrastructure building projects (Elson 1997: 224, Hart 1989: 33). In some places, as in Java for example, the upper stratum increasingly became incorporated into the state machinery as salaried government officials and minor functionaries, putting them in an even better position to secure and tend 'substantial material interests' (Hüsken and White 1989, Elson 1997: 225).

The state's relationship of patronage to the rural elite in the dual context of increasing agricultural production and securing agrarian control had major consequences for labour relations at the village level. An examination of this relationship is central to understanding particular forms of labour relations in the locality (Hart 1989: 36). In a number of cases in rural lowland Southeast Asia, certain village-level labour patterns emerged in the context of the elite's preferential access to state resources and, also, to a range of highly remunerative non-agricultural activities. Other changes in local patterns of labour have been related to the state's collaboration with the rural elite to institute social control (Hart 1986: 194-95, 200).

In the lowland Philippines, the rural elite became no less favoured clients of the state as their counterparts in other Southeast Asian countries during the period of the Green Revolution which started in the mid 1960s. They were also the favoured clients during the one and a half decades of the Marcos martial law regime (from 1972 to 1986), whose one important political agenda underpinning its agrarian policy was to counter agrarian unrest and the Communist leadership thereof and to transform the peasantry into a mass support for its own legitimisation (Wurfel 1988: 166). The Philippine rural elite's favoured status during the Green Revolution programme, particularly during its first phase, was most manifest in their preferential access to government low-interest agricultural credit under the Masagana 99 programme and to technology subsidies.[22] The large farmers and, to a certain extent, the upper stratum of tenants were the main beneficiaries of this institutional, low-interest massive credit programme which peaked in 1974-75 in the lowland agricultural areas (Esguerra 1981, Wurfel 1988: 173). Because they had privileged access to credit for purchases of inputs, they were the early adopters of IRRI seeds and consequently had the biggest gains (Fegan 1989a: 165, Boyce 1993: 138).

State patronage of the rural elite primarily through cheap and easy government credit and other forms of capital subsidies would have the most profound effect on labour arrangements in Philippine lowland agricultural areas. The flow of gov-

22 During the first phase of the Green Revolution, the rural elite derived profits and privileges in rice production. But in the later phase, beginning in the early 1980s, as rice became an unprofitable crop, the rural elite shifted to commercial activities, staying out of farming and finding niches upstream and downstream of the farm (Fegan 1989b: 176-7, Boyce 1993: 154).

ernment financial resources of which they were the main beneficiaries enabled them to operate wholly and primarily by means of hired labour. Labour-displacing technologies were employed by the rural elite (Boyce 1993: 151). Farm tractors, acquired by the rural elite in lowland villages through expansion of government rural credit programs, ushered in, for instance, the demise of reciprocal labour in soil preparation in many areas and its replacement by hired labour and farm machines (Rosario 1980: 220, Corsico 1981: 280). Moreover, availability of credit placed the rural elite in a financially secure position, enabling them to hire farm workers instead of depending on family labour and reciprocal labour groups. A large proportion of Masagana 99 loans were used to finance hired labour (Castillo 1982: 256). By the time government institutional credit dried up in the 1980s as a result of massive loan defaults (Fegan 1989b: 165), the basic profile of labour patterns in Philippine lowland farming areas had been radically altered, manifested by the rise of hired labour and the steady substitution and decline of family labour in farming (Boyce 1993: 148) and the demise of reciprocal labour exchange.

In contrast to developments in the prime agricultural lowland areas of the Philippines, since the late 1970s major agricultural changes penetrated and spread in the upland village of Duit basically without government support and without state patronage of the rural elite. Double-cropping of modern rice varieties, for example, spread among farmers in the village largely through their own initiatives, relying on informal networks to acquire and experiment with effective new rice varieties. On the other hand, government assistance in commercial vegetable gardening in the form of seed dispersal and market assistance was short-lived and had only token funding.

Lack of substantial and sustained government support and related state patronage to the local elite is most evident in the absence of a government credit program oriented towards rural producers in Kiangan municipality or in the whole of Ifugao province at a time when such assistance was flooding the rural lowlands. In an interview with the author, the former mayor of Kiangan recalled their repeated petitions to the Ministry of Agriculture in 1981 for substantial financial assistance to support local agricultural production or the expansion of the Masagana 99 credit among the Kiangan farmers. Their resolutions were flatly rejected since upland agriculture was defined as being outside the focus of the state program, consistent with the official definition of upland agriculture as a marginal and high-risk investment. Government financing institutions such as the Land Bank and the rural banks had neither the capacity nor the interest to service the demand for production loans in the uplands (Cornista and King 1988: 9).

In Duit, the elite have neither been beneficiaries of lucrative off-farm political and economic activities connected with supra-village authorities outside the village. To date, they have not enjoyed any preferential access to state resources which in fact have been scarce and marginal in most municipalities of the Cordillera.

Denied state patronage, the village elite embraced the modernisation of agriculture - adoption of modern double-cropping varieties and commercial vegetable gardening - without external financial credit or capital resources to incorporate massive wage hiring and labour-displacing mechanisation[23] such as that which characterised the implementation of the massive Green Revolution programme in the rural lowlands. Much as they might have wanted to, they simply did not have the external state capital support nor the large internally generated savings required to adopt radical changes in local labour patterns in the new agriculture.

Members of the village elite in Duit have had to rely only on their own petty cash savings as farming capital. The biggest labour hirers in the village have had to draw from modest savings from cash income sources outside the village such as, for example, salary as a petty government employee, the military pension of a deceased spouse, income from farming a self-owned modest-size irrigated farm in Lamut, Ifugao,[24] and occasional or regular petty dollar remittances from children working abroad as domestic helpers. A handful of households who acquired farm equipment such as hand tractors and threshing machines did not acquire these through loans from the banking system or through government-subsidised credits as was common in lowland farming villages. These assets were bought after long years of slow accumulation relying on various aforementioned income streams.

Lacking external capital support from the state and without self-generated large cash savings, members of the village elite have had to strategise in order to mobilise adequate labour to operate their farm holdings without the option of being able to offer and sustain high daily wage rates. Thus, they themselves have had to continue to participate in reciprocal labour-exchange to mobilise local labour. Recall in Table 6.2 that while the participation of farm-rich households in *obbo* in comparative terms is far less than farm-scarce households, it is nonetheless substantial (no less than 34 per cent in rice and 15 per cent in vegetable gardening). The most urgent concern of local big landowners in participating in *obbo* is securing adequate labour for their field especially during crucial phases of farming. A land-rich farmer who owns one of the two mechanised threshers in the village explains her own compulsion in joining an *obbo*:

23 Based on the author's random survey of 78 farming households in Duit, for instance, in field preparation for rice farming, 46 per cent use the carabao and plough; 36 per cent turn up the soil with spades (*mungaud*), while the rest (18 per cent) employ hand tractors.

24 Three families in the village own and manage three to seven hectares of farm lands in the plateau of Lamut in the lower part of Ifugao province. These unirrigated lands were acquired through the government resettlement program during the 1960s. In the late 1970s, the government constructed an irrigation project in the area, benefiting the farms of some owners who came from Duit. Some of them alternate between operating their irrigated fields in Lamut and cultivating commercial vegetable gardens in their small farms in Duit.

> Many people here do not want to work in another person's farm in exchange for a daily wage. They are often busy working in their own farms. But if they become indebted to you in labour (*naobbohan*) within an *obbo* group, then they feel compelled to reciprocate by working in your field. They may negotiate on the schedule, but to be sure they will come and work in your own field (Author's interview with Conchita Dulnuan, September 28, 1996).

As a consequence, the elite members' strategies in labour security have been largely circumscribed by the continuing strength of this traditional labour institution and its allocation, which the overwhelming majority of local farmers, comprised of poor and middle strata, have themselves been harnessed through participating in the new farming environment. It is no wonder then that even as some members of the elite have started to engage in labour-tying consumption credit to corner local labour for the operation of their fields, they themselves have had to remain active in reciprocal labour exchange in order to serve their needs of adequate labour.[25]

Furthermore, farmers in this upland village, unlike those in certain lowland areas of the Philippines and Southeast Asia, have not been the focus of social control in the counter-insurgency operations of the state. Traditional and popular forms of everyday peasant resistance in the village directed against abusive members of the local elite have not been subjected to state-initiated intimidation and harassment programs. Thus, the strong spirit of local underclass solidarity has not been effaced. In Duit, poor and lower strata farmers' solidarity to discipline members of the village elite who are known to be 'mean' and 'selfish' to date remains strong. Hence, the continuing major significance of co-operative labour in production can easily be translated into a leverage for potential community sanctions (Hall 1980: 451-2). As in the past, *obbo* has remained a convenient mechanism for this type of class solidarity and for asserting traditional economic rights and bargaining for them. As long as this mechanism remains strong, most local farmers have actual and potential power to counter the village elite and to give labour service to them basically in the former's own terms. The members of the local elite, while trying every possible manoeuvre in consumption credit transactions, do not really have much room to gain extreme advantages.

25 Labour security is not only served by being able to mobilise reciprocal exchange groups on their farms when members of the village elite join *obbo*. Creditor-employers, when they join *obbo*, are often given the opportunity to counter-check directly the truthfulness of common excuses given by the debtor-clients who fail to render a labour payment on agreed-upon dates. According to farmer informants who belong to the village elite, clients who reneged on their promise to render labour service have often argued to their creditors that they could not give labour service for the day because they had to comply to their *obbo* obligations. By being active in *obbo* work themselves, creditors are able to verify easily whether the defaulting client is just making up an excuse for payment delinquency, a co-presence acting as a strong deterrent against would be defaulters in labour payment.

Fitting Reciprocal Labour to Market-Oriented Farming

With the spread of modern rice varieties and commercial snap bean cultivation in the village, labour utilisation in agriculture has not only intensified, farm work has also been desynchronised. The double-cropping system in rice has caused the demise of rites-elaborated and community-sanctioned synchronised farming schedules. Further, separate year-round activities of households in commercial vegetable gardening also fundamentally breached the traditional rhythm of local agriculture. This combination of intensification and desynchronisation of local farm work has enhanced the value of farm labour value in livelihoods. Its use and allocation has become an important component of farmers' strategies in making a living in local farming. There is now a strong tendency among local farmers to assert control over their household's own labour time. Individual maximisation of opportunity costs in the allocation of labour shapes the labour arrangements that farmers make or enter into. The first casualty of this trend has been the traditional loose festive labour (*dang-a*) which has today come to a virtual demise. Fewer people respond and come if a household calls a *dang-a*, since they are preoccupied with a much tighter farming schedules. On the other hand, reciprocal labour exchange (*obbo*) itself has been undergoing major alterations in recent years. Local farmers have made it more efficient and attuned to meet the demands of the new farming.

The size of *obbo* has reduced considerably since the 1980s. Intensified utilisation of labour and desynchronisation in local farming have made cumbersome the organisation and mobilisation of big *obbo* to attend to the more fluid and scattered labour demands of farming in the village. Moreover, small labour exchange groups have proven themselves more attuned to the faster pace and desynchronised schedules of the new farming systems. However, specific phases in rice farming which by their very nature require bursts of energy in short periods, such as planting and harvesting, do still use the relatively larger reciprocal labour groups today. Based on the author's survey (1997) of 64 male and female respondents from different hamlets (*sitios*), all of whom participated in reciprocal labour exchange in the second crop harvest season of 1996, the average size of their groups is only 11, a far cry from the consensus of elder informants which placed the common size of a rice harvest *obbo* at 50 persons. On the other hand, *obbo* for clearing and field preparation at present has an even lower range of only eight to 10 members.

A number of local farmers are also developing new strategies to enhance the efficiency of local *obbo*. These enhancing measures are part of local farmers' response to seize livelihood opportunities in a local farming context that has diversified and become more labour intensive. One of their strategies is to improve the operations of the traditional labour-exchange arrangement in the village by maximising working time, minimising unnecessary postponement of work, observing strict equivalence in work exchange and upgrading the average skills level within a group.

Today, the various labour exchange groups follow unwritten but clear rules of conduct pertaining to work absences by members. These rules evolved from situations that farmers working in groups faced in the last two decades as they have increasingly confronted competing demands on their individual labour time, often bound to an existing reciprocal arrangement. According to farmer informants, these rules define what kinds of work absences are considered justifiable and which ones are taboo and counted as delinquency. For instance, causes of absence which are commonly regarded as valid (aside from time-honoured ones such as sickness or death in the family) are the harvesting of snap beans in one's own field,[26] peddling vegetables in Kiangan on the weekly market day[27] or childcare after all means to find an alternate carer have failed. All other absences are considered delinquencies, which in the long run may cause an individual to be excluded by many farmers in group formation. Moreover, rules also define which type of farm work gets priority in the frequent cases of two members wanting to host the work group the same day. For example, harvesting snap beans or rice is given priority over field preparation in rice or vegetable farming. Thus the person wanting to host the *obbo* for harvest work is awarded the day's schedule over someone who intends to deploy the group in less critical farming tasks.

In the past, a common cause of an *obbo*'s postponement of work, according to local informants, has been the inability of the would-be host to secure the means to buy meat to feed the work party. Constant postponements leave gaps in what otherwise should be consecutive days of work. Some farmers have recently remedied this problem by forming small regular *obbo* groups of only four or five members, all belonging to the same lower-scale economic status who have banded together as a reciprocal exchange group but have each agreed to bring his or her own food on all occasions. Thus, no would-be host is constrained by the cost of meat. With the frequency of work postponements thus reduced, these groups have maximised their labour by being able to operate uninterruptedly for many days.

26 The late harvest of snap beans is financially disastrous for the field owner. One day of delay may result in the pods being classified by the merchant buyer as second class instead of first class, a 50 per cent reduction in the farm gate price per kilo. Thus, farmers who have to start harvesting their vegetable crop, but do not want yet to host the reciprocal labour group because the harvest cuttings have not yet peaked, are excused from attending the *obbo* for the day. Their labour indebtedness to other members remains.

27 Fridays and Saturdays are usually declared by local *obbo* as official days off (*baun*). Friday is usually devoted to gathering and preparing vegetables that will be peddled in the *poblacion* market on Saturday. However, a few *obbo* might have only one or two members involved in weekly marketing of fruits and vegetables, thus a *baun* is not declared. The persons who do sell commodities in the market however are excused from participating in *obbo* work.

Moreover, certain practices directed towards upgrading the standard of skills within the group have also emerged recently. According to local informants, unlike decades ago when a member could just send any substitute worker when he or she was not available, today members refuse to accept such a substitute if they deem the person inferior to the pace and skill in farm work of the member who sent him/her. Particularly, the *obbo* host will emphatically reject the substitute's joining the group by saying 'You owe me no labour, the one who sent you owes me one'. This recently emerging strict code of reciprocation among members tends to standardise work quality at a higher level. In addition, a handful of men in the village have begun to form an exclusive *obbo* group which boldly challenges a long-held norm and popular practice.[28] The obvious aim is to form a reciprocal labour group with a superior level of work skills which can finish jobs more quickly and efficiently. This closed group came to the attention of local people due to their exclusionary conduct and the fact that obviously their members are all known to be exceptionally fast and skilled workers in the village. Though many criticisms against the exclusionary practices of this group continue to be voiced, the group has persisted. Their work no doubt has been remarkably fast and superior, yet tension between them and many members of the community has arisen.[29]

Conclusions

In their drive to modernise and commercialise their farming Duit upland peasants have relied on both market and non-market mechanisms for inputs. One such key input is labour which, to a large extent, is tied to and employed through the non-market institutions of family and labour exchange groups. In this particular upland village, family and reciprocal labour have not served as obstacles to local peasants' participation in market-oriented farming but have been their key assets for engaging in it. Today family and reciprocal labour continue to dominate the local farming scene, far surpassing hired labour in importance. Such a trend cannot be interpreted as vestigial phenomenon or mere survival of traditional labour institutions which are on the path of an inevitable decline. Rather, it is a present-

28 Elder informants affirm and popular community discourse has been explicit about *obbo* not being exclusionary. In the past and now, people who refuse other person's participation have been regarded as selfish and mean. Thus anyone can approach an organised group without running the risk of being denied participation.

29 When I left the village in 1997, a number of my informants were still high on speculation as to whether this group would dissolve itself due to social *opprobrium*, or whether other similarly gain-seeking, equally skilful farmers would follow the practice, thus probably breaching a long-held tradition of the openness of the *obbo*.

day livelihood imperative of local peasants to engage in modern and commercial farming.

Such viability of family and reciprocal labour that sharply contrasts with the common trends in lowland rural Southeast Asian farming villages can only be understood from the perspective of two important local contexts: the persistence of a small holding pattern in the upland village as a result of the 'exportation' of landlessness linked to the impact of primogeniture-based inheritance practices in post-war developments; and, the absence of state patronage of the local village elite during the late 1970s and 1980s when local agriculture was being modernised and profoundly commercialised. Emigration of low-birth order rank siblings since after the War has sustained a big mass of small holders who can be characterised as 'just-enoughs' and 'not-quite enoughs (Geertz 1993: 97) in terms of land control, and whose labour is principally committed to operating their own farms both through direct employment of family labour and via reciprocal labour arrangements with fellow local farmers. The continuing presence of such a mass of smallholders has also stymied local growth of landless waged farm workers. On the other hand, a lack of robust economic and political linkages to urban-based supra-village bureaucrats by the village elite has seriously constrained them in mechanising farming and expanding labour hiring. This has occurred in a situation where reciprocal labour exchange has remained a strong countervailing force against the village elite's control of and monopoly on farm labour, because of its potency as an organised force that can threaten to boycott abusive or unfair employers. This case thus provides counterfactual support to the view that state patronage of rural elites in Southeast Asia in recent decades has led to the demise of more egalitarian traditional labour arrangements.

Nonetheless local farmers have increasingly made important alterations to reciprocal labour arrangements to suit the requirements of flexible deployment of labour in a intensified and desynchronised farming by reducing the size of reciprocal labour groups. They have also incorporated innovations into the *obbo* to maximise working time and minimise unnecessary postponements, and to observe strict skill equivalence in work exchange, departing from the loose and 'less efficient' arrangements common prior to market transformations. Exclusionary labour exchange groups have also recently emerged.

The case of Duit suggests that in the uplands, where certain relevant indigenous cultural frameworks remain strong, and where indigenous communities have relatively enjoyed a high degree of social autonomy vis-à-vis the state in livelihood affairs, and where massive rural development programmes such as the Green Revolution have not been as intensively implemented by the government as in the lowland rural areas, market penetration and adoption of modern farming need not necessarily lead to the extinction nor decline of pre-existing non-market forms of labour. Particular elements and patterns at the intersection of local agrarian history and culture, and of state and market processes have to be carefully looked into. Studying distinct contexts is important in understanding why reproduction and adjustments of family labour and reciprocal labour may be an important part of local farmers' contemporary strategies in modern and commercial farming in certain places and times.

References

Barton, R. (1919) 'Ifugao Law', *University of California Publications in American Archaelogy and Ethnology* 15, 1, plates 1–33 (February 15, 1919): 1–186.

Barton, R. (1922) 'Ifugao Economics', *University of California Publications in American Archaelogy and Ethnology* 15, 5, plates 38–45 (April 12, 1922): 385–446.

Basu, K. (1984) *The Less Developed Economy: A Critique of Contemporary Theory*, Oxford: Basil Blackwell.

Boyce, J. (1993) *The Political Economy of Growth and Impoverishment in the Marcos Era*, Quezon City: Ateneo de Manila University Press.

Castillo, G. (1982) 'Has *Bayanihan* Gone Out of Style?', *Philippine Agriculturist* 65: 307–33.

Chulasai, L. (1986) 'Family labour, hired labour and employment linkages in rural Thailand', in S. Hirashima and M. Muqtada (eds.) *Hired Labour and Rural Labour Markets in Asia*, New Delhi: International Labour Organisation and Asian Employment Programme.

Contreras, A. (1990) *Discourse, Politics and Structure of Upland Development in the Philippines*, Policy Paper No. 29, Los Banos, Laguna: Forestry Development Center, University of the Philippines.

Cornista, L. (1986) *Land Tenure and Resource Use Among Upland Farmers*, College, Laguna: Agrarian Reform Institute, University of the Philippines at Los Banos.

Cornista, L. and King, D. (1988) *Operationalising CARP in the Philippine Uplands: Problems, Issues and Recommendations*, College, Laguna: Institute of Agrarian Studies, University of the Philippines at Los Banos.

Corsico, A. (1981) 'Changes in Traditional Forms of Co-operation in Two Barangays', PhD Thesis, University of the Philippines at Los Banos.

Dong, D. (1987) *Peasants In The Making: Malaysia's Green Revolution*, Singapore: Institute of Southeast Asian Studies.

Duhaylungsod, L. (1989) 'Confrontation With Commoditisation in a Philippine Upland Village', PhD Thesis, University of Queensland, Australia.

Dumia, M. (1979) *The Ifugao World*, Quezon City: New Day Publishers.

Eggan, F. (1967) 'Some aspects of bilateral social systems in the Northern Philippines', in M. Zamora (ed.) *Studies in Philippine Anthropology (In Honour of Henry Otley Beyer)*, Quezon City: Alemars-Phoenix Publishing House.

Elson, R.E. (1997) *The End of the Peasantry in Southeast Asia*, London: Macmillan Press.

Esguerra, E. (1981) 'An assessment of the Masagana 99 credit subsidy as an equity measure', *Philippine Review of Economics and Business* XVIII, 3–4: 168–191.

Fegan, B. (1989a) 'The Philippines: agrarian stagnation under a decaying regime', in G. Hart, A. Turton and B. White (eds.) *Agrarian Transformations: Local Processes and the State in Southeast Asia*, Berkeley: University of California Press.

— (1989b) 'Accumulation on the basis of an unprofitable crop', in G. Hart, A. Turton and B. White (eds.) *Agrarian Transformations: Local Processes and the State in Southeast Asia*, Berkeley: University of California Press.

Friedman, H. (1980) 'Household production and the national economy: concepts for the analysis of agrarian transformations', *Journal of Peasant Studies* 7, 2: 158–184.

Ganajapan, A. (1989) 'Conflicts over the deployment and control of labour in a Northern Thai village', in G. Hart, A. Turton and B. White (eds.) *Agrarian Transformations: Local Processes and the State in Southeast Asia*, Berkeley: University of California Press.

Geertz, C. (1993) *The Interpretation of Cultures. Selected Essays*, London: Fontana Press [First published by Basic Books, Inc. New York, 1973].

Goldman, I. (1937) 'The Ifugao of the Philippine Islands', in M. Mead (ed.) *Co-operation and Competition Among the Primitive People*, New York: McGraw-Hill.

Hall, R. (1980) 'Middlemen in the politics of rural Thailand: a study of articulation and cleavage', *Modern Asian Studies* 14, 3: 441–464.

Hamilton, J. (1976) *Pwo Karen: At the Edge of Mountain and Plain*, New York: West Publishing.

Hart, G. (1986) *Power, Labour, and Livelihood: Process of Change in Rural Java*, Berkeley and Los Angeles: University of California Press.

— (1989) 'Agarian change in the context of state patronage', in G. Hart, A. Turton and B. White (eds.), *Agrarian Transformations: Local Processes and the State in Southeast Asia*, Berkeley: University of California Press.

Hefner, R. (1990) *The Political Economy of Mountain Java: An Interpretative History*, Berkeley: University of California Press.

Hirashima, S. and Muqtada, M. (1986) 'Issues on employment, poverty and hired labour in South and Southeast Asia: an introduction', in S. Hirashima and M. Muqtada (eds.) *Hired Labour and Rural Labour Markets in Asia: Studies Based on Farm-level Data*, New Delhi: International Labour Organisation and Asian Employment Programme.

Horri, K. (1981) *Rice Economy and Land Tenure in West Malaysia: A Comparative Study of Eight Villages*, Tokyo: Institute of Developing Economies.

Hüsken, F. and White, B. (1989) 'Java: social differentiation, food production, and agrarian control', in G. Hart, A. Turton and B. White (eds.) *Agrarian Transformations: Local Processes and the State in Southeast Asia*, Berkeley: University of California Press.

Kikuchi, K. (1989a) 'Notes on the kinship system of the Kiangan Ifugao', in Y. Kikuchi (ed.) *Philippine Kinship and Society*, Quezon City: New Day Publishers.

— (1989b) 'Acculturation among the Kiangan Ifugao', in Y. Kikuchi (ed.) *Philippine Kinship and Society*, Quezon City: New Day Publishers.

Kunstander, P. (1978) 'Subsistence agricultural economies of Lua' and Karen hill farmers, Mae Sariang District, Northwestern Thailand', in: P. Kunstadter, E.C. Chapman and S. Sabhasri (eds.) *Farmers in The Forest: Economic Development and Marginal Agriculture in Northern Thailand*, Honolulu: University Press of Hawaii.

Lawless, R. (1975) 'Social Ecology of the Kalingas of Northern Luzon', PhD Thesis, New School of Social Research.

Lewis, M. (1992) *Wagering the Land: Ritual, Capital and Environment Degradation in the Cordillera of Northern Luzon, 1900-1986*, Berkeley: University of California Press.

Li, T. (1999) 'Marginality, power and production: analysing upland transformations', in T. Li (ed.) *Transforming the Indonesian Uplands: Marginality, Power and Production*, London: Harwood Academic Publishers.

Lopez-Gonzaga, V. (1983) *Peasants in the Hills: A Study of the Dynamics of Social Change among the Buhid Swidden Cultivators in the Philippines*, Quezon City: University of the Philippines Press.

Riedinger, J. (1995) *Agrarian Reform in the Philippines: Democratic Transitions and Redistributive Reform*, Stanford: Stanford University Press.

Rosario, C. (1980) 'Changing Rural Institutions in a Rice Growing Barrio', MA Thesis, University of the Philippines at Los Banos.

Schrauwers, A. (1999) '"It's not economical": the market roots of a moral economy in highland Sulawesi', in T. Li (ed.) *Transforming the Indonesian Uplands: Marginality, Power and Production*, London: Harwood Academic Publishers.

Scott, J. (1995) *State Simplifications: Some Applications in Southeast Asia,* The Wertheim Lecture Series, Amsterdam: Centre For Asian Studies.

— (1998) *Seeing Like A State: How Certain Schemes to Improve the Human Condition Have Failed,* New Haven and London: Yale University Press.

Simkins, J. and Wernstedt, A. (1963) 'Growth and internal migrations of the Philippine population, 1948 to 1960', *Journal of Tropical Geography* 17: 197–202.

Turton, A. (1989) 'Thailand: agrarian bases of state power', in G. Hart, A. Turton and B. White (eds.) *Agrarian Transformations: Local Processes and the State in Southeast Asia,* Berkeley: University of California Press.

Voss, J. (1983) 'Capitalist Penetration and Local Resistance: Continuity and Transformations in the Social Relations of Production of Sagada Igorots of Northern Luzon', PhD Thesis, University of Toronto.

White, B. (1976) 'Production and Reproduction in a Javanese Village', PhD Thesis, Columbia University.

Wiber, M. (1985) 'Dynamics of the peasant household economy: labour recruitment and allocation in an upland Philippine community', *Journal of Anthropological Research* 41, 4: 427–441.

World Bank (1989) *Philippine Environment and Natural Resource Management Study*, Washington: World Bank Country Report.

Wurfel, D. (1988) *Filipino Politics: Development and Decay*, Quezon City: Ateneo de Manila University Press.

7

From Resource Managers to Secondary Farm Hands: Changing Gender Divisions of Labour in a Philippine Upland Village

BERNADETTE P. RESURRECCIÓN

In recent years, much has been written and said about rural women's participation in environmental movements and the relevance of 'women and environment' concerns in both policy and research. Some analytical streams have posited women's central position in environmental conservation, while others have been more sceptical. At the heart of the relationship between women and the environment lies the gender division of labour. The Women, Environment and Development (WED) stream argues that upland and rural women are more closely associated with the environment by virtue of the gender division of labour which deploys them to gather fuel, food, and fodder, as well as grow subsistence crops for survival, whereas men are largely engaged in cash crop production (Dankelman and Davidson 1988, Rodda 1991, Sontheimer 1991). The ecofeminist argument, meanwhile, emphasises the spiritual and ideological content of women's relationship with the environment, pointing out that women had been the environment's primordial caretakers in the division of labour, until the patriarchal inroads of capitalism eroded this (Shiva 1989, Shiva and Mies 1993).

In this chapter, I depart from the foregoing and instead argue that the gender division of labour in resource use and management is influenced by historical factors, such as changing ecological, economic, and social conditions in the form of soil erosion, increasing commoditisation, and social differentiation; by power embedded in hierarchical values ascribed to gendered labour; and by people's social agency that has re-worked such values over time. In short, the gender division of labour in resource use is diverse, contested, and dynamic. The following case study on the Kalanguya, a Philippine upland group, shows that men have become today's principal resource managers: meaning, they are the major users, decision-makers, and gatekeepers of land and forest resources who actively ensure the productivity and conservation of these resources. In contrast, women's management of resources and female labour have been rechanneled to male-managed paddy rice agriculture. Their labour has been ascribed less importance compared with its prominence in swidden management in the past. While the content of the gender division of labour has not changed significantly, the hierarchy of value attached to male and female labour has been transformed, enabling men to have more access and control over resources while women are understood as men's dependants. Further, the traditional Kalanguya norm of the industrious woman continues to control female labour as it is currently deployed for male-managed agriculture and food crisis management.

Gendered resource use refers to the way resource use is *organised* – that is, women and men separately enact concrete divisions of labour, and produce distinct gender divisions of labour in various activities. In my view, the gender division of labour is organised according to (a) how work is considered female or male (constructed gender identity); and, (b) whether female work is more important than male work or vice-versa (constructed social valuation/hierarchy). Thus the gender division of labour is not a result of biologically-given or 'natural' roles of women and men, but is socially and historically constructed (Feldman 1992). For example, in earlier writing, Maria Mies (1986) has pointed out that the origins of the gender division of labour lay in the different primordial ways in which women and men worked to transform nature: women, through their bodies via childbirth and reproduction, and men, through the use of tools. Women's work has always been interpreted as a purely physiological, natural function – whereas men's work was considered social, that is, producing exchange values (Mies, 1986). Mies' insights have since then been criticised for their insistent reliance on the mode of production as that which determines gender differentiation. I have however raised her insights here to underscore the interpretative and evaluative element in discourse on female and male work, and how power is embedded in such a discourse.

Several factors also influence people as they transform or reproduce the gender division of labour in a particular social setting. For example, Mackintosh (1981) explains that the gender division of labour existing in both agricultural and urban manufacturing settings has largely fuelled the engines of capitalism, where poor women provide a source of cheap remunerated labour as well as unpaid domestic services. Changing type of cultivation, technology, employment and external intervention in productive processes have thus deployed women and men to undertake new and different tasks in response to capitalist accumulation (Deere 1982, 1995, Boserup 1970). Emerging class structures have also relegated poorer women to undertake particular activities, while wealthier women to others (Deere 1982). In particular, processes of social differentiation affect the extent to which women and men can make claims on each other's labour in interhousehold and intrahousehold arrangements.

The gender division of labour also constitutes a hierarchy of valuation ascribed to female and male work in harnessing the resources of the environment. Such a hierarchy is used to reinforce or weaken the various positions of women and men (Mohanty 1988, van Halsema 1991). One way in which power comes about between women and men is when gender divisions of labour are justified and explained by discursively positing biological and 'natural' hierarchical differences between male and female work. These differences are, however, socially and historically determined, context-specific, and are therefore changeable and vary among different groups. Hierarchical meanings attached to female and male work are also not pre-given; instead, they are produced, reproduced or changed by the repeated actions of social actors over time.

Through a case study of the Kalanguya, this chapter will attempt to show how the gender division of labour has altered over time due to environmental change, increasing linkages with the wider economy and changing gender values.[1] It will also demonstrate how ideas about gender shape resource-using activities – and how such activities, in turn, may shape new ideas about gender (Leach 1994). The natural environment will be the locus of historical social relationships, where people transform nature and simultaneously, re-define themselves as gendered individuals – specifically through their divisions of labour. The chapter will be divided according to events that occurred in chronological time, citing the pre-World War II period within American colonial rule in the Philippines as the 'historical beginning'.[2] These events, moreover, represent the principal forces of change in the people's lives.

The Kalanguya

The Kalanguya live in the upland portions of the province of Nueva Vizcaya and other adjacent provinces. The Kalanguya live in settlements within the southern Cordillera[3] region (Afable 1989) and they locate their place of origin in Tinec, a

1 Fieldwork for this study was conducted in 1996–97.

2 I have purposely marked the historical 'beginning' of this study during the American colonial period (1898 to 1946) for the following reasons: (a) a faster rate of deforestation and land conversion occurred during this period due to the American colonial state's explicit promotion of timber and non-timber forest extraction for commercial markets, and pioneer settlements and sedentary cultivation in these parts; (b) it was during this time that the colonial state aggressively began to incorporate the upland peoples of northern Luzon into the national polity more than during the Spanish colonial period; and, (c) surviving village elders still recall the old social and ecological landscape of the late colonial period and the processes which had altered this landscape.

3 The Cordillera is a mountain range located in the northernmost region of the island of Luzon, one of three major islands in the Philippines and I will continuously refer to it as the region of origin of the Kalanguya and most other ethnic groups of northern Luzon.

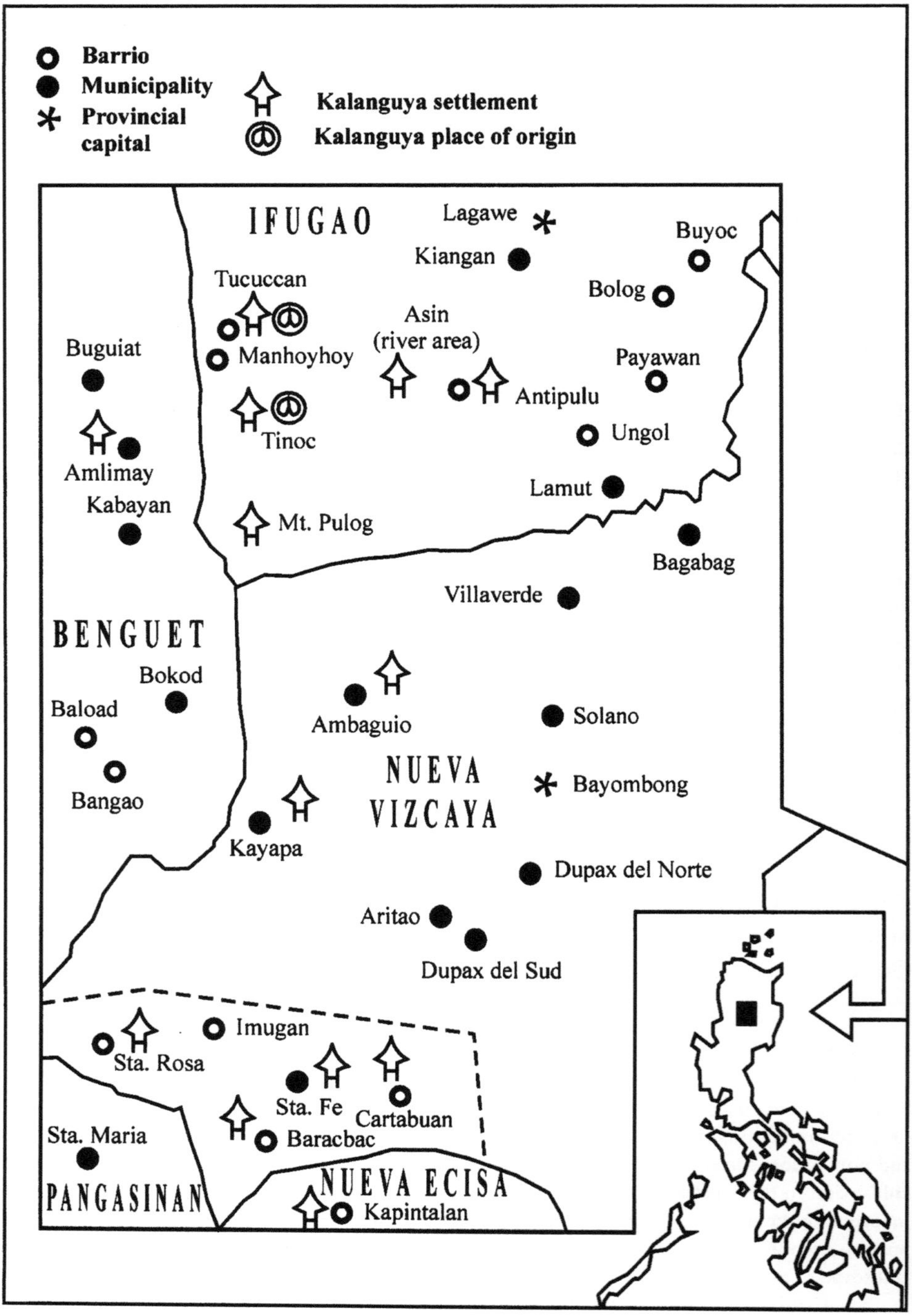

Figure 7.1: Map of Kalanguya Settlements, the Philippines

village in Ifugao province from where they had migrated southward to contiguous portions of the provinces of Benguet, Nueva Vizcaya, Pangasinan and the hilly fringes of Nueva Ecija.

The Kalanguya generally identify themselves as 'Igorot,'[4] a generic term referring largely to the upland peoples occupying the Cordillera region who were known to have resisted Spanish rule (1521–1898), thereby preserving their cultural autonomy, marking their difference from lowland, hispanised Filipinos. Today, most popular literature refers to the Igorots as the 'indigenous cultural communities' of northern Luzon. This study is concerned with the Kalanguya of Canabuan, a village in the province of Nueva Vizcaya.

The Kalanguya have been chiefly swidden and dry rice agriculturists, hunters and forest gatherers, fishers, and livestock raisers and today, engage in a different yet still diverse set of resource use activities. Continuous commercial logging in the area from 1957 to 1982 coupled with conversion of forest to agriculture weakened the Kalanguyas' sweet potato harvests, which among other reasons, compelled many of them to shift to paddy rice agriculture and vegetable gardening. The government's strict enforcement of the ban on shifting cultivation in later years also drove them to practice more sedentary forms of agriculture. Despite the ban on shifting cultivation in order to preserve the forests, it is ironic that three huge commercial logging concessions operated in these parts with the support of the Philippine government driven by the need to rev up the country's exports. Extraction of non-timber forest products, such as rattan, generated up to $138 million in export revenue by 1989. Kalanguya men earned incomes from rattan extraction by cutting and gathering these for buyers.

Today, Kalanguya engage in paddy rice agriculture of the green revolution type, livestock raising, commercial vegetable gardening, soft broom-making for which they also extract rattan from the forest, seasonal hunting of migratory birds, and sometimes forest gathering of wild orchids for sale. Absorbed by the chemical farm inputs and mechanisation markets, Kalanguya farmers today also have to raise capital in order to purchase these for their crops. Brooms, meanwhile, are sold to merchants who reside in the village and who sell them to wholesale buyers from the municipalities of Aritao and Santa Fe. These brooms are later sold in Manila and Baguio City. A number of Kalanguya also engage in commercial vegetable farming, selling their produce to wholesale merchants in the municipality of Bambang, the vegetable trade centre of northeastern Luzon that supplies local vegetable markets in Manila. Vegetable gardening also depends heavily on chemical inputs and small mechanised implements for crops to resist particular pests, the elements and declining soil fertility. As a whole, most Kalanguya have difficulties generating surpluses to cover both subsistence and production requirements. Many mire in a cycle of debt due to the need to advance the purchase of farm inputs,

4 Igorot from the word, *i-gulot* meaning 'from the hills'.

while others use loans to tide them over during periods of food scarcity due to insufficient rice harvests.

I have employed an ethnographic and historical approach to this study as a means to explore the ideas, conditions and relations that have shaped the gender divisions of labour and why. By studying social interactions historically, one is able to explore how gender relations are shaped by the complex, contradictory and uneven processes of social, economic and environmental change (Moore 1988). In order to investigate the changes in people's resource use practices and the environment in the site under study, I drew heavily from women's and men's oral histories and archival sources.

Gender, Resource Use And Debt Labour in Canabuan: The Pre-War Years, 1900–41

Resource use and management strategies before World War II convey the heavy reliance of the Kalanguya on their forests. Men and women had distinct resource use tasks, spaces and strategies. Women observed a daily routine of managing swiddens and food preparation since on these rested the sustenance of their households and livestock. Men, on the other hand, hunted and had less regimented agricultural work patterns. They claimed to know the forest and its potentials for subsistence and agriculture, and its spaces and soils to make for the choicest swidden sites. Men were also the childcarers and occasionally made and sold handicrafts.

Swidden agriculture (*inum-an*) was at the core of Kalanguya livelihood in pre-war Canabuan. The Kalanguya practised a two-year crop cycle that raised about four varieties of sweet potatoes as their major cultivar and alternatively, planted rainfed upland rice on a separate field. Sweet potatoes, the staple of both people and domestic hogs, dominated the swiddens and were consumed in such great quantity as to totally colour the memories people had of pre-war existence in Canabuan.

Men often looked for spots where two specific tree varieties stood (*alumnit* and *balete*), since these indicated a good amount of soil fertility. Ease of clearing was another criteria for site selection and secondary forests were preferred since trees were smaller and had thinner vegetative density than virgin forests. Men, who were responsible for clearing, usually preferred more easily cleared areas while the women, on the other hand, wanted more productive 'virgin' sites. However, the men's decision usually prevailed.

The Kalanguya considered the forest a male enclave since it was men who collected fuelwood and hunted, using spears and dogs to hunt wild game while women were confined to the forest periphery, cultivating their swiddens. They hunted wild deer, boar and fowls, brought their catch home and distributed these among immediate kin and neighbours.

Alingay, Dumalangay and Hibgan, elders of Canabuan, recall that during the American period, only men from a few households produced and marketed local handicrafts such as brooms and backpacks made of rattan and tiger grass straw. They carted such items to Aritao (18 kilometers away today) or to other, more distant, places. Alingay pointed out that those who sold handicrafts were regarded as the poorest (*nabitag*) in the community since they cultivated only few sweet potatoes, had few or no livestock at all, and resorted to buying rice. On other occasions, the men, Hibgan remembers, worked in road construction projects under American supervision. The women, on the other hand, very rarely went to town as they were busy tending to the fields.

In pre-war Canabuan, the Kalanguya observed an annual agricultural cycle that provided them with a steady supply of their staples, sweet potatoes and rice in alternate manner. In the summer month of March, men cleared extensive portions of the forested slopes for swidden farming. After the clearing, a waiting period of at least 10 days was allowed for the matting to dry before the clearing is put to fire. Just before planting began, men had by then built wooden fences (*alad*) around the cleared portions in order to protect swiddens from roaming wild animals. Alingay, the village elder, said there were far too many trees then to worry much over their eventual depletion.

Women began planting sweet potatoes as the first rains of May ushered in the wet season. They planted sweet potatoes and intercropped these with other cultivars in a staggered way from May to July. Elderly women said they generally benefited from their system of staggered planting since the demand for labour was distributed and the timing of the weeding and harvesting was spread out. Staggered planting prevented labour bottlenecks that provided for a steady supply of mature tubers for their households. Once sweet potatoes were planted, other crops were added within and around the fringes of the swidden. At about the same time, in an adjacent, usually smaller field, women also planted upland rice with the help of the male members of their households. However, they ate rice only when they were short in sweet potato supply, which happened quite rarely. Due to the tediousness in its preparation, rice was only a 'fallback' staple when sweet potatoes were in short supply.

Harvesting sweet potatoes was also a matter of calculated timing: leaving too many behind may result in rotting due to waterlogging, or, in the dry season, worms could attack the tubers leaving them discoloured, bitter and unpalatable. On the other hand, they also had to guard against gathering too many tubers as these spoiled easily at home when stored. Kalanguya women thus had to carefully calibrate their cropping management decisions, dutifully providing a steady food supply for their households, yet keeping in mind the limited productive capacities of the soil and the care of other crops they had planted. The Kalanguya thus believed that only their women had the skill for managing sweet potato cultivation in such manner that the supply for the staple never ran out.

Women weeded their swiddens in between clearing, planting and harvesting; these weeding intervals were referred to as *habal*. Women recall that weeding consumed the biggest portion of their labour during the entire agricultural cycle and time spent for it increased as soil fertility diminished. A full workday would consist of alternately weeding and harvesting sweet potatoes or any of the other cultivars or fruits in season from any of these fields. They lugged their daily harvests home in a *kayabang* (woven rattan basket with an elastic sling for the forehead and carried on a woman's back) for the day's food supply.

Kalanguya women always guarded against soil erosion. They employed technologies passed on to them by their mothers and decided which of these technologies best suited the fields they were cultivating. These decisions mainly had to do with how steep the slopes were. *Gen-gen* combined the methods of soil terracing and composting. The result is a series of contoured humps that look like mini-terraces and filled with composting materials which added fertility to the soil while preventing erosion (Dolinen 1995).

Day-og is done by digging a series of holes in the ground about eight or nine inches deep along canals built earlier and filling these holes with weeds and leaves from trees. The excavations were next covered with soil and on which women planted crops. The result was a fertile and productive garden where the canals provided good drainage (*ibid*). *Balkah* which means 'belt' in Kalanguya, was a form of vegetative terracing using what was commonly known as tiger grass (*Thysanolaena maxima*), later used as broom straw, which were planted following the slope's contour.

Kalanguya women decided which soil conservation technology was best adaptable to the slope conditions of their swiddens. The elder, Sasdiay, used to apply *gen-gen* on swiddens laid out on flatter areas while she applied *day-og* to those on steeper ones. The women usually worked their swiddens for two years and thereafter lay these to fallow; and once fallowed, these lands are referred to as *kinaba*. This means each swidden has undergone four sweet potato croppings and two croppings of upland rice. Another site – carefully chosen by their husbands – would have to be cleared for the new two-year cycle. The number of fallow years of swiddens in pre-war Canabuan is difficult to determine since women simply moved on to cultivate a new site without ever returning to a *kinaba*, as there was still ample land to clear in those days. None of the women interviewed ever recall having returned to one during this period. However, the community always regarded *kinaba* as land privately owned by its first cultivator. To re-cultivate it, one must secure permission from its owner.

While women were busy tending to their swiddens daily, their husbands remained at home taking care of the children to free their wives from childcare. Depending on the distance from their homes, some women visited their swiddens as much as thrice daily. Older children, girls and boys, in their adolescent years if they were not yet married, also helped their mothers weed the swiddens and sometimes harvested sweet potatoes. Mothers also brought babies to the swiddens to nurse them. Upon returning home, the women still cooked food for the family and their domesticated hogs.[5] The only time women did not go to the swiddens was when a *pedit* (prestige feast) was held in the village and the feasting stretched for as long as five days. The Kalanguya believed that their ancestors' spirits forbade them to work during *pedit*.

Religion and ancestor worship were inseparable from social rank and wealth for the Kalanguya and many other south Cordillera groups during the pre-war period (Moss 1920, Keesing and Keesing 1934, Keesing 1962, Scott 1966, Afable 1989, Russell 1989, Wiber 1989, Lewis 1992). Religion was also linked intimately with labour and land use. Wealth and status were determined by a family's propensity to hold ritual feasts since these entailed the slaughter of a good number of livestock (hogs or water buffaloes) which those of lower status could not afford. Owning livestock was thus a key index of wealth in former times. Kalanguya men found ways to accumulate animals that were often mediated by how much they had access to extra-household labour. Wealthy men cleared more land on which women could cultivate more sweet potatoes to feed a larger herd. One occasion for this was to hold a *bataris*, where the male host butchered a pig to feed and distribute among the men who had helped in land clearing and preparation for a new swidden. Women's contribution to livestock accumulation was through their labour in cultivating sweet potatoes: planting, weeding and applying erosion-control technologies on theirs and others' swiddens. They procured additional amounts of sweet potatoes by working on others' swiddens.

The industriousness of women counted crucially since enlarging one's herd was foremost the work of women who devised means and ways to obtain more sweet potatoes to raise them. The notion of industriousness was firmly based on women's repetitive tasks of planting, weeding, harvesting sweet potatoes and raising livestock. The elder, Hibgan, pointed out that the work of women in livestock raising determined how the household would figure in the community's social hierarchy. 'Hardworking women could increase livestock while the *nasadot* (lazy women) constrained the supply of their families' livestock and degraded their status,' he said.

The less wealthy and the poor (*nabitag*) also had to conform to the demands of religion. They had to appease dead ancestors to recover from disease, gain better health and harvests by sponsoring similar, but more modest rituals. This, they could only do by procuring animals on loan from wealthier neighbors, often tying female labour to the community's wealthy patrons. Women of poorer households took up the responsibility of loan repayments. They were the animal caretakers, raising the animals by feeding them until they were robust and repro-

5 Food for the hogs usually consisted of a swill of sweet potato peelings, sweet potatoes rejects and taro boiled in a cauldron daily and fed to them.

duced. They also planted, weeded and harvested the swiddens of creditors or sponsors since these were assumed to be principally female agricultural tasks. Women from richer households, on the other hand, mobilised other women's labour whose husbands incurred some form of animal debt in the past, in order to provide food for existing livestock. The more one had access to extra-household labour, the greater the chances to cultivate wider swiddens and raise more livestock.

Relations of gender were affirmed and re-affirmed through the spaces Kalanguya women and men cultivated and occupied during the swidden cycle. As men cleared and felled trees for a new swidden site, they also established themselves as the owners of this site: 'The land is the property of the person who works it first' pointed out Claude Moss in 1920, pioneer ethnologist on the southern Cordillera during the American colonial period. Male status came with the clearing of forest space, which women and younger dependants cultivated and maintained. Each swidden site 'spoke' differently after some time: former male dependants became husbands who had to carve out their own new spaces in the forest. Single or widowed women mobilised male kin or paid male labour, usually with livestock the women themselves had raised, in order to gain access to cleared spaces. Wealthy male owners mobilised poorer, indebted women to cultivate their swidden plots. Kalanguya women were also chiefly responsible for raising livestock, fed from the produce of their swiddens. A huge herd indicated the cultivation of more extensive swiddens and women's heavy labour contributions. Thus, new and old social relations cut into the forest thickness, making room for more clearings to produce more food for everyday and at the service of holding rituals. In the pre-war years, the gender division of labour was thus organised according to the obligations Kalanguya women had as household food providers, resource managers and debt labourers, while Kalanguya men were childcarers and conveyors of social prestige. These obligations were principally norm-driven: women's sense of industry validated their place in religion and society. It did not occur to them to oppose this.

After sometime, Canabuan became a mosaic of cultivated spaces and clusters of forest in various stages of growth and regrowth. These spaces 'spoke' of the mosaic of social relations that were instantiated in resource use: relations of ownership, debt and claims to labour. Thus in former times, the Kalanguya of Canabuan viewed their environment as 'spaces of the ancestors' who demanded the fruits of the land as their rituals demonstrated; and harnessed the environment by carving out clearly 'gendered spaces' for subsistence and ritual prestige.

The Advent of Commercial Logging

The people of Canabuan began to see the trees in their forest cut by outsiders in 1957. As the village opened up to commercial logging and heightened trade activities, the gender division of labour gradually altered. Most Kalanguya men were employed by the logging concessions and the Santa Clara Sawmill. As tree cutters, the men had to make daily visits to the forest to cut as many trees as they could in a single day in order to collect the equivalent payment for these from the contractors. Others were paid to clear a road into the forest interior to make the transport of logs easier.

The operations of Santa Clara Sawmill also opened some opportunities for women. They were able to bring some of their crops to sell in Santa Clara's weekly market since they could not venture as far as the town centre due to farming chores which confined them to the village most of the time. It was also during this period that women were increasingly bringing their children along to their swiddens. For example, Sultina used to bring her 11 children to the swiddens with her while her husband Hibgan was a security guard for the logging concessionaire. Others, however, had their older children or ageing parents look after the younger ones. Nevertheless men increasingly abandoned their former role as childcarers as they began to earn cash incomes through logging. Gradually men became associated with cash income and the breadwinner role, which was enhanced in their new peer groups within the largely male network of logging operations from the lowlands.

The women of Canabuan were quite ambivalent about logging and its effects on their lives. Some of them resented the influence of the lowlanders on their husbands, especially the effects of gambling and drinking on them.[6] On the other hand, logging left a lot of cleared areas which enhanced swidden farming since these newly logged-over areas produced sweet potatoes in abundance. Most women benefited from logging since it provided them with new, large clearings for potential swidden sites. This departs from the ecofeminist view that women are always victims of environmental degradation. For many of them, hardly enough male labour was available to cut the big trees for new swidden clearings. Logging however speeded up the clearing process and all the women had to do was to further clean up the logged-over spaces by ridding them of underbrush and leftover vegetation. This boosted swidden agriculture and at the beginning, gave the people good yields. Their perturbations grew worse as the ecological effects of logging were increasingly felt as the years wore on.

6 Liquor drinking in Kalanguya society was ceremonial. This changed when men increasingly socialised with lowland men for whom drinking was an occasion for leisure, male bonding or to drown one's frustrations and anxieties.

Gendered Experiences of Environmental Degradation, 1960s–70s

The situation in the 1960s was a spiral of commercial logging, more intensive land use and cultivated spaces, soil erosion and people's increasing, albeit grudging, compliance with the swidden ban. The aggregate effect on the forest was further denudation which reached 60 per cent in the 1990s earthquake (ERP/SFLGU, 1995). Almost in concert, Canabuan villagers began constructing wet ricefields as their sweet potato yields declined. The men also gathered tiger grass and rattan, which became common household crops in existing swiddens since these were used in broom-making, an increasingly marketable commodity. Moreover, the rattan furniture industry was booming in the country at the time and Kalanguya men earned income by gathering them for lowland merchants. All throughout these new resource use activities spurred by the rapid changes in their natural environment and their growing links with the cash economy, the women continued to cultivate and care for their swiddens. These still provided the bulk of their households' food supply despite their increasing dependence on cash with which to purchase rice. Still in their early stages of productivity, the ricefields were yet unable to yield sufficient harvests.

The women farmers sold their labour power and their farm and forest products (ginger, tubers and fruits) in exchange for sweet potatoes or sometimes rice. The men occasionally sold their labour power and brooms instead for cash. They gradually became more identified with the cash economy whereas women were associated with the cultivation of sweet potatoes – 'a woman is only good for [growing] *obi*!'[7] In reality, as events unfolded, Kalanguya women were also quite active economically and were engaged in petty trade, albeit irregularly, with people from adjacent villages and in the town centre of Aritao. Further, they began making brooms, were involved in the broom trade and worked on the men's expanding ricefields. By then swidden farming was already considered backward and a harmful type of agriculture by state agriculturists and foresters – and eventually by the farmers themselves. Despite women being active in paddy rice farming and petty trade, they were still, however, associated with swidden farming. This demonstrates that swidden farming, as a former social activity 'reproduces social identities. This occurs via symbolically mediated, norm-governed social practices' (Fraser 1995: 203). Such social identities, in turn, are reproduced through the divisions of work, assigning particular tasks as female, and others, as male.

Kalanguya women who were still active swidden farmers during this period remember that they had to double their efforts at making their swiddens produce the volume of sweet potatoes required by their households and ritual feasts. Female farmers employed different and sometimes multiple strategies to immediately offset the decline of their sweet potato harvests during this period including

7 *Obi* is the Kalanguya term for sweet potatoes.

erosion-control techniques which became inadequate to arrest the rate of soil erosion. Their efforts are summarised in table 7.1 below.

Table 7.1: Women's Immediate Strategies to Offset the Effects of Declining Sweet Potato Yields

	Women's Immediate Strategies
Mina	planted other root crops such as yams and taro as sweet potato substitutes; eventually learned to make compost to restore soil fertility
Sasdiay	sold ginger, yams, bananas in Beti (village near Aritao) in exchange for rice
Salome	engaged in wage labour in neighbours' dry ricefields (*bangkeg*) for a rice wage
Milya	planted other root crops such as yams and taro as sweet potato substitutes
Lurding	planted other root crops such as yams and taro as sweet potato substitutes
Milyana	urged her husband to make brooms to sell to Pablo Soryata; her husband never used to make brooms in the past
Sultina	began to gather heart of rattan and bamboo (*ubod*) from the forest and sold this together with yams in Beti

Meanwhile, the men were getting busier. As they began to build their first wet rice paddies and terraces, they squeezed in some time to make brooms to sell and at times, were employed by Ilocano (lowland) farmers in adjacent villages to repair irrigation dikes and level the rolling landscape on which Ilocanos also constructed new rice paddies. These were wage-earning opportunities for them.

The advent of sedentary rice farming in Canabuan significantly altered the labour schedules and agricultural calendar of most households (see Figure 7.2). Olalya recalls that her husband abandoned land preparation tasks in swidden farming when their ricefield was constructed since he began ploughing and strengthening the embankments between the paddies. She increasingly began to prioritise work on the ricefield over weeding her swidden. 'Sweet potato harvests were no longer sufficient, therefore we had to work longer in the ricefields to make sure our rice harvests were abundant,' she explains. Another female elder, Sultina also recalls that her daily visits to her swiddens were reduced to a single day weekly, since they began working on their ricefields. By that time, she passed on the task of weeding her swiddens to her older daughters.

Sasdiay Balasuit recalls that in this period of rapid change, a big number of village women came to work in her husband's ricefields. 'They worked on our fields because they were afraid of government men burning their huts and swiddens. They could no longer make new swiddens. We paid them *palay* (unhusked rice) after every harvest. They also had fewer sweet potatoes for their families, so they had to work for rice.' The Balasuits,[8] one of Canabuan's first rice producers and

8 The first households in Canabuan who embarked on rice paddy farming were the Balasuits,

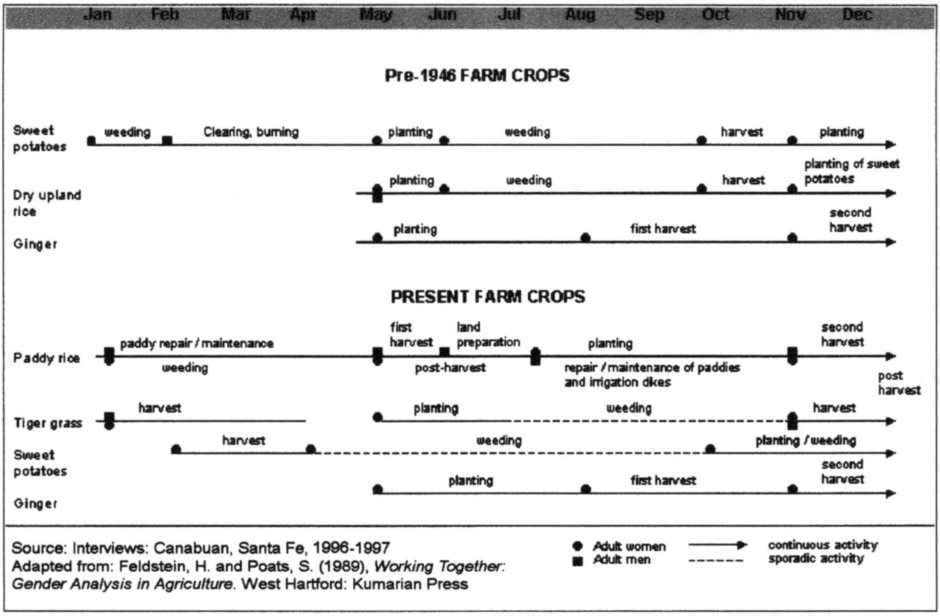

Figure 7.2: Agricultural Calendar

ricefield owners, absorbed some of the village's supply of female labour in need of rice to supplement dwindling sweet potato harvests.

The village elder, Delfinito, explains why people resorted to rice paddy farming: 'One can experience bad harvests in rice farming, but can also reinvest labour in the next cropping with a fair chance that the next one would be a better harvest. Rice farming was therefore *istedi* (steady). In *inuma* (swidden farming), succeeding harvests are insecure because of deteriorating soil fertility.' Further, the returns to labour for rice are more commensurate to the returns to labour of growing sweet potatoes according to the respondents (Resurrección 1999). In the past, they did not abandon swidden farming earlier due to their religion, the presence of still ample open-access lands and the availability of male labour. It was also less time and energy-consuming to clear forest spaces than to carve terraces and slopes for rice paddies.

The men organised *amuyo* (labour exchange) groups to build their ricefields where construction work lasted from one to two years. Delfinito recalls how work proceeded in those days:

Bugnays, Barico (Ilocano), Carreon while the others were Ibaloi and Ifugao migrants who came to settle in Canabuan in the 1960s and early 1970s.

> We brought our own food to the field sites and did not rely on the owners of the field to provide our meals as was the practice in the lowlands during the rice planting and harvesting seasons. Nobody could afford to feed a huge army of farm workers during this construction phase. During our breaks, we smoothed out strips of cut rattan so that we could make and sell brooms to Pablo Soryata, the broom trader. We could not make as many brooms as we would have wanted since our time was used up for building the ricefields.

Those who had enough livestock, were able to mobilise male labour for the construction of ricefields. The more livestock one had at one's disposal, the sooner the completion of the ricefield. Thus the construction of ricefields gradually took precedence over rituals in depleting a household's livestock. Hog-raising for ritual purposes also had to take a back seat since Christianity was making deeper inroads into the village, and villagers had to respond to the exigencies of food scarcity while they were shifting to paddy rice agriculture. In short, many individuals used their livestock to pay for extra-household labour. The women, however, had to make sure there was enough livestock for this purpose, which prompted them to find ways and means to augment their sweet potato supply to feed and raise livestock during this difficult transition period.

Aside from a heavier workload on their fields, Kalanguya women also began to learn the rudiments of broom-making and assisted their sons and husbands in the various stages of making them. Broom-making and basket-making were never women's activities, since they were often in the fields while the men stayed home to make them. Consuelo's mother, Agustina, for example, was proud that she had learned how to make an entire broom at a time when women in the village only knew how to wrap the broom handles with braided rattan strips. New activities such as broom-making and gathering rattan in the high forest were traditionally male tasks. As women increasingly performed them, these activities acquired new gender associations, discarding their former male ones.

Thus, Kalanguya women's labour largely subsidised the transition from a predominantly shifting mode of agriculture to a more permanent one during a period characterised by food scarcity and environmental change. They also became more responsible for childcare, a task men had abandoned due to the demands of constructing and cultivating ricefields and employment in logging. From being food providers, Kalanguya women gradually became food crisis managers and shouldered childcare more fully today. However, they remained associated with growing *obi*, now considered backward and a thing of the past.

Rice Scarcity, Debt and Food Crisis Management

The technologies of the green revolution introduced in the Philippines in the early 1970s have also found their way to Canabuan. These were introduced not by government extension agents but rather copied from Ilocano male farmers living nearby. The town centre of Aritao soon became a marketing hub for farming inputs such as mechanical farm implements, HYV seeds, chemical fertilisers and pesticides. For those in the low-lying portions of Canabuan, it became possible to embark on two crop seasons within one agricultural cycle, instead of only one. These technologies rapidly spread to farmers whose terraced rice paddies were in the higher slopes and who were lured to the idea that two crops could bring them more food. These concerns fell under the purview of male management.

The tasks in paddy rice farming are today considered priority tasks for both women and men. As a departure from the past where women largely shouldered crop and farming management decisions, today, men are the principal resource managers in paddy rice agriculture and more recently, in commercial vegetable gardening which a few men in the village have already embarked on.

Today, men purchase or make loans of farming implements and inputs as well as decide on the schedules of planting, harvesting and other stages of rice production. Whatever loans are made for rice farming are usually paid after the harvest. For every sack of fertiliser loaned, men have to repay two sacks of unhusked rice.[9] They also decide to accommodate sharecroppers and determine the nature of sharecropping arrangements.[10] Decisions on emergency measures such as crop failures, irrigation problems and pest management are all within the purview of the male farmer. They also have the right to dispose the ricefield for mortgage or sale, just as in the past, they did the same on former swiddens.

Men's labour has become more crucial to paddy rice agriculture than female labour. The graph below shows the extent of male and female labour in rice farming. Men participate more actively in rice farming than women in three types

9 The system of loans and repayments for rice farming itself is different from the system of loans and repayments in food crisis management where women make loans of rice from local merchants who require brooms as a payment for these loans. In rice farming, men repay all loaned inputs and services (land preparation and mechanical threshing) by setting aside a standardised amount of unhusked rice from the harvest which will go to the creditor(s). One sack fertilizer = 2 sacks unhusked rice after the harvest; for every 15 sacks of unhusked rice threshed, one sack is set aside for the owner of the threshing machine as payment for the use of the machine and services of the operator(s).

10 Usually in sharecropping arrangements, the harvest is divided in half between the sharecropper and the land owner. They both decide who is to spend for farming input requirements and who is to provide food for the labour party during planting and harvest periods. In most cases, it is the owner who is responsible for all the expenditures while the sharecropper is generally in charge of all the labour requirements.

of labour: family, exchange and hired, although in exchange labour, the number of labour days men and women spend in rice farming are almost equal. The activities which women and men engage in are land preparation tasks, gathering and bundling seedlings, transplanting, weeding, applying inputs, cutting, bundling and post-harvest tasks such as hauling, threshing and milling which all take place in one entire crop season. This graph, however, does not include the number of hours or days women spend to prepare food for the labour parties during the planting and harvest seasons. It also does not express the physical experiences of women and men as regards the types of work they perform on the ricefields.

Figure 7.3: Types of Labour in Rice Farming, by Sex

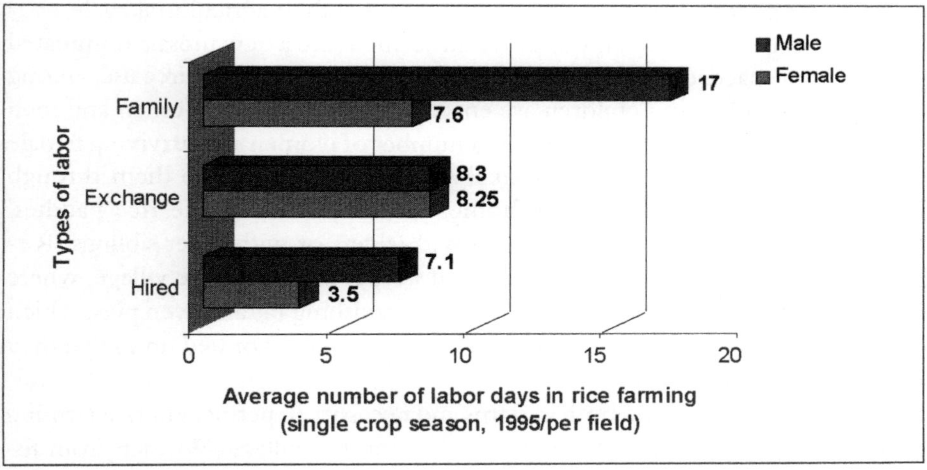

Sample size: 89 ricefields operated by 89 households with an average of 0.75 ha.
Source: Household Survey, May-June 1996, Canabuan.

A new hierarchy of land use has also emerged with the advent of permanent rice farming in Canabuan. The consensus often heard from residents today is that swidden farming is uncertain (since the soil loses its nutrients after sometime, they say), while rice paddy farming is 'steady' (*istedi*). Paddies became the spaces of men since men manage their construction and maintenance. Men also carved out rice paddies out of the contours of the hilly and mountainous slopes which required substantially more time and effort than in the lowlands due to erosion and unstable, foundering embankments. Women, meanwhile, were 'only good for *obi*!' and associated with swidden farming, and also perceived as secondary hands in rice farming. In the past, swiddens, though selected and cleared by Kalanguya men were considered women's spaces because women primarily managed them on a daily basis. In short, as more and more people practised permanent rice farming, rice paddies became men's spaces and (sometimes imaginary) swiddens or *kinaba* were understood as women's spaces. Ideas about gender shaped the divisions of labour; new resource use activities shape new ideas about gendered work.

Within the rice agricultural cycle, there were also 'women's seasons' and 'men's seasons.' Each season was gendered according to the type of labour associated with it: men were associated with heavy labour, therefore they were indispensable in the various land preparation tasks and the repair of embankments. Women were identified with repetitive, light labour, which meant they took up the tasks of weeding, transplanting and harvesting. However, post-harvest activities that require mechanisation, such as threshing and milling were men's activities, or at least managed by men. In the past, rice milling and pounding were female activities. Done with machines today, they became male tasks. Such divisions were reaffirmed year after year as villagers began and ended their agricultural cycle.

The landscape of Canabuan was thus transformed into a new mosaic dominated by permanent spaces of cultivation where altered relations of resource use, among women, men, elders and children are enacted and take place. Women and men work on these permanent spaces, while a number of women and surviving female elders re-cultivate small parcels of *kinaba* for food crops to tide them through periods of scarcity. Children stay home, lest they fall into the rice paddies' mudpools. Parents may also leave them with elders or with older siblings. Residual forest spaces remain in the higher and steeper inclines of the village, where today women and men search for increasingly vanishing rattan. Even pigs, which were allowed to roam in the past have to be placed in pens or tied up so that they don't destroy the rice crops.

Male labour, thus gaining both in status and necessity in permanent rice farming today, has not been readily accessible to some in the village. Women from female-headed households face difficulties getting access to male labour especially for the tasks in land preparation. For them, gaining access to male labour, is a question of how much social, economic and physical capital they have. The cases of Carmencita and Lita below exemplify this point.

Ifugao by ethnic origin, Carmencita came to settle in Canabuan in the mid-seventies, having sold her small ricefield in Ducligan, Banaue, Ifugao Province.[11] She used her earnings to purchase land in Canabuan where relatives have come to settle before her. About a year ago, her husband had a stroke and since then could no longer do strenuous rice farming tasks, and finally confined himself to staying at home while Carmencita sees to all his daily needs.

It sometimes takes Carmencita a week to organise a team of men for land preparation and by the time a party is organised, the rice seedlings may be too mature to guarantee an optimal yield, despite the application of fertilisers. The men also prefer to be paid in cash which she does not always have on hand. Instead, she

11 Ifugao Province lies on the north of Nueva Vizcaya. The Ifugao ethnic group inhabit this area and are known to be great rice terrace builders.

offers them remuneration in the form of *atang*.[12] Sometimes she offers her own labour in exchange for theirs – which translates into more days of labour repayment for her than for them, especially in the crucial tasks of land preparation.[13] Making her debtors repay their loans through labour is also another strategy. People make cash loans from Carmencita once word gets around that she has some cash available from her earnings from selling surplus rice or petty garment and broom trade. But to make her male debtors repay her through their labour sometimes requires great effort, imploring them with tears, on her part.

Carmencita also repairs paddy footpaths, applies fertilisers and purchases the chemical inputs needed, tasks largely performed by men in the village. It is necessary that she generates ample earnings from her trade in order to pay male labourers, otherwise, her household will have no rice. Because of the pressure to engage in trade, Carmencita cannot commit herself to labour exchange arrangements, which would secure male labour for her ricefield. Between earning cash through trade and making labour exchange arrangements which is a common strategy of other women from female headed households, she prefers the former since she is no longer too young to work for others, being in her fifties.

The case of Carmencita underscores the importance of male labour in Canabuan today. It also shows that despite coming from a relatively rich household owning prime agricultural land in the village with potential to yield comparatively abundant harvests, a woman is helpless without male labour working the land. She has had to rely on her economic and social capital to convince male neighbors to prepare her land for cultivation.

Poorer women like the widow Lita, who do not have economic capital with which to engage in trade like Carmencita and thus pay male labour with cash, have no other choice but to enter into reciprocal labour arrangements as the only way to secure access to male labour. In turn, Lita would have to repay male labour with more working days, usually by weeding, transplanting or harvesting. The

12 Payments for labour are only collected at the end of the harvest but with interest incurred.

13 For plowing (accompanied with a water buffalo or hand tractor), the amount paid is Php400, or equivalent to 8 full days (8 hours per day) of labour repayment; for repair of paddy footpaths, Php50 per day is paid or what is considered equivalent to 1 full day's work. The following are the accepted forms of remuneration and their equivalents in time:

One form of waged/remunerated labour (*lagbo*):

1 day's work (8 hours)	= 1 bundle of rice stalks, or
	= 1/2 (kerosene) can of unhusked rice, or,
	= Php40–50 per day
3 days' work (8 hours ea.)	= 2 kerosene cans of unhusked rice

Another form of remunerated labour to be paid after the rice harvest (*atang*):

1 day's work (8 hours)	= 1 (kerosene) can of unhusked rice
3 day's work (8 hrs. each)	= 3 (kerosene) cans of unhusked rice

exchange 'rate' for land preparation tasks in Canabuan (and in nearby places) is rendering three female working days for every one day of land preparation done by a man with a *carabao* (water buffalo) or a hand tractor. Thus, Lita has to devote more time working in others' fields every crop season. Her only daughter has married and now lives elsewhere, whereas her son is only eight. She has thus no one to help her in the fields. No small wonder Lita has always been ill and had to mortgage the land her mother had given her to pay for her medication. She has only her physical strength with which to secure and gain access to male labour. 'Women's inability to call on the labour of others is a function of their lack of social power, and is clearly related to their position both in the household and within a wider set of social relations outside the household' (Moore 1988: 59).

While male labour has apparently become so crucial in rice paddy farming, this, however, does not mean that women in Canabuan today have less work and that men have more. A new, although not neat, division of labour has emerged where women take up the cudgels of food crisis management during the lean, rice-deficit months while men take over the main task of cultivating rice and attending to its day-to-day requirements. But before I discuss women's responsibilities in food crisis management, I will first show the different lengths of time households experienced rice sufficiency in 1995-1996 in the following table:

Table 7.2: Frequency Distribution of Households by month/s of Rice Sufficiency* December 1995 - December 1996

Rice supply (number of months)	Absolute frequency	Relative frequency (per cent)	Cumulative frequency (per cent)
< = 1 month	3	3.4	4.5
> 1 month to 2 mos.	7	8.0	11.4
> 2 mos. to 3 mos.	5	5.7	17.0
> 3 mos. to 4 mos.	9	10.2	27.3
> 4 mos. to 5 mos.	7	8.0	35.2
> 5 mos. to 6 mos.	13	14.8	50.0
> 6 mos. to 7 mos.	13	14.8	64.8
> 7 mos. to 8 mos.	5	5.7	70.5
> 8 mos. to 9 mos.	5	5.7	76.1
> 9 mos. to 10 mos.	6	6.8	82.9
> 10 mos. to 11 mos.	1	1.1	84.1
> 11 mos. to 12 mos.	3	3.3	87.5
.> 12 months	11	12.5	100.00

N = 88 households

Source: Household Survey, January-February 1997.

* Rice sufficiency refers to the sufficiency of a household's supply of its own cultivated rice.

Table 7.2 shows that only 12.5 per cent of the sample population had a sufficient supply of rice for the entire year that came from their own rice yields (or 87.5 per cent experienced rice shortages). Fifty per cent of these households experienced rice sufficiency for only six months or less, while roughly a fourth of the entire sample produced rice that lasted them only four months or less. Meanwhile, 6 per cent of the households surveyed generated a rice surplus. Therefore, most households experience a period of rice deficiency.

Out of the 11 households (6 per cent) which produced rice surpluses, 7 sold their surpluses. These 11 households were mostly old Kalanguya families of Canabuan, or Ibalois and Ifugaos who had purchased the prime agricultural land of Canabuan's flatbelt areas from Ilocanos in the 1960s–1970s. According to village history, these parcels of land were originally Kalanguya-owned, but were usurped by these Ilocanos who produced land titles to validate their ownership.

Since members of most households in Canabuan run short of rice they had produced for a definite period, they have devised means and ways to procure rice. My survey has also revealed the kinds of food crisis strategies people in the village employ. They are the following: *lagbo*, which is understood as labour paid in kind or non-wage labour, payable usually in the form of rice; broom-making; cultivation of ginger as a cash crop; making rice loans from merchants and/or neighbors; cultivation of sweet potatoes to substitute for rice, which was the reverse in the past; and, engaging in wage labour within or outside the village. No longer can women and men rely on riverine and forest wildlife for food since many of these have already disappeared as the river's depths are now packed with silt, while the forest is no longer a haven for wildlife due to thinning cover.

All rice-scarce households engage in *lagbo* at varying degrees. In the period 1995–1996, survey results show that those who had the longest period of rice scarcity have tended to engage in *lagbo* more than the other rice-scarce households (Resurrección 1999). *Lagbo* has become the most common coping strategy for rice scarcity. Wages are often in the form of a rice wage. In a village with hardly any landless households yet characterised as largely labour-scarce, *lagbo* provides an opportunity for all to earn rice, as rice is generally the currency for exchange in Canabuan.

For example, an Ilocano woman, Anabel, who has settled on one of the ecologically marginal parts of Canabuan where thick cogon grass grows, often asked Pina to give her some work in exchange for rice. Pina belongs to Canabuan's oldest families (Balasuits) who own choice agricultural land in the village. Another woman, Ana, who has 11 children owns land but has many mouths to feed and produce from her ricefield is thus not enough. Foreseeing the quick depletion of her household's rice supply and thus the need to augment it, Ana offers members of her family, her husband and two sons aged 13 and 15, as an entire band of ricefield labourers to neighbors during the peak labour periods of transplanting and harvesting. Problems arise when she commits her family's labour at the same time that her husband has planned to set out in the forest to gather rattan for broom-making. Neighbors whisper that when her family is harvesting a ricefield, she is often not with them and is busy chatting with friends elsewhere. She also makes loans and commits her husband's labour in broom-making as a repayment for the loans she had made earlier. This has caused considerable tension between them.

Wage labour (cash-remunerated), on the other hand, is minimally practised by any of the households due to the small cash reserve in the village as well as the lack of wage opportunities immediately outside the village. Cash available is concentrated in the hands of local village merchants, notably only two of them (Rita and Basanita), who use them as their own revolving capital for their trading ventures. Access to cash incomes is today's index of wealth in the village and those who own public transport vehicles and earn salaries as petty government employees belong to the village's upper crust.

Lagbo, as it is generally understood in the village, involves the following rice farming tasks: weeding, transplanting, threshing, repairing paddy footpaths and irrigation dikes, and ploughing. The repetitive tasks like weeding and transplanting are usually done by women while those which require the use of huge implements, inputs and machines are done by the men.

Cultivating ginger, on the other hand, is not considered an 'emergency' measure during food-scarce months, in the same manner as broom-making and *lagbo*. It has been a traditional Kalanguya women's cash crop that they cultivate to a greater degree today. The village elder, Hibgan, recalls that ginger was sold in small amounts in the past not in can-fulls as it is today. With the growing absence of rattan for brooms, women are more compelled to grow ginger as a ready fallback during periods of rice scarcity, thus generating some cash income. In the 1970s, the ginger trade experienced a boom due to the heavy influx of merchants into Canabuan who bought ginger. Since then, a number of women cultivated ginger as a monocrop in *kinaba*.

Broom-making appears to be the third most employed food crisis strategy among the rice-scarce households (Resurrección 1999). Women or their husbands transact big rice or cash loans with local merchants in order to offset the food deficit. When these loans are made, they are then obliged to repay their debts by the equivalent number in brooms or cash with interest.

The case of Josephine exemplifies the strategies women employ to corner their husbands' labour in broom-making in order to protect their own labour as debt repayment. Early in her marriage, she began to help her husband Ramon in broom-making to beat their debt deadline for the repayment of rice loans. She once made a rice loan without telling Ramon. When he arrived home one day from the ricefield, he was surprised to find broom materials ready waiting for him. Josephine had already begun to make the brooms herself by the time he arrived which to her relief, cushioned any angry reaction from him. While making brooms, Ramon usually insists on a break to be able to inspect the ricefield for a while, which often causes tension between them since she worries that he may totally abandon broom-making once he finds something to do in the ricefield. She offers to go instead since he is faster at making brooms than her.

When and if, for some reason, they are not able to repay their debt on time, Josephine will have to weed and plant rice on her creditor's ricefield to repay part of the rice debt. Her labour's equivalent in cash is deducted from her outstanding loan. Thus for every loan she makes, Josephine is chiefly responsible for its repayment, whether through brooms or through her own labour in the creditor's ricefield.

Contemporary inter-household labour arrangements thus include *lagbo* and its cash and crop-based variants: *amuyo*, a reciprocal labour arrangement; *atang*, which involves a later wage repayment usually crop-based (see footnote 13 for the labour-wage equivalents). *Bataris* (traditionally, meat distribution during land clearing) is only employed rarely for non-agricultural tasks such as house repair or house transfer. There were fewer interhousehold labour arrangements in the past since swidden agriculture entailed fewer tasks, usually divided between cultivation (for women) and land clearing/fence building (for men). Today, labour arrangements are more complex and cash-based arrangements are largely male-cornered, especially the task of land preparation with draft animal or machine. This adds value to male labour already considered so crucial in rice production and management. Crop-based repayments, on the other hand, are usually given in the predominantly female tasks of transplanting, weeding and harvesting. Both women and men engage in exchange labour, *amuyo*, which adds to the list of Kalanguya women's and men's responsibilities. The Kalanguya custom of debt repayments through labour on the swiddens has been extended to rice paddy farming. Today, when couples are unable to repay rice loans by repayment in brooms, they repay these by deploying female labour in the creditor's ricefields, especially in the tasks of weeding and planting. In the past, women's labour repaid animal loans. Kalanguya women used to be chiefly responsible for livestock care for both religious rituals and loan repayments. Thus, access to extra-household labour today depends largely on a household's cash reserves, time available and capacity to grant loans whereas in the past, it depended greatly on one's capital in livestock and propensity to grant animal loans.

Women, more than men, are also the principal food crisis managers in Canabuan households. Food crisis management tasks such as *lagbo*, ginger production and marketing and broom-making are principal responsibilities of women in rice-scarce households. As their households' food providers and food crisis managers, the women are also the first to know when their supply of rice has run out. They may quickly make small rice loans from neighbors, or, make bigger rice or cash loans together with their husbands or by themselves. However, survey results have also shown that the highest incidence of women's response to food/rice scarcity was in households which had the shortest period of rice scarcity (Resurrección 1999). Such obligation and attendant tasks are unlike those of women in more rice-scarce households who would have to resort to multiple strategies to be able to get some rice, and for which they would have to enlist men as well. Thus, the contribution of husbands is hardly ever felt in households with shorter rice scarcity periods.

Digressing from the Norm

Leach (1994: 214) has also pointed out that 'just as ideas about gender shape resource-using activities, so these acts, in turn, shape [new] ideas about gender.' For example, certain resource use activities, such as searching for rattan in the high forest and broom making, have shown signs of weakening as an exclusively traditional male task. Women are increasingly performing such tasks. However, certain gendered resource-using activities persist to be identified as being either female or male. The following excerpts from Florencia's diary demonstrates this point: she is a busy woman, cultivating a ricefield, swidden and a vegetable garden together with husband, Tomas. They also have four children. The excerpts below are a short four-day diary of Florencia's activities. On September 2, Florencia took on more male tasks, like hoeing, while Tomas, her husband went to harvest on her swidden, usually considered a female task. However, when it came to pleasing her mother-in-law, Florencia had to concede to the traditional gender norms on labour in harvesting *obi*. This is also an example of the tendency for the gender division of labour to be more flexible in intra-household arrangements than in interhousehold ones. Less stringent yet more 'public' conditions prompt the observance of gendered norms of work such as in the case of Florencia harvesting *obi* for her brother-in-law. In the couple's case, however, it was a matter of achieving complementarity in workloads in the face of exigency.

A Woman's Four-day Diary (excerpts)

August 26
Florencia was winnowing rice at about 5 in the afternoon to prepare it for cooking. She later boiled the rice and cooked some river ferns she had earlier gathered after planting rice in Agapito Lawit's ricefield where she joined an *amuyo* party. She left her youngest child with her mother. Tomas, on the other hand, went to repay a loan of food (vegetables) from Alban, a neighbour, by working on his vegetable garden.

August 28
Florencia weeded her sweet potato field. Tomas was also out in search of iron roofing for his father's house. Their eldest, aged 11, took care of the youngest child. Florencia spent the whole day working on her swidden.

September 2
Florencia hoed their vegetable garden and brought along her youngest child. She could not accomplish much hoeing the entire day since her child was quite disruptive. Tomas, meanwhile, went to gather yams for their pigs in their swidden plot uphill.

September 4
Florencia had to go to her mother-in-law's (Mina) swidden to harvest sweet potatoes for her brother-in-laws' hogs. Her brother-in-law had never harvested sweet potatoes in his life before since his mother used to do it. Today, Mina is ailing with rheumatism and arthritis thus she can no longer harvest the tubers for her son.

Source: Work-day diaries of six households, Canabuan, April 1996 to February 1997.

The gender division of labour need not always be rigid; complementarity of tasks is also something women and men attempt to achieve especially in a situation of impoverishment. In my survey of household strategies during periods of food scarcity, women and men from the poorest households showed the highest incidence of co-managing the food crisis; whereas in richer households, women shoulder most of the responsibilities for food crisis management (Resurrección 1999: 201). This demonstrates that studies on the gender division of labour should also pay attention to the connections between forms and types of work in men's and women's livelihoods as these are linked with social differentiation.

Conclusions

The intent of this chapter was to trace the changes in Kalanguya female and male labour in resource use over time, and the factors that have influenced and affected such changes. Findings show that gendered labour in resource use has altered largely due to environmental degradation, changes in the types of resource use activities, increasing linkages with the wider commercial economy and the changes in the meanings and values people attach to female and male labour. These transformations reflect the dynamic nature of the gender division of labour.

The gender division of labour is also contested terrain. Throughout the pre-war to the contemporary period, we saw that the social position of Kalanguya women affected their household and interhousehold labour arrangements. In particular, women's claims to male labour have been mediated by their economic and social locations. Case studies have shown that female heads of households are particularly hard put in gaining access to male labour, while women from poorer households have to repay male labour with twice the amount of their own labour, which has a constraining effect on these women's health and other activities. Women have also been mobilised to repay debts through their labour both in the past and in the present. During the pre-war period, the imperatives of religion and livestock accumulation compelled women to cultivate more sweet potatoes in order to feed and reproduce loaned animals, as well as work on others' swiddens to procure more sweet potatoes. In the 1970s, female labour largely subsidised the transition to permanent agriculture by a heavier workload to produce food despite the increasing deterioration of the environment for swidden farming.

In all these, the Kalanguya norm of the industrious woman governed the ways by which women's labour was deployed. However, the norm also validated women's place in the dominant culture, which is why they did not oppose it. Today, female labour repays unpaid debts and rice loans by work on creditors' ricefields. Incidents have shown that women may strategise and negotiate themselves out of debt labour through covert and overt means. Kalanguya women therefore deployed their labour in the past on the basis of the social rewards they derived from observing a popular norm. In the present, they strategise to avoid that the physical burdens of debt labour fall on them. In analysing the gender division of labour, it is thus important to consider women as actors, that is, as 'experiencing selves, with powers and preferences' (Jackson 1998) in conjunction with how they are structurally located socially and economically.

Defining resource management as predominantly female or male has also changed over time. New resource use activities such as paddy rice agriculture has been recognised as a male-managed enterprise, whereas in the past, women were recognised as principal resource and erosion-control managers in their role as food providers and livestock raisers. This weakens women's current command and control over their labour, new resources, crops and earnings. Further, Kalanguya women today, are still associated with *obi* and swidden agriculture in a pejorative sense, at the same time they are also understood as secondary farm hands in paddy rice agriculture. New resource use activities thus give rise to new ideas about the gendered nature of work.

The gender division of labour in resource use and management is thus dynamic and contested. Power comes about by assigning hierarchical meanings and discourses to female and male labour. Power also comes about when women and men make claims on each other's labour arising from customary gendered norms and their unequal positions in nexuses of social and economic relations. Gender therefore shapes the way the resources of the natural environment are to be harnessed and conserved.

References

Afable, P. (1989) 'Language, Culture and Society in a Kallahan Community, Northern Luzon, Philippines', PhD Thesis, Yale University.

Boserup, E. (1970) *Women's Role in Economic Development,* London: George Allen & Unwin.

Dankelman, I. and Davidson, J. (1988) *Women and Environment in the Third World: Alliance for the Future*, London: Earthscan Publications.

Deere, C.D. (1982) 'The division of labour by sex in agriculture: a Peruvian case study', *Economic Development and Cultural Change* 30, 4: 795–811.

— (1995) 'What difference does gender make? Rethinking peasant studies', *Feminist Economics* 1, 1: 53–72.

Dolinen, L. (1995) 'Enriching upland development through indigenous knowledge systems: The case of Kalahan, Nueva Vizcaya', paper presented at the seminar-workshop: 'Application of Indigenous Knowledge Systems in Sustainable Development', held at the Institute of Forest Conservation, UPLB College of Forestry, Los Banos, Laguna.

Earthquake Rehabilitation Program and Santa Fe Local Government Unit (ERP/SFLGU) (1995) *Present Land Use Map*, Bayombong, Nueva Vizcaya: ERP.

Feldman, S. (1992) 'Crises, poverty and gender inequality: current themes and issues', in L. Beneria and S. Feldman (eds.) *Unequal Burden: Economic Crises, Persistent Poverty and Women's Work*, Boulder: Westview Press.

Fraser, N. (1995) 'The case of Habermas and gender', in *The Polity Reader in Social Theory*, Cambridge: Polity Press.

Jackson, C. (1998) 'Gender, irrigation and environment: arguing for agency', *Agriculture and Human Values* 15: 313–24.

Keesing, F. and Keesing, M. (1934) *Taming Philippine Headhunters: A Study of Government and of Cultural Change in Northern Luzon*, London: Allen & Unwin Ltd.

— (1962) *Ethnohistory of Northern Luzon,* Stanford: Stanford University Press.

Leach, M. (1994) *Rainforest Relations: Gender and Resource Use among the Mende of Gola, Sierra Leone*, Edinburgh: University of Edinburgh Press.

Lewis, M. (1992) *Wagering the Land: Ritual, Capital and Environmental Degradation in the Cordillera of Northern Luzon, 1900–1986*, Berkeley: University of California Press.

Mackintosh, M. (1981) 'Gender and economics: The sexual division of labour and the subordination of women', in K. Young, C. Wolkowitz and R. McCullagh (eds.) *Of Marriage and the Market: Women's Subordination in International Perspective,* London: CSE Books.

Mies, M. (1986) *Patriarchy and Accumulation on a World Scale*, London: Zed Books.

Mohanty, C. (1988) 'Under western eyes: Feminist scholarship and colonial discourses', *Feminist Review* 30: 61–88.

Moore, H. (1988) *Feminism and Anthropology,* Cambridge: Polity Press.

Moss, C.R. (1920) 'Nabaloi law and ritual', *American Archaeology and Ethnology* 13: 207–342.

Resurrección, B. (1999) *Transforming Nature, Redefining Selves: Gender and Ethnic Relations, Resource Use and Environmental Change in the Philippine Uplands*, Maastricht: Shaker Publishing.

Rodda, A. (1991) *Women and the Environment,* London: Zed Books.

Russell, S. (1989) 'Ritual persistence and the ancestral cult among the Ibaloi of the Luzon highlands', in S. Russell and C. Cunningham (eds.) *Changing Lives, Changing Rites: Ritual and Social Dynamics in Philippine and Indonesian Uplands*, Ann Arbor: Centre for South and Southeast Asian Studies, University of Michigan.

Scott, W.H. (1966) *On the Cordillera: A Look at the Peoples and Cultures of the Mountain Province*, Manila: MCS Enterprises.

Shiva, V. (1989) *Staying Alive: Women, Ecology And Development*, London: Zed Books.

Shiva, V. and Mies, M. (1993) *Ecofeminism*, London: Zed Books.

Sontheimer, S. (1991) *Women and the Environment: A Reader*, London: Earthscan Publications.

Van Halsema, I. (1991) *Housewives in the Field: Power, Culture and Gender in a South-Brazilian Village*, Amsterdam: CEDLA.

Wiber, M. (1989) 'The canao imperative: changes in resource control, stratification and the economy of ritual among the Ibaloi of Northern Luzon', in S. Russell and C. Cunningham (eds.) *Changing Lives, Changing Rites: Ritual And Social Dynamics in Philippine and Indonesian Uplands*, Ann Arbor: Centre for South and Southeast Asian Studies, University of Michigan.

8

Labour Practices outside the Factory: Modern Forms of Household Production in Java

JENNIFER ALEXANDER AND PAUL ALEXANDER

Many accounts of labour relations in Southeast Asian societies are written as if modern commodity production in the region is limited to factory-based manufacturing involving large, mainly female, waged-labour forces (Ong 1990, Wolf 1992). While this implicit equation of modernity with industrialisation is understandable in a region where scarce rural farmland is rapidly being converted to industrial parks and where many village daughters are becoming factory workers (Saptari 1991, 1995, Mills 1997), it is, however, far from accurate. In Indonesia, as in many other newly-industrialising nations, some of the most spectacular recent examples of successful manufacturing growth involve locally-owned and relatively small businesses, rather than multi-national factories (Hill 1994, see also Blim 1992, Hamilton 1998). Any comprehensive account of evolving labour relations in Southeast Asia should, therefore, give considerable attention to changes in the labour practices of small and medium enterprises.

Unfortunately, the intellectual tools which might be used to investigate labour relations within small businesses are, at best, rudimentary. The conventional economic explanations for the ability of local, small-scale industry to compete with transnational, vertically-integrated firms turn on the notion of flexible specialisation. In brief, the argument is that localised clusters of highly specialised, small producers which are linked into production chains by 'co-operative' contracts rather than integrated into a single firm, can adapt more quickly to economic changes (Pederson et al. 1994). In a global context, numerous – if not always compatible – reasons have been offered as to why clusters of small firms may be more efficient, or at least able to sell at lower prices, than their large transnational competitors (Zukin and DiMaggio 1990). For example, the combination of narrow specialisation with flexible contracts facilitates the collective production of a complex commodity which is beyond the financial or skill resources of an individual small firm. Co-operating clusters of small independent firms can spread development and tooling costs, as well as quickly share innovations, and because the firms are independent, each directly reaps the benefits of its own efforts. Any explanatory power of the notion of flexible specialisation thus rests on the supposed economic advantages of market-based forms of horizontal organisation as opposed to the more lineal hierarchies which characterise firms (Williamson 1975). This in turn echoes the much older, if seldom empirically tested assumption that private firms are always more efficient than public enterprises.

Even in contexts when their findings are robust, however, these narrowly economic explanations leave too many critical questions unanswered. For example, the sizeable literature analysing the role of small firms in industrialising societies as diverse as Mexico, Northern Italy, and Taiwan, agrees that a critical component in the small firms' success is their 'flexible' mobilisation of labour (e.g. Piore and Sabel 1984, Beneria and Roldan 1987, Bull and Corner 1993, Greenhalgh 1994, Rabellotti 1994). This claim resonates with recent experiences in mature industrial societies where sub-contracting some areas of production and services has sharply cut the core firm's labour costs, more often by eliminating non-wage benefits than by directly reducing wages. There is rather less agreement, however, concerning the motives for, and consequences of, such 'flexible' labour practices. Many small firms are household-based and this has been regarded as creating a positive work environment resulting in little need for supervision and, consequently, high levels of labour productivity (Goodman 1989: 6). An alternative, and rather less idyllic view, is that because small firms are shielded from State surveillance, they can avoid paying taxes and insurance fees and thus increase their profits by depriving employees of welfare benefits. Working conditions in such firms are often sub-standard, and 'sweating work has been an integral, rather than a transitional, feature of flexible specialisation' (Simmons and Kalantaridis 1994: 649). Even when the analysis is confined to Europe, the industries cited as examples of flexible specialisation vary considerably in both working conditions and the tenor of labour relations, so that any generalisations have only a weak empirical basis. The analytical problems are exacerbated when the discussion is extended to Southeast Asia where both the economy and the household structure differ significantly from familiar European forms.

When investigating the relationship between particular forms of business organisation and labour productivity or control, it is important not to adopt an unreflective 'modernisation' thesis: that is, simply to assume that historical changes in labour practices always follow lineal trajectories. One common assumption in accounts of changing labour relations is that labour organisation normally evolves around collective household and community labour, through piecework and 'putting out,' to wage labour. Another common assumption is that labour relations typically evolve from a pattern of unorganised and thus exploited congeries of individual workers to tightly organised industrial labour forces protected by sophisticated unions. This may have been the historical pattern of development in much of Northern Europe (Kriedte et al. 1981), although developments were uneven, but there is no reason to assume that innovations in labour relations will form a similar pattern in other regions. An unexamined lineal view of industrial developments is also often responsible for misleading inferences from statistical data. For example, in studies of non-European societies, evidence that a high proportion of employees are heavily indebted to their employers is commonly interpreted as a form of 'bonded' labour. In many cases this may be the appropriate interpretation, but as contemporary industrial societies demonstrate, high levels of household debt are not incompatible with circumstances where employees have considerable autonomy.

The tendency to draw unwarranted inferences from cultural and historical stereotypes is particularly marked in studies of Southeast Asian industrial development. For example, the fact that many small Southeast Asian firms are constituted by households, does not, in itself, entail the very common inference that kinship governs economic practices in these firms, let alone the stronger claim that such 'family-firms' reflect 'traditional' structures of authority based on age and gender (Mackie 1988, Redding 1990). These should always be treated as empirical questions. In some cases, family firms may be transitional forms which will be rapidly replaced by other types of business organisation. But in other cases, the rise of the 'family firm' has been accompanied by new forms of household structure in which 'reinvented traditions' are used to legitimate significant changes in the division of household labour and authority (Greenhalgh 1994, Gates 1996). Far from merely reflecting 'traditional' culture, the experience of working in such family firms changes peoples' perception of their culture, including its history. It is wrong, for example, to suggest that the economic independence of young, female factory workers in Java is a recent development (Wolf 1992), let alone to interpret it as another example of the liberating effect of modern market relations on a traditional society. Quite the contrary: individual economic autonomy has long been a feature of the Javanese household structure; the Javanese economy has been exposed to market forces for more than a century, and, as we will touch on below, modernisation is tending to restrict female autonomy rather than extend it.

As the introduction makes clear, the essays in this volume endeavour to take culture seriously, while avoiding the broad-brushed culturalist explanations which have dominated so many accounts of Asian economies (e.g. Redding 1990). Rather than being treated as a separate sphere of analysis, set apart from politics and economics and to be used only as an explanation of last resort, culture should be conceptualised as the meaning-making analytical components of all relationships, including economic and political relations. From this perspective, a statement that the form of Javanese economic institutions is determined by Javanese culture is both tautological and trivial. The more interesting analytical task is to show how specific groups of Javanese have drawn on aspects of their culture for particular economic purposes, and to examine the consequences of these innovations in the continuing process of Javanese daily life. This in turn requires that the categories conventionally used to discuss labour relations are scrutinised and the assumptions attached to these categories are made explicit.

At first glance, the Javanese furniture industry which is the empirical focus of this paper looks like a paradigm case of flexible specialisation. It is a highly localised collection of independent small enterprises, each of them highly specialised, which are co-ordinated into production chains by a series of 'contracts.' Most transactions between workshops – and many transactions within workshops – are market transactions, although most transactions also take place within relatively well-established trading, or supplier, partnerships. These partnerships often link 'relatives' and a fifth of the labour force work in workshops owned by kinsmen. The industry as a whole produces a very wide, and rapidly expanding, range of wooden products which are sold in numerous, highly segmented, domestic and global markets, but because the production units of any particular product are tightly clustered, adjoining workshops usually produce the same item.

A macro examination of the Jepara furniture industry, conducted without intensive ethnographic investigation of the production processes, would probably categorise it as yet another example of successful sub-contracting and as yet another demonstration of the efficiency of market-based institutions when they are freed from control of the State. Most recent accounts of Javanese industrial development made precisely this point (e.g. Hill 1996: 169). A sociologically informed account might in addition highlight the kinship component of workshop labour forces and point to the importance of fictive kinship relations as a transitional stage between traditional, kinship-based, household production and modern, contract-based, forms of industrial organisation (Alexander and Alexander 2000). But such interpretations are misleading: at once too powerful and not powerful enough. Too powerful because the notion of 'sub-contracting' attributes Jepara's success to a pattern of top-down flows of information, innovations, and finance, which was not, in fact, the case. Not powerful enough, because the glossing of all the varied economic relationships as 'sub-contracts,' empties these relationships of their cultural specificity. Yet the ability to vary the meanings attached to particular forms of relationships, has been a critical strategy in the development of new economic institutions in Jepara, including new forms of labour relations.

Jepara Furniture

Although the region of Jepara on Java's north coast has been famous for its finely-carved teak products since the seventeenth century, the modern furniture industry began less than two decades ago when the first reproductions of classic European styles ('antiques') were exported to Australia and Europe. The rate of growth was spectacular. In 1987, the first year for which reliable figures are available, exports from the nearest container port totalled $US1.6 million. Exports increased fourfold between 1988 and 1991, and nearly doubled again in 1992, to reach $US59 million in 1993 and an amasing US$169 million in 1997 (Kantor Perdagangan 1998). The growth in exports was accompanied by an equally rapid growth in products and by 1993 Jepara was producing a dozen distinct categories of furniture, each for a different market. European 'antiques' are now sold in forty-nine countries and comprised about 60 per cent of exports by value. Most of the exported furniture is of medium to high quality and is certainly not cheap. Production for domestic sales, mainly lower quality furniture and souvenirs, has grown equally rapidly and is probably worth more than the exports.

The term the 'Jepara furniture industry' is thus something of a misnomer because both the markets and their associated production chains are highly specialised. Although there are exceptions, each market tends to be for a single, tightly specified, product sold to a limited number of buyers. While a particular exporter may deal in several markets, each specific market has its own entry conditions and is serviced by a limited group of producers who are often located in specific villages within the Jepara region. This chapter is mainly concerned with the production of good quality furniture.

The rapid expansion of the industry was facilitated by the Indonesian government's response to the series of macro-economic changes beginning in the 1980s which are usually glossed in the literature as 'globalisation' and 'deregulation' (Booth 1992, Hill 1994). The most significant state initiatives were: improvements in the infrastructure of roads, shipping, and communications; the simplification of export procedures; and the banning of timber exports. More recently, the regional government has introduced a number of credit and educational programmes. The educational programmes have been very important in augmenting the supply of skilled workers – clerical and administrative staff as much as carvers and carpenters – but although some exporters have taken loans, the specific financial programmes were less important than a new appreciation of the value of small firms in providing employment and raising living standards. (Sandee et al. 1994: 123). In sum, the major contribution of the State to the development of the furniture industry lay in improving the infrastructure and removing some of the regulations which had inhibited exports, rather than any direct intervention. Of course, State institutions now credit themselves with a much more active role.

Although these macro-economic changes were necessary conditions for expansion, the catalyst for the initial stages of development was around ten foreign buyers. Equipped with no more than a few photographs, these buyers commissioned prototypes from local workshops who refined the quality through a long process of trial and error. By 1992, there were twenty-eight foreign buyers resident in Jepara for most of the year, but despite their important initial role, this remains predominantly a Javanese industry. Although 222 firms exported in 1997, most of them were very small, and seventy per cent of the total was exported by the twenty largest firms. Six of these firms were run by foreigners, four by Indonesian-Chinese, and ten, including the largest, by Javanese. The foreigners' initial information edge concerning Western markets was rapidly eroded. Indonesian exporters travelled overseas to trade promotions and acquired local wholesale and retail customers who did not want to spend time in Indonesia, let alone be involved with production. These relationships became easier to maintain as the Indonesians gradually acquired a more sophisticated understanding of the quality requirements of particular markets and the importers gradually lost their fear of being cheated. The bigger Jepara exporters produced lavish catalogues and elaborate show-rooms to attract buyers, and these helped to spread new designs and production standards among smaller producers very quickly. Consequently, foreigners became less critical as a source of stylistic innovations and some recent products – 'Asmat' art-carvings and a form of 'Egyptian'-style Art Nouveau furniture, for example – are local designs which later found international buyers.

It is important to emphasise that the plethora of small workshops and the relative absence of machine-tools (other than hand tools) located in large factories cannot easily be attributed to a lack of knowledge or a lack of capital. Some specialised markets, including export markets for teak garden furniture and the domestic market for school tables, are in fact served mainly by factory-based, highly-mechanised, production. In addition, specific sectors of almost all production chains are highly mechanised and use modern equipment: the cutting and milling of carving blanks is an example. Moreover, even smaller workshops have been quick to adopt modern communications such as faxes and, very recently, computers.

Workshops

Although the industry produces highly-specialised commodities for demanding and sophisticated export markets, production is concentrated in small, relatively un-mechanised, rural workshops with less than five employees each. The last comprehensive local government survey in 1994 listed 2110 workshops scattered through eighty of the 191 villages in the region with an estimated total labour force of 40,000 (Kantor Perdagangan 1994: 1). This was at least a thirty percent underestimate because very small workshops were excluded, and the numbers have probably doubled again in the past five years.

Only a few of these relatively small, and relatively un-mechanised, household-based workshops produce complete products. Most workshops are highly specialised producers of a very limited range of components, so that the production chain of a particular commodity must be mapped as a complex web of inter-linked workshops. It should be emphasised at the outset, that each node of these webs is an autonomous unit and that transactions between workshops are governed by market principles. The production chains are market chains; not a disguised form of co-operative. There is a wide variety of indigenous terms for the relationships which link workshops into production chains and the cultural nuances are important, but at this point we will gloss them as contracts.

A critical feature of this structure as far as labour relations are concerned is that all transactions between – and most of those within – workshops are at 'market' rates: a price is set for a finished item or for carrying out a specific task. This emphasis on 'piece-rates' is hidden because employees get daily 'allowances' and the smaller workshops obtain regular 'progress payments,' but the accounts are balanced eventually. Although in theory these rates can be renegotiated for each order, in practice it is difficult for the weaker party to lift the rate and this is one reason why the incomes of workers (other than skilled carvers) have increased only slowly. Another important consequence of this payment system is that even small workshops have to keep track of a complicated cash flow and a complicated set of overlapping orders.

As we have shown elsewhere (Alexander and Alexander 2000) the internal organisation of Jepara workshops bears little resemblance to the 'family firms' described in the literature. It is not simply that the corporate basis of Jepara enterprises is weakly developed, although even the large workshops operate with little legal foundation other than a simple government licence, pay no taxes, keep few public records and, thus far, have seldom survived the death of their owners. More specifically – and in sharp contrast both to the so-called 'Chinese' pattern where enterprises are the property of the household, or even larger kinship group, and to a general scholarly tendency to treat peasant households as strongly corporate units – these Javanese enterprises are owned by individuals, not households. It is significant that the closest approximation to family firms – about half the medium-sised workshops which are run as partnerships between spouses – do not usually incorporate adult children, and the wife's involvement is also often intermittent, ceasing if the business expands or if she can obtain better returns from operating her own business. Indeed, in the small and medium workshops which produce items for the cheap end of the domestic retail market there is no suggestion of joint ownership; the wife 'buys' the product from her husband's workshop and keeps whatever she can obtain on resale. This partiality for separate rather than pooled incomes between spouses has been documented for a wide range of Javanese small industries in both the colonial and post-colonial periods (Alexander 1987, Alexander and Alexander 1991a, 1991b).

The Labour Force

When placed within the conventional categories of economic analysis, there is little that is remarkable about the men and women who work in the Jepara furniture industry. The labour force is predominately male and skilled; most of the women who are employed work as relatively unskilled sanders in the finishing warehouses. The labour-force is not segmented by age and, perhaps unexpectedly, there is very little child labour. Skilled workers, conventionally divided into carpenters and carvers, are all Javanese, as are most workshop owners. However, some of the owners of the export firms, as well as a few of their senior managerial staff, are Indonesian Chinese or foreigners. Before 1990, most of the labour was obtained locally, initially from the producing villages and later from other villages in the region. But during the last decade, increasing numbers of workers have been recruited from other regions in Central and East Java.

But such bald statements about the composition of the labour force – even when produced in the form of a table with apparently more precise numerical data – tell us very little about the dynamics of labour force formation. In fact, in the absence of a specific cultural context, this type of data promotes untenable inferences based on culturalist stereotypes.

Take gender, for example. Readers unfamiliar with Java might reasonably infer that the concentration of Jepara women in the worst paid, waged jobs reflects 'traditional' Javanese ideas on the position of women. Yet in Jepara, as elsewhere in Java, it is the multi-national factories which show a strong preference for women workers suggesting that the reasons for this characteristic of female employment must be sought as much in the attitudes of the employers – including their views on what constitutes 'traditional Javanese culture' – as in the attitudes of the employees (Saptari 1995). A little empirical investigation would show that 'Jepara' views on gender are complex, variable, and by no means consistent. While it is generally true that carving and carpentry are seen as male tasks and workshops are typically owned by men, there are women carvers, carpenters and workshop owners, and there is certainly no prohibition on women taking up well-paid work in other areas of the economy (Alexander 1998).

Rather than an inflexible system of prohibitions, notions of appropriate gender and age roles, like other aspects of culture, have to be treated as an evolving, and often contested, set of preferences. For example, it was noted above that some small and medium workshops are operated as partnerships between spouses. In these workshops the woman invariably handles the accounts and pays the employees, although she is no more likely to have formal clerical skills than her husband. Employing a non-relative as a clerk is not feasible for the smaller workshops, in part because it would cost too much, but mainly because the combination of rudimentary accounting and a complicated cash-flow present too many opportunities for fraud. This efficient solution to a managerial problem required some changes in conventional Javanese views of the appropriate behaviour between spouses. But the innovation was not an increased economic role for Javanese women; the innovation was the willingness of some Javanese women to surrender the possibility of establishing an independent business of their own and enter an economic partnership with their husband. It is also significant that very recently, well-educated children, mainly girls, have begun to take-over the managerial tasks from their mothers who have in turn re-established independent businesses. As we have discussed elsewhere (Alexander and Alexander 2000), notions of appropriate gender roles are changing so rapidly and so unevenly in Java that adjectives like 'modern' and 'traditional' are almost meaningless.

The relative absence of paid or unpaid child labour within the furniture industry, which might appear to be a further step towards modernity and a recognition of the 'rights of children,' is also a product of quite specific historical and industrial circumstances and owes little to Javanese notions of appropriate employment for children. Children from the wealthier households in the producing villages have been strongly encouraged by their parents to obtain formal educational qualifications and have no economic incentive to work at manual tasks. As elsewhere in Java, children from the much larger group of poor households are usually employed for much of the day, but in Jepara they work mainly in the handicraft workshops, as servants, or in the small food-stalls. The main reason for the lack of child employment in the furniture workshops is that the way tasks are organised, leaves little space for unskilled workers other than 'apprentices' and there is considerable competition for these opportunities to learn a trade.

The distinction between skilled and unskilled workers also needs to be contextualised; while all workers are skilled, some are certainly more skillful than others. Commodity production in Java has long been characterised by 'production-line' techniques in which even quite simple objects are broken down into components which can be rapidly – because repetitively – produced (Alexander 1987). In the pre-modern Jepara furniture industry, as in contemporary craft work, production often involved preliminary work by less skilled craftsmen, with the highly skilled workers adding the final touches. In the modern industry, these simple organisational principles have been refined to an amazing degree.

Although Jepara had an initial pool of highly skilled wood-workers, expansion depended both on increasing the number of skilled carvers and on lifting their output. Some of the methods were relatively straight-forward. Within workshops, for example, differentiating carving tasks in terms of the skill required, enabled apprentices to hone their skills on the simpler work, while expert carvers concentrated on the complicated designs to reach high levels of skill and speed. At a later stage, paper templates and pre-milled carving blanks further reduced the numbers of skilled workers performing less skilled tasks within the workshop. Payment by piece rates rewarded fast and skilful work. But the increasing specialisation of workshops was even more important in increasing labour productivity. Highly skilled workers – both those capable of very complicated carving such as the portraits for French antiques, and those capable of exceptional speed in producing simple components – opened their own workshops, thus facilitating continual work on exactly the same task and, consequently, higher returns.

Over a period of time, opportunities emerged for completely new skills – clerical workers including computer operators, machinists, container-packers, truck-drivers – and, apart from the clerical workers, few were waged employees. This is one of the reasons why, outside of the factories and the finishing warehouses, it is pointless to divide the workforce into employers or managers, as opposed to employees.

Hierarchies and the Control of Labour

Hierarchies of authority, income, and ethnicity are, of course, as prevalent in the Jepara furniture industry as they are in other arenas of Javanese society. But because of the way the industry is organised, the hierarchies which are significant for labour control are not easily mapped onto terms such as 'employer' and 'employee,' or 'contractor' and 'sub-contractor.'

Working conditions in a Jepara workshop are a world removed from the production line on a factory floor. Carvers and carpenters are typically allocated work which will take two or three days to complete, and left to organise the task as they think fit. In the smaller workshops, the owner usually works alongside other men, in the larger workshops he is often absent for much of the day; but in both cases there is little direct supervision. Each man appears to work at his own pace, although the knowledge that his colleagues require the components he produces exerts a subtle pressure. Working hours are only loosely set by broad social conventions concerning mealtimes, and individuals will often work late to complete a task, or take time off for private purposes. Social interaction among these small workforces is ordered by broad systems of meaning – kinship, gender, and age – rather than regulated by specific workplace roles such as 'boss' or 'worker.' But although workers have considerable autonomy in the workplace and there is little direct surveillance, it is important not to romanticise these working arrangements: physical working conditions are often sub-standard, and payment by piece-rates reduces incentives for direct supervision of work.

Economic hierarchies, as well as the contested systems of control which accompany these hierarchies, are more apparent in relationships between workshops. Both the official statistics and the government's development programmes refer to linked workshops as *bapak/anak angkat*; a terminology which is widely applied in Indonesia to a manager and his close subordinates, or to a core business and its branches. The literal meaning of *anak angkat* is 'foster child' and the terminology thus connotes an explicitly hierarchical relationship in which the *bapak* 'father' is expected to treat his adopted son generously and the son to meet, and if possible to anticipate, his father's wishes. The use of this term thus implies that the relationship will be long term and should not be subject to strictly economic calculations. *Bapak/anak angkat* relationships might thus be seen as a form of fictive kinship which uses the traditional norms of kinship to establish relationships of trust between otherwise unrelated persons.

But rather than simply a reflection of 'traditional' Javanese culture, the concept of *bapak/anak angkat* is a innovative product of the ideological activities of the not-so-New Order State (Bowen 1986, Alexander 1989) and seldom appears in colonial accounts of Javanese small industry (Alexander and Alexander 1991a, 1991b). A common practice within this ideological process has been the appropriation of kinship metaphors to promote hierarchical and patriarchal relationships. In as much as these practices can be described as 'traditional,' they were formerly much more common among the elite than among the population of the villages.

The implications of referring to relationships as *bapak/anak angkat* can best be examined by looking at an alternative term which is more popular among medium and small workshop owners. *Langganan* is a well-established term which is grounded in Javanese, and more generally Indonesian, popular culture (Siegel 1969, Alexander 1987, 1998). Usually glossed as 'regular customer' it encompasses a wide range of relationships: a child and the tricycle driver who carries her to school each day; a market-trader and the wholesaler who supplies her; a hotel and their regular guests can all be reciprocally described as *langganan*. The common element is that *langganan* relationships are always dyadic, and they are always constituted as reciprocal, even where one party is obviously more powerful or wealthier than the other. The terms of the metaphor resonate not with kinship but with Javanese notions of *tetangga:* an unbounded but localised, household-centred, category of persons linked by a wide range of dyadic exchanges, and symbolised by participation in the major local ritual, the *slametan* (Sullivan 1994). Although *langganan* relationships often link persons who are also attached in other ways – kinsmen, neighbours, friends – they continue only as long as both parties see them as beneficial, and every exchange of goods or services takes place at market prices. *Langganan* relationships facilitate a steady flow of work, the familiarity between the partners decreases the need for complex negotiations over prices and conditions, and payment need not be made immediately after each transaction. It is also common for one party to have a considerable standing debt to the other.

Whether the relationship between two linked workshops is characterised as *bapak/anak angkat* or *langganan* thus has important economic and social consequences, and it is not surprising that the appellation is often contested. Persons who acquiesce to the term *anak-angkat* in the presence of their *bapak* or when they are seeking government grants, might well repudiate it strongly on other occasions. Apart from the hierarchical implications, no small consideration for many fiercely independent Jepara Javanese, one important difference is that whereas the term *langganan* carries no moral implications of exclusivity, exclusivity is constitutive of *bapak/anak angkat* relationships: *bapak* can have many *anak angkat*, but an *anak angkat* should have only one *bapak*. In Jepara, therefore, the latter relationship thus involves an inherent conflict of interest: the *bapak* wants suppliers to work full-time on his orders; *anak angkat* can only expand by seeking other customers and are tempted to divert labour and finance from their *bapak*'s order to secure new customers. Another important economic difference between the two relationships is the role of credit. Although Jepara *langganan* might only hope for deposits, they do expect to be paid immediately on completion – albeit with a post-dated cheque. Long term credit is inseparable from *bapak/anak angkat* contracts: deposits accompany most orders and often progress payments are made as well. Sometimes the *bapak* financed the workshop or, more commonly, its expansion, often by using his larger business to obtain bank credit which is not available to smaller workshops.

As the Jepara industry developed, there has been a steady movement away from contracts recognised by both parties as *bapak/anak angkat* towards relationships which both parties acknowledge as *langganan*. Indeed specialised workshops such as sawmills operated in this way from the beginning. For some *bapak*, a major motive for the change was to routinise administration as the business expanded: for example, to substitute a single deposit and a final payment for the weekly flow of small cash sums. In addition, many of the major economic functions earlier served by the *bapak/anak angkat* relationship, such as the rapid diffusion of innovations, the flexible use of finance, and the substantial expansion of the labour force, are now being met by other means. The change was equally welcome to many of the subalterns who saw an explicit dependency relationship as hindering the possibility of expansion and as incompatible with their new-found economic success.

Payments

Stated in very broad terms, the principles governing payments between workshops are identical to those governing payments within workshops: a price is negotiated for a particular task, progress payments are made as the task is progressively completed, and the accounts are balanced at the end. However, the application of these broad principles in particular contexts results in a very wide range of empirical outcomes. The only general statement which can be made with any confidence is that waged labour is limited to the two categories of employees at either end of the hierarchy: both male and female administrative staff are paid a monthly salary (*gaji*) while the female sanders and male labourers are paid a daily wage.

At the present time, most workers describe themselves as being paid on piece rates (*borongan*). They keep a rough tally of the work they have completed and thus the money due to them. At regular periods, usually once a day, they receive a subsistence allowance (*uang makan*) which is deducted from the amount due to them. In the medium and larger workshops, skilled workers also get a payment (*bon mingguan*) which is arrived at by deducting the subsistence allowance from their approximate piece-rate earnings for the period. Usually this is a weekly payment, but might well be fortnightly or even monthly in smaller workshops. Strictly applied this system would normally result in employees having a small credit balance with their workshop, but it is complicated by advance payments (*utang*) for special purposes. Most skilled employees in the larger workshops have drawn at least a week's income in advance, while a skilled worker returning from a major holiday may be more than a month's earnings in debt.

In addition to these payments, employees are also provided with two snacks a day, and might be allowed to sleep in the workshop, but are seldom given meals. Continuing employees are paid an annual bonus before the major holiday of Lebaran and will also be paid a bonus if exceptionally long hours are required to meet a production deadline. However, individual workers, especially those from local households with several income earners, may reject all periodic payments in favour of a single payment on completion of the job. Moreover *borongan* payments are sometimes calculated on the basis of a team which might consist of two relatively equal partners, or more commonly, a skilled worker and an 'apprentice.' The 'team' make their own arrangements for the distribution of their earnings and apart from their physical location, such 'teams' are indistinguishable from small workshops.

The practice of piece-rates paid well in arrears was one reason why producers with very little capital were able to expand so quickly. In the early years expansion was financed as much from below – by harnessing income owed to labour – as it was by cash advances from the top. In the medium workshops, deposits from the exporters were used to buy wood and to pay daily subsistence allowances to their employees, as well as providing a deposit for the portion of the orders which were subcontracted. Smaller workshops had a 'credit balance' with the larger; that is, they were not paid in full for their work until the large workshop was paid by the exporter. But employees in these small workshops were themselves only paid allowances and typically had a credit balance with their employer throughout their period of employment. As the industry expanded and a back-log of orders emerged, credit balances shifted: medium workshops began using deposits on orders to finance their current production (not always for the same customer) and skilled employees began to obtain allowances and advances in excess of the money owed to them. Higher up the production chain, exporters also began to use the deposits on new orders to finance current production, but the main source of the considerable expansion of credit after 1988 was the loans obtained by the larger exporters from the commercial banks. Because this financial system depended so heavily on a delicately balanced cash-flow, it was very vulnerable to any slowdown in orders.

The complexity of this payment system makes it impossible to arrive at an accurate figure for the income of the average worker, let alone a robust estimate of labour's share of the total proceeds. It is possible, however, to analyse those structural features which advantage employers and employees respectively when they are bargaining over prices, and say something about the ways in which this balance has changed over the past decade.

In an industry with large numbers of both employers and employees, where there are relatively few barriers to changing jobs, and where production and profits are increasing, the market should be constantly adjusting the price of labour upward. Our observations over the past seven years suggest that employee incomes have risen, but the rises have been far more sporadic and uneven than conventional economics would suggest. In particular, piece-rates for the less skilled tasks, which comprise the work of most employees and thus should be easiest to price, have been amongst the slowest to increase and appear to differ little between workshops. The reasons for the lag in these rates, as with other 'traditional' rates, such as daily-paid agriculture labour, which have also been slow to rise, have less to do with adherence to some well-established cultural norms, than with disparities in bargaining power, for it is the rates which are set by regional governments, such as the daily wage for factory workers, which have been the slowest to increase.

While the payment system is in theory based on market principles, in practice the system and the records within which it is incorporated, strongly inhibits price increases. The smaller workshops only record their cash-flow and are not in a position to calculate their profits on a specific completed order. Moreover, because these workshops are often working on overlapping orders from the same customer, they tend not to balance the account on any one order, but rather to concentrate on balancing the supply of finished goods against payments over a period of one or two weeks. This has become particularly common now that most workshops have a debit balance with the exporters and is identical with the conventions used by small traders and wholesalers (Alexander 1987). This concentration on cash-flow inhibits employee-initiated wage increases in at least two important ways: it makes it difficult for employers to calculate the potential effects of an increase on their profits, and it removes any obvious social context in which employees might seek an increase. Consequently new orders tend to be accepted without discussion at the same price as the last one. An informative contrast can be drawn with the owners of small workshops who are also uninformed about export prices or the exact cost of raw materials, but routinely request a price increase every time they deliver a completed order.

In these circumstances it is not surprising that employees negotiating efforts are more commonly directed towards obtaining an additional advance than a wage increase in the strict sense, and that small workshops often seek a larger cash payment to buy wood (*bon kayu*) rather than an explicit price increase. An additional complication is that many employees are more concerned with their total return, rather than the piece-rate *per se*. Hours of work are not regulated and smaller workshops may find it difficult to provide as much continuous work as their employees would like. Moreover, even when piece-rates are stable productivity increases would tend to lift hourly earnings.

In fact it is easier to infer why labour prices do not increase, than explain the fact that they have, albeit slowly. The catalyst for an increase in piece-rates is usually an higher offer by an established workshop to a potential employee. If the offer is accepted, it quickly becomes the standard within the local circle of workshops. This in turn sparks a general request for an increase in the prices paid to workshops and a subsequent increase in wage-rates over the wider region. Eventually the increase trickles down to the rates set by the regional government.

In a broader sense, the leaders in the process of wage increases are those employees and small workshops which are not subject to the constraints on negotiating power discussed above. These include the small, machine-based workshops producing single items such as carving blanks, skilled carvers working alone on a limited range of tasks, and skilled carpenters employed by a workshop to assemble finished items. These small firms have both very little competition and a clear understanding of their costs and returns, so that they can renegotiate prices at regular intervals. Skilled carvers and carpenters, who can easily obtain work elsewhere and whose tasks are difficult to price also obtain regular increases. The incomes of very highly skilled carvers, for whom there is a chronic shortage, have probably risen considerably faster than the profits of workshop owners.

Conflict

Although physical working conditions are still very poor, especially in the smaller workshops, and incomes are low, there are few overt signs of industrial conflict. To some extent this is a product of the way in which the workshops are organised; the owners work alongside their employees and there is little direct supervision of labour, other than young or unskilled workers. There is no doubt that many persons prefer working in this environment, although they might earn more and would have a healthier working environment in a more regimented factory. But these workplaces are not free from conflict and disputes do arise, especially over piece-rates, the allocation of tasks, the continuity of work, and personal relationships.

One possible indication of dissatisfaction with working conditions is the high degree of labour mobility; men may work for as many as five workshops in a year. Much of this mobility is related to the inability of small workshops to provide continuous work, and people may return to a particular employer on several occasions. But the ability of skilled employees to readily obtain a job elsewhere means that they can resolve disputes by leaving. In the early years of the industry, employees usually owed money and it would be reasonable to expect that this hampered mobility, although people claim that leaving to seek a new position was not problematic. It is certainly true that the debts which most skilled workers now try to establish with their employers, do not prevent mobility. Indeed, the knowledge that it will be difficult for employers to recover these debts, gives the employee some bargaining powers in negotiating a rate increase.

Industrial conflict is more obvious in the larger, more factory-like, workplaces owned by exporters. Here the labour force is sharply divided between the managerial staff, mainly males, who are paid a monthly salary, and the daily paid workers. In most warehouses, the largest and worst paid group of employees are female sanders whose wage rates and conditions are set by the local government. The three important strikes in the last years of the New Order all involved women sanders, and despite some sharp wages increases, strikes by the sanders in individual warehouses have become much more common. Several of the largest firms which are not owned by Jepara Javanese, have reacted by trying to employ an all male workforce, because they regard women as unsettling, distracting, and more prone to strike action.

Although these 'factory' workforces were supposedly unionised under the New Order, union representatives were seldom seen in the workplace and their most important role was to participate in the process by which the regional government sets minimum wage rates and other working conditions. It is too early to tell whether new governments will create space for independent, representative, and viable unions. As in the past, most of the recent industrial disputes have concerned a perceived failure by the employers to live up to industrial agreements, especially a failure to pay minimum wages. As accurate information is difficult to acquire, rumours (which are often products of competition between the indigenous Indonesian Association of Furniture Industries (ASMINDO) and foreign-owned businesses) quickly become facts. Most disputes are short-lived, however and have been resolved by the employers promising to meet the regulations.

The more serious, and probably most common, industrial problems are less accessible to research by outsiders because they involve the harassment of individual workers by their supervisors. As in other Indonesian factories (Saptari 1991) the systematic disparities of power, age, gender, and ethnicity (but not in the Jepara case) between employees and their supervisors, gives the harassed worker no choice but to leave.

Concluding Remarks

Standing on a dusty rural road outside a modern Javanese textile or shoe factory, at the time when shifts change over, encourages even the least imaginative of observers to speculate on the processes of social change. Watching thousands of women – most of them young and most wearing a simple uniform – clamber into buses and trucks for the daily trip back to their home villages, raises obvious questions about this form of labour organisation and its consequences for other aspects of Javanese daily life. Every visible aspect of production, the uniforms, the factory buildings, and the high concrete fences, epitomise the modern. Thus these large, export-orientated, manufacturing plants, present themselves for analysis as innovations in labour organisation, recruitment, and control; as intrusions driven from the outside into village life.

A visit to a Jepara village involved in furniture production would evoke quite different emotions. Although much of the densely-settled land is covered with houses and workshops, the numerous coconut and fruit-trees, the occasional garden strip, and the flowers planted in every available pot, give it a pleasant, rather rural, aspect. The production sites are scattered among the residences; the small clusters of production workers are almost indistinguishable from other householders. Some, more prosperous, households have recently built substantial brick houses with tiled roofs, internal bathrooms and kitchens, but most houses are at least partially built from split bamboo and have thatched roofs. The workshops also vary from solid, brick structures, through bamboo lean-tos to mere spaces on verandahs. The most evocative feature is the smell: the fragrant scent of freshly cut teak; the dry, musty smell of mahogany sawdust; the astringent odour of glue. Production seems to be embodied in the 'traditional' and the analytical task to show how earlier methods of production have been adapted to contemporary ends.

But the analytical trope of the passive, traditional village reacting slowly to modern ways of ordering production introduced from outside is no longer instructive In fact, Javanese villagers have had a long history of export-orientated factory labour, especially factory-based processing of agricultural crops (Boomgaard 1991, White 1991), and women have always been prominent in the factory labour forces. Conversely, the Jepara woodworking industries are only one of many recent examples of rapid industrial growth based on closely linked production networks of relatively small firms which have developed out of earlier forms of rural commodity production. The remarkable ability of these networks of small firms to adapt successfully to changing economic circumstances, including the destruction of much of the Indonesian financial system in 1997 required radical innovations in products, production methods, finance, and labour relations.

These innovations drew on both Javanese social institutions and on new knowledge acquired from external sources. For example, standard templates and minute divisions of labour are common practices in Javanese industry; what was innovative was the creation of specific templates and working patterns to produce very specialised, complex, and hitherto unknown, commodities. Beginning with little more external information than a photograph provided by an overseas buyer, Javanese artisans developed innovative methods to breakdown complex commodities into simpler, and smaller, tasks. Over a long process of trial and error buyers' and producers' expectations were aligned, although the producers' ignorance of the final markets was matched by the buyers' ignorance of the production process. Simultaneously with the innovations in production methods, workshop-owners created complex sets of dyadic, market, relationships which made it possible for small firms with few employees and fewer funds to join together in the production of complex commodities, as well as to finance large-scale production of expensive items with very little capital. They also developed markets: local conventions governing aspects of transactions including price-setting and payment. As is described elsewhere (Alexander and Alexander forthcoming), the use of differing methods to set prices at various levels of the system, and the creation of various forms of 'money' - ranging from credit, through promissory notes, post-dated checks and deposit slips, to currency - quarantined currency fluctuations, helped to keep control of production in local hands, concealed profits, and reduced book-keeping.

Labour relations in Jepara can only be understood in this context of constant innovation. Our histories of individual workshops document steady change in labour relations in the period since Independence and an escalating pattern of change in the post 1987 era of export production. It may be true that many individual aspects of contemporary labour relations would be understandable to a Javanese of twenty, or even fifty, years ago; but these elements have been combined in into a new, efficient, and modern, system of labour practices.

References

Alexander, J. (1987) *Trade, Traders and Trading in Rural Java*, Singapore: Oxford University Press.

— (1998) 'Women traders in Javanese marketplaces', in R. Hefner (ed.) *Market Cultures: Society and Morality in the New Asian Capitalisms*, Boulder: Westview Press.

Alexander, J. and Alexander, P. (1991a) 'Protecting peasants from capitalism: the subordination of Javanese traders by the colonial state', *Comparative Studies in Society and History* 33, 2: 370–394.

— (1991b) 'Trade and petty commodity production in early twentieth century Kebumen', in P. Alexander, P. Boomgaard and B. White (eds.) *In the Shadow of Agriculture. Non-Farm Activities in the Javanese Economy, Past and Present*, Amsterdam: Royal Tropical Institute.

— (2000) 'From kinship to contract? Production chains in the Javanese woodworking industries', *Human Organisation* 59, 1: 106–116.

— (forthcoming) 'Inventing money, setting prices, creating markets. Notes of the "politics of value" in Jepara, Indonesia', in P. Geschiere and W. van Bimsbergen (eds.) *The Social Life of Things Revisited*, London: Curzon.

Alexander, P. (ed.) (1989) *Creating Indonesian Cultures*, Sydney: Oceania Publications.

Beneria, L. and Roldan, M. (1987) *The Crossroads of Class and Gender: Industrial Homework, Subcontracting and Household Dynamics in Mexico City*, Chicago: University of Chicago Press.

Blim, M.L. (1992) 'Small-scale industrialisation in a rapidly changing world market', in F.A. Rothstein and M.L. Blim (eds.) *Anthropology and the Global Factory: Studies of the New Industrialisation in the Late Twentieth Century*, New York: Bergin and Garvey.

Boomgaard, P. (1991) 'The non-agricultural side of an agricultural economy: Java, 1500–1900', in P. Alexander, P. Boomgaard and B. White (eds.) *In the Shadow of Agriculture: Non-farm Activities in the Javanese Economy, Past and Present*, Amsterdam: Royal Tropical Institute.

Booth, A. (1992) 'Introduction', in A. Booth (ed.) *The Oil Boom and After: Indonesian Economic Policy and Performance in the Soeharto Era*, Singapore: Oxford University Press.

Bowen, J. (1986) 'On the political construction of tradition: *gotong royong* in Indonesia', *Journal of Asian Studies* 45: 545–561.

Bull, A. and Corner, P. (1993) *From Peasant to Entrepreneur: The Survival of the Family Economy in Italy*, Oxford: Berg.

Gates, H. (1996) *China's Motor: A Thousand Years of Petty Capitalism*, Ithaca: Cornell University Press.

Goodman, E. (1989) 'Introduction: the political economy of the small firm in Italy', in E. Goodman and J. Bamford (eds.) *Small Firms and Industrial Districts in Italy*, London: Routledge.

Greenhalgh, S. (1994) 'De-orientalising the Chinese family firm', *American Ethnologist* 21, 4: 746–775.

Hamilton, G. (1998) 'Culture and organisation in Taiwan's market economy', in R. Hefner (ed.) *Market Cultures: Society and Morality in the New Asian Capitalisms*, Boulder: Westview Press.

Hill, H. (1994) 'The Economy', in H. Hill (ed.) *Indonesia's New Order: The Dynamics of Socio-economic Transformation*, Sydney: Allen and Unwin.

– (1996) *The Indonesian Economy Since 1996: Southeast Asia's Emerging Giant*, Cambridge: Cambridge University Press.

Kantor Perdagangan (1994) *Realisasi Ekspor Kabupaten Jepara Tahun 1987 1994*, Jepara: Kantor Perdagangan.

Kantor Pedagangan (1998) *Realisasi Ekspor Kabupaten Jepara Tahun 1994–1998*, Jepara: Kantor Perdagangan.

Kriedte, P., Medick, H. and Schlubohm, J. (1981) *Industrialisation before Industrialisation: Rural Industry in the Genesis of Capitalism*, Cambridge: Cambridge University Press.

Mackie, J. (1988) 'Overseas Chinese entrepreneurship', *Asian-Pacific Economic Literature* 6: 41–64.

Mills, M.E. (1997) 'Contesting the margins of modernity: women, migration and consumption in Thailand', *American Ethnologist* 24: 37–61.

Ong, A. (1990) 'Japanese factories, Malay workers: class and sexual metaphors in West Malaysia', in J.M. Atkinson and S. Errington (eds.) *Power and Difference: Gender in Island Southeast Asia*, Stanford: Stanford University Press.

Pedersen, P.O., Sverrisson, A. and van Dijk, M.P. (eds.) (1994) *Flexible Specialisation: The Dynamics of Small-scale Industries in the South*, London: Intermediate Technology Publications.

Piore, M. and Sabel, C.F. (1984) *The Second Industrial Divide: Possibilities for Prosperity*, New York: Basic Books.

Rabellotti, R. (1994) 'Industrial districts in Mexico: The case of the footwear industry in Guadalajara and Leon', in P.O. Pederson, A. Sverrisson and M.P. van Dijk (eds.) *Flexible Specialisation: The Dynamics of Small-scale Industries in the South*, London: Intermediate Technology Publications.

Redding, G. (1990) *The Spirit of Capitalism*, Berlin: Walter de Gruyter.

Sandee, H., Rietveld, P., Hendrawan Supratikno and Prapto Yuwono (1994) 'Promoting small scale and cottage industries in Indonesia: an impact analysis for Central Java', *Bulletin of Indonesian Economic Studies* 30: 115–142.

Saptari, R. (1991) 'The differentiation of a rural industrial labour force', in P. Alexander, P. Boomgaard and B. White (eds.) *In the Shadow of Agriculture: Non-Farm Activities in the Javanese Economy, Past and Present*, Amsterdam: Royal Tropical Institute.

— (1995) 'Rural Women to the Factories: Continuity and Change in East Java's Kretek Cigarette Industry', PhD Thesis, University of Amsterdam.

Siegel, J. (1969) *The Rope of God*, Los Angeles: University of California Press.

Simmons, C.P. and Kalantaridis, C. (1994) 'Flexible specialisation in the southern European periphery: the growth of garment manufacturing in Peonia County, Greece', *Comparative Studies in Society and History* 36: 649–675

Sullivan, N. (1994) *Masters and Managers: A Study of Gender Relations in Urban Java*, Sydney: Allen and Unwin.

White, B. (1991) 'Economic diversification and agrarian change in rural Java, 1900–1990', in P. Alexander, P. Boomgaard and B. White (eds.) *In the Shadow of Agriculture: Non-Farm Activities in the Javanese Economy, Past and Present*, Amsterdam: Royal Tropical Institute.

Williamson, O.E. (1975) *Markets and Hierarchies, Analysis and Antitrust Implications: A Study in the Economics of Internal Organisation*, New York: Free Press.

Wolf, D.L. (1992) *Factory Daughters: Gender, Household Dynamics and Rural Industrialisation in Java*, Berkeley: University of California Press.

Zukin, S. and DiMaggio, P. (1990) *Structures of Capital: The Social Organization of the Economy*, Cambridge: Cambridge University Press.

9

Transforming Industrial Relations: The Case of the Malaysian Auto Industry

PETER WAD

The decentralisation of collective bargaining has been a significant trend in Western labour markets during the 1980s and 1990s, and it has challenged conventional trade union strategies and practices in many ways. In the same period we have witnessed a decentralisation of trade union organisations in East Asian market economies. The decentralisation of whole industrial relations systems, i.e. bargaining and organisational decentralisation among and between employers and trade unions, is a more unique phenomenon and very little studied. The Malaysian auto industry provides an organisational field where the trend towards double decentralisation emerged during the 1980s and continued in the 1990s, without becoming a completely decentralised system.

To understand changing industrial relations systems it is important to consider it as a system of multiple social actors, who interpret, act, and interact with other actors in accordance with their position, strategic outlook, and perception of the concrete situation. Industrial relations thereby evolve in a contextual and situational frame of political-economic power relations and socio-cultural institutions of meaning and interaction. Taking advantage of this approach this chapter aims to explore the industrial relations dynamics behind the trend toward industrial relations decentralisation in the Malaysian auto industry in order to explain the forces behind changing industrial relations and especially the role played by industrial and enterprise unions.

Taking one sub-sector (the transport equipment industry and especially the auto sub-industry) as its focus, the analysis will span the period from the late 1960s to the Malaysian crisis at the end of the 1990s, which covers more than two business cycles and a turbulent period of Malaysian political economy and trade union development (Jomo 1993, Jomo and Todd 1994, Rasiah 1995, Khoo 1997, Rasiah and Hofmann 1998). The argument is based on research evidence at the industry and organisational levels of the Malaysian manufacturing sector and auto industry during the 1980s and late 1990s. Most of the material was collected by the author during field research in Malaysia in 1995, 1996, 1997 and 1999, supplemented with material from earlier research in 1983, 1984 and 1987.[1]

The chapter is structured in the following way. The political, economic, and social history of the contemporary Malaysian industrial relations system is briefly outlined, providing the background for the development of the Malaysian auto industry, and the changing industrial relations of the auto industry. These changes are periodised by the centralisation of the industrial relations system 1971–81 and the decentralisation of the system due to the collapse of decentralised collective bargaining and the rise of enterprise unionism from 1982 onwards. This will be followed by an examination of the dynamics of Malaysian industrial relations which are explained in terms of their related social actors: labour, employers and government authorities, and more encompassing systems of political power, such as business restructuring and crisis. The final point will outline the conclusions of the findings.[2]

The History Of Malaysian Industrial Relations

Malaysia became incorporated into expanding European capitalism from the early sixteenth century. This inclusion evolved through mercantilism (1500–1850s) driven by the Portuguese and the Dutch, colonialism driven by the British (1850s–1930s and 1945–57) and the Japanese (1941–45), post-colonial industrialisation (1960s) and ethno-nationalist economic development (1971-present). A productive market economy was built during British colonialism with the establishment of capitalist plantation and mining export industries, based on immigrant Indian and Chinese labour. During the 1970s and 1980s the political-economic strategy (New Economic Policy, or NEP) sought to modernise the rural Malay population by providing jobs, housing and formal education in urban areas.

Positive discrimination in favour of the *Bumis* (comprising Malays and indigenous populations) continued in a less rigid form with the National Development Policy (NDP 1991–2000), influenced by the deregulation and liberalisation

1 Thanks to trade unionists from industrial unions, enterprise unions, and labour centres plus employers, representative for employers associations and state agencies, and researchers for invaluable information and discussions throughout the years. My deepest appreciation goes to the NUTEAIW and its officers, employees, and members. Through the years Arokia Dass, Syed Shahir and Gopalkishnam have provided me with hospitality, experience, and critical reflections on the Malaysian industrial relations system in general and the auto industry in particular, yet the responsibility for the outcome rests with me.

2 Interviews were made and transcribed and modified into written English by the author. The abbreviation 'IP' stands for 'interview person'.

measures applied during the economic crisis 1985-86 and the booming economy around 1990. In 1991 the *Bumis* came to be the dominant Malaysian labour force in agriculture, forestry and fishing (72 per cent), manufacturing (52 per cent) and services (56 per cent)(Population and Housing Census, Malaysia 1995 table 1.1). Yet, in 1995 immigrant workers probably reached 30-40 per cent of the workforce in agriculture, forestry and fishing, 13 per cent in manufacturing, and 30-40 per cent in construction (Edwards 1997: 18).

In post-colonial Malaysia industrial policies have been changing from a regime of import substitution in the 1960s to a dual policy of import substitution and export oriented industrialisation during the 1970s to the 1990s, moving into heavy and chemical industrialisation during the 1980s with Japan and South Korea as models of development. In the wake of this 'Look East' policy, which has meant a developmental re-orientation from the West (United Kingdom) to the East (Japan and South Korea), the Malaysian government introduced the policy of enterprise ('in-house') unions in 1983 (Wad 1988).

The rationale of the government's in-house union policy is the same today as it was at the time of inception. The government claims that, contrary to the Western model of industrial unionism, the Japanese model of enterprise unionism facilitates company loyalty and corporate mentality, management-labour collaboration, productivity orientation of employees, mutual sharing and industrial harmony at the enterprise level. Hence, enterprise unionism facilitates company profitability, labour benefits and national economic development.

Critics point out that in-house unions in comparison with industrial unions are 'company unions,' i.e. weak, 'yellow' or management-controlled lapdogs, more or less unable to defend and improve employees' rights and interests, and that they may even not be 'dynamically efficient' in the sense that they do not provide for concomitant wage and productivity increases (Standing 1991, 1992a, 1992b; for an alternative view Wad 1996, 1997a, 1998).

The legacy of trade unionism dates back to the formation of centralised trade unionism during British colonialism, based on the development of Chinese and Communist controlled labour organisations during the 1930s and 1940s. The trade unions were organised as general unions, based on geographical criteria across trades and industries and united under a central leadership. The general union movement became illegal in 1947-48 clashing with the returning British colonial authorities, who tried to instigate a British reformist labour movement composed of a British-like labour party and sector-wide unions (trade, industry, occupation). What were sustained were the nation-wide industrial unions, which had strongholds in the plantation estates and commercial sectors and even evolved into centralised industrial relations systems, when employers formed nation-wide associations and engaged in industry level collective bargaining.

After the fall of the centralised Communist controlled trade union movement the post-colonial government continued the British labour policy, aiming for the extermination of 'political unionism'. The Malaysian government prohibited 'outsiders' from being elected as trade union officers, demanding at least three years of work experience from the field of union jurisdiction; it required formal registration of an organisation, constituted on an economistic mission and increasingly prohibited unions from supporting political parties. The industrial relations laws regulating collective bargaining between trade unions and employers and their federations were tightened until the 1980s, providing for an enterprise regime, where management prerogatives prevailed and an elaborated system of compulsory conciliation and arbitration was developed, based on employment legislation and registered collective agreements. Finally, national labour centres were only allowed to exist in the form of 'societies' without collective bargaining rights. Although trade union centres sometimes were invited to participate in tripartite bodies, the trade union movement was mainly perceived and treated as part of the political opposition by the ruling coalition, headed by the United Malays National Organisation (UMNO).

The era of industrial unionism lasted until the late 1980s. The trend of the 1970s towards industrial unionism in the strategically important manufacturing sector changed towards enterprise unionism after the announcement of the government's legitimation of enterprise unionism, although industrial unions still dominated the trade union movement in manufacturing (Wad 1997b). Enterprise unionism proliferated during the 1980s, located primarily in the public sector, but also increasingly in the manufacturing sector.

In sum, the Malaysian system of industrial relations was decentralised in both relational and organisational terms in the long term. Centralised collective bargaining withered with the economic and employment decline of the plantation industry, and the removal of centralised bargaining in the manufacturing and service industries. Centralised unionism (and union density) declined from its peak in the general unionism of 1947-48, while enterprise unions mushroomed during the 1980s.

Yet, in absolute terms union membership grew and changed in terms of sector composition. Moreover, the trade union centre, the Malaysian Trades Union Congress (MTUC), is still dominated by the larger national unions, and the trade union field in Malaysia is today composed of pluralistic and competing union organisations, engaged in enterprise-based collective bargaining with individual employers. The economic crisis in 1997-99 did not seem to change that situation overnight.

The Development of the Malaysian Auto Industry

The Recipe for National Auto Industrialisation

The auto industry has been considered the 'industry of industries' of the twentieth century due to its scale and spin-off effects (Dicken 1998: 316). It was perceived as a core component of national economic development strategies in the North until the first oil crisis in the 1970s and in the South until recently. The strategy to form a national auto industry in developing countries had to follow more or less a particular sequence of national auto industrial development (adapted after Dicken 1998: 318):

Stage 1 Import of completely built-up (CBU) vehicles by local distributors.
Stage 2 Assembly of semi- or completely knocked-down (CKD) vehicles by subsidiaries or licensed or franchised domestic companies, importing parts and components from the brand corporation.
Stage 3 Assembly of CKD vehicles but with increasing local content.
Stage 4 Full-scale manufacture of automobiles, at first for a protected domestic market, secondly for the export market and thirdly for transplants in these export markets, meaning that the sequence is repeated by Southern auto transnational corporations.

The evolution of the Malaysian auto industry did in fact follow this sequence, which again related to the industrialisation policies of import substitution regarding transport vehicles from the 1960s and heavy and chemical industrialisation from the 1980s.

The Malaysian Auto Industry Until the Crisis 1997-99

Induced by Malaysian import substitution incentives major Western and Japanese automobile transnational corporations (TNCs) relocated auto assembly production to Malaysia from 1967 to 1977. At first the TNC auto manufacturers relied on TNC trading and/or assembling companies which were well established in the regional car market (e.g. Singapore Chinese controlled Cycle & Carriage, UK agency house Borneo Motors/Inchcape, Australian trading company Wearne Brothers). This implied that domestic companies obtained licences to sell and/or assemble TNC makes and models, and local sales companies and assemblers formed capital alliances in order to do so (e.g. Champion Motors/Assembly Services, Associated Motor Industries, Cycle & Carriage Bintang, Kelang Pembina Kerata-Kerata (KPKK), Tan Chong Motor Assemblers) (Torii 1991). A few European TNC auto manufacturers (Peugeot, Volvo) set up joined ventures with capital invested by their parent company. Capital Motor (later Oriental Assemblers), in possession of the licenses from Honda and Opel, was the only case where a domestic assembly company was set up without capital affiliation to car traders or

TNC auto manufacturers, and General Motors took over the company as a fully owned subsidiary for the period 1971 to 1980.

In the 1970s Japanese cars ousted Western cars in the Malaysian market, and the Malaysian car assembly companies began a restructuring process, which continued into the 1980s. Being an industry controlled by Western manufacturing and trading companies at the outset, the Japanese auto manufacturers had captured the market in alliance with domestic owned ethnic Chinese companies in the early 1980s. Nissan initiated this transformation as early as the mid-1970s, when it transferred the license from Swedish Motor Assemblies (Volvo) to Tan Chong Motor Holdings, controlled by the ethnic Chinese Tan family; Tan Chong provided Nissan with a minority share, and later on Tan Chong restructured the Tan Chong Motor Assemblies to include *Bumi* equity participation. General Motors sold its subsidiary assembler to Oriental Holdings, which formed an alliance with Honda to assemble Honda, General Motors and Isuzu vehicles. Lacking *Bumi* capital Ichcape Holdings lost the Toyota franchise to ethnic Chinese controlled UMW in 1981, which again formed an alliance with Toyota as a minority shareholder. In 1984 Wearne Brothers sold Associated Motor Industries (AMI) and the franchise of Ford to Ford Motor Company (Malaysia) (renamed AMIM), a joint venture of a *Bumi* majority owned company (Pernas Sime Darby, PSD) and Ford Motor Company (USA). PSD took control when Ford (USA) sold 29 per cent of Ford Motor Company Malaysia to PSD in 1986 (Interview 1987). In 1987, Pernas-Sime Darby restructured their auto companies into Tractors, owning AMIM with Ford as minority shareholder (30 per cent).

In the early 1980s, a hybrid of Japanese TNCs and ethnic Chinese family businesses evolved in the Malaysian corporate auto sector, controlling assembling, spare parts production, marketing, and distribution, but it was a sub-system of the TNCs global reach. Thereby the Malaysian auto industry was subordinated to the global and regional strategies of the auto TNCs and especially the largest Japanese auto TNCs (Toyota, Nissan and Honda). This situation was to be changed by the Malaysian government under Prime Minister Mahathir Mohamad, embarking on a heavy industrialisation strategy in the early 1980s and spearheaded by the state-owned holding company, Heavy Industries Corporation of Malaysia (HICOM). The state-led Malaysian car project, Proton, a joint venture between HICOM and Japanese Mitsubishi, succeeded in becoming the dominant market player in 1987 in the wake of the economic crisis 1985-86, the collapse of the car market, and the return to operational managerial control by the Japanese (Wad 1999). Tariffs and taxation provided Proton with a subsidised monopoly position in the domestic market.

The 1987-95 period signalled a transition period, based on an alliance between the Malaysian state and selected foreign TNCs (Mitsubishi, Toyota, and Citroen). The ethnic Chinese UMW-Toyota alliance changed to a *Bumi* PNB-Toyota alliance, when the *Bumi*-controlled trust fund, PNB, bought out UMW, which had financial troubles due to the economic crisis. In 1992 the UMW formed a joint venture (Perodua) with other companies and notably the Japanese technology supplier, the Daihatsu Motor Company (affiliated to Toyota), which thereby became the second Malaysian car project, manufacturing the Kancil. Meanwhile, Proton upgraded from the assembling of imported key components and parts to increased local manufacturing of components, introduced mechanical assembling lines and team work and aimed for just-in-time delivery from a network of local subcontractors comprising a rising share of *Bumi* small and medium sized companies. However, the more advanced technology and organisational design did not operate smoothly, the production system was not based on team production, and the production technology did not in practice include design and development of critical systems, meaning that Proton remained as a hybrid combining its own brand with original equipment manufactured by the application of Mitsubishi technology and design (*Far Eastern Economic Review* 1996.05.02, Rasiah 1996).

Both national car producers were companies within state-controlled diversified business groups, controlling car manufacturing vertically and horizontally, relating to other sectors: Proton via HICOM to steel, cement etc.; Perodua via UMW to agricultural and construction machinery, property, trade, and financing. A new state-controlled sector business system was in the making, but its major component, Proton, was subsequently privatised in line with the government's privatisation policy. In 1995 the controlling share of HICOM was bought by Yahya Ahmad, the owner of the auto assembler Diversified Resources Bhd. (DRB) and a *Bumi* businessman with auto industry competence and experience. Proton and DRB had allied with French Citroen to manufacture a new car make (Proton Tiara), based on French technology and design, in order to upgrade technologically and freeing itself from Japanese technological control.

Having bought HICOM, Yahya controlled a huge, diversified conglomerate with its core in the auto industry, and with potential for vertical and horizontal market co-ordination. The new chief executive officer took a set of initiatives, including the buying of a UK-based company (Lotus) with capability in auto design. However, a helicopter crash in March 1997 killed Yahya and his wife and brought a successful Malay business story to a tragic end, making Yahya's management an intermezzo in the history of Proton. With the death of Yahya the state returned as the controlling agency of Proton, installing a new top management, which soon faced the worst economic crisis in post-Independence Malaysia. At that time Proton had embarked on a plan to build the first genuine Malaysian designed model to be manufactured in the new 'Proton city' with the application of an advanced modular production system and in co-operation with internationally branded TNC suppliers.

The Impasse of National Auto Industrialisation

The developmental potential of national auto industries has been questioned recently (Humphrey 1998). At least three trends during the 1980s and 1990s make it increasingly difficult to establish and develop viable and international competitive auto manufacturing companies and clusters. First, the auto industry has turned into a very globalised and Northern TNC-controlled industry, demanding enormous investments for continuous innovation and product development in an increasingly liberalised and internationalised market. The recurring over-capacity of the industry has induced the formation of alliances, mergers and acquisitions, which has eradicated the British-owned auto manufacturers and has recently swept over the entire industry, subordinating large TNCs like Chrysler, Mitsubishi, Nissan, Saab and Volvo (passenger car division) to other TNCs like Daimler Benz, Renault, and Ford.

Second, auto manufacturing was an assembly industry, and standardised mass production became the paradigm of production from the 1910s (Ford's assembly line) to the 1970s. During the 1970s a flexible mass production system evolved in Japan and spread to other countries in the 1980s and 1990s. It was baptised 'lean production' (Womack et al. 1990) and was customer driven, integrating marketing, design, and production in a work organisation based on team work, and a supplier network based on outsourcing, Just-In-Time (JIT) delivery and tiering of suppliers into first, second and third grades of suppliers. This 'lean' system is now moving in the direction of modular production, while Northern TNCs are considering withdrawal from production and are instead increasingly turning to research and development, marketing, and financing.

Third, the change among Western TNCs from vertical integration to outsourcing, JIT, and supplier tiering induced the growth of auto parts and component companies into transnational companies and led the auto assemblers to divest their component subsidiaries. The outcome was the rise of first tier auto component TNCs in close collaboration with the TNC assemblers and coordinating the supplier tier down the line. The evolution undercuts the formation of Southern suppliers through localisation, because the TNC assemblers demand follow-sourcing from their first tier TNC suppliers, implying that indigenous suppliers are increasingly forced to merge or ally with TNC suppliers or exit the market.

These trends are reversing the expected development sequence of a country's auto industry from CBU import to full-scale manufacturing with CBU export. Under the present global conditions a sequence of de-indigenisation is more likely, and the East Asian financial crisis 1997-99 could be a decisive blow to national auto industries in the region, including the Malaysian national car projects.

The East Asian Crisis and the Malaysian Auto Industry

A domestic market-oriented auto industry is typically an industry which 'overreacts' to cyclical up-swings and down-swings, and this also happened in the late 1990s in Malaysia. While overall production (GNP) declined 6.8 per cent (in domestic value) in 1998, the sales value of the auto manufacturers fell by 62 per cent, and the physical production of motor vehicles (in units) fell 63 per cent with motorcycles and scooters declining by 41 per cent (DOS 1999). Among the auto companies the 'non-national' enterprises nearly vanished with a free fall of 85 per cent of production in 1998, while Proton faced a decline of 57 per cent and Perodua 43 per cent only (Wad 1999).

Employment fell considerably too, but less dramatically than production. The labour force of the auto manufacturers/assemblers dropped by 32 per cent, the auto parts/components manufacturers by 28 per cent and manufacturers of motorcycles and scooters by 20 per cent (DOS 1999). Again the national auto manufacturers only had a manpower reduction between 10-15 per cent while the labour force of the 'non-national' producers dropped by nearly 40 per cent. All in all the auto companies did not match the fall of production with a similar retrenchment of employees, but the labour costs among the auto manufacturers were reduced with paid salary and wages decreasing by 37 per cent from 1997 to 1998 (DOS 1999, the DOS-figures on auto parts/components and motorcycles/scooters are not compatible from 1997 to 1998). The cost-reduction in remuneration compared with employment indicates that the cuts hit overtime and various benefits as well as jobs. Within the unionised sector collective agreements destined for renewal were typically extended on the same terms as the old, and eventually only extended temporarily: the important thing was to save jobs.

This 'inflexible' response in a rational business interpretation makes an imprint on productivity within the auto manufacturing sub-industry. In 1997 the level lay at twenty-four units/employees/year and it went down to thirteen units/employee/year in 1998. Comparing 'non-national' companies with 'national companies' the productivity of the former decreased from eighteen units/employee/year to four, while productivity at Proton fell from thirty-four to seventeen and at Perodua from twenty-seven to eighteen (data compiled by the author 1999). These figures also reflect how both the national and the non-national auto manufacturers were unable to increase export in response to the collapsing domestic market. This inability especially concerns Proton, because it was the only company that had the opportunity and a long-term strategy for export promotion.

The turnaround of the industry and the economy in 1999 was caused by several factors in sequence or combination: the early crisis management led by finance minister, Anwar Ibrahim; the controversial currency and capital control policy, led by the prime minister Mahathir Mohamad and his chief economic adviser, Daim Zainuddin. This was combined with expanding public demand and selective support of ailing companies and industries, including the national and later also the non-national auto manufacturers. Also important were growing markets for Malaysian export (USA, Europe), and the regional economic rebound in East and Southeast Asia generally. Meanwhile, Anwar Ibrahim and his faction were ousted from UMNO and either jailed (Anwar) or reorganised in the National Justice Party, a new multi-ethnic political party headed by Wan Azizah, the wife of Anwar Ibrahim.

The Centralisation of the Auto Industrial Relations System

The development of the auto industry was followed by the formation and centralisation of an industrial relations system, generated by its two key actors in the 1970s: the automobile workers union (TEAIEU, later NUTEAIW)[3] and the automobile employers' association (the Motor Vehicle Assemblers Association, West Malaysia, MVAA).[4] An industrial union of supervisors played a minor role during the 1980s.[5]

The Industrial Workers Union

The auto worker's industrial union became registered in 1971 as the Transport Equipment and Allied Industries Employees Union, West Malaysia (TEAIEU). This event took place after an abortive attempt to unionise the Raleigh bicycle factory in 1969 by the Metal Industry Employees Union (MIEU) and industrial

3 TEAIEU is the Transport Equipment and Allied Industries Employees Union, West Malaysia. The name was changed in 1989 to the National Union of Transport Equipment and Allied Industries Workers (NUTEAIW), because the TEAIEU was often confused with another union, the Transport Workers' Union (TWU).

4 The MVAA is often mixed up with the MMVAA (the Malaysian Motor Vehicle Assemblers Association), which is the trade association of private assemblers in Malaysia. The TEAIEU is also often mixed up with the MVAA and MMVAA.

5 A new industrial union of supervisors was registered in 1981: The Motor Assemblers Supervisory Staff Union Peninsular Malaysia (MASSU). It started with seven members in 1981 (enough to register a trade union), but jumped to 195 (registered and in benefit) members the next year, the highest membership ever. At this point of time the MASSU had organised five factories: AMI, SMA, Assembly Services (ASSB), CCB, OA. The membership of MASSU decreased to 139 in 1986 and nearly collapsed in the years to come, down to sixty-seven in 1987 to bottom with twenty-nine in 1994. In 1996 the national union only had members in AMI and SMA, two factories located as neighbours in Shah Alam, Selangor. The union density is anyway 100 per cent among the supervisors at these two companies. However, the AMI management wants the supervisors to form an in-house union, but they did not provide a package of incentives which was satisfactory. Otherwise they might have agreed. The leadership of the small national union of supervisors, the MASSU, explained the membership decline by the following factors (interview 1995): the economic recession whereby more than seventy supervisors were retrenched; promotion of supervisors to executive positions (Cycle & Carriage 1988 and Oriental Assemblers 1989); formation of in-house union (Assembly Services 1991).

unrest among several auto assembly factories. The labour activists joined together and established the TEAIEU, organising 800 employees while awaiting the decision of the Registrar of the Trade Unions (RTU) for registration. Having been legalised the union soon faced external and internal problems: the formation of the employers' association (MVAA) in 1973, and factional conflicts in the union.

The founding leadership of TEAIEU was toppled by a radical and democratic-oriented group of employees, which transformed the union into an organisation with a strong workplace based structure, securing employee representatives from all major companies in the executive committee of the union, decentralised union activities and workers education programmes. This faction gained full control of the union, broadened its base, and continued to run the union with certain shifts in unionised companies, membership, and leadership. The general secretary, Arokia Dass, held the position until he was jailed for more than a year 1987–9 in Operation Lalang in November1987, whereby the Mahathir-regime suppressed opposition forces inside and outside the ruling coalition and civil society.[6] Dass recalls that the constituting principle of the union was:

> Our main code was that the power of the union had to remain always with the shopfloor workers, that the soul of the union was in the work-site committees, and that all decisions had to be taken by these committees. They were comprised of ordinary workers, elected every year by their peers on the floor. Weekly meetings of these committees were held to review events on the shopfloor. Apart from occasional disputes, the executive council concerned itself mainly with collective bargaining. If a major issue arose that necessitated the involvement of the executive council, members of the work-site committee would participate in the meetings with plant management (Dass 1991: 131).

The union successfully organised all assembly companies in Peninsular Malaysia in the 1970s: Asia Automobile Industries (AAI) (Mazda), Associated Motor Industries (AMI) (Ford), Assembly Services (AS) (Toyota), Cycle & Carriage Bintang (CCB) (Mercedes-Benz), General Motors (GM), Kilang Pembina Kereta-Kereta (KPKK) (Mitsubishi), Swedish Motor Assemblies (SMA) (Volvo), and Tan Chong Motor Assemblies (TCMA) (Nissan). Moreover, the union had also organised bicycle assembly factories, including the Raleigh Cycle company, and various component manufacturing enterprises. However, the union faced resistance from employers and reluctant employees, and the RTU sometimes opposed registration of organised factories within the union area of jurisdiction. For example, in the mid-1970s the RTU did not allow the union to represent the employees at two companies producing motor-cycle batteries and bicycle tyres and tubes respectively, although it had the majority of employees as members (Dass 1991: 43).

6 The executive secretary, Syed Shahir, has been with the union since the 1970s, and the AMI work-site committee delivered the new general secretary of the 1990s, Gopalkrishnam.

In the early 1970s the union tried to organise the UMW corporation, but the pro-tem committee at the company was exposed to the management and all members were dismissed. Union boycott of the company and demonstrations were met with union busters, and the union lost out. Later (1974) the employees established an in-house union which became member of the Malaysian Trade Unions Congress (MTUC).

At that time the TEAIEU was very critical towards MTUC, holding it responsible for the drop in union density (11 per cent compared to 67 per cent in 1947) and calling it 'a tool of capitalists for its own end' (TEAIEU 1977: 47). Together with eleven other trade unions TEAIEU disaffiliated from the MTUC in 1977 aiming to form an alternative labour centre, the Congress of Industrial Unions, but this was blocked by the authorities and the initiative withered (Dass 1991: 96, Jomo and Todd 1994: 138). Instead the union joined the international labour network, Asian Workers Solidarity Link, in the early 1980s (Dass 1991: 165), and finally, it ran a Workers Education Programme with Sahabat Alam Malaysia (Friends of the Earth, Malaysia), a very active environmental non-governmental organisation. In the early 1990s the auto workers union returned to the MTUC and became a very active member of the opposition within the labour centre.

The Employers' Association

The MVAA registered in 1973, and the first collective agreement (CA) between the MVAA and the TEAIEU was signed.[7] This CA covered the period 1973-75. The second CA was signed in November 1976 for the period January 1976-December 78, the third CA for the period January 1979-December 1981, and the fourth CA for January 1982-December 1984. The involvement of MVAA members in the CA was kept at a high level in 1976 (seven members) and 1979 (eight members; the new participant was Automotive Industries), but in 1981 the employers' federation fell apart. This brought an end to centralised collective bargaining between centralised actors in the auto industry, because the split among the employers started a process whereby the employers' association lost power and eventually faulted (see below). But other forces also generated a tendency toward a total decentralisation of the auto industrial relations system.

The Decentralisation of the Auto Industrial Relations System

Employer Driven Decentralisation

In the fourth CA of 1982-84 the MVAA participating members were reduced to five companies (AAI, AMI, CCB, OA, SMA) although actual membership counted

7 I have no exact information on the formation of the MVAA, except its registration data, and the first collective agreement (CA).

nine companies. This split among the employers was greeted as a victory by the TEAIEU:

> For the first time the 'Giants' were broken. In the 4th C.A. MMVAA[8] only represented five Assembly Plants. KPKK and ASSB/AISB signed separate agreement with the union. This is a big change since UMW group spread into the motor industry. However the terms and conditions and salaries for all Assembly Plants are the same (TEAIEU 1983: 26).

The TEAIEU managed to negotiate secretly with UMW at the same time as the CA-negotiation between MVAA and the union took place. The union achieved a better CA with the UMW, which forced the MVAA to sign a similar deal. This outcome was a blow to the employers' association, and UMW withdrew. Since then, no new CA has been bargained or signed at the industry level. TEAIEU did not regret the dissolution of the MVAA as the employers were perceived to be much stronger together. However, the employers do not seem to regret this either, as a personnel manager of one of the former MVAA members recalled:

> PW: Once you also had an employers association for the auto manufacturers?
> IP: We had one, but instead of being an assistance it became a burden. Too much paper work, too much technicality, too much government concern, so we said, we wind it up.
> PW: You couldn't achieve anything?
> IP: Nothing much. Why? Because there were very few members. People started to break away. I think the last membership was only four of us: AMI, CCB Cycle and Carrige Bintang, Oriental Assemblers Johore, and Swedish Motor Assemblies. The rest were not members, so to maintain it and to have discussions and to get all of this yearly returns done, there was a lot of paper work to be done. We said it was not worth it. If we can make it informally why do we have an association. So we wind it up.
> PW: Otherwise you should also have Proton within the association?
> IP: The Proton wouldn't come in too. They don't want to share information at that time, but now they are opening up, they are coming out, because it's their time to deal with all assemblers. They are also trying to share [...] (Interview 1995)

Policy Driven Decentralisation: the Proton In-House Union

The membership of enterprise unions in the auto industry started to rise in 1988, and this rise made for an increase of the total union membership from 1987 to 1988. The significant event was the establishment of the Proton in-house union. The TEAIEU leadership was concerned about the national car project in the early 1980s before production started, but they were not against the project as such; they worried about the whole auto industry:

8 See note 4.

IP: We have written letters to the Prime Minister and other Ministers. There was nothing serious about it. There was not much development. In fact, in that letter we repeat again that we are not opposing that project. What we are saying is that we are concerned about the workers and the whole auto industry for we are talking about billions of *ringgits* way back to the 1960s when they started assembly plans in Johore and in Shah Alam (Interview 1995).

When Proton started production and increased employment, the national union went out organising the workers, but failed. A trade unionist of the TEAIEU explained the incident:

PW: You tried to unionise Proton?
IP: Yes, we did. In fact, we almost succeeded. Almost more than 50 per cent of the employees of Proton already joined this union. That was in '87, we recruited them. We had meetings, we formed the pro-tem committee, we had the discussions, series of discussions in Shah Alam [location of TEAIEU's HQs, pw]. Probably this leaked, the management came to know about it, and they immediately started this so-called in-house union. It happened so quick and so fast. During a short period of time they managed to get it registered, and they managed to give recognition to their in-house union. I think, within one or two months they were all completed (Interview 1995).

The industrial union started penetrating Proton in 1986, and the Proton union was registered in August 1988.[9] The management initiative was authorised from above because the authorities did not want any outsider unions in control of the Proton workforce. The Proton management thereby stuck to the enterprise union policy of the government, launched in 1983. At this point in time the Proton company was not incorporated, nor publically listed. It was a state owned enterprise within the HICOM group.

The establishment of an enterprise union did not mean that there was no collective bargaining or that the collective agreement (CA) was much different from the CAs concluded by the TEAIEU. The national union, assessing the Proton negotiation and CA, says:

IP: They started negotiations with the in-house union, and they also brought a consultant from the outside. The consultant was responsible for advising the union, the in-house union. And they negotiated with their in-house union. (...) They [the leaders, PW] are quite new, the Proton industry is quite new. Then if you look at their first agreement – we managed to get their agreement – you can check the similarity, even words, what we have concluded with other assemblers. You check the other assemblers' agreements and their agreement, you can see (it). What I'm trying to say is that I think they probably copied.

9 The interference of the Proton management with the employees' rights to form a union of their own choice has been confirmed by two independent non-union sources.

PW: Did they also make better (terms) in some ways?
IP: I think not much improvement compared to the others, except maybe now we are talking about giving loans to the employees so that they can purchase a Proton car, certain loans and all that. This is different. Other than that, I think, it's almost similar or we are better in terms of adjustment of salary. I think one or two months ago they concluded an agreement with their company, and they only got 10 per cent across the board. We are talking about 12 per cent, we are talking about 11 per cent. And then if you look at the working hours, there are two shifts, day shift and night shift, so they work the plant in 24 hours[10] (Interview 1995).

The achievements of the national union have probably affected the negotiations in the Proton company and the whole structure of CAs in the industry. But this may change in time because the failure of the national union to organise the Proton factory seems to be decisive in the long run, while the national car company is increasing its market share on behalf of the other car assemblers. Moreover, history was repeated in the second national car company Perodua, where an enterprise union appeared too. In fact, it seemed to be the rule rather than the exception among HICOM companies that they formed enterprise unions, said a spokesman of the industrial union:

PW: It is my impression that many companies in the HICOM group are very difficult to unionise. Is that also your experience?
IP: Yes. We once had a situation in Sungai Petani, up in the North, in Kedah. We have a company called HICOM Honda. This company manufactures engine for Honda motorcycles in Kedah. We went there, organised the workers and all that. What happened was that the workers became harassed by the management, others were intimidated, some were sort of bought over. We have filed a report, filed a complaint. In that way, we lost in the secret ballot. People went inside the room and cast their vote, and of course they say they are not members of the union (Interview 1995).

The NUTEAIW admitted that the Proton company had a very strong company culture where the (Malay) workers were taken care of and that they have been proud of participating in the national car project. When a private businessman obtained control of Proton in 1996 the relationship between the management and the in-house union had the potential to change. A leader of the Proton in-house union stated the situation in the following way (in my summary):

IP: We are employees. We do have nothing else but our labour. If we are treated well, we'll co-operate and be loyal. If not we'll fight for the cause of our fellow members. We'll fight back if they treat us badly. If they destroy the good relationship it'll be difficult to re-establish a good one (Interview 1996).

10 Within NUTEAIW unionised plants there is only one shift and overtime work.

The Proton union leaders even characterised the management-union relationship as 'excellent' during the Japanese management 1988-93, then it went down to 'good' in 1995 and further down to 'fair' in 1996. They explained:

> IPs: The Japanese knew about the in-house unions. The present management does not have the experience. They should be sent to Japan for labour education. When the government started promoting in-house unions in the early 1980s we didn't know very much about it (Interview 1996).[11]

Labour Driven Decentralisation

The rise of the Proton company and the economic crisis 1985-86 cannot explain the whole shift from national to enterprise unionisation. Two core companies changed to in-house unions in the early 1990s: Assembly Services of the UMW group and Tan Chong Motor Assemblies of the Tan Chong group. The company Assembly Services was bought by the UMW group in 1982 and restructured in 1987 with the take-over by *Bumi* interests (PNB). The former Chinese management withdrew UMW from MVAA in order to run its own show, partly with the UMW in-house union, partly with TEAIEU. After the change in ownership and management in 1987 the car market grew again, UMW's ASSB expanded the production of Toyota cars, and new workers were hired. Then, in 1989-90 the president of the TEAIEU, who was also the chairman of the work-site committee of the ASSB, lost his position at the ASSB committee. The conflict between the president and his group and the rest of the union at local and central levels accelerated into the breakaway of the ASSB. One of the leaders of NUTEAIW explains the case:

> IP: The former president of this union was, before he became president of the union, also elected chairman of the work-site committee at Assembly Services. In 1989, in their work-site election, he was defeated. He blamed some of our colleagues from the national union that we never supported him. But we thought that this was his own area, we do not want to interfere there. He lost. Subsequently, he resigned from the presidency, and he became very close with the management. As president of the union he had more say during the period, you can see any person at any time, you can have a very close rapport with the management. But those days he did a lot of good things for the members. After this problem he started moving very close to the management, just because the national union did not support him for the work-site committee chairman election. He wanted to get away from the national union. But in the beginning the new work-site committee confronted (him) and others who initiated to form an in-house union. But over the period the management turned on the pressure. Finally after three months they became members of the existing in-house union

11 The interview was conducted before the Jahya-management group took over: the managing director during the recent period of Japanese management was a former enterprise union leader of Mitsubishi, Japan. Notes in my own words.

[the UMW enterprise union, PW]. It happened in 1990 [...]
PW: How could the management put pressure on the workers?
IP: They called group by group, five people in a group, the human resource officer called them to office to talk about the good thing of the enterprise union, what are the benefits they can get if they join the enterprise union. The work-site committee was given some good opportunities that this can happen if they join in-house union. Subsequently five members were promoted to supervisors.
PW: What about the old enterprise union. Did they try to persuade the new people to join the union?
IP: No. The enterprise union did not play much of a role. The enterprise union was under the protection of the management at that time. They did not say anything. Everything became decided by management.... You cannot blame the members, but them in the exco [executive committee, PW] were very close with the management, because they were taken well care of by the management (Interview 1995).

The breakaway from the national union by the employees of the company was very much instigated by the management's arguments about the virtues of the in-house union and its promise to improve remuneration and working conditions. By coincidence, the human resource manager of the Assembly Services entered the office where I was interviewing the work-site committee of the in-house union, and he reproved a work site committee (WSC) member, saying that 'we jumped into the in-house union,' by emphasising that 'we progressed into the in-house union' (1995).

A key actor behind the breakaway was, as mentioned earlier, the former national union officer and work site committee chairman of the industrial union in the company. He recalled the situation before, during and after the breakaway in the following way:

During the period 1972-82 the [national] union and management was always fighting, but in the national union they are also close with the management. I could sell the workers. I was there for 10 years. I got better benefits for the workers, and we had better conditions [in ASSB]. All I got from [the company] was because I was closer with the management, not because of the fighting. The national union said that they must throw me out and make new arrangement. And it is easy by the national union to do so. I did it myself. Here I lost the majority.
The management likes people with my way of thinking. National union is difficult to handle by the management. Some made national union to lay me down. So I thought, if you want to challenge me I can manage an in-house union. Management was not happy with the new work site committee. At first I tried to put my people in the work site committee, but I failed. Then I worked closer with the management, and we assembled all the workers. We did not offer anything. We did only want to change to an in-house union. The push came from the management. The national union couldn't get anything. We persuaded three line leaders in the work site committee. I don't know why the workers changed. Today I realise that I was right. All the under-

> ground I did. When I flew to Japan the management started talking group by group. At that time 10 per cent were not happy with the situation, now all are happy. I stepped out and functioned only as advisor. I was the mastermind. At the time of the national union the work site committee did not know the management. Now I can work very close with the manager. When this happened they persuaded me to become executive. I think that the union and the management must work close together.
>
> My heart is still with the union. The management knows that I address the workers. I know the workers attitude, I was a worker before. If you want something, you must also give something. Most important for the work site committee is that it must be recognised by management. Now the work site committee is recognised and they can run their own show (Interview 1996).

The human resource manager did not entirely agree with the interpretation by the 'mastermind' of the breakaway, saying that the management-worker relationship improved a lot (interview 1996). Before the in-house union took over, enterprise industrial relations were characterised by strikes, boycotts of overtime, picketing etc. After the company joined the in-house union of the mother company, the enterprise industrial relations have been calm and unproblematic. However, he did not mention that leading WSC members were dissatisfied with the outcome of the breakaway, that they had prepared to take control of the entire in-house union, and that these officers were dismissed on charges of illegal industrial action.

Asked about this dismissal case the manager brushed aside the problem arguing that it was a small group that was unhappy and stirred up the others. When asking the WSC about the same case, at first people declined to answer, saying that they were not present, one being in Japan for training. Finally they did say that the WSC had disagreements with two managers, although they did not specify what kind of grievances they had, except that it had something to do with unfulfilled expectations. In protest, the WSC decided not to wear the prescribed company cap, signalling to the members that they should also wear 'no-cap.' The management decided to dismiss the WSC chairman, the secretary, and the treasurer. The in-house union took up the case and brought it to the Industrial Court, the union officers say. After four years the dismissed persons got compensation.

Confronted with this version of the dismissal case the officer of the national union tells another story: it was a trap set up to get rid of the three persons because the management believed that they were inclined to national unionism. The national union took up their case in support of them individually because they were not members of the national union. After the case was settled out of court, the in-house union finally agreed to pay the bill of the lawyer. The former national union officer described the incident in the following way:

> These three dismissed workers were still in contact with the national union. When they became committee members they went on handling problems by way of fighting. They didn't listen to the company. Management talked to me about how to cope with them. I wanted my three people in the committee and said, we find a way. Some day they made an action, calling the workers not to wear the cap. Management took the opportunity to throw them out, and I called in my people.
> It depends on the top management whether in-house unions are good or bad. Some management you can talk to, others you can't. If we have an anti-union management it turns bad. The management [in the company] has always been easy with the workers. It is also important that the union leaders are recognised by management. If leaders only talk empty talk, it's not good. You must have leaders to create a win-win situation. What happened to the three? Management did not recognise them, they always talked (Interview 1996).

At the meeting with the work-site committee members in 1995, which the human resource manager joined, I questioned them about the benefits of becoming an in-house union: what did they get? Did the working conditions improve? The human resource manager answered that the company had better salaries than the nearby companies unionised by the national union, because they had larger volume, and because they withdrew from the employers association and signed their own CA in 1985. However, after they joined the in-house union, the company continued with the old CA running from 1991-93 and negotiated by the industrial union. In 1994 the in-house union entered into the second CA with the company. Replying to the manager's speech I noted that apparently the employees did not get anything from the shift to the in-house union. Basic salary and working conditions remained unchanged. After several questions they came up with the answer that the annual bonus was raised from two to three and a half a month's pay. Asked about promotions after the breakaway the human resource manager confirmed that after one year four out of the twelve-thirteen EXCO members were promoted. The former union officer was very sure about the benefits gained by the transition to the in-house union:

> We have the highest salary in the auto industry. We get training for people in Japan, every four months we send 30 people for training, 90 a year. We select the good people who work hard and are recommended by their supervisors. Any dinner or whatever we request is never turned down. We also get promotion (Interview 1996).

Taking all available information into consideration, the breakaway only generated meagre improvements in wage rates, a time limited extra bonus, and along the way promotions to people responsible for the transition to the in-house union. The perceived lack of progress caused dissatisfaction, and the work-site committee leaders felt cheated, went for a power struggle with the established leaders of the in-house union of the mother company, and they were dismissed when they initiated a symbolic demonstration of their discontent. The in-house union did not help them until the national union had secured compensation for unfair dismissal. The discontent continued, and a large group of employees wanted to return to the national union.

When the national union was asked by the group to assist in organising their former members, it declined at first, but after repeated applications from the internal opposition of the in-house union, the national union finally entered the scene. The concerted effort did not immediately achieve the 51 per cent signatures in need for demanding the authorities to start verifying the support of the employees and eventually change the affiliation of the workplace. The in-house union complained to the local council of the secretariat of the international federation (IMF-Malaysia), which again supported the in-house union against the national union due to internal power struggles in the MTUC between the MTUC leaders and the industrial union. When the financial crisis erupted in 1997, and the car market collapsed in 1998, the oppositional workers and the national union had still not reached their goal, and the retrenchment in the wake of the crisis eroded the base of the workplace opposition.

The other case of labour driven decentralisation took place in the Tan Chong factory within the ethnic Chinese Tan Chong group, controlled by the Tan family. The factory assembled Nissan and Datsun vehicles, and the group also made spare parts and components, turning toward original equipment manufacturing (OEM) for Nissan. Moreover, it also subcontracted the assembling of Proton cars in the 1990s. In 1991, the Tan Chong employees left the national union: an in-house union was formed after a dramatic industrial conflict. The general secretary of the NUTEAIW explains the course of the breakaway:

> The Chairman of the Union Worksite Committee of Tan Chong Motor Assemblers, elected as General Secretary of the National Union in 1988. During this period the incumbent General Secretary was detained under Internal Security Act (Operasi Lalang). I was elected as his deputy during the same term. During this tenure as General Secretary, he wanted to bring in some changes at the national union, which were failed.[12]
>
> When Arifin Idris then the President resigned, he relinquished his position to contest for President and he lost in his attempt. From than he stayed away from national union. There were occasions where he made some decision in the capacity as chairman of worksite committee without seeking opinion from national union. The relationship between him and management was very cordial during this time.
>
> However, the relationship started souring shortly. It became very severe, when the Company suspended him with another worksite committee member for instigating

12 The demands were very much related to personal gain in nature, i.e. benefits for the chairman himself and not for the union/workers in general (personal communication with the union, November 2000).

> workers not to accept overtime. Subsequently, he instigated workers to lay down tools on first day for one hour and second day for a whole day. The national union was notified on the second day.
>
> The Director of Industrial Relations Department, summoned the national union to the factory in the afternoon of the second day. The Director of Industrial Department requested the workers to start work first and let the national union handle the suspension issue. The worksite committee, being spokesman for the members in Tan Chong Motors refused to start work without two members being reinstated back.
>
> The next day the Company 'Locked Out' those 'laid down' tools on the previous day. About 316 workers were locked. During the same period there are about 200 working inside. Workers with the assistance of national union picketed at the factory for three days. Subsequently, the Minister called a meeting at his ministry. During the meeting, the Company's representative, on the advice of the minister agreed to take back all workers, however those on suspension pending domestic inquiry has to wait for the outcome of the domestic inquiry. The worksite committee did not agree to this and demanded that the two colleagues want reinstated back without any disciplinary action.
>
> Finally, the whole effort to reinstate the workers was failed. Within a week, we received resignation letter from those workers still working with the Company within short period, the Company notified the national union that they are withdrawing the recognition granted to the national union and granting another union (House-Union) who is having 100 per cent membership of the Company.
>
> Apparently, we were told that the management of Tan Chong Motors took all the initiative to register an 'in-house union.'
>
> In our investigation it was revealed that the whole problem started when the Company realised that some of the request and demands made by the Chairman of the worksite committee was not met by the management (Interview from 1995, elaborated in writing 2000).[13]

Within the Tan Chong group several auto parts makers now have enterprise unions, but it also incorporates companies that are unionised by the national union.

Countering Decentralisation

The merger of enterprise unions with the industrial union took place before and after the East Asian crisis. One case took place in a small group of companies, owned by a Japanese TNC. Three companies (called J1, J2, J3), managed by a fourth (J4), manufactures car components to several auto assembly factories, including Proton. They are located at the same site in the neighbourhood of the Proton plant. Two subsidiaries were unionised by the national union and one by an in-house union. In 1994 the in-house union joined the national union. The story is rather dramatic, and again the perception differs among the actors. The

13 The Tan Chong management declined to be interviewed, and the president of the enterprise union did not accomplish an agreement to meet.

former leadership of the in-house union has one version, but I follow the version of the general secretary of the NUTEAIW, because it has been confirmed more or less by a former work-site committee member at the company J1 and J2:

> This factory situated in Shah Alam. There are three Companies, i.e. J1, J2 (manufacturing seat for automotive industries mainly Proton) and J3 manufacturing raw material for J1 and J2. J3 was the first Company to [be] registered in Malaysia and it was located in Penang. Fifteen years ago they shifted their operation from Penang to Kuala Lumpur, and an in-house Union was formed twelve years ago. Subsequently the Company (J3) shifted to Shah Alam. During the same period J1 and J2 established in Shah Alam. While J3 maintained in-house Union, the National Union managed to organise J1 and J2. From the time the National Union organised and entered into negotiation for better terms and condition (Collective Agreement) the in-house Union was side-lined by the management. It is simply under the umbrella of the National Union the workers are united, and this gave National Union to negotiate better terms and conditions than the other union. This lead the members of house union to criticise the leadership of the in-house union. During the same period the National Union through the worksite committee J1 and J2 started talking to the members of house union in general and officers in particular to join National Union. Another important point which let the house union convert to National Union was that the management started dealing with National Union on most issues pertaining to workers issues. Within the short period we recruited more than 80 per cent of house union members and we used a provision in Trade Union Act to de-register the house union and seek recognition from the management to which they did accord recognition. Now the workers in all three companies are members of our Union, it makes easy for the National Union to negotiate for better terms and condition (Interview 1995 elaborated in writing 2000).

The election of the work-site committee in 1995 became very dramatic when the former leadership of the in-house union tried a comeback which ended in violence. They thought that they had been cheated during the work-site committee election and instead of making a complaint to the executive committee of the national union they started a fight. The police were called, and some of the people were jailed briefly. The losing group resigned from the national union, which lost about forty to fifty members. The leaders of this group also had a fight in 1993 when a dispute between a guard and a driver turned into racial accusations. These Malaysian subsidiaries of a Japanese company have not been showcases of quiet Japanese business. The Japanese management tried to be neutral, but the situation got out of hand.

This case of returning-to-the-national-union is not unique, and it indicates that the NUTEAIW succeeds when its members take control of the in-house union, close it down and join the industrial union. It is much more difficult when the in-house union is not controlled by supporters of the national union, as the case of the Assembly Services shows.

Business Driven Changes

Due to the success of the national car project during the period between the crisis in 1985–86 and 1997–99 the organisational fields between the national car manufacturers with enterprise unions and the industrial union organising non-national auto assemblers and suppliers came to overlap. The Proton factory was unable to produce and deliver the cars in demand, and the Proton management began subcontracting assembly work to a few assembling companies outside the HICOM group: Tan Chong and later on also AMI. While Tan Chong employees broke away and formed an enterprise union, the AMI was a stronghold of the industrial union. In the past the AMI was a fully owned subsidiary of Ford Motor Company (Malaysia), later being sold to local interests and finally taken over by Tractors Malaysia Holdings Bhd, one of the five core divisions of the huge Sime Darby business group. Tractors had its main activities in heavy machinery (for agriculture, construction, commercial, public and private transport, etc.) (Kuala Lumpur Stock Exchange, vol. 21 book 205–6). Through Tractors and Sime Darby AMI became related to the *Bumi* business community and the *Bumi* political elite, both of which also had heavy stakes in the HICOM and Proton corporation.

Crisis-Driven Transformation of the Industrial Relations of the Auto Industry

Other changes have been crisis-driven. The economic crisis of the 1980s effectuated a reduction in employment within the transport equipment industry: from 21,294 in 1981 and 22,281 in 1985 down to 17,026 in 1988 before it went up to 48,260 in 1993 (calculated from NPC basic material 1985–93). The car assembly factories organised by the national union witnessed massive retrenchment exercises (e.g. AMI, ASSB, SMA), but most companies stayed in the market and only AA assembling Mazda closed down. When the market picked up again, many new employees were hired, even though some companies wanted their old employees to return (e.g. AMI, SMA, CCB). This shift of the workforce to younger generations meant that the union had to socialise a new workforce into the worldview of the union.

Despite the growth in membership of the national union, enterprise union membership increased even faster. The industrial union reached its lowest membership in 1988 with 2673 members, and then rose to 5000 members in 1995 to reach 6000 members by the end of 1997, albeit interrupted by setbacks. TEAIEU lost several strongholds among their larger assembly factories: Tan Chong, Assembly Services, KPKK, Asia Automobiles. In the mid-1990s the union still organised AMI, Cycle & Carriage Bintang (CCB), Oriental Assemblers (OA) and Swedish Motor Assemblies (SMA). Besides unionising motorcycle assemblers the bulk of the union membership is spread over smaller auto parts manufacturers.

Covering thirty-four workplaces in 1995 with 5168 members makes an average of 152 members per workplace, ranging from four to 477 members per workplace. In sum, the union's industrial base has shifted from larger, foreign owned or controlled auto assembling factories towards smaller, Chinese owned and controlled transport component manufacturers.

This shift to unionise the supplier companies in the transport equipment industry was part of a strategy to revitalise the union. Besides, the union turned to a less militant and more pragmatic policy together with the assemblers in order to save the non-national auto industry. However, the union did still acknowledge that although they had to co-operate more they would participate from a position of strength and this position had sometimes to be sustained and communicated to the employers, for example through formal and informal industrial actions. The mantra for independent, democratic unions was avoid 'getting close with management.'

During the 1997-99 crisis the trade unions within the auto industry suffered with the collapse of sales and production and the loss of jobs and members, but there was again a time lag. The national union increased its membership during 1997 to around 6000, but lost 1400 members or 23 per cent of total membership during 1998 and went further down to around 4500 members in March 1999 (compiled by the author 1999). The Proton union also increased its membership during 1997 to around 4700 and improved further to around 5300 members by the end of March 1998, but then it lost more than 1000 members during the rest of 1998. The net loss during 1998 was around 500 members or 11 per cent, but the union consolidated its membership by the end of March 1999 with a little less than 4300 members. When the auto market started rebounding the national union was still slightly larger than the largest in-house union, with 4606 members and 4215 members respectively (comparable figures for Perodua have not been obtained), but together the enterprise unions held the majority of the union membership within the auto industry.

Although the crisis has impacted differentially at the various segments and companies in the auto industry the auto employees and their unions have all felt the pinch. Both the national union and the larger enterprise unions have recognised that they face similar problems and that they might gain by increasing their exchange of information and collaboration. No new breakaways have been reported, but one workplace employee collective closed down their in-house union and applied for membership of the national union.

The strategy of the national union to prioritise the organising of auto parts and components manufacturers seemed to pay off until the crisis hit. This strategy has been supplemented by a policy to form a network or even a federation of trade unions within the auto industry. In 1999 discussions were ongoing, and core enterprise unions were involved. Yet, several important questions had to be resolved, for example, what statements can be made by whom in the name of the federation? But the old myths and stereotypes about each other seemed to wither, opening up for the formation of some kind of regional 'network unionism' between auto industrial and enterprise unions in the industrial hub around the capital, Kuala Lumpur.

Explaining the Changing Malaysian Auto Industrial Relations System

The centralised industry wide bargaining system in the 1970s might be understood as a transferred IR-system initiated by the auto TNCs due to their home country system and the practices of the Western auto trading companies. In fact, it was generated by the institutionalisation of centralised industrial relations within the commercial sector prior to the evolution of a strong national auto industry workers union and an assembling industry influenced by Western-oriented employers and managers, especially Australians. However, the attempt to standardise wage and working conditions at a low level spurred the radicalisation of the national union during the mid-1970s, and tense industrial relations and confrontational bargaining prevailed until the end of the 1980s. The crisis in 1985-86 affected the auto market and private auto assemblers severely, and it made the employers of the private auto sector and the national union think twice, opting for co-operative industrial relations in order to survive.

Meanwhile the new and dominant business alliance between Japanese TNCs and ethnic Chinese businessmen undercut the centralised collective bargaining system in order to be able to follow their own strategies. This positioned the industrial union in the optimal powerful position of being able to divide the employers, but it also proved to be an unstable situation. When the employers were not united against the national union, the dominant ones went for enterprise unions, ideologically supported by the government. Being constituted on a grassroots democratic model, the national union was loosely structured and open for breakaways if worker collectives at the workplace level split, together with divisions among the top leadership.

When the state-led Malaysian car company (Proton) began dominating car manufacturing and car distribution in Malaysia, the struggle for its unionisation was on. In the end, the national union lost the struggle to unionise Proton due to management initiative and employees' support for the formation of an in-house union in 1988. This was the first serious blow to the dominant position of the national auto workers union (TEAIEU). Decisive factors seemed to be the recruitment of a new Malay workforce without former experience within the auto industry and the national union, and the deliberate exposure of this workforce to a national auto project, in which the Malay community took great pride. The second blow to the national union of autoworkers followed in 1990-91 when two important assembly companies broke away from the national union. In both cases a split within the leadership of the national union paved the way for the formation of an in-house union.

All in all, during the period of state-led restructuring between 1985 and 1995 the national union of auto industry workers declined (the MASSU did too), and enterprise unions rose not only inside but also outside the cluster of state owned companies. Enterprise unions gained the majority of the union membership from 1991 onwards. Compared to the national union with above 5000 members in 1996, the enterprise union grew to around 4000 members in 1996, following an expanding Proton workforce from 1700 in 1989 to more than 5000 in 1996 (interviews 1996). During the crisis the Proton union matched the national union with above 5000 members in 1998, but it fell behind in 1999 when it lost more members than the national union, respectively down to 4274 members and 4542 members (interviews May-June 1999). The difference may be accounted for by the retrenchment of non-unionised immigrant workers in the non-national auto industry, while the national auto companies only employed Malaysians and primarily ethnic *Bumis*.

The national union survived partly by unionising car component factories and other road transport equipment companies (motorcycle assemblers and component manufacturers), partly due to the rapid expansion of the car market in the 1990s where sales of vehicles went up from around 140,000 in 1992 to 345,000 in 1996 *Far Eastern Economic Review* 1997.05.08), the incapacity of the Proton company to fulfil demands, and the expansion of private auto makers increasing production in Malaysia 1997 to its peak: 335,000 passenger cars, nearly 110,000 commercial vehicles and slightly below 360,000 motorcycles (MIDA 1999 app. II).

Although the industrial relations of the auto industry became more pluralistic during the 1980s and the NUTEAIW no longer commanded the majority of union members of the auto industry in the 1990s, the national union still exercised great leverage on the overall terms of collective agreements. This influence is conditioned by several factors: 1) the central co-ordination and support by the national union for enterprise level negotiations, 2) the transparency of union achievements (past and present) in a pluralistic and competing area of trade unionism, 3) the work process knowledge and influence on productivity possessed by autoworkers and transformed into workplace power through the union, and 4) the capacity to persuade employees of in-house unions and even management with such unions to turn to the national union.

Because most privately-owned assemblers and the national union did survive the 1980s recession and the development of the national auto industry, the lessons learned by the leaders of the national union are still strongly in favour of national unionism. Doomsday seemed near in the second half of the 1980s and yet the union and its members stood up against the challenges and managed to maintain the union as a strong, grass roots oriented democratic union. Before the crisis in

1997, the union leaders held that the large auto TNCs will stay in Malaysian business and so will the motorcycle TNCs, that the *Bumi* conglomerates like Sime Darby are used to dealing with national unions from the plantation and trading sectors, and that there is a huge membership potential in the car parts and components industry which can be tapped. However, in-house unionism haunts and has to be considered when planning and implementing strategies for unionisation of the unorganised enterprises. The national union had to establish some kind of collaboration with the enterprise unions, subscribing to the principle that it is the workers who must choose which kind of union they prefer.

In sum, there is a process of interdependent transformation between the changes of the auto industry and the industrial relations: from the Western TNC-owned and controlled sub-assembling system with centralised industrial relations in the 1970s, via the Japanese TNC-related alliance with Chinese family businesses and the centralised-decentralised industrial relations 1982–87, towards state-supported enterprise unions and collective bargaining between enterprise-based actors within the new *Bumi*-controlled companies. However, this trend is not without exceptions and reversals. Within *Bumi* acquired older companies unionised by the national union there are not (yet) attempts to change the union structure; auto companies might even prefer standardised and integrated collective bargaining even if the negotiation will end up being the national union; and even within the *Bumi* complex of HICOM enterprises, workplaces with an enterprise union can be taken over by a national union on the initiative of the employee collective getting dissatisfied with the in-house union. Finally, the impact of the recent economic crisis has not yet worked its way through the minds and institutions of the auto industry and its industrial relations system.

Conclusion

The contemporary industrial relations of the Malaysian auto industry is very much an outcome of Malaysia's colonial legacy and process of decolonisation, the interplay between a TNC controlled auto industry and domestic industrialisation policies and restructuring, and finally the promotion of the in-house union concept by the state and the exploitation of or subscription to this discourse by the individual managers of auto companies. An actor-oriented industrial relations perspective seems pertinent and appropriate, when we consider three core trends of industrial relations disclosed by our analysis:

1. That the U-turn during the 1980s of the trend of trade unionism from industrial unionism to enterprise unionism seems to be caused by the combined actions of state agencies and business managers, adding labour-labour conflicts and ethnic-oriented loyalties to the explanatory framework.

2. That the transition from a centralised to a decentralised collective bargaining system in the Malaysian auto industry during the 1980s was driven by the rising alliance of Japanese TNCs and domestic Chinese auto businessmen.
3. That the split between the employers at first looked like a big advantage for the industrial unions, but this system of industrial relations withered and induced employers to mingle in labour-labour conflicts and support the formation of in-house unions among break away factions.

Like the former economic crisis in 1985-86, the crisis in 1997-99 may be a milestone in the development of Malaysian auto industrial relations. Although the collapse of the domestic auto market was not accompanied with a similar collapse of employment and earnings due to a concerted efforts of employers, unions, and state authorities to minimise the impact of the crisis on employment, core stakeholders do anyway acknowledge that the Malaysian auto industry must stand up to rising regional and global competition. This competitiveness may only be achieved by technological and organisational upgrading, which again calls for closer collaboration between management and labour on the one hand and intensified co-operation with one of the big global auto players on the other hand.

The technology partner of Proton, Mitsubishi Motor Corporation (MMC) probably entered the joint venture, because it was in a weak position at the Malaysian market and internationally, and today MMC is not among the big global auto manufacturers. Ironically, the disadvantage of linking up with a weaker auto TNC may now turn into an advantage, because Daimler-Chrysler recently came to control MMC. This unexpected outcome of global competition may provide the Malaysian national auto industry linkage for survival, securing workplaces and a base for trade unionism, if Daimler-Chrysler perceives Proton and Malaysia as a production platform within their global and regional strategies. Such an alliance or eventual merger would open new possibilities for labour organisation and organisational innovation, which might even invite the formation of a new network unionism, integrating Malaysian enterprise unions and national unions in an international union movement.

But such a scenario requires that the economic ethno-nationalism of the Mahathir regime is turned into some kind of cross-ethnic economic internationalism, at least for the auto industry. Such a break would jeopardise the very foundation of Malaysian politics, constituted on ethnic political parties and loyalties. And for the time being the Malaysian government has another option, which it seems to pursue. The Proton strategy for the new Malaysian designed car is to co-operate with transnational technology and component suppliers with global reputation (brands). This strategy might save the national car project for the time being, but probably it will sooner or later leave the indigenous supplier industry behind.

This scenario comprises a paradox, because the national car project was initiated in response to the resistance against increased localisation of component production in Malaysia. Moreover, the implication could be disastrous for the industrial union, if the domestic auto supplier industry is declining and ousted, because the workforce here has constituted the new membership base of the national union. However, the global principle of 'follow sourcing' among the auto TNCs may be applied to Malaysia too, providing for an expanding TNC-subsidiary supplier industry. This scenario might even provide a better platform for a revival of the industrial auto workers union than the present industry, because ethnic loyalties might disappear in relation to transnational employers, and the level of technology and scale production might be raised significantly enlarging the scope for improved wages, working conditions and eventually also unionisation.

The decentralisation of the Malaysian industrial relations is not fated, but a process of social construction and reconstruction under changing social conditions and junctures. While the present conditions do not leave much room for manoeuvre for a return to centralised collective bargaining, they do form a context for the co-existence of centralised and decentralised union organisation, which again opens up for new ways of co-operation in terms of network unionism. Such a type of unionism may even provide a better way to cope with business networking, the prevailing competitive form of inter-business organisation in Southeast Asia and beyond. But that is another story.

References

Dass, A. (1991) *Not Beyond Repair – Reflections of a Malaysian Trade Unionist*, Hong Kong: Asia Monitor Resource Centre.

Department of Statistics (DOS) (February 1999) *Monthly Manufacturing Statistics*, Kuala Lumpur: DOS.

Dicken, P. (1998) *Global Shift: Transforming the World Economy* (Third Edition), London: Paul Chapman Press.

Economic Planning Unit (EPU) (July 1998) *National Economic Recovery Plan: Agenda for Action*, Kuala Lumpur: Prime Minister's Department.

Edwards, C. (1997) 'Foreign Labour in Malaysian Development: A Strategic Shift?' IKMAS Working Papers 6, Bangi: UKM, Malaysia.

Humphrey, J. (1998) 'Assembler-Supplier Relations: Globalisation and National Development', paper presented at the DICM/CBS International Research Workshop, October 1998, Copenhagen: CBS.

Jomo, K.S. (ed.) (1993) *Industrialising Malaysia*, London: Routledge.

Jomo, K.S. and Todd, P. (1994) *Trade Unions and the State in Peninsular Malaysia*, Kuala Lumpur: Oxford University Press.

Khoo Boo Teik (1997) 'Economic Vision and Political Opposition in Malaysia, 1981–96', *Copenhagen Journal of Asian Studies* 12: 9–34.

Malaysian Industrial Development Authority (MIDA)(1999) *The Automotive Industry in Malaysia*, Kuala Lumpur: MIDA (mimeo).

Rasiah, R. (1995) 'Labour and Industrialisation in Malaysia', *Journal of Contemporary Asia* 25, 1: 73–92.

Rasiah, R. and Hofmann, N.V. (eds.) (1998) *Workers on the Brink: Unions, Exclusion and Crisis in Southeast Asia,* Singapore: Friedrich Ebert Stiftung.

Standing, G. (1991) 'Do Unions impede or accelerate structural adjustment? Industrial versus company unions in an industrialising labour market', World Employment Programme Research, Labour Market Analysis and Unemployment Planning, Working Paper 47, Geneva: WEP.

— (1992a) 'Do unions impede or accelerate structural adjustment? Industrial versus company unions in an industrialising labour market', *Cambridge Journal of Economics* 16: 327–354.

— (1992b) 'Identifying the "human resource enterprise": a Southeast Asian example', *International Labour Review* 131, 3: 281–295.

TEAIEU (1977) *1th Biennial General Report 1975–77.*

— (1983) *4th Biennial General Report 1981–83.*

Torii, T. (1991) 'Changing the manufacturing sector, reorganising automobile assemblers, and developing the auto component industry under the New Economic Policy', *The Developing Economies* XXIX, 4: 387–413.

Wad, P. (1988) 'The Japanisation of the Malaysian Trade Union Movement', in R. Southall (ed.) *Trade Unions and the New Industrialisation of the Third World,* London: Zed Books.

— (1996) 'Enterprise Unions: From backward to vanguard unionism?' IKL Working Paper 7, Frederiksberg: Copenhagen Business School.

— (1997a) 'Enterprise unions: panacea for industrial harmony in Malaysia?' *Copenhagen Journal of Asian Studies* 12: 89–125.

— (1997b) 'Enterprise Unions and Structural Change in Malaysia. Preliminary Research Findings', IKMAS Working Papers 13, Bangi: UKM, Malaysia.

— (1998) 'Enterprise unions and dynamic efficiency: the case of Malaysia', paper presented at the EUROSEAS Conference, 3–6 September, Hamburg, Panel 13: 'Changing Labour Relations in South East Asia'.

— (1999) 'Business Relations in Crisis? The Case off the National Auto Manufacturers in South Korea and Malaysia during the East Asian Crisis. Part III: The Malaysian Auto Industrial Networks in a Netholder Perspective', Occasional Paper 102 DICM/CBS, Copenhagen: Copenhagen Business School.

Womack, J.P., Jones, D.T. and Roos, D. (1990) *The Machine That Changed the World,* New York: Rawson Associates.

10

Labour Relations and Mobility in Provincial Thailand

DANIEL ARGHIROS

Rapid change in the composition of the labour force is perhaps a defining feature of industrialisation in contemporary Southeast Asia. The extent and rapidity of labour mobility both in terms of movement between agriculture and between different industrial sectors, and in terms of the spatial movement of different categories of migrant labour is remarkable. In any given context the movement of labour is guided by more than simply the supply and demand of labour. An economistic approach that relies on labour force and employment statistics to trace labour movements in rapidly changing contexts such as Thailand will inevitably fail to reveal the full and highly textured picture. Such an approach would also fail to elucidate how these movements are a response to a combination of micro and macro forces. Moreover, it is misleading to treat 'labour' as a homogenous category, as at any one time the composition of the labour force even within a particular industry is highly differentiated and can change rapidly. An approach to labour mobility that takes a multi-sectoral, longitudinal, and spatial perspective – focusing on labour movements in a single locality rather than a single sector – can reveal the source and patterns of change. This chapter illustrates the complexity of labour markets by depicting the movement of local, national migrant and immigrant labour between three different sectors – the agricultural sector, local industry and export-oriented industry – in a central Thai district. The account focuses on a period of rapid economic growth and even more sudden contraction from the 1980s and 1990s.

The nature and characteristics of labour relations within a particular industrial sector depend on a host of factors. The relative scarcity of labour and the nature of the relationship between employees and employers are key determinants. This chapter also demonstrates how labour relations, even within a single sector, are extremely diverse and reflect a combination of traditional and industrial capitalist models of social relations: labour relations range from those that draw on local paternalistic and familialistic idioms of social relations, and to those that owe more to modern forms of industrial discipline.

Most studies of labour mobility in Thailand tend to take either a broad-brush perspective as told by national labour statistics or focus on patterns of rural-urban migration. It is difficult to gain from such studies a picture of the movement of labour across and within sectors. Similarly literature on Thai industrialisation reveals a dearth of studies on labour relations in smaller, locally owned capitalist enterprises, both rural and urban. It is in these factories, often owned by first-generation entrepreneurs, that we can see the negotiation of structural relations of inequality in which former neighbours are cast into relatively enduring positions of employer-employee.

The central focus of the chapter is on movement in and out of a locally dominant rural industry: the brickmaking industry. In its infancy the brick industry relied entirely on local labour drawn out of the agricultural sector; it then came to rely entirely on Thai migrant labour, only latterly to find itself dependent on illegal workers from adjacent countries. Newer export-oriented factories drew young female workers out of the brick industry thereby contributing to a labour crisis within it. More recently still, the economic crisis has led to the collapse of the brick industry and a rapid outflow of migrant workers, while export-oriented factories have remained relatively untouched. It is important to note that the movements described below are not discrete, but represent broad trends: the picture is complicated by the fact that at any given moment, and in any enterprise, all three categories of labour may be present. In other words, there is a great deal of overlap and continuity.

After outlining the background to Thai industrialisation and the organisation of the brick industry, the paper examines the movement of labour between sectors and regions and depicts how movements have been the results of different kinds of forces. The paper draws on fieldwork in a Central Thai district that I call 'Klang' between 1989 and 1998.[1]

As almost every commentator has pointed out, Thai industrial growth between the 1980s and 1990s led by export-oriented industry has been rapid if not 'miraculous.' Prior to the economic crash of mid-1997 it was seen as a budding 'Newly

1 More precisely, this article is based on fieldwork conducted between October 1989-December 1990; July 1995-May 1997 and July-August 1998. Research conducted between 1995-97 was conducted whilst holding an ESRC Research Fellowship [H52427004094] and a British Academy Research Award. Field research in 1998 was funded by the University of Hull. The latter two periods of research were conducted in collaboration with Dr Joanne Moller, University of Hull. Research was conducted with the kind permission of the National Research Council of Thailand and affiliated to Chulalongkorn University Social Research Institute. A pseudonym is used here because some of my other writing on the 'Klang' district concerns politically sensitive data. My thanks to Mike Parnwell for providing me with sources on international migration.

Industrialising Country,' and one of the newest Southeast Asian 'tigers.' Average annual growth of GDP between 1990 and 1994 stood at an extraordinary 8.2 per cent. The share of GDP held by manufacturing rose from 16 per cent in 1970 to 29 per cent in 1994; and between 1970 and 1980 the average annual growth rate of exports was 8.9 per cent while in the period 1990 to 1994 this figures stood at 21.6 per cent (Rigg 1997: 6-7). However, economic growth came to an abrupt end in mid-1997. What began as a currency crisis led to business failure in the financial services sector and construction industry. Real GDP growth is estimated to be -0.3 per cent in 1998 (ILO 1998: 2). The construction industry has been hit particularly hard. Over half the job losses reported by industry associations by the end of 1997 occurred in the construction industry (ILO 1998: 18). In 1998 six per cent of the workforce, 1.8 million people, had been made unemployed.

Despite the massive and rapid growth in the size of the industrial workforce prior to 1997, in general Thai workers have not been active and the union movement remains relatively weak.[2] In the private sector only around six per cent of workers belong to a union, while 60 per cent of state enterprises are unionised (Hewison and Brown 1994: 503). Unionisation is lowest in private sector medium and small-scale factories owned by Sino-Thais (Limqueco et al. 1989: 39; cited in Hewison and Brown 1994: 504). The low incidence of unionised labour is not surprising given that organisation in small enterprises is particularly difficult and that the overwhelming majority of Thai enterprises (97.5 per cent) employ less than 100 workers (Sungsidh and Kanchada 1994: 221). The strategies of employers aimed at keeping labour costs flexible and low have also contributed to the inability of labour to organise. In most sectors including those described below, employers have perpetuated the insecurity of labour by providing employment on short-term contracts. Furthermore, subcontracting of production by larger firms to workshops and households ensures that workers are physically and spatially disparate and in a particularly weak position to promote their collective interests (Sungsidh and Kanchada 1994). Subcontract and independent homeworkers have recently worked with the ILO to attempt to win concessions

2 The academic literature, notes Brown, 'is pervaded by a sense of disenchantment with workers' which, he suggests is not entirely warranted (1997: 164). State action to restrict the freedom of labour to organise since the 1970s, and as late as 1992, is partly responsible for the absence of formal labour activity. Perhaps, as Brown has argued, the fact that the Thai state has in the past devoted so much attention to undermining labour 'actually attests to the increasing centrality of class relations and class politics' (Brown 1997: 176). However, conditions for labour organisation have improved since the restoration of parliamentary rule in 1992, following the end of a brief interlude of military domination. The establishment of the Ministry of Labour and Social Welfare in 1993 marks a turning point in this respect. The Labour Protection Act, enacted on 19 August 1998, has for the first time provided workers who have been employed for three years or more with statutory rights to severance pay. For an historical overview of organised labour in the Thai context, see Hewison and Brown (1994).

from the state to ensure that their incomes meet the minimum wage, and that they have the same access to social insurance as workers in the formal sector (Lazo 1996). Their efforts have not been entirely successful.

From Rice-Growing to Brickmaking: The Rise of Rural Industry in Klang District

The economy of 'Klang' district, which lies in Ayuthaya province about 120 miles north of Bangkok, is fully commercialised and economic differences between households are generally great. The district covers an area of approximately 122 square kilometres and has a population of 35,000. Some 54 per cent of households do not own or operate landholdings.[3] The district is a broad unforested plain and has alluvial soils well suited for rice cultivation and brick manufacture. As in other areas of Thailand, socio-economic conditions in the area have changed rapidly in the last decade and a half. Prior to the 1970s and as recent as 1990 no large-scale industrial enterprises, aside from one rice mill, operated in the district while by mid-1997 there were eleven factories producing mostly, but not exclusively, for export markets. A survey of two constituent subdistricts in 1969 revealed that the entire workforce was involved either in agriculture or non-farm petty commodity production: 58.5 per cent of households operated agricultural landholdings (Amyot 1976: Table 6.2). No locals worked in industry at the time (Amyot 1976: Tables 3.9, 3.10). Landless and land-poor households in the district subsisted on a combination of local and non-local agricultural labour and return or permanent migration for factory work in Bangkok.

The brick industry is an example of a branch of rural production that has become internally differentiated and has expanded rapidly in recent years with far-reaching implications. As late as 1970 enterprises were located only within the household, family members provided labour, and production was seasonal and interspersed with agriculture (Amyot 1976: 167-9). The growth of the brick industry is a direct result of national economic growth in the 1980s and the industry represents a case of 'industrialisation within industrialisation' (Cook 1984). Labour-intensive forms of industrial commodity production have expanded within a wider economy where growth is driven by the capital-intensive, factory-based sector. General economic growth has boosted the construction industry, which, in turn, has generated demand for bricks. The Klang brick industry supplies merchants and building contractors in Bangkok and surrounding provinces. Brick production has attracted a large number of entrepreneurs with capital derived from other sources to invest directly into capitalist production. In 1970 there

3 This figure and other survey data derive from a household survey of two contiguous subdistricts conducted by the author between September and November 1990.

were no mechanised brickyards; in 1989 there were thirty-two; in 1990 there were fifty-five and in 1993 their number had risen to seventy. Throughout the 1990s the number of non-mechanised brickyards has remained stable at around a thousand. The industry has generated new social and economic differences and introduced villagers to factory work relations.

Brick production in Klang District takes two forms, 'non-mechanised' and 'mechanised'. These forms co-exist: there is not an 'evolutionary' process of mechanisation, largely because hand-formed bricks have qualities mechanically-formed bricks lack, and demand for the former remains strong.[4] What defines these production methods is not the use of machinery *per se* but the method of forming bricks. In 'non-mechanised' brickyards bricks are moulded by hand. Machines are sometimes used to mix brickearth, but never for other stages of production. 'Mechanised' brickyards use machines (technically called 'extruders') to form the bricks. Whether a brickyard is non-mechanised or mechanised relates to its mode of production. Non-mechanised brickyards can produce using only household labour. On the other hand, all mechanised brickyards are petty capitalist or capitalist enterprises. The output of extruders, amounting to around 15,000 bricks a day, requires a minimum of around ten workers: no household can provide this much labour. Workers must co-operate throughout the production process and individuals or small groups cannot easily lay claim to specific outputs. Thus, by and large, mechanised brickyards pay daily wage rates. In the last few years this has changed such that these brickyards increasingly employ workers on a piece rate, by establishing work groups or contracting out particular tasks. The introduction of piece-rate regime to mechanised brickyards is a specific response to labour management issues, and is discussed below in more detail. Mechanised brickyards employ between ten and 120 workers, with the average number of employees at around forty. Non-mechanised brickyards normally employ between six and thirty workers who operate in household units. Rates of remuneration are broadly comparable: the main difference for workers is that production in non-mechanised brickyards gives workers greater freedom and flexibility (within limits they can produce at what time and pace they wish) but with greater attendant risks (for example, sudden rain can easily spoil a week's output of raw bricks).

The different wage regimes in mechanised and non-mechanised enterprises predicate different labour and employer goals. Workers in non-mechanised brickyards need to protect and enhance the piece rate wage they receive while workers in mechanised brickyards face their employers over both 'time-wages' and the use of their labour. Non-mechanised brickyards pay workers by the number of kiln-ready bricks produced, contracts are not made, and employees control their own day-to-day work patterns. Because workers are paid on a piece rate they are

4 As they are solid and have a rough exterior, hand-formed bricks remain the brick of choice for experienced builders.

generally self-motivated. Workers expressed preference for this kind of work on account of the freedom it affords. Several producers said approvingly that they were 'free' (*isara*) to work at their own pace, and that they had no one forcing (*bangkhap*) them to work in contrast to practice in mechanised brickyards: as producers said 'if you make a lot [of bricks], you earn a lot.' Another attraction of working in non-mechanised yards is that it is also possible to sustain other economic activities (basketry, raising livestock) and to fulfil household responsibilities. What is more, families can use the labour of elderly and younger household members – people mechanised brickyards were unwilling to employ. Although workers in non-mechanised brickyards are generally free to control their own work rates, owners do try to ensure a high level of production in some circumstances. It is normal practice for employers to encourage workers to draw on their wages in advance. This serves to bind workers to labouring in the employer's brickyard. The practice of binding workers with debt is so common that many family units are only able to move between employers by being 'bought' and 'sold' by brickyard owners: the new employer pays off workers' debts in the form of the employees' advances.

In the mid to late 1980s the brick industry attracted large numbers out of the agricultural workforce and from own-account petty commodity production. Former tenants found the higher incomes and reduced risks from waged brickmaking more rewarding than rice cultivation. Workers in the brick industry emphasised the fact that money was earned daily and contrasted this with the fact that rice cultivation yielded only an uncertain income once a year. In particular, brickyard work was seen as preferable to cultivating rice as a tenant because it entailed less risk: 'It's better to hire oneself out in the brickyards, you don't have to make any investment, you just use your labour.' Many local workers dropped independent petty commodity production such as raising ducks or weaving baskets, because wage labour provided higher incomes, and incomes were squeezed by rising costs of inputs and raw materials. The importance of the brick industry to local livelihoods at this time is reflected in the fact that of all households that did not operate landholdings 56 per cent had at least one member who worked in the brick industry. The brick industry also drew a minority of households out of home-based piece rate production for Bangkok factories.[5] Ironically, the brick industry increased the rate at which workers left agricultural employment at exactly the same time as local demand for agricultural labour increased. During this period local middle income farmers branched into the cultivation of more labour intensive cash crops, in particular sweet potato, for which the district had become renown. In the late 1980 and early 1990s every harvest season saw tension rise between farmers and brickyards: farmers were resentful of the fact that brickyards

5 In addition to craft production production for Bangkok-based factories (e.g. gluing leather wallets, stitching shoes and handbags) was relatively common (Arghiros 1997).

temporarily increased their wage rates to retain their workers during the harvest season.[6] Local agriculturists became increasingly reliant on non-local labour during the harvest season. Nipon's observation that Thai rural labour markets are now 'less dominated by agricultural seasonality than by the demand for non-farm employment that draws labour away from the farm' certainly applies to Klang district (Nipon 1994: 194). Daily wage labour in the brick industry also generated new tension between local workers' social obligations and work.[7] Province-wide statistics based on government surveys indicate that in the early 1990s agriculture was rapidly losing its importance and central position for the local population as a whole (Watthana 1991). By this time the proportion of farming households' income that came from off-farm activities exceeded that from agriculture (Amyot 1994). To some extent a move away from agriculture can be expected since no excess land was available for cultivation while population size had grown.

Many local employees greatly appreciated the arrival of the brick industry, and found it more rewarding than agriculture and other alternatives – such as working on Bangkok construction sites. As one worker noted 'it provides us with a stable daily income whereas you get an income from farming once a year.' However, we should not lose sight of the fact that this employment did not make for economic independence. Since wages (between 50 and 70 baht a day in 1990) provided for little more than subsistence needs employees were not able to accumulate the capital necessary to launch themselves into a more rewarding form of independent production or buy farmland or livestock. Some workers acknowledged that brickyard work represented the mainstay of their livelihood; young female workers referred to themselves as 'brick factory girls' (*saw rong it*).

By the late 1980s, however, as the number of enterprises continued to increase, and despite drawing all available labour out of agriculture, brickyards themselves started to suffer labour shortages. Poaching of labour, skilled and unskilled, between enterprises became a serious problem for entrepreneurs in the industry. The need to limit competition for labour between enterprises was so severe that it lead to the formation of an industry interest group, the Brick Manufacturers' Association (BMA) (Arghiros 1999). A rather black anecdotal joke told by a BMA member at one of their monthly meetings illustrates employers' anxiety to retain

6 Tension between industrial and agricultural production is also a product of the industrialisation of textile production in Majalaya, Indonesia (see Antlöv and Svensson 1991: 124).

7 It became increasingly common for locals to measure the immediate cash value of labour contributions that formerly were given on the basis of long-term balanced reciprocity. One landless man who stopped work in a mechanised brickyard for four days to help organise a nephew's ordination spoke resentfully of the wages he had foregone as a 'loss' (*khat*). In other words, he measured the time spent meeting the obligation to his kinspersons in terms of money. Although on this occasion the morality of kinship prevailed – after expressing his chagrin, this informant exclaimed 'you can't not help' – as households become more dependent on brickyard income and less on their kinspersons, it is inevitable that social obligations will take second place.

workers: the speaker had come across a group of young male employees sniffing glue as he was patrolling his brickyard. His first angry response was to kick them and then sack them, he said. But after a moment's reflection he thought he should go and buy them another tin of glue. Workers are too valuable, the subtext of this joke says, to sack even if they engage in socially unacceptable activities.

Owners of mechanised brickyards evolved three strategies to retain labour and increase productivity. They tried changing work regimes; they tried to reduce their reliance on labour by developing and substituting machinery; and they attempted to tie labour to them by developing reciprocal social relationships with sections of the workforce.

Some manufacturers introduced a variant of piece wage work – setting up work groups that operate individual extruders. However, several brickyards resisted operating on this basis as, they claimed, the bricks produced were shoddy. Several enterprises turned to remunerating workers based on subjective judgements of their productivity. Still wishing to use some incentive system, the owner adjusted workers' wages according to how hard they perceived them to work. Workers resented this and felt under continuous scrutiny, which indeed they were. Some employers attempted to reduce their dependence on labour by introducing new technology. Indeed, one owner, after condemning his workers as disloyal, lazy, and irresponsible, asked me to send him information about brickmaking technology in Britain: he hoped that it would allow him to do away with all his employees. Newly introduced high-capacity extruders increased productivity while reducing the number of workers needed.

Labour shortages in the mechanised branch of the industry gave rise to widespread paternalism, or what we could also call familialism. Employers attempted to bind workers to themselves through reciprocal social relationships that are essentially paternalistic and evocative of patron-client relations but also of familialistic relations. Employers are not, however, the personal patrons of employees, in the commonly used sense. Employees were expected to express their gratitude by foregoing the opportunity to take up employment elsewhere and by working conscientiously. Employers' patronage strategies aimed to obligate individual workers, households, and sometimes entire temple communities. Employers regularly acted as ritual patrons of temple ceremonies at the temples to which their work force belonged. One entrepreneur with about forty employees, told me he used 'psychology' (*jitwiththaya*) to manage his workers, managing them, in his words, 'with benevolence' (*pokkhrong duay phrakhun*). Every year between 1986 and 1996 he hosted an annual merit-making festival at his brickyard. Monks were brought in to charge brickyard and workers with auspiciousness. After the religious ritual he distributed gifts to all his employees. He began by giving rather modest items like work shirts, but started donating more valuable commodities like electric fans and electric rice pots; his 1990 gift-giving culminated with the presentation of large wooden wardrobes. He also sponsored the ordination, as temporary monks, of three of his workers in 1990, paying all expenses and feeding their kinspersons. In 1996 he had graduated to giving his best workers gold necklaces, bicycles and motorcycles. He claimed the gifts work to bind his workers to him. He said he thought his gifts would encourage recipients and, significantly, their families to think: 'If I work in Mr Santi's brickyard I get a fan/electric rice cooker/wardrobe, but if I work elsewhere for a year I come out with nothing.' He emphasised that 1990's gift of a wardrobe would be in constant view of every household member and therefore a constant reminder of the fruits of working for him. The impetus for these acts of 'kindness' does not just come from employers. Workers were aware that if they 'tell' (*bok*) their employers of a party (ordinations, weddings, and funerals) they are obliged to contribute financially to it.

Female entrepreneurs, who take care of the day to day running of most brickyards, manage workers by drawing on a familialistic model of social relations. Women downplay status differences between themselves and their employees.[8] Typically, owners expressed the employment relationship as one of mutual assistance and dependence. Some claimed that they related to their workers as same-generation kinspersons. One woman noted 'I take care of the workers as in a family: they depend on us and that is why they are loyal to their employers; I run the brickyard like a family' (see Moller 1998). Use of a familialistic idiom is also found in other comparable sectors: owners of small subcontracting garment workshops in urban areas say that they and their workers were 'like brothers and sisters,' 'we live together like a family' (Vagneron 1994: 90).

Paternalism and familialistic management strategies are likely to be found only during periods of labour shortages. Should, in future, labour be in surplus at the same time as demand for bricks is high employers will have no need to deploy such strategies. Employers do not behave as workers' patrons as a 'reflex.' Such strategies are deployed as a result of conscious decisions born of a need to retain workers. And likewise workers do not automatically play by the rules of the relationship the entrepreneur tries to construct: they often do not accept the obligations putatively imposed by an entrepreneur's paternalism. Workers are every bit as pragmatic as employers in this regard and do not hesitate to move to new employers when dissatisfied with treatment they received.

It is also true, however, that paternalism and famialism go hand in hand with more repressive measures. Many entrepreneurs used foremen who were said by workers to 'trample' on them; workers often laboured under the gaze of supervisors who sat in rooms with one-way windows evaluating their individual productivity. One 'paternalistic' owner was said to have spiked his workers drinking water with the stimulant amphetamine sulphate ('speed').[9] In most small enter-

8 I owe this insight to Joanne Moller, with whom I conducted research in 1995-97 – having myself previously been pre-occupied with male owners' strategies and presentation of relations.

9 This is the conclusion of a doctor to whom some of his workers went complaining of strange

prises such as these, labour is employed informally, without contracts: 'trouble-makers' can be easily isolated and dismissed, and it is common for employers to have more influence over workers' lives than is implied by a straightforward wage-labour relationship. It would be a mistake therefore, to characterise relations as marked only by paternalism and familialism: entrepreneurs deploy a broad range of strategies when dealing with workers, ranging from benevolent to repressive.

Even though workers all came from the locality, labour was often differentiated within a single factory. Owners of large factories, employing upwards of thirty or forty workers, cultivated relations with only a core of employees. Relations with other workers were impersonal and purely contractual while those with 'core' workers were personal and imbued with familial morality. Workers were also rewarded for their loyalty with pay bonuses which more transient workers did not receive: a differential of 30 per cent was common between new and longstanding employees.

Reliance on local labour had drawbacks for employers. Since employees of a brickyard often live in the same neighbourhood a large festival or party (*ngan*) in which kinspersons and neighbours are involved can bring production to a standstill for two or three days at a time. In a similar way, early factory owners in England were frustrated by the traditional holidays of their rural workers (Gillis 1983: 163, 167). Several owners expressed frustration at this, especially when such events coincided with periods of high brick prices. Also, if employees come from the owner's own community, as they often did, then it can be difficult for employers to treat them consistently in ways that are economically rather than morally desirable. For example, they could not turn away surplus workers when too many had appeared for work because it would be 'offensive' (*na kliat*).

In the mid-1990s as competition for labour increased some of the larger brickyards attempted to re-cast themselves as formal industries and tried to shed the image of a household enterprise: they tried to make their factories as attractive as the new export-oriented factories that started to mushroom. They introduced worker uniforms together with factory logos, required workers to attend work looking tidy with brushed hair. For many workers these changes did not have the effect of making employment more attractive. Older local workers, accustomed to the more relaxed conditions that characterise other brickyards, found these changes galling. One mature village woman could endure such conditions for only a week before resigning: she expressed her discontent in terms of the everyday conditions that distinguished work in this 'formalised' brickyard from other brickyards: 'Once the work bell went we weren't allowed to sit down and rest; if you're thirsty you have to stand up and drink; and vendors [of snacks] weren't allowed through the gates so you couldn't buy anything.'

symptoms. The Thai press has reported other cases of entrepreneurs putting amphetamine sulphate in workers' water in order to increase their productivity.

Northeasterners in the Central Plains

As labour shortages increased from the late 1980s onwards employers found it increasingly necessary to recruit migrants from other regions in the country, and in particular from the Northeast, Thailand's poorest region and the country's main source of migrant labour (Parnwell 1986). Reliance on migrant labour among brickyards increased markedly between 1990 and 1996: of seventeen mechanised brickyards I surveyed in 1990 almost a third of those still functioning (four of thirteen) that had used only local workers were entirely dependent on migrant workers in 1996; another four had substantially increased their reliance on migrants. Some employers co-operated with each other to send labour recruiters to the Northeast to find labour.

Entrepreneurs prefer to employ locals to migrants. Reliance on migrants often left brickyards with periodic labour shortages, since workers seldom stay beyond three months. Furthermore, as workers generally come in groups from a single locality the departure of a team of workers leaves an enterprise bereft of labour. Migrants often go to work in mechanised and non-mechanised brickyards as a group of up to thirty people and they are often kinspersons from a single village. When they offer their labour to a brickyard as a group they capitalise on the bargaining power their unity gives. Migrants to mechanised brickyards often use their position to ensure that all receive the same daily rates, in opposition to employers' desires to make pay reflect productivity. One can see this as a form of collective bargaining.

Likewise, migrant workers in non-mechanised brickyards who come from the same extended family petition owners collectively to obtain higher piece rates. Workers continually compare piece rates, earned in neighbouring brickyards, and seek higher rates when the price of bricks rises. Workers power lies in the fact that if they are not satisfied they will leave together, leaving the employer without a workforce. They also exploit this power to strengthen their position in disputes between individual workers and owners. Prior to the economic crisis, it was not uncommon for an entire group of migrant workers to leave in protest at the treatment of just one worker. Again, this ensures that employers treated migrant workers somewhat circumspectly.

Relations between employers and migrant workers are generally more instrumental and temporary than are those between local workers and employers and relations lack the reciprocal element described above. Employers themselves see migrant workers as outside their moral sphere, which, in their view, disarms them of the moral weapons they are able to deploy *vis-à-vis* local workers. Paternalistic strategies often fail to bind migrants in webs of mutual obligation – although workers are adept at showing the signs of respect, and giving the impression that they are playing by the rules of the relationship. The owner of one brickyard, whom I interviewed shortly after his entire workforce of migrants had abruptly left (1996), concluded that Northeastern workers 'are difficult to patronise/raise' (*liang yak*) because 'they don't know gratitude (*bunkhun*).' He declared:

> Whatever the employer does for them, and however much they show signs of respect to the employer such as calling him 'uncle' or whatever, when they want to leave they do so without a thought about the inconvenience they cause the employer.

This was contrasted with the behaviour of Central Thais: they 'work as though they are relatives; they are respectful (*krengjay*): if I'm good to them they're good to me: they've got gratitude (*khaw mii bunkhun*).'

Increasing numbers of mechanised brickyards introduced piece rate regimes as they replaced their local workers with migrants. A single family (or *jaw*, 'owners') was then given responsibility for the output of one extruder and was paid a piece rate according to output. This reduced the burden of managing the time of workers. Employers were not able to discriminate against national migrants in terms of wages because of national labour shortages and workers' consequent relatively strong position. They did not, however, receive bonuses that local longstanding workers earned.

Some entrepreneurs expressed frustration that the subsistence orientation of Northeastern workers meant they were difficult to retain: they often worked with particular savings targets in mind and they departed once these were achieved or with the arrival of the agricultural season in their home villages (many own land in the Northeast and carry out wage labour to bolster their incomes, often because their land is low-yielding). One brickyard owner expressed dismay that his Northeastern workers did not appear to want the consumer items which his local workers aspired towards obtaining – electric rice cookers and motorbikes – for example. He had no means to bind these workers more securely to employment with him. A relatively common and persistent complaint that reflects brickyard owners' view of Northeastern migrants' amorality is that they draw advances on their wages and then disappear in the night. Measures taken to prevent this include taking workers identity cards. However, this is often ineffective because workers may use false cards. One factory built high gates which it locked at night and hired a security guard to counter this problem. Northeasterners are generally denigrated by employers and were spoken about in ways that verge on the racist. Certainly, national migrants stand outside of local society and are often viewed as rather predatory. They are often blamed for thefts that occur locally, and for abusing local resources, such as over-fishing ponds.

By the mid-1990s, despite reliance on national migrant workers, the brick industry was squeezed by an absolute shortage of workers. Ironically, labour supply became a limiting factor within the brick industry while demand for bricks was stronger than ever. By early 1996, eleven of the remaining thirteen mechanised brickyards that I had initially surveyed in 1990 reported suffering labour shortages. A full ten of these ran below capacity, with most able to operate only half of their extruders. Despite massive demand for bricks, all employed fewer workers than in 1990. Moreover, wages had doubled in this period – from between 50-60 baht in 1990 to 100-120 baht in 1996.[10] The labour shortages experienced in the brick industry is mirrored by research elsewhere in the country. A survey undertaken of more than seven hundred small, privately owned enterprises revealed that half of enterprises experienced problems findings workers and that almost half of the enterprises with more than five workers were of the opinion that the capacity of their enterprise to grow was hindered by a shortage of labour, despite a positive economic environment (Oudin 1994: 100-2). Many local workers, particularly younger women, had already left the brick industry to work in new export-oriented industry where the work is lighter and in more pleasant conditions. Now there was even a shortage of migrant workers.

Invisible Workers

The local arrival of export-oriented factories, described below, with their better conditions and, initially at least, better remuneration packages, lead to an increase in the brick industry's reliance on migrant labour. However, at the same time that large-scale factories started to arrive in the district, migrant labour started to dry up. Nationally, full employment meant that workers had so many other work opportunities between 1993-97 that Thai migrants increasingly chose either to seek employment in large-scale industry that offered better conditions to those of industries such as the brick industry, or to take advantage of employment opportunities nearer to home. Even in the Northeast the growing industrial sector was unable to produce to full capacity as workers left factories to work in the mushrooming service sector – local department stores and hotels (Kermel-Torres and Veerapong 1999).

I was given a vivid demonstration of just how scarce Thai migrant labour had become when I accompanied a brickyard owner on his quest to the Northeast to recruit about twenty workers. To his great frustration, in the face of booming demand for bricks, he was operating only half of his machines due to an absolute lack of workers. Despite driving a round trip of more than a thousand kilometres and stopping at innumerable roadside settlements the owner did not manage to successfully recruit a single worker. At several places at which we stopped we learned that we were the most recent of many touring business people seeking labour. Local construction work opportunities gave workers wages almost equivalent to those they could earn in the brick industry (100 baht for men, 80 for

10 Between 1989 and mid-1997 £1 was equivalent to around 40 baht; in seems to have stabilised at 65 baht to £1 by August 1998.

women, compared for 100–120 and 95–100 in the brick industry). Even more could be earned from Bangkok based construction work.

By the mid 1990s Thai migrant workers had become so scarce that many brickyards started to rely on illegal immigrant workers, mostly from Burma but also from Cambodia. Despite their new-found importance foreign migrants were all but 'invisible.' Employers tried to prevent them from interacting with local communities and taught them to hide whenever officials were in the vicinity. Due to their illegal status it was impossible to quantify the number of workers employed.[11] Throughout early 1996 several brickyards in Klang district were subjected to repeated raids by the police, many of whom sought bribes of up to 20,000 baht. Their workers were seized and some were sent to a holding camp for eventual repatriation. Conditions in this camp were extremely poor, and inmates were reportedly physically abused. Their warders appropriated any earnings they had. A number of immigrants seized on police raids were also often either put to work in the policemen's own factories, or were 'sold' on to other factories. At this time at least ten district policemen, including the police commander, owned their own brickyards.

The Brick Manufacturers' Association, mentioned above, in an effort to solve the industry's labour shortages petitioned the provincial administration to enable it to employ foreign workers legally. The Association asked for permission to employ 400–500 workers. Businesses operating in certain sectors including the brick industry were granted permission to legally employ immigrants in September 1996: the Brick Manufacturers' Association's lobbying probably contributed in a very small way to this change. Despite the legalisation of immigrant labour many local employers did not regularise the position of their workers: they found the conditions for registration, and in particular the cash bond and permit fee due for each worker, too onerous.[12] Some employers failed to register their workers because they did not want to be held responsible for them to the authorities.

The arrival of immigrant workers meant that the workforce within a single brickyard became even more differentiated than previously (see also Saptari 1991: 128). Between 1995–97 it was common to find three categories of workers in a single enterprise: locals, Thai migrant workers, and legal or illegal immigrant workers. Generally, locals are given the most skilled and lightest tasks (operating

11 In February 1996 the Ministry of Labour assessed that there were 400 illegal workers in the province in these two industries. This is, as Stern (1998: 17) notes, likely to be a gross underestimation of the actual numbers involved.

12 Immediately after the legalisation of immigrant labour, in the three month period between September and November 1996, 503 Burmese workers who worked in either the brickmaking industry or rice mills were registered in Ayuthaya province (Stern 1998: 21). In a survey of employers of immigrant labour in a number of sectors 46.8 per cent of respondents noted that the main reason for hiring foreign labour was because of labour shortages: the second most common reason given was because Thai workers were not consistent or disciplined enough.

extruders and other machinery); national migrants were often allocated slightly heavier work, while foreign workers were given the heaviest and most arduous tasks. Foreign migrants suffered the worst conditions and were paid less than Thai workers (see Odgaard 1992: 174, for a similar scenario in rural China). The fact that entrepreneurs were able to pay immigrants between 15 and 30 per cent less than their Thai workers added to the attractions of employing them.

The Attraction of Factories

Between 1991 and 1997 several export-oriented factories were established in Klang and a neighbouring district. These sought to recruit young women in particular. Women were keen to leave the brick industry for the relatively more attractive work conditions of these new factories, which produced anything from shoes to papier-mâché ornaments. Initially those new factories that offered the best wages and conditions recruited only the better-educated locals who had a secondary education. Inevitably such opportunities were only available to women from wealthier rural households. However, as even these factories experienced progressively more severe labour shortages they reduced their educational requirements, and thus gave access to employment to women from poorer backgrounds. Thus it is possible to say that over time factory work has expanded the opportunities not only for households from the local upper stratum, but also from poorer sections of the community.[13] Macroeconomic growth, with the resultant nationwide labour shortages, is largely responsible for this spreading of benefits

The growth of industrial production in the province in which Klang district lies has been rapid and relatively sudden. At the same time agriculture has been in decline. Between 1989 and 1997 the gross provincial product of agriculture decreased by 14 per cent while the gross provincial product of industry increased a staggering fifteen fold (Ayuthaya Provincial Office 1996). In 1990, 75.9 per cent of waged workers in the province were engaged in factory work whereas by 1994 this had risen to 90.1 per cent (Amyot 1997: 6). The majority of workers are women.[14] It is also noticeable that local opportunities have led to a reduction in outmigration from the province, with a 13.8 per cent reduction between 1990 and 1994 (Ayuthaya Provincial Office 1996). It is increasingly common for enterprises to relocate from Bangkok to areas like Klang district. In the early 1990s high land prices and difficulties obtaining labour, as well as government incentives, combined to stimulate the spread of industry to what some now call the Extended

13 See Rigg (1997) Chapter 6 for a discussion of arguments regarding the benefits and disbenefits of industrial labour for women.

14 Between 1990 and 1994 the proportion of women involved in factory work increased from 81.2 per cent to 93.9 per cent; the proportion of men finding employment in factories increased from 62.5 per cent to 80.8 per cent (Amyot 1997).

Bangkok Metropolitan Region (see Luxmon 1998). A principal reason for locating outside Bangkok, and for recruiting rural labour is that rural labour is perceived by entrepreneurs as more docile, and more easily managed. As one manager of a Klang factory noted rural workers are 'easy to control' (*khum ngay*).

In Klang a process of clustering of similar enterprises has not taken place and a disparate range of products are produced. Thus there have been no opportunities for labourers to combine to represent their interests across a single subsector. However, the distinguishing features of these factories *vis-à-vis* the brickmaking industry are that they were established using external capital and management, they do not rely on local resources, they were located in this area to take advantage of cheap land and, for the most part, cheap and relatively accessible labour. Their administrative centres are located in Bangkok, and managers are from outside the locality. In this regard management does not interact with workers lives outside the factory environment so much as locally based enterprises.

It is difficult to generalise about labour relations in these enterprises. The means by which labour is recruited, retained and managed differs according to a number of factors such as the product, levels of skill requirements, and so on. Paternalism does not figure highly in the repertoire of managers' labour management strategies and few non-financial incentives are used. Labour is organised and disciplined using production quotas, line production, financial incentives, and systems of fines. Workers have not organised or formed labour unions in any factories. Just as in brickyards, movement expresses labour dissatisfaction. Prior to the economic crisis, labour mobility was very high between factories, and the establishment of a new factory often led to an outflow of workers from other factories: workers saw advantages to being among the first employees in a new factory (there are more possibilities for promotion, for example). Until the economic crisis, continually expanding opportunities served to limit the extent to which employers could impose poor conditions and pay.

Although paternalism and familialistic relations are mostly absent from the larger export-oriented factories found in and around Klang district, it is worth stressing that there is no necessary relationship between enterprise size, the level of technology used, and paternalism. In response to labour shortages and labour poaching, Kermel-Torres and Veerapong (1999: 10) have noted that even large firms in the rural Northeast utilise paternalistic management strategies: giving out social benefits – 'helping' workers meet funeral expenses, for example – rather than raising their basic wage with the explicit intention of developing a 'sense of commitment among workers.' As Montgomery has argued, although paternalism is 'readily associated with the cultural legacy of preindustrial life [...] Imagery and practices featuring the personal solicitude of a familiar boss have been emphasised by huge enterprises with elaborate managerial hierarchies' (Montgomery 1998: 1). A concrete example of this is provided by Benenatti's (1998) description of familialistic labour relations in a large Italian factory early this century.

It is important to appreciate that the most sophisticated of these modern factories offer workers non-economic rewards that brickyard labour would never provide. Export-oriented enterprises do generally provide better work conditions than do local industries such as the brickmaking sector, and a job in such a factory is seen as an improvement in status as well as in livelihood. Workers identify work in such factories as 'modern' (*than samay*), and as an opportunity to surpass rural communities: women often go to work wearing make-up; young men use their regular incomes to buy motorbikes on hire-purchase. To work in a modern factory reflects well on workers self-identity (Mills 1997). Workers are not exposed to the sun, and retain their pale complexions.

Work in such factories is also a step away from local rural society and community: workers are not necessarily able to choose with whom they will work; the pace of work is largely out of workers control; and workers are unable to stop and start work to accommodate important community or life cycle events. For the young, however, some of these attributes are not necessarily negative and it is important to realise that work in the more modern factories factory fulfils some of workers' social as well as financial needs.

The Economic Crisis and Empty Huts

The Thai economic crisis has had a catastrophic impact on the brickmaking industry. The industry has been decimated as nationally the construction industry has come to a complete standstill. The only construction work still being undertaken comprises government projects and even these were severely cut back. Throughout Thailand one can see half-completed buildings on which work has been suspended as well as rows of empty shophouses. In August 1998 none of the remaining factories I initially surveyed in 1990 were still run as profitable business concerns. Those that still operated did so at between a tenth and a quarter of their full capacity. Most still produce only in order to use up stockpiled resources, and to prevent their machinery from seizing up. Some smaller, non-mechanised capitalist enterprises have laid off their employees to revert to petty commodity production, using only household labour. The price of bricks has fallen from its peak in 1996 of 0.75 to 0.17 baht in 1998 – most enterprises estimate they break even at 0.20 baht. Ironically, entrepreneurs face a situation in which labour is now abundant but there is no demand for their product. As noted above, prior to the crisis entrepreneurs were unable to produce at full capacity despite buoyant demand solely because of labour shortages.

The impact of the crisis on labour in the brick industry has been swift and extensive. Almost all national and non-national migrant workers have been laid off – the corrugated tin shacks that lie alongside almost every mechanised brickyard lie empty. National migrants were returned to their home regions, and were forced to withdraw their children from local schools (their children were known as 'brickyard children,' *dek rong it*).[15] Registered Burmese workers have been laid off wholesale. According to Ministry of Labour and Welfare figures in 1996 there were 2,257 registered immigrant workers in the province – they worked in rice mills and the brickmaking industry. However, in July 1998 there were only 546 such workers. Workers were not given severance pay, as workers in the formal sector have generally obtained. Because most local people had moved out of the brickmaking industry prior to the economic crisis, they largely escaped unemployment: for example, in one of the district's subdistricts only two locals could be identified as people who had been made redundant and were still without work.[16] The few locals who had been made redundant from the brick industry found work in other local industries. If the brickmaking industry had crashed in 1990 we would expect almost 60 per cent of non-farming households to have lost incomes from the industry.

More generally, the Thai government, in an effort to increase work opportunities for nationals, has tried to phase out use of non-Thai workers. The government rescinded its earlier provision that enabled entrepreneurs to employ immigrants. An ongoing tussle between the government and rice millers provides an indication of the difficulties involved in promoting such a reversal. In July 1998 a fifth of the country's rice mills shut down in protest at government insistence that they get rid of their Burmese workers and recruit Thai nationals to carry the 100-kilogram sacks of milled rice between mills and wharves. Mills complained, with some justification, that locals were no longer willing or able to carry such weights. Local state authorities organised a competition to demonstrate that Thais still had the capacity for such work. The outcome, as it was shown on television, was not impressive: most entrants appeared to collapse under the weight of the sacks. As a result, rice sacks are to be reduced in weight to fifty-five kilograms. Illegal aliens in certain sectors, including rice mills have been allowed to stay (*Bangkok Post*, July 16, 1998 'Deadline on aliens put off'). Recent estimates are that there are still one million foreign workers selling their labour in Thailand, with over 750,000-800,000 from Burma: most have illegal status (*Bangkok Post,* March 15, 1998).

Export-oriented factories in and around the district have not been affected by the economic downturn to the same degree as enterprises that produce for domestic markets. Newer export-oriented industries have fared particularly well. Some of these factories have actually expanded production, and, even in mid-1998 were recruiting increased numbers of workers. Due to the depreciation of the baht, their products are cheaper on the international market, and demand is thus strong. It is not the case that workers in all export-oriented sectors are simi-

15 See Parnwell (1998) for an analysis of the situation of returnee migrants from the Northeast.

16 I am aware of this figure because the subdistrict administrative organisation was required to supply a list to the district office, and to subsequently recruit these people as labour on local works.

larly safe: workers in industries with older technology such as the textile sector are being laid off. However, in such cases the economic crisis appears to have stimulated trends that were already evident prior to the crisis.

Nevertheless, workers in large factories in and around Klang district do perceive that a change has taken place. Prior to the economic crisis they were highly aware of their value and did not hesitate to shop around for better conditions: mobility between factories was very high as workers moved to attain better fringe benefits. Currently workers are more circumspect and are prepared to accept their existing work conditions without taking the risk of moving factory. Recent school leavers are also finding it more difficult to find their first job.

Ironically, the year following the crisis saw improvements in agricultural livelihoods. Farmers generally, and central plains farmers in particular, benefited from significant crop price rises that were partly a result of the Thai economic crisis. International demand for Thai rice rose markedly in 1998 due to the depreciation of the baht and failure of rice harvests elsewhere in Southeast Asia. The prices of other cash crops also rose. Thus, paradoxically, following many years of stagnation, the agricultural sector in much of the central plains has been buoyant. In Klang district, approximately a sixth of riceland that had lain fallow during the years of the economic boom has been brought back into cultivation. Wage labour opportunities are now increasingly available in the agricultural sector in areas where cash crops are grown. Some entrepreneurs who had branched into nonfarm production returned to agriculture, and those locals who had lost job opportunities in the brick industry found new opportunities in the agriculture sector.

Conclusion

If one had taken a snapshot of the brick industry at any time between the mid-1980s and late 1990s one would have received a different impression at each moment. The rapidity of change in the composition of the labour force in the industry is remarkable. Up to the end of the 1980s the industry was built exclusively on the labour of local landless and land-poor households who were drawn out of the agricultural sector. Through the early 1990s better opportunities drew younger workers out of the brick industry, causing entrepreneurs to hunt for workers from the rural Northeast. For the first time, Northeasterners had opportunities to work in industry outside of Bangkok. But progressively full employment led to better opportunities for many Northeasterners themselves, forcing entrepreneurs to recruit illegal immigrant workers. With the economic crisis, the collapse of the industry has forced the return of national and foreign migrants to their home provinces while leaving local labour virtually untouched. The impact of the recent economic crisis on formal sector industrial labour has been more uneven.

Workers in industries that produce for domestic markets have been harder hit than those that produce for international markets. Such factories, particularly those that are recently established with modern, highly productive practices, benefit from the devaluation of the baht. In the absence of comparable data on other industrial sectors it is difficult to say how representative this process is of other industries in Thailand, and indeed elsewhere in Southeast Asia. It is likely that the experience of the brick industry is unique in one way: insofar as it is one of the first industries to benefit from growth and to suffer from downturns because its fortunes are inextricably linked with the wider economy – it represents what other industries have experienced in a telescoped time-frame, and to a more exaggerated degree.

References

Amyot, J. (1976) *Village Ayutthaya: Social and Economic Conditions of a Rural Population in Central Thailand,* Bangkok: Chulalongkorn University Social Research Institute.

— (1994) *The Structure of Employment of the Rural Population of the Central Region of Thailand,* Bangkok: Chulalongkorn University Social Research Institute.

— (1997) *The Structure of Employment of the Rural Population of Ayuthaya Province* 1994 *(Analysis of Kor Chor Chor 2 Khor 2537),* Chulalongkorn University Social Research Institute Unpublished data paper.

Antlöv, H. and Svensson, T. (1991) 'From rural home weavers to factory labour: the industrialisation of textile manufacturing in Majalaya', in P. Alexander, P. Boomgaard and B. White (eds.) *In the Shadow of Agriculture: Non-farm Activities in the Javanese Economy, Past and Present,* Amsterdam: Rural Tropical Institute.

Arghiros, D. (1997) 'Rural industry and development in Central Thailand: an alternative approach', *Journal of Entrepreneurship* 6: 1–18.

— (1999) 'The local dynamics of "The New Political Economy": a district business association and its role in electoral politics', in R. McVey (ed.) *Money and Power in Provincial Thailand,* London: Curzon/NIAS.

Ayuthaya Provincial Office (1996) *Ayuthaya Province,* Ayuthaya: Thian Wathana.

Benenatti, E. (1998) 'Americanism and paternalism: managers and workers in twentieth century Italy', *Journal of International Labour and Working-Class History* 53: 6–27.

Brown, A. (1997) 'Locating working-class power', in K. Hewison (ed.) *Political Change in Thailand: Democracy and Participation,* London: Routledge.

Cook, S. (1984) 'Peasant economy, rural industry and capitalist development in the Oaxaca Valley, Mexico', *Journal of Peasant Studies* 12: 4–40.

Gillis, J.R. (1983) *The Development of European Society, 1770–1870,* Lanham: University of America.

Hewison, K. and Brown, A. (1994) 'Labour and unions in an industrialising Thailand', *Journal of Contemporary Asia* 24: 483–513.

ILO (1998) *The Social Impact of the Asian Financial Crisis,* International Labour Organisation Regional Office for Asia and the Pacific, Technical report for discussion at the High-Level Tripartite Meeting on Social Responses to the Financial Crisis in East and Southeast Asia.

Kermel-Torres, D. and Saenjan Veerapong (1999) 'Industrial labour force mobility', paper presented to the 7th International Conference on Thai Studies, Amsterdam, 1999.

Lazo, L. (ed.) (1996) *Out of the Shadows: Practical Actions for the Social Protection of Homeworkers in Thailand,* Bangkok: International Labour Organisation.

Limqueco, P. et al. (1989) *Labour and Industry in ASEAN*, Manila: Journal of Contemporary Asia Publishers.

Luxmon Wongusphasawat (1998) 'Extended Metropolitanisation and the Process of Individual Location Decision-Making in Thailand', PhD Thesis, University of Hull.

Mills, M. (1997) 'Working for wages in Bangkok, reworking gender and family in the countryside', in V.S.S. Theobald (ed.) *Women, Gender Relations and Development in Thai Society*, Chiang Mai: Women's Study Centre, Chiang Mai University.

Moller, J. (1998) 'Gender Dimensions of Small Business Management in Thailand', Unpublished manuscript.

Montgomery, D. (1998) 'Introduction: workers' choices, company policies and loyalties', *Journal of International Labour and Working-Class History* 53: 1–5.

Nipon Poapongsakorn (1994) 'Transformations in the Thai rural labor market', in B. Koppel, J. Hawkins and W. James (eds.) *Development or Deterioration? Work in Rural Asia,* Boulder, C.O.: Lynne Rienner Publishers.

Odgaard, O. (1992) 'Labour conditions in rural private enterprises', in E.B. Vermeer (ed.) *From Peasant to Entrepreneur: Growth and Change in Rural China. Papers originating from the Second European Conference on agriculture and rural development in China, Leiden, January 14–17, 1991,* Wageningen: Pudoc.

Oudin, X. (1994) 'Small scale enterprises on the labour market', *Journal of Social Research* 17: 94–106.

Parnwell, M.J.G. (1986) 'Migration and the development of agriculture: a case study of North-East Thailand', in M.J.G.Parnwell (ed.) *Rural Development in North-East Thailand: Case Studies of Migration, Irrigation and Rural Credit*, Occasional Paper No. 12, Hull: University of Hull.

— (1998) 'Coping with crisis in Thailand: migration reversal, survivalist strategies and development implications', paper presented to conference on 'The Economic Crisis in East Asia and the Impact on Local Populations', Roskilde University, Denmark, 1998.

Rigg, J. (1997) *Southeast Asia: the Human Landscape of Modernisation and Development,* London: Routledge.

Saptari, R. (1991) 'The differentiation of a rural industrial labour force: gender segregation in East Java's *kretek* cigarette industry, 1920–1990', in P. Alexander, P. Boomgaard and B. White (eds.) *In the Shadow of Agriculture: Non-farm Activities in the Javanese Economy, Past and Present*, Amsterdam: Rural Tropical Institute.

Stern, A. (1998) *Thailand's Migration Situation and its Relation with APEC Members and Other Countries in South East Asia*, Bangkok: Institute of Asian Studies, Chulalongkorn University.

Sungsidh Piriyarangsan and Kanchada Poonpanich (1994) 'Labour institutions in an export-oriented country: a case study of Thailand', in G. Rodgers (ed.) *Workers, Institutions and Economic Growth in Asia,* Geneva: Institute for Labour Studies.

Vagneron, I. (1994) 'The integration of micro-enterprises in Thailand's growth: the case of subcontracting', *Journal of Social Research* 17: 81–93.

Watthana Wongsekiarrthirat (1991) *Kanplianplaeng Kan Chay Thidin le Raengngan Khong Chumchom Chonabot nay Cangwat Ayutthaya (2512–2532) (Changing Land and Labour Utilisation in Rural Communities in Ayutthaya Province, 1969–1989)*, Bangkok: Chulalongkorn University Social Research Institute.

11

Labour Relations in a Changing Rural World: The Evolving Thai Experience

JONATHAN RIGG

This chapter aims to embed changing labour relations in rural areas of Thailand, and particularly in agriculture, within the context of the wider economic and social transformations underway in the Kingdom. Labour relations are reflections and manifestation of more general national (and international) processes mediated and articulated through local structures. Locality, therefore, is profoundly important in moulding patterns of change. This is clear, for example, in Kelly's work in Luzon in the Philippines (1998, 1999a and 1999b), in Elmhirst's work in Sumatra (1995, 1996, 1998 and 2002), and in Hart's work in the Muda area of Peninsular Malaysia (1992, 1994).

Angeles-Reyes, in her discussion of rural change in the Philippines, poses a question that sets the stage for the discussion in this chapter: 'What does the growth of non-farm rural employment signify beyond the obvious fact of labour market differentiation?' (1994: 133). This quote is used as a spring board both to link forwards to the impacts of non-farm work on labour relations and – importantly – backwards to identify the sources of change. For labour relations in agriculture are increasingly influenced and determined by the wider labour market and Thailand's changing cultural context. As Peck argues, 'labour market "transactions" are socially encoded, socially structured and socially structuring' (1996: 344). This not only locates labour relations quite firmly within the social and cultural, but also within the local.

But while this chapter acknowledges the importance of the local, it is not possible to understand the progress and process of labour relations in rural Thailand as mere manifestations of locality. The wider political economy of agriculture, and of development, provide the lens through which the effects of locality are both received and reflected.

The Political Economy of Agriculture in Thailand

There is no space here to do more than lay out the broad historical framework regarding the political economy of agriculture. There is, it can be said, a dialectic at work when it comes to understanding the attachment of Thailand and Thais to land, agriculture, and farming. On the one hand, agriculture plays a central role in Thai historiography and remains a touchstone for what it is to be 'Thai.' From the earliest piece of Thai literature, Inscription no. 1 of King Ramkhamhaeng (dated 1292) which opens with the words 'In the time of Ramkhamhaeng this land of Sukhothai is thriving [...] there is fish in the water and rice in the fields,'[1] through to today's national school syllabus, agriculture, farming and farmers have maintained a central place in the Thai imagination. Young Thais are taught that farmers are the 'backbone' of the nation and all can recite the famous lines of Ramkhamhaeng's inscription. Thailand also remains the world's largest rice exporter and a major producer of a whole range of agricultural commodities from prawns and chickens to cassava and rubber. For a number of years it has been suggested that Thailand should carve out a niche for itself as a Newly Agro-Based Industrialising County or NABIC, playing to its competitive advantage in agriculture and agro-industries (see Simon 1996: 88).

But whilst at one level it is possible to accord farmers and farming a high status and a central position, the experience of the post-war period has been one where agriculture has become increasingly marginalised. Structurally, agriculture has seen it share of GDP decline from 50 per cent at the beginning of the 1950s to less than 10 per cent in the late 1990s. The government has, historically, taxed farming heavily (and especially rice farming), and used agriculture to subsidise industry. There are few scholars who do not see in Thai development policies, a distinct urban (and industry) bias. In their different ways, Bello et al. (1998), Dixon (1999) and Hirsch (1990) all identify a crisis in Thai agriculture which has its roots, largely, in the policies of successive Thai governments:

> For most of the post-war period successive Thai governments have explicitly promoted industry while implicitly discouraging agriculture through heavy taxation – particularly of the rice sector – and general neglect (Dixon 1999: 140).

At a popular level the crisis of agriculture today can be seen in a flurry of 'peasant' demonstrations and direct action across the country, all attempting to highlight the plight of farmers (FEER 2000). It is also clear, as the following discussion will show, that agriculture, as a way of life, is avoided by most young people, even those with farming roots.

1 There is some doubt as to the veracity of this inscription. However it nonetheless occupies a central place in the construction of Thai nationhood and identity, and this is the important point.

From Farm to Non-Farm

Scholars have noted the tendency both to view the Southeast Asian region as 'quintessentially agrarian' (McVey 1992: 7) and to '"agrarianise" the countryside' (Alexander et al. 1991: 1). In this way, Southeast Asia becomes a region of farmers and farming, and the countryside becomes equated with agricultural pursuits. While acknowledging the deep structural changes that have occurred in the economies of the region, scholars at the same time appear reluctant to accept that this has also led to an equally deep transformation in rural people's lives. This clearly has implications for labour relations in agriculture. It also helps to explain the tendency to abstract labour relations in agriculture from the rather wider question of household labour relations in rural areas. Dixon, for example, in his excellent recent review of the Thai economy writes that while Thailand might have achieved rapid economic growth during the 1990s 'observers appear to have lost sight of the fact that the country remains an essentially agricultural one [... and ...] the agricultural sector [...] remains the principal source of livelihood for some 60 per cent of the population' (1999: 140).[2] The essence of this quote, and many other similar perspectives, seems to be that while the country may have experienced economic change of some considerable magnitude, this has not undermined its essentially agrarian character. It is but a short step from here, to embracing the perspective that agricultural and agrarian change are, to a significant degree, one and the same (see Koppel and Hawkins 1994: 23).

While statistics released by Thailand's National Statistical Office and by international organisations may offer an image of a stubbornly rural and agricultural country, local level studies show that employment and residency patterns have undergone significant change. Over the years, scores of village-level studies have been conducted in Thailand. As one would expect, these recount multiple and sometimes conflicting stories about the pattern and direction of change in rural areas. However, while in their detail the narratives are importantly different (and, to be sure, the devil is in the detail), they do appear consistently to show a shift in the balance of the village economy from farm to non-farm. In many cases this has occurred to the extent that the contribution of agriculture to household income is exceeded by non-farm income (see Ritchie 1993 and 1996a, Rigg 1998, Singhanetra-Renard 1999, Chantana Banpasirichote 1993). The reasons for this difference in perspective are, in brief, linked to five main issues: inadequacies in

2 But, in an earlier discussion in the same book, Dixon questions the accuracy of the country's employment statistics, observing that the official data may mask a 'much more substantial decline in the [agricultural] sector's importance as a source of livelihood' (1999: 19-20). This is discussed in more detail below. Nipon Poapongsakorn's analysis of change in the Thai rural labour market mirrors Dixon's perspective in acknowledging the growth of non-farm work and remarking on low rural incomes while at the same time offering the view that even in the dry season the agricultural sector accounts for 60 percent of total employment (1994: 168).

household registration systems; inaccuracies in labour force surveys; static definitions of rural and urban; lack of nuance in the categorisation of rural/urban and agriculture/industry; and the failure to take sufficient account of the dispersal of industries to rural areas (see Rigg 2001).

Looking Back: Sources of Change

The Trouble with Farming

To fully appreciate the paradox which underpins this paper – namely, growing agricultural labour shortages in the context of rising rural populations – it is necessary to outline the social and cultural changes which, it is argued, have profoundly transformed the perspectives, desires, aspirations, and expectations of many rural inhabitants. While it would be wrong to extract the social and cultural from the economic and political, the tendency to see changes in labour relations essentially as responses to changing economic conditions requires an explicit discussion of the social and cultural context.

Today it is rare to find a young rural Thai with an agricultural family background who wishes to emulate her or his parents and become a farmer. In a survey of thirty-eight students at a local school in Tambon Thung Sadok, south of Chiang Mai, just one expressed a desire to work in agriculture (field research, 2000). For the rest, their horizons were likely to take them out of agriculture and beyond the village. While this is just one school in one corner of Thailand, work conducted elsewhere in the country, and more widely in Southeast Asia demonstrates the extent to which the desire to avoid farming is becoming deeply embedded (see Mills 1999, Sinhanetra-Renard 1999, Toyota 1999).

In explaining this desire to construct livelihoods that avoid farming it is sometimes difficult to disentangle the cultural from the economic. Certainly agriculture is perceived to be an occupation with little future and few prospects. Rates of return to agriculture relative to other occupations have declined, while water shortages, land degradation and land speculation, and a gradual contraction in average landholdings (Table 11.1) have also played a role in squeezing farming.[3] Bello et al. (1998) go so far as to argue that farming in Thailand is in terminal decline, and rural areas with it. It is, perhaps, worthwhile to note that the 'trouble' with agriculture, in some parts of the country at least, has a longer history than usually imagined. Anan Ganjanapan argues that farming families in the north were facing a 'crisis of subsistence' (1986: 394) in the 1970s. Significantly, given

3 The decline in the size of average landholdings is accentuated by the fact that the productivity of land has declined as more marginal land has been brought under cultivation. Furthermore, of course, the needs of farm families today are much greater than formerly.

the actual pattern of change in the area where Anan Ganjanapan worked,[4] he saw the need being to raise agricultural production (i.e. intensification) to make up for a fall in average land holdings. In the event, local people in this area embraced the non-farm economy to meet the shortfall (see below).

Table 11.1: Average Farm Land Holdings

	Whole Kingdom	*North*	*Northeast*	*Centre*	*South*
1975	27.2	22.7	28.3	33.3	23.5
1980	26.6	22.4	28.0	32.6	22.0
1985	26.4	22.7	27.1	32.4	23.2
1990	26.0	22.9	26.6	31.6	23.1
1993	25.4	22.8	25.6	31.4	22.1

Note: areas are in *rai* (1 hectare = 6.25 rai).
Source: various publications of the Ministry of Agriculture and Co-operatives.

While agriculture has declined in attractiveness so alternatives to farming have presented themselves. In places and at times, for example in parts of the Central Plains and the Northern region, these have permitted rural people to engage in non-farm work while living at home. In much of the Northeast it has created the conditions where circular migration is the norm. It is the need to engage with the non-farm sector which has made education, in many people's eyes, a necessity. Most factory employment requires, at the very least, a lower secondary level education (nine years of schooling in total). Tara Buakamsri (1997: 136) quotes an advertisement in the local press:

> Leading firm in semiconductor industry seeks a number of manufacturing workers. Female aged 18-23 in any field of study. M3, M6, vocational or equivalent. No experience required. Hiring result known at once. Ready to work within two days [...]

As one Northern Thai informant pointed out to Bencha Yoddumnern-Attig: '[i]n the past, the parents' prime responsibility and concern was to feed their children, today [... it] is to educate their children' (Bencha Yoddumnern-Attig 1992:20). To achieve this end, parents are willing to forego a great deal (see Sinhanetra-Renard 1999: 78 on Thailand and also Rodenburg 1997: 151-2, Fegan 1983: 39-40, Sherman 1990: 50-1).

But the desire for education – and, it seems, the more the better – is not purely a product of the decline of farming and the rise of non-farm livelihoods. In other

4 His study area was close to the district town of Sanpatong, about 25 kilometres south of the regional centre of Chiang Mai.

words, it is not merely driven by the relative returns to agricultural and alternative non-agricultural pursuits and the skills and level of education that each require. It is also a product of the culture of modernity which has insinuated itself, it seems, into every facet of Thai society.

Than Samay – the Culture of Modernity

There is a widely held view – supported by years of bitter experience – that agriculture is unlikely to deliver an acceptable livelihood. But farming is also perceived to be a low status occupation. This encourages children and their parents to invest time and money in education, and the process of education instills still further those beliefs that pushed them into investing in education in the first place. The process thereby becomes self-fulfilling: educating children takes them away from the field. It imbues them with the belief that agriculture is beneath them. And it provides them with skills which, because of the lack of employment opportunities for the best educated in many rural areas, serves to keep them away from home.

But behind this self-perpetuating link between education and the views held of agriculture is a more fundamental vision of lifestyle and livelihood which has been termed *than samay*, or up-to-date (see Mills 1999: 12-7). This infuses every corner of life from what are deemed desirable occupations to patterns of consumption. In turn, this culture of modernity is linked to the culture of developmentalism which has been assiduously promoted by the Thai state ever since the release of the first five year national economic development plan in 1961. This plan ushered in what has become known as *samai pattana* – or the development era (Rigg et al. 1999).

The discourse of modernity and consumerism is purveyed and promoted by the state, television, radio, and newspapers and magazines. Kazuo Funahashi writes of the 'stylish and coveted lifestyles portrayed on television' that entice young people in Yasothon province in Thailand's poor Northeast away to the city (1996: 108). The pressure to be modern is hard to resist. To rural dwellers 'the images of urban wealth and commodified progress that pervade Thai popular culture pose models of consumption and social status that, however difficult to achieve, are impossible to ignore' (Mills 1997: 42). The Thai rock band Carabao in their song *Made in Thailand*, written during the early years of the Kingdom's economic boom when it was the fastest growing economy in the world, sang of the consumer pressures on the young: 'Afraid to lose face, worried their taste isn't modern enough [...] Attach a brand label [...] It'll sell like hot cakes, fetch a good price [...] We can tell ourselves its foreign made' (Pasuk Phongpaichit and Baker 1998: 155).

Particularly striking is the speed with which a luxury can be transformed into a necessity. In Klong Ban Pho in Central Thailand's Chachoengsao province, the pick-up truck made the transition from 'status symbol' to 'necessity' in the space of just five years (Chantana Banpasirichote 1993: 58). Before 1975 this village was an archetypal (if there is such a thing) farming community. By the early 1990s most young people had opted for factory work and the motorbike and pick-up truck had become key markers of success. Once again, the pressures encouraging people, and especially young people, to embrace non-farm livelihoods are both economic and cultural. As is explored below, young women are enticed into factory work because of a desire to be modern or *than samai*, because of a certain degree of pressure to be dutiful daughters, and also because of a need/wish to earn a good living.

Gender, Class and Generation

The forces of modernity described above have differential impacts, and are embraced differentially. Nor is being modern uncontested. On the basis of her work in the Muda area of Malaysia, Hart identifies a trend among young unmarried women towards greater autonomy and independence. Furthermore she takes this one step further to argue for a 'reconceptualisation' of the household that takes into account the shift 'in the structure and exercise of power between men and women and between elders and juniors [...]' (1994: 49). While the changes in inter-gender relations evident in Malaysia (and Indonesia) are not so marked in Thailand, young rural women in Thailand are also pressuring the 'moral envelope,' taking up jobs away from home, sometimes embracing modernity against the wishes of their parents, and in general terms carving out new lifestyles and livelihoods

While treating the household as a social and economic unit is increasingly problematic, it remains the key stage on which decisions are taken, both in Thailand and in other countries of the Southeast Asian region. Household members may have different, even conflicting, interests, but those interests are articulated (generally) through and within the household (see Preston 1994). Tension and conflict, to varying degrees, are inherent in household relations. 'The household remains a stage where cooperation and conflict, corporatism and individualism, mutuality and inequality, and consensus and discordance, co-exist [...] the household is defined by dissonance' (Rigg forthcoming). The changes in rural labour relations and the effects that the cultural changes outlined above are having on inter-generational and gender relations have not destroyed the importance of the household as the social unit through which decision are mediated (even if they are contested). As Chant writes in her paper on women, the household and migration: 'even in instances where women ostensibly make their own decisions to migrate, it is hard to abstract household conditions from the process [...]' (1998: 12).

The changes which are encouraging, enticing, or forcing people out of agriculture are also differentially experienced by rich and poor. For some the process is essentially progressive and emendatory; for others it is one of degeneration and debasement (see Koppel and Hawkins 1994). For the poor, non-farm work may be highly marginal. This applies, for example, to the farmers making hats and baskets on a home-based, piece-work system in Arghiros and Wathana Wongsekiarttirat's study from Central Thailand (1996). As one villager explained, 'you can't do it quick enough to eat' (1996: 131).

Although occupational multiplicity is embraced for different reasons, it has become a defining feature of change in rural areas of Southeast Asia. Hart goes so far as to propose that the 'perpetuation of multiple, diversified, spatially-extended livelihood strategies [...] are a defining feature of late twentieth century capitalism' (Hart 1996: 269). In the past, multi-stranded livelihoods were essentially based on activities within the agricultural sector (see Rigg 1986, Grandstaff 1988 and 1992); today's diversification is founded on the expansion and diversification of non-farm opportunities.

In many cases occupational diversification is leading to spatial fragmentation as young people (especially) leave and take up work *ex situ*. Akin writes:

> In large numbers of villages in the Northeast, only old people and their daughters' children are left in the villages. The entire middle generation has gone to work in Bangkok. In Ban Talat Phra, a village in Amphoe Ban Phai, Khon Kaen province, the daughters who have gone to Bangkok to work in factories and other kind of services bring their babies back for their parents to look after (Akin Rabibhadana 1993: 20).

But while individuals may thus be spatially removed from their homes this does not mean that they are socially disembedded. They remain a component part of the household, remitting money, returning home periodically whether for key festivals or important stages in the farming calendar, and they also usually harbour the wish to settle back in their natal villages at some future date. Community and family are no longer space-bound units as they used to be. The 'household becomes less of a unit of production that operates together and more of an aggregate of consumers' (Paritta Chalermpow Koanantakool and Askew 1993: 56). Nonetheless – and again – the existence of 'shadow' households has particular impacts on labour relations. And of all the countries of the region, the degree of spatial dislocation is probably greatest in Thailand. The prevalence of villages with older people and children, but 'bereft of the vitality of youth,' has been noted in numerous studies (e.g. Sanitsuda Ekachai 1990, Tomosugi 1995, Funahashi 1996). In such circumstances, it is common for the absent wife's sisters and parents to cultivate the young couple's land while they are absent and for the couple to send money home – a system that is known as *yaek yaai kan pai haa ngaan* or 'separating out to go and look for work' (personal communication Rachel Harrison).[5] Furthermore, should the couple have children it is usual for them to be cared for by the grandparents in the village (*liang lan*).

As in many rural areas of the developing world, it has been usual to view land ownership as the critical marker delineating class and distinguishing between the

5 Funahashi refers to the term *baeng kan pai ha ngan*, or 'making money separately' (1996).

'haves' from the 'have nots.' Anan Ganjanapan in his study (1986) of Ban San Pong in the Chiang Mai valley historically differentiates poor, middle, and rich peasants in terms of land holdings. To be land rich was to be wealthy and, by contrast, non-farm work became a marker and measure of poverty. More recent work conducted in this area of the north has questioned such an association. Gray (1990) and Ritchie (1996b), for example, both note that to be landless is not necessarily to be poor. Indeed it is possible to turn the former association on its head and postulate that the landless in the area are the new rich while the new poor are those who have been marginalised in farming (see Ritchie 1996b). This can be seen to be partly a product of the role of non-farm work in providing rural people with new avenues to riches. It also, though, reflects the spatial incorporation of rural areas into the wider space economy and the infiltration of new classes (commuters, for example) into rural areas.

With land no longer the strategic resource it once was, other markers of class come into play. Education has become increasingly important because without education many of the jobs in the new economy lie out of reach (see above). *Village Chiang Mai* (Abha Sirivongs Na Ayuthaya et al. 1979) represents one of the earliest pieces of systematic fieldwork undertaken in the north of Thailand, dating from 1969.[6] The authors write that in the three villages studied 'the role of education is very limited' and that education is 'the villagers' ambition, not the villagers' needs' (1979: 43). However the study does go on to acknowledge that in the future this may change as economic development proceeds. Today the role of education and the importance of education is not questioned. It is significant that during the recent economic downturn, when many commentators were predicting a sharp fall in enrolment rates (see World Bank 1998), '[...] education outcomes [showed] little or no discernible declines from past positive trends' (World Bank 1999: 1). There was some evidence that hard-strapped families were moving their children from expensive private schools to public schools, but drop out rates did not rise. Recognising the centrality of education to their children's futures, families adjusted their spending behaviour.

Many scholars have lamented the passing of the traditional village and questioned how traditional ceremonies and festivals can continue when the young are absent. Rather less commented upon are the agricultural implications of labour loss. As the DORAS team write of farming in the Central region: 'Who, in the near future, is going to carry out agricultural activities in the Central Plain?' (1996: 197).[7] It is to this question of production that this chapter now turns.

6 Parallel studies were also conducted in the Northeast, Central Plain and in the South.

7 This, of course, resonates with work on rural change in Taiwan, South Korea, and Japan. Francks et al. note that by the early 1990s one-third of the agricultural labour force in Japan was over sixty-five years old (1999: 82). They continue: 'In the more remote and mountainous rural areas, the absence of successors has led to the abandonment of agricultural land, as household heads

Agriculture And Labour Relations In Thailand's New Rural World

The shift from farm to non-farm, and the social changes that underpin this shift have had profound implications for agriculture. Land has been abandoned or, at best, a process of disintensification has been set in train. Labour shortages have undermined co-operative work arrangements. Mechanisation has snatched traditional employment opportunities from marginal groups, forcing them to leave the countryside to survive. Women have seen their jobs evaporate as agriculture is 'masculinised.' And elderly people have found themselves struggling to maintain their farms as young people depart for the city and leave households and villages short of human resources and the vitality of youth. In different ways, and to different extents, all these changes are either products of changes in labour relations or, themselves, impact on labour relations.

Labour Short and Land Poor – Squaring the Circle

Thailand has seen its population grow from around seven million at the turn of the century to over 60 million today (Table 11.2).

Table 11.2: Population of Thailand, 1600-1995 (in millions)

1600	2.2	1970	35.6
1800	3.5	1975	42.4
1905	7.7	1980	47.0
1930	11.8	1985	51.8
1950	19.6	1990	56.3
1960	26.4	1995	59.5
1967	32.5	1998	61.5

Sources: various

In many areas of the Northern and Central Plains regions, land is in short supply and even in the formerly land-rich Northeast and West the frontier in farmland expansion has closed and holdings are declining in size as fragmentation occurs (see Table 11.1). Yet even in areas where agricultural population densities are high, local-level studies often paint a picture of severe labour shortages in agriculture (Chantana Banpasirichote 1993, Tomosugi 1995, Funahashi 1996).

In his study of ninety-seven villages across the province of Yasothon noted above, Kazuo Funahashi (1996) notes the widespread emergence of labour shortages at key points in the rice cycle. The author links this both to the absence of young people and to important changes in the practice of rice cultivation. For-

age and die, and to environmental problems, as irrigation infrastructure and field systems fall into disrepair' (1999: 82).

merly farmers would plant a variety of local and traditional rice varieties with different maturation periods and dates. But increasingly just a handful of modern varieties are cultivated, causing labour peaks to become accentuated. The common response to these labour shortages driven by the twin effects of migration and labour demand concentration has been to embrace mechanical land preparation, adopt direct seeing (broadcasting) over transplanting, and/or to hire labour to meet any labour shortfall.

The same story emerges in Chantana Banpasirichote's investigation of the village of Klong Ban Pho in Thailand's province of Chachoengsao. In the past, rice farming in this village was constrained by a shortage of credit and land. Now the chief constraint, he suggests, is a lack of labour (1993: 13). Like other studies, changes in agriculture are seen to be a response to emerging and intensifying shortages of labour, forcing households to make adjustments to their farming systems. Buffaloes have been replaced by ploughing machines, and when the cost of labour reached 100 baht per day (at that time, equivalent to US$4), households switched from transplanting to direct seeding. Rice harvesting machines and mechanical threshers were also introduced to make up for the increasingly severe labour shortfalls (Chantana Banpasirichote 1993: 14).

A similar story is evident in my own work in the sub-district of Thung Sadok, twenty-five kilometres south of Chiang Mai where labour constraints are severe and intensifying. This is linked to a number of issues and trends. First of all, households are small – reflecting the low total fertility rate and the increase in *ex situ* employment (i.e. the delocalisation of work). Second, households are ageing. Third, many household members who remain resident in the sub-district are engaged in alternative, non-farm, work. And fourth, even when there is un- or under-utilised labour these (usually young) men and women are often disinclined to take up agricultural work. This is the background which helps to inform the decisions that farmers have taken, whether that is to mechanise production or switch out of rice and in to labour saving orchard crops. But as noted above, the evidence indicates that these decisions on the part of farmers are both responses to growing labour shortages while also having important exclusionary effects for some groups in the area (see below).

Moreover this handful of examples are far from being isolated examples. For Thailand (and there are also many studies from other parts of the region), Tomosugi (1995), Rigg (1995 and 1998), DORAS (1996) and Ritchie (1993, 1996a and 1996b) recount a broadly similar story of labour shortages bringing about changes in cultivation practices and the adoption of certain labour saving technologies. But labour shortages are not merely a product of the competition for labour between farm and non-farm. On paper, and even with the proliferation of non-farm opportunities, there should still be ample labour to meet the demands of agriculture in most areas of the country. Factories may have selectively removed some people from the agricultural labour market, but not always on a sufficient level to create the widespread shortages noted in the literature. To understand the apparent paradox of labour shortages in a land-poor country it is necessary to cast the explanatory net rather wider and to place the changes that are occurring in agriculture within the wider context of *than samai* or modernity. The reconfiguration of the household and its operation, changing aspirations especially among the young, and altering relations between the genders and generations are also critical in understanding the changes that are taking place in farming systems in the region.

There would seem to be little doubt that the moving forces behind the rise of labour shortages in Thailand are multiple, rather than singular. In some places, competition between farm and non-farm is creating quite severe bottlenecks at key points in the agricultural cycle. This has created the conditions where mechanisation and various adaptations to the farming system have become necessary. At the same time there are also instances where mechanisation has displaced agricultural labour into highly marginal non-farm work. Moreover it is possible to identify both these processes at work in single villages as households with different human and physical resource endowments endeavour to juggle and manipulate these to the household's best collective advantage.

The work by the DORAS team (see DORAS 1996, Molle et al. 1999, Molle and Thippawal Srijantr 1999) in the Central Plains illustrates this multiplicity of responses. The research notes that in the 1980s the availability of non-farm work for many rural people forced rice agriculture to adapt to labour shortages by mechanisation and the adoption of various labour saving cultivation practices such as direct seeding.[8] But at the same the integration of rural and urban markets gave farmers the opportunity to cultivate high value – and labour demanding – crops such as vegetable and flowers. Thus the Central Plains came to be characterised by an apparently contradictory set of cultivation patterns and production methods: 1. low labour input, mechanised wet rice agriculture; 2. high labour input, high return market gardening; 3. and idle/abandoned land.

As the DORAS report states (1996: 156), 'a general view of agriculture [in the Chao Phraya] delta is misleading because the average situation does not exist.' Explaining the pattern requires an appreciation of factor resource scarcities at the household level. High input and risky ventures tend to be restricted to wealthy farmers. Ageing households with members working *ex situ* and remitting money tend to be linked to abandoned/idle land. Small households and large landholdings tend to be associated with labour efficient forms of rice cultivation.

8 Pandey and Velasco (1999: 7) estimate that 34 per cent of Thailand's total rice area was direct seeded in 1995.

Gender and Generational Divisions of Labour in Agriculture

An important question concerns whether the changes outlined here represent the abandonment of agriculture, or the social re-configuration of production. Does the predominance of older people in agriculture mean that when these people retire or die agriculture will cease; or is it simply that people are delaying their entry into farming until middle age? Is the 'masculinisation' of farming (Parnwell and Arghiros 1996: 21-2) which has been noted in the literature also indicative of agricultural decline?

There are some reasons to indicate that the direr predictions about the future of farming are over-done. Nonetheless, the future of farming in Thailand, given the economic and social changes outlined here, is not particularly bright. Most non-farm opportunities are selectively embraced by younger men and women. This is both because younger people are in a stronger position to exploit such opportunities (they are usually unmarried and childless and more mobile) and because employers prefer to hire younger (unmarried) men and women, and especially women. But even with the attractive wages that non-farm work may bring, along with the status that can accrue from working in the modern economy, it is nonetheless true that such work often remains marginal and unreliable (as the 1997-99 economic crisis exemplified at a regional level). Mills writes in her work on factory workers from rural backgrounds in Bangkok: 'rural women realise that a return to the village household remains their most reliable source of economic security after marriage' (1997: 48). But she also notes that many 'hoped to be more than just 'rice and upland crop farmers' (*chaaw naa chaaw ray*) when they left the city' (1997: 49).

There is, clearly, an age component as well as a gender element to these changes. For older cohorts, agriculture remains the dominant occupation, in younger cohorts it is wage labouring:

> In large numbers of villages in the Northeast [of Thailand], only old people and their daughters' children are left in the villages. The entire middle generation has gone to work in Bangkok. In Ban Talat Phra, a village in Amphoe Ban Phai, Khon Kaen province, the daughters who have gone to Bangkok to work in factories and other kind of services bring their babies back for their parents to look after (Akin Rabibhadana 1993: 20).

Some scholars suggest that this is not a life cycle shift but a permanent change in the complexion of the rural economy (e.g. Ritchie 1993: 13, Chantana Banpasirichote 1993: 38). What, they imply, will happen when middle-aged farmers retire? Who will fill the void? Putting aside, for the moment, the issue of whether those people who have left the countryside will return (and if they do, whether they will return to farming), there is also the question of whether young people have the knowledge and skills to farm. In the 'worst cases' farming knowledge has not been passed on to the younger generation and they do not know how to farm (or how to manage a farm). The arts of transplanting and harvesting, of water management, of seed selection and of land preparation, are all lost to this generation (Ritchie 1993: 14, Chantana Banpasirichote 1993: 11–2). But it is rare to find examples of parents lamenting this loss of knowledge. For them, as for their children, the future of work is seen to lie elsewhere.

'Squeezing' Agriculture

Hub Takhood (Hirsch 1992) is a coastal village close to Khao Sam Roi Yod National Park in the province of Prachuab Khiri Khan, about 275 kilometres south of Bangkok. In 1972 a road was constructed to the village as part of Thailand's Accelerated Rural Development programme. For the first time Hub Takhood was well connected with the outside world and by the end of the 1970s prawn farming had become the economic mainstay of the village economy, taking over from subsistence rice farming and coconut production (Hirsch 1992: 45–7). But it was the expansion of prawn farming itself which caused rice farming to 'all but cease' in the area. The removal of protective mangroves to make way for further prawn ponds increased salinity in fields that were already saline making them unsuitable for the cultivation of even the most salt-tolerant rice varieties.

An economistic interpretation of agricultural developments in Hub Takhood would stress the extent to which farmers moved from rice cultivation into an activity – prawn farming – offering far greater returns. But the economic changes in Hub Takhood need to be understood in terms of the space that capital and the state provided. For these two factors were also instrumental in shaping the pattern of development in the area. The state restricted (ostensibly for environmental reasons) villagers' use of the uplands while (mostly) ethnic Chinese middlemen and commercial banks provided the critical financial ingredient. Prawn farming, and especially semi-intensive prawn farming, requires considerable initial investment. In the mid- to late-1980s this amounted to 100,000 baht (US$4,000) per *rai* (6.25 *rai* = 1 hectare), or US$80,000 for a farm of 20 *rai*. In 1986–87 the average farm income of households in the South was just 20,500 baht (MOAC 1989). No local family could consider prawn farming on this scale without the involvement of outside investors. 'Capital,' Hirsch writes, 'effects control either over land itself or the way in which it is used' (Hirsch 1992: 48).

Furthermore, the pattern of development in Hub Takhood would seem to have marginalised poorer households. Rice farming has been undermined by increased salinisation; crabs and other marine life have disappeared along with the mangroves; upland, formerly used for the collection of non-timber forest products is off-limits as the state has intensified its control over forest land; and cropping of upland areas has been barred for similar reasons. It would seem, in the case of Hub Takhood, that not only have traditional agricultural pursuits been squeezed pincer-fashion by capital and the state, but poorer households have been squeezed out of agriculture and the local area. Hirsch (1992: 47) reports that some villagers work in a pineapple canning factory in nearby Pranburi but otherwise there are few locally available opportunities for villagers.

The environmental, and thus the agricultural impacts of the inter-penetration of urban and industrial activities into rural areas have been noted from several countries in the region. Land use conversion creates a cycle of environmental change and agricultural decline. Farmers abandon their land due to declining productivity brought about by urban/industrial-induced environmental change; their land either stands idle increasing pest infestation or is, itself, sold to property developers or industrial capital further undermining the environmental integrity of the land. These environmental changes and their concomitant agricultural impacts need to be seen against the forces described in the previous section. For example in the study of Klong Ban Pho noted above, the author writes that 'rural industrialisation, as indicated by the penetration of factories into rural areas, has challenged the agricultural sector, which is experiencing declines in productivity' (Chantana Banpasirichote 1993: 33). This has accelerated the process of occupational shift in the countryside which, in turn, has encouraged the labour shortage-induced agricultural changes.

But elsewhere, as in Hub Takhood, the decline of agriculture is better explained as part of a destructive process engendered by the environmental conflicts between different activities. This is the general lesson from Flaherty et al.'s work on the environmental effects of inland shrimp farming in Thailand. The decline in returns to rice have encouraged farmers to diversify into higher return agricultural activities such as shrimp farming. This, though, has created a whole series of environmental concerns. Flaherty et al. conclude that 'given the demand for freshwater, the large quantities of salt introduced, the need to dispose of enormous quantities of pond effluent, it is unlikely that inland shrimp farming can be made environmentally benign' (Flaherty et. al. 1999: 2056-7).

Labour Groups in Thung Sadok

Returning to the study in Tambon Thung Sadok, noted above, *klum rap jang mao*, or labour groups, are loose associations of wage labourers who are hired by farmers to carry out certain agricultural tasks, such as harvesting and transplanting. The groups draw their membership from poorer (usually landless) households in the sub-district who depend on *klum mao* work for a significant proportion of their income. *Klum mao* are of no fixed size and may contain between ten and twenty-five people. These are associations of relations, friends, and neighbours, include both men and women, and are fluid. There is no explicit leader as such and the return is split equally between a group's members. The size of a labour group depends partly on the task undertaken. For example, harvesting is more labour demanding than transplanting, so that while five to seven might be sufficient number of workers to transplant three *rai* in a day, twelve might be needed for harvesting.

The average age of labour group members is between thirty and forty-five years old. Older people find it difficult to take on hard agricultural work of this type, while the young are generally not interested. (Some villagers insisted the young were not up to it either!) In those instances when younger men and women do take on *klum mao* work it is invariably those from poorer, landless families with low levels of education (to *bor hok*, six years of primary level schooling). The reality that such work is only of interest to those young people with sharply constrained opportunities is recognised locally.

Landowners find it more convenient to hire groups of labourers rather than dealing with large numbers of individuals when it comes to securing workers for high labour demand – and time constrained – tasks such as transplanting and harvesting. At the same time, villagers find it easier to secure work if they are organised in this way. Because the area suffers from quite severe labour constraints at peak periods in the agricultural cycle (as noted above),[9] farmers plan their cropping decisions taking into account the likely availability of labour. Contracting of *klum mao* occurs in advance of the time when they are needed. Khun Nithi, who works with a *klum mao*, keeps a diary in which he records those days when he has agreed to work. As he explained: 'If we don't take note, we will become confused and it will be hard to manage the cultivation of our own fields.' During peak periods, labour groups will move from one job to another in the same day, so that if it takes a day and a half to complete a harvesting job, they will begin the next the same day. For day-to-day tasks such as light work in the field or orchard work, land owners prefer to hire individual wage labourers.

The costs of employing a labour group are calculated on the basis of the area to be transplanted or harvested and not according to the number of people in the group. The going rate at the beginning of 2000 was 600–800 baht/*rai* (this applies to both transplanting and harvesting) and this is paid at the end of each day. There are some differences in return between men and women. Men doing the heavier jobs, such as carrying, receive about twenty baht more per day. The average return for a day's work is about 120 baht.

On the face of it, there would seem to be some incentive to reduce the size of labour groups, make them exclusive, and therefore maximise the daily return. However some respondents indicated that there was also a moral imperative to keep labour groups open. As Khun Nithi explained: 'If someone asks me whether they can join a harvesting group tomorrow because they have no money, I reply

9 A period of the year when labour is in particularly short supply is between the end of March and the middle of April - the weeks leading up to the Songkran festival when dry season rice is harvested.

'yes'!' As he went on to say, because they too face the same problems and do the same work, how can they refuse? However, this view of the inclusive nature of labour groups in the area was challenged by some solo agricultural wage labourers. One middle-aged woman said that she was unable to join a labour group because she worked too slowly. Perhaps understandably, the members of a group are unwilling to 'carry' workers who they believe are too old or infirm to keep up with the pace.

There is also the question of whether the operation of *klum mao* in the area is indicative that the village moral economy is alive and well. Farmers noted that having hired a group for one task they were obliged to do so for another. But it would be wrong to see farmers 'tied in' to *klum mao* for some cultural reason that might be characterised as representing a village subsistence ethic. Khun Suwan remarked that if *klum mao* push their rates up too high it is easy enough to hire individual labourers. Furthermore there is no village injunction against labourers from outside the village coming to work on village fields. In this respect, it would seem that *klum mao* have not been created by the poor to protect work and incomes in a situation of labour surplus, but rather to make labour more efficient and effective in a context of labour deficit.

The relationship between labour groups and mechanisation is complex and it is not always the case that they are in competition. Rather than undermining the logic of labour groups, some types of mechanisation have bolstered them. For example, when threshing machines were introduced some years ago this made it important for harvesting to be completed in a single day. The machines are hired by the day and whereas previously manual threshing was conducted at the same pace as harvesting, and the processes spread over three or four days, the pace of the machine now sets the pace of harvesting. Only by contracting a *klum mao* can a farmer hope to harvest his rice crop in a single day and thus keep up with the machine – and therefore his rental outlays down to a single day.

However the impact of combine harvesters would seem to be unambiguous as far as labour – and labour groups – are concerned: they are destructive of work. The first combines made their appearance in the area in the late 1990s, but they proved to be less than satisfactory. However at the beginning of 2000 a new, improved combine harvester was introduced. The cost competitiveness of the combine was clear: to harvest one *rai* of rice using the combine cost 560 baht. To harvest by hand cost 600–800 baht per *rai* plus, on top of this, must be added the costs of threshing.[10]

Not only does the introduction of the combine represent a threat to the viability of *klum mao* for at least some activities, but it also had implications for the gender balance in agriculture. The people driving and working with the combine

10 The going rate in the village was thirty *satang* (0.30 baht) per kilogramme of threshed rice.

in 2000 were all men, and so too were those employed to carry the sacks of harvested rice. The work of carrying was simply too heavy for most women.

The experience of labour groups in Tambon Thung Sadok illustrates the complexities of the interplay between labour, agriculture, mechanisation, gender, class, and non-farm work. There are no simple associations and few generalisations. There is evidence that the effects of rural-urban relations have been to force farmers to rework their cropping methods and decisions to take account of labour scarcity. Forms of mechanisation have differential effects on labour relations, and on the gender balance in agriculture. At the same time, non-farm work in the area tended to selectively recruit (young) women workers, opening up avenues of employment which are not equally available to (young) men. *Klum mao* can be seen, in one sense, as a response to labour scarcities: they are one of the few ways that farmers can be assured of sufficient labour to meet the demands of labour-intensive agricultural activities.[11] At the same time there is a hint that they are also a means by which poor households can secure work, and therefore their subsistence. Without wishing to suggest that *klum mao* are all things to all women and men, there is a sense in which they are reflections of a rural situation where households and individuals face very different constraints and opportunities. They therefore reflect this complexity.

Complementary or Conflicting? Emerging Rural-Urban Relationships

The different experiences of Hub Takhood, Tambon Thung Sadok and Klong Ban Pho directs attention to the question of the complementary or conflicting relationship between farm and non-farm, agriculture and industry, and rural and urban. Bray, in her study of the rice economies of Asia hazards that:

> intensive rice-farming dovetails very neatly with petty commodity production, which requires very little capital to set up a family enterprise, and absorbs surplus labour without depriving the farm of workers at times of peak demand. It can be expanded, diversified or contracted to meet market demands, but the combination with the rice farm guarantees the family's subsistence (Bray 1986: 135).

In their work on extended metropolitan regions or EMRs, scholars like McGee (1989, 1991) and Ginsburg (1991) have suggested something rather similar when they highlight the manner in which rice agriculture and non-farm work dovetail, both spatially and in terms of the division of labour. Furthermore, these integra-

11 Hardjono explains the evolution of the *bawon* system of rice harvesting in Java as a 'production technique designed in a labour-short situation to get harvesting completed as quickly as possible' (1987: 212).

tive urban-cum-rural regions are seen to have a certain level of stability and persistence.

The notion that rural households can bridge the farm/non-farm divide with ease, indeed that agriculture and non-agriculture are complementary, overlooks many of the issues and processes highlighted here. To begin with, it ignores the social and cultural changes which have made farming, for many people, an unattractive proposition. Second, it overlooks the conflicts that can arise between men and women and between the generations. Third, it disregards the environmental costs of rural industrialisation (and some alternative agricultural practices, like prawn farming). Fourth, it tends to ignore or play down the political economy of rural change. And fifth, it tends to overlook one of the essential characteristics of the processes at work – which is their differential and, at times, contradictory, impacts.

It would seem that the most striking evidence of the changing economic priorities and opportunities in some areas of rural Thailand lies in the abandonment of agriculture and the increasing prevalence of idle or abandoned land. But the presence of such land may be the product of a number of factors. To being with, idle land may be a function of speculation rather than a lack of interest in farming. The prevalence of land speculation needs to be seen in the context of the role of the state in allowing individuals to secure ownership over land. In Thailand, the state encouraged farmers to claim title to their land. As roads made formerly remote areas accessible so land became an increasingly valuable resource to non-local people intent on its conversion to other uses. Young villagers found they could no longer buy land to farm because of its rapidly escalating price and were forced out of the village to find work (whether willingly or unwillingly). 'The "simple" act of building roads,' Ritchie writes of the North of Thailand, 'has complex repercussions sociologically and economically [...] by providing easy access to land which was formerly remote [... enabling] land speculators to go out into rural areas' (Ritchie 1993: 6).

When the legislative and political systems favour industrial development over agriculture, land speculation is likely to be instrumental in creating new agricultural geographies. Patterns of land use are shaped, in such instances, less by labour shortages and competition between agriculture and non-agriculture at the household level, than by wider political and legal processes and frameworks. To be sure, there is a tension weaving its way through the political economy of rural-urban relations, but it is a tension which has its origins outside agriculture and beyond the village.

While land speculation may be the most important reason explaining why land is left idle (aside from labour shortages), there are also other factors to consider. Year-to-year variations in climatic conditions can also have a considerable effect by taking some land – particularly if it is marginal rice land – out of production (see Rigg 1985, Grandstaff 1988). Finally, the environmental consequences of the infiltration of industrial and other activities into rural areas can also render land unsuitable for agriculture (see above). But, and notwithstanding these factors, there is also ample evidence that some land has been abandoned simply because there is not the labour, nor the economic incentive, nor the interest, to sustain its cultivation.

Conclusion

In the introduction to this chapter it was noted that increasingly work on the local configuration of the labour market stresses the degree to which labour market segmentation is a response to factors embedded in local, social, and economic space. To understand how rural people are responding, in employment terms, to the changes and opportunities that confront them is a product of global processes articulated through and within the local social setting. Thus the ability of young women to engage in non-farm work, of men to leave home for extended periods of time, of sexual divisions of labour in agriculture (should they exist) to metamorphose, and for tenant farmers to take control of land use decisions, are all a reflection of local conditions.

However, how labour relations are changing in particular localities are, self-evidently, also influenced by the forces of globalisation and by national industrialisation policies. Thus Tomosugi's (1995) account of piecework in Tonyang, a village in Central Thailand's province of Ayutthaya, emphasises the degree to which villagers' livelihoods are contingent on decisions taken by factory managers in Bangkok and by the global market for artificial flowers. Changes in labour relations thus reflect a complex interplay of cultural and economic influences operating at a variety of scales. Globalisation and national industrialisation are offering rural people – but on an unequal basis – the opportunity to take up non-farm work. The changing aspirations of rural people, and particularly the young is encouraging them to opt out of agriculture. Education and contact with the modern world is stimulating a change in the balance of power in the household between the generations and the sexes.

This vision of evolving labour relations in Thailand and, by extension, in the rest of the region, is unsatisfactory at least to the extent that it is 'empirically untidy,' to use Russell's (1993) phrase. However those aspects of contemporary change which stand out most clearly in Thailand's recent economic and social history demand such a view: the interpenetration of rural and urban; emerging and intensifying intra-household tensions; the permeability of household boundaries; and increasing spatial fragmentation. But to make the untidy even messier, while it may be possible to identify the key processes at work, the outcomes of these processes, whether in terms of production or social relations, are necessarily mixed.

References

Abha Sirivongs Na Ayuthaya, Fuhs, F. and Suthep Soonthornpasuch (1979) *Village Chiang Mai: Social and Economic Conditions of a Rural Population in Northern Thailand*, Bangkok: Social Research Institute, Chulalongkorn University.

Akin Rabibhadana (1993) *Social Inequity: a Source of Conflict in the Future?* The 1993 Year End Conference on Who Gets What and How? – Challenges for the Future, Bangkok: Thai Development Research Institute.

Alexander, P., Boomgaard, P. and White, B. (1991) 'Introduction', in P. Alexander, P. Boomgaard and B. White (eds.) *In the Shadow of Agriculture: Non-farm Activities in the Javanese Economy, Past and Present*, Amsterdam: Royal Tropical Institute.

Anan Ganjanapan (1986) 'The partial commercialisation rice production in Northern Thailand (1900–1981)', PhD Thesis, Cornell University.

Angeles-Reyes, E. (1994) 'Nonfarm work in the Philippine rural economy: an omen of change or a change of omens?' in B. Koppel, J. Hawkins and W. James (eds.) *Development or Deterioration: Work in Rural Asia*, Boulder, C.O.: Lynne Rienner.

Arghiros, D. and Wathana Wongsekiarttirat (1996) 'Development in Thailand's extended metropolitan region: the socio-economic and political implications of rapid change in an Ayutthaya district, central Thailand', in M.J.G. Parnwell (ed.) *Thailand: Uneven Development*, Aldershot: Avebury.

Bello, W., Cunningham, S. and Li Kheng Poh (1998) *A Siamese Tragedy: Development and Disintegration in Modern Thailand*, London: Zed Books.

Bencha Yoddumnern-Attig (1992) 'Thai family structure and organisation: changing roles and duties in historical perspective', in Bencha Yoddumnern-Attig et al. (eds.) *Changing Roles and Statuses of Women in Thailand: a Documentary Assessment*, Institute for Population and Social Research, Mahidol University, Thailand.

Bray, F. (1986) *The Rice Economies: Technology and Development in Asian Societies*, Oxford: Basil Blackwell.

Chant, S. (1998) 'Households, gender and rural-urban migration: reflections on linkages and considerations for policy', *Environment and Urbanisation* 10, 1: 5–21.

Chantana Banpasirichote (1993) *Community Integration into Regional Industrial Development: a Case Study of Klong Ban Pho, Chachoengsao*, Bangkok: Thai Development Research Institute.

Dixon, C. (1999) *The Thai Economy: Uneven Development and Internationalisation*, London: Routledge.

DORAS (1996) *Agricultural and Irrigation Patterns in the Central Plain of Thailand*, Bangkok: ORSTOM (Development Oriented Research on Agrarian Systems), Kasetsart University.

Elmhirst, R. (1995) 'Gender, environment and transmigration: comparing migrant and *pribumi* household strategies in Lampung, Indonesia', Paper presented to the Third WIVS Conference on 'Indonesian Women in the Household and Beyond', Royal Institute of Linguistics and Anthropology, Leiden, 25–29 September.

— (1996) 'Transmigration and local communities in North Lampung: exploring identity politics and resource control in Indonesia', Paper presented at the Association of South East Asian Studies' (ASEASUK) Conference, School of Oriental & African Studies, London, 25–27 April.

— (1998) 'Gender, culture and space: a political geography of factory labour in Indonesia', Paper presented at the European South East Asian Studies (EUROSEAS) Conference, Hamburg, 3–6 September.

— (2002) 'Daughters and displacement: migration dynamics in an Indonesian transmigration area', *Journal of Development Studies* 38, 5: 143–166.

FEER (2000) 'Uncivil society', *Far Eastern Economic Review*, 31 August.

Fegan, B. (1983) 'Establishment fund, population increase and changing class structures in Central Luzon', *Philippine Sociological Review* 31: 31–43.

Flaherty, M., Vandergeest, P. and Miller, P. (1999) 'Rice paddy or shrimp pond: tough decisions in rural Thailand', *World Development* 27, 12: 2045–2060.

Francks, P. with Boestal, J. and Choo Hyop Kim (1999) *Agriculture and Economic Development in East Asia: From Growth to Protectionism in Japan, Korea and Taiwan,* London: Routledge.

Funahashi, K. (1996) 'Farming by the older generation: the exodus of young labor in Yasothon province, Thailand', *Tonan Ajia Kenky (Southeast Asian Studies)* 33, 4: 107–121.

Ginsburg, N. (1991) 'Extended metropolitan regions in Asia: a new spatial paradigm', in N. Ginsburg, B. Koppel and T.G. McGee (eds.) *The Extended Metropolis: Settlement Transition in Asia*, Honolulu: University of Hawaii Press.

Grandstaff, T. (1988) 'Environment and economic diversity in Northeast Thailand', in T. Charoenwatana and A.T. Rambo (eds.) *Sustainable Rural Development in Asia*: Khon Kaen, Thailand: Khon Kaen University.

— (1992) 'The human environment: variation and uncertainty', *Pacific Viewpoint* 33, 2: 135–144.

Gray, J. (1990) 'The road to the city: young women and transition in Northern Thailand', PhD Thesis, Macquarie University, Sydney.

Hardjono, J. (1987) *Land, Labour and Livelihood in a West Java Village,* Yogyarkarta: Gadjah Mada University Press.

Hart, G. (1992) 'Household production reconsidered: gender, labor conflict, and technological change in Malaysia's Muda region', *World Development* 20, 6: 809–823.

— (1994) 'The dynamics of diversification in an Asian rice region', in B. Koppel, J. Hawkins and W. James (eds.) *Development or Deterioration: Work in Rural Asia*, Boulder, C.O.: Lynne Rienner.

— (1996) 'The agrarian question and industrial dispersal in South Africa: agro-industrial linkages through Asian lenses', *Journal of Peasant Studies* 23, 2–3: 245–277.

Hirsch, P. (1990) *Development Dilemmas in Thailand*, Singapore: Oxford University Press.

— (1992) 'State, capital, and land in recently cleared areas of Western Thailand', *Pacific Viewpoint* 33, 1: 36–57.

Kelly, P. (1998) 'The politics of urban-rural relations: land use conversion in the Philippines', *Environment and Urbanisation* 10, 1: 35–54.

— (1999a) 'Everyday urbanisation: the social dynamics of development in Manila's extended metropolitan region', *International Journal of Urban and Regional Research* 23, 2: 283–303.

— (1999b) 'Rethinking the "local" in labour markets: the consequences of cultural embeddedness in a Philippine growth zone', *Singapore Journal of Tropical Geography* 20, 1: 56–75.

Koppel, B. and Hawkins, J. (1994) 'Rural transformation and the future of work in rural Asia', in B. Koppel, J. Hawkins and W. James (eds.) *Development or Deterioration: Work in Rural Asia,* Boulder, C.O.: Lynne Rienner.

McGee, T.G. (1989) 'Urbanisasi or kotadesasi? Evolving patterns of urbanisation in Asia', in F.J. Costa, A.K. Dutt, L.J.C. Ma and A.G. Noble (eds.) *Urbanisation in Asia: Spatial Dimensions and Policy Issues*, Honolulu: University of Hawaii Press.

— (1991) 'The emergence of *desakota* regions in Asia: expanding a hypothesis', in N. Ginsburg, B. Koppel and T.G. McGee (eds.) *The Extended Metropolis: Settlement Transition in Asia,* Honolulu: University of Hawaii Press.

McVey, R. (1992) 'The materialisation of the Southeast Asian entrepreneur', in R. McVey (ed.) *Southeast Asian Capitalists: Studies on Southeast Asia*, Ithaca: Cornell University Press.

Mills, M. (1997) 'Contesting the margins of modernity: women, migration, and consumption in Thailand', *American Ethnologist* 24, 1: 37–61.

— (1999) *Thai Women in the Global Labor Force: Consuming Desires, Contested Selves,* New Brunswick, N.J.: Rutgers University Press.

MOAC (1989) 'Agricultural statistics of Thailand, crop year 1988/89', Bangkok: Centre for Agricultural Statistics, Ministry of Agriculture and Cooperatives.
Molle, F. and Thippawal Srijantr (1999) 'Agrarian Change and Land System in the Chao Phraya Delta', Research Report no. 8, Bangkok: ORSTOM and Kasetsart University.
Molle, F., Sripen Durongdej, Chatchom Chompadist, Joannon, A. and Yuphaa Limsawad (1999) 'Improvements of Rice Cultivation and Water Management in the Flooded Area of the Central Plain of Thailand: a Zoning of Rice Systems by Using Remote Sensing Imagery', Research Report no. 5, Bangkok: ORSTOM and Kasetsart University.
Nipon Poapongsakorn (1994) 'Transformations in the Thai rural labor market', in B. Koppel, J. Hawkins and W. James (eds.) *Development or Deterioration: Work in Rural Asia*, Boulder. C.O.: Lynne Rienner.
Pandey, S. and Velasco, L. (1999) 'Economics of direct seeding in Asia: patterns of adoption and research priorities', *International Rice Research Notes* 24, 2: 6–11.
Paritta Chalermpow Koanantakool and Askew, M. (1993) *Urban Life and Urban People in Transition*, 'The 1993 Year End Conference on Who Gets What and How? - Challenges for the Future', Bangkok: Thai Development Research Institute.
Parnwell, M.J.G. and Arghiros, D. (1996) 'Uneven development in Thailand', in M.J.G. Parnwell (ed.) *Thailand: Uneven Development*, Aldershot: Avebury.
Pasuk Phongpaichit and C. Baker (1998) *Thailand's Boom and Bust*, Chiang Mai: Silkworm Books.
Peck, J. (1996) 'Lived labour markets', *Antipode* 28, 4: 343–345.
Preston, D. (1994) 'Rapid household appraisal: a method for facilitating the analysis of household livelihood strategies', *Applied Geography* 14: 203–213.
Rigg, J. (1985) 'The role of the environment in limiting the adoption of new rice technology in Northeastern Thailand', *Transactions of the Institute of British Geographers* 10, 4: 481–494.
— (1986) 'Innovation and intensification in Northeastern Thailand: Brookfield applied', *Pacific Viewpoint* 27: 29–45.
— (1995) 'Errors in the making: rice, knowledge, technological change and "applied" research in Northeastern Thailand', *Malaysian Journal of Tropical Geography* 26, 1: 19–33.
— (1998) 'Tracking the poor: the making of wealth and poverty in Thailand (1982–1994)', *International Journal of Social Economics* 25, 6–8: 1128–1141.
— (2001) *More than the Soil: Rural Change in Southeast Asia*, Harlow: Pearson Education.
— (forthcoming) 'Evolving rural-urban relations: changing patterns of life and livelihood', in Chia Lin Sien (ed.) *Southeast Asia Transformed: a Geography of Change*, Singapore: Institute of Southeast Asian Studies.
Rigg, J., Allott, A., Harrison, R. and Kratz, U. (1999) 'Understanding languages of modernisation', *Modern Asian Studies* 33, 3: 581–602.
Ritchie, M.A. (1993) 'The "village" in context: arenas of social action and historical change in Northern Thai peasant classes', Paper presented at the 5th International Thai Studies Conference, SOAS, London, July.
— (1996a) 'Centralisation and diversification: from local to non-local economic reproduction and resource control in Northern Thailand', Paper presented at the 6th International Conference on Thai Studies, Chiang Mai, 14–17 October.
— (1996b) *From Peasant Farmers to Construction Workers: the Breaking Down of the Boundaries between Agrarian and Urban Life in Northern Thailand, 1974–1992*, Ann Arbor: UMI.
Rodenburg, J. (1997) *In the Shadow of Migration: Rural Women and Their Households in North Tapanuli. Indonesia*, Leiden: KITLV Press.
Russell, M. (1993) 'Are households universal? On misunderstanding domestic groups in Swaziland', *Development and Change* 24, 4: 755–785.
Sanitsuda Ekachai (1990) *Behind the Smile: Voices of Thailand*, Bangkok: Post Publishing.

Sherman, D.G. (1990) *Rice, Rupees and Ritual: Economy and Society Among the Samosir Batak of Sumatra*, Stanford: Stanford University Press.

Simon, J-C. (1996) 'The Thai manufacturing sector: new patterns of expansion', in M.J.G. Parnwell (ed.) *Uneven Development in Thailand,* Aldershot: Avebury.

Singhanetra-Renard, A. (1999) 'Population mobility and the transformation of the village community in Northern Thailand', *Asia Pacific Viewpoint* 40, 1: 69–87.

Tara Buakamsri (1997) 'Spatial mobility and health risks among factory workers in the Northern Region Industrial Estate', MSc Thesis, Chiang Mai University (in Thai).

Tomosugi, T. (1995) *Changing Features of a Rice-growing Village in Central Thailand: a Fixed-Point Study from 1967 to 1993*, Tokyo: Centre for East Asian Cultural Studies.

Toyota, M. (1999) 'Cross border mobility and multiple identity choices: the urban Akha in Chiang Mai, Thailand', PhD Thesis, University of Hull.

World Bank (1998) *Social Consequences of the East Asian Financial Crisis,* Http://www.worldbank.org/poverty/eacrisis/partners/library/socconsq/index.html.

— (1999) *Thailand Social Monitor: Coping with the Crisis in Education and Health,* Bangkok: World Bank.

12

Labour Restructuring in Vietnam Since the Economic Reform

XAVIER OUDIN

Vietnam is presently undergoing an economic transformation that has a strong impact on labour relations. When the *Doi Moi* policy was decided in December 1986, the Vietnamese government opened up the country to foreign private investment and allowed domestic private enterprise as well as self-employment. Briefly, this process can be described as a 'de-socialisation' of labour relations, with the rise of community and market-based labour relations or self-employment.

This transformation of labour relations is accompanied by a new distribution of human resources by educational level, industry, gender, as well as increased mobility. Although the transformation is in progress and it is difficult to forecast its evolution, the change was, and still is, influenced by demographic factors; the labour situation is unsatisfactory because labour supply is not matched by demand.

We shall examine the impact of population change on the labour force in recent decades and study the flows that have shaped the present labour situation. The labour situation is part of the total population, hence the importance of the demographic structure to understand the labour system today. In the first part we describe the entire system in relation to population features. In the second part we investigate how the system works and the significance of the *Doi Moi* policy in this respect.

In examining non-farm occupations since 1976, we focus on 1988 to 1996, along with original data from a survey we performed.[1] These years saw a signifi-

1 Survey conducted by the MOLISA (Ministry of Labour, Invalids and Social Affairs, and ORSTOM (now IRD, Institute of Research for Development, from France) on a sample of 3,500 individuals in non-farm families in 12 provinces or cities of Vietnam (rural or urban, with a multi-stage sampling method), in 1996.

cant change in the labour situation: collectivisation was abandoned, the state sector was restructured, and individual and family enterprises mushroomed. At the same time there was a radical change in Vietnam in when it joined the world economy.

Demographic Evolution And Dependency

The Mobilisation of Labour after the War

With the fall of the South Vietnamese regime in April 1975 the austere soldiers of the North discovered a wealthy society there that most of them had probably never dreamt of. For the DRV (Democratic Republic of Vietnam), the reunification of the country was the accomplishment of a 30-year war and the attainment of an objective that had always been proclaimed as the main one: a unified country, free from any foreign power. Economically it meant access to the rice surplus of the Mekong River delta and the end of food shortages in the North. Despite the devastation of the country at the end of the war, optimism reigned among communist leaders who thought that winning the war was the most difficult task and that bringing the country to prosperity would be a formality (Vo Nhan Tri 1992).

For them, socialism was the best way to boost production through an efficient mobilisation of 'productive resources,' i.e. capital, land, and labour. Northern politicians did not listen to the Southern communist leaders who advised a longer transition. Socialism was proclaimed in 1976 in South Vietnam, and the entire country became the Socialist Republic of Vietnam. All economic activities was to be collectivised; private land ownership was abolished; most factories were nationalised (private enterprises with fewer than ten workers were tolerated for a while); and private trade, except for petty trade, was forbidden. In particular, the rice trade and management of the rice surplus were to be within the purviews of co-operatives and public enterprise. As in 1959 in the North, the system of socialist labour relations was a three-stage system, with, from bottom up, small family enterprises and self-employment, then co-operatives (consisting of several types), and at the top state enterprises.[2] Socialism was supposed to ensure a better allocation of labour and capital than market forces. Commercial capital (i.e. the profits from rice and other trades) would be directed toward productive activities, especially manufacturing.

The purpose of the system of socialist labour relations was twofold. On the one hand, it was supposed to eradicate labour exploitation, and on the other, it was meant to upgrade the level of productive forces. This last aspect was concretised in the state enterprises that concentrated most of national investment. Vietnam

2 See Post (1989) and Kerkvliet (1995) for a description of the different kinds of co-operatives.

had to be reconstructed and was in great need of financial capital as well as labour, especially skilled labour. In the few years that followed the end of the war, both these resources were impossible to mobilise.

Even if the U.S. government had never fulfilled its commitments from the Paris agreement to pay for reconstruction of North Vietnam, the Vietnamese had been able to gain a great deal of credit in the Western world, as well as from the Chinese. Soon after the liberation of Saigon, doubts arose and it became clear that the Vietnamese government did nothing to raise confidence among potential donors or investors. Privately-owned factories (many of them Chinese) were nationalised at ridiculous prices. The Southern Piaster was devalued, suddenly depriving the Saigon bourgeoisie of its wealth (Terzani 1997). In general, the Vietnamese authorities did not seem to bother much about creating favourable conditions to attract and retain financial capital in the country. In following years the situation worsened, and international as well as bilateral foreign assistance (except from Eastern Europe and the Scandinavian countries) was completely cut when in January 1979 Vietnamese armies invaded Cambodia.

If the government of the unified Vietnam did not do anything to attract capital, its policy proved to be as disastrous for the mobilisation of labour. The structure of the population, marked by a deficit of young adults and numerous cohorts of children from the high fertility rate, was not favourable to mobilisation of labour. The rapid march to socialism aggravated the situation because it discouraged rather than encouraged the mobilisation of labour. Peasants, artisans, and traders of the South, whose assets had been collectivised, were not very zealous in supporting the new political system. An economic situation that had been difficult in 1975 became catastrophic in the following years because of bad harvests, and this caused one of the most tragic exoduses of the end of the twentieth century. Despite some economic reforms between 1979 and 1981, the situation remained critical, and when Gorbachev announced that the USSR would stop subsidising Vietnam, a radical movement was begun. It was known as *Doi Moi* (renovation).

The Demographic Framework

When the *Doi Moi* policy was proclaimed in December 1986, Vietnam was in a period of such rapid expansion of labour supply that the centrally planned economy could hardly match the demand. This was mainly a result of demographic factors, although there were some other features (relative decline of the share of agriculture, change in schooling rates, and the rate women participated in the labour force) that shaped the supply of labour.

Since the mid-1970s, Vietnam has been in a period of demographic transition,[3] with a yearly population growth rate of 1.7 per cent for 1989-1999, which was

3 The demographic transition is the passage of a population with high birth and mortality rates to low rates. Mortality rates decline first (first stage of the demographic transition), followed by a drop in fertility (second stage).

down from 3.2 per cent in 1976. The total fertility rate is commonly 2.4 children, down from 6.1 in 1976 and 3.8 in 1989 (Barbieri et al. 1995, US Dept of Commerce 2000).

The change in fertility and mortality rates has a significant impact on the age structure of the population. At first mortality usually declines, especially infant mortality, while fertility remains high. As a result, young cohorts are numerous, and the percentage of total population under 20 can rise to 60 per cent. This is usually combined with a high growth rate (more than 3 per cent). At a later stage fertility starts to decline, along with the percentage of the youngest to total population, while children born in the preceding period reach adulthood. In this period the population growth rate slows down, but the growth rate of the working-age population (15-65 years old) remains high. In the last stage of the transition the population stabilises and the percentage of population under 20 is below 25 per cent.

In Vietnam the percentage of youth was 54 per cent in 1979, 50 per cent in 1990, and 44 per cent in 2000.[4] The total population is presently around 80 million, up from 49 million in 1976. Since the mid-1980s, Vietnam has been in the second stage of demographic transition, with declining fertility but a high growth rate for its working population.

Fall of Dependency

The age structure of a population is well rendered by dependency rates. For demographers the dependency rate is calculated from the number of people outside working age in relation to the working age population.[5] In Vietnam the demographic dependency rate was 90 in 1979 (Banister 1993), but went down to 75 in 1989. It is calculated at 60 in 2001 and forecasted to be 48 in 2010 (US Bureau of Census). This means that in 2001 there will be only 60 people under 15 or over 64 for every 100 people between 15 and 64, compared to the 90 in the dependency range of 22 years earlier. This provides some idea of the burden the young and elderly relatives present for the working age population.

It is more significant to measure this burden in relation to those who are actually employed. To gauge this we use a different ratio called the economic dependency rate, which is defined as the ratio of non-active and unemployed relatives to those employed. It provides a better picture of the burden of dependents (children, students, disabled, unemployed) borne by those who are employed.

4 Data from US Bureau of Census, except 1979 (adjusted results of the Census by Banister 1993). Unless specified, other statistical data are taken from different yearbooks of the General Statistical Office (GSO).

5 Different ratios can be used to measure dependency, for instance the portion of population under 15 and over 65 of the total population (see Williamson 1993 for a discussion of dependency rates in Asian countries).

Further, it also reveals the context for the main social investment and re-distribution choices that a government has to face. In effect, public investment is paid by taxes, and taxes depend on economic activity. If the dependency rate is high, a government must make considerable efforts in education and health, because the many children and other dependents are supported by a relatively small part of the working population. These investments are made at the expense of other kinds of investments, such as infrastructure. When dependency rates decline, it means more workers pay taxes for social investment for a relatively smaller part of the population. Educational investment per student can then increase, allowing longer or more extensive training. This in turn will increase the skills of the youth and improve the quality of their labour when they join the labour market. In addition, declining dependency rates favour saving and investment.

Up to 1979 the economic dependency rate of Vietnam has been rising: in that year it reached 170 dependents for 100 employed. Thereafter it fell rapidly, to 120 in 1988, and it continues to decline, but less precipitously. In 2000 it was around 100, meaning that half of the population of Vietnam works, or that each worker has to support himself and one other person. This dramatic change is mainly (but not only) due to the relative decline of the population under 15 and to the fact that the large cohorts born in the 1970s are now reaching working age.

After the war the cost of reconstruction (in the midst of international tensions that forced Vietnam to maintain a large army) has put a serious strain on rapid development. Collectivisation largely disorganised production and favoured the flight of capital as well as labour. Paddy production per head diminished from 270 kg a year in 1976 to 260 kg in 1979 (Nguyen Trong Nam Tran 1991). During that period dependency rates were on the rise, and food production was not able to grow at the same rate as the population.

In the 1980s the decrease of the dependency rate, mainly caused by the family planning policy, puts Vietnam in a more favourable position for economic development. Despite the reforms of 1979 that allowed families to have a plot of land for their own production, however, the economic situation continues to deteriorate, especially since 1984. Yet family production and the fall in dependency rates (with smaller families) bring improvements in food supply, and in 1986 the yields from a paddy was up to 301 kg per head (Nguyen Trong Nam Tran 1991).

Although there is a correlation between paddy yields and dependency rates, demographic pressures were not the main causes of economic difficulties in Vietnam up to 1988. Although these did aggravated the situation in the late 1970s, economic policy was primarily responsible for the economic crisis, even if bad harvests were the direct result of unfavourable weather.

Explosion of the Labour Supply

Dependency rates fall when the labour force grows faster than does the total population. When large cohorts reach working age, the conditions in which they can enter the labour market are very important, and these determine the evolution of economic dependency. If young people cannot find jobs, unemployment will rise and the burden of unemployment will replace the burden of young cohorts.

From the mid-1980s there has been a rapid expansion in the labour supply, mainly because large cohorts born when fertility was high are entering the labour market. The labour force in Vietnam increases at a rapid pace every year (between 2.5 and 3 per cent), with more than one million newcomers entering every year. In addition, between 1988 and 1994, a flow of former migrant workers from Eastern Europe, boat people returning from the camps,[6] and (above all) demobilised soldiers (following the departure of the Vietnamese from Cambodia) have added more than one million people to the labour force. So, since 1985, Vietnam has faced the challenge of having to provide jobs for all these newcomers on the labour market. The 15 to 34-year olds (accounting for most job seekers) comprised nearly 37 per cent of the population in 2000, compared with 29 per cent in 1970 (ILO 1997). This should reach a peak around 2005 and then start declining. The coming years will be a critical period for Vietnam in its ability to manage the labour market.

In a socialist economy there is no labour market. After leaving school or university, people are assigned a position. The state is responsible for the allocation of jobs, either through its central body or through its enterprises at different levels (provinces, districts). As in most socialist countries, self-employment had been tolerated, although how much tolerance there was in different periods is not clear. The tolerance probably depends on the capacity of the state to offer jobs to everyone. In the beginning of the 1960s in Northern Vietnam almost all labour was socialised, i.e. in state enterprises or co-operatives (Vo Nhan Tri 1967). But since then there has been a trend towards permitting self employment, showing some weaknesses in the system. In 1974 employment statistics show that 14 per cent of the non-farm employed population of Northern Vietnam were self-employed (General Statistical Office 1977).

Implementation of co-operatives at different levels (work-group, village, commune, district) has not been enforced in the same way everywhere. Although all workers were supposed to work in co-operatives, there are examples of peasants who left the co-operatives as early as the mid 1960s (Kleinen 1999), and we have also met artisans who have been self employed since the 1960s. The implementation of socialist labour relations depended on local conditions. Nevertheless, the rare niches of private production that existed through the 1980s were confined to low technical levels and sold their products in neighbourhood markets.

6 Although there are no statistics on the social characteristics of boat people, it seems that the share of people in age of work and the share of skilled people among them was more than the average for the country.

After 1976 collectivisation encountered strong resistance from the population of South Vietnam. Even so, the state did not provide jobs to all. Small enterprises (with only family labour) and petty trade were tolerated. Since many former collaborators of the Southern regime and their families were barred from all positions, they had no choice but to become self employed. Hundreds of thousands of people (including children of mixed unions) had to survive on their own. In the beginning of the 1990s, when Vietnam opened up to the western world, street workers, cyclo drivers, and many other petty jobs were still typical occupations filled by former civil servants of the Southern regime.

At that time self employment was not a free market activity because the market for goods and services was very restricted. The supply of raw materials was under the control of state enterprises or co-operatives, and permissions were required in many fields. Self employed workers and family enterprises were severely controlled by local authorities, especially when they were considered politically incorrect. They often had to resort to the underground economy to buy raw materials and sell their products.

Greater tolerance became inevitable because the growth of labour supply was becoming unmanageable in the framework of socialist labour relations. Up to 1986 most of the labour increment was directed to agriculture. The remainder was employed in the state sector, which increased from 2.2 million in 1976 to 3.7 million in 1987. Yet the economic crisis forced the government to tolerate more private activities for workers in factories alongside their positions as state wage workers. In effect, their salaries had become too low to feed their families, and many workers had to resort to semi-legal activities to get additional income.

The *Doi Moi* reform legalised a situation that had gotten out of control. The system of socialist labour relations was shaken to its foundations, as were the labour representatives that were part of it. Especially affected was the hierarchy of the labour system that accorded civil service and wage labour in state enterprises a supreme labour status. This type of position not only carried a life time guarantee, but also social protection, a better income, and, above all, access to those benefits for other members of the family. As early as the mid-1980s the position of state worker became less attractive because the wages were too low. When more freedom was given for self employment and family enterprises, many state workers resigned and created their own 'jobs.'

The reform of *Doi Moi*, which allowed people to work on their own or in the private sector, corresponds to the rapid expansion of the labour supply because of demographic factors. In 1986 it became obvious that the economy would not develop enough to provide jobs for everyone in the state sector or co-operatives. Instead, the Sixth Congress of the Communist Party decided to reform the state sector so it would not be technologically backward, and to let the rest of the population manage on its own. The explosion of labour beyond the agricultural market was entirely absorbed by self employment and small family enterprises. Non-farm labour grew from 6 million in 1986 to 11.5 million in 1997.

Together, *Doi Moi* and the reform of state enterprises, caused employment in the state sector to decline to 2.5 million; later, when foreign investment contributed to modernisation of these enterprises through joint ventures, employment rose to 3 million in 1997. Over the last 25 years employment in the state sector has been relatively stable, remaining around 3 million - but the non-farm labour force has more than doubled.

Dynamics Of The Labour System

The transformation of the labour situation can be studied by analysing the career pattern of individuals, which sheds new light on the changes now in progress. Demographic pressure on the labour system is felt through the growing number of people emerging from the educational system (schools, universities, vocational training). Yet most new entrants to the labour market are people who have had no previous work. Only a few individuals in non-farm activities have experience in farming. The main characteristics of the labour situation in the first decade of *Doi Moi* have been the rise of non-socialist labour opportunities and the changes in labour in the state sector.

Feeding the Labour Market: Education

Schooling rates have a tremendous impact on labour supply. A drop of 5 per cent in the schooling rate for the 15 to 24-year cohorts would increase labour supply considerably.[7] Conversely, improvement in schooling for that age group, releases the tension on the labour supply.

The recent change in schooling rates has been very rapid. While there was a sharp drop in secondary school enrollments between 1990 and 1994, the trend has since been reversed. By contrast, in tertiary education, there has been a steady growth of enrollment in universities, with the number of students more than tripling between 1991 and 1995. This was partially counterbalanced by a drop in some areas of vocational training, but in all, enrollment has grown in the 15 to 24-year-old population (World Bank 1996). One reason for this trend may be the

7 The 15-24 years old population is over 16 million people. A 5 per cent drop in schooling rates would free 800,000 individuals (but not all school leavers would try to work) while the increase of schooling rates, especially for the 15-year olds and over, diminishes the labour supply. Yet, the improvement of schooling also has an indirect and positive impact on labour force participation rates, especially for women. Many studies have shown that women with a higher education tend to participate more in the labour force (see for instance Meng 1997 or Duryea and Székely 1998). Therefore, a rise in the schooling rate for the population over 14 will have a negative effect on labour supply in the short term, but a positive effect in the long term.

difficulty of finding a job after school. After 1995 this trend has continued, with more recent reports showing a sharp increase of enrollment in tertiary education, as well as a greater availability of training, especially from private institutions.

In the sample this trend is not yet significant, although part of the sample that entered the labour market in the last years has stayed in school longer. But another part dropped out of school early (they are non-active). The survey reveals that the main result is a growing gap between the less and the more educated, and this is also reflected in the labour market.

Most people employed in non-farm activities did not start their working life directly after school. They became non-active or unemployed (the difference between unemployment and non-activity is explained below). The share of those who obtain a job immediately after school is an indication for the efficiency of the education system as well as for the efficiency of the institutions that regulate labour entry. In this respect the survey shows that the conditions of passage from education to activity have changed with the *Doi Moi* policy in the late 1980s and the early 1990s.

Table 12.1: Types of Employment for School Leavers, 1977-95 (in percentages)

Date of first work experience		*77-81*	*82-86*	*87-89*	*90-92*	*93-95*
Have job	Non-state sector	15.2	21.4	28.3	36.6	40.9
	State and co-op	31.8	27.2	28.3	14.9	30.1
	Activity (not sp.)	5.3	4.7	4.3	4.6	1.2
No job	Unemployment	3.0	4.0	6.9	9.9	11.0
	Non activity	44.7	42.7	44.1	34.0	16.7

Source: ORSTOM-MOLISA survey.
Note: Non-state includes the private sector (registered enterprise), household or family enterprises and self-employment. Employment in foreign companies is not important (under 3 per cent of non-farm labour).

The fact that up to 1990 half the school leavers become non-active after leaving school is at the first glance a sign that the school system was not efficient. It also shows that the socialist system of labour does not appear to have been functioning properly and was not very efficient in providing jobs. By allowing people to take charge of their own activity, the *Doi Moi* policy has released the tension on the labour market. The 'informal sector' (household enterprises and self employment that constitute the bulk of non-state labour) is the main outlet for people who leave school. Since 1993 state employment has been expanding again and is the main outlet for the most educated people in the sample.

Between 1976 and 1996 the average age for obtaining the first job has risen by nearly one year for males, and more than one and a half years for females. This is not because schooling lasts longer, but because there is a longer period of non-activity between school and the first work experience. It is more difficult to get a job, and it takes a longer time. Thus, although it is less rigid and more open (everyone can start their own activity), the labour system has not gained efficiency with the new 'institutions' (i.e. the set of mechanisms that regulate the 'labour market').

Table 12.2: Average Age of First Job, End of Education and Duration of Non-Activity or Unemployment Before First Job

	Males			*Females*		
	First job	*End school*	*Non-activity*	*First job*	*End school*	*Non-activity*
1979–81	20.5	16.9	3.6	20.1	16.4	3.7
1982–84	20.7	16.6	4.1	20.3	15.8	4.5
1985–87	20.2	16.1	4.1	21.0	16.2	4.7
1988–90	20.3	16.1	4.1	21.8	15.1	6.7
1991–93	20.8	15.9	4.9	21.2	15.9	5.4
1994–96	21.3	15.7	5.5	21.8	16.3	5.5

Source: ORSTOM-MOLISA survey.

Those who leave school early (before 15) necessarily become non-active for a while. For this part of the population, the less educated (with less than 9 years of schooling), the average time of non-activity has increased (from 5.5 years in 1980 to 7.3 in 1995) more than for the better-educated part of the population.

These data apply to those who have jobs. But a significant part of the population has no job and is presently (at the time of the survey) non-active. Only 22 per cent of the population aged between 15 and 19 years old, 67 per cent of the 20 to 24-year olds, and 80 per cent of the 25 to 29-year olds are in the labour force. This is a clear sign of the weaknesses of the labour market and the tension brought about by demographic pressure.

Flows in the Institutional Sectors

The growing educational gap is now clearly visible in the employed population and is a major effect of the *Doi Moi* policy. When state-owned enterprises were restructured, life employment was eliminated (see Nørlund 1996 for details). More than 1 million employees from the state sector were made redundant between 1988 and 1992 (World Bank 1995). The ORSTOM-MOLISA survey reveals that lay-offs have hit the lowest educated state employees massively, while only a few educated employees were dismissed or decided to quit on their own. In the last 15 years, but mainly between 1989 and 1992, 90 per cent of the uneducated state employees (without a primary school certificate) were laid off or voluntarily left the state sector. Only one quarter of this number were laid off among those with higher education or an advanced technical level (university or vocational schools). Besides, more of those who had been dismissed and had some educational background became self employed than those with no educational background, who generally withdrew from the labour force.

Table 12.3: Present Position of People Who Have Been in the State Sector, by Educational Level (in percentages)

	Still in state sector	*Left to self-employment*	*Became non-active*	*Total*
No diploma or primary certif.	3.1	16.4	39.7	18.0
Lower secondary certificate	18.9	34.3	20.1	23.4
Upper secondary certificate	26.5	27.1	27.8	26.9
University or vocational school	51.6	22.2	12.4	35.5
Total	100.0	100.0	100.0	100.0
Incidences	981	531	378	1890

Source: *ORSTOM-MOLISA survey*.

Table 12.4: Percentage of Educated Labour Force,* by Age and Type of Enterprise

Age	*Civil service*	*State enterprises*	*Private enterpr. ≥10 emp.*	*Private enterpr. <10 emp.*	*Self-employed*	*Casual labour*	*All*
15-24	89.3	39.7	34.8	23.2	21.1	7.1	29.1
25-34	91.7	69.4	56.3	39.9	39.2	11.8	51.7
35-44	91.5	65.9	46.3	40.6	34.6	8.0	51.4
45-64	83.5	63.7	50.0	24.6	26.7	21.1	40.8
Total	89.4	63.1	46.5	32.8	31.7	11.0	45.3
Total incidences	482.0	609.0	172.0	650.0	1504.0	109.0	3526.0
Educated	431.0	384.0	80.0	213.0	477.0	12.0	1597.0

Source: *ORSTOM-MOLISA survey*.
* With a lower secondary certificate or more. Non-farm labour force only.

The educational gap shapes a heavily segmented labour market. Educated people enter the state sector immediately after finishing university. Less educated people go in private enterprises or work for themselves, while the least educated work in casual activities or remain non-active. There is now a clear hierarchy by type of work, from civil service at the top to casual labour at the bottom.

Before *Doi Moi* the most qualified part of the labour force was already concentrated in the state sector. The restructuring of this sector emphasised this human capital concentration by the dismissal of the less qualified. Moreover, the state sector attracts most of the investment, and its share in the GDP is growing. Any gains in productivity that this brings is at least partly determined by the concentration of educated workers in this sector.

Women's Participation

Rising rates of non-activity or unemployment should hit the female population more than the male population, if Vietnam follows the traditional Asian pattern. The ORSTOM-MOLISA survey shows that more women than men were dismissed from state enterprises in the beginning of the 1980s, but their performance is not significantly different from that of males, and whatever differences there are may be owing to differences in educational attainment. With similar levels of education, there is no gender discrimination in this matter. This survey also shows that in 1996 labour force participation rates for women (60 per cent of the population between 15 and 64 years old) are well under those of men (71 per cent).

The 1979 population census shows an overall female labour force participation rate of 69.5 per cent (for the population 15 years and over); in the 1989 census a more favourable age structure shows a rate of 74 per cent, but age specific rates seem to be downward oriented (ILO 1997). Subsequent surveys do not provide a clear image of female labour force participation rates. The ORSTOM-MOLISA survey shows lower rates, especially for the prime working age, which is also the fertility age. The 1997 labour force survey shows a rate of 68.5 per cent (MOLISA 1997), which is an important step backward compared with the 1989 census. Despite the lack of precision of some of these statistics, the trend of female labour force participation is downward oriented at the present time. Explanations can be advanced, but some are hypothetical.

First, the labour force participation rates for women in the period of the centrally planned economy were exceptionally high by international standards, coming after a long tradition of women's participation in rural work. The government has encouraged enrollment in labour for women by setting up kindergartens and social welfare associated with the work unit (co-operative or enterprise). During the war, when many young men had to leave their homes to join the army, women were encouraged to participate in all aspects of social life, especially labour. Wartime really ended in 1988 when the Vietnamese withdrew from Cambodia.

Females constituted half of the work force in 1989, but their participation was higher in agriculture. The female labour force participation rate (population 15 years old and over) in urban areas was 65.1 per cent (77 per cent for males) compared with 77 per cent (83 per cent) in rural areas. The decline in the number of agricultural workers as part of the total labour force now contributes to the decline of the average labour force participation rates (more for women than for men).

Moreover, the change of economic policy and the dismantling of co-operatives have left many women without a job, and some of them have decided to withdraw from the labour force instead of seeking a new job. In addition, the end of co-operatives deprived many families of social services such as child-minding for which they now have to pay. More generally, a return of traditional family values is discernible, and the recent evolution in women's status is questionable. Cultural change and the revival of tradition might also have an impact on the occupations of women. Some of these rituals signify a return to male domination. Along the same line the return of men to top positions in many institutions after the war is a sign of the reverse tendency in the position of women in public life (see for instance Kleinen 1999 for examples in a northern village). The share of women in local and provincial people's committees has decreased since the mid-1970s (UNDP 2000).

Even when they have stayed in the labour force, women may have suffered under the *Doi Moi* reform. More of them have entered petty trade rather than secure wage labour, and above all, they have 'lost benefits such as maternity leave allowance and childcare provision. Women's retreat into the household also means that they have less social contact, an increased burden of productive and reproductive labour, and fewer opportunities to improve their skills and decision-making capacity' (Beresford 1997, quoted by UNDP 2000).

Unemployment and Underemployment

In all the censuses and surveys the rates of unemployment are rather low. In the two Vietnam Living Standard Surveys, in the labour surveys as well as in the ORSTOM-MOLISA survey, recorded rates of unemployment are under 7 per cent of the labour force in urban areas. They have declined since 1989 when the unemployment rate for the population aged 15 and over was 13 per cent, with a very high rate of 45 per cent for the 15 to 19-year olds, and 20 per cent for the 20 to 24-year old groups in urban areas. This decline is concomitant with better enrollment in school, but also with rising non-activity.

The adjustment mechanism for the labour supply towards a strong demand is a rise of labour force participation rates in so far as the stock of population allows it. Since the 15 to 24-year old cohorts are the most numerous, this stock is very important, even more so if one considers only the demand for non-farm jobs and the surplus workers in agriculture as a possible reserve. Conversely, when the demand is weak, some people withdraw from the labour force and young people delay their entry in the labour market.[8] Other people will stay unemployed. Unemployment is an adjustment buffer between supply and demand for labour, but cannot be analysed independent of the change in the labour force participation rates.

In this respect the line between non-activity and unemployment is not distinct, as is the case in other countries where unemployment is not strictly registered and does not bring any benefit. The difference between the two concepts relies only on a subjective perception of respondents in surveys, where those who declare they are looking for a job are classified as unemployed, while the others are classified as non-active. In the ORSTOM-MOLISA survey, the characteristics of the unemployed are not much different from those who declare themselves as non-active, at least for males (more females declare they devote their time only to housework). The unemployed have been without jobs for a long period (the average is three years in the sample), and there is no evidence of an active job search. The point is that the government now recognises unemployment because it can no longer guarantee a job for everyone.

A dynamic analysis of unemployment from the ORSTOM-MOLISA survey shows that the balance of unemployment is 'positive,' with more people entering unemployment than leaving. This growth in unemployment reached its peak in 1990 to 1992 but has slowed since 1992. The origin of the unemployed is also changing, with more people having previous work experience in the last period (1993 to 1996) than before. They generally come from the individual or private sector activities. This is a sign that the 'informal sector' cannot absorb the labour supply as much as it has in the recent past.

Farming Work and the Shift from Agriculture

Vietnam has experienced growth in the rate of the working population engaged in farming in the last 20 years. From 67 per cent of the total labour force, the share of farmers went up to 73 per cent in 1985. This proportion remained nearly unchanged up to 1992. This very unusual statistic (nearly everywhere in the world the share of the labour force engaged in agriculture tends to decline) reflects the resettlement of urban refugees in rural areas after the war and the migrations to the new economic zones. More recently the redistribution of land to families may have encouraged some people to resettle in their home village.[9] It has most prob-

8 Malarney (1997) states that in the village he studied 'political leadership, despite the revolutionary agenda, still remains an almost exclusively male domain in Vietnam.' Only in the late 1970s was there a woman who acceded to the position of president of the commune for several terms.

9 There is evidence of resettlement in the home village among people who were let go from state enterprises in the beginning of the 1990s. Many of these workers wanted to be in their village

ably restrained some from leaving for urban areas. Finally, the need for a residence permit has limited migration to urban areas up to recently.

As a consequence the shift from agriculture to non-farm activities has played a minor role in shaping the present non-farm labour force, at least up to 1996. In the years 1993 to 1995, under 5 per cent of the new entrants came from agriculture. This flow, however, only shows those who started their working life as farmers and then moved to a non-farm occupation. The decline of labour in agriculture is more a matter of a generational move, with children of farmers increasingly entering non-farm occupations at the expense of farming upon finishing their schooling. In 1996 17 per cent of workers under 35 years old and 42 per cent of those 35 and over came from a peasant family (ORSTOM-MOLISA survey).

Now, however, there is a change because of an increase in the seasonal and casual work in cities, along with the component of the non-farm labour force, which is not well measured; it is fed by people coming from rural areas. It might signal a passage to permanent non-farm work, as there is an acceleration in the decrease of the share of farmers in the labour force (measured at 69 per cent in 1997).[10]

The shift from farm to non-farm activities takes many forms and cannot be seen as only the desperate move of poor peasants toward cities. This shift was moderate in the first years of the *Doi Moi* period because of the de-collectivisation in agriculture that helped keep farmers on their land. This is one of the most important challenges Vietnam will face in the future. Between 1976 and 1986, 84 per cent of the increase in the labour force was absorbed by agriculture. The decade after the share of agriculture in incremental labour absorption fell to 57 per cent, and in the last years (1993 to 1996) to 37 per cent.

This has important consequences for the non-farm labour market. While the total increase of the labour force has been on average 1 million people a year, non-farm employment grew by 135,000 from 1976 to 1986. Today the increase is over 700,000 per year (average 1993 to 1996). It is interesting to note that incremental employment in agriculture is almost entirely comprised of women (93 per cent of incremental growth in farming between 1992 to 93 and 1997 to 98 - see Bales 2000). This shows the rise of a sexual division of labour in rural areas where men engage in services or construction activities while women remain in charge of the farm.

when collectivised land was reallocated to private households. Generally, the number of members of the household was a criterion for land allocation. However, there are no quantitative data about this.

10 Data from GSO yearbook 1998, to be considered cautiously since it might be only a projection. The 1999 labour force survey gives a figure of 63.6 per cent workers in agriculture (MOLISA 2000).

Conclusion

The change in the population structure in contemporary Vietnam has two corollary effects: a decline of dependency rates on one hand, and an explosion of labour supply on the other. The first effect promises a more favourable development because it lightens the burden of education and health, or improves the efficiency of investment in these sectors. The second effect is, in the short term, the main challenge the government must face. Despite rapid growth, labour demand is not strong enough to match labour supply. Adjustments are made through a decline in the labour force participation rates in certain categories: youth, who are better enrolled in secondary and tertiary education, and women of fertile age, who participate less in the labour force than they did in the past.

The explosion of labour supply has shattered socialist labour relations, especially co-operatives. It now causes some tension in the labour market, one of which is rising unemployment. The bulk of the population must now to use its own savings to create jobs, while the state drains most of the financial resources from international donors and investors. The segmentation of the 'labour market' that arises is rendered by flows into the labour system according to educational level. The state sector is nearly closed to those who have little education (less than 9 years). The less educated part of the population oscillates between non-activity, casual work, and self employment, showing a more chaotic working career. These characteristics point to a process of segmentation in the labour market, although it is not possible to say if this trend will continue. In effect, it depends on the ability of the state sector to attract a skilled labour force, and it relies mainly on foreign investment. As the flow of foreign investment in joint ventures with state enterprises declines, these features in the labour force might change.

The situation of labour will be critical in the next decade, since the growth in the labour supply will still be high. In addition, the absorption capacity of agriculture is at its limit, and the urban informal sector also seems to be saturated. Job creation will now depend on the capacity to attract foreign investment and to raise domestic savings.

References

Bales, S. (2000) 'Vietnam's Labour Situation and Trends – Analysis Based on 1992-93 and 1997-98 Vietnam Living Standards Data', background paper for the Vietnam Development Report 2000.

Banister, J. (1993) *Vietnam Population Dynamics and Prospects*, Berkeley: Institute of East Asian Studies, University of California.

Barbieri, M. et al. (1995) 'La situation démographique du Vietnam,' *Population* 3: 621–652.

Dureya, S. and M. Székely (1998) 'Labor markets in Latin America: a supply side story', Inter-American Development Bank, working paper 374.

General Statistical Office (1976) *Dan so Nuoc Cong Hoa Xa Hoi Chu Nghia Viet Nam* (Population of

the Socialist Republic of Vietnam), Hanoi: Statistical Publishing House.
— (1996) *Statistical Yearbook 1995*, Hanoi: Statistical Publishing House.
— (1997) *Statistical Yearbook 1996*, Hanoi: Statistical Publishing House.
— (1998) *Statistical Yearbook 1997*, Hanoi: Statistical Publishing House.
— (1999) *Statistical Yearbook 1998*, Hanoi: Statistical Publishing House.
ILO (1997) *Economically Active Population* 1950-2010, Geneva: International Labour Organisation Bureau of Statistics.
Kerkviet, B.T. (1995) 'Village-state relations in Vietnam: the effects of everyday politics on decollectivisation', *Journal of Asian Studies* 54, 2: 396–418.
Kleinen, J. (1999) *Facing the Future, Reviving the Past: A Study of Social Change in a Northern Vietnamese Village*, Singapore: Institute of Southeast Asian Studies.
Malarney, S.K. (1997) 'Culture, virtue and political transformation in contemporary northern Vietnam', *Journal of Asian Studies* 56, 4: 899–920.
Meng, X. (1997) 'The economic position of women in Asia', Paper presented at the Manila workshop, CLARA, October 1997.
MOLISA (Ministry of Labour, Invalids and Social Affairs), General Statistical Office (1997) *Status of Labour-Employment in Vietnam*, Hanoi: Statistical Publishing House.
— (1998) *Status of Labour-Employment in Vietnam, 1997*, Hanoi: Statistical Publishing House.
Nguyen Trong Nam Tran (1991) 'Les politiques agraires Vietnamiennes', *Revue Tiers-Monde* XXXII, 128: 791–810.
Nørlund, I. (1996) 'Democracy and Trade Unions in Vietnam', *Copenhagen Journal of Asian Studies* 11: 73–99.
Post, K. (1989) *Revolution, Socialism and Nationalism in Vietnam*, Worcester: Dartmouth Publishing Company Ltd.
Terzani, T. (1997) *Saigon 1975: Three Days and Three Months*, Bangkok: White Lotus.
U.S. Department of Commerce (National Trade Data Bank) (2000) '1999 census results', www.tradeport.org/ts/countries/vietnam/mrr/mark0100.html (December 2000).
U.S. Bureau of Census International Data Base (2000) www.census.gov/ipc/www/idbagg.html (December 2000).
Vo Nhan Tri (1967) *Croissance Économique de la République Démocratique du Vietnam*, Hanoi: Editions en Langues Étrangères.
— (1992) *Vietnam's Economic Policy Since 1975*, Singapore: Institute of Southeast Asian Studies.
Williamson, J.G. (1993) 'Human capital deepening, inequality and demographic events along the Asia-Pacific rim', in N. Ogawa, G.W. Jones and J.G. Williamson (eds.) *Human Resources in Development Along the Pacific Rim*, Singapore: Oxford University Press.
World Bank (1995) *Vietnam Poverty Assessment and Strategy*, Washington D.C.: World Bank.
— (1996) *Vietnam Education Financing Sector Study*, Washington D.C.: World Bank, Human Resources Operations Division, East Asia and Pacific Region.
UNDP (2000) *Gender Briefing Kit*, Hanoi: United Nations Development Programme.

13

Domestic Workers and Transnational Migration: Perspectives from the Philippines and Singapore

SHIRLENA HUANG, BRENDA S.A. YEOH
AND RICHARD T. JACKSON

On 5 October 1994, Foreign Secretary Romulo of the Philippines called on the United Nations to hold an international conference on the effects of global migration on development as the 'transnational migration of workers is an increasingly important phenomenon and the rights of migrant workers must be protected' (*Migration News* 1994a). The salience of these issues is clearly evident for the Philippines, a significant exporter of migrant workers since the 1960s and which is today, the leading exporter of labour in Asia and the world's leading exporter of female workers, of whom well over half are domestic or sex workers.

Romulo's call is interesting from many viewpoints. Why was it issued at that particular moment? Why do international flows of labour receive so little attention from political leaders? Are migrant labour rights part of a wider human rights package or, possibly, the deliberately overlooked by-products of the human rights agenda? What has been the impact of the overseas contract worker (OCW) phenomenon on the Philippines to date? Why are so many of the Philippines' OCWs female? We will attempt to address some of these issues in this paper.[1] We begin by briefly outlining the quantitative aspects of the export of labour from the Philippines, paying special attention to female domestic workers, with the aim of demonstrating how many aspects of this phenomenon can be related to historic patterns of female employment in the Philippines. We then examine the structural conditions within Singapore which have resulted in the demand for foreign domestic helpers, foremost among whom are Filipinas. Finally, using data col-

1 This chapter was originally published in French as 'Les migrations internationales des domestiques Philippines: contextes et expériences aux Philippines et à Singapour', *Revue Europeene des Migrations Internationales* 1999, 15, 2: 37-67. We are grateful to the publishers for allowing a translated version to be reprinted here.

lected in the field, we investigate how the migrant workers themselves perceive their situations.

One of the great contradictions evident in the process of the globalisation of the world economy is the contrast between the energy displayed by the world's leading economies (selectively targeted though this energy is in terms of particular products) in their efforts to remove trade barriers and obstacles to the free, global movement of capital on the one hand, and their studied disinterest in any moves to allow similarly free international movements of peoples. Clearly, any such liberalisation of population movement comparable to that afforded to goods or capital would have the potential to create enormous social tensions – but so do the existing disparities in economic opportunities between nations. The lack of official interest is itself interesting for two contrasting reasons: one basically economic in nature, and the other social and legal. Simple economics tells us that if one factor of production (capital) and the product itself (goods) are increasingly mobile but the labour factor of production remains immobile, one may expect with reasonable confidence that, over time, economic activity will tend to gravitate towards those areas which, for a specific form of economic activity, offer the optimal combination of locational costs, including a mix of low-cost and highly-skilled labour. Economic activity will leave inefficient areas to rust into oblivion whilst creating new centres of activity, particularly in an era when transportation, communications networks, and types of economic activity are undergoing rapid change and old patterns and networks are slow to adapt to such innovations.

With recent relative changes in the international mobility of goods, capital and labour, it is reasonable to expect the world's capital-rich but increasingly labour-poor economies to have become increasingly concerned about, and paid more attention to, the freeing up of labour movement as a means of ameliorating the effects of an ageing domestic populations and rising dependency ratios. However, almost all the economically better off countries have erected rather severe barriers to formal immigration. This studied ignorance is interesting because it flies in the face of reality: most of these countries have also admitted, on a short-term basis, large numbers of relatively poorly-paid workers from less well-off parts of the world to bolster their diminishing labour supplies (particularly in the least attractive occupations). Admitting supposedly short-term migrants as workers but becoming increasingly restrictive on permanent migration has indirectly encouraged the illegal trafficking of both migrants and workers, and their abuse by criminal elements. While the exact circumstances differ, Japan's Peruvians and Iranians, Germany's Turks, France's black Africans, Britain's Pakistanis, and Singapore's Thais, and Filipinas are of the same generic class. By condemning such illegal movements on the one hand but continuing to license labour recruitment agencies on the other, many of these governments are reaping the economic benefits of such workers' productive efforts without paying much attention to their welfare (see Sassen 1988, Huang and Yeoh 1996), while simultaneously satisfying their domestic electorates' hostility towards the newcomers.

A report by the United States Commission for the Study of International Migration and Co-operative Economic Development recently 'concluded that although free trade and investment were the best mutually beneficial policies that emigration and immigration countries could adopt to accelerate their development and eventually reduce unwanted immigration, such migration would not be reduced quickly, and may even increase temporarily' (*Migration News* 1994b). Such a conclusion, one might reasonably say, is blindingly obvious. In the case of a poor country and its inhabitants which, for whatever reason, has not seen its income increasing as a result of free trade and capital movement, international flows of people trying to improve their lot in life will occur given a clear demand for labour in the better off or rapidly developing countries, and the availability of relatively cheap transportation to facilitate cross-border movements. If free trade and freer capital movement are merely a device to 'eventually reduce unwanted immigration', they will fail in that goal.

This is not to say that globalisation is a 'bad thing'. It offers to many previously excluded economies the possibility of competing successfully with already wealthy, and possibly decreasingly efficient, economies and their labour forces. But it is to say that, far from heralding the death of geographical location (and its influence on any society's potential for economic progress), global competition, facilitated by the absolute reduction in the cost of overcoming distance in the manufacture and marketing of any tradable good, has only highlighted the relative and differential advantages and disadvantages of all locations. In an increasingly competitive world (which is what globalisation is fundamentally all about), relativities become more, not less, important. Whilst modern transportation and communications technology has improved all places' accessibility – and therefore their potential for participation in the global economy – it has also improved the economic potential of selected foci in the new international networks which it has created far more than it has improved that same potential in the rest of the world. It has not destroyed geography; it has created a *new* geography of the world. Globalisation has not eliminated differences; it has created *new* differences in the ability of places to compete economically with one another. Just because some of what were previously the world's economic also-rans have gained spectacularly in significance in this new world geography (and, equally, others previously important, are sinking into relative obscurity) does not mean that all previously peripheral regions will also gain. New relativities do not mean the end of the periphery; they create new peripheries with somewhat, but not entirely, different, memberships. As Brah (1991: 168) claims, 'All our fates are linked within this [global economic] system but our precise position in it depends on a multiplicity of factors such as our gender, class background, colour, ethnicity, caste, whether we live in a rich industrially advanced society of a poor country of the Third World'. The difference in this new situation is not that there is no longer a centre or series of centres and a periphery, but that the periphery is in absolute terms very much closer to the centre and that individuals in the periphery can now make the leap to the centre very much more easily – whether they are 'unwanted immigrants' or not. Indeed, much has been written about the process of 'globalisation' as a dominant force in the latter decades of the twentieth century and its impact in producing new 'geographies with quite different breaks and borders from what went on before' (Thrift 1994: 368).

Migration from the Philippines

Thus, Romulo's call is a timely one in an age of globalisation. In particular, the challenge presented by the international flow of labour is one of the most important confronting the Philippines. This, of course, is precisely why the Foreign Secretary of the Philippines made the call: hardly any other nation state is as affected by the trade in labour as his. Approximately ten per cent of Philippines citizens live overseas and, over the past decade, about half a million Filipinos (just under one per cent of the country's resident population) have left each year, although not necessarily permanently (Vasquez, Tumbaga and Cruz-Soriano 1995: 5).

The precise volume of this annual flow and the stock of overseas Filipinos are matters of conjecture. There are very few countries in the world where one would not find Filipino workers, but many are illegal migrants and thus unlikely to be enumerated in any official estimates of their numbers. Romulo himself estimated that between 1985 and 1993, a total of 3.69 million legally processed workers left the Philippines on contracts and that altogether there were six million of his compatriots then (October 1994) resident abroad of whom close to two million were undocumented and, therefore, illegal emigrants to a greater or lesser degree (*Migration News* 1994a).

The emigrant stream is composed of three unequal tributaries. The smallest subgroup is of legal, permanent emigrants who have, for the last decade, totalled between 50,000 and 70,000 annually. As of the end of 1993, there were 1.76 million of such emigrants of whom 772,000 had migrated since 1981. Nearly three-quarters had emigrated to the United States, with a further 12 per cent going to Canada, eight per cent to Australia and three per cent to Japan. The bulk of these emigrants are families, but a significant proportion is of females migrating as fiancees or newly married spouses of foreign males. Between 1989 and 1994, 95,000 of such Filipinas emigrated of whom 44 per cent went to the USA (many as wives of ethnic Filipinos who were already US citizens), while 29 per cent and ten per cent to Japan and Australia respectively (almost all of these marrying non-Filipinos). Since 1992, under Republic Act No. 6955, it has been illegal to match

Filipinas for marriage to foreigners through the 'mail order' system. However, a few seconds search on the InterNet will indicate that the law is not readily enforceable. Of the overall stream of such permanent emigrants since 1981, 59.1 per cent were females (Samonte et al. 1995: 97).

The second subgroup of emigrants is of unknown size because it is, in one form or another, illegal and therefore undocumented. Forms of illegality vary. A common form is that of staying on overseas after the expiry of the original legal contract without reconfirming the new contract with authorities. Alternatively, the original departure from the Philippines and entry to an overseas country may themselves have been illegal, or they may have been legal (*via* a genuine tourist or student visa) but status was changed after arrival. Third, the emigrant may have thought their move was legal but their sponsor or recruiting agent may have acted illegally. One of the present writers has interviewed over 40 Filipinas who had migrated to Japan thinking they were legally married to Japanese males (a marriage ceremony had taken place in Manila prior to departure). On arrival they found that not only were they not married according to Japanese law, but they had in fact inadvertently signed up as factory workers. In some cases, their illegal status was regarded as being of so little consequence in Japan that their teacher in the Japanese language programmes they undertook was the wife of the local mayor (Jackson, unpublished field notes). Fourth, the original move may have been legal but on arrival the nature of the occupation had changed from licit to illicit, the most common transformation being from either teacher, sales representative or singer to sex worker, or from domestic worker to assistant in a family business.

It is germane to bear in mind that even though such illegal activities expose Filipinos to very considerable danger and exploitation – and as the examples above suggest, most of these emigrants are female – many individuals are extremely reluctant to return to the Philippines. For example, in 1989 Philippines newspapers reported that several hundred Filipina dancers had been expelled from Cyprus (which has often acted as a staging point for the distribution of Filipina sex workers throughout Europe and the Middle East (see De Stoop 1992) and were living in difficult circumstances in Beirut. In Lebanon at the time, there were 4,000 Filipinos working as domestic servants and entertainers; since, however, the Philippines government had banned export of labour to that country for several years they were all, presumably, illegals. In July 1989, a rescue mission to Beirut found 'the women living in miserable conditions in third rate hotels... could hardly pay their rent and had to leave their belongings as payment so that they could be allowed to leave' (Anon. 1991: 74). Despite this, most of those for whom the rescue mission was designed were very reluctant to leave and, eventually, only 190 did so. When the Philippines' Senate Committee on Women and Family Relations interviewed some of the 'rescued' they discovered that, prior to the mission itself, 300 had been interviewed by the Philippines Consul in Beirut who 'asked them specifically if any one of them wanted to go home or be repatriated, but everybody refused. *Not a single one of them offered to be returned home*' (Philippines Senate Hearings on Resolutions No. 555 and 556, July 7 and August 9, 1989; emphasis in the original). Moreover, most of those who were rescued and interviewed on their return expressed a wish to go back overseas, some to Beirut. One is given cause to reflect on the nature of these women's prospects within the Philippines under such circumstances.

Whilst exact numbers of illegals are impossible to specify, it is certain that they are large (see Hoffman 1996). For example, in November 1996, the United Arab Emirates threatened to jail all illegal workers within its boundaries. Consequently, 23,280 Filipino workers were reported to have departed of whom around 3,000 were illegals by virtue of either overstaying valid work permits or who had illegally entered the country; all proceeded to enter Kuwait or Saudi Arabia without any further documentation (*Philippines Daily Inquirer* Dec. 1, 1996). Almost all were female domestic workers. In Hong Kong it has been alleged that there are 'over 100,000 Filipinos employed illegally' mainly as domestic workers (*Migration News* 1996). One reliable Philippines estimate is that 'there are 300,000 unauthorised Filipinos working in neighbouring East Asian nations, so that illegal Filipino migrant workers in East Asia outnumber legals' (Tigno 1994). In these and many other reports, the undocumented and illegals are usually sex workers or domestic workers, and overwhelmingly female.

The third subgroup of emigrants is of legally contracted workers who have passed through official channels. In recent years, documentation of such workers within the Philippines has greatly improved so that statistics relating to them are now relatively reliable. This does, however, mean that comparisons with earlier, less reliable data are hazardous. For example, remittances from overseas Filipino workers appear to have increased from US$600 million in 1984 to US$2.3 billion by 1992 (Samonte et al. 1995: 102) and to US$5 billion by 1994-95 (*Migration News* 1995b). The latter figures may be accurate, but those for the early 1980s almost certainly do not tell us the true size of remittances since most OCWs at that time would not have entrusted their savings to the inefficient, and often corrupt, banking system then operating in the Philippines.

The Scalabrini Migration Center of Manila, which has consistently been the most reliable source of data on Philippines' OCWs, indicate that since the late 1980s, females have closed the gap with males amongst land-based OCWs. Indeed, by 1994, female OCWs overtook males to account for 60 per cent of the total land-based OCWs newly deployed that year (Table 13.1), up from 30 and 47 per cent in 1975 and 1987 respectively (Gonzalez and Holmes, 1996: 306). Particularly noticeable is their increasing dominance amongst new hires, which means that in future years their overall dominance will become even clearer. The rise of females as the major force in overseas contract work has coincided with the increasing importance of Asia as a destination for such workers. Most of the women are concentrated in domestic service, entertainment and nursing.

Table 13.1: Data on legal Overseas Contract Workers, Philippines, 1992-94

	1992	*1993*	*1994*
A Total OCWs	549,695	550,872	565,226
of whom: B Rehire	258,436	276,567	296,515
% Female	44.4	51.3	37.8
C New Hires	291,219	274,305	268,711
C1 % Female	50.7	54.9	60 0
Of C1: maids %	48.1	53.2	49.6
numbers	71,048	80,070	79,985
entertainers %	35.5	28.5	32.6
numbers	52,400	42,890	52,496
% OCWs to (1) Asia	26	33	38
(2) Middle East	66	59	55

Source: *Asia and Pacific Migration Journal* 1995.

The largest single group, comprising approximately half of Filipina OCWs, is of domestic workers. The export of female domestic workers from the Philippines is by no means new. In the 1960s, the presence of Filipinas as domestic workers in the households of wealthier Britons in the United Kingdom was so well known that the satirical magazine, *Private Eye,* ran a feature column weekly entitled 'Filipino Fanciers' which gave details of which eminent households (usually those of persons professing leftwing ideologies) employed Filipina maids. Such maids also appeared in other parts of Europe during this time, albeit in small numbers. However, in the 1970s, with the soaring of oil incomes in the Middle East, this type of employment began to take on much larger proportions (Arcinas 1986). At first, domestic helpers from the Philippines irrespective of their religion were drawn to the Middle East; this in effect meant recruitment was predominantly from Manila and Luzon. During the late 1970s and early 1980s as Middle Eastern employers became aware of the Muslim populations of Mindanao, in the southern Philippines, recruitment from that area increased. Simultaneously, the increasingly rich economies of Singapore and Hong Kong set out to encourage their skilled female populations to enter the workforce by allowing the recruitment of domestic help from the Philippines (and also from Sri Lanka, Thailand, Indonesia and Bangladesh). In Hong Kong, Filipinas have (until now) been officially preferred to mainland Chinese since the latter, it was felt, would not be repatriatable. In November 1996, in the course of the APEC summit held in the Philippines, the Chinese leader Jiang Zemin purportedly assured his Filipino counterpart, President Ramos, that Filipinas would continue to be employed in Hong Kong after July 1997 (*Philippines Daily Inquirer,* 28 November, 1997).

In brief, in all the migrant streams leaving the Philippines, females now constitute a majority, with the biggest single group of Philippines' OCWs being that of domestic workers.[2] This has had major repercussions both within the Philippines and for the country's stance in international labour matters.

Reactions within the Philippines

It is generally accepted that the export of overseas workers from the Philippines commenced, as a semi-official policy, in the early 1970s when the then President, Ferdinand Marcos, encouraged such migration as a short-term means of generating foreign funds for the country. In most years since then, migrant remittances (generally much higher than official estimates, as noted earlier) have exceeded the value of direct foreign investment into the country. As a percentage of the country's gross national product (GNP), OCW remittances have steadily increased from less than 0.5 per cent in 1975 to four per cent in 1993 and 1994 (Gonzalez and Holmes 1996: 304). Such remittances, provided they have not been siphoned off by an intermediary *en route*, go directly to the migrant's family; there is no waiting for aid or foreign investment to 'trickle down'. According to the 1994 *Family Income and Expenditure Survey* of the Philippines, 6.8 per cent of all households depended on 'cash receipts, gifts and other forms of assistance from abroad' for their main source of income. This represented 860,000 families or over four million people (up from just under 600,000 families in 1985) (Jackson 1990). However, it is likely that as many as three times this number of households are, or have been, in receipt of some support from overseas sources in recent years. While foreign remittances include war pensions from the US and dividend payments from overseas, the overwhelming bulk are from Filipino migrants, usually OCWs. The highest dependencies on such income were reported from Ilocos (the first area in the Philippines from which workers heading overseas – Hawaii to be precise – were recruited around 1908) and interestingly, Manila itself where one in nine households listed overseas funds as their main source of income (National Statistics Office, 1996). What used to be a city where landed gentry lived off the rentals from their rural Philippines property, is fast becoming a city of middle income, single (often male) parent households relying on funds sent by the other parent working overseas.

2 It does not seem to be a coincidence that females have now emerged as the dominant sex in all types of international migration streams and, simultaneously, have also increasingly become far more mobile than males within the Philippines. According to the 1990 Census, females are 10.5 per cent more likely to be intraprovincial migrants than males (in gross terms) and 11.8 per cent more likely to be interregional migrants (also in gross terms). Moreover, because their 'effectiveness quotients' (calculated by dividing the nett migration between any two points by the gross migration between the same points) are higher than those of males, females are 35.8 per cent more likely to be nett migrants than males. Finally, in nett terms, of the total of migrants gained by the capital city (i.e. Manila and its National Capital Region, or NCR) between 1985 and 1990, 76.3 per cent were female.

Although migration has historically been a common demographic response of Filipinos to social and economic problems (Carino 1995: 259), the extent (the continually increasing numbers) and form (involving rising numbers of women on short-term contracts for jobs often considered demeaning) of current migration streams has aroused mixed feelings within and outside the Philippines. Negative views of the problems faced by migrant Filipinas are often given full prominence in the popular press and discussed in the legislature. In the Manila press, barely a day goes by without there being a new story of violence against or exploitation of Filipinas overseas. Headlines such as 'Dreams that were Shattered' or 'Domestics Face the Home Truth' (*South China Morning Post* 11 November, 1996: 25) are also common in the overseas press. Similarly, politicians within the country express deep concern: 'of special concern to the [Senate Committee on Women and Family Relations] are the reported exploitation of our women workers abroad in terms of inadequate pay and intolerable working conditions, as well as their maltreatment and even sexual harassment by foreign employers' (Philippines Congress 1991). On overseas trips their concern is similar: 'Senator Sergio Osmena, in Hong Kong recently, said labour export is "wreaking havoc" in the community [...] "The social cost of migration is a problem no matter what you try to do [...]" said Mr. Osmena' (*South China Morning Post* 11 November, 1996: 25).

There are two problems raised by such popular and populist views. First, if conditions are so bad, why do tens of thousands of Filipinas go overseas to work in such occupations every year? Are they acting irrationally? The political view is that they are simply poorly informed. If so, why do so many choose to be rehired? Clearly, such individuals who undertake subsequent contracts are not poorly informed about overseas conditions relative to those current in their homeland; even first-time migrants are not ignorant about the latter. Thus, the more horrible the portrayal of the fate of overseas domestic workers in the Philippines press and legislature, the more disquieting become the implications of such reports for life *within* the country. Second, social science research within the Philippines on the impacts of overseas migration has not come to the same conclusions as the press and politicians. Many leaders of sociological research (Eviota 1992: 142–5) have come to more balanced conclusions that although emigration 'has deep social consequences because it often results in the disintegration of family-households', it has also meant that 'women are able to seek a way out of situations they find subordinating or oppressive and to exercise options for themselves. By means of remittances women have also begun to play a central role in the maintenance of their families'. Other researchers (Go et al. 1983, Cruz and Paganoni 1989) openly disagree with some of the more pessimistic conclusions cited above.[3] Vasquez (1992: 60), for example, specifically states:

3 It is true that there are some publications (for example those of the Catholic Institute for International Relations) that are compendia of misery.

> While the media has drawn attention to cases of marital problems and infidelity due to contract migration, this is not the trend. Studies indicate that marriage and family life have generally remained stable.

In other words, academic opinion on the overall impact of overseas migration is by no means unanimous within the Philippines. Indeed, on balance it would appear that those specialising in this area of research have concluded that emigration has not had altogether negative impacts.

Ultimately, however, weighing the costs and benefits of exporting overseas workers is not a purely academic exercise but one strongly conditioned by political factors. In recent years, the Philippines government has created, both internally and externally, a number of initiatives aimed at improving the lot of its overseas female domestic workers. Undoubtedly, part of the impetus for this has its roots in the 1994 arrest, trial and sentencing for murder of Flor Contemplacion, a Filipina domestic worker in Singapore.[4] Romulo's call for UN action came after her sentencing. When the death sentence was executed on March 17, 1995, a series of demonstrations began in Manila which had the dual purpose of attacking both the Singapore decision and, more alarmingly for the Philippines government, the latter's involvement in the labour trade. Not surprisingly, the government metaphorically hosed down the demonstration by taking a very strong anti-Singapore line to the point of recalling its ambassador to Singapore and banning further deployment of domestic workers thither (*Migration News* 1995a).

However, it is clear that the Ramos government, unlike most of its predecessors, also took to heart the public disquiet about its own role in the labour trade and called a special meeting of the Philippines Congress in May 1995, as well as having earlier established a commission (the Gancayco Commission) to examine all aspects of labour migration. The special session both ratified the UN Convention for the Protection of the Rights of Migrant Workers and Their Families and debated four bills proposed by its members. Previous congresses had often debated bills and resolutions. No fewer than 35 affecting overseas Filipinos had been filed in the Eighth Congress but only three had been signed into law (one banned mail order marriages). Similarly, most of the 95 bills filed in the Ninth Congress, did not go 'beyond their first reading' (Samonte et al. 1995: 8).

Among its recommendations, the Gancayco Commission advocated that women workers are not to be deployed to Middle Eastern countries after the year 2000 and 'women entertainers, except musicians and artists' be banned for travel to Japan, Greece and Cyprus for employment purposes. The special meeting of the Philippines Congress legislated a new Migrant Workers and Overseas Employ-

4 Contemplacion, a Filipina domestic helper in Singapore, was charged and convicted for the double murder of a fellow Filipina (also a domestic helper) and the three-year-old son of the murdered maid's employer. She was hanged in Singapore on 17 March 1995 (*The Straits Times*, 11 March 1995).

ment Act which came into effect on 16 July 1995. The next day, 'an alliance of 500 overseas recruitment agencies stopped sending Filipino workers abroad to protest the new law' (*Migration News* 1995b). In response, aspects of the new law were modified or held in abeyance. Coincidentally, in 1995 the volume of workers proceeding overseas fell by 2.5 per cent, prompting some to suggest that perhaps a turning point had been reached and that President Ramos' vision for 'Philippines 2000' which, among other things, aims to ensure that most overseas Filipinos will have returned home by the end of the century, might have some chance of becoming reality.

While it might be expected that recruitment agencies would resist any new regulation of their business, it has been more disappointing for government officials to find that their proposals have also not been entirely acceptable to the migrants themselves. Most see the new attempts to 'protect' them more as being attempts to get them to pay 'protection' money. For example, Remy Borlongan, president of the Hong Kong Asian Domestic Workers Union, attacked proposals to establish private legal insurance schemes for OCWs on the grounds that her members already paid US$50 or more on insurance annually, US$80 for every contract renewal and, income taxes, out of the minimum monthly earnings of US$470, directly to Manila. Many migrants feel that the sudden urge to protect them is in fact 'inventing new ways of extracting money from us' (Regalado 1996). Thus, the Philippines government is placed in a difficult situation between its radical domestic opponents who see the OCW issue as a useful club (almost as useful as environmental issues) with which to beat it over the head and the workers themselves who, on this issue as on so many others, seemingly want as little government control over their decisions as possible.

It is apparent that the migration phenomenon is complex and is the outcome of larger political, economic and social forces operating at the global, regional and domestic levels. As Eviota (1992), among others, have argued, the conditions which generate the outflow of Filipino workers are embedded in the unequal economic and political relationships between the Philippines and labour importing countries. However, we do not agree with Eviota's (1992: 42) assertion that 'the nature of the migratory flow depends on these conditions, and not on the individual decisions and actions of migrants themselves, these being a consequence of these conditions'. Instead, we contend that international levels of inequality alone cannot explain the extent to which particular sectors of employment, the ages and sex of migrants, and which areas within the Philippines supply the international workforce. To fully understand the export of labour from the Philippines, the experiences of the individuals involved must also be contextualised within the historically evolved values, internally regulated conditions and inequalities of both sending *and* receiving countries. We do this in the next section by focussing on the particular case of migrant female domestic workers from the Philippines to Singapore.

The Export of Domestic Workers from the Philippines

Domestic Service in the Philippines

As Scott (1986) has noted, few occupations can rival domestic service for subordination, docility, immobility, domestication or cheapness nor, judging by the frequency of reports of servants being sexually abused by their employers, for the potential for sexual harassment. However, it would be a serious error to imagine that such subordinating occupations have only sprung up for Filipinas with the recent onset of globalisation. For example, the inuring of so many Filipinas to occupations in the sex industry has not occurred purely as a consequence of the global economy.

The proposition that the widespread *occurrence* of prostitution 'is largely due to the historical presence of US military personnel and to ex-President Marcos's concerted drive to promote international tourism in the 1970s' (Chant and McIlwaine 1995: 211–12) is difficult to maintain, although its *rapid recent growth* (the focus of Chant and McIlwaine's study) may be explained by these factors. As Gilandas 1982 (cited in Eviota 1992: 134) has noted, even 'in the 1970s it was estimated that between 30–70 per cent of married men kept mistresses'. Thus, it is necessary to relate the occupational choices of Filipina OCWs not only to extra-national factors, but to internal domestic structures such as the Philippines' female occupational structures which have historically tended to 'embed women further within their traditional gender-assigned activities' (Chant and McIlwaine 1995: 291). Like other occupations that Filipina OCWs predominate in, the choice of working as a domestic helper overseas must also be understood in relation to the occupational opportunities, structures and conditions within the Philippines, such as the range of jobs available to women.

Domestic service at the beginning of this century was by no means exclusively female (Eviota 1992: 131). Only in Manila, Central Luzon and Mindanao did females outnumber males in the occupation at the time of the 1903 Census. The destruction of the handicraft, informal retailing and (literally) manufacturing activities – all of which were dominated by females – by the economic transformation occasioned by the Philippines' occupation by the United States from 1898 onwards combined with the male dominated resettlement of the country's frontier lands, together increasingly pushed women into domestic service.

By 1948, domestic service was a 'female' occupation. At that time, only 16 per cent of the female population aged 10 years and over were in 'gainful employment', but of these one million women, over 210,000 were domestic servants or *lavenderias* (laundrywomen). Intercensal variations in occupational classifications do not make it easy to establish exact numbers of domestic workers over time. However, the 1975 Census, whose completion roughly coincided with the beginnings of the OCW phenomenon, gives relatively clear information, as shown in Table 13.2.

Since 1975, it has been more difficult to isolate female domestic workers in the general census publications. However, it is possible to identify 213,090 females employed in the broader category of 'personal and domestic services' in Manila by 1980. There were around 231,000 domestic helpers at the 1990 Census, including males; the female total was probably closer to 200,000.

These figures suggest that the absolute numbers of female domestic workers in Manila has actually declined since 1975 and, given that the capital's population has increased by 60 per cent since then, it is certain that the number of domestic workers per household has fallen substantially since maids started going overseas.

Table 13.2: Female Occupations in 1975, Philippines

		Metropolitan Manila	*Remainder of Philippines*
A	Females 10 yrs and over	1,921,828	12,635,079
B	Females in gainful employ	611,913	2,432,742
C	B as per cent A	31.8	19.3
D	No. females employed as:		
D1	Domestic servants	195,312 (31.9%)	337,294 (13.9%)
D2	Clerks	99,476 (16.3%)	103,528 (4.3%)
D3	Sales assistants	57,149 (9.3%)	212,758 (8.7%)
D4	Tailors	47,478 (7.8%)	172,431 (7.1%)
D5	Professors/ teachers	40,623 (6.6%)	246,246 (10.1%)
D6	Farmers	n. a.	165,994 (6.8%)
D7	Farm workers	n. a.	593,531 (24.4%)
D8	Others	171,875 (28.1%)	600,960 (24.7%)

Sources: *1975 Integrated Census of the Population and its Economic Activities; vol. I Metropolitan Manila, vol. II Philippines.*

Apart from raising the question as to the effect of the export of domestic servants on their supply (and cost) to Filipino families, others have imputed more cynical undertones in the attitudes of legislators, bureaucrats, journalists and other leaders of public opinion towards the regulation of Philippines' overseas domestic workers. For example, Pertierra (1992: xv) has stated that:

> while there is considerable and justifiable outrage in the media and other sectors about the horrendous and exploited conditions of many domestic workers abroad, there is relatively little interest in improving the conditions of local domestics.

In view of the local politicians' and media concern over sexual molestation of Filipina domestics overseas, it is worth mentioning what is very rarely mentioned in the debate within the Philippines on the mistreatment of domestic workers by overseas employers: that within the Philippines 'the nature of the work has made domestic servants vulnerable to physical and mental abuse by female employers and to sexual harassment and abuse by male employers' (Eviota 1992: 131). Pertierra (1992: xv) has even harsher criticism of the opinion makers of Manila:

> Much of the media outrage about Filipinos working overseas is directed as much to the fact that they are working as maids than that they are potentially exploitable [... it] undoubtedly reflects the views of the Philippine elite who resent that the country's image is shaped by their social and cultural inferiors.

To this might be added the resentment that not only are such inferiors much better paid than they would be in Manila (and are thus climbing the social hierarchy) but they are not available as servants to the elite.

To make matters worse, the bulk of the domestic workers going overseas would probably not enter the same occupation if they remained at home. Data on the educational qualifications of Filipina domestic worker migrants from surveys we have conducted in Hong Kong (by Jackson) and Singapore (by Huang and Yeoh) support findings in other studies (Beltran and de Dios 1992; Vasquez et al. 1995) which have found that these migrants have relatively high levels of educational qualifications. Jackson's as yet unpublished survey of 324 domestic workers in Hong Kong in 1996 of whom no fewer than 55 per cent had university degrees and more than half the remainder had post-secondary qualifications; four in ten had degrees in education or nursing. Most regarded themselves as 'tutors' or 'nurse' rather than domestic servants. Only thirty of the respondents had been domestic workers (for wages) prior to coming to Hong Kong and even these individuals stated that if they returned to the Philippines they would not be prepared to take on similar work. Similarly, in Singapore, Huang and Yeoh's survey of 86 Filipina domestic helpers found that almost 70 per cent had either university, high-school or vocational qualifications; this was much higher than domestic workers from Indonesia (of whom 18 per cent were so qualified) and Sri Lanka (35 per cent). Only 14 per cent of the Filipinas had prior experience working as a domestic helper; the others had either never worked at all (23.3 per cent) or had been employed in occupations ranging from nursing, teaching, clerical and adminstration to jobs in production, sales and service (both formal and informal) sectors. In Europe, Filipina degree holders with jobs in domestic service 'earn close to six times what they would earn in the Philippines if they practised their professions' (Eviota 1992: 144). The lack of job opportunities at wages commensurate with the respective occupations within the Philippines itself reflects 'the continued lack of articulation between the education system and human resource development on one hand and the needs of a basically agricultural economy on the other' (Carino 1995: 271).

Thus, it would seem that the majority of those working overseas as domestic servants are actually well-educated; they are not simply *probincianas* or poor relations from a distant branch of their employer's family as many of Manila's domestic workers appear to be. Without detailed information on their educational qualifications we cannot be sure that this is the case, but it does fit rather neatly with findings relating to other female migrants and internally despised, female occupations. For example, it should not be assumed that sex worker migrants are poorly educated, especially if they were recruited from Manila. As Eviota (1992: 137), citing Evangelista (1974) and Wihtol (1982) states:

> The prostitutes in Manila seem to be recruited from a slightly different socioeconomic group to prostitutes at American airbases: some do come from relatively poor rural families, but many have urban origins and, as a group, have a higher level of educational attainment than the female population as a whole.

Another group of female emigrants regarded with some suspicion in their own country, those who migrate for marriage, are also known to have very high educational qualifications: in the late 1980s, 29 per cent of Philippines-born females in Australia (the great majority of whom bear the opprobrium in both Australia and their homeland of being labelled 'mail order brides') had university degrees compared to only three per cent of Australian females, with a further 21 per cent having other post-secondary qualifications (Jackson and Flores 1989: 44). This makes these emigrants' demonstrated need to move overseas even more tragic for the Philippines: the country is losing highly educated women, to work as others' servants.

It also makes it plain that it is not, in general, people who would have become domestic servants in the Philippines who are going overseas in such a capacity. From our personal interviews with these women, it is clear that they regard themselves less as 'servants' than as pre-school tutors, cooks or child specialists. Although acculturated in a society where domestic help is a normal accepted part of life, many, like the sex workers they are so often bracketed with, have problems justifying their choice of occupation beyond the economic opportunities it opens up for them.

Thus, while the attempts of the Philippines government in recent years to increase the protection available to their overseas domestic workers are undoubtedly genuine, the context in which they have occurred is by no means as transparent as might appear at first sight. Fundamentally, it is not merely that the Philippines is a poor country being exploited by richer countries; additionally, the poor in the Philippines have long been exploited within their own country. While unemployment and underemployment is widespread in the Philippines,[5] women

5 According to Gonzalez and Holmes (1996: 305), the high levels of unemployment and underemployment are tied to the slow rate of economic development in the Philippines relative to its neighbours. Most of the 1980s and the first half of the 1990s produced double-digit unemployment and between 1985 and 1993, underemployment averaged 23.4 per cent.

in particular have found the opportunities and range of employment available to them – not to mention both the conditions of work and the pay available – entirely unsatisfactory and have been quick to venture abroad as an additional route of entry into waged work, and a means to improve their economic, if not necessarily the social, conditions of employment. In the next section, we examine the conditions in Singapore which have turned it into a popular destination of Filipinas seeking work as overseas domestic helpers.

The Demand for Filipina Domestic Workers in Singapore

Singapore's by now well-known industrialisation programme of the 1960s and 1970s engendered a rapid influx of women into its formal labour force. Women's participation in the formal economy continued to climb steadily as the country consolidated its role as a major financial, transportation and communications centre in the 1980s. Today, at 50.3 per cent (1990 Census), Singapore's female labour force participation rate (FLFPR) is relatively high, especially as compared to other Southeast Asian countries, having risen from 19.3 per cent in 1957, 24.6 per cent in 1970 and 39.3 per cent in 1980. Despite her increasingly active role in the formal labour force, the Singapore woman has continued to bear the main responsibility for domestic work in the home (Singam 1991, Wong and Leong 1993). However, the social and demographic shifts – in particular, the unwillingness of locals to undertake work as domestic workers, the dwindling stocks of 'black and white *amahs*'[6], and the rise of the nuclear household – which accompanied Singapore's rapid economic transformation, resulted in the gradual disappearance of traditional sources of help in the reproductive sphere.

First, as with other developed economies, Singapore has largely depended, since the early 1970s, on less developed countries for labour to fill the ranks of jobs regarded by the locals as menial, initially for work on factory assembly lines and construction sites and, more recently for jobs in the service industry, including domestic service. With the expansion of employment opportunities in the service sector that accompanied Singapore's economic expansion, blue-collar jobs in the manufacturing sector and other forms of manual labour characterised by low skills, low pay and low status – a category which includes domestic service – rapidly became unattractive to the local citizenry. The shortage of locals willing to work as domestic helpers in the 1970s was compounded by the problem of dwindling stocks of *amahs* in Singapore.

The *amahs* were women, often members of an anti-marriage movement, who had originally migrated from China in the 1930s to seek employment overseas. Those arriving in Singapore often found work as live-in domestics for British

6 The '*black and white amahs*' were women who originally migrated from South China in the 1930s. As they were commonly dressed in 'black, baggy, silky trousers and starched white cotton *samfoo* tops' (Gaw 1988: xvii), they came to be widely known as the '*black and white amahs*'.

colonial and Chinese middle-class families. Their supply was not replenished after World War II partly because of more stringent immigration conditions but also as a result of major social and economic upheavals in the postwar era. The advent of an industrial economy in the Chinese hinterland as well as better education and increased social awareness, expanded job opportunities for women (Gaw 1988: 165). Careers in domestic service soon acquired the stigma of a low status job and many who might previously have gone into domestic service now no longer did so. With the withdrawal of the British armed forces from Singapore in the late 1960s, many *amahs* were left in search of employment which they managed to secure fairly easily due to the increase in demand for domestic servants among the local population (Gaw 1988: 165). However, by the 1970s, many *amahs* had retired or returned to China. The few who were still able-bodied enough to work were already in their late sixties or seventies but, well-known for their loyalty, most normally stayed with the same household until retirement or death.

A third factor which contributed to changing domestic practices in Singapore has been the concommitant rise of nuclear households and dual-income couples since the early 1980s. The proportion of single family nucleus households in Singapore climbed steadily from 63.5 per cent in 1957 to 78.0 per cent in 1980; by 1990, 85.1 per cent of Singapore's half a million households were single family nuclei (Quah 1993: 60). Dual-career households also became more common through the 1980s, rising from 111,800 (27 per cent of all married couples) in 1980 to 215,300 (40 per cent of all married couples) in 1990; thus, by 1990, the number of dual-career households almost equalled the approximately 244,000 households (in both 1980 and 1990) where only the husband works (Department of Statistics 1994: 2 & 4). As such, the traditional family support for childcare – usually grandmothers, aunts and other female relatives living in extended family households – has been increasingly difficult to sustain (Yeoh and Huang 1994).

Together, these factors have resulted in an increasing dependence on foreign women as reproductive labour substitutes since 1978, when the state first allowed a limited recruitment of women from neighbouring countries, initially from mainly the Philippines and Thailand, to work as domestic servants in Singapore. Currently, there are about 90,000 foreign maids in Singapore (*The Straits Times* 24 October 1996) having increased three and a half times from an estimated 20,000 in 1987 (*The Straits Times* 7 February 1987). To dampen the rising demand for foreign domestic helpers, the state in Singapore has imposed stringent legislation governing their employment. These measures include the imposition of a monthly levy (currently S$330),[7] payable by all employers of foreign maids; the issuance of

7 Meant primarily as a mechanism to dampen the demand for foreign workers, the levy has risen with the number of foreign maids: first set in 1982, it remained at its initial level of S$120 per month until January 1989 (reflecting the relatively slow take-off in demand for foreign maids in Singapore until that time) but has since steadily and rapidly risen to its present rate.

two-year work permits (usually renewable on application up to a maximum of eight years) on the condition that maids do not marry Singaporeans or get pregnant; a compulsory six-monthly medical check-up to test for pregnancy and venereal diseases; the payment of a security bond of S$5,000 by employers which is forfeited should any of the conditions be broken; and, newly legislated from 1 March 1997 onwards, a personal accident insurance policy of at least S$10,000 for the maid (with beneficiaries being the maid or her next-of-kin) (*The Straits Times* 24 January 1997).

While the demand for Filipina maids in Singapore has fluctuated from time to time, they have consistently constituted the largest proportion of foreign maids in Singapore since the late 1970s. A decline in demand for Filipina maids usually coincides with changes in governmental policy of either sending or receiving country concerning the financial cost of employing a Filipina maid (such as when the Singapore government has increased the maid levy, or when the Philippines government imposed an additional security bond on agencies bringing in maids) or when constraints have been imposed on Filipinos working overseas (such as when the Philippines government banned its women from working in Singapore). Following the hanging of Flor Contemplacion and the downgrading of diplomatic ties between the Philippines and Singapore, the Philippines not only banned Filipinas from coming to work in Singapore but also arranged to fly home Filipina maids already in Singapore (*The Straits Times* 23 March 1995). Although only an estimated 280 out of the then 50,000 maids in Singapore took up the offer to fly home (a number which approximates the normal attrition rate), the monthly intake of two to three thousand Filipina maids to Singapore dropped to zero with the ban (*The Straits Times* 15 April 1995). However, according the Foreign Maids Employment Agencies Association (*The Straits Times* 15 April 1995):

> We were more or less prepared, and have managed to get an average of about 1,500 maids from countries like Sri Lanka, Indonesia and India. We can't fill the vacancies immediately but the situation should be back to normal in about two to three months.

Despite the curbs imposed by both governments, Filipinas have remained the most popular choice as maids in Singapore households because many employers claim that they (the employers) 'don't have a choice' because they 'need someone who speaks English'; besides the lack of communication problems, Filipinas also have a reputation for being fast learners (*The Straits Times* 10 November 1994). Currently, Filipinas comprise approximately three-quarters of the foreign maid population in Singapore; another one-fifth are from Indonesia and the rest mainly from Sri Lanka and a few other countries such as India, Myanmar and Thailand (*The Straits Times* 8 July & 13 May 1995).

The Filipina Migrant's Experience

> Literally hundreds of thousands of women from Third World countries are cleaning the homes and minding the children of *other* Third World women. (Enloe 1989: 193)

Given the highly publicised cases of abuse, the apparently disadvantageous conditions of employment, the emotional trauma for themselves and their families, and the lack of social status of domestic service, what has drawn these large numbers of women to migrate overseas to work in the homes of people of a foreign culture? How do these women feel about their situations? We investigate these issues through the eyes of the Filipina domestic workers themselves, drawing mainly on data gathered through a questionnaire survey of 86 Filipina domestic helpers, seven of whom were followed up with in-depth interviews, each lasting from two to four hours.[8] Our findings concerning the profile of these women confirms those of others (see, for example, Asian and Pacific Development Centre (1989), Heyzer et al. (1994)): the migrant stream of domestic workers to Singapore tends to be dominated by young (1.2 per cent were below 20 years old, 45.4 per cent were between 20 and 29, 39.5 per cent were in their thirties, and 13.9 per cent were in their forties), single (67.4 per cent; 17.4 per cent were married and 15.1 per cent were widowed, divorced or separated) and, as noted earlier, relatively well-educated women.

Most of these women did not make the decision to work overseas blindly; almost all had specific reasons for coming to Singapore. Our findings clearly show that there is little support for the argument made by some Filipino politicians that the Filipinos who migrate overseas are ignorant of working conditions abroad. The majority of the women in our survey had received reports, both positive and negative, of working conditions in the different labour receiving countries. For example, 43.2 per cent of the domestic workers interviewed said that they would never work in the Middle East because they had heard of the dreadful conditions of employment. Others (17.9 per cent) noted that while Hong Kong (and Canada) offered better pay, work hours in Hong Kong were long. Thus, the women had thought through their decisions and had clear rationale for working overseas as well as choosing Singapore as a destination.

As suspected, the economic conditions within the Philippines weighed heavily on the decision to work overseas: an overwhelming majority (91.9 per cent) of the women surveyed cited the higher pay that working as a foreign domestic helper accorded in contrast to the lack of employment opportunities and/or jobs

8 The questionnaire survey and in-depth interviews were part of a much larger survey of 162 pairs of foreign domestic helpers and their employers (all matched) and in-depth interviews with fifteen domestic helpers and fifteen employers (thirteen matched pairs; the others were unpaired) conducted between June and December 1995.

in the Philippines which could pay a sufficient wage to support their families (75.6 per cent) (Table 13.3).

Table 13.3: Reasons for Working as a Foreign Domestic Helper (n=86)

Reason	%
The pay as a maid is higher overseas	91.9
Poor employment situation back home	75.6
Chance to travel/for adventure	41.9
It's all I know how to do/poor educational qualifications	7.0
Running away from family problems	5.8
Other reasons	1.2

Note: Percentages do not add up to 100.0 per cent because respondents were allowed to give more than one reason each.

The financial incentives of overseas contract work was a common refrain among the women:

> Because in the Philippines, I earn so little. I must educate my children. Not enough for them, so I come here. If I can find a factory [to work in], very far from my place. It takes eight hours you know, how to go there? (Milly, who earned just under S$100 a month as a tailor in the Philippines.)

> We can find jobs [in the Philippines] but the thing is, the salary is very low. There are a lot of factories [in my town], only thing, the salary is very low. (Rosa, who earned S$40-50 a month in each of her jobs as a factory operator paid on piece rates, and then as maid in the Philippines.)

Because almost half of all the Filipinas we interviewed had at least a high school degree, only seven per cent of them saw working as a domestic helper overseas as their sole economic (rather than most economically attractive) option of earning a wage. It is important to note, however, that beyond purely economic motivations, a job overseas was also seen as a chance for travel and adventure that these women would otherwise have little chance of experiencing (41.9 per cent). Only a handful (5.8 per cent) were primarily driven to leave the Philippines because of family problems, including difficult marital circumstances.

In Singapore, salaries earned are relatively higher than those in the Philippines. Almost two-thirds earned between $250-350 per month, but a significant proportion (31.0 per cent) had monthly salaries of $350-449 (Table 13.4). Most regularly send substantial proportions of their salaries home to support their families. Of the 73 maids who had worked long enough in Singapore at the time of the survey (i.e. more than one year) to have sent money home on a regular basis, only three claimed to send no money home at all. Of the other 70, 14.3 per cent remit up to 20 per cent of their annual income; 35.7 per cent remit 21–40 per cent; 20.0 per cent remit 41–60 per cent; 7.1 per cent remit 61–80 per cent; and 18.6 per cent claimed they remit more than 80 per cent of their annual earnings home.[9]

Table 13.4: Salaries Paid to Filipina Domestic Helpers (n=86)

Salary Range (S$)	%
150 – 199	-
200 – 249	3.6
250 – 299	27.4
300 – 349	38.1
350 – 399	15.5
400 – 449	15.5
≥ 450	-

Considering that almost half of the women remit a large part of their earnings home, it is not entirely clear that they will be significantly more economically independent at the end of their overseas stint. However, during the period of gainful employment, they do hold a position as an important contributor to their family's financial betterment.

The remittances home, however, do not begin until after the women have paid off their loans which most had to take to finance themselves as OCWs, and the salary from the first few months are spent mainly on repaying their recruiting agency. Among the maids we surveyed, the amounts owed ranged from as little as $100 to as much as $2,000 (Table 13.5) at the time of their arrival in Singapore: two-thirds (65.1 per cent) claimed they had outstanding debts of $800–2,000, the largest sum compared to other nationalities working as domestic helpers in Singapore.[10] Some (about one-quarter) did not know what the money they paid the agents went towards paying. The rest largely guessed that it went towards training and housing costs, airfares to Singapore[10] and immigration processing fees.

9 The other 4.3 per cent preferred not to divulge the value of their remittances home.

10 Our survey found that Indonesians and Sri Lankans seldom had debts totalling more than $800.

Table 13.5: Amounts Owed to Agents by Maid at Start of Contracts

Amount Owed (S$)	%
0	5.0
400 or less	11.3
401 – 800	18.7
801 – 1,200	38.7
1,201 – 1,600	20.0
1,601 – 2,000	6.3

Heyzer (1994: xxv) has argued that the very fact that these women have taken loans from friends, relatives and, more often, agents implies that the women have been 'persuaded to think of overseas employment as an investment' which, in the long-run, will earn them enough to accumulate a surplus; 'such expectations have led to family pressures being put on women to migrate so as to earn big money for the benefit of the family'. Indeed, most of the women had specific goals, usually economic, aimed at ensuring a better future for themselves and/or their families – usually a piece of land on which to build a house, seeing children or siblings through school, or earning enough to start a business – sometimes because they saw no other option. However, unlike Heyzer's argument above, the women in our study often migrated overseas not at the urging, but despite the reluctance, of their family members, and it was mainly the conviction of the economic virtues of their decision that helped many, especially those with young children, bear the difficulties and pain of separation in the stoic and pragmatic manner that struck us repeatedly at the interviews.

Sandra, for example, whose father was strongly opposed to the decision, waited until he passed away before applying for Singapore. Milly, on the other hand, managed to persuade her husband despite his (and their children's, then ten and eight years old) objections because, after much discussion, he too realised that:

> If I don't go, if we want to educate our children, not enough our money. Ya. So I let my husband decide if I can come here to work. So he say, depend on you. So I try. To go far way from my love ones, my family, is very difficult. [Milly then asks the interviewer:] You are married? You have children? [After receiving affirmations to both questions, Milly continues:] Ahh, then you know [...]

For Lucy, the decision was equally difficult but also motivated by pragmatism and aspirations to secure a more certain future for her family. A high school graduate, she was a housewife when her husband passed away in 1980 leaving her with two children aged nine and five years old. She then worked as a clerk in Manila (she was paid the equivalent of about S$60 a month) but in 1986, decided to leave her children with her mother so that she could work as a domestic helper overseas because:

> I don't have enough money, *lah*. I need to earn money because, ah, I'm alone. I'm the father, I'm the mother, and then how, if the children grow up, I have no money. Aiyah, then now my son is in school already, then high school already, then er, college, then what to do? I'm thinking of the education.

Having overcome her own feelings of anxiety over her children and extreme homesicksickness, Lucy recalled (with great amusement and some condescension) the story of her sister-in-law who left after three months in Singapore because the latter had become:

> so homesick, ya, cannot *tahan* [local colloquailism for 'tolerate' or 'withstand'] already. Wanted to climb the window and then jump! I said, 'Okay, *lah*. Go home' [...] But I, when I [used to] thinking and thinking like that, I lie to myself, *lah*. I think how is my children's education, the schooling. Must be practical, *lah*!

Lucy, like the others with younger children, while acknowledging the pain of separation, voiced confidence in the necessity of leaving the raising of their children in the hands of their husbands and female relatives. This practical attitude has seen Lucy through ten years of working as a maid in Singapore with the same employer. Similarly, Rosa's husband, whom she married in between contract renewals, only relented to her returning to Singapore on the promise that it would be her last two years. She feels that working overseas has not affected her relationship:

> It's okay, my husband always write me once a week, call on the phone. I feel normal [having to leave him so soon after our wedding].

While the women's stoicism does not wane, their goals, however, do change with time, family circumstances and personal aspirations – although they remain largely economic – and explain why many of these women continue to work as maids even after original aims have been achieved. Lucy, having seen her children through school, is now working to pay off a housing mortgage and hopes to be able to renew her contract for a final two years (even if it means returning to Singapore under an assumed name). Having fulfilled her initial objective of seeing her sister through the university during her second contract in Singapore, Rosa's pay is now going to help her husband pay for their new house. Similarly, Sandra who had also originally worked to put her sister through high school, decided after her sister's graduation, to continue working towards accumulating sufficient savings to start a small business for herself.

Singapore is generally perceived as a 'good place to work as a maid': 81.4 per cent of our respondents agreed to this when asked outright (Table 13.6) and, in fact, three out of every five Filipino maids we spoke to felt that Singapore employers do prefer maids from the Philippines over and above those from other countries.[11]

Table 13.6: Maids' Assessment of Singapore as a Place to Work (n=86)

Statement	*strongly agree*	*agree*	*neutral*	*disagree strongly*	*dis-agree*
Singapore is a good place to work as a maid	51.2	30.2	11.6	4.7	2.3
Your employer treats you like a member of the family	62.8	25.6	8.1	1.2	2.3
Singaporeans are not as nice to you as they are to other Singaporeans	4.7	24.4	26.7	30.2	14.0

Approximately half came to Singapore to work based on the recommendation of friends and relatives; having friends and relatives already working in Singapore drew another 24.4 per cent (Table 13.7). Rosa, for example, who had been working as a factory operator in the Philippines was persuaded by her cousin to work as a maid in Singapore. Her cousin who, at that time, had already worked in Singapore for five years and assured her that 'Singapore is very clean and if anything [goes wrong], the government can protect us'. This contrasted with the 'bad stories' Rosa had heard of other destinations:

> In our place [village], there's a lot came from Hong Kong and more than one came back because of raping, abuse [...] that's why I'm scared [to go there ...] Some of my neighbours work in Hong Kong and then after, work in Singapore because they say no good to work there [Hong Kong], they sleep at two o'clock in the morning. I don't know if it's true, lah, that's their story. I don't know, but it is all the same story [...] In Saudi, I have an auntie, now is no more there, but they lock her up, no food.

When asked why, having heard stories such as these, she was not afraid to work overseas, she laughed and said, 'Because I know my cousin is working here, five years already before I come, that's why'.

11 This was the highest percentage among the three different nationalities of maids surveyed: only 40 per cent of Indonesian maids and 30 per cent of Sri Lankan maids were of the opinion that Singapore employers in general have a preference for Indonesian and Sri Lankan maids respectively.

Table 13.7: Reasons for Working in Singapore (n=86)

Reason	%
Friends/relatives recommended it	48.8
Singapore is a safe place to work in	38.4
It is near my home country	25.6
I have friends/relatives working here	24.4
Speed at which application was processed	22.1
Similar culture and language	9.3
Good employment conditions (e.g. pay, work hours)	18.6
Similar climate/weather	7.0
Good place to learn English/stepping stone	7.0
Other reasons	1.1

Note: Percentages do not add up to 100.0 per cent because respondents were allowed to give more than one reason each.

Similarly, Rina came to Singapore because both her sister and cousin were already working here, while Sandra was seeking (at the time of the interview) a maid's position in Canada – with her Singapore employer's blessings – through a friend who was already working as a maid in Vancouver and who had informed her of the shorter working hours and better pay available there. This supports what others (e.g. Radcliffe 1990: 382) have found in other contexts: that domestic service is largely maintained through family and fictive kin whose reports are given more credence than those put out by the media.

Hence, despite the furore over the Contemplacion case, Singapore is still seen as 'safe', both from the abuse of employers as well as from crime (38.4 per cent) (Table 13.7). Milly's feelings about the incident are indicative of most maids we spoke to:

> Because it is my co-Filipina, of course I feel very upset about it, lah, and I feel what the family feel, and how upset they are. They lost their mother, their wife. Only thing is upset only. We [she and the other Filipina maids in the neighbourhood] weren't angry. Not frightened.

Because of this, many Filipina maids felt no qualms about staying on in Singapore despite the Philippine Embassy's offers to fly any maid back to the Philippines for free (*The Straits Times* 23 March 1995) and the view that there are Singaporeans who do treat them as second-class members of society (See Table 13.6 above).[12]

12 The social spaces of foreign domestic workers in Singapore are discussed in Yeoh and Huang (1996).

More important is the treatment they receive from their employing household: an overwhelming 88.4 per cent said that they were treated like a member of their employer's family (Table 13.6). Dora, while acknowledging that:

> sometimes I get scolding [from my employer] because something is wrong, of course [I am] not perfect, what. But the houses is so big, how to clean? And she [the employer] say, 'Why not clean?'

also maintained that:

> she [the employer] treat me like family. Sometimes, okay, she brings me out, together with the children, and go all the places to swimming, like that. Like Raffles Marina [an upper-class private yacht club in Singapore]. Sometimes I watch TV with them, sometimes I go outside together [with them] to the restaurant. If dinner at home, sometimes I join, sometimes, ah, nothing to do at the kitchen and so I join.

For Milly, her weekday 'chit chat' sessions when she sits down alone with her employer for lunch have, in her opinion, helped them to better understand each other. During these chats, Milly talks about her problems and friends, television programmes, and asks about her employer's friends with whom she is familiar. Milly also values her close relationship with the employer's school-age children; paradoxically, having them to talk to and cuddle makes her 'think less' of her own children. She contrasted it to her situation at her previous employer (her present employer's sister), which she found harder because the children there were in their late teens and had little interaction with her.

Singapore's proximity to the Philippines is also an important drawing factor (25.6 per cent) for this group of migrant labour (Table 13.7), as is the reputation Singapore has gained as a 'training ground for Filipino maids because at the end of their two year contracts here they speak English, are considered to be well-trained and have a reputation for being good with children' (*The Straits Times* 6 November 1986). These factors perhaps explain why, despite the importance of economic factors which motivate the women to work overseas, they still choose to work in Singapore where employment conditions are not generally regarded as attractive as those in Hong Kong (and Canada).

Conclusion

We dream of a society where families are not broken up by the urgent need for survival. We dream of a homeland where there is opportunity for everyone to live a decent and humane life (*Tulay Ng Tagumpay*[13] Vol. 2, no. 3: 15).

Although, as Colen (1989: 172) points out, 'migration and domestic work are part of an international solution to women's problems of carrying out their responsibilities for themselves and their kin within a world economic system', migration is nevertheless an 'alternative employment strategy' that presents some contradictions that each woman who takes it on has to grapple with in reality. Ironically, for Filipinas, employment as a foreign domestic worker usually means stepping down the occupational ladder while increasing one's earning power. Although earning wages more commensurate with what her educational qualifications are worth, she finds that the job itself has low social status – although it should be pointed out that reduced occupational status exchanged for a higher income is by no means uncommon in permanent Filipino migration overseas (see, for example, Jackson and Flores 1989). While a form of productive labour, domestic work also further embeds the women in what society perceives as the natural role of women – these women are expected to step into their roles as paid reproductive labour without much specific training for the work involved. Thus, although employment overseas supposedly frees the women from the constraints of patriarchal structures of their society, the women continue to be bound by 'the logic of gender' (Castro 1986: 18). Ultimately, the realities of domestic work are more mundane and ordinary than the sensational stories often circulated by the Philippines media and politicians. For the women, however, there is a certain sense of personal pride and conviction about the role they have taken on to provide for their families and their own futures which provides the foundation of coping with the emotional, and sometimes physical, hardship that comes with the job.

Our discussion has clearly shown that the Philippines' migration phenomenon cannot be fully understood simply as the outcome of the politics and economics of inequality at the international or even regional level. The decisions and actions taken by the migrants, more than just being a consequence of global conditions, are also context-specific: to the individual, as well as the values and conditions of the various societies involved. Instead, we need 'to clarify the significance of both the social context [...] and the structures of authority and legitimation in the wider society' (Eyles and Smith 1988: 228) and, at the same time, understand the indi-

13 This is a locally-published monthly magazine, distributed free-of-charge, and targeted primarily at Filipina domestic helpers in Singapore. Articles are written in both Tagalog and English and cover a wide range of topics such as employer-employee relationships, announcement of social (especially religious) activities, helplines, and bible study guides.

vidual's interpretation of the migration process. The decison to become a domestic worker, leave home for a foreign land and cope with the inevitable social and spatial dislocations intrinsic to migration, is ultimately located at the nexus between public accounts of the socio-economic conditions which provide the broad canvas underlying human motivations and actions, and private life-narratives interpreted from a personal perspective.

References

Anon. (1987) *The Labour Trade*, London and Mandaluyong: Catholic Institute for International Relations.

Anon. (1991) 'The plight of Filipinas overseas', *Review of Women's Studies* 2, 1: 61–102.

Arcinas, F.R. (1987) *Asian Migrant Workers to the Gulf Region: The Philippines Case*, Quezon City: University of the Philippines.

Asia and Pacific Migration Journal 1995, 4, 4.

Asian and Pacific Development Center (1989) *The Trade in Domestic Helpers: Causes, Mechanisms and Consequences*, Kuala Lumpur: Asian and Pacific Development Center.

Beltran, R.P. and de Dios, A.J. (eds.) (1992) *Filipino Women Overseas Contract Workers: At What Cost?* Manila: Goodwill Trading and Women in Development Foundation Inc.

Brah, A. (1991) 'Questions of difference and international feminism', in J. Aaron and S. Walby (eds.) *Out of the Margins: Women's Studies in the Nineties*, London: Falmer Press.

Carino, B.V. (1995) 'International migrants from the Philippines: Policy issues and problems in the sending country', in J.H. Ong, K.B. Chan and S.B. Chew (eds.) *Crossing Borders: Transmigration in Asia Pacific*, Singapore: Prentice-Hall.

Castro, M.G. (1986) 'Migrant women: issues in organisation and solidarity', *Migration World* 1, 2: 15–19.

Chant, S. and McIlwaine, C. (1995) *Women of a Lesser Cost: Female Labour, Foreign Exchange and Philippine Development*, Manila and London: Ateneo de Manila and Pluto Press.

Colen, S. (1989) '"Just a little respect": West Indian domestic workers in New York City', in E. Chaney and M.G. Castro (eds.) *Muchachas No More: Household Workers in Latin America and the Caribbean*, Philadelphia: Temple University Press.

Cornwell, J. (1988) 'A case-study approach to lay health beliefs', in J. Eyles and D.M. Smith (eds.) *Qualitative Methods in Human Geography*, Cambridge: Polity Press.

Cruz, V.P. and Paganoni, A. (1989) *Filipinas in Migration*, Quezon City: Scalabrini Migration Center.

Department of Statistics (1991) *Census of Population 1990: Advance Data Release*, Singapore: Department of Statistics.

Enloe, C. (1989) *Bananas, Beaches and Bases: Making Feminist Sense of International Politics*, London: Pandora.

Evangelista, S.P. (1974) 'Massage Attendants in the Philippines: a Case Study on the Role of Women in Economic Development', MA Thesis, University of the Philippines.

Eviota, E.U. (1992) *The Political Economy of Gender: The Sexual Division of Labour in the Philippines*, London and Manila: Zed Books and St. Scholastica's College.

Gaw, K. (1988) *Superior Servants: The Legendary Cantonese Amah of the Far East*, Singapore: Oxford University Press.

Gilandas, A. with (C. Gastardo and Judy C. Sevilla (1982) *Sex and the Single Filipina: the Omega Women*, Manila: Philippines Educational Company.

Go, S.P., Postrado, L.T. and Ramos-Jimenez, P. (1983) *The Effects of International Contract Labor: Community Studies,* Manila: Integrated Research Center, De La Salle University.

Gonzalez III, J.L. and Holmes, R.D. (1996) 'The Philippine labour diaspora', *Southeast Asian Affairs* 22: 300–317.

Heyzer, N. (1994) 'Introduction: Creating responsive policies for migrant women domestic workers', in N. Heyzer, G. Lycklama à Nijeholt and N. Weerakoon (eds.) *The Trade in Domestic Workers: Causes, Mechanisms and Consequences of International Migration*, Kuala Lumpur: Asian and Pacific Development Center and London: Zed Books.

Hoffman, E. (1996) 'Administrative Records and Surveys as a Basis for Statistics on International Labour Migration', Geneva: ILO, found at: http:// www.stjr.is/st...s/papers/2~hoffma.html).

Huang, S. and Yeoh, B.S.A. (1996) 'The ties that bind: state policy and migrant female domestic helpers in Singapore', *Geoforum* 27, 4: 479–493.

Jackson, R.T. (1990) 'The cheque's in the mail', *Singapore Journal of Tropical Geography* 2, 2: 76–86.

Jackson, R.T. and Flores, E.R. (1989) *No Filipinos in Manila,* Townsville: James Cook University.

Migration News (1994a) (November) *Philippines Overseas Workers.*

— (1994b) (September) *Development and Migration in Asia.*

— (1995a) (April) *Philippines to Restrict Overseas Workers*

— (1995b) (August) *Philippines Tries to Protect Overseas Workers.*

— (1996) (August) *Female Migrants in Asia.*

National Statistics Office (of the Philippines) (1996) *The 1994 Family Income and Expenditure Survey*, Manila: NSO.

Pertierra, R. (1992) *Remittances and Returnees*, Quezon City: New Day Publishers.

Philippines Daily Inquirer Dec. 1, 1996.

Quah, S. (1993) 'Marriage and family', in A. Wong and W.K. Leong (eds.) *Singapore Women: Three Decades of Change*, Singapore: Times Academic Press.

Radcliffe, S.A. (1990) 'Ethnicity, patriarchy and incorporation into the nation: female migrants as domestic workers in Peru', *Environment and Planning D: Society and Space* 8: 379–393.

Regalado, C. (1996) cited in *South China Morning Post (vide infra).*

Samonte, E.L., Maceda, C.P., Cabilao, M.I., del Castillo, B.P. and Zulueta, M.P.F. (1995) *Issues and Concerns of Overseas Filipinos,* Quezon City: University of the Philippines Press.

Sassen, S. (1988) *The Mobility of Labour and Capital*, Cambridge: Cambridge University Press.

Scott, A.M. (1986) 'Women and industrialisation: examining the "female marginalisation" thesis', *Journal of Development Studies* 22, 4: 649–680.

Singam, C. (1991) 'Redesigning work: Redefining corporate concerns', Paper presented at the Singapore Council of Women's Organisations Forum on *Work and Family – The Challenges Ahead,* Singapore, 28 September 1991.

South China Morning Post 11 November 1996: 25.

de Stoop, C. (1992) *Ze zijn zo lief, meneer (They Are So Sweet, Sir: The Cruel World of Traffickers in Filipinas)*, Leuven: Kritak Publishers.

The Straits Times, Singapore, various issues.

Thrift, N. (1994) 'Globalisation, regulation, urbanisation: The case of the Netherlands', *Urban Studies* 31, 3: 365–380.

Tigno, J. (1994) cited in *Migration News* 1 (5) May, Philippines Proposed Labour Agreement.

Vasquez, N.D. (1992) 'Economic and social impact of labor migration', in G. Battistella and A. Paganoni (eds.) *Philippines Labor Migration*, Quezon City: Scalabrini Migration Center.

Vasquez, N.D., Tumbaga, L.C. and Cruz-Soriano, M. (1995) *Tracer Study on Filipino Domestic Helpers Abroad: The Socio-Economic Conditions of Filipino Domestic Workers from Pre-Departure until the End of Their First Two-Year Contract in Hong Kong*, Geneva: International Organisation for Migration.

Wihtol, R. (1982) 'Hospitality Girls in the Manila Tourist Belt', *Philippines Journal of Industrial Relations* 4 (1 and 2).

Wong, A. and Leong, W.K. (1993) *Singapore Women: Three Decades of Change*, Singapore: Times Academic Press.

Yeoh, B.S.A. and Huang, S. (1994) 'Between tradition and modernity: childcare arrangements among Malay women in Singapore', *International Journal of Comparative Family and Marriage* I/II: 100–118.

14

Labouring Communities: Women's Roles in the Ombilin Coal Mines of Sumatra (1892-1965)[1]

ERWIZA ERMAN

In focusing on the proletarianisation process of male miners and their entry into the masculine world of the mining community, historians have tended to neglect women's roles and the gendered nature of workers' communities (Rothermund 1978: 1-19, Simeon 1995, Klubock 1997: 232). Indeed, mining communities have often been portrayed as reflecting ideologies of masculinity at various levels, but in doing so, scholars have often understated the ways in which gender ideologies have structured the formation of mining working classes, transformed relations between men and women, and generated specific ideas about masculinity and femininity.[2] This article will look at the way men and women from the Ombilin mining community have been defined by management and how they have responded to workplace and national politics. The shifts in the miners' response

1 The opportunity to write this article was provided by a three-month research fellowship (February-April, 2001) in the 'Changing Asian Labour Relations' (CLARA) programme, a collaboration between the International Institute for Asian Studies (IIAS) in Leiden and the International Institute of Social History (IISH) in Amsterdam. My thanks to the IIAS, IISH, and CLARA, which have funded my three-month stay in the Netherlands. The first version of this article was presented at a seminar organised by the *Werkgroep Indonesische Vrouwen Studies* (WIVS) in March 2001 in Leiden. Criticism and challenging questions on gender issues from participants during that discussion helped me improve this article. My special thanks go to Ratna Saptari for her invaluable comments and sharp criticism of the early version of this article. I also wish to thank Marcel van der Linden for introducing me to the literature on labour history in the mining industries in West European countries.

2 Nevertheless, there were at least two studies that dealt with women's involvement in defining the politics of men in the mining sector. See Nash (1979) and Robinson (1986). For comments regarding the neglect of women's role in Indonesian history, see also Locher-Scholten (2000: 13-37).

from resistance to accommodation and to political protest and confrontation should also be seen in conjunction with the social position of women as workers, 'entertainers,' and wives. Changes in women's social position are also inseparable from shifts in labour force recruitment policy by management. The problem is to identify the kind of ideology behind the changes in labour force recruitment policy that were imposed by the company.

As other studies have shown, the gender composition of enclave communities such as plantations and mines have followed identifiable courses. In the early period of their formation the labour force would mainly consist of single male (and often) migrant workers. Recruitment of female labour was very limited. Women were part of an employer's attempt to tie male workers to the plantations longer. At first female labourers were positioned as 'entertainers' for the men. Eventually, however, the expansion of the enterprise and shortage of labour led to the need for a more stable and permanent work force. Employers shifted from recruiting single males to recruiting married workers, which meant that establishing families and stable communities became a priority. In the process of family formation by the enterprises 'the family' was not only viewed as an economic unit or kinship structure, but it became an ideological configuration resonating far beyond the narrow definition of family. Labourers cannot be regarded as passive subjects, simply as objects of shifts in colonial policy (Stoler 1979: 43, Stolcke 1988). Workers respond to changes in recruitment policy as well as to attitudes of family formation, often using the family as a means to ensure survival and for enhancing political alliances. This chapter will address the following questions: to what extent were these conditions true for the Ombilin coal mines? What were the miners' reactions to state labour recruitment policy following the various shifts in policy? What types of actions did women or female labourers take with regard to the male-dominated world? Can we trace the effects of the economic development of coal to the survival strategy of the household, to the gender hierarchies, and the ideology of family solidarity? How did the male-dominated policy of the colonial state influence social relations among mining families?

This paper is divided into five sections. The first section deals with the historical background of the Ombilin coal mines and the labour force formation in this area. This will be followed by an examination of the politics of resistance of the miners and their families from 1892–1927. The third section will cover the period of 1928–42, focusing on the politics of the miners' accommodation during the Depression and the years afterwards, especially when family and mining community had been established. The fourth section will discuss the Japanese occupation and the period of Revolution (1942–49), after which the politics of resistance and accommodation emerged. Discussions of radical changes in the miners' politics and the women's involvement in the public political sphere during the period of 1950–65 are taken up in the fifth section, as both men and women were involved in various informal and formal representations.

Entering the World of the Ombilin Coal Miners

Located in Sawahlunto about 115 km from Padang, the capital city of West Sumatra, this coal was discovered in 1868, and its coal deposits were estimated at about 200 million tons (Van Diest 1871, R.J. van Lier 1915). After a long debate in the Dutch Parliament on whether it should be exploited by the state or by a private company, in 1892 the colonial government finally decided to create a state mine (Colombijn 1992: 437-58). The decision was based on the importance of coal as a source of energy for the Dutch navy and for most state-owned companies such as railways, and for various industries. In the early years of the exploitation coal production from the Ombilin coal mines met about 95 per cent of the colonial state's demand for coal. Although this declined to 65 per cent in the 1930s, its contribution remained a significant amount of the total coal production in the Netherlands East Indies.[3]

The Different Categories of Labour

A cheap labour force could not be obtained by recruiting local people. Besides the fact that contract work was not a familiar pattern, the status of a miner was low (miners were regarded as less than human, and are still viewed that way). Apart from this, the area's low population density and the availability of other economic opportunities strengthened the bargaining position of the local populace. The local people were mainly Minangkabau and the inhabitants of Nias (called '*Melayus*' in the Dutch reports). They only sought work sporadically, when their rice harvest failed or when they needed cash to participate in traditional ceremonies. Recruitment of casual workers was unsatisfactory because the supply was irregular and uncertain. Consequently, the management was continually complaining about the shortage of labour.[4] This was not new: the estate plantations in West Sumatra had experienced the same problem previously and had to import contract labourers from outside West Sumatra. Thus, not long after coal reserves were found, Dutch local officials in West Sumatra advised their superiors in Batavia to import labour from outside the region (Stibbe 1884: 698-700).

To ensure a permanent, regular labour force, the colonial government recruited convicts and then contract labourers from outside. The convict labourers were recruited from the Department of Justice, and were political prisoners and criminals mainly from the prisons in Java such as Cipinang and Glodok in Batavia to

3 There was not sufficient capital to accommodate the high demand of the colonial state for coal. The colonial budget was at that time mainly directed towards supplying the war effort against Aceh.

4 As did also the engineer, Th.F.A. Delprat, in 1898. See Mining Archives (Bandung), *Dwangarbeiders te Ombilin Steenkolenmijnen*, VI-A/85. Letter by Delprat, 11/2/1899 no.127 to the Governor-General.

work as convict labourers at the Ombilin coal mines.[5] But there were not enough of them, because many convict labourers from Sawahlunto were brought to Pidie in Aceh to transport goods in the war against Aceh, Jambi, and other regions. In order to solve the labour problem, the company also recruited contract labourers, first from China and then from Java. They worked for at least three years and were subject to penal sanctions (laid down in the 'Coolie Ordinance'). These groups were called contract labourers A, to distinguish them from the free labourers (called contract labourers B), who were free to define the duration of their own contracts, usually one or two years, and were not subject to penal sanctions. The third category of workers were the casual labourers. These were local people who worked without any contract. In later years casual workers included other ethnic groups (such as Sundanese and Javanese who had finished their previous contract with the company) as well as members of the local populace.

Convict labourers would be punished by flogging if they ran away, shirked work, participated in a protest against their foremen, or fought with other workers or with the foremen. The contract labourers covered by the Coolie Ordinance were punished by flogging if they did not fulfil the requirements of the contract (for example, running away or shirking work), but the other convict, contract, and free labourers were also controlled by police officers who could be described as semi-military. The officers wore a black uniform and were recruited from the Minangkabau and Batak areas.[6] Colonial officials introduced strict state control to counteract the 'lazy mentality' of the local populace society, whom they deemed to be lacking in a proper 'work orientation.' Miners were mostly seen as criminals who could only be productive under strict control and discipline.

In 1896 there were 1,234 labourers, all of them convicts. Along with the increase in the number of mines, the total amount of the labour force also increased. In 1921 the number of labourers rose to 11,046, the majority of which were convict and contract labourers (Erman 1999: 41). The company preferred to recruit convicts rather than contract labourers because it was cheaper to maintain them and their productivity was higher than the contract labourers. The daily cost of convict labourers averaged 34.9 cents per day, whereas contract labourers were 60 cents per day. In the following years, this discrepancy became even more striking.[7] The background of the labourers was very fragmented. Not only were their work contracts different, but so were their social and cultural backgrounds. They were typically young males, physically strong and unattached, unaccompanied by any family members. There were also several different sub-cultures and sub-ethnic groups: Javanese, Sundanese, Buginese, Madurese, Makassare, Chinese,

5 Arsip Nasional, Jakarta (ARNAS), Register 1891-1907: 412.

6 *Hoa Po*, 13/2/1915.

7 In 1916 the daily cost of convict labourers was only 53.4 cents, and contract labourers were

Minangkabau, and Nias. The convict labourers consisted of two different groups, sentenced to different penalties. The first group were criminals recruited from the prisons of Glodok and Cipinang in Batavia. The second group were political prisoners jailed for political actions against the government. The duration of sentences varied from one to five years or five to twenty years. Differences in the categories and cultural backgrounds of the labourers influenced their social relations and politics with regard to management.

Up to the third decade of the twentieth century there were very few women in this world, whether they were wives accompanying their husbands or working as labourers in their own right. These women functioned as mine workers, wives, or 'entertainers.' The first category were labourers recruited by the company from Java as contract or free labourers. No women or female prisoners were recruited as convict workers for this mine. The cost of recruitment was the same for both male and female labourers, and like males, the women labourers were recruited by recruitment agencies in Batavia and Semarang (Soesman, Hilderbrands, and Algemeen Delisch Emigratie Kantoor, or ADEK) to work on plantations and mining industries in the Outer Islands. Little is known how the recruitment of women was carried out. Family members of the recruited women tell that most of the recruiters for women were also women. Jobs available to the women were transporting coal from open-pit mines to the area of collection, sorting coal in three sizes: large, middle, and small, or cleaning the mine hospital. Table 14.1 shows the percentage of female to male contract and free labourers from 1910 to 1930. The highest percentage of female labourers was 4.2 per cent in 1911; although the percentage varied in the subsequent years, it remained under 4 per cent. (Unfortunately, no information is available about why the recruitment of female labourers varied.) The highest percentage of female labourers was 4 per cent. This may have come about because in 1910 the Labour Inspectors suggested that more women be recruited from Java. Nevertheless, as a whole, there was little increase in the number of women recruited from Java whether they were labourers, wives, or entertainers. Only in 1929 and 1930, did the percentage of female labourers increase compared to 1926 and 1927.

86.8 cents. See Mining Archives (Bandung), *Steenkolenpolitiek*, no. IV-32B. Letter of the Mining State Companies Director to the Governor General, 27/2/1918.

Table 14.1: Percentage of Female to Total Male Labourers (Contract and Free Labourers), 1910–30

Year	*%*	*Year*	*%*
1910	...	1921	1.5
1911	4.2	1922	0.4
1912	2.7	1923	0.5
1913	2.1	1924	1.0
1914	3.2	1925	...
1915	2.8	1926	...
1916	1.3	1927	1.4
1917	0.9	1928	1.9
1918	1.0	1929	3.4
1919	2.7	1930	3.1
1920	4.2		

Source: *Verslagen van den Sumatra-Staatsspoorweg en de Ombilinmijnen 1910-1916* (Batavia 1911–1917). *Verslagen van de Ombilinmijnen 1917-1923/24* (Batavia/ Weltevreden 1918–1925). *Jaarverslagen van 's lands kolenmijnen 1925-1930* (Weltevreden 1926–1931).

The number of female contract labourers increased 6 per cent from 1926 to 1927. In 1926 female contract labourers were only 17.1 per cent of the male contract labourers. In 1927 the percentage increased to 23.1 per cent., because there had been a decrease in the total number of male contract labourers. Many contract labourers were dismissed because of their involvement in a series of strikes in 1925, 1926, and the communist uprising in 1926–1927. As is shown in Table 14.2, the total number of male contract labourers was reduced dramatically from 4,170 in 1925 to 2,783 in 1927.

Table 14.2: Comparison Between Female and Male Contract Labourers 1923–28

Year	*Male contract labourer*	*Female contract labourer (%)*
1923	4.196	17.7%
1924	4.801	16.0%
1925	4.170	21.3%
1926	3.839	17.1%
1927	2.783	23.1%
1928	2.839	22.4%

Source: KITLV, Korn Collection OR 435. No. 368, 'Het Ombilin Steenkolen Bedrijf door een bestuursambtenaar bezien', 1931: 97–8.

The second category consisted of women who functioned as wives or 'partners' for the male labourers. They went to Sawahlunto with their husbands who worked as contract or free labourers there. Some were also former female contract or free labourers who did not return to Java but got married in Sawahlunto. The yearly company reports do not provide any information about the total amount of female labourers repatriated to Java, which suggests that the former female labourers had become wives or partners for male labourers or housekeepers or 'bed-servants' of the European staff on the East Sumatran plantations. Nor is any information available on the married labourers and those who stayed with their families in Sawahlunto. Only very few Javanese male contract labourers married local women because they were regarded as having low status by the local people. Only the Javanese foremen who had high status and much money could marry local women.[8] Javanese labourers preferred to stay at their wife's house or construct a new house in the vicinity of the mines.

The third category consisted of women who acted as entertainers, either as traditional *ronggeng* or *tandak* dancers or prostitutes. *Ronggeng* and *tandak* dancers[9] entertained the miners and were contracted to stay a longer period with the company. They were recruited for six months at a time. The dancers were beautiful young women. Two or three times a year (or following completion of the work contract) the company recruited new, more beautiful, younger dancers. Generally speaking, they were also prostitutes. Some former dancers did not return home, but remained in Sawahlunto and were married with contract or free labourers. Others who remained reverted to prostitution. It would be misleading to categorise these three different types of women as one.

The *ronggeng* and *tandak* dancers had come to the attention of Dutch officials and Labour Inspectors. Van Kol, for example, who visited Sawahlunto at the beginning of the twentieth century, reported that many *ronggeng* dancers were recruited along with 439 contract labourers in 1901 (Van Kol 1903: 37). Van Kol was concerned about the emergence of 'bad elements' because the *ronggeng* dancers' relationship with the male labourers was very vague. He warned the Dutch officials that dangerous elements might emerge if the women were sold to convict labourers. In the following years recruitment of the *ronggeng* dancers as entertainers occasioned heated discussions among state colonial officials. A Labour Inspector, D.B.W. van Ardenne, who was investigating labour conditions in the Ombilin

8 Interviews with Pak Warso and his son Pak Suwardi Kisut, 22/8/1995. According to Pak Suwardi Kisut, up to the end of 1970s, mixed marriages between local people and Javanese workers in Sawahlunto very seldom happened. See also Joustra (1923: 27). Joustra reported that the Javanese men who married local women tended to change their occupation from miner to peasant.

9 *Ronggeng* and *tandak* are traditional dance performances. *Ronggeng* is found in West Java, whereas *tandak* is from East Java. For a story on a *ronggeng* dancer's life, see Tohari (1982).

coal mines in 1921, reported that there was not enough entertainment for the miners. There were only five groups of *ronggeng* dancers, and he believed that fifteen groups were needed to entertain the 1,500 Sundanese labourers.[10] This did not even include the other kinds of entertainment such as gamelan (a Javanese musical group), gambling, and opium. In the following years the recruitment of *ronggeng* dancers continued apace, and by 1928, B.H.F. van Heuven, the Assistant-Resident of Solok seized in Sawahlunto, reported that there were fifty groups of *ronggeng* dancers to entertain labourers.[11] Heuven pointed out that this number was far more proportional to the male labourers, noting that it would have a calming effect on the labourers because *ronggeng* dancers also acted as prostitutes.

The previous policy of recruiting only unmarried workers was also in effect for the European staff. Recruiting Europeans along with their families would increase the cost of production, because the management would have to prepare facilities such as housing and schools as well as provide the costs of family returns to Europe for vacation. Stoler, in her study on East Sumatran plantations, showed that this would greatly increase the cost (Stoler 1992: 319–52). Thus marriage was prohibited to all incoming European plantation employees. As a result many European employees took Javanese women as concubines (*nyai*). In the Ombilin coal mines the European employees preferred to oversee the Javanese, Chinese, and Nias women. These partners bore Indo-European children who later became mine overseers.

Government Responses to Women as Members of the Mining Community

H.G. Heyting, Assistant-resident of Tanah Datar in 1903, was aware that the lack of women was a problem for male labourers. He suggested that management recruit twenty-five unmarried Javanese women from the southern part of Kedu. They were expected to marry male contract labourers and provide an incentive for recruiting other married male contract labourers.[12] Engineer-director A.H. van Lessen agreed to this and tried to convince his superior, W. de Jongh, the Chief of the Sumatran Railways and exploitation of the Ombilin coal mines, that there was no need to be concerned about an increase of population in Sawahlunto because of the recruitment of women and their marriage to male labourers. He

10 16 ARA, MvK, MR 1924/2608.

11 KITLV, Korn Collection OR 435. No. 368 (1931: 98).

12 This is not only true for the Ombilin coal mines. In 1864 the Billiton tin mining company on the Island of Belitung tried to recruit 137 Javanese women from Batavia and Semarang to 'marry' Chinese coolies. This was intended to encourage permanent settlements among the Chinese male contract coolies on that island. Only a few of the women returned to Java; the rest formed partnerships, as intended. Attempts to provide the basis of a settled population had almost no effect. Five years after the project more than one hundred women had given birth to only twenty-six children, eleven of them males. It is not known what eventually happened to the women. In any case, most miners could not afford to maintain a family. See Somers (1991: 6), de Groot (1887: 356–8).

believed that about 80 per cent of the married male labourers would return to their homeland after finishing their contract.[13] There is no data on whether the 25 women from Kedu actually married male labourers, as neither local Dutch officials nor labour inspectors wrote any reports on this subject in the following years; even the Ombilin company staff did not report on this. Heyting also suggested building a coolie village for 200 contract labourers in Sawahlunto to create a social environment for the miners, provide miners with the opportunity and incentive to form a family and produce a future generation of miners that in the long run would reduce the difficulty of recruiting labour from outside. The Engineer-director did not agree with these suggestions. He argued that the construction of the coolie village would need a great deal of capital.

In 1910 and 1917 labour inspectors again suggested creation of a village. Engineer-director Van der Kloes said that the state had forced the company to create a Javanese colony as a reserve labour force in Sawahlunto. In 1918 the company sent an administrator at the suggestion of the central government. This administrator, A. Stark, wrote a comparative study for East Sumatra. But the company decided not to do this in Sawahlunto because land was too scarce there and it was afraid that the Javanese labourers would stop functioning as miners and become peasants.

Although local colonial administrators commented on the absence of female labourers and family members (wife and children), the company remained convinced that bringing in women would be unprofitable and too expensive. Female labourers were only permitted to engage in a few specific occupations (see above). More than solely economic motives were behind this labour policy, and the abnormal life of the Sawahlunto coal miners was maintained up to the second decade of the twentieth century. It is also not surprising that only a few female labourers were ever recruited to work, and then only at very limited jobs, in the Ombilin coal mines.

Gender Differentiation in Hiring Policies

In the early years of exploitation the company did not differentiate in the way male and female and contract and free labourers were paid. In 1911 Female contract labourers, like their male colleagues, received twenty cents a day for the first contract year for working on the surface, as well as three meals a day. In 1921 female labourers were paid thirty cents a day (five cents lower than their male colleagues). The company's annual reports for subsequent years reveal no differentiation in pay between male and female labourers. Differences in pay were based only on the place of work: underground miners were paid more than those who worked on the surface.

13 ARA, MvK, Mr 1904/1151. Letter of A.H. van Lessen, 3/6/1904 to the Chief of Exploitation, W. de Jongh.

The company's discriminatory policy with regard to women was especially apparent in the system of promotion. Promotion of female contract labourers was very limited because they were only recruited as partners for male labourers after completion of their contract, although a male labourer could pay a ransom of 80 guilders for a female labourer (1911) still on contract with the company. If the female contract labourer had already completed her contract, she could become the wife of a contract or free male labourer. One labour inspector admitted that this price was too high, so not many male labourers were interested in ransoming a female contract labourer. Later the ransom was reduced to 50 guilders to provide an incentive for marriages to increase, encouraging establishment of proper family life. It was hoped that this would cause the men to remain longer at the mines. But management policy was unsuccessful, not only because the recruited women were too few in number, but also because they preferred to remain single.[14] Some former miners believed that being unmarried provided women with many opportunities to engage in financially profitable illicit relations with male labourers. The fact that there were so few women put the women in a very good bargaining position.

The Miners' Politics of Resistance and the Hidden Role of Women

The institutionalised system of controlling the miners by beating them with canes was unsuccessful because it did not result in the disciplined labour force as the Dutch officials hoped for. Proof of its ineffectiveness was the high rate of desertions and work avoidance from 1892 to 1925 (Erman 1999: 45, see also van Empel 1999: 158–79). In 1922 the average convict labourer had deserted more than once, and by 1924, this had increased to three times a year.[15] The workers' show of resistance by running away and avoiding work was also true for contract workers: for example, between 1907 and 1909, contract labourers tried to escape from the mines an average of 2 to 2.5 times a year.[16] This meant that a contract labourer received punishment by caning about 2 to 2.5 times a year.

No female labourers attempted to escape or avoid work, nor were any involved in the series of strikes and protests in 1925, 1926 and 1927. Although this could suggest that women were more politically passive, that is not necessarily true because it fails to take into consideration the underlying factors of the miners' resistance. The miners' political resistance was not only directed at the misuse of power

14 Interview with Pak Warso, 4 May 1995, Pak Rusman, 5 May 1995.

15 Verslag over de Hervormingen van het Gevangeniswezen over 1921 t/m 1925, Batavia: G. Kolff and Co, 1926: 6, Bruinink-Darlang (1986: 143).

16 ARA, MvK, Mr 1911 no. 218. Report of Labour Inspector, Stibbe, 12/11/1910.

by state agents, but also at the insecure and vulnerable position of the miners themselves. The insecurity and vulnerability of the coolies' barracks and the mines resulted in ethnic conflicts, an embedded culture of violence among convict labourers, and conflict and competition within and between various categories of labourers in their efforts to gain scarce resources such as food, money, and women. Thus, the Ombilin case suggests the importance of a nuanced understanding of the miners' resistance as well as the hidden role of women.

Two interesting points should be noted here. First, the limited number of women in the mines caused conflict in the social relations among male labourers because they competed to gain access to women. Second, women found their own ways to respond to the labour policy imposed by the company or the state. Female contract labourers preferred to remain unmarried rather than be ransomed by male labourers, even though the company reduced the ransom from eighty to fifty guilders in 1911. The company's annual reports show that no female contract labourers returned home after finishing their working contracts. There was no indication that women who finished their contract wanted to marry. Figures for married male labourers up to the third decade of the twentieth century remain very low, and even in 1924 only 600 children were born to the miners' families in Sawahlunto.[17]

Thus, women had a strong bargaining position in this world dominated by men. Women preferred to become partners to male labourers or *nyai* for European personnel. Prostitutes and gambling were essential means for keeping male labourers indebted and indentured because they encouraged male labourers to spend more than they earned, ensuring that male labourers worked for the company even longer.

After 1925 the politics of resistance changed from individual, unorganised resistance to collective, organised protests. Labourers were able to express their demands through a series of trade union strikes in 1925 and 1926. Their struggle culminated in the communist uprising of 1926-27. The changes were linked to formation of a miners' trade union, the Persatuan Kaum Buruh Tambang (PKBT) in 1925. The PKBT was established on the initiatives of the leaders of the Sarekat Rakyat and the Indonesian Communist Party or PKI in Sawahlunto. The leaders of the political parties were successful in uniting the differing interests of the indigenous people inside the mines (foremen, clerks, police officers, coolies) and outside (petty traders, teachers, local peasants, and religious and political leaders). They spread the ideology of class struggle among different groups in the mining town (including labourers, teachers, hajis, petty traders, and peasants). The labourers saw the PKBT as a vehicle for the struggle against injustice and a means to build a better life in the future. The PKBT also reduced the social distance be-

17 Mining Archives, *Arbeid aangelegenheden Mijnbedrijven* VI-A/5. Report of Labour Inspector Deibert , 3 July 1924.

tween various categories of labourers and the clerks, petty traders, and local populace, because such an organisation bridged ethnic differences.

Although no specific information is available about the gender and background of the strikers, we should not assume that women were completely passive in this context. My interviews with the former miners' wives reinforced the argument that women were indeed active behind the scenes in the political activities. Many women from the coolies' barracks prepared meals for strikers. Women who were servants for European families were regarded by Dutch colonials officials as dangerous, which caused most European families to dismiss their indigenous help before the uprising broke out. They were afraid they would engage in radical political activities. Women servants had indeed become a social force in the mining society.

The Politics of Accommodation and the Emergence of the Family (1928-42)

After the communist uprising of 1926-27, the miners' politics shifted from resistance to accommodation, or collaboration. This politics of accommodation took the form of increased rates of work attendance. There is no strong evidence that the accommodation politics were simply a result of the political pressure exerted by the state, especially after the communist uprising in 1926-27. The conciliatory attitude was not only associated with the absence of strong leaders in radical political parties, as shown by Ingleson in the case of Java (Ingleson 1981: 485-502, 1986), but was also linked to the effects of the economic depression and the changing face of mining society.

Since the leaders of the political parties involved in the communist uprising had been imprisoned or executed, labour movement momentum in West Sumatra and Java declined. This was followed by repressive state actions that made it impossible for the miners to protest openly in their struggle for justice. In 1932 and again in 1933 management was forced to restrict mine production and reduce the labour force. These factors suggest that the politics of accommodation was a rational decision by the miners, taken after considering the pros and cons of the situation.

What was the role of women in this politics of accommodation? If women had played a marginal part in political activities previously and had been a source of conflict among male labourers, after the 1930s, women played an important part in defining miners' politics. Before delineating what the women's contributions to the accommodation politics were, we need to appreciate the growing presence of women and married miners in the context of changing management policy.

The scarcity of women and its effect on work discipline has been discussed from the beginning of the twentieth century, but it had been a closed discussion until the 1920s. The opening of the discussion coincided with the liberal rule of Governor General Fox in the Netherlands Indies, both in the Volksraad and the mass media. Attacks were directed at companies that ignored the social welfare of the miners. Reports by labour inspectors about miners' complaints that they missed their family, that they had no moral support for work, that there was a great deal of homosexuality and conflicts over women strengthened the argument for a change in management labour policy. At the same time international pressures were growing to abolish slavery in countries that still used penal sanctions for contract labourers as well as those that used convict labourers in production.[18] The company was also confronted by a high demand for coal and very low discipline among miners, which led to significant economic losses.

In addition to international pressures, internal attacks from politicians and journalists in the Volksraad and the mass media, the management was itself motivated to change policy. The move to replace convict and contract labourers was at least partly motivated by the difficulty of recruiting convict labourers from Batavian prisons after 1927. (Most of the prisons in the Netherlands Indies had used convicts for productive jobs.) Second, recruiting contract labourers without allowing them to come with their families had led to poor discipline among the labourers. This led the company to recruit more women and male labourers with families. By 1934 management no longer recruited contract labourers under penal sanctions, and contract labourers were replaced by free labourers. In 1937 convict labourers were no longer supplied to Ombilin, and in 1938 only free labourers were employed. The company's main policy was to recruit free labourers with families and create a mining community. It was expected that establishing a mining community would bring favourably affect reproduction of future generations of labourers.

The percentage of female contract labourers rose from 17.7 per cent to 22.4 per cent in 1928 (Table 14.2). This was intended to reduce the unequal ratio between males and females. From December 1929 to March 1930 9.9 per cent of the total labour force was married, and 30.7 per cent was female. Furthermore, the average number of married male labourers rose from 40.7 per cent in 1931 to 56.44 per cent in 1933, and reached 62 per cent in 1934.[19]

The increase in female labourers and wives was intended to serve the needs of the male labourers and to keep them from political activity. This policy was successful (attested to by the large presence of labourers). The rate of attendance for the various categories of labourers rose between 1929 and 1934. The lowest attendance was in 1929, especially for contract labourers who had signed their contract under the penal sanction (67 per cent). Compare this with the rate of attend-

18 For a discussion on international pressure for the abolition of convict and contract labourers in Indonesia, see Keppy (1998: 29-50).

19 Mining Archives, Jaarverslag van de Ombilin Mijnen 1934, no. 2502.

ance of convict, free, and casual labourers, which was above 88 per cent in the same year.[20]

It is the traditional male attitude of the company that restricted the role of women to serving men. One indication of this is the fact that after finishing their contract female labourers were expected to remain in the town, marry male labourers and become mothers for their children. The company also established a family allowance that became a crucial stimulus for men and women to marry. The family allowance was a bonus paid to married miners with children. In addition, the company also distributed staples in an amount defined by the company. These included rice, oil, and salted fish, which were distributed to each member of a miner's family, and was intended to reinforce a husband's responsibility towards his family. In short, the company's attitude increased women's dependence on their husband's wage from the very creation of the mining community.

The company's predominantly male attitude was also evidenced in the case of entertainment. Various kinds of entertainment such as gambling, *ronggeng* or *tandak*, football clubs, etc. were more directed at entertaining men than other family members. The company tended to subordinate the position of women and the family to the men. Not only did these entertainments leave the miners in debt, but by spending the money on the various kinds of entertainment, the miners could not give all their wages to their wives. Bu Ruiyah (76 years old) described how her father and first husband went gambling straight after work. She said the habit was common in Sawahlunto. 'Every Saturday and Sunday, or after receiving their salary, my father or my husband went directly to the gambling rooms or watching *ronggeng* or *tandak*.'[21]

The family's dependence on a miner's wages encouraged miners to work without protest, even though it was a time of state pressure (after 1927) and poor economic conditions (the Depression affected everyone since 1929). My interviews with former miners suggest that the miners did not protest because they were afraid of being dismissed. It was also difficult for men to look for additional income outside the mine, because the company had closed opportunities for working extra jobs not related to the mine. The presence of family encouraged the collaborative politics by the miners, and establishment of the mining community can be seen as an early attempt at the formation of a mining culture. The adaptation process to the world of the mines started earlier among the children of miners. It should not be surprising that many in the mining community viewed working in the mines as a status symbol.[22]

20 Mining Archives, *Arbeidersvoorziening van de Mijnbedrijven II*, no.1 V. Secret letter of Engineer-Director V.H. Ploem, 10/8/1929 no. 14 to the Head of State Mining Companies.

21 Interview with Bu Ru'iyah, 22/5/1995.

22 My interviews with some families of former miners are the basis for this argument. Many former miners hoped that their children could work at the Ombilin coal mines, even up to the present day.

What were the survival politics women engaged in under the layers of repression by state, management and their husbands? Women or wives had their own strategies to survive. They prepared and sold traditional Javanese food, either at the barracks or in the Sawahlunto market. They collected firewood in the forest, planted vegetables and worked as housemaids for Europeans.[23] Bu Semi (92 years old) described her role in the household economy three years after arriving at Sawahlunto in 1926. Bu Semi's experience as a miner's wife who came to Sawahlunto with her husband and daughter provides an interesting example. When I met her in her daughter's house in the village of Teleng, Sawahlunto, in October 2000, she described her experiences as follows:

> I told my husband that he did not need to go on strike, because I was afraid that he would be punished by having his salary withheld. You know many people were dismissed and repatriated to Java, because they went on strike several times. His salary was 30 cents per day at that time. That was not enough. When my daughter was six or seven years old, I thought that I could leave her to look for additional income. In Java I was also familiar with selling various kinds of food at my mother's food stall. In Sawahlunto I started to buy *krupuk singkong* (cassava chips) made by the miners' wives in the barracks. My husband permitted me to do this kind of work because he knew that we did not have enough money. My daughter helped me collect the *krupuk singkong* from other women, and I took them to Padang. I cooperated with five women. I stayed there for a few days and then would return to Sawahlunto, bringing back other basic necessities to be sold on credit to people in the barracks (Sawahlunto, 20 October 2000).

We can conclude from Bu Semi's story that women were not only important in helping to alleviate the economic difficulties of the household, but also in defining the forms of their husband's political participation. Nevertheless, women were confined to a more limited social sphere than were men. The company did not form any associations to channel women's interests or hobbies as they did for men – at least until Indonesia proclaimed its independence.

The Japanese Occupation and the Period of Revolution (1942–49)

The Japanese occupation and the Indonesian Revolution were turbulent periods for the mining society. The society endured ongoing destruction of the mines by the Dutch (before the Japanese occupation) and by the Indonesian populace (before the Dutch returned to Sawahlunto in 1948). Oil and coal were two mining commodities regarded by the Japanese as especially important, and were subsequently exploited by the Japanese military as well as by a semi-official govern-

23 Interview with Bu Ru'iyah, 22/5/1995, Mrs Ketty Urban, 13/12/1994.

ment company, the Hokkaido and Steamship Co., Ltd. There were also some changes in the management system during this period. The lack of skilled labour caused the Japanese to promote many Indonesians to higher positions than they had enjoyed before. The position of director was occupied by a Japanese engineer, Kobuta, while the position of deputy-director was held by Roesli, a graduate of the mining school at Sawahlunto. Some other former students of the mining school including A. Aziz, Sjahbuddin Sutan Radjo Nando, and Baharson were also promoted to higher positions. Those advanced were mostly Minangkabaus who held important positions in the company following Indonesian independence.[24] The company also changed the status of workers from free labourers to convict labourers, or *romusha*, employed not just in the mines but also for projects vital to Japanese war needs. Although the miners were under the iron discipline of the Japanese company, they were no longer confined in the cage of production. They could have social contacts with local people, especially after finishing their jobs in the mine. But they could no longer watch the *ronggeng* or *tandak* dancers or gamble, because the company did not provide these diversions.

Work and living conditions were very poor, especially in the final years of the Japanese occupation. On the one hand, the labourers were forced to produce as much coal as possible for the war effort, and on the other hand, there were few social amenities. It is easy to imagine how the lack of food and medical treatment affected working and living conditions. Many workers died, falling victim to mine accidents and worn out by the impossible workload. Apart from these hazards they also fell ill with malaria, typhus, various other diseases, and suffered from malnutrition.

Under such circumstances it should not be surprising that some labourers tried to break their contracts and escape from the mine. In 1942, 123 labourers ceased working or escaped to other places within and outside West Sumatra. Eight of these labourers ran away. In 1943, 153 labourers stopped working in the mine and moved elsewhere, and 104 ran away completely. As a result, supervision was increased and strict controls were imposed by the Japanese military, which reduced the number of people who stopped working to thirty and twelve who ran away in 1944 (Erman 1999: 138).

Mainly unmarried labourers followed the politics of resistance. It was easier for those who had no family to stop working or run away from the mine, and to earn a living in other places within or outside West Sumatra. Those who were married could not afford to stop working. They were forced to survive in the mine under harsh working and living conditions. To overcome economic difficulties they worked together with their shift mates or in work groups growing cassava, sweet potatoes, and other vegetables.

24 PTBA-UPO Archives, Buku Register, 1942–1948.

The working and living conditions of labourers during the Indonesian Revolution (1945-49) were even worse. The Ombilin coal mines had a dual function, as they produced coal as well as guns for the struggle. The labour force was also divided in two: working in the mine or following the guerilla groups fighting in the jungles. Those who stayed in town and worked in the mine continued the same survival strategy they had pursued in the previous years.

Political Protest and the Unity of Interest (1950-65)

The development of the mining sector in general and coal mining in particular between 1950-65 cannot be separated from political and economic developments in Indonesia. The economic recovery following the Indonesian Revolution was very slow and uneven. Apart from the lack of capital and strong dependence on foreign sources of finance, the state faced separatist movements such as *Darul Islam* in West Java and Aceh. It also had to deal with the Revolutionary Government of the Republic of Indonesia (PRRI) rebellion. These separatist movements totally absorbed the government's attention.

At this time the Indonesian coal mines also experienced difficulties. Much of the machinery had become old and was breaking down. In addition, the state-owned railway companies that had been the greatest coal consumers faced rising debts. Moreover, the state was unable to repair or modernise the mines, and coal began to compete with oil as the main source of fuel. All this led to a collapse in coal production. The company suffered continual losses, especially in 1951 and the following years, and in 1958 the PRRI local rebellion caused further difficulties. The company became an arena for various political groups and military factions of both supporters and opponents of the PRRI and the central government. Although there were plans for renewal in 1954, and again in 1964, coal production was unable to regain the production figures of the pre-Independence years.

Table 14.3 below shows the fluctuations in the labour force, including all levels as well as labourers. In 1950, there were only 1,526. By 1953 this number increased to 2,214 as new labourers were recruited together with their families (especially from Java). After 1953, the number decreased to 1,371, because many labourers were dismissed by the managers as punishment for their involvement in the strike. Between 1955 and 1958 the total number of labourers remained fairly constant. But in the years 1958, 1959, and 1960 the total number of labourers dropped each year, because many labourers, especially non-Javanese, left the mine to join the PRRI as a regional movement against the central government.

The labour force again increased from 1,946 in 1960 to 3,082 in 1965. This increase was caused by the recruitment of new labourers from Jakarta and other cities in central Java. For example, on 8 March 1963, 200 unemployed people from Jakarta were hired for the Ombilin coal mines. A second and third group

Table 14.3: Fluctuations in the Labour Force, 1950-65.

Year	*Total number in labour force*	*Year*	*Total number in labour force*
1950	1,526	1958	2,199
1951	1,565	1959	2,088
1952	2,001	1960	1,946
1953	2,214	1961	2,025
1954	1,371	1962	2,083
1955	2,064	1963	2,269
1956	2,026	1964	2,472
1957	2,199	1965	3,082

Source: PTBA-UPO Collection, *The Yearly report of the PTBA Ombilin* 1995.

followed their countrymen. In all, there were 319 people. They were *preman*,[25] or unemployed people, and a group of 'volunteers' (*sukarelawan*) from the Indonesian army, recruited to fight for the liberation of West Irian. Some of them had been sent to Kendari (Southeast Sulawesi) and Irian, while others had remained in Jakarta, where they waited for an indefinite period of time.[26] Both *preman* and the volunteer s were young men and unmarried. In 1964 the company recruited 23 men with families from Central Java through the office for Allocation of Labour Force located in Yogyakarta. This recruitment system sent Javanese men who had remained a long time in Sawahlunto to central Java in order to attract more Javanese to work in the Ombilin coal mines. These recruits were labourers under contract for three years. They included both day and monthly labourers, and were mostly men. Indeed, there were a few women, but they were hired only to sort coal or perform subordinate administrative tasks in the office.

The Natsir cabinet banned strikes and lockouts in vital undertakings under a prohibition issued on 13 February 1951 – not by the Ministry of Labour but by the Ministry of Defence. The strike ban could not stem the wave of strikes and strong protest actions by the unions. There was an eventual compromise in the Sukiman period under Emergency Act no. 16, in 1951, which stated that the state did not prohibit strikes but did restrict them (Feith 1962: 187). Thus, the state aimed at minimising the number of strikes through careful regulation. In addition, to solve labour disputes the state also created the P4P (*Panitia Penyelesaian*

25 The group of *preman* could also be divided into two categories, the criminal *preman* and those who were regarded as *preman* by police because they had no identity cards. Both categories were recruited mercilessly when the central government in Jakarta mounted 'cleansing' operations, or *sapu bersih*. The police rounded them up from the streets or food stalls. They were arrested, put in a truck, and taken to a collection place located in Bekasi. For this story, see Erman (1999: 177).
26 Antara, Berita Ekonomi dan Keuangan, 13/3/1963: 8.

Perselisihan Perburuhan Pusat, or The Central Labour Disputes Committee), or an equivalent institution for the different state institutions. The Central Labour Disputes Committee had branches on regional and local levels. The mechanism for resolving labour disputes was made more complex, enabling interference by a wider range of parties or state bureaucracy (Saptari 1995: 50). In 1957 martial law was declared. The military and the Ministry of Labour became more repressive, and in August 1957 the state banned strikes in vital industries and in the government-owned companies (Hawkins 1971: 233). The Ombilin and Bukit Asam coal mines, as state-owned companies, were included among the vital mining industries. After nationalisation of foreign companies, the government set up the *Dewan Perusahaan* (Company Board). The *Dewan Perusahaan* was set up in 1964 in the Ombilin coal mines, and representatives of labour trade unions were chosen.

If the miners had been more accommodating in the 1930s when the their families were formed, what happened after 1950 when the mining community was experiencing social and cultural changes? Workers had more social contacts with local people and were involved in formal and informal representations. Although the Indonesian coal mines were experiencing difficulties, the state was relaxing its controls on political parties and trade unions. This was especially felt by the contract labourers who stayed in the barracks. Political leaders also went into the mines, appealing to the collective consciousness of the mining society and encouraging workers to be more daring. Under such conditions the boundary between the world of politics and the world of work, between political control and labour control became blurred and in some case the two overlapped (Erman 1999: 172). In these circumstances the mining community before 1942 became involved in formal politics.

The formation of political parties and trade unions in the Ombilin coal mines can be divided in two periods: before 1960 and afterwards. Table 14.4 shows the contrasting picture of political parties and trade unions within the company in the two periods.

While the Masyumi and the PSI were strong parties in 1960, afterwards both were completely eclipsed, disgraced by their involvement in the PRRI rebellion. A new balance of political power emerged that was born of the fusion of three ideological streams: Nationalist, Islamic, and Communist, or Nasakom. Subsequently these streams were represented by the Indonesian Nationalist Party, or PNI, the *Nahdhatul Ulama*, or NU for religious traditionalists, and the PKI.[27] Before 1960 the PSI and the Masyumi vied for power with the PKI, but after 1960 its main competition was the Functional Group (later called *Golongan Karya*, or Golkar).

27 For a good introduction and review about Soekarno's ideas on nationalism, Islam, and marxism, see Mc Vey (1963: 113-22, 1970).

Table 14.4: Development of Political Parties and Trade Unions at the Ombilin Coal Mines, 1950-65

Year	Political Parties	Trade Unions
1945-59	Indonesian Socialist Party (PSI)	Indonesian Miners' Trade Union/ All-Indonesian Congress of Workers, SBTI/KBSI
	Indonesian Communist Party (PKI)	All-Indonesian Workers' Central Organisation (SBTI/SOBSI)
	Masyumi	
		Indonesian Islamic Trade Union (SBII)
1960-65	Indonesian Communist Party (PKI)	All-Indonesian Workers' Central Organisation (SBTI/SOBSI)
	Indonesian National Party (PNI)	Marhaenist Workers' Union (KBM)
	Nahdhatul Ulama (NU)	Indonesian Muslim Trade Union (Sarbumusi)
	Functional Group	Coalmine *Karyawan* Union/Central Organisation of Socialist White Collar *Karyawan* (PKBT-SOKSI)

Source: Erman 1999: 145, 187-8.

In the period between 1945 and 1959 the SBTI-SOBSI had the most members. Its strength lay in the modest attitude adopted by its leaders and their willingness to give labour problems a central place. The SBTI's concern for labour problems is evidenced in the demands it made of management. These demands included strikes (in 1953) as well as demands for improvements in the nine basic needs: food, clothing, wage increases and others. Other trade unions such as SBII and Sarbumusi did not pay much attention to labour problems, but concentrated instead on religious issues. The KBM-PNI was more elitist, and not interested in any concessions to labour that would endanger the comfortable positions of its members in the company. Finally, support for the SBTI-KBSI and PKTB-SOKSI had never been strong among the miners.

Outside the company the miners and their families were involved in social and cultural organisations, some of which were affiliated with the PKI (e.g., People's Youth (*Pemuda Rakyat*), the Association of Indonesian Farmers (*Barisan Tani Indonesia*-BTI) and the Indonesian Women's Movement (*Gerwani*). The mining community also established various musical, sports, and religious groups. The musical groups included *Ketoprak*, *Kuda Kepang*, *Kecapi Sunda*, *Randai*, and *Keroncong* – but *ronggeng* and *tandak*, which had been formed by the Javanese community and recruited by company, disappeared from the mining community. The associations created solidarity among the miners.

What differed from previous years was the emergence of formal representations for women (miners' wives and daughters). Many women became members of *Gerwani*, the *Pemuda Rakyat*, and other social-cultural clubs. *Gerwani* not only provided helpful strategies in domestic matters and social survival, but also created a consciousness within the working class community. The leaders of *Gerwani* were very active in supporting SBTI-SOBSI, the *Pemuda Rakyat*, and the BTI, by continually seeking additional members, spreading the ideology of class struggle, and promising a better life for the future.

At Sawahlunto some women became the leaders of *Gerwani*; these included Djalinus, Subranti, Martini, Satidjah, and Gadis. Djalinus, a well-known member of the PKI in Sawahlunto, led *Gerwani*. She was from Minangkabau and worked in the Department of Information office at Sawahlunto. She co-operated with several educated women that included Subranti, Martini, Satidjah, and Gadis. They represented the second generation of the Javanese contract labourers. For the most part their husbands were also workers at the Ombilin coal mines. These women actively mobilised others for various activities in Durian, Surian, and Sikalang villages such as *arisan*, a voluntary savings association that provided mutual assistance in times of need (such as deaths, births, and marriages), literacy courses, co-operative shops, sports, and political courses. *Gerwani*'s activities intensified after 1964, adding military training to its programme. About twice a week, twenty or thirty women from each village reported for military training, wearing long shirts and trousers and holding bamboo spears. They were led by the Pemuda Rakyat. Moreover, Djalinus and her friends successfully placed about twenty-five women in jobs in the mines (Erman 1999: 152).

The involvement of miners and their families in formal and informal representations also changed the forms of their responses to company. The politics of protest was marked by a set of strikes from April to July, 1953, which was two years after the Minister of Defence announced the law against strikes.[28] Table

Table 14.5: Strikes in 1953

Date of strike	*Duration*	*Total Strikes*
18 April	2 hours	144
9 May	24 hours	1,200
17-23 May	6 days	933
23 May-30 May	8 days	856
31 May-15 July	48 days	760
16 July	?	400

Source: *Haluan*, 8-6-1953, *Sumatera Tengah* 1953: 17.

28 As a whole, in fact the attempt by the state to restrict the strike was successful. No more than 11 per cent of the Indonesian labourers went on strike in 1956. On this, see Hawkins (1971: 239).

14.5 shows the strikes that took place from April to July, 1953, which involved the majority of the labourers. In total, the company lost over 60 working days.

The strikes of 1953 were not simply a protest by the Javanese workers, but were also a reflection of conflicts between the two trade unions and political parties that were exacerbated by ethnic and class tensions. The strikers were Javanese labourers, members of the SBTI-SOBSI. They demanded an end to the power abuses of the Minangkabau, socialist manager, Sjahbuddin Sutan Radjo Nando and the overseers, as well as an end to arbitrary mistreatment, wage cuts and taxes on company land used by labourers to construct their houses. This group was from the socialist trade union (SBTI-KBSI) and mostly Minangkabau. The leaders of the SBTI-SOBSI – Sugino M. Wiguno, Ramali, and Ronojudo were all sons of former contract Javanese labourers, and were very vocal in their slogans and demands. Their posters were plastered on the walls of every miners' barracks, with slogans such as 'Move! Fight for honesty and truth!'[29]

The miners' politics of protest through the 1953 strikes were not only a collective conflict between the Javanese miners from the communist trade union and their Minangkabau socialist manager and overseers, but also a battle between a mining working-class community and the company. What we see in this instance is the emergence of class consciousness among the mining community – a consciousness that was bound up with class and ethnic conflicts. Perhaps even more important was the presence of mining working-class community in the strikes, where the role of informal associations shaped the political consciousness of the miners. In addition, there was the involvement of women in the public political sphere. The role of women played was complex and fragmented. Women were not only involved in the politics of survival for their own households (like the 1930s), but also in formal representations, and informal associations. These associations had become a locus of communication among the townspeople and also a place where political choice and actions were defined. Arisan, a very active association among women in each of the barracks in Sawahlunto, functioned as a bridge for their political actions.

The role of women in supporting the miners' struggle under the SBTI-SOBSI can be seen clearly in the preparation for strikes and in the 1953 visit by the member of Parliament, Werdojo. Women or miners' wives had prepared food for meetings of the leaders of SBTI-SOBSI and Werdojo in Sawahlunto. Their involvement was an important stimulus, deriving from their own husbands' involvement and the leaders of Gerwani. What motivated the women in their activities can be seen from the following statement by a miner's wife:

29 PTBA-UPO Archives, letter by Sugino to Aminoeddin, the leader of the Durian village branch of SBTL, 20/8/1952.

> I had to prepare and bring some snacks to the branch office of the SBTI-SOBSI in the village of Durian. I was ordered by my husband to do this. I did not mind because I felt it helped my husband in the struggle for our future. I had to help the organisation because it had helped me so much, and my husband, especially when our daughter passed away (anonymous, 19 April 1995).

The above statement indicates there was a reciprocal relationship between the men, women, and trade unions. Members of the trade union would obey their leaders so long as the organisation provided protection. In this respect the SBTI-SOBSI and other organisations affiliated with the PKI were indeed more concerned with the labourers' interests.

Werdojo's visit renewed the enthusiasm of the SBTI-SOBSI and the PKI leaders both in Sawahlunto and West Sumatra in their efforts to gain greater political influence. Their demands contained two main themes: the need to replace the socialist manager, Sjahbuddin Sutan Radjo Nando, and improvement of miners' living conditions. The latter included concerns such as health care, housing, and wages. The miners were successful, especially after a visit to Sawahlunto in July 1953 by a member of the P4P, two high officials from the Ministry of Court, and the Head of mining industry from Jakarta. They were charged with the task of solving the labour conflicts in the Ombilin coal mines.

The women's support for their husbands' struggles through the trade union (SBTI-SOBSI) increased after 1960. They helped collect contributions of rice and money from barracks residents, attended meetings of their husbands' organisations and their own associations, followed political courses and para-military training, and attended the meetings of *arisan*. Women also accompanied their husbands, demanding improvements in working and living conditions from the company. Although there were no strikes during the 1960s, the miners' remained vocal in their demands, which were sometimes successful. What was different from previous years was the women's involvement in military training, which was intended to help in the struggle for West Irian. About twice a week twenty to thirty women reported for military training, wearing long shirts and trousers and holding bamboo spears. They were especially eager in the villages of Durian and Sikalang. The training was led by members of the *Pemuda Rakyat*, which planned that the women would be sent as female volunteers, helping the Indonesian military struggle for West Irian.

This chapter describes the politics of the miners and its relation to the role of the women who were involved in the communist organisations. Apart from the unity of interest between the miners and their wives in the miners' struggles, women also played a more complex and fragmented role than before. The lives of both the miners and their wives became more varied. The miners not only performed their jobs in the mines, they also sought to take additional jobs to make ends meet – as well as attending meetings of informal and formal organisations.

Like their husbands, the women or wives also performed more than one task: they now had both domestic and public roles. They not only took care of their children, husbands, cooking, and washing, but they, too, sought additional income by preparing snacks, planting vegetables, and attending meetings, courses, *arisan*, and military training. This unity of interests in the struggle for their rights during the period of democracy was certainly not the intent of the company when it created a community of stable households. In contrast with the events of the Depression period, when state control was strong and the miners, with the support of their families, were more accommodating, in the period of democracy state control and the Indonesian economy were both weak, and the miners, with the economic and political support of their families became more militant. The democratic political climate allowed them to protest more openly, struggling to improve their future by means of labour strikes. Thus, married labourers and their wives began to plan for improved lives in the barracks.

Concluding Remarks

It is too early to make any definitive conclusions because there is a dearth of information on gender response to state control. We do not yet know how the negotiation process between women and their husbands will develop, or between Gerwani and the SBTI–SOBSI. We can, however, draw some preliminary conclusions based on the preceding description of events in the Ombilin coal mines. First, not only did the social-political and economic pressures by the state and management lead to a similar response by men and women, but these pressures also determined the demographic, social, cultural, and economic nature of the miners themselves. The history of the mines: the imbalance between men and women, the formation of the mining community, socio-political and cultural organisations and associations were important factors influencing the forms and intensity of gender response to state and management control.

Second, the gendered response to state control was not a linear process. In the first years of mining exploitation miners used a politics of resistance and maintained this up to the second decade of the twentieth century. Afterwards they changed to a politics of accommodation. The change in the miners' politics was caused not only by a shift in management and state labour policies, but also by the changing social composition of the miners. Women had an important role in defining the politics of resistance and accommodation of the miners. Third, after Indonesian independence, when state control was weak and the role of society became stronger, women started to become involved in formal organisations, strikes, and protests, which suggests that their struggle was the same as that of their husbands in the trade union.

References

Archives

Algemeen Rijks Archief (ARA), Den Haag, Ministerie van Koloniën.

Mailrapport (Mr) 1904/1151, 1911 no. 218, 1924/2608.

Mining Archives (Bandung)

Arbeid aangelegenheden Mijnbedrijven VI-A/5. Report of Labour Inspector Deibert, 3 July 1924.

Arbeidersvoorziening van de Mijnbedrijven II, no. 1V.

Dwangarbeiders te Ombilin Steenkolenmijnen, VI-A/85.

Jaarverslag van de Ombilin Mijnen 1934, no. 2502.

Steenkolenpolitiek, no. IV-32B.

National Archives (Arsip Nasional), Jakarta.

Register 1891-1907: 412.

Mining Archives (PTBA-UPO, *Perusahaan Tambang Batubara-Unit Produksi Ombilin*), Sawahlunto, West Sumatra.

Letter by Sugino to Aminoeddin, the leader of the Durian village branch of SBTI, 20/8/1952.

Interviews

Ketty Urban, 13/12/1994.

Pak Oejoeb, 23/5/1995.

Pak Suwardi Kisut, 22/8/1995.

Pak Rahmat, 15/5/1995.

Bu Ru'iyah, 15/5/1995.

Pak Rusman, 5 May 1995.

Pak Warso, 4 May 1995.

Oriental Collections

KITLV, Korn Collection OR 435. No. 368, 'Het Ombilin Steenkolen Bedrijf door een bestuursambtenaar bezien', 1931.

Newspapers

Hoa Po, 13/2/1915.

Haluan, 86, 1953, 31/12/1953.

Sinar Sumatra, 12/2/1914, 11/4/1914, 13/11/1922, 16/6/1926, 16/6/1927.

Sumatera Tengah, 1953.

Tjaja Sumatra, 13/8/1917, 23/8/1917, 21/9/1920.

Utusan Melayu, 10/11/1922.

Official reports

Antara, Berita Ekonomi dan Keuangan, 13/3/1963.

The Yearly Report of the PTBA (Perusahaan Tambang Bukit Asam) Ombilin 1995.

Verslag over de Hervormingen van het Gevangeniswezen over 1921 t/m 1925, Batavia: G. Kolff and Co, 1926.

Verslag over de Hervormingen van het Gevangeniswezen over 1926, Batavia: G.Kolff and Co, 1927: 24.

Verslagen van den Sumatra-Staatsspoorweg en de Ombilinmijnen 1910-1916, Batavia 1911-1917.

Verslagen van de Ombilinmijnen 1917-1923/24, Batavia/Weltevreden 1918-1925.

Jaarverslagen van 's lands kolenmijnen 1925-1930, Batavia/Weltevreden 1926-1931.

Articles, Books

Bruinink-Darlang, C.A.M. (1986) 'Het Penitentiair Stelsel in Nederlands-Indië van 1905 tot 1940', PhD Thesis, Rijksuniversiteit Utrecht.

Colombijn, F. (1992) 'Uiteenlopende spoorrails. De verschillende ideeën over spoorwegaanleg en ontginning van het Umbilin-kolenveld in West Sumatra 1868-1891', *Bijdragen en Mededelingen betreffende de Geschiedenis der Nederlanden* 107: 437–458.

Diest, P.H. van (1871) *De Kolenrijkdom der Padangsche Bovenlanden en de Mogelijkheden van de Voordeelige Ontginning*, Amsterdam: Stemler.

Empel, C. van (1999) 'Dark mines: labour conditions of coolies in the state coal mines of West Sumatra', in V.J.H. Houben and J.T. Lindblad (eds.) *Coolie Labour in Colonial Indonesia: A Study of Labour Relations in the Outer Islands, c. 1900-1940*, Wiesbaden: Harrassowitz.

Erman, E. (1999) 'Miners, Managers and the State: A Socio-political History of the Ombilin Coal-mines, West Sumatra, 1892-1996', PhD Thesis, University of Amsterdam.

Feith, H. (1962) *The Decline of Constitutional Democracy in Indonesia,* Ithaca: Cornell University Press.

Groot, C. de (1887) *Herinneringen aan Blitong, historisch, lithologisch, mineralogisch, geographisch, geologisch en mijnbouwkundig*, The Hague: H.L. Smits.

Hawkins, E. (1971) 'Labor in developing countries: Indonesia', in B. Glassburner (ed.) *The Economy of Indonesia*, Ithaca: Cornell University Press.

Joustra, M. (1923) *Minangkabau: Overzicht van Land, Geschiedenis en Volk*, 's-Gravenhage: Nijhoff.

Ingleson, J. (1981) 'Worker consciousness and labour unions in colonial Java', *Pacific Affairs* 54, 3: 485–502.

– (1986) *In Search of Justice: Workers and Unions in Colonial Java, 1908-1926*, Asian Studies Association of Australia, Singapore: Oxford University Press.

Keppy, P. (1998) 'Labour relations in late-colonial Indonesia: the case of the manufacturing labour regulation of 1941', *Masyarakat Indonesia* xxiv, 1: 29–50.

Kol, H. van (1903) *Uit onze koloniën: Uitvoerig reisverhaal*, Leiden: A.W. Sijthoff.

Klubock, M.T. (1997) 'Morality and good habits: the construction of gender and class in the Chilean copper mines, 1904-1951', in J.D. French and D. James (eds.) *The Gendered Worlds of Latin American Women Workers: From Household and Factory to the Union Hall and Ballot Box*, Durham: Duke University Press.

Lier, R.J. van (1915) *Voordracht over de Ombilinkolenmijnen ter Sumatra's Westkust*, Amsterdam: J.H. de Busy.

Locher-Scholten, E. (2000) *Women and the Colonial State: Essays on Gender and Modernity in the Netherlands Indies 1900-1942*, Amsterdam: Amsterdam University Press.

McVey, R. (1963) 'The strategic triangle: Indonesia', *Survey* 54: 113–122.

— (1970) *Nationalism, Islam and Marxism: The Management of Ideological Conflict in Indonesia: Introduction to Sukarno, Nationalism, Islam, Marxism,* Ithaca: Cornell University Press.

Nash, J. (1979) *We Eat the Mines and the Mines Eat Us: Dependency and Exploitation in Bolivian Tin Mines*, New York: Colombia University Press.

Phimister, I. (1994) 'Lashers and Leviathan: the 1954 coal-miners' strike in colonial Zimbabwe', *International Review of Social History* 39: 186–187.

Ritz, A. (1935) 'Mijnpolitiek en Financiën', *Koloniale Studiën* 19, 2: 319–352.

Robinson, K.M. (1986) *Stepchildren of Progress: The Political Economy of Development in an Indonesian Mining Town*, New York: State University of New York Press.

Rothermund, D. (1978) 'The coalfield: an enclave in a backward region', in D. Rothermund and D.C. Wadhwa (eds.) *Zamindars, Mines and Peasants: Studies in the History of an Indian Coalfield*, Delhi: Ramesh Jain.

Saptari, R. (1995) 'Rural Women to the Factories: Continuity and Change in East Java's Kretek Cigarette Industry', PhD Thesis, University of Amsterdam.

Simeon, D. (1995) *The Politics of Labour Under Late Colonialism: Worker, Unions and the State in Chota Nagpur 1928-1939*, Delhi: Manohar Publisher & Distributors.

Somers Heidhues, F.M. (1991) 'Company Island: a note on the history of Belitung', *Indonesia* 51 (April): 1-20.

Stibbe, S. (1884) 'Werkvolk ter westkust van Sumatra', *Indische Gids* 6, II: 698–700.

Stolcke, V. (1988) *Coffee Planters, Workers and Wives: Class Conflict and Gender Relations on Sao Paulo Plantations, 1850-1980*, Oxford: Macmillan.

Stoler, A.L. (1979) *In the Company's Shadow: A History of Plantation Women and Labor Policy in North Sumatra*, Amsterdam: s.n.

— (1992) 'Rethinking Amsterdam: s.n. colonial categories: European communities and the boundaries of rule', in N.B. Dirks (ed.) *Colonialism and Culture*, Ann Arbor: University of Michigan Press.

Tohari, A. (1982) *Ronggeng Dukuh Paruk: Catatan Buat Emak*, Jakarta: PT Gramedia.

15

Labour Politics in Migrant Communities: Ethnicity and Women's Activism in Tangerang, Indonesia

REBECCA ELMHIRST

One of the most notable aspects of labour politics in Indonesia over the past decade has been a dramatic rise in the incidence of labour activism, culminating in strikes and protests, particularly in Java's export-oriented industrial zones. Since the mid-1990s, prior to the political turmoil surrounding the ousting of Suharto and subsequent presidential transitions, strikes and labour-instigated demonstrations have been an almost daily feature of industrial life in areas such as Tangerang and Bekasi in West Java, Surabaya in East Java, and Medan in North Sumatra (Manning 1993, Hadiz 1997, Kammen 1999, Ford 2001). A singular feature of contemporary labour activism among factory workers in Indonesia has been the increasing militancy of women workers. Far from being the docile, compliant young factory girls harnessed by global capital, as portrayed in populist accounts and reproduced in the New International Division of Labour literature (Pearson 1986, Safa 1986, Wolf 1992), women have been active players in the surge of labour activism over the past few years (Saptari 1995, Tjandraningsih 1995, Andriyani 1996, Hadiz 1997, Smyth and Grijns 1997). This phenomenon has been attributed to a growing worker consciousness among female factory workers as large numbers of women have been drawn into waged factory work and as they confront the exigencies of state labour policy. More specifically, their propensity to resist *as workers* has come about as they have been increasingly linked into activist networks and labour-oriented non-governmental organisations (NGOs) active in industrial areas (Manning 1992, Hadiz 1997, Pangestu and Hendytio 1997).

Ethnographies of women factory workers in Indonesia have sought to produce more nuanced accounts of gendered labour politics, emphasising the ways in which the prospects for and nature of women's activism are located within frames of meaning and action that lie beyond the factory (Mather 1985, Wolf 1992, Smyth and Grijns 1997, Saptari 1995, Silvey 2000, 2001). One area of interest has been the connection between women's labour activism (or its lack) and different women's home-based priorities, both economic and socio-cultural. The argument is that women's resistance as workers is shaped by the interplay of various factors, one of which is the nature of workers' communities (Saptari 1998). Such accounts have envisaged 'community' in a variety of ways. One of the most influential has been the interplay between women's position in the family (as mothers or as daughters) and the consequent gender interests that intersect with and shape their subjectivities as workers. Both Mather (1985) and Wolf (1992) suggest parental influence and a desire to be a 'dutiful daughter' was an important factor in suppressing worker resistance among young women in West and Central Java respectively, whilst others have suggested that older women are less likely to be militant where this can jeopardise important family income (Smyth and Grijns 1997, Tjandraningsih 1995). Outside the household, women's embeddedness in family networks may also influence labour activism in complex ways (Saptari 1995, 1998; Silvey 2001).

Beyond the family and familial networks, research has also pointed to the importance of women workers' communities: the social groups in which they participate and inter-household community networks in and around factory areas. In different circumstances, such communities can stifle women's labour activism, as Mather (1985) reports for Tangerang in the early 1980s, where an 'Islamic patriarchy' worked in conjunction with factory managers to ensure young women workers in the locality remained 'docile'. By contrast, Andriyani's research shows how social activities and the presence of activist role models within workers' communities have led to a growing worker consciousness among women factory workers in West Java (Andriyani 1996). As Saptari points out, the interplay of worker communities and women's activism depends greatly on the nature of the communities themselves, and in particular, local histories of women's work and labour activism in particular places (Saptari 1998). Whilst reaching slightly different conclusions, all of these contributions point to the importance of highlighting the terms upon which women are able to express their militancy as workers, and each problematises the analytical separation between work and community so that attention is directed towards the multifarious ways that women carry specific domestic and community entanglements that shape their identities as workers and, following from that, their willingness and capacity to take part in various forms of workplace resistance at different historical moments.

This chapter shares a concern with the ways community and workplace politics intersect, but focuses on a specific kind of community: the spatially-extensive migrant networks that link young female factory workers in the West Java city of Tangerang with their home village in Lampung province, Sumatra.[1] In doing so,

1 Research was conducted in conjunction with staff and students from Pusat Studi Wanita,

a social network perspective is adopted, that challenges the equation of spatial proximity with social interaction, and instead traces connections between the locality and wider contexts (Rogers and Vertovec 1995), in this instance, young women's villages of origin. Since the mid 1990s, young women in their late teens from the study village of Tiuh Indah in North Lampung have travelled to Tangerang to take up work in garment and textile factories. A notable feature of this migration is that these young women maintain strong ties with their parental homes in the village, and envisage returning to North Lampung permanently when the time comes for them to marry and have children. The maintenance of these ties has been facilitated by the founding of an organisation in Tangerang with the explicit aim of looking after the interests of people from Tiuh Indah for the time that they are in the city. The *Ikatan Buay Serunting Sakti* (literally, family ties of the descendants of Serunting Sakti) was founded by a member of the village elite, who has long been in residence in Tangerang, but who owns land in Tiuh Indah and thus maintains interests in its community affairs. One consequence of the way rural-urban ties are being maintained in this instance has been the generation of a strong sense of common origin-based identity among migrants, who regard themselves first and foremost as *orang Lampung* – Lampungese people. This process of ethnicisation has been reinforced by rural North Lampung's status as a receiving area for Javanese people who have been resettled under the transmigration programme. Tensions between local Lampung people and Javanese migrants over land and other resources has been expressed in cultural terms (Elmhirst 1999) and this heightened awareness of cultural difference has been carried through to Tangerang. Thus the community discussed here is one that is marked by its 'ethnicity'.

In focusing on this kind of migrant community, the chapter brings to the foreground the question of ethnicity: an issue that is elided in many recent accounts of women, industrial work and labour politics. It challenges the idea of women workers as a homogeneous group with shared interests and objectives, looking instead to the ways ethnicity carries particular resonance amongst this group of proletarianised, urban women workers. In the context of an increasingly politicised awareness of cultural identities in Indonesia in general (Tirtosudarmo 1997), looking at the ways ethnicity, class and gender intersect in given circumstances would seem to be an important concern. In this chapter I consider the links between migration, ethnic relations and women's labour activism, focusing on the trade-offs that young women make as they negotiate the potential costs and benefits of participation in migrant community networks. I suggest that the observed lack of militancy among this group of young female factory workers was not due to some sort of primordial cultural propensity – as Lampung women – to be docile. Rather, it relates to their embeddedness in ethnicised social networks that

Universitas Lampung, Pusat Studi Kajian Wanita, Universitas Indonesia and ICRAF-Indonesia. Field work was funded by Economic and Social Research Council Award Number R000222089.

are constructed, in and through the practices of these women workers, their families and members of their village elite. In focusing on ethnicity as a process, the chapter challenges earlier conceptions of ethnicity and labour that imply that 'culture' is a 'given' from which all else flows.

The chapter draws on empirical material gathered in two separate periods of field work, in 1994-95 and in 1998 in Tiuh Indah and Tangerang. This time scale is significant as it covers the period when Indonesia's economy was at its height (in 1994), followed by the period around the economic crisis of 1997-98, when growth was reversed and when economic contraction, job insecurity and unemployment characterised urban labour markets. Other research conducted at this time has highlighted the ways in which the pressures brought to bear on urban incomes and employment prospects drew many workers to rely on their social safety nets – community networks and links with areas of origin – in order to cope with the exigencies of the economic crisis (Silvey 2000). From an empirical point of view, this reinforces the importance of considering the links between workplace and community in forging worker consciousness and practices of resistance among women.

Ethnicity And Labour In Indonesia

Given that so many introductory accounts of Indonesian development begin with observing that the country is made up of more than 300 distinct ethno-linguistic groups spread over 13,000 islands, it is perhaps surprising that ethnicity has received so little attention in either recent accounts of labour and labour politics (Manning 1993, Hadiz 1997, Kammen 1999) or within the labour movement itself. Moreover, this omission is all the more surprising when in West Java's industrial areas, marked as home to Sundanese people, it is increasingly the case that much of the workforce comprises migrants from outside the province and indeed from outside Java itself. The implications for labour activism of both retaining ties with areas of origin and of the consequent cultural diversity that such ties imply have yet to be explored in relation to the West Java work force.

In part, disregard for ethnicity relates to the very distinct ways that cultural constructions of labour have been examined in the literature on Indonesian labour history. Here, particular attention has been given to the ways that colonialism posited lines of difference between white, Chinese and 'native' or *pribumi* workers (Furnivall 1944, Stoler 1986) with relatively little regard for self-defined differences within this latter category (for an exception see Ingleson 2001). Even those accounts that draw on postcolonial theory have tended to focus particularly on the ways these broader differences have been constructed in and through the discursive practices of the colonial encounter (Stoler 1991). Indeed, given the historical links between Indonesia's labour movement and nationalist struggle, notions of cultural difference might have been seen as contrary to both working class interests and attempts to secure Indonesian independence (Ingleson 2001).

A second factor accounting for the omission of ethnicity in contemporary Indonesian labour studies relates to the ways that recent accounts of labour politics have emphasised the process of proletarianisation, and in doing so, have privileged class above all other social divisions and sources of identity (see for example, the collection in Harris 1995, Hadiz 1997). Even in accounts that have sought to challenge an overemphasis on class conflict the focus has been on political and economic regimes (e.g. Kammen 1999), thus eclipsing the implications that ethnic politics have for labour relations more generally. Finally, the invisibility of ethnicity from accounts of labour politics relates to the ways that cultural diversity has been envisaged in Indonesia, both in the literature and through state discourses. Rather than being seen as a political process, culture (or more specifically, ethnic diversity) is cast as an 'object': moulded into forms designated by government in the course of 'nation-building' (Bowen 1986, Widodo 1995). In unpicking this process, Pemberton's exploration of the links between 'culture' and interiorised repression has indicated the ways that 'a rhetoric of culture enframes political will and secures political horizons' (Pemberton 1994: 9, Errington 1997). In other words, this 'official' perspective on culture has effectively set limits on the ways that ethnicity is viewed in Indonesia, emphasising rituals, dress and language, and displacing politicised processes of cultural difference such as claims and entitlements to resources and political recognition.

Whilst ethnicity has been elided in discussions of proletarian labour politics, it has been of some concern to those examining other kinds of work in Indonesia, and most particularly, in the literature on the urban informal sector. In contrast to research on Indonesia's working class where factory workers are envisaged as a homogeneous group of (cultureless) workers, the informal sector literature has given considerable attention to issues concerning ethnicity and culture that give shape to labour markets and patterns of residence in urban areas. Early accounts that built upon notions of a dualistic economy in which pre-capitalist forms were conserved emphasised the links between ethnic identification and participation in particular kinds of 'traditional' economic activity (Furnivall 1946, Boeke 1953, Geertz 1963b). Such differences were interpreted as resting on primordial sentiments: 'the assumed givens...of social existence: immediate contiguity and kin connection mainly, but beyond them the givenness that stems from being born into a particular religious community, speaking a particular language, or even a dialect of a language and following particular social practices. These congruities...are seen to have an ineffable, and at times, overpowering, coerciveness in and of themselves' (Geertz 1963a: 259). The difficulties with this position is that it is at once univeralist and ahistorical, failing to take account of the mutability of ethnic categories in the face of social change. In particular, studies of migrants in the urban informal sector, such as Bruner's (1974) account of Batak migrants in

Bandung, have illustrated the ways that cultural identities may be transformed as individuals and groups emphasise or play down particular dimensions of their historically-constructed identities as occasion demanded. The rational choice implications of this perspective are countered by those that show how ethnicity is structured through the exclusion or positioning of particular groups of people in processes of commoditisation, particularly in the plantation sector (Liddle 1973) and in resource extraction (Robinson 1986).

Such accounts provide a corrective to the limitations of both a primordial and a populist approach to culture and ethnic diversity in Indonesia. However, there remains an underlying assumption that ethnicity and cultural difference represent vestiges of tradition that are being conserved within particular sectors of the economy that have yet to be fully commoditised and among groups that have thus far been excluded from proletarianisation. Given that there are considerable difficulties in maintaining the conceptual distinctions between the working class (i.e. factory workers) and the urban poor (i.e. the informal sector) (Pinches 1987), there is an imperative to examine how ethnicity is both constructed in and expressed through (factory) labour politics in Indonesia, particularly at a moment where the ideological and material uncertainties of post-New Order Indonesia are promoting notions of primordial culture as objects of political struggle (c.f. Comaroff and Comaroff 1992, Brown 1993). This raised awareness of a particular version of ethnicity in Indonesia is being fuelled by political initiatives such as decentralisation and the formation of organisations with the explicit goal of securing the rights of defined (and territory-based) cultural groups (see Li 1999). How these large-scale movements might intersect with working class politics remains to be explored and is beyond the scope of this chapter. However, historical studies of worker politics in the 1920s and 1930s reveal the importance of socially-constructed ethnic divisions in workplaces and factories, particularly where these are forged through specific networks of patronage and kinship in ways that condition the course of labour activism as groups are played off against each other (Ingleson 2001). This begs the question as to whether ethnic groupings (and associated networks) are significant in shaping contemporary labour politics in similar ways. Here, I take a small step towards examining the links between cultural identity and labour politics among a particular group of people, in this case, young female factory workers from Lampung. Rather than drawing on the primordialism that seems to underpin most recent discussions of ethnic diversity in Indonesia my interpretation is informed by a more nuanced account of subject formation. Here, ethnicity is seen as an embodied process that develops through a sense of common origin and common kinship, and embraces processes of exclusion and inclusion integral to the social networks associated with migration, factory work and day-to-day living in Tangerang.

Gender, Ethnicity And Social Networks: Lampung Migrant Workers

Since the early 1980s, when Indonesia embarked on a course of export-oriented industrialisation, there has been a mushrooming of factory development in Tangerang. In the beginning, labour for factories was drawn from local communities in and around the factory zone (and from Jakarta's urban fringes). More recently, migrants from regions beyond West Java are increasingly being drawn into the Tangerang workforce, taking up residence on a semi-permanent basis in order to secure waged work and, at least in the first instance, augment limited agrarian livelihoods. Lampung province in particular has paid an important role in this migration, as communications links have improved and as the province has increasingly been drawn into the Jakarta-Bogor-Tangerang-Bekasi (JABOTABEK) regional economy. According to Soegiharto et al. (1997), who base their analysis on official census data, *recorded* numbers migrating from Lampung to West Java increased from 15,851 in 1980 to 84,290 in 1990. With respect to the study village of Tiuh Indah, integration into this regional dynamic has come about quite recently. Until the early 1980s this part of North Lampung was relatively isolated, with movement in and out of the area largely by boat. Livelihoods were derived from swamp rice cultivation on fertile flood plains, from fishing and from trade in forest products including timber and rattan from the area's extensive forests. In the late 1970s, the provincial government earmarked the area for local transmigration: to receive 'forest squatters' from protected forests elsewhere in Lampung. Over the course of the 1980s, more than 500,000 Javanese migrants were resettled in North Lampung, increasing the region's population sevenfold in the space of just 10 years, transforming agro-ecological landscapes, land tenure structures and livelihood possibilities in the process. The perceived threats to local Lampung peoples' livelihoods that these changes posed meant that work in the city acquired a greater importance for the community as a whole, and migration generally was facilitated by the improvement of roads that transmigration brought, particularly during the early 1990s. Today, Tangerang may be reached in less than 18 hours overland and by ferry, thus smoothing connections between the city and village, and establishing the infrastructure for migration to take place.

Factory Work and Lampung Identity

It is in this wider context that Lampung women's migration to Tangerang's factory zone should be seen. Young women's participation in factory work began in the early 1990s when a young woman, originally from Tiuh Indah but living in Lampung's provincial capital Tanjung Karang, went to work in Tangerang. Effectively, this initiated a steady stream of young women, mostly this woman's relatives and close friends from the village, to follow suit. By 1994 (the first period of fieldwork on which this study is based) around a third of all young women aged 15 to 20 were going to Tangerang to work. By late 1997, prior to the monetary crisis, all but four women in this cohort of the total village population were working in the city. The participation of these young women in migration and factory work has been remarkable in the light of local gender and kinship ideologies that imply considerable mobility and employment constraints, particularly for unmarried post-pubescent women. All female household members are under the guardianship of male household members, whatever their age. Women are expected to obey their husbands, and daughters to obey their fathers, particularly when it comes to life decisions, such as education, marriage and work. Restrictions on women's work relate to normative constraints on their mobility and for unmarried, young women, these prescriptions are particularly strong (Elmhirst 2000). On reaching puberty, daughters are not allowed to go out of the house except with parents or older brothers. Thus, they have no role whatever in the farming system as they are precluded from taking part in any activity that takes them away from the confines of the house until after they have married and borne their husband a child. Particular considerations appear to be both aesthetic and moral: a protection of young girls' pale skin and delicate constitution and a protection of their honour, as agricultural work is associated with the possibility of being 'bothered' by young men. Thus, on the one hand, there is little expectation for daughters to assist their mothers beyond household duties, or of their being able to support themselves through their own efforts, were they to remain in the village. On the other hand, the position of daughters is entirely dependent on them making a suitable marriage, as they will have to look to their future husband for their future welfare.

In view of this, daughters (and their families) need to negotiate a line of expected behaviours (and aesthetics) which will maintain their respectability and standing in the eyes of others in the village. One of the socio-cultural impacts associated with the arrival of Javanese migrants in the locality in recent years has been for such prescriptions to gather strength, as Lampung people have become ever more concerned to distance themselves from a symbolically and materially threatening 'Other' and as they attempt to deflect gossip about their conduct in relation to migrants with their supposedly looser morals. Factory work must therefore be accommodated within this framework: it must be perceived by parents (and young women themselves) to pose no threat to prestige considerations. Factory work enables daughters to maintain their aesthetic appeal (they can keep their skins pale and avoid building muscles), and parents consider young women to be effectively 'supervised' while they are in Tangerang: prevented from engaging in behaviours that would compromise family standing. Factory work also presents a very public way that Lampung people can distance themselves from their Javanese neighbours. Within the transmigration community there was only one household from which young women had gone to work in Tangerang, and they were the daughters of a middle class school teacher and market trader. Barriers to Javanese transmigrants working in Tangerang included generally lower education attainment than their Lampung peers (most factory jobs required high school education, which few transmigrant women had) and difficulties in raising the capital to make the journey to Tangerang. Other issues were demand for their labour as agricultural workers in the transmigration settlement and, importantly for the argument being developed in this chapter, an inability to take part in and command the generally Lampungese social networks that linked Tangerang with North Lampung. The interweaving of class and cultural identity in this way, as revealed in the contrasting lives of young women in each community, was frequently commented on by both groups, and again provided a discursive mechanism through which Lampung people could reiterate their cultural (and material) distance from their migrant neighbours.

Migration, Identity and Social Networks

If a particular notion of Lampung ethnicity is being reworked through perceptions of female factory employment and its symbolic and aesthetic appeal, there is another more material sense in which factory migration is revisioning contemporary ideas of 'Lampungeseness' in ways that may have implications for labour politics. The development of an established, and increasingly institutionalised, social network linking those working in Tangerang with their family, friends and neighbours in Tiuh Indah has been one of the defining features of the way in which participation in factory work has developed amongst young Lampung women. However, the maintenance of rural-urban ties is not a simple case of urbanised women holding on to vestiges of rural tradition whilst in the city. Rather, the very establishment and operation of these ties, and the practices of those involved in maintaining ties, is creating particular ideas of Lampung identity, that revolve around but that are not reducible to a sense of common origin, common language and difference from other groups of workers in Tangerang.

The beginnings of a network linking daughters working in Tangerang with peers, parents and relatives in Tiuh Indah may be located in the early 1990s, when young women began to look for factory work in Tangerang. In the absence of a formal system of labour brokerage by factories or middlemen, following protracted negotiations with parents, young women borrowed money from friends and relations already working in Tangerang in order to pay for travel and initial expenses, and moved to Tangerang, generally accompanying relatives already working there. Villagers recall 'bursts' of migration activity, generally immediately after the *Lebaran* holiday, when a number of migrants would return to the village with presents, new clothes and new ways of talking, and encourage sisters, cousins and friends to come with them at the end of their holiday. The return of those already working in factories meant that young women in the village were able to point out to their parents that their 'cousins' were working in Tangerang, to no observable ill-effect.

Over the course of the early 1990s, as more and more young women began to head towards Tangerang, the negative connotations of factory work and salacious stories about life in the city that circulated in Tiuh Indah began to subside. An informal kinship-based peer group network of young women had emerged, so that by the early part of 1998, 25 of the 30 young women in the village aged between 15 and 20 were working in Tangerang. According to one father: 'The main thing is the trend in this era, which is for [young women] to go to Tangerang. If that's what you feel you must do [...] I don't know [...] they are all talking about it. The main thing is this is the village fashion'. The existence of a network based on kinship and common identity (belonging to the same clan) enabled factory work to be accommodated within prevailing ideologies concerning young women's work and their obligations towards their natal household. Effectively, it allowed young women to influence and manipulate their parents into allowing them to work in Tangerang.

Ties between Tiuh Indah and Tangerang had important material consequences for the daily lives of those that went to find work in the city. Kin-based peer group connections enabled young women new in Tangerang to find places to live, generally staying in the same hostels and rented houses as peer-group relatives already working there. They also followed the advice of these relatives and friends originally from Tiuh Indah who helped them approach the personnel departments of the various factories in which the majority of people from Tiuh Indah were working. In this way, small clusters of women from the village lived together and worked together, and although friendships did develop between these young women and migrant workers from elsewhere, most social interaction was among others from Tiuh Indah (and some neighbouring North Lampung villages). Being part of this social group was an important motivating factor in encouraging young women to go to Tangerang in the first place, but it also meant that there was little inducement for young women to break away from their kin-based networks even after settling into working life in the city. As Herna (18) put it: 'I have met other people, Javanese, Sundanese, but mostly my close friends are from Tiuh Indah, also Negri Besar (the neighbouring village in North Lampung). We help each other out, I can talk to them. It is hard to be close to Javanese people'. Noticeable from this quote (and from others like it) is how young women position themselves in relation to others in terms of cultural difference, and how cultural stereotypes about the qualities of, for example, people from Java are invoked.

This sense of common origin, common identity and difference from other workers appears not to subside, even after a period of several months in the city. In part, this is because of the importance young women attach to maintaining ties with their home village. There are several dimensions to this. First, prevailing ideas among young women about their responsibilities towards their families looms large as they negotiate their lives in Tangerang. In the early 1990s, this sense of responsibility was couched very much in terms of ensuring that they did not stray beyond the boundaries of what was regarded by their parents as socially acceptable behaviour. This is not to say that such boundaries were never transgressed. However, young women compared themselves with other people around them: the 'flirtatious' Sundanese, the 'loud' Batak, and were at pains to demonstrate their own elegant, quiet and 'polite' behaviour characteristic, in their view, of Lampung women. Later, family responsibilities revolved more around the material demands parents began to place upon their daughters, particularly as prolonged drought and rural restructuring brought agrarian livelihoods under pressure. Sending small amounts of money to their parents was at the discretion of women themselves: 'parents don't ask us for the money. Well, they have done, but usually it is us that offers it. I feel better if I can help my family', said Yuli (19). Whilst some of this money went towards buying food or paying for school uniforms for siblings, most of the earnings that were sent home were used to buy gold jewellery (for the worker herself), furniture and linen items used when setting up home: the kinds of goods handed over by the woman's family as 'bride price' when she marries. Over the 1990s, this spending pattern became more entrenched as more Lampung women began to follow suit and as it became expected cultural practice.

Secondly, the importance of this sense of responsibility towards family is strengthened by the fact that the majority of young women plan to return to the village once they have gathered sufficient experience of the wider world, saved up for the items needed for a successful Lampung wedding, and are ready to find a husband. Return to the village is not so much about returning to a rural livelihood so much as about finding a suitable husband from within the wider Lampung clan. Most women who had gone to work in Tangerang at the age of 17 had, by the time they were 22, returned to Tiuh Indah to get married. A small proportion of these, with husbands working outside agriculture, returned as a couple to Tangerang, where both sought factory work. But the majority of those that had returned by the time of the second period of field work in 1998 had taken up their role as farmers' wives. The good name and material resources that women were able to carry back to the village from Tangerang thus stood them in good stead for their future married life. Whilst there were instances of young women marrying people from outside their Lampung village, this was rare: stereotypical views of an apparent propensity for divorce among people from West Java struck fear among parents and young women alike, as divorce is taboo in Tiuh Indah.

Finally, during the course of young women's sojourn in Tangerang, the maintenance of links with the village links offered something in the way of a social safety net, particularly during the economic crisis of 1997-98, when factory contracts were uncertain and some women went through short periods of unemployment. There was always the possibility of return to the village, at least on a temporary basis. However, for the most part, ties involved small gifts of food being sent from village-based family members to young women in the city.

These rural-urban ties and the peer group network linking Lampung women have been reinforced very powerfully through an institution set up to look after the interests of Tiuh Indah people working in Tangerang. The *Ikatan Keluarga Buay Serunting* (literally, the family ties of Buay Serunting – the ancestral founder of the village centuries ago), was set up in the mid-1990s by a member of the village elite, who had been resident in Tangerang for more than 20 years, but retained land and other assets in the village. As a member of a *penyimbang* line (i.e., an aristocrat, with considerable power over matters of community custom), Pak Selamat carried much authority, both within Tiuh Indah, and in Tangerang. Furthermore, he was a successful figure in 'modern' terms, with a relatively well-paid job with a government utility company, and a home in a middle class housing estate in Tangerang. The *Ikatan Keluarga* involves regular meetings of young migrants (male and female) at the founder's home, where they have the opportunity to discuss issues associated with life in Tangerang (e.g. problems with accommodation), receive messages and gifts from parents, eat traditional Lampung food and sing Lampung folk songs.

This institution shares many features set up by other Sumatrans now living in Jakarta, including middle class and professional people, and relates to the primarily male practice of *merantau*: migration to seek one's fortune and worldly experience. As a culturally-inflected form of social support, the *Ikatan Keluarga* cements ties with home for young women in various ways. The founder of the organisation has taken on a parental role in the style of a Tiuh Indah father, guiding the behaviours of those now in his charge. 'Parents are happy to know that there is someone they trust, a relative [i.e. from the same blood line], who can look after their daughters,' he said. 'When these girls come to the city, they are very young, very inexperienced. It is important that they are taken care of, to ensure they do not make mistakes, or find themselves in trouble'. In regular meetings of the *Ikatan* women were continually reminded of their familial role and their responsibilities towards their parents as couched in Lampung custom.

One specific way in which the *Ikatan* was able to ensure young women's material responsibilities towards their families were realised was through a rotating credit savings system (*arisan*). Rather than using a bank account, daughters were encouraged to place a small amount of cash into a common pot that they would be entitled to 'win' once every few months. This gave daughters the opportunity to have access to a lump sum of money. In meetings, there was much discussion of what was going to be bought, peer group influence was very important, but more crucial was the influence exerted by Pak Selamat himself, in his self-appointed parental role. Whilst there was much reinventing of 'tradition', in this case, versions of Lampung *adat* or customary practice, in the conduct of the *Ikatan* and its meetings, other dimensions revealed that this was in fact a very 'modern' organisation. Specifically, surveillance of young women was highly organised, in ways that mimic New Order government practices. Pak Selamat kept a book with passport size photographs, personal details and employment history of all members of the *Ikatan*: as young women arrive in Tangerang, they are 'invited' to register, and as they leave to return to the village, their entry is deleted. The counterposing of tradition and modernity in this way attests to the ways that ethnic identity has been enframed within the organisation: objectified and depoliticised, yet at the same time, socially constructed through the relationships linking factory migrants with each other and with their families in Tiuh Indah.

Social Networks and Political Activism

The emergence of this network of women workers from North Lampung coincides with a dramatic increase in levels of protest action among Indonesian workers generally (Hadiz 1997, Kammen 1999). According to Hadiz, women were at the forefront of labour activism, and particularly visible in the strikes and demonstrations that dominated industrial life in Tangerang (and elsewhere) over the 1990s. Andriyani's study of women activists in North Jakarta factories attests to this growing militancy. She suggests that female passivity of the sort portrayed in Mather's (1985) account of Tangerang women workers is either a misinterpretation of female agency, or else a depiction of gendered labour relations characteristic of an era that has since passed (Andriyani 1996). In May 1998, as interviews were being carried out for this study, strikes and protests in Tangerang were an almost daily event, coinciding with loud demands for reform in Indonesia as a whole. Newspaper articles and interviews with activists at this time suggested that most of these were protests over severance pay, and over disputed minimum wage levels. In addition, workers were venting their frustration with the officially recognised All-Indonesia Federation of Workers Unions (FSPSI) for its failure to deal adequately with worker's concerns as people were being laid off.

Yet interviews with the young women that made up the network linking North Lampung suggest that female worker militancy cannot be seen as a universal within Indonesian labour relations. None of the 25 young women interviewed regarded themselves as labour activists, and only six had ever taken part in strike action. In these instances, the strikes in question had involved all the workers from the factory striking en masse. So what accounts for such a lack of militancy among these young Lampung women in the face of a generally high level of labour activism? Early research on women workers in Indonesia noted similar patterns of inactivity among young women working in Tangerang. Beyond the obvious question of repression, some researchers pointed to cultural reasons 'behind the lack of industrial strife', particularly among those hailing from the strongly Islamic

Tangerang area. For example, Mather's work shows how a prevailing ideology encouraging young women to be shy (*malu*) and afraid (*takut*), and therefore easily exploited by capital that drew on cultural expectations.

The women interviewed for this study share many characteristics with Mather's interviewees. They are young (aged between 17 and 25) and from a relatively strong Islamic background. All are unmarried, and all are relatively recent participants in factory work, having arrived in Tangerang within the last three years. However, they could hardly be regarded as docile, shy or afraid. In initiating the move to Tangerang from North Lampung these young women are regarded as *berani* (brave) by their peers, a word which has connotations of challenging authority. Furthermore, most of them were acutely aware of their employment rights, particularly with regard to the minimum wage and severance pay, and of the fact that many of these rights were being flouted by their employers. This accords with work by Pangestu and Hendytio (1997), whose survey of women workers in the garment and footwear industries indicated that although there was a low level of worker knowledge about work place entitlements, workers were knowledgeable about minimum wage regulations. Lampung women were also knowledgeable about pay and conditions at different factories, and thus were quick to move on if they felt they were being exploited. Around half of the women worked in what they themselves referred to as 'export' factories: generally South Korean clothing and sports shoes subcontractors, supplying internationally branded goods to companies such as NIKE. The remainder worked in smaller factories producing manufactured goods for the domestic market. Discussion among women about the relative merits and problems of particular factories and managers, and their willingness to change jobs belies lack of consciousness, passivity and shyness in the face of exploitation.

A closer look at the experiences of young women from North Lampung suggests that their reluctance to engage in labour activism is closely related to the ways in which they have sought to maintain ties with their home village and with other Lampung people in Tangerang. Labour activism is conditioned by the importance young women attach to their Lampung social networks, and this was particularly the case during the 1997-98 economic crisis. Factory closures, short-term contracts (rapid hiring and firing) and social unrest during this period led to young women increasingly being drawn to the support offered by their links with parents and friends, as formalised through the *Ikatan Keluarga* (family ties) organisation. It appeared that they were willing to accept the norms and restrictions on their agency that involvement in the *Ikatan* implied, rather than look towards involvement with labour organisations and non-governmental advocacy groups.

In her work on migrant social networks in a South Sulawesi industrial area, Silvey (2000, 2001) points to the local geographies of unrest, linking this to kinds of social networks women were embedded within. The ability to fall back on parental contributions of rice meant women were able to risk unemployment by engaging in labour protests. However, in the context of severe drought and depleted harvests, the direction of support among young women from North Lampung was from city to village, engendering a strong sense among factory migrants that they should avoid actions (such as factory protests) that could jeopardise their jobs as the following exchange suggests:

> Q: Have you ever been involved in a strike?
> A: No, never.
> Q: Why is that [...] why might that be, in your opinion?'
> A: Maybe because of the factory, maybe down to us - we are not modern [laughs a little], although we work in an export factory [regarded as better work and more stable], food is not so certain [...] we need the work.

That such women regarded themselves as being 'not modern' was also borne out in their acknowledgement that work in Tangerang was only a brief sojourn in what would otherwise be a rural life in North Lampung. Women said that as they were only planning to work in Tangerang for a short time, there was no point in making themselves unemployable by being 'trouble-makers'. Putting up with difficult circumstances in the short term was regarded as a better course of action than engaging in activities that might make other factories less willing to take them on as workers. Most young women were sceptical about their capacity to challenge factories failing to comply with labour regulations, preferring to leave and seek other employment (at least, prior to monetary crisis), to cope, or to return to the village.

As well as being a conduit enabling factory workers to send small remittances home to the village, the *ikatan* also brought practical support to young women during the economic crisis. Newly unemployed women remaining in Tangerang used the *ikatan* as an important information source for tracking down factory jobs, which (at that time) still existed, but with factories recruiting when orders come in, and laying workers off when there were no orders (i.e. rapid hire and fire). In such circumstances, information counted for a great deal, and the *ikatan* network was important to this end. Secondly, the *ikatan* represented a form of social insurance for the newly unemployed, enabling young women to borrow small amounts of money to meet subsistence needs while they looked for new work, and, importantly, to cover medical expenses. While the *ikatan* was unlikely to offer sufficient material assistance for daughters and their families to enable them to overcome the difficulties they faced, it had nevertheless been an important source of moral and material support in the face of crisis.

However, being able to draw on the resources offered through the *ikatan* meant foregoing other sources of social and political support, and thus direct involvement in the labour movement. Whilst there was no evidence to suggest that the *ikatan* leader was employed by factories to curtail labour activism in the way that

Mather (1985) found, Pak Selamat did stipulate rules of conduct for young women that impeded their involvement in strikes:

Pak Selamat:	I state it like this. If it is outside the law, we cannot be responsible. It is already decided, if they break the law, it is not the responsibility of the group, of this organisation. If they have a problem or something that they need, then yes, we can help. But if they stray outside the law, then we cannot help.
Q:	What do you mean by breaking the law, for example?
Pak Selamat:	Like stealing, violence [...]
Q:	What about strikes?
Pak Selamat:	I feel that is included. That is also contravening the law, don't you think? There is always another way out...discussion or some other way. Maybe I can go to the boss of their factory, I can ask them about the issue, if they ask for my help.
Q:	Ya [...]
Pak Selamat:	But don't take the route of striking. I don't want that [...]

Young women appear to have capitulated to this, drawing upon the resources of the *ikatan* rather than seeking the support of advocacy groups and labour activists in Tangerang. Keeping on good terms with the *ikatan* has been seen as critical, for it is of central importance in maintaining ties with home (which might be needed in times of crisis). Its role extends beyond the realm of work and income – through the *ikatan* links, marriage partners are found, and women's own standing in the village might be enhanced or compromised. Effectively, Lampung women factory workers have made a trade-off between the *ikatan's* rather authoritarian approach towards their behaviour, and the benevolence it can offer in the form of small loans, advice and information: all of which are critically important in the face of political instability and economic uncertainty.

Beyond the direct impact of the *ikatan* leadership on militancy, participation in such a specific and culturally-inflected social network has also effectively led young women away from the wider networks of labour activism present in Tangerang. Just as Portes and Landolt (1996) note in their review of the 'downside' of social capital, involvement in such a tight social network has meant young women have been unable and unwilling to 'scale up' their concerns and participate in those wider social networks that embrace various forms of labour organisation in Tangerang. This exclusion from activist networks relates both to the nature of labour organisations and labour activism in Tangerang and to the desires and motivations of young women themselves.

At the time of research in Tangerang (in early 1998) whilst state repression of formal trade unions was particularly powerful, much labour organisation was conducted through non-governmental organisations (NGOs). These were small organisations that were able to operate by representing labour issues as human rights issues, and by their location within global networks of financial support from international organisations that shielded them (to a degree) from state repression (Ford 2001). Ford points out that this structural location affected their priorities, with labour being one of a number of social issues upon which they focused. Interviews with labour NGOs in Tangerang in 1998 concur with Ford's observation that their agendas emphasised enlightenment and empowerment of workers, and their aim was to give voice to workers' concerns. Whilst activists suggested that suspicion, fear and a lack of self-confidence seemed to hinder young female factory workers' desire to work with NGOs, Lampung women themselves regarded these largely middle-class activists as belonging to a different world that held little relevance to their needs. NGO activists and Lampung women moved in different social circles, rationalised their situations in different ways and articulated their concerns through completely different vocabularies. The social distance between these activists and young Lampung women was compounded by the non-engagement of these very young factory workers in the social group activities that Andriyani (1996) found to be so important in making collective resistance possible.

Similar processes distanced young Lampung factory women from fellow workers that were active in organising strikes (and who themselves regarded NGO activists as 'outsiders'). Lampung workers were very young, some no more than 17 years old, and had only two years of work experience in the factory. In a sense, their inexperience meant they were less likely to have forged connections with labour organisers. Furthermore, they moved within different social networks from those workers that came from Java; they lived in different places and socialised with fellow Lampung migrants (e.g. through the *ikatan*). Strike organisers were regarded as culturally 'other' as the following quote suggests:

Q: At your factory, have there ever been strikes?

A: Often. It was because the wages had not risen, so in the end there was a strike. [The term used was *unjuk rasa*, literally, display of feelings. Smyth and Grijns suggest this is the term commonly used to refer to strikes in Java and indicates discursive efforts to depoliticise such forms of protest].

Q: Did everyone in the factory follow?

A: Everyone followed, men, women, everyone. It was organised by kids on the assembly line – Javanese people.

Proximity to other groups and raised awareness of ethnic difference fostered through the *ikatan* served to dissolve the potential for solidarity with other workers among Lampung factory women. The capital offered through the Lampung social network meant that for young Lampung women, cultural and linguistic distance from other workers (and labour activists), coupled with the possibility of return to the village, counted against their direct involvement in labour militancy. Interviews suggest that this was less to do with a lack of consciousness as workers, and more a result of the kinds of social trade-offs women had made through their involvement in culturally-inflected migrant networks such as the *ikatan*.

Conclusion

This analysis of the practices of young female factory workers from North Lampung has pointed to the importance of challenging a homogeneous view of female agency in the context of labour activism in Indonesia's industrial zones. Whilst it is possible to make the general observation that female militancy has been on the rise since the early 1990s, the experiences of these women suggest that the picture is more complex than blanket generalisations would allow. The chapter has offered a more nuanced account of gendered labour relations by seeking to contextualise labour activism within the communities through which women live their lives. With respect to migrant workers, the notion of 'community' may imply networks of individuals separated geographically, through which women workers must negotiate competing material and symbolic demands from parents and fellow workers. Evidence presented here reinforces the point made by Saptari (1998) and Silvey (2001) that the links between workplace and community are critical in shaping practices of worker resistance among women.

Examination of this particular community of migrant workers has introduced the question of ethnicity and cultural difference into the literature on worker communities and labour politics. By outlining the social construction of cultural difference through rural-urban networks, this chapter has suggested that a heightened sense of cultural difference among Lampung women in the context of economic crisis is being forged through practices associated with the maintenance of ties with their rural kin and peers. This has had the effect of drawing these women away from wider networks of labour activists, and has cemented a sense of their distinctly Lampung identity in ways that appear to undermine solidarity with fellow workers. This process should not be interpreted as representing a lack of female agency or unformed worker consciousness among women. Rather, it points to the ways that female worker identities are multifarious, fractured and contradictory, and the potential implications for women's militancy as workers. More generally, the analysis here points towards the important work that needs to be done in examining the consequences of recent struggles over ethnic identity and cultural recognition in post-New Order Indonesia for working class politics more generally.

References

Andriyani, N. (1996) 'Women Labour Activists in Indonesia', MA Thesis, University of Newfoundland.

Boeke, J.M. (1953) *Economics and Economic Policy of Dual Societies: as Examplified by Indonesia*, New York: Institute of Pacific Studies.

Bowen, J. (1986) 'On the political construction of tradition: gotong royong in Indonesia', *Journal of Asian Studies* 45: 545–561.

Brown, D. (1994) *The State and Ethnic Politics in Southeast Asia*, London: Routledge.

Bruner, E. M. (1974) 'The expression of ethnicity in Indonesia', in A. Cohen (ed.) *Urban Ethnicity*, London: Tavistock Publications.

Comaroff, J. and Comaroff, J. (1992) *Ethnography and the Historical Imagination*, Boulder: Westview Press.

Elmhirst, R. (1999) 'Space, identity politics and resource control in Indonesia's transmigration programme', *Political Geography* 18: 813–835.

Elmhirst, R. (2000) 'Negotiating gender, kinship and livelihood practices in an Indonesian transmigration area', in J. Koning, R. Saptari, M. Nolten and J. Rodenburg (eds.) *The Household and Beyond: Cultural Notions and Social Practices in the Study of Gender in Indonesia*, London: Curzon Press.

Errington, S. (1997) 'The cosmic theme park of the Javanese', *Review of Indonesian and Malaysian Affairs* 31: 7–36.

Ford, M. (2001) 'Challenging the criteria of significance: lessons from contemporary Indonesian labour history', *Australian Journal of Politics and History* 47 (1).

Furnivall, J.S. (1944) *Netherlands India. A Study of a Plural Economy*, Cambridge: Cambridge University Press.

Geertz, C. (1963a) *Agricultural Involution: The Processes of Ecological Change in Indonesia*, Berkeley: University of California Press.

Geertz, C. (1963b) *Peddlers and Princes: Social Change and Economic Organisation in Two Indonesian Towns*, Chicago: University of Chicago Press.

Hadiz, V. (1997) *Workers and the State in New Order Indonesia*, London: Routledge.

Harris, D. (ed.) (1995) *Prisoners of Progress: A Review of the Current Indonesian Labour Situation*, Leiden: Indonesian Documentation and Information Centre.

Ingleson, J. (2001) 'The legacy of colonial labour unions in Indonesia', *Australian Journal of Politics and History* 47, 1: 85–100.

Kammen, D. (1999) 'Mogok: Labour and Industrial Strikes in the Late New Order', The Berkeley-Harvard Center for Labor Politics, Berkeley Working Paper 1999, Institute of Industrial Relations. Online at http://ist-socrates.berkeley.edu/~iir/laborpolitics/.

Li, T. (1999) 'Compromising power: development, culture and rule in Indonesia', *Cultural Anthropology* 14, 3: 1–28.

Liddle, R.W. (1973) 'Ethnicity and political organisation: three East Sumatra cases', in C. Holt (ed.) *Culture and Politics in Indonesia*, Ithaca: Cornell University Press.

Manning, C. (1993) 'Introduction', in C. Manning and J. Hardjono (eds.) *Indonesia Assessment 1993: Labour: Sharing in the Benefits of Growth?* Political and Social Change Monograph No. 20, Research School of Pacific Studies, Canberra: Australian National University.

Mather, C.E. (1985) '"Rather than make trouble, it's better just to leave": behind the lack of industrial strife in the Tangerang region of West Java', in H. Afshar (ed.) *Women, Work and Ideology in the Third World*, London: Tavistock Publications.

Pangestu, M. and Hendytio, M. (1997) 'Survey responses from women workers in Indonesia's textile, garment, and footwear industries', World Bank policy research working paper 1755, Washington DC.

Pearson, R. (1986) 'Female workers in the first and third worlds: the "greening" of women's labour', in K. Purcell, A. Waton and S. Allen (eds.) *The Changing Experience of Employment: Restructuring and Recession*, London: Macmillan.

Pemberton, J. (1994) *On the Subject of Java*, Ithaca: Cornell University Press.

Pinches, M. (1987) 'All that we have is our muscle and sweat', in M. Pinches and S. Lakha (eds.) *Wage Labour and Social Change: The Proletariat in Asia and the Pacific*, Clayton: Centre for Southeast Asian Studies, Monash University.

Portes, Alejandro and Landolt, P. (1996) 'The downside of social capital', *American Prospect* 26: 18–22.

Robinson, K. (1986) 'Stepchildren in their own land: class and identity in an Indonesian corporate town', *Mankind* 16, 2: 85–98.

Rogers, A. and Vertovec, S. (eds.) (1995) *The Urban Context: Ethnicity, Social Networks and Situational Analysis*, Oxford: Berg Publishers.

Safa, H. (1986) 'Runaway shops and female employment: the search for cheap labour', in E. Leacock and H. Safa (eds.) *Women's Work in Development and the Division of Labour by Gender*, Boston, MA: Bergin and Garvey Publishers.

Saptari, R. (1995) 'Rural Women to the Factories: Continuity and Change in East Java's Kretek Cigarette Industry', PhD Thesis, University of Amsterdam.

Saptari, R. (1998) 'Workers' politics and gender in Indonesia: some preliminary notes', Paper presented at the European Southeast Asian Studies conference, Hamburg, 3-6 September.

Silvey, R. (2000) 'Stigmatised spaces: gender and mobility under crisis in South Sulawesi, Indonesia', *Gender, Place and Culture* 7: 143–161.

Silvey, R. (2001) 'Migration under crisis: disaggregating the burdens of household safety nets', *Geoforum* 32: 33–45.

Smyth, I. and Grijns, M. (1997) 'Unjuk rasa or conscious protest? Resistance strategies of Indonesian women workers', *Bulletin of Concerned Asian Scholars* 29, 4: 13–22.

Soegiharto, S., Herawati, T. and Wagiran (1997) 'Migration patterns and migrant characteristics in the province of Lampung (1980 to 1990)', Final report to Centre for Research and Development, Ministry of Transmigration and Forest Squatter Resettlement, Alternatives to Slash-and-Burn (ASB) consortium, and Agency for Agricultural Research and Development, Ministry of Agriculture, Jakarta.

Stoler, A. (1991) 'Carnal knowledge and imperial power: gender, race, and morality in colonial Asia', in M. di Leonardo (ed.) *Gender at the Crossroads of Knowledge: Feminist Anthropology in the Postmodern Era*, Berkeley: University of California Press.

— (1986) 'Plantation politics and protests on Sumatra's East Coast', *Journal of Peasant Studies* 13, 2: 124–143.

Tjandraningsih, I. (1995) 'Between factory and home: problems of women workers', in D. Harris (ed.) *Prisoners of Progress: A Review of the Current Indonesian Labour Situation*, Leiden: Indonesian Documentation and Information Centre.

Widodo, A. (1995) 'The states of the state: arts of the people and rites of homogenisation', *Review of Indonesian and Malaysian Affairs* 29: 1–35.

Wolf, D. (1992) *Factory Daughters: Gender, Household Dynamics, and Rural Industrialisation in Java.* Berkeley: University of California Press.

INDEX

For Product Safety Concerns and Information please contact our EU representative GPSR@taylorandfrancis.com
Taylor & Francis Verlag GmbH, Kaufingerstraße 24, 80331 München, Germany

www.ingramcontent.com/pod-product-compliance
Ingram Content Group UK Ltd.
Pitfield, Milton Keynes, MK11 3LW, UK
UKHW020023200926
475702UK00014B/2034
* 9 7 8 0 4 1 5 4 0 5 9 9 7 *